Makamsız:
Individualization of Traditional Music on the Eve of Kemalist Turkey

ISTANBULER TEXTE UND STUDIEN

HERAUSGEGEBEN VOM
ORIENT-INSTITUT ISTANBUL

BAND 39

Makamsız: Individualization of Traditional Music on the Eve of Kemalist Turkey

Martin Greve

WÜRZBURG 2017

ERGON VERLAG WÜRZBURG
IN KOMMISSION

Umschlaggestaltung: Taline Yozgatian

Umschlagabbildung: Dem Trio (Murat Salim Tokat - tanbur, ney; Derya Turkan - kemençe; Cenk Güray - divan sazı, bağlama). Foto: Alper Taşçı

Bibliografische Information der Deutschen Nationalbibliothek
Die Deutsche Nationalbibliothek verzeichnet diese Publikation in der Deutschen Nationalbibliografie; detaillierte bibliografische Daten sind im Internet über http://dnb.d-nb.de abrufbar.

Bibliographic information published by the Deutsche Nationalbibliothek
The Deutsche Nationalbibliothek lists this publication in the Deutsche Nationalbibliografie; detailed bibliographic data are available in the Internet at http://dnb.d-nb.de.

ISBN 978-3-95650-278-1
ISSN 1863-9461

 Gedruckt mit Unterstützung des Orient-Instituts Istanbul, gegründet von der Deutschen Morgenländischen Gesellschaft, aus Mitteln des Bundesministeriums für Bildung und Forschung.

Ergon-Verlag GmbH
Keesburgstr. 11, D-97074 Würzburg

Gedruckt auf alterungsbeständigem Papier

Contents

I Introduction

In 2010, Istanbul was crowned by the European Union as the "Cultural Capital of Europe," together with Pécs, Hungary and Essen-Ruhr, Germany. Following some scandal and resignations, Mehmet Güntekin, Director of the *Istanbul State Classical Turkish Music Choir* was appointed as the Director of the music program. During the year 2010 numerous events, festivals and concerts took place in Istanbul, including the first *Yorgo Bacanos International Ud-Festival*, the *First International Istanbul Opera Festival*, a harp concert series, the *Festival of Youth Choirs* of the Boğaziçi University and the *Contemporary Music Sonic Festival*.[1] The main focus of the "Cultural Capital of Europe" program was not "European culture" in Turkey, but rather the culture of the Ottoman Empire, or more precisely, its contemporary cultural heritage (i.e. that culture which meets European orientalist expectations). Major parts of the festival budget were invested in the renovation of historic Ottoman buildings and in the music program, many concerts presented Ottoman-Turkish music. The concert series, *Music of Istanbul's Architecture* (*İstanbul Mimarisinin Müziği*) featured Mehmet Güntekin's *Istanbul State Choir for Turkish Classical Music*,[2] with Ottoman-Turkish music performed at historical venues; another concert series with the ensemble *Bezmara* was dedicated to the 400th anniversary of Ali Ufukî's birth. Other projects were intended to have an impact of greater longevity. Under the art directorate of Doğan Dikmen, the classical edition of Ottoman art music, *Darü'l-Elhân Külliyâti*, printed in the early Republican era, was re-edited into four DVDs, containing replica of the notations together with new recordings of the pieces (Dikmen & Türk Musikisi Vakfı 2010). A collection of 70,000 notations of Turkish music was made available publicly available on the websites of the *Turkish Music Foundation* and the *Istanbul State Classical Turkish Music Choir*. Finally Cüneyd Kosal's archive and library, consisting of more than 80,000 notation sheets and around 120 notation books, including autographs of several famous musicians from the late nineteenth and twentieth century, was bought for the Islamic Research Center Library (ISAM). Some of the book series edited as part of the program included music history; for example the memoirs of Neyzen Süleyman Erguner (b. 1957), a book on musicians of Istanbul written by Mehmet Güntekin himself and two volumes on Armenian music in Istanbul.[3] Noteworthy was also the publication in English of books on *makam* and on traditional Turkish instruments, as well as an edition of folksongs collected in Istanbul between 1936 and 1951 in a fieldwork project by

---

1 Istanbul 2010a, b; Hein 2010; Öner 2009.

2 Meanwhile: Choir for Classical Turkish Music of the Presidency of the Republic (*Cumhurbaşkanlığı Klasik Türk Müziği Korosu*).

3 Erguner 2010, Güntekin 2010; Kerovpyan & Yılmaz 2010; Bora 2010

the Ministry for Education.[4] Even the reconstruction of the *laterna*, the barrel piano, popular among the Greek population of Istanbul around 1850-1920 received financial support from the Istanbul 2010 program (CD *Pera Güzeli Laterna*, 2010). The eminent Armenian music scholar and composer, Gomidas was honored on the 140th anniversary of his birth and 75th anniversary of his death, in several events organized by Istanbul's Armenian community. Islamic music occupied a particularly important role in the program, for example with more than 50 publicly held performances of *Mevlevi* (an Ottoman mystic brotherhood) *sema* ceremonies.[5] During Ramadan a separate program offered concerts at venues such as the historical *Feshane* and the *Bağlarbaşı Culture Center Garden* (Istanbul 2010c). Another series reconstructed the historical tradition of *enderûn terâvihi*, religious singing during Ramadan (Şahin & Kemiksiz 2010), while *Jazz in Ramadan* featured internationally renowned Muslim jazz musicians. This festival has been performed on an annual basis since.

However, many of the concerts included original, sometimes even bizarre programs or ensembles without any obvious or direct historical predecessor. On November 22 for example, I attended a concert in the historic pavilion, *Sepetçiler Kasrı* (located at the entrance of the Golden Horn), entitled, *An Italian in Istanbul: Callisto Guatelli Paşa*. During the first part the *Tahir Aydoğdu Ensemble* played instrumental interpretations of *şarkı* (urban songs) of the late nineteenth century, performed on *kanun*, *ney*, *kemençe*, *tanbur*, cello and *daire*. More interesting, however, was the second part: Again *şarkı* by nineteenth century composers such as Şevki Bey, Rıfat Bey, Karabet Ağa and Giriftzen Asım Bey, but now harmonized by the then director of the Ottoman court orchestra, Callisto Guatelli (1819–1900) and published by Hacı Emin Bey (1845-1907). Surprisingly these songs were not performed in their notated form for piano, but rather on *kanun* and guitar – hence they were rearrangements of historically reconstructed arrangements of Ottoman art songs (CD Küçükay & Aydoğdu, 2006).

Actually the creation of new "hybrid" ensembles, arrangements or repertoires is far from new in Turkey. Popular Ensembles such as *İncesaz*, *Yansımalar* and *Kardeş Türküler* (all founded in the 1990s) are known for their combinations of Western and Ottoman or Anatolian instruments. In recent years several Turkish ensembles also tried to cooperate with Western symphony orchestras or chamber orchestras. In 2010, however, when I tried to attend as many concerts as possible, I realized that "hybrid" music has become the mainstream music in Turkey. After a period of excitement and curiosity, I became tired of this general obsession with hybridity. Even entirely convincing new ensembles, arrangements or compositions were soon replaced yet again by new concepts on a subsequent concert

---

4 This fieldwork was conducted by Muzaffer Sarısözen, Halil Bedii Yönetken and Rıza Yetişen; Şenel 2010; Aydemir 2010; Altınay 2010.

5 One special concert presented Islamic sufi and Byzantine music together: *Terirem/Terennüm* with the groups *İncesaz* and the *Romeiko Ensemble*.

or CD. Notwithstanding a few stable ensembles, almost every concert or new CD in Turkey today presents a new mixture or music performed by a new type of ensemble: a trio with *kemençe*, bass and cello; a combination of Ottoman and Baroque music in the form of a fictional opera from Handel; a concert with 40 *ney*-flutes, or a duo of *bağlama* and Iranian *kamanche* (bowed fiddle) and many others. In recordings of popular folk music the use of keyboards, electronic drums and bass has been almost obligatory since at least the 1990s. Combinations of *bağlama* and guitar are also common practice today, similarly *bağlama* and *ney* or *bağlama* and *kemençe*. Today, even Turkish composers of contemporary international music often use instruments and/or musical elements from traditional music.

I

This book describes the story of the extremely vibrant musical life of Istanbul in the early 2000s. It describes the confusing, contradictory and individualized musicscape in Turkey around the turn of the twenty-first century, including its prehistory throughout the twentieth century and sometimes beyond. One focus lies on the recent tendency towards disintegration of musical traditionals into internationalism and multiple musical hybrids. Instead of a tendency towards unification and standardization, intense Western influence has caused Turkish music to open up to the point where it becomes difficult to see any common foundation. However, the stylistic diversity mainly concerns arrangements and performance styles and far less, new compositions. Turkish music has expanded, both geographically and in terms of musical variety; yet its main traditional repertoire has been exhausted, and is hardly perpetuated by new compositions. As Bülent Aksoy (2008: 220) pointed out: "*Ottoman Music has not seen the rise of important composers since the 1950s.*"

For the analysis of more or less traditional music in Turkey today, a range of theoretical frameworks could be applied, including globalization, glocalisation (Robertson), cross-cultural, trans-cultural (Welsch), hybrid (Pieterse), creole (Hannerz), third space (Bhabha), cultural collage or bricolage (Slobin).[6] Since the 1980s the developing theoretical discussion has turned away from essentialist concepts of culture as coherent units. However, the overwhelming trend in theory writing impedes a rational approach. A detailed discussion of related theories would fill a book by itself (of course many such books have been written), while the recent consensus tends to the opinion that all cultures are "hybrid" (trans- or cross-culture) anyway.

6 To mention just a few important writings, see Kim 2016; Siebert 2015; Utz 2014; Greve (2002) 2016; Pieterse 1995; Featherstone 1995; Robertson 1995; Kartomi & Blum 1994; Welsch 1992; Slobin 1992; Abu-Lughod 1991; Bhabha 1990; Hannerz 1987, 1989.

> However, if we follow the results of postcolonial studies, like those of Stuart Hall and Homi K. Bhabha, who stated a fundamental hybridity as the starting point of all cultural processes, then we realize that the term "cross-cultural" is in fact tautological. For every culture, in whatever form it may be constituted otherwise, is in essence "cross-cultural" and by no means "mono-cultural. (Kim 2016)

Meanwhile, no serious contemporary academic discussion argues for the existence of essential cultural units, such as the West, Turkish culture, East Asia etc. (Kim 2014). In this situation theoretical approaches as mentioned before increasingly lose their analytical and differentiating quality; while the growing use of them in popular discourse weakened them further (Solomon 2015: 319; Lo 2000: 156). Today, public (and partly also academic) discourse tends to the use of either hyphenated terms, such as European-Turkish, Ottoman-Turkish; or composite expressions based on the metaphor of "post" or "beyond", an approach beginning with concepts such as post-modern, post-structural, or recently, post-migrant. For several years while working on this book, I considered "post-traditional music" as an appropriate term for the musical situation in Turkey at present. Sofia Kompotiati told me that she had used the expression "post-traditional music" in her (Greek) Ph.D. thesis (*Music, Identity, Globalization and Nationalism in modern Turkey*, University of Athens, 2005), in particular for groups such as *Baba Zula*. However, already the term "tradition" provokes serious theoretical problems (Coplan 1993). Since Eric Hobsbawm's eminent book, at least in academic contexts, the word is hardly understood separately from his concept of "invented traditions" (Hobsbawm & Ranger 1983). Of course numerous aspects of contemporary Turkish music could easily be described as "invented traditions" in Hobsbawm's sense, for example the Arel-Ezgi-Uzdilek pitch system, *saz* orchestras or today's *mehter* (Janissary) bands. In the Turkish context, however, the term "tradition" would be used in its more general meaning. In Turkey expressions like "*gelenek*" and "*geleneksel*" (tradition, traditional) are common in daily use and also in reference to music, e.g. *geleneksel halk müziği* (traditional folk music) or *geleneksel Türk müziği* (traditional Turkish music). This notion of "tradition" is hardly discussed in Turkey, though in many cases of obviously invented or at least recently transformed music traditions, one might be tempted to refer to this widespread approach as "imagined traditions." In a general sense, however, "tradition" might further imply an opposition to "modern" and the title therefore indicates a eurocentric, or even culturally imperialist position. The western "world music" market for example regularly refers to "traditional music," excluding all kinds of traditional Western music (such as opera, string quartet etc.). Here exotistic associations are quite obvious and often even intended, and a notion of "timelessness" as being implicit to the term "tradition," impedes a sources-based historical approach.

The actual title of this book, "*makamsız*" attempts to focus the idea of "post-traditional" on music. In a strictly musical context *makamsız* means "without *makam*," hence "without the traditional melodic concept called *makam*." It is borrowed from a composition by Evrim Demirel and a CD containing this composition. However, the term "*makamsız*" as used by both Evrim Demirel and myself, goes beyond its direct musical-technical meaning to be understood as a metaphor which emphasizes the consciousness of a bygone musical tradition. The notes on the Evrim Demirels CD read:

> The title makes clear that Evrim Demirel is acutely aware of his own cultural heritage in how he conceives and perceives his work. All five pieces [of the CD] refer quite emphatically to his background, Turkish elements having been woven into the music.

In this sense both expressions "*makamsız*" and "post-traditional" (which I ultimately decided to omit), share a common meaning: a musicscape in which traditions are more or less abandoned, though not completely destroyed, and whose fragmented elements still, in some way, influence and possibly even dominate most artistic music in Turkey today. At the same time the use of the term *makamsız* instead of the more general (and problematic) "(post-) traditional" emphasized the focus on music and aesthetics.

For the analysis of artistic music in Turkey today, however, yet another category seems to be much more appropriate, that is "individual": individual musicians, individual music pieces, individual life experiences, identities and approaches to music, individual musical projects, individual CDs and concerts, even individual concepts of music theory, conferences or research projects. A general theory of individualization as a social process was put forward by Ulrich Beck as early as 1983. Beck describes the dissolution of social classes, family models, gender roles and other social forms in Western industry societies after the Second World War as a consequence of an individualization of the labour market. The main aspects are the expansion of education and the need for personal selection within it; further mobility, particularly concerning work; and growing competition, which forces individuals to develop personal abilities and profiles (Beck 2007). In 2001, Abu-Lughod proposed an *ethnography of the particular*. In fact, individuals had already became a particular focus within ethnomusicological studies. As a result of their analysis of ethnomusicological monographies published between 1976 and 2003, Ruskin & Rice (2012, 316) realized that "*the study of individuals is now a norm in the discipline.*" Almost half of the books in the main parts of the study focused on individual musicians as innovators of a given musical tradition, as prominent key figures, as musicians "normal" or "typical" for a tradition, or even as non-musicians, usually anonymous auditors. However, this growing focus on individualization has hardly been theorized in musicology or even in cultural studies. The concept of religious individualism, proposed by Martin Fuchs and Jörg Rüpke, is at least close to what I have in mind here. We simply replace the terms "religion" and "religious" by "music" and "musical:"

> A focus on processes of religious individualization puts the experiences and activities of individuals center stage: how individuals interact with religious ideas and institutions; engage with religious practices; choose options and take decisions; critically reflect on

> their experiences, their being, their positionalities and their leeway for action, and on their relationships with larger reality; and how they develop new religious practices and new religious ideas. More specifically, the eyes are on such constellations in which the individual personality becomes a central focus of religious activities (which does not mean that this would have to apply to all actors in a given social context). There may be different shapes and grades of individualization in a given context, as also not all dimensions of individual agency encountered here must necessarily congregate around one mode of individualization. Viewed this way, 'religions' appear not so much as unified, but rather as diverse, complex and unruly. (Fuchs & Rüpke 2015: 324)

Similar to the persistence of discreet religions, musical styles (hence "traditions") such as classical Turkish music, *bağlama* of the Arif Sağ school, or Romantic piano music as well as political, aesthetic, religious and other discourses continue to exist – even in a growing number. However, hardly any musician nowadays would perform or compose exclusively in one style, and if they did, then only for a limited period of his or her life. In addition, the approach to "traditions," or whatever is understood by that again differs across individuals. My understanding of individuum hence also appeals to Heiner Keupp's concept of patchwork identities (Keupp 1999). Musical traditions in contemporary Turkey, to put it in other words, are seriously disintegrating.

In the case of Turkish music several factors lead to this individualization: A growing rate of and importance of migration and international mobility; the availability of almost all Ottoman-Turkish, Anatolian and global musical styles, instruments and other elements via media; the increase of cross-cultural encounters and experiences; the opening up of identity discourses. To summarize, all the elements which have long been discussed under the headlines of globalization or glocalization.

The perception of a culturescape which mainly consists of individuums and disintegration, rather than of stabile traditions, poses serious challenges for everyone involved, that is musicians, the audience, media, managers, venues and culture politicians. The main risk is that the audience might become bored, both by purely traditional music (now perceived as old fashioned and simple) and by the overheated and incomprehensible totality. The general atmosphere of commerce and entertainment in Turkey today anyway promotes the attraction of popular music while artistic music (of any style) is losing its prestige and appeal.

In fact music in Turkey has experienced a dramatic fall in its political importance. The ideologization of music, the political project of the early Republic period to "Westernize" Turkish music and at the same time to strengthen its national "roots," which were supposed to be "Turkish folk music," has lost most of its force. Over the course of the last few decades, it became possible to appreciate traditional Ottoman-Turkish music without being perceived as an enemy of the Republic. In contemporary Turkey, Western music is established enough to allow its younger musicians to re-encounter traditional music too. Hüseyin Saddeddin Arel's (at that time clearly nationalistic) idea of a unity of "Turkish music," today, has become at least partly a reality and partly lost its former ideological baggage. Within the great ideological and political debates of recent years (over the sale of alcohol, the headscarf, the struggle against the Fethullah Gülen network, issues of democratic rights, independence of the judiciary, the Kurdish issue, relations with the European Union etc.) the field of music did not play any role at all. Only some well-known polemicists such as the pianist and composer, Fazıl Say or the (music) historian, Murat Bardakçı initiated occasional and short-lived public discussions on music. In his column in the daily *Habertürk,* on November 8, 2010 for example, Murat Bardakçı forcefully claimed that the Kemalist musical reforms (*inkılâb*) had been a complete failure. Over the following weeks violent responses appeared in blogs, on *Facebook,* or on the nationalist website *OdaTV.* Murat Bardakçı's most prominent opponent became Cihat Aşkın, at that time Director of the State Conservatory for Turkish Music at the ITÜ (Bardakçı 2010; Aşkın 2010). Similarly Fazıl Say regularly initiates public discussions. He is known for his harsh criticism of popular music (in particular of *arabesk*) and his polemics against the AKP.

While there is hardly any serious debate in Turkey on what I would call an aesthetic crisis of Turkish music, there are endless debates in musicological publications, at conferences and panels, on basic concepts of Turkish art music, including pitch system, *makam* and notation. There is an obvious struggle to maintain or even to establish standards within a growing chaos. These attempts to fix (at least partly) and standardize Turkish music and its education have existed since at least the early Republic of Turkey. They have (and this is the second argument of the present book) overall completely failed.

The difficulties inherent in perceiving and understanding an individualized musicscape also affect researchers (who of course also work as individuums), including the present one. The main problem here is the challenge in creating a narrative of this incoherent field, even more problematic if this narrative tries to integrate a historical dimension. Though the present book will also include some short personal stories of individual musicians, an apparently random selection of individuals for closer attention would of course not form a convincing narrative (Stock 2001).

The general approach of this book is the search for precursors of the present, or predecessors of elements prevailing today, rather than a historical march from, say, the late nineteenth century till today (as for example Paçacı 1999; Aksoy 1985; Oransay 1973), while trying to understand each period according to its own values and conditions. The primary aim of this book is to understand the present. However, no linear structured narrative is able to describe this process of individualization. Of course the writing of a history of a given discourse or issue (e.g. Turkish nationalism, or the violin etc.) is still possible (according to the availability of relevant sources). A general periodization however, is difficult. No new period will be described here, nor the end of a former one; rather the musical situation in Turkey (in particular that in Istanbul) at present, together with a plethora of fragments of prehistory. These fragments are disunited, highly diverse strips of prehistory, some of them only beginning in the 1990s, others going back to the early nineteenth century. The dominance of the individual does not signify a new period whose inception might be dated, but rather has developed in a long, complex and from the 1990s, intensifying process.

The 1990s in fact, represent a crucial period for these changes in Turkey, as these years followed the general political, social and cultural decline of the 1980s, caused by the military coup on September 12, 1980. The 1980s in general were marked by structural adjustment, economic liberalization, and privatizations. The deregulation of the media began in the early 1990s. On a global level of course the collapse of East European Socialism, the fall of the Berlin wall in 1989 and the ensuing "new order," caused deep changes in the world's political and economic landscape. In Turkey this affected relations and business with Russia and the Central Asian Turkic Republics. In Turkey musical life grew again during the 1990s, and the decade became a fairly creative period, during which some new important music groups, musicians and musical approaches emerged, including *Kardeş Türküler*, Erkan Oğur, *Bezmara*, and *Ince Saz*. At the same time some influential books, in particular on Ottoman music history, were published, including Cem Behar's analysis of the traditional *meşk* education and transmission (1989), Owen Wright's edition of Cantemir's *edvâr* (1992), and Walter Feldman's groundbreaking book, "Music of the Ottoman Court" (1996). The record label *Kalan* music, founded in 1991, released numerous widely unknown historical recordings of Turkish art, folk and western music as part of its "archival series." In 1993, the "Copenhagen Criteria" of the European Union seemed to open Europe to the possibility of full Turkish membership, at the same time calling for (among other issues) the "protection of minorities" as a condition for Turkey's membership. In particular the late 1990s and early 2000s were dominated by a liberal multicultural discourse and many ethnic and religious minorities in Turkey formed new identities, and sought to revive their cultures.

Many of the described changes occurred simultaneously and with various interrelations. In addition, most of the musical changes in Turkey which have become important recently had already begun much earlier, though the scope of this prehistory differs according to musical styles and socio-cultural context. Despite the suggestive subheading ("On the Eve of Kemalist Turkey"), I do not perceive this process as a result of Kemalism or of its failure. The historical roots of this disintegration of musical traditions go beyond the Republic of Turkey and Turks as a people, and are spread over a large international area. On the contrary, I suggest that the impact of Kemalism and in particular that of the person Mustafa Kemal on contemporary musical life in Turkey is widely overestimated.

Another challenge in writing this book is the extremely broad field it has to deal with. For instance it is impossible to track all developments over their full international remit, including for example Iran, Azerbaijan and Georgia. Similarly the almost endless musical hybrids in Turkey stretch all possible strategies of description, and the field of music theory in Turkey today is full of extremely complex and sensitive issues, whose description would alone fill a book.

Another limitation should be highlighted. The focus of the present book is the recent developments in the field of artistic music, in particular in Istanbul (as the main musical center of Turkey). The economic dimension of music, and connected with it the huge and dynamic world of popular music in Turkey is beyond its scope. I will focus on music that in any way perpetuates or reflects elements of Anatolian folk music and / or urban Ottoman-Turkish music. Purely Western music, as also performed and composed in Turkey will not be discussed here.

Finally I can only try to describe the situation as perceived by a foreigner. About thirty years after my first visit to Istanbul and after nine years of regular residence in the city, I actually don't feel a stranger anymore. Nevertheless, I did not grow up in Turkey, Turkish is not my mother tongue, and I am not a musician.

II

This book is the result of several years of practical experience with Turkish music, followed by historical and theoretical research. After completing my book on German-Turkish musical life in Germany more than fourteen years ago (Greve 2003), I was working on practical issues, such as the integration of the *bağlama* into the annual German music competition *Jugend Musiziert* (Youth Making Music), or giving training programs for cross-cultural competency and music education. From 2005 I was in charge of the re-organization and management of the first regular study course of Turkish music outside of Turkey, at the *World Music Academy, Codarts Rotterdam* in the Netherlands. Together with the academy's artistic director, Leo Vervelde, and the artistic director of the Turkish music program, Kemal Dinç, we developed and tested curricula for *bağlama*, improved and extended them, and enlarged the program with further instruments such as Turkish percussion, voice or *ney*, with Kudsi Erguner as master teacher. In order to compensate for our lack of experience in teaching Turkish music, we invited the musicologist Melih Duygulu from Istanbul as a regular guest teacher and musicians from Turkey such as Erkan Oğur and Barış Güney gave additional lessons in adhoc workshops. Official cooperation was established with the State Conservatory for Turkish Music of the Technical University Istanbul (ITÜ). Later, I mirrored the first steps of some music academies in Germany (Berlin, Cologne, Mannheim) to prepare comparable programs for *bağlama* and other Turkish instruments.

The more I learned about music education in Turkey, the more I realized that even in Istanbul, teaching traditional music in an institution of predominantly western origin was a difficult and much debated issue. A professional education in Turkish folk music singing for example, is without any historical model and only a few decades ago would have attracted no interest. Whoever had a beautiful voice (or was supposed to have one), would simply sing. The only exception was the *aşık* tradition: In several Anatolian regions young men could accompany well-known *aşık*s for a number of years (as their *çırak*s) and learn by more or less intentional imitation. The traditional education for Turkish art music (*meşk*) never separated theory, practice, repertoire and performance techniques as western academies do, but rather taught music in a holistic approach.

In 2013 the *Landesmusikrat Berlin*, an umbrella organization for music in Berlin officially announced the *bağlama* as *Instrument of the Year 2013*. While working at the *Orient-Institut Istanbul*, I took part in the organization of workshops, concerts, a congress for *bağlama* teachers in Berlin and finally the first symposium on *bağlama* in Germany, again in cooperation with the State Conservatory for Turkish music of the ITÜ (Çiftçi & Greve, forthcomming 2017). In 2006 the Berlin *Philharmonie* concert hall assigned me to the new concert series, *Alla Turca*.[7] The basic idea of the series was to organize joint concerts with excellent examples of both traditional musicians from Turkey and international non-Turkish musicians. Over a period of five years I took part in planning and organizing these concerts, experienced multiple communication problems and sometimes overwhelming musical encounters.

In 2008, I moved to Istanbul, henceforth traveling regularly between Istanbul, Rotterdam and Berlin. Working for two outstanding music institutions, *Codarts Rotterdam* with its (at that time) unique *World Music Academy*, and the *Philharmonie Berlin*, provided me encounters with the best musicians in Turkey. Finally, a position as Research Fellow at the Orient-Institut Istanbul began in 2011, giving me the opportunity to systematically analyze the confusing situation of (post-) traditional music in Turkey. Back in the field of musicology – but now in Turkey – I followed academic discussion in conferences and workshops, took part in the organization of some of my own and worked on the editing of some related books.[8] At the same time I tried to observe Istanbul's musical life over several years, developing contacts with musicians, musicologists and producers.

Moving from small and peaceful Berlin to Istanbul in 2008 confronted me with the daily experience of a megalopolis. Since the mid-twentieth century Is-

7 Initially together with Shermin Langhoff and in communication with Vladimir Ivanoff, Director of the ensemble *Sarband*, later only in cooperation with the Director's assistant, Sara Braun.

8 Conference "Writing the History of 'Ottoman Music'," in cooperation with the State Conservatory for Turkish Music in 2012; "Hören Sie – Erfahrungsaustausch Deutsch-Türkischer Musiktherapie" on music therapy (Istanbul 2012); "Erstes *Bağlama* Symposium in Deutschland" on the *bağlama*, in cooperation with the Landesmusikrat Berlin and the Universität der Künste Berlin; "Transfer and Diversity" (Berlin and Istanbul, 2014); "Integrative Approaches to Contemporary Cross-Cultural Music Making" (Rome, 2016) in cooperation with the German Historical Institut Rome and Bahçeşehir University Istanbul. Kalaitzidis 2012; Greve 2015; Jäger, Olley & Helvacı 2016; Yıldız 2016; Çiftçi & Greve 2017.

tanbul has rapidly expanded in size and population. In 1960 it had 1.5 million inhabitants, in 1984 (during my very first visit there) it numbered about 5.5 million, today the official figures declare some 15 million residents, with an unknown number of unregistered inhabitants. During these decades the population structure also changed dramatically, and today the vast majority of Istanbul inhabitants are of Anatolian origin. Beginning in the 1950s, migrants from Anatolia settled in improvised *gecekondu* neighborhoods, which with time became regular parts of the city. A second wave of immigration arrived during the 1980s and early 1990s, propelled by the terror of the Kurdish PKK and the civil war of the Turkish army against them. In the 1990s the high-risers of Maslak signaled a new phase of urban concentration (Esen 2005).

During these years Istanbul's character changed "*from a typical Third World sprawl to a global city*" (Keyder 2010). Together with growing tourism, Istanbul became attractive for international business, arts and science.

> There is no doubt that Istanbul's success in capturing a share of the global dazzle is due in large part to the world economy, since the 1980s, favoring the resurgence of the metropolis: this was a period in which the control and management functions of global capital shifted to the great cities of the world and those sectors which are specifically urban gained ground. (Keyker 1999b: 26)

In the early twenty-first century the international hype over Istanbul changed the image of the city to *Cool Istanbul* (so declared the title of *Newsweek,* August 29, 2005).[9] During my initial years in Istanbul I was constantly besieged by visitors from Germany or the Netherlands. Almost everybody seemed to be attracted by the rising metropole of Istanbul. International media regularly wrote on Istanbul, and the city itself began to perceive itself as an international center rather than part of an imagined periphery. Within Turkey, Istanbul was always a central hub for IT, design, mode, media and music (Enlil & Evren 2011), and similarly for political, social or culturally alternative movements or underground arts (e.g. hiphop, LGBT, comics). The *gezi* movement in the summer of 2013, protesting initially against the destruction of the *gezi park* at the *Taksim* square, with its striking creativity, demonstrated a strong Turkish civil society and was perceived, at least internationally, as a culmination of this *cool Istanbul* – however, also as the beginning of its forced decline.

III

This book is composed of three essays focusing on three factors of central importance to Turkish music today, that is: internationalisation, historisation and hybridisation. These three aspects are interrelated to a degree that even the sequence of reading might easily be changed. In the end, I decided to begin with

[9] Göktürk, Soysal & Türeli 2010: 1; Özkan 2014.

internationalisation in chapter II mainly because this point includes my own position as an observer from more or less the outside. At the same time this chapter will recall the situation of music life in Turkey today, in addition I tried to include all important aspects of globalization as necessary for an understanding of today's Turkish (post-) traditional music. Chapter III will deliver the prehistory of this recent musicscape, though not plainly described in a historic narrative, but rather as a short recapitulation. The main emphases will be on changes in the perceptions of the past as a precondition to understanding the present. This chapter therefore deals with historiographic concepts and sources, popular narratives of music history, and historical reconstructions and revivals. Chapter IV focusses on the music itself, hence on the musical consequences of the developments described before. In a basically systematic approach several strategies of musical hybrids will be described in their respective historical development, looking back from the present rather than following a historical continuum. The fifth chapter is intended as a short reflection on the question of how this unprecedented musical expansion could have happened within an authoritarian state and society such as the Republic of Turkey.

The publication of this book falls in a period of fundamental change in Turkey. The "New Turkey" of President Recep Tayyip Erdoğan and the ruling AKP turned away from the Kemalism, which dominated the state for most of the twentieth century. The story of this book hence seems to end around 2016. After the Gezi riots, and in particular after the general elections of 1 November 2015, the political athmosphere in Turkey changed dramatically. Current political discussions are dominated by debates over the renewed rise of Turkish nationalism and Islam, the distrust of the AKP government towards the EU and the USA (also spread by the major media outlets), a growing political censorship, numerous terror attacks and war in Syria and Iraq, discusions about a political reorientation from the West towards Rusia and the Eurasian Shanghai Pact, and even a possible break with the EU. The consequences of these state-level developments for music and musical life are not clearly visible yet. In particular since the failed coup on July 15, 2016, and in the context of widespread political arrests of opposition groups and journalists, a possible economic crisis and the change towards a presidential system where political power is concentrated in a single person (that of President Recep Tayyip Erdoğan), music life in Turkey seems to be substantially reduced. The thrilling athmosphere of the early 2000s with its almost overheated creativity gave way to a general feeling of depression and insecurity. Today, Beyoğlu is losing its central position in the cultural life of Istanbul, while many intellectuals and artists have moved to neighborhoods such as Nişantaşı, Beşiktaş or Kadıköy. The *dengbêj* house in Diyarbakır, the symbol for the revival of Kurdish music has partly been damaged during the fights between PKK fighters and the Turkish army in 2016.

In parallel to these political developments the concept of this book changed several times; while simultaneously new individual musical projects constantly appeared (and often disappeared again after a short time). However, it is important to reiterate the crucial point that many apparently recent tendencies were in fact already discernible even before the founding of the AKP, or even before the early Republican period, i.e. the tendency to combine and intermingle "musical traditions." During the 1920s and '30s, Ottoman-Turkish musical traditions in particular were forced to struggle against the impact of Kemalism. Today, in the early twenty-first century, while a post-Kemalistic political atmosphere is growing, again musicians are under political observation, though the AKP barely exhibits any explicit music policy (yet), and in general seems hardly interested in music at all. On May 3-5, 2017 the Ministry for Culture and Tourism organized a much discussed council on music (*III.Millî Kültür Şûrâsı Müzik Komisyonu*), and even announced plans for the foundation of a University of Music, possibly a model for further political influence on music and music education in Turkey. This unclear situation might be reminiscent of the founding years of the Turkish Republic, where only ten years after the founding of a new Turkey a serious cultural policy was implemented. Today, the political project of Recep Tayyıp Erdoğan's "New Turkey" still lacks a vision concerning music. We therefore do not yet know when – or if at all – a new and distinct musical period will be established in Turkey (or within any broader framework), nor how long this present period of transition will continue. Even the end of political Kemalism, though highly advanced, has not yet been completed and might be reversed at least to some degree. It is possible that President Erdoğan, once he has secured power, might be tempted to repeat Mustafa Kemal's mistake and overestimate his ability to influence and adjust what he imagines to be the appropriate music for his country. In the worst case imagineable then, for a given period of, say, one or two decades music life could be partially blocked or dominated by state control and ideology. In particular "Islamic music" could gain further importance over the coming years, with for example the growing popularity of the *ney* over the last ten years as a potential indicator of this development (Senay 2015a). "Islamic music" as a concept, however, is hardly less ideological than its "Turkish" counterpart, and similarly unclear concerning its musical implications, as might be seen for example in the German-based rap group, *Sert Müslümanlar* or interpretations of the Koran and *ilahi*s on piano (as by Tuluyhan Uğurlu). A complete roll-back to Ottoman music traditions is hardly imaginable anyway. A purely ideological approach to Ottoman history and its music, would have no chance of convincing serious Turkish musicians. Historical research on Ottoman music has already advanced too far for simply ideological or political approaches. Further, the tradition of *meşk* on a large scale, crucial for Ottoman music, has disappeared, most probably to a irreversable degree, and even after a potentially forced shut-down of conservatories in Turkey the mainly private-based *meşk* could not be revived simply by order of the state. Western music on the other hand, is widely established in Turkey (though less than in Europe). Even if the new state would withdraw its financial support for institutions such as orchestras and operas, musicians, composers and most importantly the audiences will not change their musical preferences simply to follow political directives.

Opening the focus again to an international perspective, we might perceive the situation of (post-) traditional Turkish music as only one case within the phenomenon of world-wide music globalisation. If no serious global disaster (such as a global economic crisis or even a war) harms, decimates or even deletes the field of culture, cultural globalisation will most likely continue anyway, and together with it the individualization of music – whatever a single government might do. Also in Turkey the extent of globalisation with its medialisation, migration and general mobility is probably irreversible. Turkish musicians abroad, in Europe, Greece, the USA and elswhere, are much less effected by the political and psychological situation in Turkey anyway. Also "New Turkey" is internationally active (Aksoy 2009), possibly with a changing focus on Russia, Arabic countries, and in general Asia. Even in Africa Turkey tries to push back the influence of the Fetullah Gülen movement and expand its own influence and trade. The worldwide decline of physical music albums (CDs and audio cassettes) and their replacement by digital availability of music online will further open the international musicscape.

In this larger context, the specifics of the Turkish case are merely colored by local factors, that is the structure of its traditional music and music life, and, most importantly its particular structure of nationalism and the Kemalist cultural policy during the early twentieth century. The individualization of the field of music, however, might be understood as a general, international and cross-cultural development of the late twentieth and early twenty-first century.

Acknowledgements

This book owes its existence to the generous support of the *Orient-Institut Istanbul* and the *Max Weber Stiftung*. In particular I would like to thank my colleagues, Elif Damla Yavuz, Alexandre Toumarkine, Barbara Pusch, Sara Nur Yıldız, the staff of the library, the Institute's Director, Raoul Motika and its Vice Director, Richard Wittmann. During the years 2004-2013, I benefited greatly from the creative atmosphere and the experience and knowledge of my colleagues at the *World Music Academy* of *Codarts,* Rotterdam, in particular from my colleagues and friends, Leo Vervelde and Kemal Dinç. Similarly from 2006 to 2011, I drew on the *Berlin Philharmonie* concert hall, Pamela Rosenberg, Sarah Braun, and Gerhard Forck, also on Alba Kultur and Birgit Ellinghaus. Finally, I benefited greatly from two conferences, the first one, "Writing the History of 'Ottoman Music,'" organized together with the State Conservatory of the ITÜ and its then Vice Director, the late Şehvar

Behşiroğlu; the second organized together with the DHI Rome and Markus Engelhardt, Director of its Department for Music History together with his colleague, Sabine Ehrmann-Herford, entitled "Integrative Approaches to Contemporary Cross-Cultural Music Making." Long before, during and after this second conference I had numerous suggestive and more than pleasant conversations with Michael Ellison and Ulrich Mertin, the co-Directors of the *Hezarfen* Ensemble.

It is impossible to mention all musicians, musicologists and other colleagues from whose confidence, experience, advice and friendship I have benefitted over the last ten years, I should at least mention (in alphabetic order) Bülent Aksoy, Ahmet Aslan, Süleyman Aslan, Nevzat Çiftçi, Evrim Demirel, Melih Duygulu, Kudsi Erguner, Walter Feldman, Wendelmoet Hamelink, Ralf Martin Jäger, Kyriakos Kalaitzidis, Rıza Okçu, Erol Parlak, Hasan Saltık, Ülker Uncu, Yaprak Melike Uyar, Elif Damla Yavuz, Burcu Yıldız, and the State Conservatory for Turkish Music of the ITÜ, in particular Şehvar Behşiroğlu, Belma Kurtişoğlu and Cihangir Terzi. A very short talk with Charlotte Seither at the very end of the before mentioned conference in Rome helped me to find a new vision for this book (and I am sure she would be surprised to see her name here).

For comments on earlier versions of parts of this book I am more than grateful to Elif Damla Yavuz, Banu Şenay, Burcu Yıldız, Judith Haug, Ersin Mıhçı, and Kyriakos Kalaitzidis.

Without the language editing skills of Sarah Mandel, the English of this book would have retained its original strong and hard German accent. Chapter four was finally once again corrected by Sarah Atkinson.

Special thanks must go to Evrim Demirel for the title! The virtually endless friendship and hospitality of Hüseyin and İbrahim Üregil enabled me to finish this book in an inspiring and peaceful atmosphere. For support during all these years I am indebted to Özay Şahin, Nurcan Uyanık, Arzu Kılıç, and to my parents.

II International Turkish Music

During my work for the Berlin Philharmonic concert hall I cooperated regularly with the Istanbul-based booking agent Rıza Okçu, the owner and director of the agency *Stage Art*, which specialized in Turkish traditional music. I once complained to him about my ever growing collection of phone numbers (German, Turkish and Dutch). He laughed and opened a small box, which he carried in his jacket. It contained at least 40 SIM cards. Rıza took out one after the other, looked at them and explained; this is for Belgium; this for Sweden; this must be Bosnia, this is Spain, this Greece, Finland, the UK, etc.

Today, Turkey is deeply connected to the global world – politically, economically, through its media, in the arts and many other fields. Actually for Istanbul, this situation is far from new, as Çağlar Keyder put it, "*unlike other global cities, Istanbul has always been a* world city."[1] As the capital of the Ottoman Empire for centuries, Istanbul was an international metropolis, which attracted visitors from both Islamic and European countries, in addition to numerous waves of migration and refugees (Erdoğan & Kaya 2015). In the field of music, Iranian musicians were particularly active at the Ottoman court until the seventeenth century, with intense musical exchanges between Arab countries and Istanbul emerging later, in particular with Cairo during the nineteenth century (Behar 2006; Feldman 1996: 39-44, 65-67; 2015). Long-standing and close contacts also connected Istanbul and Europe, fostered by a range of agents, including travellers, embassies and the Italian and Levantine communities in Galata / Istanbul.

> One can also conclude that the majority of European musical instruments which had been incorporated into common musical circulation in Turkey (such as the violin, the viola, the viola d'amore, the clarinet or the European lauta) came predominantly through the channel of the Venice-Istanbul connection. (Aksoy 2010: 65)

We know about Western operas, Italian musicians, concerts, church music and a *Società Operaia Italiana* in Istanbul. In the other direction, for example, the *colascione* (an instrument similar to the Turkish *bağlama*) was adapted in Venice and Padua already in the sixteenth and seventeenth century (Baydar 2010; Aksoy 2010; And 1989). The first known Turkish opera and operetta composer Dikran Çuhacıyan (1836-1898) received his musical training in Milan.

In the first half of the nineteenth century, political relations developed further, and a cosmopolitan lifestyle including European culture and entertainments, emerged in particular in Istanbul's Galata and Pera districts. Also European musicians began to travel to Istanbul, for concerts or even longer residence. By the 1890s, non-Muslims constituted the majority of the city's population

1 Keyder 1999b: 3. This could similarly be said about Thessaloniki / Selanik and Izmir / Smyrna, see Kaliviotis 2002 / 2013.

though in 1914, after the arrival of refugees from the Balkan Wars, the portion of Muslims increased to 55 percent.[2] Non-Muslim minorities in particular developed good contacts with Europe, for example the Ottoman Jews were part of the Paris-based *Alliance Israélite Universelle*, founded in 1860. Around the mid-1870s, the Greek "Literary Society of Constantinople" came into contact with French composers and musicians (Erol 2009: 204f). "*At the beginning of the twentieth century, the Ecclesiastical Music Society members became interested in investigating their common musical heritage with Russia and got into contact with Russian musicians.*" (Erol 2009: 279) During the Hamidian era Bohemian and later Russian musicians arrived in Istanbul and Izmir, influencing the entertainment music market too (Alimdar 2016: 183; Fuhrmann 2009; Deleon 1995).

During the twentieth century however, and in particular at the turn of the 21st century, the level of internationalisation increased to an unprecedented degree. Several factors led to this development. First, the sharp rise of migration and travel inside Turkey and later, to and from Europe (Castles & Miller 1993; Dündar 2014). Beginning in the 1960s, transnational migration and growing international markets deeply changed the economic and cultural landscapes worldwide. As a result there was an increase in the influence of the growing Turkish diaspora on the musical life of Turkey. Second, the relations with Turkey's neighbouring countries improved, and they also began to influence Turkish musical life. Third, the emergence of so called "world music," a new transnational musical field which increasingly interacted and mingled with the music scene inside Turkey.

This chapter will describe the internationalisation of Turkish music, hence the emergence of new international musical projects, collaborations between musicians, pedagogical practices, as well as the consumption of music. After a scetch of the situation in Istanbul around 2010, I will dwell upon the emergence of a public music live in Istanbul and Turkey as a precondition of the later internationalization. The following parts analyse the international migration and its consequences for Turkish music and the intensifying musical relations between Turkey and its neighboring countries. The last part deals with the implementation of Turkish music in the emerging Wolrd music scene and market.

Istanbul – the Global Music City

No reliable figures are available on cultural activities and musical preferences in Turkey, neither in the past nor the present. We do not know exactly what kind of music is popular within different social groups, nor the amount of music production of the numerous popular and artistic musical styles in Turkey. In a survey on cultural activities conducted in 2006, Turkish citizens reported that they

2 Keyder 1999b: 10; Christian population in 1914: 450 000, however in 1927 dropped to 240 000.

watch an average of 63 hours of television per month, while time spent on concerts, museum visits and other artistic performances averaged just 30 seconds.[3] In Turkey today, much more important than live music, is the listening to music on CDs, the internet, television (in particular music channels such as *Kral TV*, *Dream Türk*, *Number 1*, *Number 1 Türk*, *Powertürk*, *TRT Müzik* etc.) or on radio. During the first half of the year 2009 more than 50 million CDs were sold in Turkey, more than in Italy or Spain, which does not include downloads and pirate copies (Yazıcıoğlu 2010: 241). Since then, however, the CD market worldwide collapsed due to the possibility of copying and downloading music from the internet – a common practice in particular in contemporary Turkey. This commercial music is clearly dominated by Turkish popular music with its numerous styles.

At the same time Turkish cultural life is still concentrated in Istanbul. In 2009 ten percent of all Turkish theatres and twenty-five percent of all cinemas were situated in Istanbul (Ada 2009: 99). Let us take a short glance at Istanbul's music venues of the early 21st century. In contrast to the media industry which had been located in Babıâli since the1870s, but from 1980 left the centre of Istanbul and moved to the Ikitelli district (Yücesoy 2011), the musical life of Istanbul is still concentrated at the very heart of the city. It thrives particularly in the traditional entertainment neighbourhood Beyoğlu, with its restaurants, bars, clubs, recording studios, *türkü bars* (folk music bars), rock bars, discos, and night clubs (Bates 2008: 137ff; Beken 1998: 32ff); but also in Beşiktaş, Şişli and much less in Fatih, Üsküdar or Kadıköy. Besides the well-known concert halls such as *Cemal Reşit Rey* concert hall, *İş Sanat*, *Borusan Müzik Evi*, *Süreyya Opera*, *Babylon*, *Ghetto*, *Nardis Jazz Club*, *Akbank Sanat*, *Barış Manco Kültür Merkezi*, *Garaj Istanbul* (the well-known *Atatürk Kültür Merkezi* has been closed since 2008), the abundant music scene in Beyoğlu around İstiklal Street (the former *Haymatloz*, *Hayal Kahvesi*, *Peyote*, *The Mekan*) offers numerous venues for all kinds of music ranging from Anatolian folk music and jazz to heavy metal. Some of these venues focus on particular styles, such as western music (e.g. *İş Sanat*), world music (*Babylon*),[4] avant-garde (*Borusan Müzik Evi*), or Jazz (*Nardis*, *IKSV Lounge*). Others offer a wider repertoire, for example the prestigious *Cemal Reşit Rey* concert hall. In addition the five conservatories of Istanbul need to be mentioned (ITÜ, Mimar Sinan GS University, Istanbul University, Yıldız Technical University, Haliç University), in addition to numerous private music schools, studios and music associations.

The main reason for this geographical concentration is Istanbul's disastrous traffic situation, which makes peripheral areas simply difficult to access. The situation is self-perpetuating as the intensity of cultural life in the centre makes it

3 www.turkstat.gov.tr/icerikgetir.do?istab_id=171 (accessed December 15, 2015).

4 Babylon was twice voted among the best 100 jazz clubs of the world (2002 and 2004) by the music magazine, Down Beat. (Değirmenci 2013: 19, fn 47)

attractive for national and internationals tourists. Over the last several years the centre of Istanbul has undergone a strong process of gentrification (in particular the districts of Beyoğlu, Galata, Tophane, Balat and Tarlabaşı), and areas such as the historical peninsula, the area around Taksim square and Galata have turned into a kind of open air museum, attractive only to hotels and representatives of national and international companies. The AKP-controlled (Justice and Development Party / *Adalet ve Kalkınma Partisi*) municipality tried to break the monopoly of the central area, and during the last few years several cultural centres have opened in other neighbourhoods (some of them administrated by CHP), most of them offering mixed cultural programs of all genres and traditions.[5]

In addition to these regular venues, throughout the year a growing number of music and other festivals attract tourists and local audiences. The main actor is the private *Istanbul Foundation for Culture and Arts* (*Istanbul Kültür Sanat Vakfi*, IKSV) founded in 1973 (and financed by its main sponsor Dr. Nejat F. Eczadebaşı and others), which organizes a number of important festivals, including the *Istanbul Müzik Festivali*, *Istanbul Film Festivali* (since 1982), the (arts) *Biennale* (since 1987), *Istanbul Tiyatro Festivali* (since 1989) and the *Istanbul Jazz Festivali* (since 1994). Beginning in 2004 IKSV became active internationally, with festivals in European cities,[6] and occasionally even organizing music and other conferences such as the *International Modal Music Congress* (1985) or *Contemporary Performance in Turkish Music* (1988). In addition other private festivals take place over the year, many of them during the summer and focusing on popular music, for example *Rock'n'Coke* since 2003, or the *Pera Festival*, which offered a mixed program. In autumn 2012 the *5th International Body Music Festival* took place in Beyoglu, organized by the Istanbul-based ensemble *KeKeCa* together with *Crosspulse* (USA). Public street festivals include *Hidrellez* (since 1997), which takes place in Ahırkapı in May and features Roman music from Istanbul and Trakya, as well as several local festivals (Ada 2011; Erdoğan 2011). From 2010–2013 the first of May was celebrated peacefully in the Taksim square, including a concert of left wing musicians and groups (e.g. Timur Selcuk, *Kardeş Türküler*, *Grup Yorum* and others). After 2013, on the eve of the *gezi* protests, the meeting was forbidden which resulted in riots.

Nevertheless, traditional Ottoman-Turkish music today is in a difficult position. Only during the month of Ramadan does the state sponsor numerous concerts with religious art music (Stokes 2013), while during the rest of the year such concerts often attract less people in the audience than musicians on stage. Sev-

5 E.g. *Caddebostan Kültür Merkezi*, Bülent Ecevit Kültür Merkezi, *Atakent Kültür Merkezi*, *Altunizade Kültür ve Sanat Merkezi*, *Cem Karaca Kültür Merkezi*, *Başakşehir Kültür Merkezi*, *Emir Efendi Kültür Merkezi*, *Erdem Bayazit Kültür Merkezi*, *Sultanbeyli Kültür Merkezi*, *Tuzla Idris Güllüce Kültür Merkezi* and others more.

6 E.g. Berlin 2004, Brussels 2004, London 2005, Stuttgart 2005, Amsterdam / Rotterdam 2007 and 2012; Russia 2008; Vienna 2008 and 2009, France 2009 and 2010.

eral state ensembles offer high quality concerts for a shrinking audience, as well as a regular income for many traditional musicians. Such musicians, instrumentalists in particular, often depend on the international market, and try to build up a personal international network.

Official biographies of Turkish traditional musicians as presented on CD covers, concert programs, as information on websites or by their booking managers, regularly describe an impressive number of countries in which the respective artist has already performed. In addition numerous international musicians, reflecting a wide range of musical styles, are mentioned as former musical partners. For example the biography of the *ud* player Yurdal Tokcan:

> Yurdal Tokcan was born in Ordu, on the Black Sea Coast of Turkey in 1966. He is a 1998 graduate of Istanbul Technical University's Turkish Music Government Conservatory. While completing his Masters program there, he joined the faculty as an *ud* instructor. In 1990, he joined the Culture and Tourism Ministry's Istanbul Government Music Ensemble under the artistic direction of Tanburi Necdet Yaşar. As a member of this ensemble, Yurdal performed in France, Holland, Belgium, and Spain. He is a member of the Istanbul Fasıl Ensemble and the Istanbul Tasavvuf Music Ensemble, and a founding member of the Istanbul Sazendeleri (Musicians of Istanbul), a group dedicated to presenting Turkish instrumental works. Tokcan has participated in many recording sessions and has performed internationally, in Germany, France, Belgium, Netherlands, Spain, Greece, Japan, Turkmenistan, Israel, Tunisia, Lebanon, USA, Bosnia, and Northern Cyprus.
>
> As a soloist, Tokcan performed in the Netherlands with the Amsterdam Percussion Group and Chamber Orchestra in a program entitled European Music Around Oud, and with the Tekfen Philharmonic Orchestra in Turkey, the United Kingdom, France, Germany and Belgium. (...)
>
> Tokcan represented Turkey in several international festivals and celebrations, including the 3rd International Oud and Lavta Festival in Dresden, Germany and the 2002 International Oud Meeting in Thessaloniki, Greece (along with oud players Ara Dinkjian, Simon Shaheen, Haig Yazdjian, and Omar Bashir). In 2003, he performed at the Oud Festival in Jordan, gave two concerts at the Arabic Music Festival at the Cairo Opera Hall, and performed during celebrations of the 2003 Turkish Year in Japan. Tokcan was invited to perform in Kudus in a pan-Mediterranean music festival (along with Selim Güler, Ross Daly, Zohar Fresko and Yinon Muallem). He has performed with the Mercan Dede Ensemble in various festivals, including the Akbank International Jazz Festival in Istanbul. (...)[7]

Turkish folk music in Istanbul on the other hand, is alive and full of vitality, performed in numerous *türkü* bars, at concerts and privately at home. Many young people learn how to play a little *bağlama* or folk dancing, others play Turkish folk tunes on guitar. A deep change in the traditions of folk music, however, has been prompted by the migration towards large cities, in particular to Istanbul, Ankara, Izmir, Adana or Diyarbakır. Many Anatolian villages nowadays are almost emp-

7 Promotional biography of Yurdal Tokcan (2012). Since the release of this version of his biography Yurdal Tokcan added several international projects, CDs, and concerts to this list.

ty, at least during the winter. Turkish folk music has therefore become predominantly urban music. Just as with art musicians, folk musicians also focus on international experiences in their biographies.

Western music is deeply established in Turkey today. In several Turkish cities opera houses and symphony orchestras exist, the school education on music normally focuses – on whatever level – on Western music and music theory. Most well-known international orchestras, conductors and soloists have already given concerts in Turkey (mostly in Istanbul). As an example, the year 2013 saw the following performers in Istanbul: pianists Martha Argerich and Katia and Marielle Labèque; violinist Gideon Kremer, Itzhak Perlman, Christian Tetzlaff, and Joshua Bell; the New York Philhamonic; baritone Thomas Hampson; composer Krzystof Penderecki; and tenor Roberto Alagna, just to mention the most well-known Western musicians (Ivanoff 2013). Western music in Turkey, from its earliest incarnations, was deeply influenced by migration and international exchange. The most well-known Turkish musician in this field is Fazıl Say (b. 1970), who studied piano in Ankara and Düsseldorf (Germany). His international career began in 1994, when he won the international "Young Concert Artists" competition in New York. As a regular guest at leading festivals and orchestras aroung the world, Say has performed on all continents, together with conductors such as Kurt Masur, Itzhak Perlman, Shlomo Mintz and Yuri Bashmet.

The audience for contemporary Western music in Turkey is even smaller, at the same time even more international. Some of the professors for composition, Ahmet Yürür or Hasan Ucarsu, studied in the USA, many others in Europe. Several Turkish composers are still based in countries such as Germany or the Netherlands (for example, Meliha Doğuduyal, Füsun Köksal, Zeynep Gedizlioğlu, Mahir Çetiz).

World music first became known in Turkey during the 1990s. Turkish musicians began to sing music from the Balkans, from Central Asia or Arabic countries, Latin music and others.[8] The cultural hype surrounding Istanbul attracted a growing number of international musicians to Istanbul. On the Istiklal Street (similar to other European cities) musicians and groups from Europe, Iran, Peru and many other places of the world came to play for tourists. Today Tango, Flamenco, Salsa, African Dance and many other international music styles are performed in Istanbul, in smaller venues but also at the frequent world music con-

8 Some examples are the album *Düğün ve Cenaze* by Sezen Aksu (Plaza, 1997) including compositions of Goran Bregovic (Stokes 2010: 137), the cover version of usbek singer Yulduz Usmanova by Candan Erçetin (*Yalan*, on her album *Çapkın*, Topkapı 1997) or a rai song from Faudel Beloua in a Turkish version sung by Levent Yüksel (*Hayrünnisa* on the album *Adi Menekşe*, Plaza, 1998). In 2000 the album *Pasaporte Latino. Latin türküler* (DMC, 2000) was anounced to be the first Turkish Latin-Pop; the first known Turkish Reggae band Sattas was foundet in 2004, their first album was released in 2012. In 2000 Sezen Aksu released an album together with the Greek singer Haris Alexiou.

certs in the Cemal Reşit Rey Concert Hall.[9] In addition international music festivals bring music of different styles to Turkey, for example "International *Ney* Meetings" organized by MediMuses and Süleyman Erguner in 2003, another one by Kudsi Erguner in 2007,[10] an "International Istanbul *Ud* Festival" in 2010,[11] or the International *Kanun* Festival in 2012 and 2015.[12] During the annual "Mystic Music Festival" in Konya numerous international musicians and ensembles perform all kind of religious music to the highest standard.

Most Turkish musical institutions, both private and state, are well connected to other international music bodies. The State Conservatory for Turkish Music of the Technical University Istanbul (DTMK) for example, the most important institution for the education of Turkish music, has an extended network of international partnerships, reaching from Europe and North America to Asia, in particular to Central Asia. Several of its teachers have international experience. Cihat Aşkın for example, Director from 2008-2012, graduated with an MA and PhD from the Royal College of Music and the City Univercity of London respectively, and has performed with numerous international well-known musicians. Aşkın's then Vice Director, the late musicologist and *kanun* player Şehvar Beşiroğlu, did research at Harvard University in 1999. The conservatory organized numerous cooperative projects and concerts with institutions in Sweden, Azerbaijan, the Netherlands, Japan and other countries. On the other hand, only a few non-Turkish musicians are members of the teaching staff of the DTMK.[13]

In 1999 an adjunct to the DTMK, the "Center for Advanced Studies in Music", MIAM (*Müzik İleri Araştırmalar Merkezi*), was founded. Equipped with an excellent international library and a tone studio, the MIAM offers English-language MA and PhD programs in music and musicology. Academic teachers were recruited

9 See for example Abtuman 2012, an article in The *New Yorker* on İnci Turan, Istanbul's first African dance instructor. In 2010 several concerts presented international encounters, e.g. the Istanbul meeting of Turkish-Japanese drums; another one featuring foreign Istanbul-based musicians including Yinon Muallem (Israel), Brenna MacCrimmon (Canada), Nathalia Mann (New Zealand), Bob Bear (USA), Ruth Hill (Greece), Arslan Hazreti (Iran), Laurent Clouet (France), Chris Moser (Switzerland). Since 2010 an annual international Flamenco festival takes place in Ankara.

10 Including many international musicians such as Muhammed Mosavi, Mohammed Ali Kaini, Hasan Nahit, Ali Jihad Racy, Qadry Serour, Mahmoud Effat, Sabir Siblini, Rascid Zeroual, Mosoud Jahed.

11 Directed by Necati Çelik, 25. – 31. October, with workshops and concerts with musicians including Elia Khoury, Georgios Marinakis, Haig Yazdjian, Josef Tawadros, Kyriakos Kalaitzidis, Münir Nurettin Beken, Naseer Shamma, Omar Bashir, Perikles Tsoukalas.

12 Other international festivals where for example the "Swiss Festival" in October 2014 (including a course for *Alphorn*), or the "Ruhaniyat" Sufi & Mystic Music Festival, presented by the Mumbai-based cultural organization *Banyan Tree* at Istanbul Technical University, Istanbul on 17 May, 2014.

13 E.g. the American perkussionist Jarrod Cagwin, who had learned south indian drumming in Ontario, and conducted several field studies in the Middle East and North and West Africa; https://jarrodcagwin.wordpress.com/biography/ (accessed Feburary 26, 2015); or Sandra Sindsch, German barock oboe player.

from the United States and the UK.[14] Its director was initially the American-Turkish composer Kamrân İnce (b. 1960; Memphis) together with Cihat Aşkın, and since 2015 Şehvar Beşiroğlu has fulfilled this role. In addition international musicians and musicologists regularly offer workshops at the MIAM.

Conferences in Turkey, including those on music, are often keen to include international guests (though the number of these non-Turkish speakers is often limited to a few individuals).[15] Participation at international conferences is highly esteemed among Turkish scholars, and even smaller Anatolian universities offer generous financial support to enable their teaching staff to participate in conferences abroad. Since at least the 1970s a number of foreign musicologists, anthropologists and historians come regularly to Istanbul for research trips of varying lengths (e.g. Eugenia Popescu-Judetz, Irene Markhoff, Kurt and Ursula Reinhard, Owen Wright, Eckhardt Neubauer, Walter Feldman and Ralf Martin Jäger, not to mention the numerous doctoral students). Both international and Turkish scholars are highly interested in long term cooperation and exchanges. Even musicologists working on Anatolian folk music, leave Turkey from time to time for longer stays abroad; in 2015 for example Süleyman Şenel travelled to the United States and Erol Parlak to the UK.

Today, some Turkish ensembles have members from several countries, including *Sarband*, *Pera*, *Hezarfen* and Metin Kemal Kahraman. Even if all musicians are based in Istanbul their numerous individual concert trips abroad require coordination to allow for mutual rehearsal time and concerts. Eliot Bates describes the production of the album "*Yıldızlar Kuşandık*" by *Grup Yorum* in 2006 as follows:

> The creation of arrangements was managed by the two de-facto project arrangers – Inan Altın in Istanbul, and Ufuk Lüker in Köln, Germany – and group and studio musician performances were recorded at three professional studios (ZB and Sistem in Istanbul and Per Sound in Köln), mixed at three studios, and finally mastered at Monoposto, a German mastering facility. Up until the mastering stage, music charts, lyrics, mixes (on CD-R, flash drive, and mp3 players), session files (on hard disk and DVD-R), and ideas were continuously circulated between spaces. (Bates 2008: 128)

Several international programs currently support student exchanges, for example, Erasmus, Marie Curie fellowships, "Cultural Bridges", "Civil Society Dialogue: Istanbul 2010" or the Al Farabi Program (covering Islamic countries).

> In 2009, nearly 36,000 Turkish students, academics, and artists went to the EU not only to improve their professional skills but also to experience living in a different country, to interact with its people and to understand its culture. (…) In addition, around 4,000

---

14 For example Michael Ellison, Tom Solomon, later Robert Reigle, Pieter Snapper, Paul Whitehead, Reuben de Latour, Jane Harrison and Amy Salsgiver.

15 In addition to the already mentioned International *ney* and *ud* festivals in Istanbul, in 2012, an international *Kanun* Symposium and Festival was organised by the State Conservatory for Turkish Music of the ITÜ, with performances of a number of non-Turkish musicians including Mohammed Saadaoui (Algeria), Manolis Karpathios (Greece), Julien Celalettin Weiss (France), Jamel Abid (Tunesia), Anahit Valesyan (Armenia).

> Erasmus students from the EU now come annually to do their year abroad in Turkey. (Pierini 2011: 160)

Some non-Turkish NGOs and institutions offer international cultural, academic or political programs in Istanbul, including the British Council, Cervantes Institute, French Cultural Institute, Goethe Institute, Italian Cultural Institute and the Turkish-Japanese Association. The ensemble *Bezmara* for example, was instigated and supported by the French Research Institute in Istanbul (*Institut Français d'Études Anatoliennes*, IFEA), and for many years the ensemble used to rehearse in their rooms. The Turkish Ministry of Foreign Affairs runs a number of Turkish cultural centres abroad, in particular the "Yunus Emre Institutes."[16]

According to official statistics in 2013, a total of 456,506 foreigners lived regularly in Turkey, among them 135,726 (29.7 percent) citizens of the European Communıty (Kaiser 2013: 224), In Istanbul alone, 135,018 foreigners (35,677 European citizens) were resident (Balkır & Kaiser 2015). Some are married to Turks, some Turks with German citizenship, businessmen, or retirees (in particular around Alanya) (Kaiser 2013: 228). A recent trend is the so-called transmigration of German-Turks of the second or third generation to Turkey, for improved economic opportunities. In addition, for many years the number of foreign tourists in Turkey has grown steadily, for example German tourist numbers have risen from 67,000 (1984) to 2.5 million (1997) to 5.58 Million (2015). In 2006, "*In 2006, 19,8 million foreign tourist visited Turkey and income was 12,5 billion USD, which is nearly 1/7 of Turkeys export.*" (Sarı 2010: 2) Today Turkey is also a transit country as well as a destination for refugees (İçduygu 2015), and several waves of refugees have entered Turkey, including from Bulgaria in 1989, and Kurds from northern Iraq in 1991. In 2016 about 3 million refugees from Syria, Iraq, Afganistan and many other countries were residing in Turkey.

Among the foreigners, some musicians (and musicologists) for one reason or another moved to Istanbul, including Julien Weiss (*kanun* player, in 2005), Stefan Pohlit (composer, 2007), Ulrich Mertin (viola, co-director of *Hezarfen* Ensemble; 2008), Bob Beer (baglama, main translator of Kalan Müzik, 2000), Sandra Sindsch (oboe player, 2011), several teachers at the MIAM as mentioned before, Jarrod Cagwin (percussionist), and Yinon Muallem (percussionist, 2002). The perception of foreigners in Istanbul can range from almost exotic fascination to suspicion of them as potential foreign agents (according to one of the many conspiracy theories popular in Turkey). Sometimes I felt unclear about how I was perceived, yet I never experienced openly expressed reservations or suspicion towards me as a contemporary orientalist. Turkish naturalization is a difficult and lengthy process which only a few foreigners achieve.

---

16 Berlin, Frankfurt, Sarajevo, Tirana, Cairo; to be opened in Algeria, Belgium, Brazil, France, India, Spain, Japan, Kosovo, Libyi, People's Republic of China, Russia, Serbia, Spain, the UK and the USA.

Stefan Pohlit:

> Today, I see Istanbul more as the centre of the last eleven years, in the sense that we all end up at a place, where we, due to our active structures of personality and thoughts belong to at best. From 1993–1999 the central city in my life was Paris. (...) Actually I was always travelling in the Arab world, and in 1999, as a backpacker on my way to Jordan, I came for the first time to Istanbul. It was Islam, in particular Sufism which fascinated me. From 2000 on I learned Arabic, as an amateur with good success. (...) At that time I found a perfect teacher in Sandeep Bhagwati to help me develop this interest. In 2003 I received a fellowship from the *Landesstiftung Baden-Württemberg* for another stay abroad, which I planned to spend in Jerusalem. Due to the growing troubles in Israel at that time, I decided to change my residence to Turkey with the help of already existing contacts. Officially I was a student of Nevit Kodalli (1924-2009) in Mersin, but in fact I spent most of the time traveling to Eastern Anatolia or in Istanbul. My Turkish friends helped me a lot, most of the time I stayed at the conductor Murat Kodalli. (...) In Istanbul I was introduced to Ottoman music by Cihat Aşkın and Şehvar Beşiroğlu, who still today, together with Ruhi Ayangil, advise me on my PhD thesis [completed in 2011]. In 2006, it became evident that for a permanent position I had to do a doctorate, and I searched for an appropriate place for my PhD study. Instead of continuing my visits to London (with musicologists such as Owen Wright or John Baily), I found myself in Turkey. Again several aides became decisive, in particular musicologist and composer Yiğit Aydın, who at that time was a PhD student in Marburg (Germany). Actually I never had a serious interest in becoming a composer in Turkey. I use to see it as a place for my research, in a kind of blend of Parsifal and Indiana Jones.[17]

Following the *Gezi* protests in 2013, Istanbul's image as a "cool city" became tarnished by pictures of police violence, accusations of corruption against leading politicians, extensive purges and the direct intervention of the government in the justice system. In 2015 both the government and the Kurdish Terror organisation PKK declared the cessation of the peace process, which had brought peace to the country for the past four years. As a result, violence from both sides returned, in particular to South-eastern Anatolia, and a series of suicide bombs in 2015 and 2016 in Ankara and Istanbul almost put a stop to tourism.

The Emergence of Public Music Life

The precondition for the international scope of Istanbul's musical life in the early 21st century is the development of a public music life in Turkey during the nineteenth and twentieth centuries. Beginning in western Ottoman cities, in public concerts, music schools and academies, almost all kind of music became available for growing parts of the population. Similarly media, including printed

---

17 Pohlit, born in Heidelberg (Germany), studied composition with Wittinger, Brandmüller, Müller-Siemens and Wolfgang Rihm. He began teaching in Karlsruhe, in 2008 at the conservatory in Ankara, later at ITÜ. He graduated with PhD on Jelal ed Din Weiss at MIAM, at present he lives in Izmir. Interview von Moritz Eggert, in: http://blogs.nmz.de/badblog/2011/02/25/in-der-fremde-1-stefan-pohlit/; Bad Blog of Musick, 25.2.2011.

booklets and books on music, radio, television and eventually the internet, became commonplace public spaces. In the late twentieth century this public Turkish music even expanded its reach beyond Turkey's borders to become international. While in the eighteenth and nineteenth centuries almost all Ottoman musicians we know about today lived in Istanbul, contemporary Turkish musicians are distributed evenly between Ankara, Paris or Athens, and listeners of Turkish music can be absolutely anywhere on the planet.

Already in Ottoman times *makam*-based music was partly a public affair. As in particular Cem Behar (2012: 52ff) pointed out, Ottoman music was much more than a court tradition but rather an urban music, practiced in several Ottoman cities, including Istanbul, Bursa, Edirne, Selânik, Izmir or Diyarbakır. Long before the first concert halls, music was accessible to almost everyone in *meyhane*s and *çalgılı* coffeehouses, schools, and at dervish lodges (*tekkes*) of brotherhodd such as Mevlevi, Halvetiyye, Gülşeniyye, Kadiriyye, and Cerrahiyye. The education system in Ottoman-Turkish art music (*meşk*) also depended solely on the student's acceptance by a master, and numerous examples show that even musicians of lower social status could fashion a musical career.

> More specifically, *meşk*, apart from its private form *(meşk-i hususi)*, was also practiced publicly *(meşk-i umumi)* in the various müzik cemiyets (music societies) and *meşkhanes* (practicing houses), that were located either in the religious houses of Sufi orders, such as the Mevlevi, or in the palaces of the Ottoman elite (Behar 1998: 52–53).

Singers might initially receive their education as koran readers or *muezzins*, from any good *müezzin* or *hafiz*. In some cases this humble beginning opened the way to a career as a singer of art music, even to the Ottoman court.

The concept of commercial public art music, however, only reached Turkey together with Western music in the early nineteenth century. *"Before the arrival of European influences, a raised platform was never used as a stage by these performers."* (And 1976: 135). From 1840 theatre pieces and operas were performed in the famous *Naum* Theater,[18] the *Dolmabahce Saray Tiyatrosu* which was opened in 1859 (and burned down in 1863) (Ölmez 2008:26; Emre 2006:124), after 1881 at the *Tepebaşı Bahçesi* (*Petit-Champs*) and at the *Taksim Bahçesi*. Most of the early local protagonists in this process were non-Muslims, in particular Greeks and Armenians, the latter playing a particularly central role in the development of Ottoman theatre.

During the later nineteenth century the first public concerts of traditional art music similar to the European model took place in coffeehouses in Istanbul neighbourhoods Şehzadebaşı, Vezneciler and Beyazit. Around 1900 only a few concert halls existed in Istanbul (Baydar 2010: 267ff; Alimdar 2016: 238ff, 358ff), most of them in *Pera* (today's *Beyoğlu*), including the French and Italian theatre *Concordia*, the "Municipal Garden" (*Jardin Municipal*) and "Municipal Theatre" (*Theatre Municipal*), the *Tepebaşı Tiyatrosu* (called *Petit-Champs*), the *Odeon Tiyatrosu*;

---

18 Yöre 2011; Aracı 2010; Ölmez 2008:26; And 2004.

and the venues of *Teutonia* and *Union Francaise*. In addition concerts took place in some associations' rooms or at consulates (Baydar 2010: 269). From 1908 concerts were organized in theatres, where, in contrast to coffeehouses, the audience came solely to listen to music (Alimdar 2016: 377ff; Greve 1995: 71ff). Famous concerts, which would later become models for many others were Tanburi Cemil Bey's concert at the *Moda Apollon Theater* on November 19, 1920; and the legendary concert of Münir Nurettin Selcuk at the French Theatre (*Fransiz Tiyatrosu*) on February 22, 1930 (O'Conell 2013: 109ff; Paçacı 1999: 326f; Beken 1998: 99). Regular concert halls, however, remained rare, and until the 1960s, concerts (of both Western and Turkish art music) regularly took place in cinemas, in popular *gazinos* (music nightclubs or restaurants, though often with good musicians) or at the state radio station (*radio evi*) (Aytar & Parmaksızoğlu 2010; Beken 1998). Only from the mid-twentieth century did the Turkish state eventually begin to build opera and concert halls. Today concerts of Turkish music are usually organised similarly to Western classical concerts. Program books have become standard, at least for serious concerts of Turkish art music, containing biographies of composers, historical explanations, lyrics of performed songs and possibly with explanations and translations of less well-known Ottoman expressions.

In addition to concerts, public access to art music was facilitated by the accelerating development of media, beginning with printed scores, books and journals (Paçacı 2014: 31).

> During the Tanzimat period, relevant publications covering music theory (such as Haşim Bey, 1864) and music biography (such as Hızır İlyas Ağa, 1857) were disseminated in the form of monographs and articles. With the expansion of music education outside of the imperial court after 1876, there was a concomitant increase in music publications especially in the areas of theoretical discourse (for example Cağatay, 1895) and historical research (for example Midhat Efendi, 1885). Further, music dictionaries (such as Kazım Uz 19894/95), music methods (such as Töre 1885) and music anthologies (such as Konuk, 1899) were published to address the didactic requirements of an amateur audience. In addition to the propagation of musical scores in popular publications (like *Kadın*) or by popular publishers (like Şamlı Iskender), journals like *Malumat* (for music theory), *Şehbal* (for music history) and *Peyam* (for music criticism) catered to a growing intellectual interest and yet also engendered a burgeoning critical appraisal of alaturca. (O'Connell 2013: 142)

From 1875 on notation sheets were printed in Istanbul, as well as books on music and teaching books on instruments or music theory. Around 1900 the first practical method books for auto didactical studies of instruments were published, beginning with translations from French, for example at the end of the nineteenth century *Alaturka Keman Muallimi* ("Alaturca Violin Teacher") by Kemanî Zafirâki, *Ud Metodu* (Ud Method) by Hafiz Mehmed, Selanik 1318 (1901) (Alimdar 2016: 326ff; Pacaci, 2010: 154, 159; Oransay 1973: 1501f). Some of these early publications were obviously written in the environment of early music associations (*cemiyetis*) and focused on popular instruments such as violin or *ud*, which were played mainly in coffeehouses.[19] Method books for *ud* in particular, would be written throughout the twentieth century.[20] Around the same time the first general books on music were printed in Istanbul, including Tanburî Cemil Bey's (1871/73-1916) *Rehberi Musikî* (Guide to Music, 1902) or Mu'allîm Ismâ'îl Hakki Bey's (1866-1927) *Solfej Nota Dersleri* (Lessons on Solfège and Notation, 1341/1925). In this period a number of shops in Istanbul already offered printed scores, practical method books and other books on music (Pacaci 2010: 31f). Significantly later, method books for Ottoman art music instruments were published, including *tanbur, kanun* and *kudüm*,[21] and eventually method books for *cümbüş* and folk music instruments such as *davul* or *kaval*.[22] Until more recently only the *ney* remained limited to direct lessons; Süleyman Erguners *ney* method was published as late as 1986.[23] Since the 1980s, several books have been published focusing on the conducting of choirs.[24] Also method books for the Anatolian long-necked lute *baglama* began to be published only from 1959 on (after some few exceptions most books in fact were written beginning in the late 1980s; Akdağ 2017). Most of them actually consist of collections of scores, preceded by short explanations of staff notation, tuning systems, playing techniques and sometimes regional styles (*tavir*). Only recently have more elaborated method books been written, for example by Erol Parlak (2001, 2005) or the one published by Arif Sağ and Erdal Erzincan (2009).

Similarly a number of books have been published on music theory aimed at autodidactic studies on music. While around 1900 it was difficult to gain substantial knowledge of music theory, today a couple of books offer basics on Turk-

---

19 Alimdar 2016: 314ff. Further method books for *ud* include: Hafız Mehmet Efendi: *Ud Muallimi*, 1901 (Kalender 1978: 23); Ali Salahi (1878-1924): *Hocasız ûd öğrenme usûlü*, Istanbul 1910 (H. 1326), Ali Salahi: *İlâveli ûd mu'allimi*, Istanbul 1924 (H. 1346); Abdülkadir [Töre, 1873-1946]: *Usûl-i Ta'lîm-i keman*, 1331 H (1915); *Şerif Muhiddin [Targan]* began to write another method book for *ud* which remain uncompleted (Cevher 1993: 17-21); Fahri Bey [Kopuz, 1882-1962]: *Nazarî ve Amelî ud dersleri*, ²1336 H (1920).

20 S.Erten: *Ud Metodu*, Istanbul 1956; Iskender Kudmani: *Ud Metodu*, Istanbul n.Y.; Hacı Kadri Şençalar: *Ud Öğrenme Metodu*, Istanbul 1974, ²1978; Onur Akdoğu: *Ud Metodu*, Izmir 1991.

21 S. Ezgi: *Tanbur Metod* (uncompleted), 1.part in: *Musiki Mecmusası* 17, 1949; Laika Karabey: *Tanbur kılavuzu*, in: *Musiki Mecmuası*, p. 23 ff , 1950; Ümit Mutlu: *Kanun Metodu* (c. 1980s); Ahmed Lütfü Taşçı: *Kanun Öğrenme Metodu*, Elazığ Musiki Konservatuvarı Derneği [1980s]; Haluk Recai Menemencioğlu: *Kemençe hakkında Etüd*, Istanbul 1970; Sadun Aksüt: *Tanbur Metodu*, Istanbul 1971, ²1994; Emin Akan: *Tanbur Metodu*, Eylül Üniversitesi, DTMK yayınları, No 89, Izmir 1989; M.Hurşıt Ungay: *Türk Musikisinde Usuller ve Kudüm*, Istanbul 1981.

22 Z.A. Cümbüş: Cümbüş Metodu; Salim Ağırbaş: *Davul Metodu*; Burhan Tarlabaşı: *Kaval Metodu* 1988.

23 Behar (2012: 109f) mentions earlier attempts for written *ney* methods, e.g. by Ziya Santuri (1868-1954), Emin Yazıcı (1883-1945), Hayrı Tümer (1902-1973), Süleyman Erguner (1902-1953) and Ulvi Erguner (1924-1974). Burcu Karadağ: *Meşkte Ney Eğitimi. Teaching the Ney with the Meşk Method*, Istanbul: Pan 2013.

24 Saip Egüz: *Koro Eğitimi ve Yönetimi*, Ankara 1981.

ish music theory together with lists of *makam* and *usul*, ranging from specialized and detailed books (e.g. Onur Akdoğu's "What is a Taksim and How to make it?", 1989b; or Alaaddin Yavasca's book on composition of Turkish art music, 2002), to introductions or simple prints of popular *şarkı* combined with short explanations of the use of *makams*.[25]

The first known music journal of the Ottoman Empire was *Kınar Haykakam* published in the 1860s by Nikoğos Taşcıyan and Kapriel Yerenyan (Paçacı 2010: 180), From 1910 on *Saz u Söz* by Âfet Efendi followed. While Western concerts were reviewed regularly in late Ottoman newspapers, critics of *alaturca* music were only rarely published (O'Connell 2013: 143ff). It was only from the mid-twentieth century that discussions of music and the aesthetics of this music were debated publicly by writers, musicians and theoreticians in daily newspapers or in journals such as *Musiki Mecmuası* (since 1948), *Türk Musikisi Dergisi* (1947/49), or *Musiki ve Nota* (since 1969).

Around 1900, 78rpm records entered the Turkish market, again at first in Istanbul, for both Western and Ottoman-Turkish art as well as for popular music.[26] Numerous international record companies (including Odeon, Beka, Lyrofon, Favorite, Grammophone Co / His Masters Voice, Columbia) produced records of *taksim*, *peşrev*, *saz semai*, *gazel*, *şarkı*, *semai*, *mani*, or marches, but also several more or less hybrid entertainment music styles, including *kanto*, polka, tango or mazurka.[27] With the introduction of the gramophone, which eliminated the direct contact between audience and musicians, a new perception of music emerged in Turkey. A music listener could now hear his selected music where and whenever he preferred, of course depending on whether he was able to buy the record disc.

The impact of sound recordings were multiplied by mass media such as radio or television, which followed slightly later. In 1927 the Company for Radio Telephone (*Türk Telsiz Telefon Şirketi*) broadcasted the first radio programs in Turkey. On the radio, in addition to live concerts, it was mostly records that were broadcasted. The combination of different types of music made a significant contribution to the spread of music styles and to the dissolution of divisive social boundaries. In 1939 *Ankara Radyosu* began its service, which motivated many musicians to move from Istanbul to Ankara – though most of them returned in 1950 when *Istanbul Radyosu* was founded. Several local radio stations followed later, culminating in the nationwide network TRT (*Türkiye Radyo ve Televisyon Ku-*

---

25 E.g. Muallim Ismail Hakkı: Türk Musikisi (1919, 2 1959); Emin Ongan: *Türk müziği solfej metodu*, Izmir n.y.Ö Hüseyin Sadeddin Arel, Arel, *Nazariyati Dersleri* (1943-48, 21991); Karadeniz 1965, 21984; Özkan 1984; Emin, Bedia & Hakan Ünkan, *Türk Sanat Musikisinde Temel Bilgiler*, 1984; *Türk Sanat Müziği Makamları ve Örnekleri*, n.y.; Zeki Yılmaz: Türk Musikisi Dersleri, Istanbul 21988 (1973).

26 Alimdar 2016: 233ff; Ünlü 2004; Akçura 2002; Seeman 2002: 211ff; Greve 1995: 146ff; Strötbaum 1992.

27 Seeman 2002: 227; Beken 1998: 47; Strötbaum 1992. For the record industry and its effects on music, see Racy 1977.

rumu) founded in 1964 (Kocabaşı 1980). The first Turkish television programs were broadcast in 1954 (Istanbul) and 1966 (Ankara) respectively, a regular program began in 1969. Beginning in the late 1950s the radio began to conquer Anatolia, and during the 1970s it was the television.

In the years 1954-55, the record company *Grafson Plak* introduced the 45rpm technology into Turkey (Seeman 2002: 243). However, it was the introduction of audio cassette technology in the 1970s which made music available for almost everybody, everywhere in Turkey, even outside of Istanbul and other major cities. As a result even Anatolian music became commercially attractive for producers of cassettes. "*During the 1960s, owners and producers increasingly turned to regional artists to serve regional markets outside of urban centers.*" (Seeman 2002: 247). From the early 21st century onwards, the internet gradually facilitated access to all kind of music worldwide.

Following the coup against Abdulhamid II in 1908, there was a liberalization of education in general, which also affected musical education in Istanbul. It gradually opened to a broader audience, facilitated in particular by the foundation of new music schools, for example *Musikî-i Osmanî* or *Dârü'l Mûsikî Osmani*. In 1914 the municipal theatre academy *Darü'l Bedâyi* opened, including a music department; three years later this department was enlarged. Under the name of *Dârü'l Elhân* (House of Melodies) it became the first music academy in Turkey. During the First World War further private music schools opened (e.g. *Dârü't Tâlim-i Mûsikî)*, offering education, organizing concerts and printing notation. During the second half of the twentieth century further music associations were founded, now also in other cities (e.g. Gaziantep 1952, Afyon 1955, Kastamonu 1960s). In 1986 Turkey there existed about two hundred music institutions, state and municipal conservatories or music associations (Say 1985: 1226).

Teaching methodologies and didactics, however, did not change immediately. In fact *meşk* was practiced in most *cemiyeti*s, at the Ankara Radyosu, and partly even at the state conservatories founded in the late 1970s. During this later period, which saw the establishment of radio, TV, music academies and state ensembles, the first trade union of musicians was even founded (*Türkiye Müzisyenler Sendikası*), as well as an association of Turkish composers and lyricists *(Türk Bestekâr ve Güfte Yazarları Derneği*). Since the 1980s further institutions have been founded, including the Society for Music Copyright *Mesam* (*Musiki Eseri Sahipleri Meslek Birliği*) and the Society of Music Producers *Mü-Yap* (*Musiki Yapımcıları Derneği*).

Beginning at the latest in the 1950s, Ottoman-Turkish art music began to expand over Anatolia, with a peak during the 1970s and 1980s, when in several cities new state choirs and conservatories were founded. In 1959, the Symphony Orchestra of the State President (CSO) (*Cumhurbaşkanlığı Senfoni Orkestrası*) with its director Hikmet Şimşek, gave concerts in Anatolian cities for the first time, including Sivas, Malatya and Diyarbakır (Okyay 2009: 118 ff). In 1959 Nazife Aral Güran founded the *Diyarbakır Filharmoni Derneği*, in 1965 the "Music Society of Diyarbakir" followed. On the other hand numerous musicians from Southeast Anatolia moved to Istanbul to become successful musicians, even of Ottoman-Turkish music (from Urfa and Gaziantep for example Necdet Yaşar, Alaeddin Yavaşça or Ihsan Özgen). Most migrants, however, brought folk music from rural Anatolia to Istanbul, where it began to merge with urban music styles. Only after the 1960s did Anatolian folk music become international – with the noteworthy trailblazers of the Anatolian Armenians, who had already migrated to the USA in the 1890s and took their music with them. Today, a huge number of *türkü bars* in all major Turkish cities regularly offer folk music.

A final example for the ongoing process of public availability of music might be the Alevi renaissance, beginning in the 1980s, which transformed the once hidden *cem* ceremonies to public, regular services and huge festivals. Commercially successful religious Alevi songs even came to dominate the Turkish folk music market since the 1980s, for example the cassette series *Muhabbet*.

The Turkish Diaspora

Migration

International migration away from Turkey to a great extent began in the nineteenth century, and reached its peak in the second half of the twentieth. It led to the establishment of ever growing transnational spaces, which also deeply affected the field of music.[28]

During the nineteenth century the first waves of migrants left the Ottoman Empire. Between 1820 and 1920 about 1.2 million people departed for the Americas, in particular the USA. Most of them were Armenians and Arabs, with an additional approximately 50,000 Turks (Karpat 1995: 233). From the late 1880s until the genocide of 1915, tens of thousands of Ottoman-Armenians escaped to the United States, to Russia and to neighbouring countries of the Ottoman Empire. After the failed revolts of 1925 and 1929 several groups of Kurds flew to Georgia, Lebanon, Russia, or America.

In addition, since the late nineteenth century Turkish students, some of whom would later became influential in Turkey, also started to enrol at European Uni-

[28] Within the extensive literature on Turkish migration, most of the existing musicological research concerning the music of the Turkish diaspora engages with the situation in Germany (Yavuz 2014, Nevin Şahin 2009, Wurm 2006, Greve 2003, Uysal 2001, Öztürk 2001, Kaya 2000, Schedtler 1999: 125-136, Reinhard 1987, Baumann 1985, Anhegger 1982) and Austria (Saglam 2017). As for other European countries, only a few case studies have been published for Belgium (Liselotte Sels 2014), Sweden (Lundberg 1994, Hammarlund 1993), the United Kingdom – in fact London (Tkachenko 2009) – though further research does exist on the Turkish diaspora of North America (Hall 1982) and Australia (Marett 1987). The first international conference about music in the Turkish diaspora took place in Vienna in 2007 (Hemetek, Saglam 2008), Berlin 2013; Çiftçi & Greve 2017; Documentary by Müjde Yazıcı: Gurbetin Sesi: *Das ist Musik* (2013).

versities. Saffet Bey [Atabinen] (1858-1939), for instance, who lived in Paris in 1876, later became the conductor of the Ottoman court orchestra (*mızıkay-ı hümâyûn*) in 1908. The eminent Ottoman-Armenian musicologist and composer Gomitas Vardabet studied from 1896-1899 in Berlin, and even published several articles in German. Later, back in Istanbul he became the most influential Armenian musician, his influence persisting until today. With the genocide in 1915 his career in Turkey ended brutally and he left for Paris to remain in hospital for the rest of his life.[29] Another student in Germany was Musa Süreyya Bey (1884-1932) who studied in Berlin at the beginning of World War I and later became the director of the *Dârü'l Elhân* (Istanbul Conservatory). In 1917/18 the *mızıkay-ı hümâyûn* together with its conductor, Osman Zeki Üngör (1880-1958), did a first concert tour throughout Europe, performing in Vienna, Berlin, Dresden, Munich, Budapest and Sofia. During the 1920s the musicologist Mahmud Ragıb Gazimihal (1900-1961) and the musician and composer Mesut Cemil (1902-1963) again studied in Berlin, while the musicologist Halil Bedii Yönetken (1901-1968) learnt in Prague. In 1924, the *ud* and cello player Şerif Muhiddin Targan (1892-1967) travelled to New York, where he met among others the pianist Leopold Godowsky (1870-1997), as well as the violinists Jascha Heifetz (1901-1987) and Fritz Kreisler (1875-1962). Targan gave successful concerts on both *ud* and cello. Only in 1934 did he return to Istanbul (though from 1936 till 1948 he taught in Bagdad) where he remained until his death in 1967 (Cevher 1993: 5ff).

The number of Turkish musicians with international experience grew during the early Republican period. The new Turkish state offered grants for Western oriented Turkish musicians to study in Paris, Wien, Berlin, Prague or Budapest (Şarman 2005; Oransay 1983: 1520). In 1948 the so-called "wunderkind law" (*harika çocuklar yasası*) facilitated several young musicians to study abroad (including violinist Suna Kan, pianists Idil Birit, Selman Ada and Gülsin Onay, Kahramankaptan 1998: 214). Almost all Turkish composers of this period received their musical education in Europe, including the so-called Turkish Five (*Türk Beşler*): Cemal Reşit Rey (1904-1985), Ahmet Adnan Saygun (1907-1991), Ulvi Cemal Erkin (1906-1972), Necil Kazim Akses (1908-1999) and Hasan Ferit Alnar (1906-1978). Saygun's *Yunus-Emre-Oratorium* was later successfully performed abroad – in Paris (1947) and in New York (1958).[30] More than 20 years after his studies, Necil Kazim Akses returned to Europe, than as cultural attaché in Bern, Switzerland (1954) and Bonn, Germany (1955-1957) (Başeğmezler 1992).

In 1935 the German composer Paul Hindemith (Hindemith 2013; Pack 1977), then official advisor charged with building up Western musical life in Turkey, invited German musicians such as Eduard Zuckmayer and Ernst Praetorius to Ankara. A few years later refugees from Nazi Germany became music teachers in Is-

29 Begian 1964; Kuyumjian 2010; Yıldız 2016; Bilal 2013.

30 For performances abroad see Refiğ 1997: 52f.

tanbul and Ankara. Until the 1950s German musicians remained influential in the Western musical life of Turkey. Consequently, and until the 1960s, this influence encouraged many young Turkish music students to begin or continue their studies in the homelands of their teachers. From 1950-1957 the later historian and music historian Yılmaz Öztuna studied in Paris (Akdoğu 1990: 11f).

From an international perspective between the foundation of the Turkish Republic in 1923 and the 1950s, music in Turkey remained closed and isolated. It was only towards the end of the 1940s that Turkey began to open up again, becoming a member of NATO in 1952 and hence part of the political "West". In the course of the political rapprochement with the USA during the 1950s, North America again (mirroring the late nineteenth century) became attractive for Turkish (Western) musicians and composers as a study trip destination.[31] While most of these composers returned to Turkey after their years abroad, after the 1950s a few remained in the USA. From 1959 Bülent Arel for example, studied with a grant of the Rockefeller Foundation at the new "Columbia-Princeton Electronic Music Center" in New York. 1962 he returned to Turkey and tried for two years to set up a studio for electronic music at the Middle East Technical University in Ankara. In 1964, Arel returned to the US, became a teacher at Yale University and from 1971 a Professor of Composition at the State University of New York. In addition he directed the university's associated studio for electronic music.[32] Kamran Ince was born in 1960 in Montana (USA) as the son of a Turkish father and an American mother. He studied in Izmir, but primarily at the Oberlin Conservatory and at the Eastman School of Music. In 1999 he was appointed as Director of the "Center for Advanced Studies in Music" (MIAM) at the ITÜ Istanbul.[33] The *tanbur* master Necdet Yaşar (b.1930) was appointed artist in residence of the University of Washington in 1972/73 and 1979 and also inspired the foundation of the Turkish Art Music Society in Britain (Pohlit 2011: 4). In his PhD thesis Frederick W. Stubbs mentions his first lessons with Niyazi Sayın in New York in 1980, and again in 1983 and 1986 in Boston (Stubbs 1994); Eliot Bates began to learn *ud* with Necati Çelik in 1993 in Turkey and continued in 1994, 1995 and 2000 in California.

The 1960's marked a new era of Turkish emigration to Europe. Several factors might explain the enormity of this new type of migration: The strong economic growth in Western Europe, the immense losses in its male population during

---

31 Köksal, Nemutlu & Şenürkmez 2015; Ali 2002; Karpat 1995; Altschiller 1995: 1364.

32 Similarly Ilhan Mimaroğlu came in 1955/56 with a Rockefeller grant to New York, studied at Columbia University and became a student of Vladimir Ussachevsky and Edgard Varèse. In 1968 he worked at the *Groupe de Recherches musicales* in Paris, and again in 1971/72. Later Mimaroğlu moved to New York where he remained until his dead in 2012.

33 Founder and President of "Atlantic records," one of the most important music producers of the USA, was Ahmet Ertegün (1923-2006), son of a former Turkish ambassador to the USA. His brothers Nesuhi Ertegün (1917 – 1989) and Arif Mardin (1932 – 2006) also worked at "Atlantic Records".

World War II and finally the Cold War, which blocked access to countries in Eastern Europe who had supplied workers for Central and West Europe in the past. In this context many central European countries began to recruit workers from Southern European countries such as Italy, Turkey, Yugoslavia and Spain. Turkey's economy at that time was still weak and unemployment rates high, prompting recruitment agreements with Germany and the UK (1961), Austria (1964), the Netherlands (1964), Belgium (1964), France (1966), Sweden and Australia (1967), Switzerland (1971), Denmark (1973) and Norway (1981) (Perchinig 2008). The majority of these "*Gastarbeiter*" (guest workers), as they were called in Germany in these early years, came from rural areas of Anatolia, although many of them had lived in Turkish cities before their migration to Europe. In this first period in particular, many Turkish workers aimed to save as much money as possible for a later return to Turkey, or to send to family members who remained in Turkey.

The history and structure of migration differed from country to country. In the UK for example, most Turkish migrants came from Cyprus rather than from mainland Turkey (O'Connell 2008). Switzerland never signed a recruitment agreement with Turkey and hence migrants came either undocumented or as political refugees. In many regions migrants of particular regions of origin concentrated as a result of the chain of migration. In Belgium for example, the majority of Turkish migrants came from the western Anatolian province of Afyon, a region hardly represented among migrants to any other European county. In the small Northern German city of Celle almost all migrants were Kurdish *Êzidî* from Southeast Turkey (Sels 2014: 175-176; Greve 2003: 159ff).

Around 1973 most European countries ceased to recruit Turkish workers. The following years saw minimal employment migration to Arabic countries such as Libya und Saudi Arabia, Iraq (1981-1990), and from the 1990s onwards to the states of the CIS (Unbehaun 1995). In Europe 1973 marked another turning point: Turkish workers who suspected that the legal channels of family unification could soon be stopped, called upon their families to follow them – others decided to turn back to Turkey. From the late 1960s onwards, therefore, a regular Turkish family life began to develop in Europe, with slowly improving housing conditions and the establishment of entrepreneurial activities such as *kebab* takeaways, Turkish grocery shops and small handicraft enterprises. As part of this process of establishment taking place throughout the 1970's, a Turkish entertainment market also began to emerge, including music restaurants and *gazinos*. Here amateurs, emerging semi-professional and professional musicians played and sang folk music, and later also *arabesk* and *taverna* music. From the 1970's onwards Turkish weddings became a lucrative market for professional musicians in Europe.

European-Turkish life became diversified. While in the 1960s almost all Turks in western Europe had been unskilled workers, at least from the 1990s onwards European-Turks occupied almost all professions and social strata. Initially most migrants came to Europe with the idea of returning to Turkey. However only some of them put this plan into practice. Many others postponed their return again and again, and ultimately gave up their plans completely. While for most Turkish migrants their time in Europe was perceived as a period of transition, a longing for a glorified past in Turkey began to develop. Since the end of the 1960s this desire for a far-away home found its expression in *arabesk* (Stokes 1992; Güngör 1990). Also in Turkey, *arabesk* emerged together with the increasing internal migration to the major cities. Among European-Turks it became the most popular music, spread by the new musical tapes that made recorded music affordable even for poor migrant families.

Concurrently with the migration of Turkish workers, Turkish musicians also arrived in Europe with a strong interest in contact with the European music scene. Paris in particular, launched the international careers for the diverse Turkish musicians of Tülay German (1966) and Timur Selçuk (1964–1975), the rock group *Moğollar* (late 1960s), the *ney* player Kudsi Erguner (since 1975) and the *bağlama* player Talip Özkan (since 1977).

After the military coup in Turkey on September 12, 1980, a number of intellectuals and artists escaped to Europe, in particular to Germany, Sweden and Switzerland. They included the musicians, Selda Bağcan, Melike Demirağ, Sanar Yurdatapan, Fuat Saka, Sümeyra, Nizamettin Arıç, Cem Karaca, Şiwan Perwer and Zülfü Livaneli. Some of these refugees returned to Turkey after the political situation improved, for instance Cem Karaca, Sümeyra, Nizamettin Arıç, Melike Demirağ, Sanar Yurdatapan, Selda Bağcan, and Zülfü Livaneli. Others, including Sümeyra, Fuat Saka and Şiwan Perwer stayed in their new home countries. Searching for international political solidarity with the persecuted in Turkey, these musicians gave concerts at political events, often together with politically active German and other non-Turkish musicians.

Since the 1980s the size of the Turkish populations in Europe has remained more or less constant, with a slow increase due to birth rate. A Turkish diaspora has emerged in Europe, more or less adapted to the local daily life and at the same time strongly connected to Turkey. According to the Turkish Ministry of Foreign Affairs, today more than 5 million Turks live abroad, around 4 million of them in Europe.[34] However, official statistics do not include the many naturalised people of Turkish origin and their children and grandchildren, who may only have one Turkish (or naturalised) parent. Three quarters of European Turks live in German speaking countries with the majority in Germany itself. Nominal Turkish minorities live in the USA, Canada, Australia as well as in some Arabic and Central Asian countries (de Tapia 1995, Unbehaun 1995).

Today the structure of the Turkish population differs significantly in all these countries. In countries such as Germany, Austria or the Netherlands, second ge-

---

34 www.mfa.gov.tr (accessed May 15, 2015.)

neration Turks are the dominant group. In Switzerland or Sweden there is a much higher percentage of Kurdish and Turkish refugees (Coggins 1995). In addition complex migration movements are still ongoing. Refugees, visting students and marriage partners come from Turkey to Europe, while retired workers of the first generation or people of the second generation, with a high level of education move to Turkey or to other countries.

Transnational Connections and Music

Transnational connections between Turkey and Turkish migrants in Europe are facilitated by and reinforced through travel, as well as by media (Glick-Schiller 1997; Pries 2010; Faist 2000). Newspapers such as *Sabah*, *Zaman*, *Hürriyet*, *Milliyet* or *Türkiye* are present in almost every central European city, although many younger European-Turks of the second generation prefer newspapers in German, Dutch, or French. In the early 1980s, Turkish videos and video-shops boomed in Europe; in 1984, about one hundred Turkish video shops existed just in Berlin. One year later the first German-based Turkish TV channel, TD 1, started broadcasting, and in 1990 the national Turkish television channel TRT INT was broadcast via the German cable network. In 1992 TRT Avrasya (in 2002 the name changed to TRT *TÜRK*) was launched, intended to target the Turks of Central Asia, i.e. Kazakhstan, Uzbekistan, and Kirgizstan. In 1992, the acceptance of private channels in Turkey together with the development of satellite technologies resulted in rapidly growing Turkish TV exposure in Europe. Several major TV channels from Turkey established partner channels in Europe (*Euro D*, *Euroshow*, *atv-INT*), some of them still active today. In 2005, more than a hundred Turkish TV channels were available in Europe, several channels of TRT, private commercial programs, music channels (like *Kral TV*), channels from special Anatolian regions (such as *Karadeniz TV*) or religious channels (Berliner Institut für Vergleichende Sozialforschung 2005). Some of the bigger channels have studios in Germany, a few minor channels are mainly produced in Germany (*TD 1* in Berlin, *Kanal Avrupa* in Duisburg, *Düzgün TV* in Lünen, *Yol TV* in Köln, *Su TV*, TV 10). A unique case is the Kurdish *Roj TV* and its successors under different names, broadcasting initially under the name *Med TV* from Belgium and later officially from Denmark (Hassanpour 1997: 246). Radio programs from Turkey, also available in Europe via satellite or internet, never matched the importance of television. Europe-based radio stations include *Metropol FM* (Berlin and Southwest-Germany) or London Turkish Radio (*Londra Türk Radyosu*) (O'Connell 2008; Tkachenko 2009).

During the 1980s and 1990s the most striking peculiarity of Turkish-European music life was the overwhelming production of CD's (in earlier times MC's) by Euro-Turks. Already since the 1960s music records, tape cassettes and later CDs were imported from Turkey to Europe. In 1963 Yılmaz Asöcal established the tape company "*Türküola*" in Köln, which dominated the German market over many years. In addition several minor and small Turkish tape companies rivalled for this market. Many European Turkish amateur musicians invested significantly in producing CDs, dreaming of becoming famous in Turkey. However, only a few European-Turkish musicians actually succeeded in this approach, for example Özlem Özdil or the group *Yurtseven Kardeşler* (Germany). By far most of these CDs by European-based Turkish musicians contain Anatolian folk music, whereas Turkish pop remained the domain of professional producers in Turkey. CDs with *arabesk* or Turkish art music were also rarities. On the other hand, before the beginning of the rise of religious Islamic music in Turkey in the 1990s, recordings of *ilahi* and *Mevlevi* music were produced almost exclusively in Europe, mainly by international companies. Many of the folk music recordings by European-based Turkish musicians were made in Europe, at the Turkish Studios which existed in many European cities. The music managers selected and arranged the songs and organized guest musicians. Only the production and distribution were usually done in Turkey due to its higher prestige. Over decades the production of European-Turkish musicians provided an important income for the Turkish music industry. However, many inexperienced amateur musicians also lost a lot of money in this process and remained unknown, with nothing but a bad experience and a bunch of unsold copies of their own CDs.

Families in Europe and Turkey maintain intense contact via regular phone calls or internet chats. Anatolian villages became connected to the telephone network, later cell phones further facititated personal communication. From at least the year 2000, the internet became the most important transnational media. Music is transferred via *youtube*, numerous private websites or blogs or social networks such as *Facebook*. At the Eurovision Song Contest for instance, candidates from Turkey regularly received higher scores from countries with large Turkish communities.[35]

The second crucial factor for transnational connections is the growing feasibility of travel. Since the 1970s a major part of the European Turkish population have spent their summer holidays in Turkey, to enjoy the beach and to meet relatives and friends. Inversely, Turkey-based businessmen, politicians and musicians regularly visit Europe, for periods of hours, days or even many weeks. Family celebrations like weddings, circumcisions or funerals and also private business matters frequently lead to travel between Europe and Turkey. European Turkish pensioners often live in two countries, staying six months in one home and six months in the other. Travelling has become cheap and easy, although flight prices to Turkey differ widely between European countries and cities. Whereas flights from Germany are quite cheap, in particular outside the holiday seasons, flights from France, the Netherlands or Great Britain are more expensive.

[35] Solomon 2007. In 2013 Turkey withdrew from the contest.

Increased transnational interaction also became noticeable with regards to the production of music. Studio musicians fly from Turkey to Europe, singers and groups come to record in Istanbul. Moreover, various Turkey-based musicians, involved in all sorts of music, regularly give concerts in Europe. For young musicians in Turkey it has become common to stay for some time in Germany or another European country. At the same time, Turkish-European associations and businessmen regularly invite musicians from Turkey. Many popular singers in Turkey have in the past worked for a long time in music restaurants in Germany, for example Mahsun Kırmızıgül and Özcan Deniz in Berlin, or Ceylan in Munich.

Over four decades Turkey has thus remained an important point of reference for Turks in Europe. All official Turkish holidays are also celebrated in Europe; all major banks and companies, all Turkish political, religious, social or economic organisations have some kind of representation in Europe. In the field of music, however, the Turkish state, remained almost inactive, with the exception of some cultural centres (*Türk Kültür Merkezi*, *Türk Evi*, recently *Yunus Emre Enstitüsü*) which are affiliated with the Turkish state.

The developing transnational connections changed the attitude of European Turks towards Turkey. The first generation tended to compare their daily lives in Europe with an idealised picture of Turkey they had left. Also in European-Turkish music life, this attitude prevailed until at least the 1990s: instruments, even strings, were not considered as good as when they have been bought directly in Turkey. Since the 1980s, however, the nostalgic longing for a lost home became increasingly obsolete. New developments in Turkey concerning ideological and political issues, as well as changes in the language immediately lead to similar developments within the European Turkish diaspora. Every innovation in Turkey, every political bent, new fashion, ideas or debates today appear in the Turkish European communities immediately. Similarly new musical styles, instruments or songs are instantly adopted in the diaspora.

During the 1980s, Arif Sağ and the *bağlama* group *Muhabbet* became popular in Turkey and impressed a whole generation of young *bağlama* players to prefer the short-necked *bağlama* over the traditional long necked variant; similarily in Europe this shorter *bağlama* soon displaced the long necked instrument. When musicians such as Arif Sağ, Erdal Erzincan and Erol Parlak developed the so called *şelpe* playing technique (without plectrum), young *bağlama* players in Europe competed over who would master it first in their country of residence. Since at least the 1980s a number of well-known folk singers and *bağlama* players were (or still are) based in Europe, for example, Güler Duman or Neşet Ertaş. Since the 1990s in many cities all over Europe, and in Germany in particular, private Turkish music schools primarily offer *bağlama* lessons, and many also regularly invited famous musicians from Turkey for workshops and master-classes.

Growing transnational connections are also obvious in the rise of classical Turkish music (*klasik türk müziği*) in Europe, again during the 1980s. Only in the mid- and late 1970s did the Turkish state lift its rejection of the Ottoman musical heritage, and began to support choirs and orchestras for classical Turkish music as well as to found conservatories. Soon after the foundation of the first state choirs in Turkey, the first private Turkish choirs in Germany also emerged. Subsequently, music graduates from Turkey came to Europe – most of them by marriage – and improved the general musical level of this musical tradition. Most members of these choirs, as well as of folk music choirs, were amateurs, who began to make music without substantial knowledge of Turkish music traditions. Some choirs are attached to associations, culture centres or consulates, others just meet privately. Similar to the private Turkish music schools, the growing musical life for Turkish art music in Europe attracted numerous musicians from Turkey, to travel for concerts, workshops or recordings to Europe.

Similarly, the rise of Kurdish and slightly later Zaza nationalism since the 1980s and 1990s developed almost in parallel in Turkey and Europe. For the development of Kurdish and Zaza culture and literature in particular, the influence of the European diaspora can hardly be overestimated. Many well-known Kurdish musicians live in Europe, such as Şivan Perwer, Nizamettin Arıç, Ciwan Haco, Naso Rezazi or Temo. The music of Dersim (today Tunceli), a province in eastern Anatolia inhabited mainly by Alevi Zaza, developed mainly as a diaspora culture (e.g. Mikail Aslan, Ahmet Aslan, Kemal Kahraman, Ferhat Tunç, Yılmaz Çelik) (Greve & Şahin 2017; Skalla 1999). In the 1980s most Kurdish and Zaza music cassettes were produced in Europe and secretly distributed in Turkey. In addition recordings were published by Unesco Edition and other international labels (Reigle 2013). Only after 1991, when the ban of Kurdish language in Turkey was lifted, did most Kurdish, Zaza and other non-Turkish music productions moved to Istanbul.

Comparably important was the influence of the European diaspora on the renaissance of Alevism and Alevi music in the 1990s. In almost all European cities Alevi associations became important centres for Anatolian folk music. Most European Alevi associations offer *bağlama* lessons, some also have folk music choirs or dance groups. For musicians and music managers Alevi centres and festivals offer networking opportunities. Since 1994 huge annual Alevi festivals in Europe, including concerts of numerous Alevi singers, remember the deaths in the massacre in Sivas. In 2000 the German Federation of Alevi Associations organised the "Saga of the Millennium" in Cologne (Director: Necati Şahin, musical conductor: Zafer Gündoğdu), a monumental event with 1246 *bağlama* players from all over Germany.[36] Two years later the concept was repeated for the first time in Turkey.

Transnational spaces affected not only religious or political discourses, but also musical styles, genres or singing and playing techniques. In the 1990s, a musical youth culture emerged in Turkey for the first time, connected with a new music

[36] Almanya Alevi Birlikleri Federasyonu 2000. On October 5, 2002 a similar concert was organized in Istanbul.

style (*pop müzik*) and supported by the still new private TV channels (Solmaz 1996). Again, the new culture was immediately transmitted to Europe, in the heart centres of large cities (hence away from the suburbs) new clubs opened (Çağlar 1998: 49). It was in this context that both Turkish and international record companies made their first serious attempts to facilitate the international marketing of popular Turkish music. For a number of Turkish pop stars of the 1990s, part of their public image was the fact that they grew up, or even still lived in western Europe (or North America); for example, Bendeniz in Switzerland, Ragga Oktay from the Netherlands, Tarkan and Rafet El Roman from Germany. Numerous Turkish pop groups from Germany similarly tried to succeed on the Turkish music market, ignoring the German audience.[37] From the mid-1990s several international labels tried to expose the European market to compilations of Turkish pop music.[38] At the same time Turkish labels tried to connect themselves with the international market. The main challenge to this cooperation, however, was the large gap between the respective price levels in Turkey and Europe. The most successful international singer was Tarkan in 1998, when his first international album was released containing songs which had already been released in Turkey earlier.[39] At the same time some European-Turkish musicians succeeded in the European pop business. In 2000 Mousse T. (Mustafa Gündoğdu), living in Hannover (Germany) wrote the international hit "Sex Bomb" for Tom Jones; and in 2003 Sertab Erener wan the "Eurovision Song Contest" with the song, "Everyway That I Can". The film "Crossing the Bridge," by Fatih Akın (Hamburg, Germany), was produced in 2005, directly after his prize-winning film, "Gegen die Wand" ("Head On") made Istanbul famous as a cutting edge centre for Rock and Hip-Hop.

The first Turkish popular music which emerged completely in Europe and was only later exported to Turkey, was Turkish rap. Alread in the 1980s hiphop became popular among European youngsters of migrant background (Elflein 1997). Many identified themselves with Afro-Americans in the US and perceived hiphop as an articulation of the identity of discriminated minorities. Even the first ever rap song with German lyrics ("*Ahmed Gündüz*") was published by a Turkish-German rap group, that is Flash Family (Verlan & Loh 2000: 134). Simultaneously in Germany the first Turkish rap songs were written. In 1991 in Nuremberg the rap group, "King Size Terror" released the album "*Bir Yabancının Hayatı*" ("The life of a for-

37 E.g. Hakan: *Naz Yapma* (Inter Müzik, 1998); Tamer: *Renkler* (Raks, 1998); Elgin: *Elgin* (Raks, 1998); *Kimbunlar: Dağlar Kızı Reyhan / Atabari* (Prestij, 1999); *Grup Yade* (Berlin): *Işte Yade Geldi* (Prestij, 1999).

38 Şıkıdım. The Best of Turkish Pop (Universal, 1999); Şıkıdım 2 (Universal, 2002); Pop Turkish. Les Plus Grands Artistes Turc de la Pop Orientale (Atoll/EMI, 1999); Bodrum nights. The Finest of Turkish Pop (BMG, 1999); Turkish Suprême (PolyGram, 1999); Süper. The Best of Turkish Dance and Pop Music (BMG, 1994).

39 Tarkan: *Tarkan* (Istanbul/Polygram, 1998). In Belgium, Norway, Portugal and the Czech Republic the single topped the charts, in the Netherlands and France receiving no.3, in Switzerland No 5, in Russia Tarkan became the most-sold foreign musician.

eigner")(Elflein 1997: 289). Four years later, in 1995, the group Cartel (Nürnberg, Kiel, Berlin) achieved anunexpected succes in Turkey.[40] The hype around "Oriental Hiphop" lasted only for a short time in both Germany and Turkey. The next generation of German-Turkish rappers (such as Kool Savaş) became mainstream in Germany, but with English or German lyrics.[41]

Turkish Music as European Music

The serious integration of Turkish artists into mainstream European media and public cultural institutions began in the early 2000s, with Turkish actors, speakers and commedians in private German (and other) TV channels. Today, Turkish actors feature in most German daily soaps, reality and casting shows. In 1999 the Turkish-German group "*Sürpriz*" represented Germany at the "Eurovision Song Contest," and at the millenium party the Turkish-Swiss singer Erkan Akı sang at the Brandenburg Gate in Berlin. In other arts Turkish artists have also integrated. In literature for example, writers of Turkish origin writing in German, such as Emine Sevgi Özdamar, Feridun Zaimoğlu and Yadé Kara have won some of the most prestigious awards for German literature. In 2004 Fatih Akıns film "*Gegen die Wand*" (Head on) was awarded the Golden Bear at the Berlin International Film Festival (Yavus 2014).

The integration of non-commercial Turkish musicians into Europe's cultural life, however, has progressed more slowly and haltingly. The success differs widely, less between European countries but rather between musical styles. Western oriented musicians, composers, singers, instrumentalists and conductors do not usually encounter difficulties integrating into European orchestras, music academies or music schools. Betin Güneş, for example, was born in 1957 in Istanbul, and studied piano and composition at MSÜ in Istanbul with Ilhan Usmanbaş and others. In 1980 he moved to Cologne as a Fellow of the German DAAD to continue his studies of composition (with Joachim Blume and Günther Fork), conducting and trombone. His "Symphonie Orchestra Köln," founded in 1983, regularly performs contemporary music of Turkish composers (Greve 2003: 325). Other Turkish composers based in Europe include Zeynep Gedizlioglu (Berlin) or Meliha Doğuduyal (Amsterdam).

For musicians of Anatolian folk music or Ottoman-Turkish art music, however, the situation was completely different. Their music was predominantly per-

---

40 *Cartel* (Spyce/Mercury, 1995).

41 Hip-Hop shows in an exemplary way the change of identity discourses among youngsters with a migration background who were (and still are) turning away from any formal national identity in favour of a European or global identity. See Greve & Kaya 2004; Greve 2003; Verlan & Loh, 2000:134; Elflein, 1997. Orthodox Islamic identity discourses also have an impact on music products, such as for instance the genre of the so-called Green Pop, with Yusuf Sami (London) or HipHop groups like Sert Müslümanlar (Hard Muslims; Frankfurt a.M.) (Solomon 2006).

ceived in Europe as a social issue, rather than artistic, and over decades traditional Turkish music was excluded from state education and concert halls.

The growing fear of Islamic terror following the September 11, 2001 attacks on the World Trade Center in New York, changed the attitude of many Europeans. This fear prompted a growing awareness of the lack of knowledge about Muslim minorities, their daily lives and ultimately also about their music. In 2005 UNESCO issued the "Convention on the Protection and Promotion of the Diversity of Cultural Expression" as a binding international legal instrument, followed in 2006 by the "*2. Berliner Apell*" of the German Music Council entitled "Those who don't know their own will not be able to recognize the other" ("*Wer das je Eigene nicht kennt, kann das je Andere nicht erkennen*"). In Europe musical diversity became an important issue for articles in newspapers, journals and books.[42]

In the following years public institutions in both Germany and the Netherlands made noticeable efforts to incorporate Turkish music (Greve 2007). The basic idea in most cases was to begin with the largest group of immigrants, that is with Turks, and to proceed with other minorities later. First attempts were on the level of single institutions, initiated mostly by individual protagonists. Only in 2014, with the conference, "Transfer and Diversity. Music and Transcultural Practice: Turkey-Germany" held in Berlin and Istanbul, was there a first attempt to conceptualize and evaluate the experience made in the Turkish-German musical exchange.[43]

A first milestone for concerts with Turkish music in established European concert halls, was Arif Sağ's Concert in the Berlin *Philharmonie* concert hall in 1995, followed only one year later by another concert at the same venue with Arif Sağ, Erdal Erzincan and Erol Parlak. Since about 2000 European concert promoters have increasingly tried to attract Turkish and non-Turkish audiences to Turkish music. The Amsterdam-based agency *Kulsan* for example, organised ambitious Turkish concerts in many important concert halls in Holland for almost 30 years. Today their office is situated in the prestigious *Muziekgebouw aan 't Ij* in Amsterdam. In Germany more and more festivals with Turkish music take place with official financial support, including – as one of the first – "Berlin-Turkey without borders. Cultural encounters with Turkey" ("Berlin Türkei. Grenzenlos. Kulturelle Begegnungen mit der Türkei") in 1998. In 2004 the London management company, Harrison & Parrot in cooperation with the Istanbul Culture and Art Foundation organised the festival "Şimdi Now" in Berlin. Directly preceding the decision of the EU concerning Turkey's official candidacy for the EU, the event was

42 Bachir-Loopuyt 2013: 339ff. Congress of the German Music Council 2005: *Musikland Deutschland. Wieviel kulturelle Vielfalt wollen wir?* ("German Music Country. How much cultural diversity do we want?").

43 Organized in the framework of the "German-Turkish Year of Science 2014, in cooperation with Humbold University Berlin, Landesmusikrat Berlin, Center for Advanced Studies in Music (MIAM) of the ITÜ Istanbul, Orient-Institut Istanbul and others.

almost an application to join Europe. In 2005 a similar festival, "*Şimdi* Stuttgart" took place in Southern Germany, in 2009 in Vienna, and since 2006 is hosted regularly as "Turkey Now" in Amsterdam and Rotterdam. Other festivals with Turkish culture took place in 2001 in Munich, 2003 at the Kemnade (near Bochum), 2004 in Karlsruhe and 2005 in Bochum (Hoffmann 2007). During Autumn and Winter 2015/2016 an encompassing "Turkish Arts Festival" was organized all over Belgium by the *Europalia* festival management.

In 2007 Berlin witnessed almost simultaneously the beginning of two concert series including Turkish music: "Alla Turca – a Cultural Dialogue" (*Alla Turca – Ein Kultureller Dialog*) in the *Philharmonie* Berlin, and "Sound Cultures/Sound of Cultures" (*Klang Kulturen / Kültürler Sesi*) by the "*Rundfunk-Sinfonieorchester Berlin*" in cooperation with the private "Conservatory for Turkish Music Berlin." In 2010 the "*Komische Oper*" opera house in Berlin started a program called "Selam Opera!" to attract Turkish audiences (Komische Oper Berlin 2014; Yavuz 2014). In particular the state of North Rhine-Westphalia tried to integrate Turkish music into public institutions, especially in the run-up to the "European Cultural Capital Essen 2010." In this context, among others, the festival "*Melez – Festival der Kulturen*" (Festival of Cultures) took place. Essen and the Ruhrgebiet area explicitly emphasized its national and ethnic diversity in its application. During recent years the number of Turkish music and cultural festivals in Europe has grown further, and Turkish musicians regularly perform their music in all the main European concert halls (Greve 2008).

As early as the 1970s discussions began in several European cities on the integration of Turkish and other migrant children into the regular school system, and as part of this also on an appropriate music education for schools. Today a vast literature exists on cross-cultural music education. While in the 1970s Turkish music was perceived as "foreign" music, the distance decreased over the years. Teachers learnt about Turkish music in special education programs and books, audio cassettes and records were published as teaching materials (Merkt 1993: 145; Fohrbeck 1983).

In Germany and the Netherlands the first efforts to integrate the education of Turkish music were made by municipal music schools. In numerous music schools in Germany and the Netherlands, today, Turkish music has become a well-established part of the regular teaching program,[44] while in smaller towns, the topic of intercultural integration is still a distant vision, often linked with fears and stereotypes. In 2000, the popular nationwide German music competition "*Jugend Musiziert*" (Youth Makes Music) started in Berlin with an annual competition for *bağlama* at regional level, and the federal state of Nordrhein-Westfalen followed four years later. In 2015 a nationwide *bağlama* competition took place in

44 At the *École Nationale de Musique de Villeurbanne* (Lyon), Marc Loopuyt offered a program for the short-necked lute *ud* combining Turkish and Arabic art musics.

Germany for the first time. From 2005 until 2010, North Rhine-Westphalia supported *bağlama* courses at municipal music schools in the framework of the project, "*Bağlama* for Everyone" (*Bağlama Für Alle/ Herkese Bağlama*) (Fließ 2008: 34). Within the frameworks of this project, *bağlama* courses have been financially supported by the state at municipal music schools since 2005. The project "Every Child an Instrument" (*Jedem Kind ein Instrument, JeKi*) supported elementary schools in North Rhine Westphalia to offer instrumental lessons, including those for *bağlama*. *JeKi* also initiated the development of an official curriculum for *bağlama* lessons at municipal music schools. Written in German on the basis of existing curricula for guitar and other instruments, the curriculum was adapted for *bağlama* by a group of regional *bağlama* teachers and didactic experts from *JeKi*, after regular discussion meetings over one year in 2009/2010.[45] Later also a teaching book for *bağlama* was edited again in German (Yıldırım 2013). Meanwhile an introductory book on the *bağlama* in Dutch and a couple of *bağlama* teaching books are available in English or German.[46]

Until recently only European music academies remained as institutions which completely blocked the integration of traditional Turkish music (Neuhoff 2017). The earliest music academy which eventually opened up to Turkish and other non-Western instruments was the "World Music Academy," part of the conservatory in Rotterdam (today: *Codarts*) (Vervelde & Greve 2008). In 2000, for the first time outside of Turkey, a regular study program of Turkish music began. Initially, Talip Özkan (Paris) served as Musical Director, the basic courses of the program were held by lecturers from Rotterdam, in particular by Nahim Avcı. After internal difficulties, the program restarted in 2006 with Kemal Dinç (Cologne), Alper Kekeç (Amsterdam) and later Kudsi Erguner (Paris). Codarts still offers both Bachelor and Masters level programs for Turkish folk and art music with *bağlama*, voice and percussion as main subjects, as well as for Ottoman-Turkish art music. Students are mostly Turks who have grown up in the Netherlands and Germany and who are interested in an accredited Bachelor degree in their country of residence. In its first years students from Turkey also enrolled, but later changes in the regulation of university fees for non-European citizens blocked this group. In addition a number of Greek students enrolled.

During recent years some European music academies have begun to include at least a few lessons on Turkish music, including SOAS London and the Sibelius

---

45 Organized by *Jeki, NRW Kultursekretariat* and *Landesverband der Musikschulen NRW* (Verband deutscher Musikschulen 2012). For two meetings guests from Turkey were invited, musicologist Melih Duygulu, and Erol Parlak.

46 De Zeeuw2009; Erzincan & Sağ 2013; Parlak 2011; Yusuf Caner: *Benim Bağlama / Meine Bağlama*, Duisburg Verlag Hubertus Nogatz 2009; Özgür Ersoy: *Lehrbuch für Bağlama*, Berlin: Ries & Erler 2013; Kenan Tülek: *Şelpe Lehrbuch* (in preparation); Kemal Dinc: *Kelebek in Konzert. Rhythmische Übungen für die Musikpraxis mit Kindern.* Already in the 1980s some method books for *Bağlama* were published in Germany, most remained widely unknown though, e.g. by Attila Yakut in 1987; Sabri Uysal (1989), Sadık Ziypak (c. mid 1990s).

Academy Helsinki. Regular workshops on *ney* have been given by Kudsi Erguner and his former student Giovanni de Zorzi, at the Ethnomusicology department of the Conservatory "*Cesare Pollini*" of Padua (Italy) since 2002; since 2005 similar lecture workshops are held at the Institute for Intercultural Music Studies (IISMS) in Venice; and since 2008 at the Conservatory "*Arrigo Pedrollo*" of Vicenza, partly also in Palermo (de Zorzi 2008). In Germany only after 2010 did a few universities and music academies accept the importance of such programs to improve intercultural skills. At the Berlin University of the Arts (*Universität der Künste*, UdK) regular courses on Turkish music have been held since 2000 by the private music school "Conservatory for Turkish Music" (*Konservatorium für Türkische Musik Berlin*) of the late Nuri Karademirli.[47] In 2013, the UdK officially accepted *bağlama* as a main subject instrument for music teachers' education. In 2014 Erdal Erzincan held a first summer school master class at UdK Berlin, which has since continued annually with various teachers. Some other German music academies (including Cologne, Wuppertal, Hannover, Hildesheim and Rostock) also plan to open up to a broader cultural spectrum, some of them including Turkish music. In 2015 the music academy Cologne, in cooperation with the *Landesmusikakademie NRW* offered a certificate program for *bağlama* teachers. In the same year the Mannheim Pop Academy in cooperation with the private music school "*Orientalische Musikakademie Mannheim,*" offered Bachelor programs for *bağlama*, *ud* and "oriental percussion". Finally Turkish music has been discussed in several international conferences in Europe since 2007, including in Vienna, Berlin, Heek (Germany), and Ghent (Belgium).[48] In 2013 the Berlin Music Council selected the *bağlama* as the "instrument of the year" and organized numerous workshops, concerts and two conferences, and commissioned a composition for *bağlama* and orchestra by Sinem Altan.

Old Neighbors

Having seen the impact of migration (in particular to Europe) on Turkish music we will now continue with the much older international relations between Turkey (or the Ottoman Empire) and its neighboring countries. Over the last decades, and in particular since the 1990s, joint musical projects involving musicians from Turkey and its neighboring countries have substantially increased. This includes both neighbors with an existing, historical relationship (e.g. Iran)

---

47 In return the UdK gave lessons on Western music theory at the Music Academy for Turkish Music.

48 Hemetek & Sağlam 2008; DVD *Baglama: Ersten Bağlama-Symposium in Deutschland / Manufacturing of a Bağlama with Carvel-Built Body*, Ethnologisches Museum Berlin. Staatliche Museen zu Berlin 2014. Çiftçi & Greve 2017; November 7, 2014 congress *Die Bağlama im Kontext von Pädagogik, Musikschule, Jugend musiziert und Konzertwesen* ("The Bağlama in the Context of Pedagogy, Musik Schools, Jugend Musiziert (Competitions) and Concert Business", Heek, Germany.

and those which were in the past part of the Ottoman Empire (e.g. Greece or Bulgaria). It even also includes countries, such as Armenia and Israel, which were founded by former Ottoman minorities. Though the history of political and cultural relations between these countries and Turkey differs widely, in general the collapse of the Ottoman Empire (along with the Russian and the Habsburg Empires) in the First World War, led to heightened nationalization and the foundation of nation states in former parts of the Empire (as well as in its neighboring countries). In the early twentieth century this growing nationalism prevented deeper cultural exchanges with the (similarly nationalistic) Republic of Turkey. Over decades most of these new nation states denied the common traits of their musical traditions with Ottoman traditions.

> With few exceptions, Balkan narratives of national memory interpret the multi-ethnic Ottoman past anachronistically as a struggle between the repressive Turkish culture and the suppressed national cultures of the non-Turks or non-Muslims. (Pennanen 2008: 128)

The rich Ottoman musical heritage was rather perceived as particular national culture, which entailed a corresponding negation of its impact on the Balkans and in the Levant,

> [i]n the Balkans, that culture had many branches; a large part of the music café repertoire in Greece before the Second World War consisted of Ottoman popular pieces and new compositions in that style. Other Ottoman-influenced traditions are Greek *rebetika*, Macedonian *čalgiska muzika*, Bosnian *sevdalinke*, the older strata of *gradski* pesni or *starogradske pesme* (old town songs) of Bulgaria, Macedonia and Serbia, and the corresponding styles of Albania, Kosovo and Walachia. (Pennanen 2008: 129; cf. Samson 2013)

Similarly,

> the Greekness of indigenous cultural practices that drew significantly upon Eastern traditions – such as Greek shadow theatre, the *café-aman* and later on the *rempétiko* – has been called into question throughout the twentieth century. (Kallimopoulou 2009: 16)

In contrast in Turkey, musicians from the Balkans for instance, remained important in popular music such as in the entertainment scene of Beyoğlu.

Both the collapse of Eastern European socialism and more recent changes in Turkish foreign policy opened the way for a new mutual interest and openness.

> Against the background of the 'new order of things' occasioned after the 1989 events in the Balkans, the question of legacy – the influence a previous political and cultural arrangement has on its successors – comes to center roughly around two poles: the currency of the socialist and the Ottoman past. (Pennanen, Poulos & Theodosiou 2013: vii)

While the so-called Neo-Ottomanism, which operated on a political level (connected in particular with the then foreign minister Ahmet Davutoğlu) aroused suspicion, at the same time all over the Balkans a great number of Turkish TV series were aired, indicating a parallel and growing interest in cultural heritage (for example, *Magnificent Century*). In 2010, the Turkish government established a "Presidency for Turks Abroad and related Communities", attached to the prime ministry.

For practical reasons I will devide the countries to be discussed here into three parts, that is Muslim countries, reaching from Central Asia over Iran to the Arabic world; than Greece as a particular and important case; and finally Israel and Armenia, where in addition to the contemporary countries large international diaspora communities have to be taken into acount.

Muslim Neighbors

Iran and Central Asia have a particularly strong historical connection with early Ottoman music and the origin of Anatolian folk music is often assumed to be in Central Asia.[49] Musician-researchers such as Mahmut Ragıb Gazimihal, later Rahmi Oruç Güvenç and Erol Parlak searched for Central Asian instruments comparable to those in Anatolia. Recently the *Mahoor* Institute of Culture and Art in Tehran released several CDs focusing on the common Persian-Ottoman musical heritage. For example the CD "*Ajamlar. An Anthology of Pieces by Persian Composers and their Contemporaries at the Ottoman Court from the sixteenth and seventeenth Century*," compiled and arranged by Ârash Mohâfez (2013), included composition as preserved in the collections of Cantemir and Ali Ufukî, ascribed to Persian composers.

More recent musical collaboration with Iranian musicians, however, is rare and only a few musicians try to bridge Iranian and Turkish music. Today the internationally most well-known Iranian musician is the *kamanche* player, Kayhan Kalhor, born in1963 in Tehran of Kurdish origin.[50] In 1982, at the age of 18 he spent 6 months in a hotel in Istanbul, before he embarked to Italy and the United States. Since 2002 he has been based in Tehran again. His first album was released by the American Label, "Traditional Crossroads." With the help of the young musician Ulaş Özdemir (b. 1976, Kahramanmaraş), who had done fieldwork in Maraş and among *Ahl-Haqq* in Iran,[51] Kayhor encountered the famous *bağlama* player Erdal Erzincan. Their meeting led to numerous joint concerts, two CDs and one DVD with "*improvisations based on Persian and Turkish music.*"[52] Ulaş Özdemir also participated in some of their concerts, in addition to pro-

49 In Turkey often it is ignored that for example, Celaleddin Rumi (Mevlana) was born in Balkh (today Afghanistan) and that all of his poems are in the Persian language rather than in Turkish.

50 Kalhor for example has cooperated with the Kronos Quartet and Yo-Yo Ma's Silk Road Project; Yedig 2007.

51 Özdemir studied Political Sciences and was awarded his master and Ph.D. degrees in Ethnomusicology at Yildiz Technical University Istanbul. His Ph.D. thesis addresses alevi *zakir* musicians in Istanbul. Over the years he has worked at *Kalan* music. He published the book *Su diyar-i gurbet elde* on Aşık Mücrimî in 2007; CD *Bu Dem / This Breath*, Kalan, 2008; CD Ulas Özdemir: *Ummanda. Maras Sinemilli Deyisleri*, Kalan 1998. Together with the ensemble Forabandit he has released two albums (www.ulasozdemir.com).

52 Linear notes to the CD, Erdal Erzincan & Hayhan Kalhor, *The Wind*, ECM 2006; DVD Erdal Erzincan & Kayhan Kalhor: *Life in Tehran*, Kalan 2012.

grams with other Iranian musicians, including Ali Akbar Moradi, Sussan Deyhim, Mamak Khadem and the Montreal based Iranian group *Niyaz*.[53] In Istanbul the Azeri-Iranian singer Cavit Mürtezaoğlu, born in Tebriz and raised in Baku, became popular in the early 2000s, within the scene of *Kardeş Türküler* for his singing technique workshops. Later Mürtezaoğlu, together with the singer Feryal Öney and other musicians from *Kardeş Türküler* developed the project, "From Tabriz to Taurus / *Tebriz'den Toros'a*."[54] Siavash Shahani (b. 1972), another Iranian musician, released a CD together with well-known Turkish musicians, including Göksel Bakdagir, Eyyüp Hamiş and Muammer Ketençoğlu.[55]

Other Iranian musicians involved in Turkish music are the two brothers Kiya Tabassian (*setar*, voice) and Ziya Tabassian (percussion). Based in Canada, they are members of the Ensemble *Constantinople*, together with Pierre-Yves Martel (viola da gamba), Didem Basar (*kanun*) and others. The ensemble plays European Renaissance and Mediterranean music. Both are also members of Kyriakos Kalaitzidis' ensemble *En Chordais*, and both have taken part in several projects involving Turkish music, e.g. *Çeke çeke* – Goute à goutte (2010): Love songs from Anatolia and Persia, with Özlem Özdil and Sinan Celik.[56]

In contemporary Istanbul several Iranian musicians offer lectures on Iranian music, for example the *Hunya Bahar Müzik Kampi* (2015); or the *Khonya* Persian Music Camp Summer 2015 (*setar*, *tar*, *shoorangiz*) in Sazköy, Düzce, about 230 km from Istanbul, with Hossein Vali.

Several Arabic countries, which today are independent states, were once part of the Ottoman Empire, including Syria, Lebanon, Iraq, Jordan, the Arabic Peninsular and wide parts of North Africa. Arab minorities, on the other hand, are still living in Turkey, mainly in the regions of Adana, Antakya, Şanlıurfa, Mardin and Siirt. Ottoman genres such as *peşrev*, *saz semaisi* and *taksim* are still performed in particular in Egypt and other North African countries (Feldman 1990/1991). Unfortunately, interactions and mutual influences between music in the Ottoman Empire and in the Arabic provinces have hardly been researched (Maraqa 2015). We know for instance about *Mevlevi* lodges in the Balkans, in Syria, Iraq, Egypt or Medina, but almost nothing about their music. In the nineteenth century several important musicians from Istanbul travelled in particular to Egypt, e.g. Zekai Dede (1824-1897), Aziz Dede (1835-1905), Ahmed Celalleddin Dede (1835-?) and Giriftzen Asim Bey (1852–1929). Even the folk singer Âşık Dertli spent ten years in Cairo before he came back to Istanbul (Çiftçi 2011). In 1908 Neyzen Tevfik (1879–1953)

---

53 Later the kaval and fretless guitar player Sinan Cem Eroğlu became member of *Niyaz*. Ali Akbar Moradi & Ulas Özdemir: *The Companion*, Hermes Records 2007.

54 CD *From Tabriz to Taurus / Tebriz'den Toros'a*, Cavit Mürtezaoglu & Feryal Öney, Kalan 2012.

55 CD *Derya*, Kalan 2014.

56 CD *La Sublime Porte / The Sublime Port*, 2009 mit Mercan Dede, Mısırlı Ahmet, Kyriakos Kalaitzidiz.

escaped to Egypt for political reasons and only returned in 1913. In is uncertain how Mısırlı Ibrahim Efendi acquired his nickname *Mısırlı* "from Egypt" – he had spent time in Egypt before 1923, and gave concerts in Egypt later in the 1930s (Jackson 2013:187, fn 67). In 1932, Rauf Yekta and Mesut Cemil Tel traveled to the famous congress on Arabic music in Cairo (Özyıldırım 2013:19-27).

During the early Republic, several Turkish musicians went to Arabic countries to build up education programs or simply for concerts. Violinist Haydar Tatlıyay (1890–1963) spent seven years in Aleppo and Egypt, Serif Muhiddin Targan (born 1892 as son of the last Ottoman Emir in Mecca, d. 1967) helped to found the Baghdad Conservatory in 1934, and stayed until 1948. Mesut Cemil Tel (1902-1963) worked at the same institution from 1955-1959, also the violinist Cevdet Çağla (b. 1902), Necdet Varol, and the *kemençe* player Cüneyd Orhon, who, in 1961 came at least for a few months (Aksoy 2009: 121). Refik (1893–1964) and Fahire Fersan (1900-1997) were founding members of the Conservatory of Damascus in 1948 (Bardakçı 1995: 47ff; Özyıldırım 2013:96ff) and Ruşen Ferid Kam (1902-1981) was active in the reconstruction of the Cairo Conservatory in 1967. In addition a number of musicians regulary traveled to Egypt (and other arab countries) for concerts (Özyıldırım 2013). On Turkish musical activities in Lebanon I unfortunately do not have any information.

During the 1930s and 1940s Egyptian music films became popular in Turkey (Özyıldırım 2013: 137ff), from 1938 on with Turkish songs, performed by singers such as Münir Nurettin Selcuk or Sadettin Kaynak. Kaynak's *fantezi* style is said to have been inspired by early recordings of *muwashshahat* and *adwar* in Egypt.[57] Both, Egyptian film music and *fantezi* later became main sources for Turkish *arabesk* music (Stokes 1992; Özyıldırım 2013:213ff).

In recent times, however, there are few examples of joint Turkish-Arab musical productions,[58] with the few exceptions facilitated by French-Arabic relations. The French *kanun* player Julien Jâlal Eddine Weiss founded his "Al-Kindî Ensemble" in 1983 in Aleppo, and he later moved to Istanbul to play with important Turkish musicians. Kudis Erguner – based in Paris – also performed together with Arabic musicians.[59] The folk music group, *Kardeş Türküler*, with their focus on the numerous Anatolian languages and religions also performed Arabic songs.

---

57 Stokes 1992; Racy 1977; For the early Arab recording industry see the podcasts, recordings and transcriptions available on the AMAR Foundation's website (www.amar-foundation.org/podcasting/). O'Connell 2017.

58 For example a concert on December 5, 2011 in Doha, Qatar entitled "Magic Lutes," including the Qatar Philharmonic Orchestra, Erdem Şimşek (*bağlama*), Mısırlı Ahmet (percussion), Nevcihan Özel (*tar*), Teodosii Spasow (*kaval*) and Debanjan Bhattacharjee (*sarod*). In 2012 a concert at the Cemal Reşit Rey concert hall presented „Sufi hymns from Andalusia to Istanbul" performend by Ender Doğan and Rachid Gholam.

59 Another concert took playce on October 25, 2011 at the Cemal Reşit Rey Concert hall, Istanbul entitled *Şark Bülbülleri* ("Nightingales of the East") including the singers Ghada Shbeir (Beyrouth) and Meliha Gülses.

Political and cultural relations between Turkey and Azerbaijan only became tense after the collapse of the Soviet Union, and Azerbaijan's subsequent independence in 1991. Both Azerbaijan and Ottoman music historians perceive Abdülkadir Marâghî (d. 1435) as their main ancestor, and we know of several Azerbaijan musicians at the Ottoman court (Inalcık 2010: 47ff; Agayeva 2006). Contemporary Azerbaijan art music, however, is nearer to Iranian than to Ottoman music, both in performance style and musical structure. The main instruments are frame drum (*def*), long-necked lute (*tar*), bowed fiddle (*kemenche*), all similarly in use in Iran, Armenia and East Anatolia (Djani-Zade 1998). After the Second World War the Azerbaijani singer Resid Behbudov became famous, giving celebrated concerts in Iran, Turkey, India and even in South America.

Folk music of North Eastern Anatolia shares many common traits with Azerbaijan folk music. The Turkish city Kars is situated near to the Armenian and Iranian borders, and many Azerbaijanis live in the province (as well as Kurds and Caucasians). In the nineteenth century Kars was besieged three times by Russian troops (1828, 1855 and 1877). The Russian occupation of 1878-1918 in particular, caused migrations both from the region westward and from the east to Kars. "*Because of geographical proximity the ashiks in the northeast, especially those in the province of Kars were always in close contact with the aşıks of Azerbaijan. When the province of Kars became a part of the Russian territory (1878-1981) it was especially easy for the aşıks in Kars to travel to Azerbaijan and exchange ideas with aşıks there.*" (Erdener 1995: 32) The most important of them was Aşık Şenlik (mid-nineteenth century – c. 1912) who traveled to Baku, Tblisi and Yerevan in order to meet other *aşık*s (Artun 2009: 334; Erdener 1995: 32). As a result the Azerbaijan tradition of duet songs also spread in Kars and Erzurum.[60] "*Today, the historical connection of* aşıks *in northeastern Turkey with Azerbaijan ashiqs and Azerbaijan culture still continues.*"[61] Similarly close relations exist between Kars and Iğdır, and Azerbaijan-Nakhchivan (Salomoni 2014: 149). Today Baku has its Jazz and nightclub scene and since 2005 even an international Jazz festival.

The migration from Azerbaijan to Turkey had already begun in the late nineteenth century, but today the numbers of migrants are still low (Ünver 2015). Nevertheless a number of Azerbaijani musicians – mainly western musicians – left the country. In many Turkish conservatorys Azerbaijani teachers found better economic conditions than in their home country. Teachers at the Bilkent Conservatory (Ankara) include Elhan Bakihanov, Naile Mehdiyeva, and Server Ganiyev. Similarly in many other Anatolian cities, for example in Erzurum you find Rauf

60 Finally in 1966 also to Konya; Erdener 1995: 30ff; Reinhard & Pinto 1989.

61 Erdener 1995; In particular in the east of Azerbaijan aşıks are accompanied by long-necked lutes (*saz*) but also with double reed instruments, *balaban*. Meanwhile the tradition is even mixed with the art music (*mugan*), though the vocal techniques do differ. From the 1930s onwards, Soviet propaganda declared *ashiqs* as proletarian, and *mugam* as bourgeois. Just as in other Soviet republics, also in Azerbaijan great orchestras of folk instruments emerged, which performed songs of the *asiq* or praises of Lenin or Stalin.

Kerimov, Cavid Asadov and Ayna Isababayeva (since 1999); in Eskişehir Prof. Dr. Zohrab Adigüzelzade (d. 2012); in Kayseri Afak Caferova (since 2000).[62] Applications to Turkish institutions are facilitated by the almost common language and the high standard of Azerbaijan education, in particular in Western music.

Frangiz Alizadeh (b. 1947, Baku) for example, studied piano and composition in Baku until 1972. In 1989 she was awarded her PhD and shortly after, began to teach contemporary music and orchestration. From 1993 to 1996 she directed the choir at the Opera of Mersin (Turkey) and subsequently became Professor for piano and music theory at the conservatory Mersin. At the end of 1998, Frangis Alizade returned to Baku and one year later she became composer-in-residence at the *Internationale Musikfestwochen Luzern* (Switzerland). Eventually, in 1998, she left for Germany, initially equipped with a DAAD fellowship, later living there as freelance composer.

Ilyas Mirzayev (b. 1961) is the son of the well-known Azerbaijan composer Musa Mirzayev. He studied composition in Baku and Moskau (with Cevdet Haciyev, Edison Denisov and Alfred Schnittke). In 1992 he moved to Istanbul, where he now lives (Arna 2006). His jazz compositions combine classical, traditional and pop elements. His symphony entitled "Sufi" was written in cooperation with the Turkish *ney* player, Ercan Irmak, as was the concert for *ney* in 2002.[63]

Among internationally active traditional musicians the *mugam* singer, Alim Qasimov (b. 1957) must be included. Since the 1990s Qasimov has traveled for festivals and concerts to Europe and the United States, and his albums have gained top positions in world music charts. Qasimov has cooperated with musicians from Mongolia and Mali, with Yo-Yo Ma and eventually with the Kronos Qartett.[64] In Turkey he has given concerts together with Derya Türkan and Erkan Oğur.

In Turkey the most successful Azerbaijan pop musician is probably Sami Yusuf. He was born in 1980 in Teheran, where his grandparents had fled from Baku in fear of the Red Army. Yusuf now lives in London. His religious pop songs in English, Arabic, Persian, Azerbaijan and Turkish are popular all over the Islamic world, including in Turkey.

Greece

Probably most intense, but also most sensitive are the relations between Turkey and Greece. Due to the long history of close contacts beginning in Byzantine

---

62 I would like to thank Nejla Melike Atalay for this information.

63 Premiered by Tekfen Philharmonic Orchestra, conducted by Saim Akçıl at the International Music Festival Istanbul. Later it was performed in Ankara, Bursa, Izmir, Thesassaloniki, Baku, Cypris, Kasachstan, Kirgisistan and Uzbekistan.

64 The promotional biography of Alim Qasimov mentions a great number of other international cooperative projects.

times, the musical traditions of Turkey and Greece are deeply connected with each other. In his recent book Kyriakis Kalaitzidis filled a total of 4,200 pages with post-byzantine notations originating from between the fifteenth and early nineteenth centuries, containing songs from the Constantinople-Phanariot tradition (most well-known Petros Peloponnesios) and Ottoman art music.[65]

> The material, although appearing heterogeneous at first sight, must be seen in the context of the *psaltic* world's regard of Eastern music as being akin and familiar. According to their aesthetic and knowledge, the *psaltai* and scribes understood Eastern music as part of their Byzantine and post-Byzantine heritage. (Kalaitzidis 2012: 310)

In particular from the eighteenth century on, Greek musicians worked at the Ottoman court; its most important theorist, Dimitrie Cantemir (1673–1723), son of the voivode Constantin Cantemir was educated in Greek church music before he came to Istanbul. Already during the eighteenth and nineteenth centuries several Greek scholars compared Greek modes (*echo*) and Ottoman *makam*s – important books include *Euterpe* (1830) and *Pandora* (1843/46). A number of printed Greek music collections were edited in the Ottoman Empire. The few Ottoman *ud* makers of the late nineteenth and early twentieth century that we know about, were either Greeks such as Manol (Manolis Venios), or Armenian such as Onnik Karibyan (Bates 2011: 36). In Istanbul popular instruments such as lute (*lavta*) or *kemençe* were played mainly by Greeks, including the family Kyriazis, that is Lavtacı Andon (d. 1925), Lavtacı Civan (d. 1910) and Lavtacı Hristo (d. 1914) (Élias 2012: 23). Folk music on both sides of the Aegean Sea still exhibits basic similarities in terms of instruments, forms, dances (in particular the *zeybek / zeibekiko*) and songs.

As part of the population exchange that Turkey and Greece agreed upon in 1922 (involving about 1.2 million Rums (Ottoman Greeks) and more than 400,000 Turks),[66] many Greek as well as some Jewish and Armenian musicians left Constantinople / Istanbul or Smyrna / Izmir to Greece. These included Stella Chaskil, Roza Eskenazi and Marika Ninu, who dominated the Greek popular music scene for over a decade (Kallimopoulou 2009: 24). In Greece *rembetiko* emerged as a new music style similar to urban Ottoman music, from which a great number of historical recordings exists (Yiangou 2005). During the dictatorial rule of General Ioánnis Metaxás (1936-41), this music was censored and declined in the late 1930s. Until 1955, however, several musicians continued to travel from Greece to Turkey. For example in the 1930s and 1950s, the Armenian *ud* player Agápios Tompoúlis and Jewish singer Roza Eskenazi toured and recorded in Turkey (Pennanen 2004: 8; Kallimopoulou 2009: 25).

---

65 Erol 2015; Apostolopoulos & Kalaitzidis 2015; Kalaitzidis 2012; Bardakçı 1993; Brandel 1989.

66 Even before 1922, a large-scale migration began from the Ottoman Empire to Greece. Pennanen 2004: 6; Macar 2015; Dündar 2014; Andrews 1989: 142-147.

> Post-1922 history writing [in Greece], as it turned its interest to the Greek-Orthodox populations of the Ottoman Empire, adopted a rather nostalgic approach. (...) The phenomenon [of Greek voluntary societies in Constantinople and Asia Minor] was seen as describing the struggle of the unredeemed Greeks of Asia Minor, fighting against despotism and ignorance, and at the same time competing with the nationalism of other groups. (Erol 2009: 50)

Constantinople remained a symbol for the "*megali Idea*", the nationalistic vision to re-conquer Istanbul / Constantinople and form a Greek state encompassing all territories with Greek populations (or minorities). Izmir / Smyrna on the other hand became the symbol for its failure (Zelepos 2010).

In Turkey at that time Christians remained central in the entertainment sector in Istanbul.

> Until the middle of this [20th] century, the most well-known performers in the *piyasa* (market) were Armenians and Greeks. (...) Some of the Armenian *piyasa* musicians mentioned in the sources were Nubar Tekyay, Kemani Aleksan, Udi Serkis, Tatyos Efendi, Udi Afet, Garbis, Karekine, Lavtacı Ovrik, Udi Hırant, Hırant Lusikyan, Bimen Şen and Agyazar, and famous Greek musicians included the Bacanos brothers, Vasilaki, Nikolaki, Kemani Andon, Lavtacı Andon, and Kemençeci Anastas. (Beken 1998: 155)

The Wealth Tax of 1942, however, divided the citizens of Turkey between Muslims and non-Muslims – the latter had to pay higher taxes. In particular the pogroms against Greeks in Istanbul on September 6 and 7, 1955 led to the emigration of many Istanbul Greeks. The Cyprus crisis 1964-1965, and finally the Turkish occupation of North Cyprus in 1974 brought Turkish-Greek relations to a low-point. In Istanbul, Greek and Armenian musicians were replaced by gypsies from Adana or Izmir. Also in Greece the transmission of Ottoman-Greek music was increasingly abandoned (Kallimopoulou 2009: 8).

A revival of this Greek-Ottoman musical tradition began only in the 1970s – the following description is mainly based on the Ph.D. thesis of Eleni Kallimopoulou (2009).[67] After the end of military dictatorship in Greece (1967–1974) a debate on the nature of Greek identity, and, politically over the membership of the European Economic Community (EEC) arose –and eventually in 1981 Greece entered the EEC as full member. Part of this debate was the question of the possibility of incorporating the *Romioí* (pl of *Romiós*, i.e. Byzantine and Turkish Christians) and Byzantine into the dominant Western-oriented Greek identity.

In this context, during late 1970s Greece, a revival of *rembetiko* began, and 78rpm records of the 1920s were released, along with written song collections or autobiographies of *rempétes*.[68] Greek writers now began to suggest a more intimate link between "*Smyrnaic rempétiko*" and "Turkish music" (Kallimopoulou 2009: 27). Similarly *paradosiaká* (pl. from: "traditional") emerged, an urban musi-

---

[67] Cf. also Kalaitzidis 2005; Erol 2017.

[68] Kallimopoulou 2009; Greve 1995: 83-85; Dietrich 1987: 10ff; Holst 1979: 24ff.

cal style, which led to an importation and appropriation of a number of "Eastern" instruments.

> The novelty of the use of Eastern instruments such as *sázi* and the *oúti* (...) cannot be overstated. In the late 1970s and early 1980s even getting to know about such instruments was hard, let alone finding one. (Kallimopoulou 2009: 28)

The *paradosiaká* revival brought a number of these forgotten instruments, now labeled as "oriental" (*anatolítika*), "Byzantine" (*Vyzantiná*) or "Smyrnaic" (*Smyrnáika*) back to Greece, including *oúdi* (*ud*), *tampourás* (=*sázi*, saz), *kanonáki* (*kanun*), *L'yra polítiki* (*Lyra* of Istanbul), klasik *kemençe*, actually still played as Crete viole, (*kritiki lyra*), *néi (ney)*, *tampour* (*tanbur)*, and *laoúto polítiki* (*laoúto* of Istanbul, *lavta*).[69] In Greece a syncretic musical idiom emerged, which drew from a variety of folk and urban styles and repertoires of Greece and Turkey, and also incorporated new compositions, improvisation, and experimentation with the playing technique of the Eastern instruments (Kallimopoulou 2009: 85).

In this context Ross Daly (b. 1952) became the most influential musician of the revival (Kallimopoulou 2009: 58ff). Of Irish origin, Ross Daly began to learn *sitar* at an early age. During the 1970s, he traveled to India, Afghanistan and later to Istanbul (to learn from Ihsan Özgen). In 1975 he settled in the village of Houdetsi, 20 km south of Iraklion, the capital of Crete.[70] Daly plays an impressive number of instruments, including *tanbur*, *bendir*, *yaylı tanbur*, klasik *kemençe*, *ud*, *kudüm*, *lavta*, but also Greek *laoúto*, Crete *lyra*, Afghan *rabab*, Indian *tabla* and *sarangi*. From 1982 on, at the age of thirty, when *paradosiaká* was more or less in full swing, he began to organize the annual "Labyrinth Musical Workshop," which became one of the most important centers for modal music in Europe.[71] Over the years numerous Greek, Turkish, Azerbaijan, Arabic, Iranian, Indian and Afghan musicians gave lectures for international students, for example on *makam* (Derya Türkan, Sokratis Sinopoulos), Bulgarian singing technique (Tzvetanka Varimezova), Afghan *rabab* (Daud Khan Sadozai), *ney* (Ömer Erdoğdular), Iranian *tar* (Hamid Motebassem), *bağlama* (Erdal Erzincan), Irakian *maqam* (Anwar Abu Dragh), Greek clarinet (Alexandros Arkadopoulos) and others. In 2007 the Labyrinth Music Workshop already encompassed 27 seminars.[72]

Over the years several music ensembles emerged out of the workshops, uniting prominent musicians of different modal music traditions. For example, the "Labyrinth Modal Ensemble," which combined Greek and Turkish traditions;

---

69 Élias 2012: 57ff; Kallimopoulou 2009: 3.

70 Also Ross Daily's collection of more than 250 musical instruments of modal music traditions are stored there.

71 www.labyrinthmusic.gr

72 In 2012 for example, lectures included Erkan Ogur (fretless guitar and *kopuz*); Murat Aydemir (*tanbur* and *makam*); Derya Turkan and Socratis Sinopoulos (*kemençe*); Ömer Erdoğdular (*ney*); Ahmet Erdoğdular (Ottoman singing); Cihan Türkoğlu (*saz*); Yurdal Tokcan (*ud*), Göksel Baktagir (*kanun*).

later, *Seyir* with the Turkish *ud* player Yurdal Tokcan, *kanun* player Gökçen Baktagir, Ross Daly (lyra), Kelly Thoma (b. 1978, lyra) and the Israeli percussionist Zohar Fresco. Ross Daily himself made numerous records with both his own compositions and traditional arrangements, together with several international ensembles and musicians, including Jordi Savall, Eduardo Niebla, *Huun Huur Tu*, Habil Aliev, *Dhoad* Gypsies of Rajasthan, Mohammad Rahim Khushnawaz, Trio *Chemirani*, Adel Selameh and many others. In summer 2004 Ross Daily was Artistic Director for the cultural program of the Olympic Games for the Olympic city of Heraklion on the island of Crete, entitled "Crete, Music Crossroads." The concept of international music workshops in a village atmosphere was later adopted by others, for example in Vollos, a small village in Mount Villion; or another one in Agios Lavrentios since 2007.[73] Recently also in Turkey a music village was founded near to Fethiye (*Müzik Köy Fethiye*).

Parallel to the revival of music, musicological research facilitated increasing awareness of the Ottoman-Greek past and its music.

> In the 1990s, as a result of the turn in the theoretical orientation of Greek historians, the communities of Asia Minor began to be studied on the one hand with a focus on the question of identity, belonging etc. and on the other, through analyzing cultural representations and discursive formations. (Erol 2009: 50f)

Musicologist Simon Karás (1903-1999) studied ancient Greek, Byzantine and post-Byzantine music, and later he also conducted fieldwork in Greece on folk music. Karás propagated the idea of continuity from ancient Greece to the Byzantine period until today. Under this schema, even the music of Muslim populations followed Greek traditions (Kallimopoulou 2009: 35ff). From the 1980s onwards, a number of comparative treatises or/and musical compilations, written in the nineteenth and early twentieth centuries by *Romioí* chanters of Istanbul were reprinted in Greece. They treated comparatively ecclesiastical music and so-called *exoterikí mousikí* (secular Ottoman music), hence *echos* and *makam*. (Kallimopoulou 2009: 40) Other Greek scholars also emphasized a supposed Byzantine origin of instruments known in Turkey, including *tampourás* (*saz*), *tanbur*, or *kanun* (Kallimopoulou 2009 , 53ff). As far as I know the earliest reconstruction of the phanariot repertoire (still without reconstructing instruments or the use of Ottoman instruments) are the three CDs, “Pandora. Music of the Post-Byzantine High Society”, 1991–1993, directed by Christodoulos Halaris (who previously also reconstructed Byzantine secular music and even ancient Greece music).[74]

---

73 http://www.music-village.gr/en/music-village (accessed August 24, 2015). In summer 2012 lectures included *taxim* with Socratis Sinopoulos; Ottoman music and *yaylı tanbur* with Evgenios Voulgaris; Minor Asian song and dance, with Katerina Papadopoulou (song), Socratis Sinopoulos (Ensemble direction), and Christianna Katsarou (dance).

74 CD Christodoulos Halaris: *Pandora. Music of the Post-byzantine high Society*, Vol. II, Orata, Athens (n.y.)

Travel between Turkey and Greece was, however, still rare. In the 1980s Turkey was almost taboo for Greeks, though the political situation did improve slowly. Rare exceptions of direct musical contacts at that time were for example, the cooperation of the Greek composer Mikis Theodorakis and the Turkish singer Zülfü Livaneli (Kallimopoulou 2009: 114). At the same time (late 1970s and early 1980s), the violinist Senih Ündeğer came to Athens as one of the first Turkish musicians.[75]

It was the Bosphorus Ensemble directed by Ihsan Özgen which opened the door for closer musical cooperation between both countries. The ensemble was formed by Nikifóros Metaxás, who had been in Istanbul in 1984 to study the relationship between Greek and Turkish music; actually the group mainly performed in Greece rather than in Turkey (Kallimopoulou 2009: 120; Erol 2017). In 1987 Bosphorus produced its first LP entitled "*Romioí* Composers of the City [i.e. Istanbul]", recorded in Istanbul, but produced and published in Greece (Kallimopoulou 2009: 118f). One year later Metaxas organized the first concerts of Bosphorus in Athens, Thessaloniki and Heraklio, followed by further concerts in 1989 and 1990 in Athens, some of whom later were released as CDs.[76] The concerts each attracted two to three thousand visitors– much more than would have been possible in Turkey at that time (Kallimopoulou 2009: 9; Feldman 1989).

> Bosphorus caused a sensation among the people of Athens and Thessaloniki already involved in the revival and would, in the late 1980s, provide the final spur to a more direct exploration of Turkish culture. (Kallimopoulou 2009: 113)

Mihalis Holevas (*ney*, *yaylı tanbur* and *tarhu* player, teacher at Codarts, Rotterdam):

> I was in the concert in Athens. Ömer [Erdoğdular] was one of the musicians playing from the Turkish side, and many Greeks and Sokratis (Sinopoulos) were there. It was a very interesting event to see at that time. Bosporus was at that time a huge event for Greece. (Interview, December 14, 2011, Rotterdam)

These first live concerts were purely instrumental, to avoid difficulties caused by the different languages, while instrumental music was also preferred by the "world music" audience in general (see below). The performance was innovative, also by Turkish standards. Instruments included one *kemençe*, three *ney*, *ud*, *kanun*, two *tanbur*, cello, panflute, *bendir*/*davul*/*kudüm*, and three singers. During their concerts the ensemble also performed music by non-Greek composers, including composition by Ihsan Özgen on Alevi poems (Âşık Veysel, Pir Sultan Abdal), *zeybek*, popular tunes of Istanbul, and a Mevlevi *ayın*. Emphasis was pla-

---

75 Kallimopoulou 2009: 28. Accordung to Kyriakos Kalaitzidis (personal information), until the 1960s Turkish musician were occasionally invited to Thessaloniki.

76 CD Vosporus: Romioi Synthetes tis Polis, EMI 1998; CD Bosphorus in Athens, United Nations High Commissioner for Refugees, 1990; CD Osmanli Imparatorlugu'nda Müzik. Music in the Ottoman Empire. Live 31 May 1990 Herod Atticus.

ced on individual and group improvisation, as had been introduced by the trio of Niyazi Sayın, Necdet Yaşar and İhsan Özgen in the late 1970s – early 1980s (Poulos 2005: 139f).

Subsequently additional projects with Ottoman music took place in Greece. For example by Ross Daly in the early 1990s, with a program including the *mevlevi bayatı ayın* by Mustafa Dede (mid-seventeenth century), with mainly younger Greek musicians playing Ottoman instruments. Only recently, however, have Greek singers (especially from Thessaloniki) also gone to Turkey to study specifically Ottoman-Turkish vocal techniques (Kallimopoulou 2009: 10).

During the 1990s several young *paradosiaká* musicians became formidable professional performers (Kallimopoulou 2009: 147ff). The Thessaloniki based ensemble *En Chordais* became active internationally. *En Chordais* was founded in 1993 by the *ud* player Kyriakos Kalaitzidis (b. 1969, Thessaloniki) and specialized in Mediterranean and Byzantine music (regularly inviting leading Turkish guest musicians). Kyriakos Kalaitzides' family is of Pontos (today the Turkish Black Sea Coast) and Capadokia origin; he studied Byzantine music and musicology, and learned *ud*. Kalaitzides published a teaching method for *ud* (1996), wrote many of the extensive liner notes for their CDs[77] and became Artistic Director of the broad project of MediMuses, including research and study, re-composition and promotion of elements of the Mediterranean musical heritage.[78] Part of the project was the edited series, "Works of Great Mediterranean Composers", including among others, music of Kemânî Tatyos Efendi, edited by Vassilis Tzortzinis; Tanbûrî Cemil Bey (1871–1916), edited by Necip Gülses (2005) and Zakharia Khanendeh (eighteenth century), edited by Kyriakos Kalaitzides (2005). Furthermore, international meetings took place, including an International *Oud* Meeting in Thessaloniki (2002), International *Qanun* Meeting in Beirut (2003), International *Ney* Meeting in Istanbul (2003), International Percussion Meeting in Tunis (2004), International Violin Meeting in Amman (2004), International Voice Meeting in London (2005) and an International Lute Meeting in Athens (2005), all of them including prominent Turkish (and other) musicians.

Kallimopoulous describes the 1990s as a period of indigenization and musical hybridization (Kallimopoulou 2009: 133ff). Periklís Papapetrópoulos, a former

77 CDs *Yorgos Bacanos / Yiorgios Batzanos* (1997), *Zakharia Khanendeh* (2001). Guest Turkish musicians include Süleyman Erguner, Melihat Gülses, Necip Gülses, Vahit Anadolu, Özer Özel, Neva Selda and Özgen and others. CD *Music of Asia Minor and Constantinople* (Ocora 2008). CD En Chordais: *Tanbûrî Isak,* 2004.

78 European Union Programme: Euromed Heritage II MediMuses Project – Action for the History of Music of the Mediterranean Corpus Series with works of Great Mediterranean Composers, encompassing 11 concerts, 7 International Music Meetings, 75 Visiting Lecturers, 6 CDs in the Great Mediterranean Masters series, 6 CDs in the Great Mediterranean Composers series, 6 Anthologies with works of Great Mediterranean Composers, 2 Workgroups, 10 Workshops, / 3 Symposia / 2 Volumes for the History and Theory of Mediterranean Music.

student of Ross Daly, for example, arranged traditional Greek music for *saz*, including music from Crete (where the *boulgarí*, a small, long-necked lute similar to the *saz* occurs), Peloponnese and other regions. Tuning and finger techniques remain according to the Anatolian tradition, ornamentation according to the Greek one (Kallimopoulou 2009: 152).

Already from 1988, secondary education music schools were founded with a curriculum including Greek traditional music; many of its teachers were influenced by Karás (Kallimopoulou 2009: 48ff; Apostolopoulos 2005: 482).

Mihalis Holevas:

> I started with this (Greek-Ottoman) music at first in Musical High School, the first music high school that was established in Greece. It was in Athens, Peleni, and was founded in 1988. I was in the second generation of students in 1989. In that high school (...) we would have daily music courses on Byzantine music, traditional Greek music, Ottoman music, musicological issues, Western music harmony and theory, and three individual classes per week on three instruments. We had to pursue piano lessons, and *tambura*, the Greek equivalent for *saz*. That was compulsory for the first three years, and we could also add an extra instrument of our choice. (...) We had a lot of teachers. Some of them were students of Ross Daly or other musicians. I was studying *kanun* at that time, and my teacher was an Armenian from Istanbul, who is now working in Istanbul, Her name is Anje Sagopyan. There were people from Greece, who had studied abroad, in Turkey, or in the Arab countries. (...) Turkish musicians were not there because not many Turkish musicians connected with Ottoman music were in Greece. There were Greeks connected with us that had studied in Turkey, but they were not living in Istanbul. They were coming back and forth and having lessons with people like Salih Bilgin, Fahrettin Çimenli or Sokratis. (...) Every class year had one hundred students in it. When we had six classes in total at the high school, that means around six hundred students.
>
> (Question: What do all these peoples do when they graduate?)
>
> Well, good question. With these musical high schools and other high schools that came into existence – there are now something like 36 music high schools all over Greece – they have both normal classes and musical classes. They either became teachers, or they became professional, because nowadays there is a need for that music. (Interview, December 14, 2011, Rotterdam)

A short time after the success of Bosphorus in Greece, around 1993, the Turkish label *Kalan* Music began to release historical recordings of *rembetiko* music from Greek, followed with a CD of historical recordings of Pontos Greek Songs from the 1930s; a set of five CDs with 78 rpm recordings from Orfeon-Odeon (1914-1926) of the then *protopsaltos* from the patriarch of Constantinople, Iakovos Nafpliotis, and finally a reconstruction of the *laterna* tradition in 2010.[79] From the late 1990s several music groups from Turkey rediscovered Greek music of western Anatolia or Constantinople / Istanbul, for example the popular group *Yeni*

[79] MC *Remebetika*; *Rembetika II „Izmir ve Istanbul'dan Yillanmis Sarkilar"* 1996; *Songs of Pontos. Recordings of 1930s*, Kalan 2003. Further recordings of Pontos Greek music (made by Nikos Michailidis) was published by Güvercin (2013): *Selanik'tan Trabzon'a Köprü*.

Türkü. In particular after the 1999 earthquake in Izmit and the direct Greek aid for the victims, the atmosphere between Turkey and Greece improved, which had an impact on musical exchanges. Today Turkish musicians including Mehmet Erener, Erdal Erzincan, Yurdal Tokcan, Salih Bilgin, Ömer Erdoğdular and Necati Çelik frequently travel to Greece for workshops or concerts.

Mihalis Holevas:

> (Question: Nowadays it is not so unusual that Turkish musicians perform in Greece?)
>
> Especially after Ross' workshops, after Labyrinth there are so many good Turkish musicians coming back every year, and we make concerts for them every year.
>
> (...) Now it is easy, because there is so much notation, if you go to websites like neyzen.com you get everything notated by makam, then all the books of the TRT are of course known in Greece. There are Greek books on Ottoman music notation. And there are many people transcribing stuff from recordings. And I think there is the same more or less going on in Turkey. (Interview, December 14, 2011, Rotterdam)

Today, a great number of excellent Greek musicians are active in the international field of Ottoman-Turkish music, for example.

Alexandros Papadimitrakis (*ud*, *lavta*);
Sokratis Sinopoulos (b. 1974, *lyra*, *lavta*);[80]
Martha Mavroidi (voice, *lavta*; Élias 2012: 63);
Periklís Papapetrópoulos (*sazi*, *lavta*);
Sophia Lampropoúlou (*kanun*) (Kallimopoulou 2009: 179ff, 183);
Markos Skoulios (*ney*, *ud*);
Evgenios Voulgaris (*yaylı tanbur*);
Michalis Holevas (*yaylı tanbur*, *ney*, *tarhu*);[81]
Harris Lamprakis (*ney*);[82]
Katerina Papadopoulou, percussion;
Hrístos Barbas (*ney*, *kaval*, b. 1980; Kallimopoulou 2009: 193f).

In addition there are also some musicologists, such as Miltiadis Pappas,[83] or Kyriakos Kalaitzidis. Buzuki Orhan (Orhan Osman) was born in Germany of a Turkish family who had lived in Greece.[84]

---

80 Élias 2012: 61f; CD *Letter from Istanbul*, Golden Horn Records, Istanbul 2001, together with Derya Türkan; later also published in Greece (Melodiko Karavi, 2002).

81 Student of Ömer Erdoğdular in Crete and Kudsi Erguner in Italy and Rotterdam, since 2011 teacher at Codarts Rotterdam;

82 Harris Lambrakis plays *ney* since 1991 and since then he has worked with numerous well-known artists and participated in numerous albums in Greek and international discography as a performer and composer. In 2006 he founded Harris Lambrakis Quartet and recorded the album Théa (2010). Since 2000 he has been teaching *ney* in conservatories in Athens.

83 Ph.D. thesis at the state conservatory of the ITÜ on the theory book of Apostolos Konstas (1820).

Meanwhile, a growing numbers of mutual concerts and recordings with both Turkish and Greek (and possibly other) musicians deal with the musical heritage of almost the whole area, including Istanbul / Konstantinopolis, Izmir / Smyrna, Saloniki / Selanik, Cyprus, or even the Princes Islands near Istanbul:[85]

- CD Bospohorus: *Balkan Düşleri* (Ada, 1996) with Turkish and Greek art songs, folk songs. The Art Director is Nikiforos Metaxas.
- CD Kırıka: *Kaba Saz* (Baykuş 2008).
- CD Kudsi Erguner Ensemble, *From Phanar to the Ottoman Court* (Equinox, 2008): Turkish and Greek musicians interpreting compositions from Greek-Ottoman composers such as the Zaharya /Zaccarias (d.1730), who was both cantor at the Phanar Patriarchate and singer in the palace of Ahmed III; Ilya Efendi, Petraki Lampadarios and others, performed in the traditional Turkish art music style.
- *Tatavla Keyfi*: an international Istanbul-based group which performs *rembetiko* songs from Istanbul, Smyrna and Piraeus, founded in 2008.
- CD Vasiliki Papageorgiou: *Ellino Tourkika* (Kalan 2009), again Nikiforos Metaxas as Art Director. Turkish Art and Anatolian music.
- Katerina Papadopoulou, CD *Kıyı / Aktes* (Akustik Müzik 2009), instrumental music, musical director was the Turkish *ud* player Yurdal Tokcan; mainly well-known Turkish musicians around the ensemble "*Istanbul Sazendeler*".
- The Galata Spirit, music group founded in 2012 in Istanbul, specialized in Greek composers form Istanbul.[86]

Armenia and Israel

Both Armenia and Israel could be seen as Turkey's neighboring countries and even more as new homes for former Ottoman minorities. Until the early twentieth century Jewish composers and musicians could live and work in Istanbul without serious problems. Well-known Ottoman-Jewish composers are for example, Tanburi Isak (1745-1814) or Isak Varon (1884-1962). The emigration of Ottoman Jews began in the early years of the Republic. The general Turkish nationalization, the pogrom in Trace 1934, and the Wealth Tax (*varlık vergisi*) in 1942

---

84 http://www.orhanosman.net/bio.html (August 15, 2015)

85 Muammer Ketençoğlu (who had worked on music from the Balkans before) in his CD *Smyrna Recollections* (Kalan, 2007) interpreted songs of the Izmir region of Turkish, Greek and Jewish traditions. The liner notes document the interwoven repertoires.; CD *Music of Cyprus*, Kalan 2007; CD Yarınistan / Vassiliki Papageorgiou / Taner Öngör: *Bizim Adalar*, Ak 2014; CD Dilek Koç: *Souvenir de Salonique*, General Music / Sony 2015.

86 www.facebook.com/TheGalataSpirit (August 24, 2015); members of the group are Georgios Marinakis (*ud*, artistic director), Katerina Papadopoulou (percussion), Stathis Koutouzos (percussion), Aris Siskakis (crete kemençe, violin),Fotini Kokkala (cello).

forced many to leave the country, to the USA, to South America, and from 1948 to Israel.[87]

> In the early 1930s, following a decade of musical flourishing, some Jewish hazanim, highly valued by their communities, began to leave Turkey. Algazi immigrated to Uruguay through Paris (1933), Benaroya to Switzerland, then Seattle, Washington (1934), and Moşe Kordova to Palestine (before 1935).[88]

During the past two decades antisemitism in Turkey rose (in 2003 the Neve Shalom and Bet Israel Synagogue in Istanbul were bombed), while relations between Turkey and Israel, in particular under the rule of the AKP deteriorated. Eventually the war in Gaza, the following Israeli blockade of Gaza and finally the deadly confrontation of the Turkish ship *Mavi Marmara* with Israeli commandos in 2010 brought the relations to a low for the following five years.

Among the worldwide Sephardic-Jewish diaspora many musicians still practice music of the Ottoman-Jewish heritage. When Necdet Yaşar came to the US in the early 1970s to teach at the University of Washington, Seattle,

> [h]e met the late Samuel Benaroya, who was born and raised in Ottoman Edirne in the early twentieth century, emigrated to Seattle through Switzerland in 1952, and was serving as hazan (prayer leader, or cantor) at one of the two Sephardic synagogues in the city. (Jackson 2013: 17)

Necdet Yaşar later remembered the encounter in an interview which he gave in 2006:

> Later I saw him beat a long *usul* (rhythmic pattern). He beat *devir kebir*. I was surprised. He beat a long *usul* on his knees, Ottoman-style, *meşk usuls*, and he recited a piece for me. He really surprised me. He beat *usuls* incredibly well. (Jackson 2013: 18)

The percussion player Zohar Fresco was born 1969 in Israel to a family of Ottoman descent. He became enamored with Oriental music, played in particular *darbuka* and frame drums (such as *bendir* and *riqq*) and began to play with older musicians who had immigrated to Israel from Arab countries, as well as with internationally well-known musicians including Phillip Glass, Glen Velez, Zakir Hussain, and Noa. In addition, he became a teacher and head of the Oriental percussion department at the Jerusalem Music Academy.[89] His playing techniques include influences of Arabic, Indian, Persian, and Turkish music, as well as Jazz.[90] At

87 Bunzl 1989; recordings of the singer Bienvenida Aguado (b. 1929 in Çanakkale, later migrated to Israel) are on the CD *Judeo-Spanish Songs from Eastern Mediterranean* (Inedit, 1994); Victoria Rosa Hazan, b. 1898 in Turkey, migrated in the 1920s in the USA and continued to sing judeo-spanish songs (Cohen 1999).

88 Serroussi, introduction to *Maftirim* (Istanbul: Gözlem 2009); Jackson 2013: 62; Ishak El Gazi (b. 1889 in Izmir) for example was cantor in Izmir and from 1923 in Istanbul, in addition he also recorded Ottoman art songs. In 1933 he left for Paris, 1935 he moved from France to Uruguay where he died in 1950 (Seroussi 1989).

89 www.zoharfresco.com (accessed May 23, 2016).

90 www.zoharfresco.com/ (accessed September 29, 2016).

the *ud* Festival in Jerusalem in 2009, a concert for three *ud* plus percussion was organized (among others), featuring Yurdal Tokcan, the American-Armenian Ara Dinkjian and the Christian-Arab from Israel, Taiseer Elias, together with Zohar Fresco.[91]

Since the 1970s Sephardic folk music has also attracted growing attention, initially in particular among collectors, musicians and scholars in Israel (e.g. Israel Katz, Judith Cohen, Susana Welch-Shahak and Edwin Seroussi).[92] "*Turkish Jewish cultural productions in general, and religious music in particular, participate in worldwide transnational trends today*" (Jackson 2013: 137) In Turkey since the late 1980s, in particular Jak and Janet Esim as well as the group *Los Paşaros Sefaradis* are known for their Sefardi songs. Several musicians from Israel stayed (or still stay) in Istanbul, for example the singer and musicologist Hadass Pal-Yarden. The percussionist Yinon Muallem came for the first time in 2000, later he studied *ud* in Istanbul and recorded several CDs together with Turkish musicians.[93]

Turkish-Armenian relations are overshadowed by the ongoing political-historical discussion on the genocide of Armenians in 1915/1916. Already during the nineteenth century many Armenians left the Ottoman Empire, most of them for North America (Karpat 1995). With the massacres of 1880, 1895 and 1915/1916 the numbers of refugees rose. In American cities such as Chicago and New York an Armenian music scene emerged with music night clubs and Armenian record companies (Gronow 1981: 5; Arzruni 2001: 97). Preceding the First World War however, the majority of Armenians lived within the borders of the Ottoman Empire, until the events of 1915/1916 in which most of the Ottoman-Armenians were killed. In Turkey about 60000–65000 remained, mostly in Istanbul, in addition to an unclear number of converted and Turkified or Kurdified Armenians in Anatolia (Özdogan et al. 2009: 462).

The USA has welcomed on the numerous occasions, the Istanbul based Udi Hrant (Udi Hrant Kenkülyan, 1901-1952), an Armenian *ud* player who survived the genocide in Konya and later became a successful musician in Istanbul in the 1950s and 1960s (Bilal 2013: 18f). Throughout the later 20th century Armenian musicians from around the world occasionally visited Istanbul (Bilal 2013: 30). When the Armenian percussionist, singer and composer Arto Tuncboyaciyan moved from Istanbul to New York in 1981, he soon found local Armenian musicians, including the *ud* player Ara Dinkjian. Ara Dinkjian's father Onnik Dinkjian

91 www.youtube.com/watch?v=wAPlgkmuNYo (accessed September 29, 2016).

92 Jackson 2013: 204, fn10; As an example for an edition of field recordings see Susanna Weich-Shahak (ed.), *Judeo-Spanish Songs for the Life Cycle in the Eastern Mediterranean*. (Anthology of Music Traditons in Israel), The Hebrew University of Jerusalem. Jewish Music Research Center, including sefardic songs from Ottoman Juwish traditions.

93 Çelik 2013; in 2002 Muallem recorded an album together with Istanbul sazendeleri; CD Yinon Muallem: *Klezmer for the Sultan*; Oriente Music 2005; CD Yinon Muallem: *The Way it is*, Kaf 2008; since then he has published almost one new CD per year.

was born 1929 in Paris, where his family had fled to from Diyarbakır / Dikranagert. At an early age Onnik Dinkjian moved to the USA, and became a singer both in the church and of Armenian folk songs (Yıldız 2016: 127ff; 2012). Arto Tuncboyaciyan's (b. 1957 in Istanbul) family came from Sivas (Central Anatolia), but migrated to Istanbul in the 1950s (Yıldız 2016: 150). In 1998 Arto Tuncboyaciyan went to Armenia where in 1999, he formed his "Armenian Navy Band" (Yıldız 2016: 157).

Contemporary Armenia is hence only one of several countries were the Ottoman / Turkish Armenian Diaspora lives. Today, of an estimated 7.5–8 million Armenians worldwide, only 2.5 million reside in Armenia, the rest in Russia, United States, Europe (in particular in France), Canada, and other countries. Armenia itself became part of the Soviet Union in 1936, and hence fell under the strong influence of the Russian-Soviet cultural politics and aesthetics (Berkman 2012). The importance of Radio Yerevan, with its regular Kurdish music programs for Kurdish music in Turkey can hardly be overestimated.

> Radio Yerevan started broadcasting a program in Kurmanci in 1955. Part of the program was devoted to music, and the voices of Kurdish *Dengbêj* performing from Yerevan became famous throughout the region. The radio had an enormous influence on the evolving awareness of Kurdish language and culture, and the *Dengbêj* played an important role in this. The tradition became less local, people heard songs from many regions. (Hamelink 2016: 26; İnanç 2016)

In the Republic of Turkey the genocide left a deep gap in the country's musical life. In many Anatolian cities, as well as in Istanbul or Izmir, Armenians had been important musicians, in particular instrumentalists. Still the 1920s several Armenian musicians had lived in Istanbul (Bilal 2013: 26), for example Edgar Manas (1875-1964), who was one of the teachers of Hüseyin Sadettin Arel. Armenian producers and instrument makers also played important roles. They were among the first Istanbul jazz musicians in the 1920s, and featured prominently in other parts of its entertainment world up to the upper middle class, (Bilal 2013: 27).

In Turkey in general, however, the genocide and most Armenian culture (except for church music) remained a closed issue over decades. Most Anatolian Armenian music was destroyed and forgotten. The eminent composer and musicologist Gomitas Vardabet (1869-1935), who was active only until 1915, became a symbol for the genocide, and his musical work remained dominant within the Armenian communities abroad, in Turkey and in Armenia. Notation collections by Armenian scholars, in particular the five volumes of Mihran Toumajan was never translated into Turkish (nor any other language).[94]

[94] Toumajan 1972; for armenian sources of the (later) nineteenth and twentieth centuries, see Bilal 2013.

> After many years of avoiding the open display of Armenian identity within broader Turkish society, in favor of a more introverted community life, the Armenian community began making its voice heard from the mid-1990s on. (Yıldız 2016: 68)

It was mainly the internationalization, in particular contacts with Armenia and Armenians in the USA, which began to challenge the public amnesia.

> My informants spoke of their surprise when they realized the existence of secular, non-sacred Armenian music, via records imported from Beirut, Soviet Armenia or other diaspora communities. Recordings by musicians such as Hovannes Badalyan, Tatul Altunyan, Khachadur Avedisyan, Parsegh Ganachyan, Aram Khachaduryan, Rupen Matevosyan, Ophelia Hampartzumyan and Edgar Hovhannesyan, who were trained under the Soviet system, have been the determining models influencing the developing musical aesthetics of Istanbul's Armenian community since the late 1960s. They began collecting records of Armenian songs, learned to sing them, and realized that the Armenian world was not confined to Istanbul. It may sound absurd at first, but many people were not even aware of the existence of Eastern (Soviet) Armenia. As a result of those records, the borders of Armenian ethnicity broadened for Turkey's Armenian community of Turkey, leading to cultural interaction with other Armenian communities in the late 1960s. (Yıldız 2016: 71)

The independence of Armenia in 1991 also implied the opening of its borders. Between 1988 and 2005 nearly a million Armenians left the country, most of them to Russia, the EU and the United States. About 10,000 Armenian citizens live in contemporary Turkey (Salomoni 2014: 125f). The assassination of the Armenian-Turkish journalist Hrant Dink broght the issue of Armenian-Turkish relations back on the political agenda. In 2008 Abdullah Gül was the first Turkish President who visited Armenia, officially invited by Armenias President Serzh Sargsyan to attent the soccer match of both national teams for the qualification for the World Cup. Today the private Hrant Dink Vakfi supports travel between Turkey and Armenia for artistic or academic purposes. Several Armenian musicians regularly give concerts in Turkey, most famous is the *duduk* player Djivan Gasparyan (b. 1928), who has performed in concert with *Kardeş Türküler*[95] and who released a successful CD together with Erkan Oğur. Another *duduk* player, Suren Asaduryan, realized a common project together with the group *Yansımalar*.[96]

New Markets: "World Music"

The following large part will describe the expansion of Turkish music into the emerging field of "world music". Partly this development might be seen as parallel to the migration from Turkey to and the ongoing integration of Turkish music in Europe, but also numerous musical projects as decribed in the previous part ("Old Neighbors") at the same time are part of the "world music".

---

95 CD Erkan Ogur / Djivan Gasparyan: *Fuat*, Kalan 2001.

96 CD Yansimalar & Suren Asaduryan: Serzeniş, 2000; 2010 concert program *Barışa Çiçekler*.

Since the 1960s European and American jazz musicians became interested in music of non-European origin, beginning with North Indian art music (for example the 1976 group Shakti with guitarist John McLaughlin, L. Shankar on violin, and Zakir Hussein on *tabla*); followed by Arabic, African, Brazilian and other music culture.[97] The label "world music" was introduced by some record companies in 1987 for all kinds of music which is neither European nor North American (Bachir-Loopuyt 2013: 4; Frith 2000). In 1989 the former rock singer Peter Gabriel founded the first label specializing in world music, *Real World*, and other labels followed later. In 1991 German radio journalist Johannes Theurer initiated the "European World Music Charts," selected by an international group of radio journalists. The term "world music" was often criticized for several reasons (which will not be discussed here; cf. Peres da Silvia 2017). From 2006 on the West-German radio channel *Funkhaus Europa* skipped the term in favor of "global pop". Four years later, the German music competition, the "Creole Award for World Music from Germany" ("*Creole Preis für Weltmusik aus Deutschland*") was re-named to the "Creole Award for Global Music from Germany" ("Creole Preis für globale Musik aus Deutschland") (Bachir-Loopuyt 2013).

Though obviously still characterized by a certain degree of exoticism, world music differed from the orientalism of the seventeenth until the nineteenth centuries at least in one important aspect: in the later 20th century it was musicians of non-European origin themselves who presented their music to European and American audiences rather than, as before, European orchestras playing "oriental" or "alla turca" music. Already at an early stage, world music festivals such as Peter Gabriel's WOMAD-Festival or Serif Khasnedar's "*Festival des Musiques Traditionelles*" in Paris brought non-European musicians and ensembles to Europe. Today, the European Forum of Worldwide Music Festivals EFWMF represents 45 world music festivals Europe wide.[98] A number of journals (including the "Global Rhythm", "Folker!", "Blue Rhythm" and "Songlines") inform their readers about traditional music from all over the world.

Turkey and Turkish music only later entered the field of world music. While the first edition of *The Rough Guide to World Music* for example, did not mention Turkey at all, the second, enlarged edition (1999) included a comprehensive article by the musicologist Martin Stokes.[99] During the early years of "world music" Turkish musicians were hardly active in the field. In 1999, only one exhibiter from Turkey (among a total of 150) was present at the most important fair for

---

97 For an overview on world music literature in relation to Turkey, see Değirmenci 2013: 4-14.

98 www.efwmf.org (assecced January 6, 2015)

99 Broughton, Ellingham & Trillo, 1999: *World Music. The Rough Guide*, Bd. 1, London: Rough Guides; including as part of *Middle East* (rather than *Europe*): Martin Stokes: Turkey: Sounds of Anatolia (pp. 396-410), a encompassing overview; Harold Hagopian: Armenia: The Sorrow Sound (pp. 332-337); Eva Skalla, Jemima Amiri: Kurdish Music: Songs of the Stateless (pp. 378-384).

world music, WOMEX ("Worldwide Music Expo"; Greve 2003). Thirteen years later, in October 2012 in Thessaloniki, the WOMEX opened with an official concert entitled *My Sweet Canary*, dedicated to Roza Eskenazi (c. 1895-1980), the legendary *rembetiko* singer who was born in Istanbul to a sephardic family in the last years of the twentieth century, later moving to Thessaloniky in her early childhood. The concert featured musicians form Greece, Turkey and Israel together, including the singers Mehtap Demir, Mor Kabasi, Savina Yannatou. At the fair itself numerous Turkish groups and exhibiters were present, such as *MUYAP* (Phonogram Producers Collection Society representing several labels[100]), *MESAM*, *MSG* (Musical Work Owners Society of Turkey), *MUYORBIR* (Music Performers Society of Turkey), the groups *Café Aman Istanbul*, *Arifa* (The Netherlands) and *Gevende*; in addition some record distributers and booking agencies offered Turkish music.[101] The Womex-CD (Charmworks, 2012) contained Turkish ensembles such as *Café Aman*, *Kardeş Türküler*, *Mercan Dede*, Şivan Perwer, Ahmet Aslan, Omar Faruk Tekbilek, and Gulistan Perwer.

Over the last years several festivals in Europe focused on music from Turkey, including:

- Festival *Alla Turca. Musique de Turquie*, October, 2012, Genève, Switzerland.
- *Babel Med* Music, March 2013, Marseille, France (the 9th World Music Forum), Director: Sami Sadak.
- *Festival De Orient*, September 2014, Deventer, the Netherlands.
- *Schleswig-Holstein Musik Festival*, 2011[102]
- *Bodenseefestival: Türk Kültürü 2013*

Initially only a few Turkish pioneers entered the new market, in particular the labels *Kalan Müzik* and Doublemoon. *Kalan* was founded by Hasan Saltik in 1991, and produced left wing groups like *Grup Yorum*, but also music of Kurds, Zaza and other minorities.[103] In an interview Kalan's owner Hasan Saltik related:

> The turning point was my visit in Germany in 1992. In their music market, I saw the albums of Tanburi Cemil Bey, Udi Hrant, and many other Turkish masters, the recording of whom were reproduced from the gramophone records by an American label. We asked ourselves why we should not do such things. (Değirmenci 2013: 36)

---

[100] Ada Müzik, Kalan Müzik, Doğan Müzik, Mert Müzik.

[101] *Pasión Turca*: a booking agency in Madrid, representing Aynur, *Baba Zula*, Mercan Dede, Burhan Öçal, Galata Dervishes, Gevende, Ilhan Erşahin, Istanbul Calling, *Kolektif Istanbul*, Selim Sesler and others; *Molpé* music: a record distribution representing Gül Hacer Toruk (France); Titi Robin; *Ajs* music, a record distribution in Turkey.

[102] Including numerous prominent musicians such as Pera Ensemble, Fazıl Say, Sarband, Marc Sinan & Dresden Symphony Orchestra, Aynur; Selim Sesler; Burhan Öcal; Gülsin Onay and Ferhan & Ferzan Önder.

[103] In his book Koray Değirmenci (2013: 36) describes the rise of world music in Turkey, and the rise of Turkey within the world music.

Kalan's CDs are produced with extensive booklets, written by specialists (see below), including English translations (only MC and CDs produced in *Kalan*'s first years were not fully translated). *Doublemoon* was founded 1998 as an offshoot of *Pozitif* Music (Değirmenci 2013: 23-34), which organized festivals such as the *Efes Pilsen* Blues Festival (1990), Akbank Jazz Festival (1991), later Rock 'n Coke Istanbul, and Fuji Film World Music Days.[104]

From the 1990s onwards, many European-based Turkish musicians and managers also became active in world music, in particular those of the second generation of migrants, who were familiar with European orientalism, and tried to meet those expectations even in their name, e.g. "*Dervish Kulturmanagement*" (Bochum) or "*Oriental Media Network*" (Berlin). Also many music groups or solo musicians trying to attract a non-Turkish audience were naming themselves more or less ironically as "oriental," such as for instance the groups *Orient Express*, *Orient Connection* or *Orientation* (all Berlin; Greve 2003: 390). However, it was as late as 2011 that for the first time a group with Anatolian music (*Kavpersaz*) won the German Creole world music competition.

World music led to the emergence of a plethora of individual musicians and ensembles, among them also many who performed more or less Turkish music. Roughly five approaches might be identified, which will be described in the following parts: Islamic music as world music; rhythmic music in particular the asymmetric Anatolian rhythms; cross-cultural encounters; early music; and contemporary western music.

Islamic Music as World Music

The music of the *mevlevi* already roused the interest of European travellers already in the nineteenth century. Most travelogues and early tourist guides until the 1920s recommended the public ceremonies of the "whirling dervishes," in particular those of the Galata lodge.[105] After the abolishment of the mystic brotherhoods in Turkey, international interest persisted. From the 1960s international tours began to bring musicians of the *mevlevi* heritage to Europe and America.[106] The American musicologist Karl Signell performed together with highly regarded *mevlevi*-musicians in Istanbul during the 1970s.[107] The *ud*-player and

[104] Doublemoon was awareded by WOMEX and World Music Charts Europe (WMCE), ranked among top twenty labels in the world in 2007, chart toping albums: *800* by Mercan Dede, *Taksim Trio*, *Trakya Dance Party* by Burhan Öcal and Trakya All Stars (2007), *Breath* by Mercan Dede. (Değirmenci 2013: 49, fn 29). Doublemoon was the first Turish label with a catalog in Apple's iTune and Napster. (Değirmenci 2013: 26).

[105] Feldman 1996:203; Aksoy 2008a; Greve 1995:266ff.

[106] Kişmir 1967; Kudsi Erguner 2000; Süleyman Erguner 2010.

[107] For example *Aras Quintet: Mevlana Instrumental*,Aras, c. 1970, with Akagündüz Kutbay, Doğan Ergin, Karl Signell, Fahrettin Çimenli and Nezih Üzel.

composer Çinuçen Tanrıkurur remembers a tour through the USA in 1994, where to his surprise, he met two American *ney*- and *tanbur*-players (Tanrıkorur 1998). As mentioned before, until the 1990s most recordings with sufi music were produced in either Europe or the USA (Greve 1995: 299f). During the early 1990s in Turkey instrumental (and later also vocal) versions of *ilahi* and *ayın* were released, directed by Nezih Üzel and including the participation of Kudsi and Süleyman Erguner. To attract an international audience most of the cassettes had both Turkish and English titles.[108] Among the *mevlevi* group *Çağdaş Mevlana Aşıkları Topluluğu* of Dede Hasan Çıkar, which in the 1990s for the first time included women in its *sema* performance at the former lodge in Galata, also a female American and a Japanes *sema* dancer took place (Görgün 2000; Vicente 2007: 235). Currently one spiritual leader of the *mevlevi*, Kabir Helminski, lives in the US.[109] Today dozens of *ney* makers produce instruments in Istanbul and *ney* lessons are available via internet all over the world. A number of non-Turkish *ney* players are active in the field of world music, including Harris Lambrakis (Greece), Giovanni de Zorzi (Italy),[110] Christos Barbas (Greece), Mihalis Holevas (Greece, The Netherlands), Maren Lueg (London). Until today world music shops offer music from Turkey, in particular "Sufi Music" (Senay 2014; 2015). Similarly concerts with Sufi music attract much more interest from European audiences than even the most famous Turkish folk music singers.

Internationally one of the most well-known Turkish musicians (himself a hard critic of the commercialization and popularization of the *mevlevi* tradition) is the *ney* player and composer Kudsi Erguner (b. 1952). His grandfather Süleyman Erguner (1913-1955), was *müezzin* at the Sultanselim mosque, student of Sadettin Kaynak and later one of the best *ney* players of his generation. His son (Kudsi's father) Ulvi Erguner (1924-1974), also became famous as a *ney* player. During the 1940s Süleyman Erguner's house in Istanbul was an informal centre for musicians of traditional late Ottoman art music. Later sufi musicians would meet in

108 MC Nezih Üzel: *Ilahiler (Sufi Music)*, Kent, late 1980s; further audio cassettse were published under the name of *Erguner Toplulugu*, e.g. *Sufi Music. Türk Tasavvuf Musikîsi*, Kalite, early 1990s. Beginning in the mid 1990s the repertoire was enlarged, e.g. MC Nezih Üzel: *Mevlana Rubailer. Selected Masterpieces of Mevlevi Music*, Kent, early 1990s; MC *Zikir. Islamic Ritual Music*, Kent, 1993; MC *Tekbir, Durak, Naat ve Salatlar. Islamic Religious Music*, Kent, 1993; MC *Klasik Bektaşi Nefesleri / Bektaşi Hymns*, EMI-Kent, 1995.

109 http://sufism.org/kabir-camille/kabir-and-camille-helminski-threshold-society-founders-2 (accessed September 27, 2016).

110 Giovanni De Zorzi: *Musiche di Turchia*, Mailand: Ricordi 2010; De Zorzi 2005. Giovanni De Zorzi received a *DÉA* (*Diplome d'Étude Approfondi*) with *EHÉSS* (*École des Hautes Études en Sciences Sociales*) of Paris in 2001 with his thesis on *Le* ney *dans la Turquie contemporaine. Situation actuelle d'un instrument 'passéiste'*. ("The *ney* in contemporary Turkey. Actual Situation of a 'Traditionalist' Instrument"). He currently teaches *ney* flute at the Conservatory "Arrigo Pedrollo" of Vicenza and organizes regular seminars with Kudsi Erguner at the *Istituto Interculturale de Studi Musicali Comparati*, Venedig.

the *Özbeklerin Tekkesi* in Üsküdar.[111] In 1944, Süleyman Erguner took part in the inaugural broadcast of Radio Istanbul, continuing to perform in the first regular radio programs throughout the 1950s. After his death, Ulvi Erguner continued to host the music meetings that his father had established. In 1967 he became the Director of Art and Folk music at Radio Istanbul, where he directed choirs and for the first time included religious Ottoman music in his programs. Kudsi Erguner, having grown up with Ottoman-Turkish music, went to Paris in 1975 at the age of 23 (Erguner 2000). Already in 1970, a group of Istanbul *mevlevi* musicians had played at the *Théâtre de la Ville* in Paris, and had toured to the UK and America in the following years. Kudsi Erguner soon discovered the European interest in Sufi culture and music. Over the years he gave concerts all over Europe and America, at all major concert halls and festivals, and edited up to 100 albums, in particular for French labels such as *al sur*, *Inedit – Maison des Cultures du Monde*, *Arion* und *Ocora* (Senay 2015; Erguner 2000; Greve 2003: 395). Noteworthy are his regular *ney* courses in Venice and Vicenza (Italy) organised by his former student Giovanni De Zorzi (Kudsi Erguner speaks Italian, English and French fluently).[112] Since 2011 Erguner is teaching at Codarts, Rotterdam.

The scope of Kutsi Erguner's musical activities is impressive, and only a fraction can be included here: He recorded parts of the soundtrack for the Peter Brooks Film, "Meetings With Remarkable Men" (1979) and of Peter Brooks' theatre piece and film, "Mahabharata" (1989); in the 1980s, together with Peter Gabriel he took part in creating the soundtrack for Martin Scorsese' film *The Last Temptation Of Christ*. During the 1990s, together with Nezih Üzel, Süleyman Erguner, Hasan Esen and others he released several albums with religious Islamic music including *ilahi*, *ayın* and *taksim*.[113] In the same period he composed two ballets, *Neva* with Carolyn Carlson for the *Théâtre de la Ville de Paris* (1991) and *Le voyage nocturne* with Maurice Béjart for the *Théâtre des Champs-Elysées* (1997). In 1997/98 he took part in a production of Mozart's, "The Abduction from the Seraglio" at *Salzburger Festspiele*. Since the mid-1990s Kudsi Erguner played together with jazz musicians, including saxophonist Christof Lauer, tuba and serpent player Michel Godard, guitarist Nguyên Lê, and later with the trumpet player Markus Stockhausen;[114] he worked with Indian musicians, string quartets, Fla-

---

[111] In this environment a generation of excellent musicians grew up, including the *ney* players Niyazi Sayın and Selami Bertuğ, the singer and composer Alâeddin Yavaşça, and Nevzat Atlığ, who in the 1980s would become one of the most influencial art musicians in Turkey.

[112] De Zorzi 2008; most students are Italians, many of them former saxophone and transverse flute players.

[113] CD *Osmanli Davullari*, 1992; CD *Ferahfezâ Mevlevî Ayini*, 1992. CD *Sufi Music of Turkey*, 1990 with Suleyman Erguner, Mahmoud Tabrizi Zadeh, Bruno Caillat; CD *The Turkish Ney*, 1990 with Salih Dede and Süleyman Erguner; CD *Whirling Dervishes from Turkey*, 1991, with Kemal Evren, Tugrul Inancer, Aram Kerovpyan, Muzzffereddîn Ozak, Hafiz Kemâl Ozmutlu, Mahmud Tabrîzîzade.

[114] CD *Ottomania. Sufi-Jazz-Project*, Act 1999 with Christof Lauer (Saxophon), Derya Turkan (*kemençe*), Michel Godard (tuba, serpent), Mehmet Emin Bitmez (*ud*), Yves Rousseau (dou-

menco musicians, the Hilliard Ensemble and many others.[115] In July 2016, Kudsi Erguner was officially declared the *UNESCO Artist for Peace*.

In Istanbul Kudsi Erguner presented a project called "*Ilahiname*" ("Book of Hymns") which brought together Greek, Armenian, Jewish and Muslim liturgical music of Istanbul; in another project in 2008 he composed Goethe's, "West-Östlicher Divan" in Ottoman style but sung in the original German language. In addition he produced numerous CDs with traditional Ottoman-Turkish art music without any cross-cultural element. Many successful contemporary Turkish musicians owe their international careers to him, for example Derya Türkan, Hakan Güngör, Aziz Bahriyeli and Yusuf Bilgin. On the other hand, a number of Turkish musicians today criticize Kudsi Erguner on the basis of musical arguments and personal envy.

In contrast to Kudsi Erguner, his younger brother Süleyman Erguner never left Istanbul for an extended period. In 1975, he was accepted to the TRT İstanbul State Radio and Television as a *ney* player. In 1980, he started teaching *ney* and music theory at the İstanbul Technical University Turkish Music Conservatory. In 1997 Süleyman Erguner completed his Ph.D. on the history of Turkish mystical music at Marmara University. In 1995 he became the leader of the İstanbul Mevlevi Ensemble (founded in 1980). Currently, he is teaching in various universities and in the "*Süleyman Erguner Ney Atölyesi*," and he gives international and national concerts. Süleyman Erguner wrote the first method book for *ney*, published in 1986 with a new edition in 2002. In 2007, he worked as the artistic and the administrative director of an international *Ney* Festival held in Istanbul, with the support of the European Union. Further music groups and albums presenting at least partially "Sufi Music" include *Yansımalar*, with *ney* player Aziz Şenol Filiz, the album *Zikr* by Okay Temiz together with *ney* player Aka Gündüz Kutbay (1989), or the cooperative project of Süleyman Erguner and Butch Morris in 1992 (Senay 2014: 418).

Turkey also benefited financially from the international interest in Islamic music. "*Whirling Dervish Ceremonies are now being performed in restaurants, bars, at open-*

ble bass), Hakan Güngör (*kanun*), Bruno Caillat (*bendir, zarb, tabla*), Necib Gülses (*tanbur*), Mark Nauseef (drums); *Islam Blues*, Act 2001 with the jazz gitarrist Nguyên Lê and turkish musicians including Yunus Balcıoğlu (voice), Derya Turjan (*kemençe*); CD *Gazing Point*, 2003, with Markus Stockhausen and Mark Nauseef; CD *No Matter*, 2008, with Markus Stockhausen.

115 Some examples include CD Kudsi Erguner & Xavier Bellenger: *Ney et Kena. Conférence de Roseaux* (Ocora, 1984); CD *Music from the Arabian Nights*, Air Mail Music 1991, with Bruno Caillat, Tabrizi Mahmoud Zadeh; Mahmoud Tébrizizadeh & Kudsi Erguner: Oriental Dreams, Sunset Playa 1991; CD *L'Orient de l'Occident. Tasavvuf'dan Flamenko'ya*, Topkapı, 1995 with Yusuf Bilgin (voice), Mehmet Emin Bitmez (*ud*), Tamer Pınarbaşı (*kanun*); Enrique el Extremeño (voice), Salvador Gutiérrez (gitar), Pedro Soler (gitar), Bruno Caillat (percussion); CD *Taj Mahal*, Equinox 2001, with Bruno Caillat (*zarb*), Renaud Garcia-Fons (bass) , Hakan Güngör (*kanun*), Sultan Khan (*sarangi*), Fazal Qureshi (*tabla*), Derya Turkan (*kemençe*), Ken Zukerman (*sarod*).

ing ceremonies, circumcision feasts, in hotel lobbies and in many tourist venues" (Uyar & Beşiroğlu 2012: 145; Senay 2014: 419). According to Vincente (2007: 106), the "Mevlana Cultural Centre" in Konya, which opened in 2004 with numerous exhibitions, symposia, public performances and out-door *sema* performance spaces, tries to "*serve as a sort of headquarters for the lucrative Mevlana pilgrimage and tourism industry.*" The centre is furthermore connected with the "Mystical Music Festival" which presents international religious music from different religions every September (Vicente 2007: 284ff; 295ff). "*Visitors are mainly from Europe and North America, but during the 2004 Mevlana Festival pilgrims arrived from all four corners of the earth.*" (Vincente 2007: 286; Sarı 2010) The number of domestic and foreign visitors to the Mevlana museum rose from nearly six hundred thousand in 1985 to 1.5 million in 2004, and two million in 2006 (Vicente 2007: 118). Furthermore, Mevlana was the subject of several operas and orchestral and choral works, including the *Mevlana Oratorio* of Ali Doğan Sinangil (1973), and two other works entitled *Mevlana Oratorio* were composed for Mevlana's 800th birthday in 2007 (Vicente 2007: 288ff; Lewis 2000: 616ff). The libretto of a Mevlana opera by Robert Willson and Philip Glass is based on Collman Barks, "Essential Rumi". For the same occasion the municipality of Istanbul sponsored the edition of eight CDs with Mevlevi *Ayin-i Şerif* (Uyar & Beşiroğlu 2012: 145).

Sheik Nail Kesova (b.1939) was accepted as Mevlevi by Hafiz Sadettin Heper and studied music with the *semabaşı* Ahmet Biçan Kasaboğlu. From 1970 to 1982 he was *semazen*, becoming *postnişin* or *dede* in 1994. Since 1995 he conducted numerous workshops, concerts and *sema* performances in Europe, managed by the German based world music management *Alba Kultur.*[116] In 2003, he was involved in the music for the French film, "Monsieur Ibrahim" by Francois Dupeyron, based on the novel by Eric-Emmanuel Schmitt and produced in cooperation with the International Mevlana Foundation as part of a research project for the UNESCO program, "Masterpieces of the Oral and Intangible Heritage of Humanity: The *Mevlevi Sema* Ceremony" (October 2004).

Many CDs produced in the context of world music, however, combine sufi (and other religious) traditions with new age sounds (the most well-known is the CD series *Buddha Bar*).[117] The most well-known musicians with this approach are US-based Omar Faruk Tekbilek and Montreal-based Mercan Dede (Arkin Ilıcalı, aka Arkin Allen) (Senay 2015). Mercan Dede's albums *Su* (2004) and 800 (2007) reached at the top of the European World Music Charts. They are among his total eight albums, many of which focus on sufism, including "Sufi Dream" (1998)

---

116 CD Galata Mevlevi Musik und Sema Ensemble: *Lost in Ecstasy*, Heaven and Earth 2005; CD The Music of Islam, Vol. 9, *Mawlawiyah. Music of the Whirling Derwishes*, Celestial Harmonies 1997 and other CD in this series more.

117 Vicente 2007: 228ff; Uyar & Beşiroğlu 2012: 145f; Derğirmen 2013: 93-107; e.g. CD Destination: *Istanbul*, Dynamic/Bar de Lune 2006; CD Buddha Bar: *Oriental Lounge*, 2006; CD Minor Empire: *Second Nature*, Z Yapim, 2014.

or "Journey of a Dervish" (1999). He uses "*taksim-like ney improvisations as in* neyname *(The Book of the* Ney*) from* Seyahatname *to* zikr*-like passages in* Semaname *(The Book of* Sema*) from the same album and* Nar-i Cem *(Fire of Communal Union" from* Nar." (Vicente 2007: 274)

Successful in particular in Germany and Austria, though again with a completely different approach was Oruç Güvenç. With his music therapy, based on Central Asian shamanism and the Islamic heritage of music therapy, he has developed a large network of former students and followers. Both in Turkey and Europe he has organized numerous workshops, concerts and symposia. Together with his wife Aziz Güvenç (who is of German origin) he published three books in German and numerous booklets in Turkish.

World Rhythms

In order to facilitate an international perception of worldwide musical traditions, world music has tended to prefer (though not exclusively) either vocal music based on European languages, or dance-like music with a strong emphasis on rhythm. Among the first musical styles from Turkey which met this expectation was the instrumental music of the Roma. The West German Broadcaster WDR produced a CD with the clarinet player Mustafa Kandıralı in the 1980s and in 1991 Kandıralı played at the New Jazz Festival Moers (Germany).[118] Later he worked with Okay Temiz.

Among the first Turkish musicians active in world music, many in fact were percussionists. Their experience with the asymmetric Anatolian *aksak* rhythms, unusual in Western music, but loaded with discourses of Anatolian or Turkish identity gave them a particular competence, which turned out to be highly interesting for European musicians. Once inside the world music scene many Turkish percussionists learnt to play other non-Western percussion instruments including conga, *djembe* or *berimbao*. Most successful in this field were artists such as Okay Temiz in Sweden and Burhan Öçal in Zurich. Okay Temiz migrated to Stockholm in 1967 and began to play with jazz musicians such as trumpet player, Don Cherry and pianist, Dollar Brand. During the 1980s Temiz returned to Turkey but continued to work with international artists, for example in a dance project with Roman Bunka and Grace Yoon, with African musicians and with the Indian *Karnataka College of Percussion*.[119]

Burhan Öçal (b. 1953, Kırklareli) became a drummer in his youth, playing jazz, international beat and rock, but also dance music of the Roma (although not being Roma himself). In 1977 he left Turkey and stayed until the end of the

---

118 CD Mustafa Kandirali & Ensemble: *Caz Roman*, Network Medien 1992 (recorded 1984).

119 Seeman 2002: 340, see for example MC Okay Temiz – Karnataka College of Perkussion: *Mishram*,Raks, 1997; MC Okay Temiz & Group Zourna: *Karşılama*, Ada, 1997.

1990s in Zurich. During the 1980s he played with numerous jazz musicians, including Werner Lüdi, Pierre Favre, Urs Blöchlinger, Joe Zawinul, Maria João and Steve Swallow. Later Öçal was a member of the group, "Family of Percussion" of the Swiss percussionist Peter Giger, and played in George Gruntz', "Concert Jazz Band". During the 1990s Öçal turned to Turkish musical traditions, stylistically based on a range of forms from Anatolian folk music to art music of the sufis.[120] After his return to Turkey he founded the "Istanbul Oriental Ensemble," together with Roma musicians, which was successful particularly on the international stage, with numerous concerts and several albums.

Other musicians of Roma music from Turkey were also present on the world music market (Değirmenci 2013: 60ff; Seeman 2002: 322). Canadian singer Brenna Mac Crimmon began to learn music from the Balkans; later she stayed in Turkey, and cooperated in particular with the Roma musician, Selim Sesler (b. 1957, Kesan, Thrace).[121] Together with the musicologist Sonia Tamar Seeman, Brenna McCrimmon formed the group *Karşılama* (Encounter) whose first album was released in Canada in 1998 and one year later in Turkey by *Kalan* Music (Derğirmen 2013: 61). Selim Sesler's subsequent album was again released by *Kalan*, entitled "*Kesan'a Giden Yollar*"" with the English subtitle "Regional and Roman (Gypsy) Music from Trace"(1999) (Derğirmen 2013: 63). The album contained a book on daily lives, customs, and ceremonies in the Kesan region. Following the release of these albums Selim Sesler moved his publishing company to Doublemoon Records, hence transforming from a "local" musician to "world music" (Derğirmen 2013: 63). During this time he also played in the Fatih Akıns films, *Gegen die Wand* ("Heat on", 2004), and "Crossing the Bridge" (2005). His next album at Doublemoon, *Oğlan Bizim Kız Bizim* was entitled "Anatolian Wedding." It reached international markets in 2006 and contained music from different regions of Turkey, not necessarily Roman.

Koray Değirmen commented that this rise of Roma music and in particular that of the Turkish clarinet (*girnata*), signalled a "gentrification of *girnata*" (Derğirmen 2013: 58ff). During the first decade of the 21st century several companies emerged that manufacture the instrument to a high quality and at equivalent prices – until about a decade ago, the *girnata* had still been produced solely by local manufacturers (Derğirmen 2013: 59). In 2006 an article in the Guardian

---

[120] CD Burhan Öçal & Classical Ensemble of Istanbul: *Orient Secret*, L'Empreinte digitale, 1998; CD Burhan Öçal: *Demedim-mi, Musique savante et musique soufi*,Amori, 1995; CD Burhan Öçal & Istanbul Oriental Ensemble: *Sultan's Secret Door*, Network, 1997; CD Burhan Öçal & Pete Namlook: *Sultan – Osman*, PW, 1998; CD Burhan Öçal & Seda Oriental Band: *Seda Oriental Band*, Konnex, 1998; CD Burhan Öcal: *Turkish Folk Music Vol. 1*, Soundways, 1992; CD Burhan Öçal & Istanbul Oriental Ensemble: *Caravanserai*, Network, 2000; CD Burhan Öçal & Jamaaladeen Tacuma, featering Natacha Atlas: *Groove alla Turca*, Double Moon, 2000.

[121] CD Brenna Mac Crimmon & Selim Sesler: *Karşılama*, Kalan 1998; Brenna MacCrimmon: *Kular Misafiri*, Kalan 2009.

called Selim Sesler one of the greatest clarinettists in the world, eventually even "the Coltrane of the clarinet" (Derğirmen 2013: 60). Today the most successful Turkish clarinettist is Hüsnü Şenlendirici (b. 1976, Bergama). His father Ergün Şenlendirici has been involved in many international projects within Okay Temiz's "Magnetic Band." In the early 2000s Hüsnü Şenlendirici played in several internationally successful groups including *Laco Tayfa* and "Brookly Funk Essentials;" his first solo album *Hüsn-ü Klarnet* was released in 2005. From 2007-2009 the *Taksim* Trio (with Ismail Tunçbilek *bağlama*, and Aytac Doğan, *kanun*) gave numerous international concerts. In an interview with Koray Değirmen in 2007, Hüsnü Senlendirici stated:

> I have a Greek bassist who is a doctoral student at Berkeley, a drummer from Canada who also attends Berkeley, a clarinettist from Macedonia who is of Turkish decent, a Turkish *kanun* player, and finally a Macedonian percussionist. (Derğirmen 2013: 53)

In 1997 even Turkish pop singer Sezen Aksu cooperated with Goran Bregović for her album, "The Wedding and The Funeral" (*Düğün ve Nenaze*), featuring the Macedonian Roma brass band *Kočani* (Seeman 2002: 351).

Cross-Cultural Encounters

The international world music scene's postmodern, eclectic character (and often orientalist exoticist naivety) makes it fertile ground for the theme of cross-cultural encounters. Many festivals initiate, promote and sometimes almost force musicians to play together with others of completely different musical traditions (for a concert program at the Berlin Philharmonic concert hall the present writer participated in this approach). At world music academies such as in Rotterdam or Helsinki / Malmö, most students are primarily interested in musical cross-over rather than in deeper studies of one single tradition.

Of course not all of these encounters are successful or convincing, either musically or in terms of personal understanding. Implicit rules for improvisation differ widely between music cultures (as far as a concept of improvisation exists at all) and only experienced musicians are able to maintain their own musical language on a high level while listening openly and with respect to another music culture, while also finding a common musical way. Vladimir Ivanoff, Director of the ensemble Sarband for many years, told in an interview:

> It took years and years until the European musicians were able to play – badly – Turkish music. The crucial point for European musicians is the intonation. It is difficult to internalize the *makam* system, as long as one has not be born and grown up with it, and even more, when you play together with highly qualified musicians. (...) In the end our home remedy that crystalized over the years was that: the more Western the Western musicians remain and the more Eastern the Eastern musicians, the better the cooperation works. Meanwhile I keep away from actual cross-over trials as I once tried to realize them from time to time – for example by letting a shawm play the irak peşrev. You skate

> on thin ice and accept compromises on both sides, actually this is not nice. (...) Everything else, these musical compromises, that is often very tough and in general not very productive.[122]

On the other hand, such encounters open up a wide field for musical experiments. The earliest and still most wide-spread encounters happened with the participation of Western jazz musicians, who were experienced in improvisation (Tekelioğlu 2011; Meriç 1998). Important Turkish musicians in this approach are Kudsi Erguner (CDs *Ottomania* 1999; *Islam Blues* 2001) and Erkan Oğur. In Kudsi Erguner's respective projects the Ottoman-Turkish part in general is strong, and the musicians almost switch from Ottoman to jazz music rather than blend both together. Several Ottoman-Turkish art musicians later worked with similar approaches, for example *kemençe* player Ahmet Kadri Rizeli (known for his membership in *Sarband*) with a Turkish jazz quartet.

Erkan Oğur on the other hand unites jazz and Anatolian music within himself as a person: as fretless guitar player he is mainly a jazz musician, who played with numerous international well-known jazz musicians,[123] or in his own group *Telvin*; with *kopuz* however, he is a successful performer of Turkish folk songs (most well-known is his duo with Ismail Demircioğlu [*bağlama*]). Similar combinations of jazz and Turkish music had already been tried by Turkish jazz musicians, for example with the album "JazzEastern" – an "Osman Ismen Project," including musicians such as Ercan Irmak (*ney*, *zurna*, *mizmar*) and Halil Karaduman (*kanun*) (Columbia 1998).

Other projects have tried to bring together Turkish and Flamenco music (Dawe & Eroğlu 2013). On his last two CDs the *ud* player Mutlu Torun partly plays *ud* using Flamenco playing techniques, which he learned in Spain from Pepe Rodriguez, Rafael Nogales and Nino Ricardo.[124] However he has also written a *saz semaisi* for classical guitar.[125] Ahmet Aslan learned Flamenco Guitar in Rot-

---

122 Interview with Vladimir Ivanoff April 30, 2000 in Berlin. CD Sarband: Cantico, JARO, 1990; CD *Music of the Emperors*, JARO, 1992; CD *Llibre Vermell de Montserrat. Medieval Pilgrim Songs from Spain*, JARO 1994; CD *Sepharad. Songs of the Spanish Jews in the Mediterranean and the Ottoman Empire*, BMG, 1995; CD *Sephardic Songs. In the Hispano-Arabic Tradition of Medieval Spain*, JARO, 1996; CD *Fallen Women. Women as Composers and Performers of Medieval Chant*, JARO, 1998; CD L'Orient Imaginaire: *Yehudi: Jewish Music from the Seraglio*, Teldec, 1996; CD *Gerusalemme Liberata*, Teldec, 1999; *Alla Turca*, Teldec, 1999; CD *Fantasies from Hindoostan*, Teldec, 2000; CD *Danse Gothique: Music by Satie & Machaut*, JARO, 2000.

123 E.g. MC *Istanbul Connection* with Erkan Oğur (fretless guitar), Dick de Graaf (saxophon), Baki Duyarlar (piano), Ruben van Rompaey (percussion), Erdal Akyol (double bass), Joost Kroon (drums), Kalan 2006.

124 http://www.muziksoylesileri.net/cms/index.php?option=com_content&task=view&id=224&Itemid=45 (20 August 2015)

125 *Bulusmalar*, 2001. *From Spain's flamenco to the horon of Blacksea*: *Flamenco Alaturka* is a common project of Spain and Turkey with Spanish and Turkish dancers and musicians, performing with a synthesis of Flamenco and Turkish local music, accompanied by an orchestra formed of Flamenco and Turkish musical instruments.
http://www.dailymotion.com/video/x9xtmm_flamenco-turkoetnik34_creation

terdam and adapted its picking technique for *bağlama*. Further combination of flamenco guitar and *bağlama* include:

- Arif Sağ & Gerardo Nuñez Flamenco group, which performed in concert in 2002 in Istanbul (Kalkan 2004: 191ff);
- Erkan Oğur (*kopuz*, fretless guitar), Ismail Altunsaray (*bağlama*, voice), Paco Peña, Flamenco guitar), Miguel Ortega, (voice), performed in concert in Berlin, 2009;
- Erdal Akkaya (*bağlama*) & Jeronimo Maya (Flamenco guitar), concerts and CD in 2914.[126]

Some projects involving larger ensembles:

- Kudsi Erguner: *Tasavvuf'tan Flamenko'ya / L'Orient de l'Occident*, concert at the Summer Festival Barcelona, 1995.[127]
- *Sufi Müzik'ten Flamenko'ya* / From Sufi Music to Flamenco, initiated by Kulsan for a concert series in the Netherlands in 1999[128]
- On her CD *Hevra* / Together (2013) the Kurdish singer Aynur Doğan cooperated with several Spanish musicians, the arrangements of the songs were written by the Spanish musician, Javier Limón using among others Flamenco guitars together with *tembur* (a small version of the *bağlama*) in Tunceli/Dersim, Flamenco voice, piano.[129]

Other Iberian or Latin music styles have also been combined with Turkish music, for example:

- Fado singer Ana Moura together with Turkish folk singer Gülay, held a concert in Bursa in 2008;
- Fado singer Katia Guerreiro and Ahmet Aslan (contemporary songs from Dersim), held a concert in Berlin in 2010
- "*Ederlezi* – Turkey in Madrid," music project by Eva Monro and Aurora Montero together with Turkish and Spanish Dancers and Musicians performed in Madrid in 2014.[130]
- "*Turquía Latina* – From philharmonic Bolero to Istanbul Tango" (*Vom philharmonischen Bolero bis zum Tango aus Istanbul*) concert with *Bolero Berlin* & Incesaz in Berlin in 2009;

---

http://www.facebook.com/video/video.php?v=53189702220
http://www.dailymotion.com/video/xa1gr4_isil-reina_creation
http://www.dailymotion.com/video/xa192f_one-night-in-ghetto_music

126 CD Erdal Akkaya & Jeronimo Maya: *Endülüs & Anadolu Buluşmalar*, 2014.

127 CD Kudsi Erguner: *Tasavvuf'tan Flamenko'ya / L'Orient de l'Occident*, Al Sur 1995.

128 CD Sufi Müzik'ten *Flamenko'ya / From Sufi Music to Flamenco*, Kalan 2000.

129 CD Aynur: *Hevra / Together*, Sony 2013.

130 Ederlezi promotion video: https://www.youtube.com/watch?v=PeqjoIHSZjo
Ederlezi Serkan Polat & Eva Monro : https://www.youtube.com/watch?v=3F2UiCSRuvM
Ederlezi Turkish Ritm Show: https://www.youtube.com/watch?v=CdLps2v_O1w

The search for unusual sounds in world music have resulted in a growing number of cross-cultural encounters which bring together several non-Western musicians without any Western participation. Examples include Turkish-Yiddish groups such as *Katakofti*, a common project of *De Amsterdam Klezmer Band* & the Galata Gypsy Band, initiated by Kulsan in Amsterdam in 2002.[131] Çiğdem Aslan for example, is an Istanbul-born singer, with Kurdish Alevi background. In Istanbul she initially sang *rebetiko*, sephardic and other music from Turkey. In 2003 she moved to London (to study at Goldsmith's College) and joined the *Dunav* Balkan Group, and in 2008 she joined the Klezmer group *She'Koyokh*.[132]

Other encounters including Turkish-Indian music:

- CD Kudsi Erguner: *Taj Mahal* (2004)
- Süleyman Erguner gave a concert in Berlin in 2008 together with Ali Rıza Şahin (*hafiz*), Murat Cemalettin Necipoğlu (*hafiz*), Alev Erguner (*kanun*), Selim Ergen (Indian *sarod*), Gürkan Özkan (*tabla*, *bendir*);.
- "*Hindistanbul*" with Mısırlı Ahmet (percussion), (Egyptian) Roman Bestion (piano), Özgür Abbak (guitar), Neyveli S. Radhakrishna (violin); concert in Istanbul in 2012.

Turkish-Japanese collaborations include:

- "*Ney-Zen*," a project of Kudsi Erguner (*ney*), Akikazu Nakamura (*shakhuhachi*), Michiyo Yagi (*koto*), Maki Isogai (*koto*), Hakan Güngör (*kanun*); Bruno Caillat (percussion); concerts and CD from 2002–2009.

Eventually a few ensembles emerged which include a complete mix of instrumentation:

- Group *Forabandit* with Sam Karkienia (*mandolonchelle*, voice), Ulaş Özdemir (*bağlama*, voice), Bijan Chemirani (*zarb*, percussion). This group has been playing Occitan and Anatolian songs with Persian percussion since 2009.[133] Further cross-cultural Turkish world musicians include, just to name some examples from the Netherlands, the percussionist Sjahin During,[134] Mehmet Polat, [135] and the group *Arifa*.[136]

Even the Turkish ensemble *Kardeş Türküler* was perceived internationally as a kind of cross-cultural group, singing in several languages and combining songs of different Anatolian ethnic and religious groups. Since 1998, the group has taken part in a variety of tours, festivals and other activities all over Europe.

---

131 CD De Amsterdam Klezmer Band & Galata Gypsy Band: *Katakofti*, Kalan 2003.

132 Her debut album was released in 2013: *Mortissa*, Asphalt Tango Records.

133 CD *Forabandit*, Buda Musique 2012; *Port*, Buda Musique 2014.

134 CD Sjahin During: *Afro Anatolian Tales*, Doublemoon 2008.

135 CD Mehmet Polat: *Desire*, Reinmusic 2011; CD Mehmet Polat: *Desire*, Reinmusic 2011; Mehmet Polat Trio: *Next Spring*, Brussels: Homerecords 2014.

136 CD Arifa: *Anatolian Alchemy*, Mundus 2012.

Western classical musicians are more rarely involved in comparable encounters. As part of the program at the Berlin *Philharmonic* concert hall several chamber ensembles of the Berlin Philharmonic Orchestra played together with Turkish ensembles, as well as the a-cappella vocal quintet *Amacord* with the chamber ensemble of the State Choir for Classical Turkish Music Istanbul (director Fatih Salgar) in 2009. This concert was even repeated in Istanbul as part of the program, "Cultural Capital of Europe" in June, 2010. In 2008 the famous baritone Thomas Quasthoff sang together with Turkish folk singer Sabahat Akkiraz (who had already cooperated with Jazz musicians in London in the 1990s).[137] In the same year Derya Türkan Minstrel's Era trio (*kemençe*, cello, double bass) met the viol quintet *Sirius Viols* (Director, Hille Perl); in 2009 Burhan Öçal's Istanbul Oriental Ensemble played with the percussion ensemble of the Berlin Philharmonic Orchestra. In all these cases the musicians exchanged some easy notations of songs beforehand, none of them saw this encounter as a major part of their concert. During the joint rehearsals differences of mentality occasionally became obvious – the Western musicians being used to rehearsing over long periods and focussing on details of interpretation, and then avoiding changing them; while the Turkish musicians were much more flexible in their interpretation or even the selection of their repertoire.

Early Music and Music of the Middle East

The movement of historically informed performance of early Western music (mainly of the Middle Ages, Renaissance and Baroque) led to several large and extensive music projects combining Western and Middle Eastern musicians. The pioneer of this idea was the ensemble, *Sarband* founded in 1986 by the Bulgarian-German lutenist and percussionist, Vladimir Ivanoff and the Munich based *ud*-player Mehmet Yeşilçay.[138] Mehmet Yeşilçay (b. 1960) came from a family of sufis in Istanbul, which had close contacts with well-known sufi musicians, including (his oucle) Seyyid Nusret Yeşilçay, Kani Karaca, Aziz Bahriyeli and Ali Gülses. He himself lived in Germany from the age of eight, and later became a student of Çinuçen Tanrıkorur, meeting musicians such as Ahmet Doğan, *tanbur* player Necip Gülses, Mustafa Doğan Dikmen, *kanun*-player Mehmet Ihsan Özer and *kemençe*-player Ahmet Kadri Rizeli.[139]

---

[137] During the mid-1990s she was the first Turkish folk music singer who entered the international world music market, for example at the London Jazz Festival, with concerts in France, the Netherlands and Brazil. She cooperated with world msuic groups such as Orient Expressions.

[138] Similar approaches already on the LP *Kecskes Ensemble: Ancient Turkish Music in Europe*, Hungaroton, 1984.

[139] Greve 2003: 427; Interview with Mehmet Yeşilçay August 28, 2011 in Istanbul; www.sarband.de.

Ivanoff, as with many other musicians of early music, combined historical research with practical performance from an early stage of his career. In order to improve his understanding of monophonic music, Ivanoff contacted Turkish, Iranian and Arabic musicians in Germany, including Mehmet Yeşilçay and Fadia El-Hage, a Lebanese singer who studied singing at the Richard-Strauss-Conservatory in Munich in the 1980s. *Sarband*'s repertoire consists of early music from both Europe and the Middle East. The CD, *Music of the Emperors* (1992) for example, contains music from the courts of both Frederick II of Sicily (1272-1337) and the Central Asian Emperor Tamerlan (d. 1404). In 1998, as part of the memorial year for Hildegard von Bingen (1098-1179), the *Fallen Woman* project combined Arabic-Byzantine vocal traditions with poems and music by Hildegard von Bingen, and music of the Spanish codex *Las Huelgas* (c.1300). *Sarband* have an additional two albums with Sefardic music from Middle Age sources as well as from oral tradition in the Balkans, Turkey and North Africa. They were released in 1995 und 1996, demonstrating how important traditional Turkish art music had become as part of the ensemble's repertoire. The style of the CD, "*Yehudi – Jüdische Komponisten am Osmanischen Hof*" (Jewish Music at the Ottoman Court) does not differ substantially from a (high quality) production of Istanbul art music. Later the musical encounters of *Sarband* became more experimental. In *Alla Turca*, *Sarband* combined musical reconstructions of notated sources of Ottoman music with music created before the European *alla turca* imaginations of the eighteenth and nineteenth century.[140] In *Danse Gothique* (2000) the ensemble arranged songs from Guillaume de Machaut (c.1300-1377) and piano pieces by Erik Satie (1866-1925) for both European early music and Ottoman-Turkish instruments. A later project picked its storry from the visit of an Ottoman delegation to Prussia 1763-1793, covering music form c.1700-1850. Together with the "*Berliner Barock Solisten,*" *Sarband* gave music concerts with music of the court of Frederick II, including composers such as Louis Ferdinand or Johann Joachim Quantz.[141] It is noteworthy that over decades only a very basic verbal communication between the Arabic, Turkish and the European musicians was possible, since both Vladimir Ivanoff's Turkish and his main Turkish partner Ahmet Kadri Rizeli's English is limited (only Ihsan Özer speaks German).

After the year 2000, personal reasons prompted the separation of Mehmet Yeşilçay and Vladimir Iwanoff. As a result, today two ensembles with a comparable aesthetic and repertoire exist, Ivaoff's *Sarband*, and Yeşilçay's *Pera* Ensemble, founded in 2005 together with Ihsan Özer. *Pera* has performed in numerous

140 CD L'Orient Imaginaire: Alla Turca, Teldec; including reconstructions following Giovanni Battista Donà: *Della letteratura de' Turci, Osservazioni* (...), Venice 1688; Charles Blainville: *Histoire générale, critique et philologique de la musique*, Paris 1767; Giovanni Battista Toderini: *Letteratura Turchesca*, Venedig 1787 and others more.

141 CD Concerto Köln &Sarband: *Dream of the Orient.* Deutsche Grammophon 2003. CD Concerto Köln & Sarband: *The Waltz. Ecstasy and Mysticism*, Archiv Produktion 2005.

concert halls and festivals[142] in cooperation with ensembles such as *Hesperion XXI* and *Concerto Köln*. *Pera's* most extensive project was the fictive Handel opera "Armida," a collage of music from several Handel operas and historical Ottoman court music. "Trialog – Music for One God" combined Assyrian and Baroque church music, with music by Ali Ufukî, Zekai Dede, Itrî, Hâfiz Post, Praetorius, Pergolesi and others.

Meanwhile a number of projects or ensembles tried to combine European Baroque, Renaissance or Medieval music with Ottoman music. Similarly to Sarband, an historical approach was applied solely to the European part (using historical instruments such as viola da gamba or harpsichord), but the Ottoman music was mostly performed in contemporary Turkish style.[143] These include:

- The Ensemble *Musica Historica*, which was founded in Budapest in 1988 by Rumen István Csörsz (b. 1974) who sings, and plays *koboz*, *duda*, *zurna*, cello, percussion, jews' harp, *bağlama*, lute, violine, and flute. The group has developed its interpretation through the study of classical and early music, as well as traditional music from Hungary and Eastern Europe, their repertoire includes Solakzade (sic), Ali Ufukî, Balassi Bálint (1554–1594), Wathay Ferenc and others.[144]
- Since 1998 the Montreal (Canada) based ensemble *Istanbul*, directed by Kiya Tabassian (who is also a member of the Greek ensemble, *En Chordais*), has performed medieval and renaissance European music, but with the Iranian lute *setar* as the leading instrument (along with gamba and percussion).[145] The CD *Terres Turquoise* (2004) is dedicated to Turkish music, including Judeo-Spanish romances, Ottoman art music, and music from Salonika, Izmir and Alexandria.
- *Izmir Baroque* was founded in Izmir by double bass (and viola da gamba) player Bülent Oral and (Baroque) violinist Hakan Özaytekin. The ensemble plays music of the European and Ottoman courts from the sixteenth until the first half of eighteenth century on original instruments, e.g. Jean Babtiste Lully, Gazi Giray Han, Claudio Monteverdi, Ali Ufukî etc. Members include Atilla Oral (voice, baroque flute), Erica Fossi (harpsichord), Şehvar Beşiroğlu (*kanun*, *çenk*), Mehmet Rafik Kaya (*rebab*) and Hüseyin Tuncel (percussion).
- "Three Alla Turca Baroque Pasticcios," played by Guitarist Melih Güzel on his album *Sounds of Anatolia* (Aura, 2000).

---

142 E.g. at Händel Festspiele Halle, Schleswig Holstein Music Festival, Festtage Alter Musik Innsbruck, Rheingau Musikfestival, Berliner Philharmonie, Kölner Philharmonie, Konzerthaus Dortmund, CRR Istanbul and many others.

143 In February, 2012 for example in Venice a "*Festival di Musica Balcanika Dimitrie Cantemir*", including Jordi Savall & Esperion XXI (Spain), Ensemble *Meragi* (Italy), Ensemble *Bezmara* (Turkey) and Ensemble *Anton Pann* (Rumänia).

144 www.musicahistorica.hu/inndex-eng.html (accessed March 19, 2014).

145 Their first CD was *Musique du Moyen Âge et de la Renaissance*, Atma Classique 2001.

- The *Cantemir Ensemble* with Ihsan Özgen (*kemençe*) and Linda Burman-Hall (harpsichord), combined European Baroque and Ottoman music, and also contemporary compositions, including Lou Harrison: "In Honor of Prince Kantemir" (1996), for *kemençe*, baroque viola, viola, *kudüm*, tambourine; Yalçın Tura: Andante (a movement of his Concerto per *kemençe*, *tanbur*, harpsichord, early guitar, baroque flute, baroque violin, viola, 2000). They also perform orientalizing European Baroque, including pieces by composers such as Thomas Shwo (1738), Marin Marais (1725) and Jean-Baptiste Lully (1670); further a "Moldavian Dance: Syrba" and collective improvisations. Instruments include Baroque gamba, Baroque violine, Baroque flute, lute, *tanbur* (Murat Aydemir), and *kemençe* (Neva Özgen).[146]
- *Ensemble Galatia* was founded in 2003 in Ankara by F. Kaan Bahadir und Selcuk Dalar. The group plays medieval music, including *Cantigas de Santa Maria* (Spain, thirteenth century), *Cantigas d'Amigo* (Portugal, 1220-1350), *Llibre Vermell de Montserrat* (Katalonia, fourteenth century), but also Sefardic songs, Italian songs and dances, *muwashshahat* (Arabic-and Alusian poetry eleventh-twelfth century) or Abd al-Qadir Merâghî. Among the instruments used are *kanun*, *ud*, *lavta*, *setar*, *santur*, *ney*, *kabak kemane*, *kudüm*, bendir, def, as well as vielle, rebec, *setar*, psaltery and recorders.[147]
- CD *Les Fin'Amoureures: Marions Les Roses. Chansonss & Psaumes de la France à l'Empire Ottoman* (Alpha 2005). A French trio composed of two viols and one singer interprets Franch folk and renaisance music, maronite and landino music and one psaum as notated by Ali Ufukî.
- The CD, *From Byzantium to Andalusia* by Oni Wytar's Ensemble in 2006 (Naxos), played Mediterranean, Christian, Jewish and Islamic music of the Middle Ages, including Italian *Laude* (from the *Laudario di Cortona*, thirteenth century), hymns by Yunus Emre (*Bir Gece Muhammed'e, Ey Dervisler, Ey Kardesler*"), Andalusian Judeo – Sephardic romances, Christian-Arabic music from Syria, music of the "Andalusian school" in Morocco, and Christian-Spanish music from the *Llibre vermell de Montserrat* (fourteenth century).
- "Itri in the East, Bach in the West" (*Doğu'da Itri Batı'da Bach*), a concert in Istanbul in 2010 with Göksel Baktagir, Yurdal Tokcan, Selim Güler, Emrullah Sengüller (cello), Eyüp Hamış (*ney*) and Ümit Atalay (percussion)
- *Osmanlı Barok Müziği* ("Ottoman Baroque Music", Kalan, 2011) was a project of the harpsichord player and expert on (European) Baroque music, Leyla Pınar, realised in 2011. The repertoire included music in Istanbul as notated by Europeans visitors such as Ch.H. Blainville, G. Toderini, F.J. Sulzer, as well as compositions notated in Dimitir Cantemirs *edvâr*, or contemporary composers from much later sources (up to TRT notations). In the liner notes Leyla

146 CD *Cantemir Ensemble*, Golden Horn Records 2004.

147 CD Ensemble Galatia: Ortaçağ Şarkıları / Medieval Music from 13th – 15th Century, Kalan 2013.

Pınar writes: "*We don't know how the works of this composer (Ebubekir Ağa) – a contemporary of Händel and J.S.Bach – or composers such as Hafiz Post, Mustafa Çavus, were performed; in my view they should be interpreted in the context of research findings as well as the globalism of the Baroque world.*" Leading instruments in this approach are the harpsichord, in addition to the bass recorder, Baroque trumpet, singers (including the counter tenors Kaan Buldular and Celal Eldeniz), *kemençe* and Ottoman-Turkish percussion. Notably the singers use Western voice technique including vibrato in the style of Baroque opera arias.

- *Alla Turca Kollektif* was founded in 2011.[148] At that time German Baroque oboist Sandra Sinsch moved to Istanbul, where she teaches early music at the Istanbul Technical University Turkish State Music Conservatory. One of the ensembles projects was "Bach in Istanbul – The oboe in the Serail". The press text reads:

> 1709: The Ottoman Empire was giving protection to King Charles XII when he had to flee from his Russian enemies. Together with the king came also an oboe player, Johann Jacob Bach, Johann Sebastian Bach's younger brother. Records show that Bach has performed concerts for the Sultan and Ottoman intellectuals. There are also references that the oboe entered into the *Muzika-i Humayun* (the ensemble of the Ottoman Empire Palace "Saray") in the eighteenth century along with the other Western instruments that we use in the program. We invite you to join us on our journey through the old Istanbul on the eve of the Tulip period, during which the Ottoman Empire lived an intellectual Renaissance inspired by foreign trends. The music of Bach's environment will meet the sounds of the Imperial palace, the Janissary Band, the lodges of the Whirling Dervishes and also the music of Istanbul's baroque expat community. Works from the Ali Ufkî collection, Tanburi Mustafa Çavus, Zurnazen Ibrahim Ağa, Johann Sebastian Bach, Jean-Philippe Rameau, Giuseppe Toderini and others.

- *Ney* and Cello, was a concert in Istanbul 2012 with Eric Maria Couturier and Kudsi Erguner.
- *Bab-i Saadet*, was a concert in 2012 at the Istanbul music festival, featering the Kudsi Erguner Ensemble and the *Doulce Mémoir* Ensemble with European and Ottoman music of the fifteenth and sixteenth centuries.
- *Camerata* Baroque Opera Ensemble (*Opera Barok Topluluğu*) with Sintem Doğan (harpsichord), Burak Ayrancı (cello), Ceren Dik (flute), Burak Kayan (violine).
- *Passage* (by Imago Mundi), Ottoman art songs combined with troubadour songs and Telemann, Ottoman-Turkish art music singer Mustafa Doğan Dikmen and lute player Sofie Vanden Eynde.
- CD *Bach & Itrî* (Kalan, 2013), a project with Ertan Tekin (*duduk*), Murat Aydemir (*tanbur*) and Çağ Erçağ (cello), combining Ottoman art music and Johann Sebastian Bach (e.g. Flute Sonata in E flat major No. 22 BWV 867, transcription in D minor).

[148] http://en-allaturca.weebly.com/ (August 24, 2015).

- *Bach'tan Dede Efendi'ye*, was a concert program in 2014, including the cello quartett *Cellistanbul*, pianist Hakan Ali Toker and the *ney* player Burcu Karadağ.

Probably the most well-known concert and CD project in this field was Jordi Savall's interpretation of notations transmitted by Dimitrie Cantemir.[149] The Spanish conductor and viola player Savall (b. 1941), one of the major figures in the field of early European music, came across Cantemir's collection in 1999 during a project on Isabella of Castile.[150] In Owen Wright's 1996 edition he found a reliable and readable source for the notation. Savall's realisation of selected pieces, included his international ensemble Hesperion XXI,[151] and a number of well-known Turkish musicians, including Kudsi Erguner, Hakan Güngör, Murat Salim Tokaç, Yurdal Tokcan, Derya Türkan and Fahrettin Yarkın. Savall selected three anonymous compositions from the Cantemir collection, one by Cantemir himself, and three by his contemporaries Baba Mest, Edirneli Ahmed and Neyzen Ali Hoca. Later, in order to reflect the cosmopolitan character of Ottoman court culture, Savall added some Jewish-Sephardic songs (*La rosa enflorece*, *Maciço de rosas*, *Sépharade*, as collected by Alberto Hamsi, which were far from Ottoman court tradition) as well as Armenian songs, the latter from Gusan Ashot (1907–1989) and Sayat Nova (1722–1795). Instead of forming an historical Ottoman *fasıl* cycle, Savall hence constructed a completely free composition of pieces. Similarly in the instrumentation Savall included instruments of different provenience and historical periods, such as the *kemençe* (which was never used at the Ottoman court), *ud* (which was not in use in Cantemir's time), *santur* (in fact played at the court in the sixteenth century), the *duduk*, the double-reed instrument of Armenian folk music and of course the European gamba. In order to emphasize the musical form Savall changed the instrumentation between stanza and refrain – a practice foreign to the Ottoman tradition. Jordy Savall's free and unhistorical handling of Cantemir's notation was much discussed and criticized among Turkish musicians: the change to the tempered pitch system, the fast tempo, his embellishments, transpositions, even changes of modes, which combined to allude more to Spanish Renaissance rather than Ottoman court music. Still, due to his international success a second album with a similar concept was devised, though only Hakan Göngör, Murat Salim Tokaç and Fahrettin Yarkın contributed again.[152]

---

149 CD Hesperion XXI & Jordi Savall: *Istanbul. Dimitirie Cantemir, 1673-1723*, Alia Vox 2009, with Hakan Güngör (*kanun*), Yurdal Tokcan (*ud*).

150 CD Orient-Ocident 1200 – 1700, Alia Vox 2006.

151 Haïg Sarikouyoumdjian (Armenia), *ney*, *duduk*; Dimitri Psonis (Greece), *santur*; Driss El Maloumi (Marokko), *oud*; Pedro Estevan (Spain), percussion; Jordi Savall, *vièle à archet*, *lira*, *rebab*.

152 CD Hesperion XXI & Jordi Savall: *La Sublime Porte. Voix d'Istanbul 1430-1750*, Alia Vox 2011.

World Music in Contemporary Western Art Music

In order to understand the huge potential of avant-garde music from Turkey, it might be helpful to take a quick glance at other contemporary arts. Some eleven years ago I interviewed the young video artist, Fikret Atay, who at that time was completely unknown internationally and was on his second trip abroad passing through Berlin. In the age of 26 he had débuted at the Istanbul Biennial one year before, and to his great surprise had been invited to exhibitions in Kassel, Berlin and Paris, and even to London, Los Angeles, and Sydney. At amazing speed an artist from the southeast Anatolian city of Batman was catapulted into some of the most important museums of the world. The main catalyst for this amazing success was obviously the Istanbul Biennial. While state art academies in Istanbul initially taught purely conservative concepts of art, from 1987 the Biennial brought the international innovative scene to Istanbul, and consequently connected formerly isolated Turkish artists to the international art scene.

In 2008, some months after I had moved to Istanbul, I experienced the Istanbul Biennale for the first time. The opening event was spectacular. A huge venue (the *Depo* at *Tophane*), packed full with important international guests, artists, art critics, sponsors, and scholars. Small talk in English, German, Turkish and many other languages abound. The Biennial was as one of the most important international exhibitions for contemporary art in that period. During the early 2000s, in particular in Tophane and Beyoğlu some new art centres opened, financed by Turkish sponsors, in addition to private galleries for Turkish and international contemporary art.[153] Several art fairs took place in Istanbul over recent years, including *Artist Sanat* (held annually, 265 artists in 2009); *Artistanbul* (held irregularly, 180 artists in 2009); *Contemporary Istanbul* (an annual event, in 2011 it was held in the Lütfi Kirdar congress centre with more than 500 artists,); *Art Bosphorus Sanat Fuarı* (held annually, 101 artists in 2011); *Art Show* (held annually, 43 artists in 2011).[154] In 2009/2010 contemporary Turkish art sold better than classical art for the first time ever. On November 15, 2009 the most expensive work (by Burhan Doğançay) fetched 2.2 million Turkish Lira. In 2009 Sotheby's organized its first ever auction solely for contemporary Turkish art (Erten 2010: 20).

Comparably successful during recent years was Turkish contemporary literature, in particular after 2006, when Orhan Pamuk was awarded the Nobel Prize for Literature. In 2008, Turkey was the visiting country at the *Frankfurt Book Fair* (the world's largest and most important trade fair for books). Meanwhile all im-

153 In Beyoglu around the Istiklal Street for example *Aksanat* (*Akbank*), *Salt Galata* (*Garanti Bankası*), *Salt Beyoglu* (*Garanti Bankası*), *Yapı Kredi Bankası* (publishing house, galery), *Arter* (Vehbi Koç Foundation). Several privately owned museums for contemporary art include Sakıp Sabancı Museum (2002), Istanbul Modern (Eczadebaşı; 2005); Pera Museum (Koç, 2005), Tütün Deposu (*Anadolu Kültür*).

154 Bakbaşa 2011; anonymus: Sahne Çağdaş Sanatın, Radikal 24.11.2011.

portant Turkish writers have had their work translated into European languages. Even earlier, beginning in the 1990s, Turkish film makers (including Nuri Bilge Ceylan, Zeki Demir Kubuz, Semih Kaplanoğlu, Reha Erdem and Kutluğ Ataman) gained an international reputation. In 2008 Nuri Bilge Ceylan was awarded with the *Best Director Award* at the *Cannes Film Festival* for his film *Üç Maymun* ("Three Monkeys"); in 2011 with the *Grand Jury Prize* for *Bir Zamanda Anadolu'da* ("Once Upon a Time in Anatolia"); and in 2014 with the *Golden Palm* for *Kış Uykusu* ("Winter Sleep"). In 2010 Semih Kaplan won in Berlin with the *Golden Bear* for *Bal* ("Honey"), just to mention a few examples.

The discrepancy between the international success of Turkey's avant-garde art, literature and film scene and the international profile of Turkish music, with its focus on "traditional" Turkish music, is striking. The prestigious *Istanbul Music Festival* hardly attracts any international audiences. It presents important international orchestras and musicians of classical European music, but only a few contemporary Turkish composers such as Fazıl Say or Kamran Ince), which could attract the curiosity of foreigners. In the international Western music world only a few Turkish composers are known, for example, Fazıl Say, Kamran Ince, Ilhan Mimaroğlu, Bülent Arel, Ilhan Usmanbaş etc.

Over recent decades however, cross-cultural interest has grown, including among Western contemporary musicians (Utz 2015). This openness by Western composers of course has its roots in the exoticism of the nineteenth century, which grew even further in the early twentieth century when composers started to look beyond the boundaries of their own conventions. Claude Debussy (1862-1918) tried to emulate the sound of the Javanese *gamelan* orchestras by means of Western instruments; Béla Bartók (1881-1945) researched the folk music of his own native Hungary, then studied Romania and beyond. Several composers searched for universalism in music, for example Karlheinz Stockhausen (1928-2007) in *Hymnen* (1965). North Indian music was particularly influential for composers such as La Monte Young (b. 1935), Terry Riley (b.1935) and Philip Glass (b. 1937); later György Ligeti (1923-2006) was inspired by African music. In addition several composers have worked with microtonal music, e.g. Alois Hába (1893-1973), Ivan Vishnegradsky (1893-1979), Harry Partsch (1901-1974), La Monte Young and many others. Composers like Lou Harrison (1917-2003) wrote for Javanes *gamelan* ensembles since the 1970s. Today, Western avant-garde music is both composed and performed almost worldwide, including by composers from Asia, Africa or South America.[155]

One pioneer of cross-cultural encounters with contemporary Western music was the Kronos Quartet, founded in 1973 by David Harrington in Los Angeles. The ensemble began with interpretations of works by experimental composers such as George Crumb, Philip Glas, Terry Riley, Henryk Mikolaj Górecki and

---

155 Mack 2004; Utz 2002; 2014; Ryker 1991.

others. On the more conventional side, the quartet also played arrangements of jazz pieces by Ornette Coleman, Charles Mingus or John Zorn, and later even Pop and Rock, including Jimi Hendrix. In 1992 the CD, "Pieces of Africa" was released with music of African composers, in 2002, "Nuevo" with Mexican music. Over the years Kronos cooperated with numerous non-Western musicians and composers, including the chinese *pipa* (lute) player Wu Man, Bollywood singer Asha Bhosle, Inuit singer Tanya Tagaq or the Romanian Gypsy band *Taraf de Haïdouks*. As part of these efforts Kronos encountered the *makam* based music of the Middle East. For the CD, "Night Prayer" (1993) the Azerbaijani composer Firengiz Alizade (Franghiz Ali-Zadeh, born 1947 in Baku) composed the piec,e "*Mugam sayagi*," which actually was her first composition which dealt with Azerbaijan *muğam*. The piece, however, does not include any traditional melody or *muğam* structures but rather is a free composition of melodic layering with short, expressional melodies. In 2005 the Kronos Quartet devoted a whole CD to the composer.[156] Kronos' later CD's, "Floodplain" (Nonsuch 2009) and "Rainbow" (Nonsuch 2010) were devoted to musicians of the Middle East and Central Asia, including arrangements of Egyptian, Iraqi and Iranian songs, Indian *raga*s, Turkish and Kazakh instrumental pieces and Greek *rembetiko*. In 1999 Turkish percussionist Burhan Öçal composed the piece, *Dance of Rhythm* for the quartet.[157] The main arranger of the quartet, however, was the New York trombone player and composer Jacob Garchik.

In 2008 Kronos embarked on an intense collaboration with the traditional Azerbaijan singer Alim Qasimov. Qasimov selected appropriate songs, most of them well-known twentieth century songs, written by Western educated composers such as Cahangir Cahangirov (1921–1992) and Şəfiqə Axundova, but also the famous *Getme, getme* ("Don't Leave, Don't Leave") by the *tar* player Səid Rüstəmov (1907–1983). Recordings of these songs as performed by Qasimov's traditional ensemble (including *kamança* [bowed stringed instrument], *tar* [lute], *balaban* [double-reed instrument] and *def* [frame drum]) were sent to New York to Jacob Garchik, who wrote a version for a string quartet, adding some new sections, partly in late romantic harmony and partly in motoric ostinati allusion to Philip Glass. The music therefore went through a double transformation: from composition to free arrangements, including improvisation and from there back to fixed, precomposed pieces. During the rehearsals in San Francisco the Azerbaijan musicians usually played without notation and hence changed the interpretation each time, while the string quartet tried to maintain conformity to the notation.[158]

---

156 CD Mugam Sayagi: *Music of Franghiz Ali-Zadeh*, Nonesuch.

157 A version for orchestra is recorded on the CD, Burhan Öçal & Istanbul Oriental Orchestra / Züricher Kammerorchester: *Concerto Alla Turca*, Universal Music 2006.

158 http://kronosquartet.org/projects/detail/alim_qasimov_ensemble (accessed April 28, 2016).

Several international ensembles followed the cross-cultural approach of the Kronos Quartet, including Yo-Yo Ma's *Silk Road Project* (founded 1998), or the Dutch *Atlas Ensemble*. In 2001 Silk Road commissioned the piece, *Eski Istanbul'un Arka Sokaklarında* ("In the Side Streets of Old Istanbul") from Hasan Uçarsu; in 2014 the ensemble cooperated with Aynur Doğan. The Atlas Ensemble (and academy) was founded in 2002 in Amsterdam by the Artistic Director of the *Nieuw Ensemble*, Joël Bons, and consists of members of the latter group in addition to (revolving) musicians from several Asian countries including China, Iran, Azerbaijan, Armenia, Turkey and others. In 2004 Evrim Demirel wrote *Four Folksongs from Anatolia* for the ensemble. Another cross-cultural ensemble from the Netherlands, *Ziggurat*, was founded in 2003 by the composer and saxophonist Theo Loevendie. Loevendie, an expert on Turkish art music, became a composer later in his career. Inspired by the Atlas Ensemble he started this latter ensemble, which combines instruments and musicians from different traditions, such as an *erhu* from China, a *kanun*, an Armenian *duduk*, a viola da gamba and his own soprano saxophone. Evrim Demirel's composition *Makamsız* ("without *makam*", 2005) was written for *Ziggurat*. In 2006 the *Nederlands Blazers Ensemble* developed another project with the singer Aynur Doğan, and compositions / arrangements by the American-Turkish composer Kamran İnce.[159] In Istanbul the *Hezarfen* Ensemble is the best and most active ensemble for contemporary Western music, including Turkish instruments.

A number of music festivals in Europe have included cross-cultural contemporary music in their programs, e.g.

- "Music of the Centuries" ("*Musik der Jahrhunderte*") in Stuttgart/Germany has been running since 2005.
- Congress "Microtonality: Practice and Utopia", Stuttgart, 2011.[160]
- Music Festival *MaerzMusik*, Berlin 2013 with the focus, "*(Um)Brüche: Türkei. Levante. Maghreb*".[161]
- *Yakamoz* Festival Turkish Music and Culture Today ("*Türkische Musik und Kultur Heute*"), Hannover/Germany, 2011.[162]

---

159 CD *Turquoise*, NBE. In 2004 the CD *Zeikekiko. The Greek Concert* (NBE 014) was released in cooperation with Greek musicians. See also the project of the New York based string quartett *Brooklyn Rider* with the Iranian *Kamanche* player, Kayhan Kalhor, CD *Silent City*, World Village 2008.

160 With papers by Michalis Cholevas (Rotterdam) and Julien Jalâl Eddine Weiss (Istanbul).

161 Including *Hasretim* by Marc Sinan; Erdem Helvacıoğlu & Ulrich Mertens: *Planet X*; sound installation by Cevdet Erek; *Ensemble Adapter* and *Hezarfen*; a concert with early Turkish and Arabic composers for electronic music and a symposium on New Music in Arabic-Turkish mediteranean.

162 Including Alper Maral, Murat Coskun & *Ensemble Fisfüz*, Fazıl Say & Borusan Quartett, Taner Akyol; Burhan Öcal; a symposium entitled "New (?) Music at the Bosphorus – Germqan-Turkish Perspectives" (*Neue (?) Musik am Bosporus – deutsch-türkische Perspektiven*).

- Music festival *Kreuztanbul* (composers from Kreuzberg, a neighbourhood in Berlin) and Istanbul), annual from 2007-2009[163]
- Music festival “Sound art Istanbul” (Klangkunst Istanbul), Zurich, 2012.[164]
- Project of the *Komische Oper* Berlin opera house over several years, “Turkish. Opera can do that” (“*Türkisch. Oper kann das*”), later “Selam Opera”, including the commission for a children’s opera from Taner Akyols: “Ali Baba and the Forty Thieves” (“*Ali Baba und die 40 Räuber*”), 2012, libretto Çetin Ipekkaya and Marietta Rohrer-Ipekkaya.
- The festival *Akzente* in Duisburg/Germany 2009 included a workshop (with commissions for compositions) for two composers from Duisburg together with two Turkish composers (Gerhard Stäbler, Kunsu Shim, Can Aksel Akın und Ahmet Altınel).
- The conference, “*Rewriting of Turkish Traditions*” was held at Codarts, Rotterdam in 2007 with composers and musicians from the Netherlands, Germany and Turkey.
- “Global Music. Contemporary Expression” was an international composers competition organized by the Association for New Music, Brandenburg/Germany (*Internationaler Kompositionswettbewerb des Brandenburgischen Vereins Neue Musik e.V.*) in 2007. Candidates submitted a composition of up to 15 minutes, for a chamber ensemble plus either *sheng* (chinese mouth organ), *bağlama*, *ajaeng* (korean zither) or soprano voice or electronics. The advisor for *bağlama* was Taner Akyol.

This still emerging musical field is characterized by intense cooperation between composers, musicologists and musicians. Similar to practitioners of early music, where musicians often conduct historical research, a number of composers have published books or articles on post-colonial contemporary music. Some Western composers include:

- Swiss composer Klaus Huber (b. 1924, Bern, Switzerland), a former professor at the music academies of Basle and Freiburg. He became interested in Arab music once his academic career had already finished. With the Second Gulf War of 1990/1 and the image of an aggressive Islamic world being propagated in Western news, Huber started to explore Arab literature. Huber composed a chamber cantata entitled, “*Die Erde dreht sich auf den Hörnern eines Stiers*” (“Earth turns on the Horns of a Bull”) for a Sufi-singer, three Arab instrumentalists, viola, guitar, and electronics. He premiered with the participation of

---

163 In 2008 presenters were Mısırlı Ahmet; Erdal Erzincan; Taner Akyol Trio; İlahn Mimaroğlu, Pieter Snapper; Metin Kemal Kahraman; Mercan Dede; Alper Maral; Erdem Helvacıoğlu. In 2009, Alper Maral, İlhan Mimaroglu, Onur Türkmen, Stefan Pohlit, Kudsi Erguner & Markus Stackhausen, Renaud Garcia Fons, Alexander Hacke & Brenna McCrimmon.

164 Presenters were *Baba Zula*, Tuna Base (electroacoustic world & visuals), Metin Ülkü (piano), Aynur Dogan.

the ensemble, Al-Kindi in 1994 at the *Tage für Neue Kammermusik* in Witten (Germany). Here as well as in several subsequent works *makam* is used by Huber simply as tone material.[165]

- Amsterdam based composer and saxophone player Theo Loevendie (b. 1930) cooperated with the well-known *kemençe* player Ihsan Özgen;[166] in 1995 he composed *Six Turkish Folk poems.*
- During the project, *Into Istanbul* in 2008, supported by the *Siemens Arts Program*, the composers Mark André, Beat Furrer, Samir Odeh-Tamimi and Vladimir Tarnopolski stayed in Istanbul for several weeks. The compositions they wrote during this time were later performed by *Ensemble Modern.*[167]
- Palestinian composer Samir Odeh Tamimi (b. 1970, Tel-Aviv) was active for several years in ensembles for traditional Arabic music, before he studied musicology in Kiel, Germany and composition with Younghi Pagh Paan and Günter Steinke in Bremen.
- In 2009, American composer Christopher Trapani wrote a piece for the French *kanun* player, Julien Jalâl Ed-Dine Weiss (Pohlit 2011: 182).
- The German-Turkish-Armenian guitarist and composer Marc Sinan (b. 1976) composed "*Hasretim* – Journey to Anatolia" in 2010, including video recordings from traditional Turkish musicians together with newly composed contemporary music for orchestra; his subsequent project was *Dede Korkut* (2015) with music from Central Asia, and eventually *Komitas* (2016). The projects were realized in cooperation with the Dresden Symphony orchestra, plus guest musicians from Turkey and Central Asia respectively.
- Israel Neuman (b. 1966) wrote "Normal Mode" for Chamber Orchestra and Electronics in 2010 in Iowa, using microtones as employed in Turkish music (though no other Turkish musical influence is discernible)
- Helmut Zapf (b.1956), *Albedo IX* (2003) for *bağlama*, flute, clarinette, horn and piano

Finally some Western, non-Turkish composers are (or were) based in Istanbul, including Pieter Snapper (b. 1967), Michael Ellison (b. 1969) and Stefan Pohlit (b. 1967).[168] Since 2016 the Istanbul based *Hezarfen* Ensemble, in cooperation with

---

[165] Pohlit 2011: 197ff.; Utz 2014: 69ff; www.klaushuber.com.

[166] CD *Inspirations*, Kalan 1995, the basis of most of the pieces is religious Ottoman music (*nefes*, *ilahi*, *saz semai*) including free jazz improvisations.

[167] Mark Andre: *üg*; Beat Furrer: *Xenos*; Samir Odeh-Tamimi: *Cihangir*; Vladimir Tarnopolski: *Eastanbul.*

[168] Michale Ellison composed (among others) a *Turkish Concerto* for Turkish instruments, cello and orchestra (2008). Ethnomusicologist and saxophone player Robert Reigle is active mainly in spektral music aktiv. Reigle & Whitehead 2008, Stefan Pohlit wrote his Ph.D. thesis at the MIAM Istanbul after having completed his study in Germny (with Wolfgang Riehm among others), and taught composition and music theory at the ITÜ. Over the years he conducted research on Ottoman music and some of his compositions are related to it, e.g. *Ikaros* (2006) and *Der zerrissene Orpheus* (2006) both for orchestra.

the University of Bristol conducts a five year research program on the interaction of contemporary music and traditional Turkish music.

Non-Turkish Musicians performing Turkish Music

Early in the development of world music, European and American musicians began to learn traditional music, at first primarily Indian or Arabic, but later also Turkish music; often many styles one after the other. Musicians including Don Cherry, Charlie Mariano or groups such as Codona and Oregon eventually claimed to perform music of the whole world.

In particular collaborations took place in folk music ensembles of Turkish migrants based in Europe. Two technical problems constrain these musical cooperations. Firstly, language: Both Anatolian folk music and Ottoman Turkish art music are primarily vocal. Turkish is very different to Indo-European languages and thus difficult for Europeans to learn, with the consequence that most non-Turkish musicians are forced to remain in the background, only accompanying Turkish singers. The second challenge is the different tone system which makes exact intonation for non-Turks very difficult. Most cross-cultural ensembles are thus forced to play in tempered tuning. One of the rare exceptions is the French singer Françoise Demir (b. 1957), accompanied on a *bağlama* by her husband Mahmut Demir (b. 1960).[169]

Even more difficult is the issue of intonation in Turkish art music, a precise intonation of its microtones is almost impossible for foreigners who didn't grew up with this music. Only a few non-Turkish musicians have successfully met the challenge of *makam* beyond *arabesk*-like art music, and even then only as instrumentalists, not as far as I know as singers.[170] The most well-known non-Turkish musicians in Ottoman-Turkish (and other) music are Julien Weiss and Ross Daily (mentioned above).

[169] MC Mahmut & Françoise Demir: *Garip ile Senem*, Bayar, 1987; MC *Ağlama Bebeğim*, ASM, 1993; CD *Turquie Musique des Troubadours*, Ethnic Auvidis, 1992; CD *Yar Bağında*, Kalan, 1995. In 1996 Françoise Arnaud-Demir published the folk song anthology *Littérature Populaire: En Suivant les Âşık*, Montreuil: Anka.

[170] MC *Inspirations: Rotterdam Concert*, Kalan, 1995 a project of the *kemençe* player Ihsan Özgen together with Dutch musicians including Theo Loevendie (saxophone), Guus Jansen (piano), Martin van Duynhoven (drums) with jazz versions of *bektaşi nefes* and *ilahi*. Two further hardly known but remarkable exceptions include the Finn based group *Nefes*, where since 1990 Turkish musicians (*kanun*, *ney*, clarinet, *ud*, percussion) and Finnish musians cooperate, including Panu Helke (recorder), Kai Olander (*ney*, bulgarian *kaval*), Ismo Piipponen (percussion); MC *Nefes: Fasl-ı Nefes*, Güvercin, 1996; the Dutch ensemble *Çalgija* was founded in 1969 by musicologist Wouter Swets (synthesizer, accordeon), Roel Sluis (voice, *kaval*, recorder), Joost Rekveld *(ney*, *tanbur*, *rawap*, *dutar*, *daf)*, Kamil Abbas (violin, *gidschäk*, *rawap*), Janni Kyriakidhis *(ud)*, Magnus Robb (viola); MC *Çalgija: Music of the Balkan and Anatolia 2*, Pan, 1992. Further see the CD Sylvain Rappaport (piano) & Youval Micenmacher (percussion): *Turkish Songs*, Al Sur, 1997; Vincent Courtois & Gilles Andrieux: *Turkish Blend*, Al Sur, 1995.

> The Swiss-Alsatian born Bernard Weiss (born 1953), graduate of the École Normale de Musique (Paris), started his musical career as a classically trained guitar player and also, occasionally, performed as a Jazz musician. The decisive experience that led Julien [Jalâl Ed-Dine] Weiss (...) to break with his inherited musical roots occurred in 1976: He was invited to a reception with the Egyptian Minister of Culture, Farouk Hosni, where he was given the occasion to listen, for the first time, to a recording of Munir Bashir. He was equally fascinated by scholarly descriptions of Arab musical theory, the phenomenon of *tarab* and microtonal pitches in which he was initially instructed by the ethnomusicologist Jean-Claude Chabrier. (...) He subsequently travelled the Middle East to study with teachers in Tunis, Baghdad, Beirut, Cairo and Istanbul. He met Munir Bashir for the first time at a festival in Fés in the early 1980's and would later visit him regularly in Amman. (Pohlit 2011: 10f)

Weiss later switched to *kanun* and in 1983 founded the ensemble, *Al-Kindi* in Paris. In Aleppo, *Al-Kindi* worked with renowned Syrian masters of Arab religious chants, in particular with Sheykh Hamza Shakkûr (1944-2009), Sabri Moudallal (1918-2006) and Sheykh Ahmad Habboush.[171] In 2010, Mohamed Gomar (Iraqi *joza*) and the Turks Aslıhan Özel (*kemençe*) and Özer Özel (*tanbur*) joined the ensemble (Pohlit 2011: 12). In 1986, Julien Weiss converted to Islam, learned Syrian Arabic and adopted the Muslim name of Jalâl Ed-Dine, in remembrance of Mevlana Rumi. Julien Weiss resided in Aleppo until 2005 and then moved to Istanbul (Pohlit 2011: 12).

A number of contemporary international workshops offer lectures in Turkish (and other) music for non-Turks, including the above mentioned Labyrinth workshops in Crete, and similar workshops in Greece; but also regular music summer workshops in Turkey, for example, the "Turkish Music Workshop Days" in June 2011 in Antalya organized by the "Ottoman Music Centre" (Emine Kolivar);[172] or the "International Summer School of Turkish Music" of the OMAR (Istanbul University) in June 2015.[173] Many Turkish musicians in Istanbul today have at least occasional international students. Regular workshops take place in Italy, the USA, BA and Masters degrees in Turkish music are offered in Rotterdam and Mannheim (Germany). In addition several method books for autodidactic study of Turkish music have been published, including.

- Sağ, Arif; Erzincan, Erdal: *Bağlama Metodu* / Baglama Method (2 volumes), Englisch / Turkish, 2009

171 At its foundation the group comprised (besides Weiss) of the Syrians Ziyâd Kâdî Amin (*nay*) and Muhammad Qadri Dalal (*ud*), and the Egyptian Adel Shams el-Din (percussion); other names accompanied by "Al-Kindi" have included the singers Adib Dayikh and Omar Sarmimi (Aleppo), Husayin Ismail al-Azami (Iraq), Loutfi Bouchnak (Tunis), and Doğan Dikmen (Turkey).

172 Teachers included Derya Türkan (*kemençe*), Mehmet Erenler (*bağlama*), Murat Aydemir (*tanbur*), Murat Bagdatli (*ud*), and Yavuz Akalin (*ney*).

173 İnci Cayirli (repertoire, style), Sadrettin Özçimi (*ney*), Murat Aydemir (*tanbur*), Derya Türkan (*kemençe*), Göksel Baktagir (*kanun*), and Yurdal Tokcan (*ud*).

- Murat Aydemir (translation: Erman Dirikcan): Turkish Music Makam Guide, 2010 (Greek translation 2012; German translation in preparation)
- Altinay (2010): *Turkish Musical Instruments.*
- Parlak, Erol: *Bağlama* Schule, Acoustic Music, Oldenburg 2011, German / English / Turkish
- Burcu Karadağ: *Meskte Ney Eğitimi.* Teaching the *Ney* with the Meşk Method, Istanbul: Pan 2013
- Eric Ederer, *Makam and Beyond*, 2015.
- Fahrettin Yarkın, *Türk Müziğinde Usuller / The Usul in Turkish Music / Τα Ογσογλ Στην Τογϱκικη Μογσικη*, Istanbul, Pan, 2017.

As an example of European musicians who play Turkish music, let us focus briefly on the products of one particular European country, Spain:[174]

- Efrén López (b. 1972, Valencia)[175] studied in Crete in the 1990s and later travelled to Turkey, to work with Erkan Oğur, Erol Parlak, Ross Daly, Yurdal Tokcan and Necati Çelik. López plays several Turkish instruments including *bağlama*, *ud* and *kanun.*
- The ensemble, *Milo ke Mandarini* was founded in 2008 and was based in Villanueva de la Vera (Spain), with Isabel Martín (vocal, percussion) and Charlos Ramírez (*lavta*, *saz*, *tanbur*); It performs the music of Greece, Bulgaria, Turkey, and the Sefardic-Jewish tradition. The musicians studied in Crete.[176]
- The ensemble, *La Banda del Pepo* has combined popular flamenco with "oriental sounds," "world music," and "oriental music" since 1999. Musicians include Pepo Sánchez (voice), José Antonio Aarnouste (*guitarra española*), Diego López (drums and *percusiones mediterráneas*), Jaume Pallardo (*bajo eléctrico*), Abel García (*bağlama*, Greek lute), Sara Guirado (dance, percussion) and Christos Barbas (*kaval*, *ney*).[177]

Eric Bernhard Federer describes how non-Turks have adapted the *cümbüş*:

> Outside of Turkey, the cümbüş has been incorporated into the works of American musicians, Steve Vai, David Lindley, Carmine Guida and Ry Cooder; multi-instrumentalist Lu Edmonds (both solo and with the pop group 3Mustafa3), ex-Pink Floyd guitarist David Gilmour in Britain; Italian guitarist Roberto Zanisi and Algerian-French artist Rachid Taha; Israeli composer Arie Shapira; a variety of Sephardic music groups (e.g., L'Ham de Foc and Aman Aman of Spain, Flor de Kanela in the U.S.); Syrian-Swedish folksinger Sabri Yousef, Armenian-Syrian singer Haig Yazdjian, and Armenian-American Ara Dinkjian. (Ederer 2007: 115)

---

174 For these examples I am indepted to Sara Islan!

175 http://www.efrenlopez.net/web_angles/angnoticies.htm (accessed August 25, 2015)

176 www.facebook.com/milokemandarini (accessed August 25, 2015)

177 www.facebook.com/pages/LA-BANDA-DEL-PEPO/137529397035?fref=photo&__mref=message (accessed August 25, 2015)

Well-known international musicians who have cooperated with Turkish musicians include the singer, Loreena McKennith,[178] double bass player Renaud Garcia-Fons and many others.[179]

Conclusion

The internationalisation of Turkish music, as part of the general phenomenon of globalisation, has developed steadily since at least the early nineteenth century. In fact, even much earlier Istanbul was a global city attracting visitors and migrants from both the Islamic world and from Europe. Urban Ottoman music and even Anatolian folk music traditions reflect numerous influences from neighbouring countries and music traditions.

The main catalysts for globalisation were twofold. Firstly the development of a public music life since the nineteenth century, with public concerts and educational institutions (*cemiyet*is, *Darül-Elhân*, municipal and later state conservatorys); combined with the growing importance of media, including notation (since the nineteenth century), which facilitated the printing of notation (1876), books on music, method teaching books, newspapers, journals and since around 1900, 78rpm records.

The second factor enabling the internationalisation of Turkish music is the increase in population mobility. Emigration from the Ottoman Empire to America and Europe, i.e. out of the Islamic world, began in the later nineteenth century. Until the mid-twentieth century migration mainly influenced Western Turkish music. After the 1930s many Western musicians escaped from Nazi Germany to Turkey and became teachers in the emerging Western music life in Ankara and Istanbul.

Both contributing factors to globalisation – media and international mobility – expanded and grew continuously over the early and middle-twentieth century. The foundation of the Republic of Turkey in 1923 reinforced the importance of Europe, though its impact on internationalisation in general is limited. After some two decades of international isolation in the early republican period, Turkey's international profile and participation re-emerged following the Second World War.

Musical relations with Iran and some Arabic countries continued in a reduced form throughout the twentieth century. In parallel, employment migration to several European countries began in the 1960s, reaching its peak in the early 1970s. In Europe a Turkish community life emerged, followed by social and musical diversification. After the coup in 1980, additional political refugees migrated to Europe, including numerous artists, intellectuals and musicians. Since

---

178 CD Loreena McKennith: *An Ancient Muse*, 2006, including Sokrátis Sinópoulos, Haig Yazdjian and others, Kallimopoulou 2009: 200.

179 CD Renaud Garcia-Fons: *Oriental Bass*, Enja 2002.

then, the Turkish population in Europe has remained roughly constant at around 4 million people. The Turkish diaspora in Europe adapted to the daily life in their new home countries but at the same time remained strongly connected to Turkey through travel and media, such as telephone, TV and internet. European Turkish communities became a market for music and musicians from Turkey. During the 1980s and 1990s the most striking peculiarity of this Turkish-European music life was the overwhelming production of CD's (in earlier times MC's) by Euro-Turks, from which the Turkish music industry in Kumkapanı benefited to a large extent. Studio musicians regularly fly from Turkey to Europe, European-based singers and groups come to Istanbul for recording sessions, and Turkey-based musicians travel for concerts throughout Europe. Since the 1980s new musical styles, instruments or songs from Turkey are instantly adopted in the diaspora, for example Arif Sağ's style of the short-necked *bağlama*, classical Turkish art music (*klasik türk müzigi)*, Kurdish and Zaza music, Alevi culture and music, and many more. In the 1980s the development of international Turkish music accelerated. In Greece a revival of Greek-Ottoman musical traditions (including *rembetiko* and *paradosiaká*) began and a number of "Eastern" instruments where reintroduced, which had been forgotten over decades. From the late 1980s concerts and workshops with Turkish musicians were held in Greece. Shortly after, around 1993, the Turkish label *Kalan* Music started to produce historical recordings of *rembetiko* and other (Ottoman-)Greek music in Turkey. Since the 1990s, joint musical projects involving musicians from Turkey and its neighbouring countries substantially increased. These includes both historic neighbours (e.g. Iran), countries, which in the past were part of the Ottoman Empire (e.g. Greece, Bulgaria; and finally countries such as Armenia and Israel, which were founded partially by former Ottoman minorities.

Since the late 1980s the so-called "world music" market developed as an attractive forum for all kinds of traditional music in Europe and America. The world music genre also became known in Istanbul in the 1990s. Approximately five approaches to the integration of Turkish music into world music became apparent: Islamic music as world music; rhythmical music, in particular the asymmetric Anatolian rhythms as world music; cross-cultural encounters (including Indian, Flamenco and many other music traditions) including Turkish musicians; early European music in dialogue with Middle Eastern traditions; and contemporary Western music integrating elements of traditional Turkish music. As part of the world music genre, a growing number of non-Turkish musicians (mostly instrumentalists) have also begun to learn and perform Turkish music all over Europe and North America. This has opened up another avenue for Turkish musicians, that is lessons and workshops for foreigners, both abroad and in Turkey. Today, a great number of excellent Greek, Armenian, Israeli, European and other musicians are active in the international field of Ottoman-Turkish music. Over the last twenty years the world music market has become a substantial source of income for Turkish musicians. Labels such as *Kalan* and Doublemoon successfully market Turkish traditional music internationally as world music.

In general, migration, international mobility and the growing global mediascape has expanded accessible individual experiences and available musical styles to an unprecedented extent. In particular the growth of world music has led to the emergence of a plethora of individual musicians and ensembles, among them many who perform more or less Turkish music. In the early 21st century Istanbul is a global music city where numerous individual musicians live and work, most of them internationally well-connected.

III Tradition becomes History

Ottoman culture has increasingly attracted the Turkish public interest over the last two decades. Films with historic themes such as "Conquest 1453" ("*Fetih* 1453") by Faruk Aksoy (2012) have become successful; similary popular are television soap operas such as "Magnificent Century" ("*Muhteşem Yüzyıl*"), which details the life of Süleyman the Magnificent (2011–2014), novels on historic subjects (like *Aşk*, 2009, or *Ustam ve Ben*, 2013, by Elif Şafak[1]) and even restaurants offering traditional Ottoman foot in an historic ambiance (Karaosmanoglu 2009). Numerous historic buildings in Istanbul have been restored, for example as early as 1984 the house of the nineteenth century composer Dede Efendi in Istanbul's Cankurtaran neighborhood was removated and today it serves as a venue for concerts and workshops. In addition, three historic *Mevlevi* lodges have bee restored: Yenikapı (2005–2009), Eyüp-Bahariye (2008–2010), and Galata (2010–2011) (Waltron 2010). The former house of Dimitrie Cantemir (Kantemiroğlu) in Fener, meanwhile hosts the *Dimitrie Cantemir Museum*, in 2003 a park in Macka was officially renamed *Dimitrie Cantemir Parkı* (Eker 2011: 71). In particular in 2010, when Istanbul received the designation as "*Cultural Capital of Europe*," numerous historical buildings in Sultan Ahmed (the historic peninsula) and elsewhere were renovated. As part of the music program a concert series entitled, "Music of Istanbul Architects" (*Istanbul Mimarısının Müziği*) presented music at historical venues featuring the *Istanbul State Turkish Classical Music Choir* with Ottoman-Turkish art music.[2]

In politics and culture this new attitude towards Turkey's past has been discused as the AKP's "Ottoman Revival" or "Neo-Ottomanism." In 2015 President R. T. Erdogan initiated the official practice of receiving international guests with the formality of a group of soldiers dressed in traditional uniforms representing Turkish empires of the past. In the same year the AKP proposed compulsory Ottoman language classes in high schools.

In Istanbul's live music scene the increasing awareness of the historical dimension of music is visible in concerts or other events labeled as "anniversaries" of important composers. For example, a concert on the 101st anniversary of the death of the composer, Reşat Aysu in 2011 in the *Cemal Reşit Rey* concert hall or, at the same venue, the concert of the *Cumhurbaşkanlığı Klasik Türk Müziği Korosu*

---

1 A great number of more or less serious Turkish novelists have written on historic subjects in recent years, including Orhan Pamuk, Nedim Gürsel, Ayşe Kulin, İskender Pala, Zülfü Livaneli, Ahmet Ümit, Okay Tiryakioğlu, Nazım Tektas, İhsan Oktay Anar and many others (Tüfekçioğlu 2016).

2 Concerts took place at *Aynalıkavak Pavilion*, *Topkapı Palace*, *Yenikapı Mevlevi lodge*, *Kumkapı Armenian Church*, Istanbul Radio, *Dolmabahçe* Palace, *Feshane*, *Sepetçiler Pavilion*, Archeology Museum, *Yıldız Chalet Pavilion*, *Süleymaniye* mosque complex, *Yenikapı Mevlevi Lodge* and *Taksim Armenian Catholic Church*.

on October 31, 2013, marketed as a celebration of the foundation of the Turkish Republic 90 years ago and the the anniversary of the death of the composer and choir director, Mesut Cemil, 50 years ago. As part of the Cultural Capital of Europe program in 2010 the Armenian community of Istanbul honored the Armenian composer and musicologist, Gomitas on the 140th anniversary of his birth and the 75th anniversary of his death with several projects.[3] In 1996 the Istanbul municipality organized a composers' competition to honor the 150th anniversary of the death of Dede Efendi and the 80th anniversary of the death of Tanburî Cemil Bey (Tanrıkorur 2001: 60-62). 2007, being the 800th anniversary of Mevlana Rumi's birth, was branded "Mevlana Year" by UNESCO. That year saw symposia in both Konya and Istanbul, exhibitions, national and international concert tours with Mevlevi, *sema* ceremonies organized by the Turkish state; concerts with Mercan Dede in the *Aya Ireni* concert hall as well as an "International *Ney*-Meeting" (*Uluslararası Neyzenler Buluşması*), organized by Süleyman Ergüner in Istanbul.[4] In the following year the lounge musician Mercan Dede released his chart topping album, "800", and the municipality of Istanbul published a set of eight CDs with *ayins* (ceremonial hymns) of the Mevlevi composed by Dede Efendi.[5] The most spectacular event took place in Mevlana's city, Konya with a gigantic ceremony in the city's sports stadium, with the participation of more than 300 *sema*-performers wearing traditional clothes, accompanied by a symphony orchestra. The night ended with a laser show and fireworks above Rumi's mausuleum.[6] For the same historical occasion of Mevlana's 800th anniversary Can Attila (born 1969) wrote a "*Mevlana 800. Yıl Oratoryosu*" and Sabri Tuluğ Tırpan (born 1970) his senfonic poem "*Mevlana-Simyacı*" (Mevlana the Alchemist)[7].

---

3 For example, a concert entitled, *Gomidas'a Saygı: Bu Toprağın Şarkıları* ("In Honor of Gomidas: Songs of These Lands"), whose organizers included Anadolu Kültür, İstanbulahay, the Gomidas Platform and the Armenian Patriarchate of Turkey; a dance and improvisational performance entitled, *Gomidas'la Yolculuk* ("A Journey with Gomidas"); a *Badarak* concert by the *Kusan 2010* chorus, a collaboration of Istanbul's active Armenian choruses dedicated to Gomidas' *Kusan* chorus, and a subsequently released album; a book entitled, *Deliliğın Arkeolojisi: Gomidas* (An Archaeology of Insanity: Gomidas), published by Birzamanlar Publishing; and the "Two Polyphonic Concerts by Three Choruses" project.

4 www.mfa.gov.tr/mevlana-celaleddin-rumi_nin-800_-dogum-yildonumu-.tr.mfa (accessed November 11, 2013)

5 CD Istanbul Büyükşehir Belediyesi (ed.): *Dede Efendi Mevlevi Sesler*, Istanbul 2007.

6 See http://www.youtube.com/watch?v=ly4UXdUDlDg&feature=related or http://www.youtube.com/watch?v=zdLL-h7zZX4 (accessed May 12, 2016). This monumental show might have been inspired by the even bigger "Epos of the Millennium" (*1000 Yılın Türküsü*), organized by the European Federation of Alevi Organizations for the first time in 2000 in Köln, Germany and later on several occasions in Turkey.

7 Değirmenci 2013: 49, Fn 29; Vincente 2007. Mevlana was further the subject of a few opera projects and projects for orchestra and choir. These included *Mevlana Oratorio* of Ali Doğan Sinangil, written again in honor of the 700th anniversery of Mevlana's death; and two other works entitled, *Mevlana Oratorio* for Mevlana's 800th birthday in 2007 (Vincente 2007:288f).

Figure 1: CDs released in comemmoration of the 300th anniversary of Itrî's death, based on the collection of Abdülbâki Baykara (d. 1935), today owned by his grandson Nâsir Abdülbâki Baykara. The extended booklet (written by Hakan Talu) contained historical photographs (from the Yenikapı *Mevlevîhanesi*, the *kudüm* (kettledrum) of Dede Efendi etc.), articles on the history of the Yenikapı lodge, facsimile of manuscripts with lyrics and notation in Dede Efendi's handwriting.

Only one year later, in 2008, the 200th anniversary of the death of Selim III prompted concerts, an exibition in the Topkapi palace museum (Beşiroğlu 2008), as well as the publication of books, notation editions and a related CD by the municipality of Istanbul.[8] 2012 was declared by UNESCO as the 300th anniversary of the death of Buhurizâde Mustafa Itrî (c. 163?-1712), a musician, composer, calligrapher and poet, although there is no source to prove either the year of his birth or of his death. In 2009 Turkey had already issued a 100 *lira* banknote with Itri's portrait (as Murat Bardakçı (2012) scornfully noted with an imaginary picture, since no true picture survived). Two international conferences on

8 CD Ayangil Türk Müziği Orkestra ve Korosu Solistleri: *Bestekâr III. Selîm Hân*, İstanbul Büyükşehir Belediyesi, 2008.

Itrî were held in Istanbul in 2012, several CDs released, books and notation editions, and several concerts took place.[9]

In 2013, packaged in a luxury designed box, six CDs with recordings from compositions ascribed to Itrî (musical director: Murat Sâlim Tokaç) were released by the municipality of Istanbul, sponsored by Turkish Airlines.[10] In the same year the "Itrî-Prize for Classical Turkish Music" (*Itrî Klasik Türk Musıkisi Ödülleri*) was awarded for the first time by the municipality of Beyoglu and the *Türk Musikisi Vakfi* across ten categories. In 2014, a CD with recordings of music ascribed to 'Abd al-Qâdir Marâghî was released on the 600th anniversary of his treatise *Makâsidü'l Elhân*.[11] One year later, the "Ensemble for Historical Turkish Music İstanbul" attached to the Ministery for Culture released a CD commited to the 150th Aniversary of Muallim İsmail Hakkı Bey, and a symposium at the ITÜ on the 80th anniversery of his death, focused on Ali Rifat Çağatay. In 2016 the 100th anniversary of the death of Tanburi Cemil Bey led to the publication of a luxury and complete edition of his original recordings on 78 rpm records, a number of concerts (among them one concert series organized by members of the Choir for Classical Turkish Music of the State President), and finally a symposium organized by İstanbul Şehir University.

The expanding interest in music history is further evidenced by the increasing number of popular books on this issue, the growing number of Turkish music historians and in the enlarged departments for musicology / (Turkish) music history[12]. Several journals (more or less succesfully) deal with Ottoman-Turkish music history, for example *Musiki Mecmuası* ("Music Collection"; since 1948), *Kadem* (every three months since 2010) and *Musıkişinas* ("Music Lovers", since 1996; Uslu 2006: 49ff). It is noteworthy that international musicological reasearch on music in Turkey has also focused on the history since about the

---

9 Symposium *Itrî ve Dönemine Disiplinlerarası Bakışlar* / 'Interdisciplinary Perspectives on Itrî and his Period' (3 December 2012, Istanbul Üniversitesi Kongre Kültür Merkezi) organized by IKSV, curated by Gönül Pacacı (OMAR). International Symposium: "Great Composer Itrî" (23 – 24 November 2012, Haliç Sütlüce Congress Center & FSMVÜ Yenikapı Mevlevîhânesi), organized by the Fatih Sultan Mehmet Vakıf University. (CD, Book, Multimedia CD) T.C. Kültür ve Turizm Bakanlığı & Güzel Sanatlar Genel Müdürlüğü (eds.), Cumhurbaşkanlığı Klasik Türk Müziği Korosu: *Itrî*, Istanbul, Kaf 2012; CD *Söz Saz Istanbul, Yenikapi Mevlevîhanesi 1597 – 1925. Itrî 300. Yılı anısına*, Istanbul, TFM Müzik 2012; Ali Altan, Nilgün Doğrusöz & Recep Uslu, *Itri Izleri*, Istanbul, Balat Yayınları 2012.

10 CD Istanbul Büyüksehir Belediyesi, Buhûrizâde Mustafa Itrî Efendi. Bilinen ve Bilinmeyen Yönleri ile, 2013.

11 CD Gülçin Yahya Kaçar: *Abdülkâdir-I Merâgî Besteleri*, Atatürk Kültür Merkezi Başkanlığı, 2015.

12 At the State Conservatory for Turkish music of the Istanbul Technical University (Director: Songül Karahasanoğlu), Istanbul Sehir University (Cem Behar); Istanbul University (Mehtap Demir, "Center for Research and Practice of Ottoman Music" – *Osmanlı Dönemi Müziği Uygulama ve Araştırma Merkezi, OMAR*) of the Istanbul University; Gönül Pacaci), and until 2016 Fatih University (Rûhi Ayangil); to mention only those in Istanbul.

Figure 2: CD Cover of the Project *Ilk Renk* ("First Color") by Güç Başar Gülle (Ak, 2010) showing a collage of a picture from Charles Fonton's *Essai sur la musique orientale*, Paris 1751, in red color. The linear notes of the CD begin "*This project aims to prove that Ottoman-Turkish Music is more than a historic artifact and still carries the potential to establish its own aesthetic standards for the future.*" All compositions on the CD, however, were composed anew and arranged for *ud*, double bass and percussions.

1980s,[13] while folk music has almost completely lost it's former attraction for international musicologists. Today research at least on Turkish art music is almost always historically based.

We might suppose that most professionel Turkish musicians today have at least some knowledge about Turkish music history. In general this past is imagined as a combination of a far prehistory followed by a timeless Ottoman tradition. Historical research and numerous editions of notations today offer a growing repertoire of music of the past (in whatever form); while meanwhile the awarness of music history slowly replaces the notion of a direct connection to what was once perceived as an ongoing tradition. Many musicians and ensembles who are aware of the historical distance, endeavor to reconstruct and revive lost music traditions. The growing interest in music history hence opened a wide range of new fields for musicians, and in the end enlarged the scope music practised in the present.

13 Similarly recently historical research has been conducted on the music in Persia (Lucas 2014) or Egypt (Racy 1977) For recent overviews on Historical Ethnomusicology see McCollum & Hebert 2014; Bohlman 2013.

Musicians of the Past

Despite the great tradition of Ottoman historiography, the history of music as a description of historical development was never the focus of Ottoman music theory (and other) writers. In general the musical past was conceptualized as an idealized origin on the one hand, and comprising the living stories of direct teachers and those teachers' teachers on the other. This divided perception of the past reflects the historical conciousness as Jan Vansina (1985) and Jan Assmann (1997) described it with respect to oral traditions: direct memories encompassing some 80-100 years, combined with an imagined "origin" of the respective culture. Between both Vansina saw a "floating gap" (Assmann 2011: 34; Vansina 1985: 23f), while Jan Assmann's book on cultural memory (1997: 35) posited that in cultural memory both levels of the past are directly and mutually linked. Ottoman music tradition, though of course not strictly an oral tradition (Poulos (2011: 171) described the situation as "in-between orality"; similar Behar 2012: 95), shows both approaches side by side: an almost genealogical attachment to individuals teachers, their teachers and further back to other musicians in the past (*silsile*), combined with the idea of an "origin" of music. This general structure remained stable over the early Republican time, partly until today. In Ottoman writings, the musical past was highly personalized, focusing on individual people, while abstract notions of stylistic periods never became an issue. In Ottoman *mecmû'as* (song text anthologies) many compositions were transmitted together with the names of their composers (and poets), in addition knowledge about musicians was transmitted orally. The literary genre of biographical dictionaries (*tezkere*), however, seems to have ignored musicians until the eighteenth century. The first and until the twentieth century only exception was Es'ad Efendi's *Atrab ül-asâr fi tezkire-ti urefâ'il edvâr*, written in the late 1720s.[14]

Several music theory treatises mention Greek philosophers including Pythagoras (*Hekim Fisagoret*), Plato, Aristotle and Ptolemy in connection with the "origin of music" (Popescu-Judetz 2007: 21). As founder – at least as a main figure – of the theory of music, writers refer to al Fârâbî (sometime even as the inventor of musical instruments such as the *kanun* or *ud*), similarly to Ibn Sînâ, Safi al-Dîn Urmavî, and, as the most important, to 'Abd al-Qâdir Marâghî (d.1435), who until the nineteenth century is regularly labeled as either teacher (*hâce*, *hoca*), or second teacher (*hoca-i sâni*, after Pythagoras as the first).[15] In Ottoman song-text anthologies regularly compositions are attributed to Marâghî.[16]

---

14 Behar 2010; Yekta 2000; Uslu 2008.

15 Yekta 1318/1902 (2000); Feldman 2015: 87.

16 Feldman 2015:130ff; as an example for recent performance of compositions attributed to Merâgî see CD Gülçin Yahya Kaçar: *Abdülkâdir-I Merâgî Besteleri*, Atatürk Kültür Merkezi Başkanlığı, 2015.

Each approach engenders a different form of legitimisation. While looking back to one's own direct teacher legitimates the individually performed music as proven and accepted by a respected teacher, the narrative of an "origin" of a musical tradition aims to secure the music tradition as a whole. Agayeva and Uslu explain the reasons behind the incessant mentioning of names such as al-Fârâbî, Safî al-Dîn Urmavî and Ibn Sînâ in *edvârs* (music treatises): 1. The desire to show that music is honourable and sacred; 2. The desire to demonstrate that the science of music is in accordance with religion; 3. The intention of the *edvâr* writers to claim a close connection to these masters by showing affinity to them through reading their texts (Agayeva & Uslu, 2004: 8; Doğrusöz 2012: 25).

On the other hand, several Ottoman theory writers have obviously been aware of different historical layers, Abdülbâkî Nâsır Dede (1765-1821) for instance, distingished

> several generations of masters in chronological order: the most Ancients *(akdemun)*, the Ancients *(kudema)*, the predecessors of the Moderns *(kudema-i müteakhirrin)*, the Moderns *(müteakhirin)* and the precursors of a vague period *(müteakhirin-i selef* or *eslaf)*.[17]

What exactly Ottoman writers thought about their musical past is still unclear due to the lack of respective sources. Cantemir and Es'ad Efendi also speak about "elder music," in particular referring to the early seventeenth century, hence the time before the emergence of an independent Ottoman music style. In particular the opposition of *kadîm – cedîd* (old – new) has been a frequent topic in theory works.[18] Moreover, Feldman mentions the existence of three earlier *ayîns*, known as "*beste-i kadîmler*" (ancient compositions). The Mevlevî did not speculate concerning their composers, but rather "*tolerated the existence of compositions by unknown composers, and even allowed them to remain fragmentary*" (Feldman 2001: 51).

Nevertheless, the sources do not evidence a conciousness of the historical development of music and persons from the past are mentioned rather as figures of a timeless tradition. Music has been perceived as "*monolitic, essential and unchanging*" (Feldman 2014:149), rendering music of the past as basically identical to contemporary music. Musicians in history have not been imagined with the awarenes of historical difference – as musicians living in earlier periods, under different social or political circumstances, and expressing different aesthetic values – but rather as persons of just another generation, as imagined teachers, who derserve respect, and who could be regarded as direct predecessors.

In traditional Ottoman education (*meşk*), teachers also transmitted biographical knowledge of composers and musicians of the past, while dates of their lifetime or musical "periods" were hardly given. "*The lack of distance can also be seen in the fact that cultural history was never based on actual sources, musical documents, although these were known at least by some experts*" (Feldman 2014:107). Still today elder musicians

---

17 Popescu-Judetz 2010: 200 2007a: 70; Doğrusöz 2015: 83f.

18 Behar 2010: 61ff; Popescu-Judetz 2007: 72.

sometimes speak about musicians of the past as if they had met them in person, praising their musicality or even quoting dialogues. For these kind of information no sources or other prooves will ever be asked for.

The music itself was transmitted by *meşk* (lit. practice; practicing; Behar 2012). In the context of Ottoman calligraphy (*hat*), the term refers to the copying exercises given to students by their teacher.

> In musical terms, *meşk* accounts for the learning process in which a student memorizes the repertoire of his teacher by rote, that is, through the aid of repetition of basic structural components of a composition, such as the poetic text, the rhythmic cycle *(usûl)*, and the melodic structures based on the modal system of *makam*. The element of repetition in *meşk* also has an important physical aspect, which is manifested in the practice of students repeatedly 'beating' the rhythmic cycle on their left and right knees, distinguishing between heavy and light strokes, in resemblance to the percussion instruments playing technique (Behar 1998 [2012]: 16). This physical participation, known also as *'düm-tek'* style [...], functioned as a bodily-verbal mnemonic device of the transmitted repertoire; it helped students to internalize the rhythmic structure of the composition they were trying to memorize and served as a means for recalling it in *performance* (Poulos 2011: 167f).

Music hence was transmitted in a holistic way, including performing techniques and style, melodic ornamentation and aesthetics. Education was imbedded in close relations of master and student (*usta-çırak*) with mutual affection and deep respect from the pupil to his teacher. This respect also prevented the student from intentional changes to compositions he learned from his teacher. This "fidelity" (*sadakat*) to the teachers repertoire and style eventually led to the formation of musical quasi-genealogical chains of authority (Poulos 2011: 170), called *silsile* (practicing chains). Until today these chains are highly esteemed among musicians (Behar 2012: 87ff). Sadettin Kaynak (1895-1961) for example is connected over several lines with Kazim Uz (1872-1938) – Zekâi Dede (1825-1897), finally until Tanburi Isak Efendi (1744-1814); with Zeki Arif Araergin (1896-1964); and with Rauf Yekta – Şeyh Celâleddin Dede (1849-1907). In his music encyclopedia, Öztuna lists over five pages of *silsile* chains of numerous important Ottoman musicians. The claim his own *silsile* chain would go back over seven hundred years to the thirteenth century theorist Safî al-Dîn (as Behar [2012: 136] noted) of course cannot be taken serious.[19]

In spite of all the efforts at loyality, however, as a consequence of the oral transmission no completely fixed version of compositions existed. Musicians tried to defend original versions but at the same time were aware of changes.

> Many seventeenth- and eighteenth-century traditional Ottoman/Turkish musicians took note of the existence and the circulation of multiple variants of the same musical work. (Behar 2013b: 5)

[19] Ayas 2015: 352ff; Öztuna 1990: I, 47ff; Istanbul: Ergüner 2002: 24 on *silsile* of *ney* players.

Owen Wright (1988) has demonstrated the extent of changes in compositions which have been transmitted since Cantemir's time (c.1710) until today. Not only minor melodic elements but even longer passages might have changed, disappeared or be added anew. Instead of one single and universally accepted standard version of a given composition, a variety of versions exist, or, how Jäger puts it, an "opus cluster" (Jäger 2015:42). Even composers themselves generated differing versions (Behar 2013b: 9).

Sources from the late nineteenth century indicate a growing historical awareness. When Ismail Hakkı Bey (1866-1927) claimed to have discovered ancient pieces (which in fact he composed himself), such as a *peşrev* by Cellaleddin Rumi's son, Sultan Veled, or the *peşrev* by Al Farabi (d. 950; Behar 2012: 144ff), all of them bore a striking resemblance to items in the Cantemir Collection, to which he had access (Feldman 2014:148). We can assume that Hakkı Bey composed them in a style, which he (and his contemporaries) must have perceived as "archaic," hence as different from the contempory style.

Furthermore, during the nineeenth century, European ideas of the "prehistory" of music reached the Ottoma Empire. Instead of the invention of an already complete music culture, in this thinking the musical past was imagined as the gradual development from earlier, less developed states ascending from "culture" to "culture" to finaly reach the present. The early European music histories of the eighteenth and nineteenth century tended to describe non-European music traditions as the latter's prehistory, hence as cultures of the past in an essentialistic view, rather than as contemporary music performed or composed by individual musicians.[20] In European musicology the question of an "origin" of music only later became an issue, that is towards the end of the nineteenth century under the influence of Darwin's theory of evolution and with the beginning of a comparative musicology (the predecessor of ethnomusicology). In the Ottoman Empire, the impact of the idea of non-personified cultures as prehistory, might be seen for example in nineteenth century Ottoman-Greek music histories, which "*referred [to] accounts about music in the Bible and in Greek mythology, narrated anecdotes showing the importance of music for the ancient Greek musicians.*"[21]

The beginning of Ottoman-Turkish music historiography is connected with the person of Rauf Yekta Bey (1871-1935). From 1914 on, Rahmi Bey, Ismail

20 Greve 1995:5ff; Bohlman 1987; M. de Blainville: *Histoire Générale Critique de la Musique*, Paris, 1767; Johann Nikolaus Forkel: *Allgemeine Geschichte der Musik*, Leipzig 1788; Knowledge of music of the Ottoman Empire of the time was based on books such as Cantemir (1734), Charles Fonton (1751), Franz Josef Sulzer (1781), Giovanni Battista Toderini (1789) and Guillaume Villotteau (1809). Further music histories of the nineteenth century include H. Mendel, *Konversations-Lexikon*, 1875; A.W. Ambros: *Geschichte der Musik*, Leipzig 1862-1878.

21 Archimandrite Hrisanthos: Narration of the Beginning and the Advancement of Music, Trieste 1832; Theodore of Focaea: Foundations of Theory and Practice of Ecclesiastical Music, Constantinople 1842; G.I. Papadopoulos: Contributions to the History of Our Ecclesiastical Music 1890; Erol 2009: 257.

Hakkı Bey and Hafız Ahmet Bey taught Turkish Music History (*Türk Mûsikîsi Tarihi*) at the *Dârü'l Bedâyi*, which was the first theater academy of the Ottoman Empire. After the opening of the first conservatory (*Dârü'l Elhân*) in 1917, Rauf Yekta gave lessons there on the "History of Eastern Music" (*Şark Mûsikîsi Tarihi*) and Turkish music theory (*Türk Mûsikîsi Nazariyatı*).[22] Obviously during this time he began to write his overarching, "Music History of the East" (*Şark Mûsikîsi Tarihi*), which was published in 1343/1924 (Paçacı 2010: 172f). Already in 1915 Yekta Bey published an article entitled, "Research on Ancient Turkish Music," whose first chapter discussed "roots" (*kökler*). Even his famous encompassing article in the *Encyclopedia Lavignac* (1913) includes a chapter "*De l'opinion des Orientaux sur l'origine de la musique – Son historique – Coup d'oeil sur l'histoire de la musique chez les Turcs.*" (Yekta 1915; 1913-22: 2971) Yekta Bey's writings exhibit an ongoing conceptual transition. In these earlier writings he "*always conforms to the general mystic history of Ottoman music that we know from much earlier sources*" (Feldman 2014: 129), that is with Pythagoras, al Fârâbi, Avicenne (Ibn Sina) and 'Abd al-Qâdir Marâghî as personalized "origin;" the Lavignac article instead begins with Mohammed (Yekta, 1913-22: 2975). His book on music history, on the other hand, includes as a musical "prehistory" the "music cultures" of ancient Egypt, Assyria, Phoenicians, Indian, Hebrew, China, Japan, Birma, Siam, Ceylon, ancient Greeks, and Persian music (Paçacı 2010: 172). This approach is clearly resonant of European global music history writings of the nineteenth century. Yekta, in this book, obviously tried to integrate Turkish music into contemporary European music historiography (Jäger 2013:8). The approach to Western music history from Ahmet Muhtar Ataman (1928) was similar: In his first chapter, "Music in the First Period" (*Ilk Çağda Mûsikî*) he writes on Egyt, Assyria, Phoenicia, Israel, China, India, Greek, Rome, and early Christianity (Akdoğu 1989: 64; Paçacı 2010:174).

For Ottoman music history, however, Rauf Yekta Bey critizices European writers, such as Kiesewetter, in a way similar, though still less sharp, to Hüseyin Sadettin Arel's treatment of them twenty years later. Later Rauf Yekta wrote biographies of musicians in his personal teachers' chain. The first of the three volumes of *Esâtîz-i Elhân,* published in 1318/1902, was dedicated to Rauf Yekta's teacher, Zekâî Dede (1825-1897) who had passed away five years earlier.[23] The second volume (again 1902) dealt with Merâğî, the third volume (1925) with Zekâîs Dede's teacher, Ismail Dede.[24] Also in other books and articles, as for example in the *Lavignac* article Rauf Yekta primarily names teachers, musicians or composers, while he never discusses the historical development of music.

22 Erguner 2003: 30. Şevket Gavsi Danışzâde: *Tarih-i Musik-i Sultan Selim*, Peyam Dergisi 1914: 45.

23 Yektâ 2000; Paçacı: 168-171; Jäger 2013: 8.

24 Feldman 2015: 129. Further volumes on Cantemir and Nâyî Osman Dede were no to be realized. Erguner 2003: 66ff.

The foundation of the Republic of Turkey in 1923 led to further changes in Turkish music historiography, in particular concerning the concept of origin. The nineteenth century European idea of cultures as prehistory was modified to the ideologically loaded theory of the origin of "Turkish music." Thereby, for the first time, folk music replaced Ottoman music as the main subject of historical research.[25] The trigger for this shift was the findings of European Turkism in the nineteenth century concerning the Central Asian ancestry of Turks, leading to a growing notion amongst the Ottoman intelligentsia of the existence of a Turkish world and Turkish culture beyond the boundaries of the Ottoman empire (Stokes 1992: 22ff). Together with the emerging Turkish nationalism of the late nineteenth century the idea also developed that Anatolian folk music (previously ignored among the educated Ottoman elite as primitive) was the genuine "Turkish" music, in opposition to "foreign" Ottoman music (Aksoy (1987) 2008: 139-156; Şenel 2000). This ideological approach was particularly propagated by the highly influential sociologist, Ziya Gökalp (1876-1924).[26]

In the early Republic of Turkey historiography became a political project, with the basic aim to create a continuous "Turkish history," reaching from a Central Asian origin (Türk-Hun Empire, Göktürk Empire etc.) to Anatolia, which was simultaneously declared as a land of Turks since its pre-history, from the Sumerians and Hittites up to the present (Üngör 2011: 229; Ayhan 2012). The general framework was the "Turkish History Thesis" (*Türk Tarih Tezi*)[27], developed in the 1930s by the Turkish Hearts' (*Türk Ocakları*) Committee for the Study of Turkish History and the subsequent Turkish Historical Society, which included prominent historians and intellectuals such as Yusuf Akçura, Reşit Galip, Samih Rıfat and Afet İnan (Ersanlı 2003). A number of new institutions were founded by the state in order to develop and propagate this new model of national history.[28] Turkish nationalists dated the "origin of Turkish music" back to the time of an original, "first" Turkish people; the history of "Turkish music" hence was extended to at least 6000 years.[29] This assumption was not the result of new historical findings or newly accessed sources but rather a shift of ideology. Whatever might have happened after this "origin" of "Turkish music," and how music from this "origin"

---

25 For music policies in Turkey during the Republican period, see Ayas 2014; Balkılıç 2009; Hasgül 1996; Paçacı 1999; Şenel 1999; Stokes 1992: 22ff; Tekelioğlu 1999; Öztürkmen 1998.

26 Gökalp 1923; Okan Murat Öztürk 2015; Stokes 1992: 25ff; Markoff 1986; Greve1995: 59ff; Behar 1987: 93ff. Öztürkmen 1998; Ülkütaşır 1973; Gökalp even collected folklore material including songs since 1912 (Yüksel 2011: 83).

27 Akkoç 2015; Balkılıç 2009; Behar 1992.

28 In 1930, the Association for the Study of Turkish History (*Türk Tarihi Tetkik Cemiyeti*) instituted by Atatürk in 1930, published "Outlines of Turkish History" (*Türk Tarihinin Ana Hatları*), ed. Afet Inan et.al. (other volumes followed).

29 Feldman 1990/91: 101; Emin, Bedia & Hakan Ünkan 1984; Aksoy 1989: 5f mentiones further quotes for this approach including Ergun (1942), Arel (1944) Öztuna (1976) and Karadeniz (1965, [2]1984).

later developed was of minor interest. On the contrary, unaltered traits of music, still similar to this remote past now became the subject of research for historians and music historians. Since no sources existed to document the mystical prehistory, these theories could hardly be proved nor contradicted.

In the early Republican period, consequently, a new form of music research emerged, which in both its main focus and methodology completely differed from all Ottoman precursors. Turkish musicologists such as Mahmud Ragıb Gazimihal (1900-1961), Ahmet Adnan Saygun (1907-1991) or Halil Bedii Yönetken (1899-1968) now searched for the Central Asian roots of Turkish music.[30] The Anatolian long-necked lute *bağlama* was interpreted as a descendant of the Central Asian lute *kopuz* (about which hardly anything was known at that time; Öztürk 2015: 184), similarly the spike fiddle *kabak kemane* as one of the Asian *iklığ*. In particular Gazimihal was a polyglot and well informed about European musicological methodology. He compared instruments over a wide range of times and cultures, and analysed both Europen and Asian sources. The model for this new Turkish music historiography was obviously European comparative (folk) music research. Ahmet Adnan Saygun still saw Turkish music as "older" and less developed (hence as part of a "prehistory"), as might be seen in his melody typology, *Töresel Musiki, Okuma Kitabı op 40* ("Costumary Music, a Reading Book", 1967). In 1936 the Hungarian composer and folklorist Béla Bartók was invited to Turkey by the Ankara *halkevi* for both fieldword and seminars (Vikár 1976; Bartók 1976). Bartók was also interested in the Asian "roots" of Turkish music, which he claimed to have parallels to the origin of "Hungarian music." During his short field work trip to southern Turkey (Osmaniye, near Adana), the composers Ahmed Adnan Saygun, Ulvi Cemal Erkin and Necil Kazım Akses accompanied Bartók. The focus of the fieldwork was the music of the Turkish Yörük nomads, supposedly particular "archaic."

Influenced by the so called sun language theory (*güneş dil teorisi*), developed in the 1930s, according to which all human languages are descendents of a proto Turkish, Turkish musicologists discussed the role of pentatonicism in Turkish folk music, supposing a comparable role as archaic ground for all music worldwide (Saygun 1936; Arsunar 1937a, b). The fundamental idea had been developed in Hungary and Germany, still as part of an essentialistic conception of culture, in particular concerning those cultures, which were interpreted as "prehistorical." In the 1930s, German musicologist Werner Dankert assumed that pentatonicism belonged to the "matriachic dominated cultural area" ("*mutterrechtlich geprägter Kulturkreis*"), from where it migrated to the "shepherd cultural area" ("Hirtenkulturkreis"; Schneider 1976: 199). In 1935 Bence Szabolcsi described several stylistic layers of pentatonicism, claiming that the pentatonicizm he had found in Hungary was of Central Asian origin (Schneider 1976: 184ff). Also around the same

[30] Behar 1987; Gazimihal 1927; 1928; 1958; (1958) 2001; Altınay 2004: 354ff.

time Turks, such as Gazimihal, Saygun or Ferruh Arsunar published articles in which they tried to describe music in Dersim (Tunceli) or Eğin (Erzincan) as archaic pentatonic (Saygun 1936; Arsunar 1937a, b). Saygun later (1935) claimed the pentatonic scale as a Turkish scale.[31]

From the 1940s the narrative of the "origin of Turkish music" had completly replaced the idea of an invention by individual musicians. Hüseyin Sâdeddin Arel's (1880-1955) approach to Turkish music history, which was published in these years, was not only motivated by Turkish nationalism and the attempt to save Ottoman-Turkish art music from Kemalist attacks. He also tried to integrate several concepts of music history: the theory of a "Turkish origin", the concept of cultures as prehistories, and the leading role of particular people, who in Ottoman writings (with which Arel was intimately familiar) had been praised as inventors or teachers of music. In 1939/40 Arel (1880-1955) published a series of articles in his journal *Musiki Mecmuası*, under the title, "To whom does Turkish music belong?" (*Türk Musikisi kimindir*? Arel 1969), where he countered the Kemalist history thesis that Ottoman music was not part of the national Turkish culture (Aksoy (1987) 2008: 149ff). Arguing primarly against nineteenth century European musicologists such as Kiesewetter or Fètis, Arel tried to prove that, what he refered to as "Turkish music" – now mainly implying music at the Ottoman court – in fact was of Central Asian and Anatolian origin, rather than formed by Byzantine, Iranian or Arabic predecessors. According to Arel, on the contrary, Arabic and Iranian music was deeply influenced by this "Turkish music," which would explain the obvious similarities. Islamic mediaval writers such as al-Fârâbî or Safî al-Dîn could now be labeled as "Turkish" theoretists, and their importance further strengthened the idea of a Turkish origin. Following this concept Arel began to write a "History of Early Music" (*Eski Musiki Tarihi*). In the only completed part, "Origin" (*Başlangıç*) he dealt with the music of Sumerian, early Greece and India, and thereby interpreted these cultures as a kind of prehistory of Turkish music. Until today most Turkish popular books on music history follow this general outline, without taking any possible influence of non-Turks into account.[32]

The chapters on the prehistory of Turkish music in some popular books on Turkish music history might demonstrate this approach:

Ahmet Şahin Ak: *Turkish Music History*, 2003

After two introductory chapters the third chapter "Turkish music from the beginning until the sixteenth century": shortly sketches the music cultures of Sha-

31 Saygun 1936:6. A similar idea of pentatonicism as a pre-historical tone system was put forward concerning andian music of the Inca (Mendívil 2009: 30-47).

32 International research on the history of Central Asian music hardly is hardly noticed, e.g. Kishibe 1940; Karomatov, Mesˇkeris & Vyzgo 1987.

mans, Huns, Gökturks, Uygur, Karahanlis, followed by paragraphs on theorists of the muslim middle age, including al-Fârâbî, Ibn-i Sînâ, Sultan Veled, Safî al-Dîn, Qutb al-Dîn Şirâzî. For the history of Ottoman music Ak organizes his chapters according to centuries, each exclusively with biographies of respective composers.

Ogün Attilla Budak: *Roots and Development of Turkish Music*, 2006

Similarly to Ak's book, Budaks book beginns with introductory reflections, followed by six chapters on the "Proto Turkish Music Culture of the Altay Period"; "Shamanistic Music"; "Turkish music in the periods of Huns"; "Turkish music in the periods of Gökturks"; "Turkish music in the periods of Uygurs" and eventually one on "Turkish music Cultures of the period of Karahanlilar, Gazneliler and Selcuks". One chapter covers "Turkish Music Culture of the Ottoman Period", another one "Turkish and Western Art Music Cultures"; and eventually two chapters on "Turkish Music Culture of the Republic of Turkey".

Feyzan Göher Vural: *Culture and Music among Pre-Islam Turks. Huns, Kök-Turcs, Turkish and Uygur States*, 2011

This is an extended general history of Turkish – actually only Turkish – Central Asia. The structure of the chapters is arranged around the theme of musical forms: 1. Religious Music, 2. Military Music, 3. Heroism and Epic Music, 4. Meetings, ceremonies and festival music, 5. Music in daily life, 6. Laments; instruments, musical structure and musical particularities.[33]

This narrative may be seen as the historical backgroud of most Turkish musicians until today.[34] The *ud*-player and composer Çinuçen Tanrıkorur (1938-2000) for example wrote in 1989: *"les premières traces [de la musique turque] connues remontent aux Huns"* (Derviş 1989: 257). In Sadun Aksüt's, *Tanbur Metodu* (1994) an introduction on the *tanbur* describes the instrument's history since the Sumerians (following Arel), than mentions the *pandura* of ancient Greece; his early Islamic instrumental history follows Henry George Farmer. Erol Parlak's book on playing techniques on long-necked lutes without plectrum (2000) opens with a history of the *kopuz* mainly based on Gazimihal, including photographs of reconstructed instruments, while historical sources are hardly discussed. The basic approach is that of a typology interpreted as historical development, from simple bow to

33 Even Ayhan Sarı's (2012) *Introduction to Turkish music instruments* (*ud*, *tanbur*, *kanun*, *kemence*, *ney*, *kudüm*) refers to the history of these instruments from a cross-cultural perspective, including Central Asian, Arabic, Chinese and others, including pictures of sources, citations, lists of instrument makers and players (without giving sources).

34 Similar also to the curricula for music lessons in Turkish schools; see Mîllî Eğitim Bakanlığı 2009.

bağlama, and comparisons with Central Asian lute types (based on Oruç Güvenç's collection).

For the historiography of specifically Ottoman-Turkish music the focus on biographies within this framework of an unchanging music culture remained dominant, while historical development continued to be ignored. A number of text anthologies, which were published since the 1940s (e.g. Ergun 1942; Anıl/ Zakoğlu 1979; Üngör 1981; Ünkan 1984) continued to erase historical differences and presented Ottoman art songs written over centuries in alphabetic order, as though elements of one single culture. Turkish theorists, on the other hand, preferred to discuss the tonal system, *makam* and *usûl*, much less musical forms, and hardly any music history. Suphi Ezgi reserved only three pages for history in his monumental five volume work on Ottoman-Turkish art music theory, while throughout the work he included numerous biographies of composers of the past.[35] Most theorists of Ottoman-Turkish music never regarded Anatolian music as being worthy of serious study, neither it's presence nor it's history.

Today, most popular writings on Turkish music history are biographical lexica of Ottoman-Turkish composers. The pioneering "Encyclopedia of Turkish Music" was published for the first time in 1969 by Yılmaz Öztuna (b. 1930), a student and admirer of Hüseyin Sadettin Arel.[36] It contains an overall view of Ottoman-Turkish art music, again consisting mainly of biographical articles. Until today, despite its many critics due to both the numerous mistakes in details and insufficient specification of sources, this dictionary remains a standard reference book, republished several times. Later Öztuna (1988) published (among several general books on Turkish history) detailed biographies of composers such as Itrî (1987), Dede Efendi, and 'Abd al-Qâdir Marâghî. Later biographic encyclopedias included those of Mustafa Rona (1960 and 1970), B.S. Edipoğlu (1962), Sadun Kemal Aksüt (1967), Melâhat & Gültekin Oransay (1969), Salâhattin Göktepe (1971), Sadun Kemal Aksüt (1993) and Mehmet Gürler (2015).[37] Also the two general music encyclopedias by Vural Sözer in 1964 ([2]1986) and Ahmet Say (1985) are based mainly on biographical articles. Part of the program, "Cultural Capital of Europe" in 2010, Mehmet Güntekin published a book containing biographies of 100 musicians from Istanbul. In addition to these encyclopedias a growing number of monographic books on individual composers have been written since, some in the series of the Ministry for Culture's, "Great Turks" (*Türk Büyükler Dizisi*), others following the pattern, "Life and work of...", includ-

35 *Türk Musikisi Tarihcesi. Bugünden mazinin kararlıklarına doğru* (Ezgi 1940, Vol. IV: 137-139).

36 Form an early age Öztuna worked in Arel's (second) library, and from 1948 till 1950 – hence in the age of 18 to 20 –,he began to publish his "Dictionary of Turkish Music" (*Türk Musikisi Lûgati*; Akdoğu 1990), based on Arel's collection (in Arel's journal *Musiki Mecmuası*). Already in 1958 Inal published his biographical lexica on musicians.

37 The first part of his book, "Music in Islamic civilization" Arslan (2015) contains an overview on theorists and their works, while the second parts includes systematic articles.

ing biographies and extensive work lists.[38] At Turkish music conservatories numberous BA and MA theses have been written according to this model. Süleyman Erguner's, *Ney Metod* (2002) includes a chapter with biographies of Ottoman ney players. Emine Bora's book on Armenian and Ottoman music (2010) offers biographies of Armenian composers in Ottoman art music. Today in concerts of Ottoman-Turkish art music, program sheets inform the audience primarily about the biographies of composers, perhaps with only the lyrics added (sometimes with modern Turkish translations).

The small book "Ottoman Sounds. Magnificent Ottoman Composers" published in 2008, might be an example for a contemporary popular book on Ottoman music history. The advisor for the historical parts was the respected music historian, Gönül Paçacı. Together with some short remarks on the general historical background, but with only a few rough remarks on music development, biographies of the following composers form the historical framework: Buhûrîzâde Mustafa Itrî Efendi (1640–1712) / Selim III (1760–1808) / Hammâmî-zâde Ismail Dede Efendi (1878–1846) / Hoca Mehmed Zekâî Dede (1825–1897) / Hacı Arif Bey (1831–1885). The book is well illustrated by numerous pictures, though most of them are unhistorical paintings, which where made decades or even centuries after the death of the respective composer.

The biographical approach of musical historiography was already adapted during the early Turkish republic, in particular with respect to the *aşık* (folk singer-poets), who represent the only tradition in Anatolia where names of past musicians have been transmitted (i.e. in the last stanzas of their songs). Recently Okan Murat Öztürk (2016) proposed a model of four master generation of *bağlama* players:

1. First Generation (born before 1919), e.g.Tanburacı Osman Pehlıvan, Aşık Veysel, Hisarlı Ahmet, Muharrem Ertaş);
2. Second Generation (born 1920-1939), e.g. Bayram Aracı, Ramazan Güngör, Davud Suları, Nida Tüfekçi, Rıza Konyalı);
3. Third Generation (born 1940-1959), e.g. Murat Çobanoğlu, Arif Sağ, Musa Eroğlu, Mehmet Erenler, Yavuz Top;
4. Fourth Generation (born 1960-1979), e.g. Erol Parlak, Cihangir Terzi, Okan Murat Öztürk, Cengiz Özkan, Hasret Gültekin, Erdal Erzincan.

Even the history of Western music in Turkey was conceptualized accordingly. Almost all books on this issue describe the development of Western-Turkish music as a sequence of four (or more) generations of composers, rather than as the development of musical styles or aesthetics:

[38] For example see Ferid 1933; Ertaylan 1958; Akdoğu 1990; Yazıcı 2011; Ergür 2011; Şekeryan 2012.

1. Turkish Five (b. 1904 -1908)
2. Ekrem Zeki Ün (1910–87), Bülent Tarcan (1914–1991), Kemal Ilerici (1910–1986)
3. Bülent Arel (1919–1991), Ilhan Usmanbas (1921), Ilhan Baran (1934-2016) etc.
4. Turgay Erdener (1957), Betin Günes (1957), Perihan Önder (1960) Hasan Ucarsu (1965), Özkan Manav (1967) etc.

Biographical dictionaries and overviews are also available (Oransay 1965, Say 1985; İlyasoğlu 1989/2007).

Relics from the Past

It was the technology of recording music, in written form and later audible, which led to further changes in the notion of the past and its music. Notation, the technique of writing music down in order to store or transmit it over time and space, was known and practiced in the Islamic world since at least the ninth century. Early Arabic theorists used letters representing tones for the exemplification of their theories, later similar notations (even with written melodies) were used in the treatises of the thirteenth century (Qutb al-Dîn Sirâzî, Safi al-Dîn Urmevî) and the fourteenth century (Marâghî), again for theoretical purposes. Beginning in the mid-seventeenth century, some few singular Ottoman manuscripts included large collections of notations (in different notation systems), hence obviously written at least partly for a practical use; including *Mecmû'a-i Saz ü Söz* by Ali Ufukî Bey (Albert [Wojciech] Bobowski, ca. 1650), *Kitâb-i 'Ilmü'l mûsikî 'alâ Vech'il Hurûfât* by Dimitrie Cantemir (c. 1710); a collection by Nâyî Osman Dede (ca. 1652–1730) and the *Kevserî Mecmû'ası* (Nâyî Ali Mustafa Kevserî Efendi (d. c. 1770).[39] It is noteworthy that the majority of the notated music was instrumental, which was much more difficult to memorize than vocal music (whose lyrics where written in *mecmû'a*s; Behar 2012: 39ff). However, it was only from the early nineteenth century that notation in the Ottoman Empire was in practice used for the transmission of music. Around 1810-1812 both Armenian and Byzantine church music notations were radically reformed, which enabled them to record also non-Christian music, hence even Ottoman art music. In particular the so-called Hamparsum notation became widely used over the following decades among Ottoman musicians (Olley 2017; Jäger 1996a; b). Around the same time Western staff notation also became generally accepted in Istanbul. As a forth notation system, the one developed by Abdülbâki Dede needs to be mentioned, though it hardly reached any practical relevance. All these notations systems of the nineteenth century, ignored the sound of music, focused on the notes, and hence diminished its aesthetic importance. Also the character of *usul* began to change from a continuously repeated rhythmical and

[39] Tohumcu 2006; Popescu-Judetz 1996.

structural frame, which was frequently depicted in theoretical writings as circles, to a linear and countable measure. On the other hand notation strengthened the idea that music could have an existence of its own, rather than just being something audible, which inevitably passes away once the sound ends.

Unfortunately little research has been conducted so far on the use and perception of notation manuscrips during the nineteenth century.[40] We do not know exactly why, how and for whom the first collections of notation were written. During the nineteenth century the number of notation collections grew, well-known examples include those of Necip Paşa (1815-1883), Abdülhamid Paşa (1830-1894), Ethem Paşa (1830?-1886/94), Piyanist Mimar Esad Efendi (d.1895), and some collections of Mevlevi lodges, e.g. that of the *Yenikapı Mevlevîhanesi* (Yavasca 1994: 529; Jäger 1996a; b; Olley 2017). Beginning in the 1850s anthologies of song texts were printed in Istanbul, from 1875 also collections of notations.[41] From 1975 Notacı Hacı Emin Efendi (1845–1907) edited notation in the journals *Ma'lûmat* and *Servet-ı Fünûn* (Paçacı 2010: 218-224). Popular music printers around 1900 include Arşak Çömlekçiyan, Onnik Zadoryan, Kutmânîzâde Şamlı Selim, Kutmânîzâde Şamlı Tevfik, Kutmânîzâde Şamlı Iskender, after 1916 the *Dârü't-ta'lîm-i Musıki* printed about 200 notations, the comprehensive editions of the *Dârü'l Elhân*, printed during the 1920s eventually gained acceptance as "classical" sources.

Similarly limited is our knowledge on the imagination of music of the past among musicians and music scholars in the late Ottoman Empire. Some connoisseurs obviously collected and esteemed old manuscripts, though again we do not know to what extent either as representations of the elder, hence highly respected music teachers, or as sources of a lost past. Süleyman Erguner (2003: 57-62) described the library of Rauf Yekta, which included among others the famous treateses *Nota-i Türkî* and *Rabt-i Ta'bîrât-i Mûsikîsi* as well as manuscripts from Safî al-Dîn Urmavî, Marâghî, Kirşehrî Yusuf, Lâdikî Mehmed Çelebi, Ali Nutkî Dede, Cantemir, Nâyî Osman Dede and the Kevserî collection. In addition, Yekta mentions further manuscripts in several libraries in Istanbul. Nilgün Doğrusöz prepared a first (still unpublished) catalogues of Yektas extensive bequest. Similary we have an idea of Sâdeddin Arel's second library (the first one burned down during the occupation of Istanbul in 1922; Öztuna 1986). It included a broad selection of issues and languages, as well as the notation collections of Yesârî-zâde Ahmed

40 The project, Corpus Musicae Ottomanicae (CMO) of the University of Münster, Germany, directed by Ralf Martin Jäger aims to edit all available Hamparsum notations of the nineteenth century; https://www.uni-muenster.de/CMO-Edition/en/index.html; Olley 2017.

41 The earliest known printed *mecmua* was the *Biblios Kaloumeni Evterpi*, published in the1830ers (Behar 2012: 43). Early printed *mecmuas* include Hasim Beys 1269 (1852/53)Nineteenth century printed songtext collections include the *Mecmu'a-ı Şarkı*, 1268 (1852), Hâşim Bey's well known *Güfte Mecmuası* 1269 / 1853 (*Mecmua-ı Kârhâ ve Nakşhâ ve Şarkiyyât* in 1269, (Paçacı 2010: 44ff); Bolahenk Mehmet Nuri Bey's collection *Mecmu'a-ı Şarkiyyât ve Kârhâ ve Nakşhâ* (1290), or Hacı Arif Bey's lyric anthology published in 1873-74 (Paçacı 2010).

Necip Paşa (1815-1883; on which obviously most of Arel's notation editions are based, Öztuna 1986: 49), Müşir Dâmâd Mahmûd Edhem Paşa (1830?-1886), Abdülhalim Paşa (1830-1894), Levon Hanciyan (1841-1947) and Mehmed Vahîdeddin (1861-1926, reg. 1918-1922). In his forth volume (1953) Suphi Ezgi mentiones as his sources Cantemir, the collection of Necip Paşa (in Hamparsum notation); the collection of Necmettin Koca Paşa (in Hamparsum notation); notations from the *Yenikapı Mevlevihanesi* (in Hamparsum notation); further manuscripts of Abdülbaki Dede and the collection of Mustafa Nezih Albayraks, which he found in Arels library. Ezgi was familiar with the notation systems of Cantemir, Abdülbakî Nasir Dede, and of course with Hamparsum notation.[42]

Further collections of the early twentieth century today are stored at TRT; including the collection of Ismail Hakki Bey (1866-1927), and one by Dr. Hâmid Hüsnü (1868–1952) (Öztuna 1986: 52). By mid-twentieth century the theorist and musician, M. Ekrem Karadeniz gathered a collection of notations of Turkish art music of all genres, comprising 66 volumes and stored at Süleymaniye library (and catalogued by Murat Bardakçı; Popescu-Judetz 2010: 33). Still today an unclear amount of Ottoman music manuscripts (both notations and theoretical writings) are stored in private archives, closed to the public and in some cases even to scholars.

In the early years of the twentieth century writers such as Rauf Yekta, Suphi Ezgi and Hüseyin Sadettin Arel began to publish articles or books for the first time directly based on these written sources, both notations and *edvârs*.[43] Among other manuscripts Arel owned the original of Cantemirs (1773-1723) *edvâr*, the "*Kitâb-i 'Ilmü'l Mûsîkî 'ala Vechi'l Hurûfât*"[44], written around 1700, which includes notations of 351 instrumental compositions. Between 1909 and 1913, Arel printed parts of it in *Şehbal* for the first time.[45] Similarly, since 1907, Yekta published articles on Cantemir in the French journal *La Revue Musicale*.[46] Another book on Cantemir was written in 1911 by the Romanian ethnologist Teodor T. Burada. Later Suphi Ezgi also included some of the melodies in his five volume book, *Nazarî ve Amelî*

---

42 Ezgi 1940 Vol. IV: 27-37; 137-139; 526-7; 528-530; 530-535.

43 In particular in the culture journal *Şehbâl*, edited from 1909-1914 by Arel (e.g. on Marâghî, 1327/1911; 1328/1913) or *Ikdam* (again on Marâghî, 1898).

44 Arel's autograph of the manuscript is today in the Türkiyat Enstitüsü, another copy in the Istanbul University; a third one was discovered recently in the National Library of Iran (Ekinci 2015a).

45 *Şehbal* No. 12-85, 1909-1913; Aksoy 2015: 29; Wright 1992 a; b; for the earlier history of Cantemir's perception (including Kevserî, Charles Fonton 1751, Muallim Ismail Hakki 1895 in *Mahzen-i Esrar*) see Popescu-Judetz 2010: 34. Already in the late nineteenth century A. Mandoli (d.1880) collected some of the compositions of Cantemir's collection in Hamparsum Notation, Kiltzandidis even printed some as early as 1881, however in hebrew psalmic notation.

46 Gölçen 2007. Rauf Yekta published biographical notes on Kevserî (Revue Musicale 1907: Musique Orientale. Le Compositeur du Péchrev dans le mode Nihavend; Musique Orientale: Le mode Nihavend; Musique Orientale: les Modes Orientaux; Correspondance: La vraie Théorie de la Gamme Majeure.

Türk Musikisi (1933-53). Similarly Sadettin Nüzhet Ergun's (1942) anthology of song lyrics was based on the knowledge of numerous notation collections.

We can suppose that at least these experts underwent a gradual realization that historical manuscripts contained music that differed from music of their own time, with the inevitably consequence that the music had changed since. Together with this latter idea, the concept of given and unchanging cultures lost its unquestioned position, and differences within music cultures began to attract the interest of researchers. The eminent pioneer of research on Ottoman music history, Henry George Farmer (1882–1965), who since the 1920s wrote on Arab music history, in 1937 began to publish on musical instruments mentioned by Evliya Çelebi, hence not on the still recent nineteenth century but rather on a period already 300 years ago, to which the historical difference was more obvious.

While until the 1970s most Turkish books on music were written by educated musicians or intellectuals, since the 1960s, more and more educated historians became active in this field, e.g. Yılmaz Öztuna, Ismail Hakkı Uzunçarşılı, Ruhi Kalender, Murat Bardakçi, later the economic historian, Cem Behar and others. Parallel to this, among international musicologists historical research began to dominate the research on Turkish music, with music historians such as Owen Wright, Eckhard Neubauer, Eugenia Popescu and Walter Feldman. Gültekin Oransay's Ph.D., finished in 1964 in Munich (Germany), was based on numerous primary and secondary scources. He developed a first theory and terminology for the analysis of Ottoman-Turkish melodies and proposed a framework for a history of this tradition (1966; 1964). Only a few muscians remain in the field of Ottoman music history, for example Yalçın Tura (b. 1934) or Onur Akdoğu (1947-2007). Together with this shift towards greater involvment of historians, the main focus of research became written sources, in particular *mecmûa*s (anthologies) and *risâle*s (treatises).

A general race for critical editions began (Popescu-Judetz 2007). Eight years after Eugenia Popescu-Judetz already mentioned facsimile and Romanian translations of Cantemir's *edvâr* (1973), an English version followed, in 1999 a Turkish edition. In addition, from 1976 Yalçın Tura began to edit a facsimile, transcription and translation of the manuscript into contemporary Turkish, a complete edition was published in 2001 (Popescu-Judetz 1999). In 1992 / 2000 Owen Wright published the first complete scientific edition of the treatise together with the notations. After the 1990s more Turkish musicologists / music historians published on Ottoman music history, including Recep Uslu, recently Nilgün Doğrusöz, Cenk Güray and others.

The following table gives an overview of the recently accelerating publication of treatises, travelogues, lyric anthologies and similar manuscripts as sources for Ottoman music history in facsimile, edition, translation or analysis (unpublished masters or PhD theses or smaller articles as in the journal *Musiki Mecmuası*, are not included):

Year of Publication	Source	Date of the source	Author
1977/1980	*Bedr-i Dilşad*	15th century	Halil Ibrahim Şener & Mehmet Ali Sarı
1979	*Hafiz Post Güfte Mecmû'ası*	17th century	Osman Nuri Özpekel
1985–1989	Charles Fonton: *Essai sur la musique orientale*	1750	Eckhard Neubauer, Thomas Betzwieser, Cem Behar (1987), Robert Martin (1988/1989)
1986	Monography on music theory writer 'Abd al-Qâdir Marâghî	15th century	Murat Bardakçı
	Fethullah Mümin Sirvânî: *Mecelle fi'l-Mûsikî*	15th century	Eckhard Neubauer[47]
1990	Ali Ufukî: Psalter	Mid-17th cenutry	Cem Behar
1992	Mirza-Bey: *Risale-i Musiki*	Early 17th century	Gültekin Shamilly
	Ahmed-i Dâî: *Cenknâme*	15th century	Gönül Alpay Tekin
	Cantemir edvârı	Early 18th century	Owen Wright
	Four *mecmû'as'*	15th – 16th century	Owen Wright
	Nâyî Osman Dede: *Rabt-i Tâbirât-i Mûsikî*	Early 18th century	Onur Akdoğu
1993	Hâfız Post's *Mecmû'a*	17th century	Nilgün Doğrusöz
1994	Article on 'Abd al-Qâdir Marâghî and Ali B. Muhammad Bina'i	15th century	Owen Wright
	Hüccetü's-Semâ'	Early 17th century	Bayram Akdoğan (1996)
1997	Mehmed VI Vahideddins compositions	Early 20th century	Murat Bardakçı
1999	*Edvârs*		Suraya Agayeva

47 A French translation had already been published in 1939 by Baron Rodolphe D'Erlanger: *La Musique Arabe*, Vol. IV, Paris, Librairie Orientaliste Paul Geuthner, p. 1 – 255.

Year of Publication	Source	Date of the source	Author
2000	Panayiotes Chalatzoglou and Kyrillos Marmarinos	1720s and 1749	Eugenia Popescu-Judetz
	Notation collections by Rupen Hagopiyan	19th century	Ralf Martin Jäger
	Derviş es-Seyyid Mehmed Efendi	c. 1770	Murat Bardakçı
	Syrian and Egypt sources		Eckhard Neubauer
2001	Mehmet Hafid Efendi	Late 18th century	Recep Uslu
	Panayiotes Chalatzoglu; Kyrillos Marmarinos	1724; 1749	Popescu-Judetz & Sirli 2001
	Qutb Al-Dîn al Shîrâzî's Music Notation	13th century	Fazli Arslan 2001
2002	Tanburî Kücük Artin	After 1735	Eugenia Popescu-Judetz 2002
	Ahmed Oglı Sükru'llah	15th century	Murat Bardakci
2004	Seydî	c. 1500	Popescu-Judetz & Eckhard Neubauer
	Rûhperver	15th century	Cevher
2005	Gevrekzâde Hâfız Hasan Efendi	18th century	Ahmet Hakkı Turabi
	Ruhperver	15th century	Agayeva
2006	Mu'allîm Ismâ'îl Hakki Bey: *Mûsikî Tekâmül Dersleri*	1926	Nermin Kaygusuz
	Kadızade Mehmet Tirevî	Early 17th century	Keskiner
	Abdülbâki Nâsır Dede: *Tedkik ve Tahkık*	1794/95	Yalçın Tura
2007	Turkish translation of the *Neynâme* from Abdurrahmân Câmî by Hoca Neş'et	Late 18th century	Üzeyir Aslan
	Music in the time of Mehmet II The Conquerer	15th century	Recep Uslu

Year of Publication	Source	Date of the source	Author
	Anonym *Kitâb el Edvâr*	1477	Deniz Ertan
	Harîrî bin Muhammed: *Kirsehrî edvâri*	15th century	Nilgün Doğrusöz
2008	Ruhperver: *Kitab-ı Edvâr*	15th century	Recep Uslu & Sureya Agayeva
	Es'ad Efendi: *Atrabü'l-Âsâr'i*	1728/30	Recep Uslu
2009	Abdülbâkî Nâsir Dede: *Tahrîriye*	1794	Recep Uslu & Nilgün Doğrusöz
	Hızır bin Abdullah, *Edvâr*	1441	Bayram Akdoğan
	İsmâil-i Ankaravî: *Mûsıkî Risâlesi*	16th century	Bayram Akdoğan
	Safî al-Dîn-i Urmevî	13th century	Fazlı Arslan 2009
2010	Es'ad Efendi: *Atrabü'l-Âsâr'i*	1728/30	Cem Behar
2011	Şevki Bey: *Yâdigârı Şevk* (*mecmû'ası*)	19th century	Sadun Aksüt
	Music in Seljuk Empire	10th – 15th century	Recep Uslu
2012	Four musical treatises	15th and 18th century	Nilgün Doğrusöz
	mecmû'as	17th & 18th century	Ali Altan, Nilgün Doğrusöz & Recep Uslu
	Kevşerî *mecmû'ası*	After 1750	Mehmet Uğur Ekinci
	Post-Byzantine Manuscripts	15th-19th centuries	Kalaitzidis
	Hasan Tahsîn: Gülzâr-ı Mûsikî	1905	Yahya Kaçar
2015	Marâghî: *Makâsidu'l-Elhân*	15th century	Recep Uslu (2015a)
	Kemânî Hızır Ağa: *Tefhimü'l Makâmât fî Tevlîdi'n Nagâmât*	1749	Abdülkadir Tekin
	Kevşerî *mecmû'ası*	After 1750	Mehmet Uğur Ekinci (2015b)
2016	Hâşim Bey *Mecmuası*	1864	Gökhan Yalçın

Year of Publication	Source	Date of the source	Author
2017	Minas Bžškean: *Eražštut'iwn*	1812	Jacob Olley
	Ali Ufukî: Paris Manuscript	17th century	Judith Haug

An unknown number of manuscripts and collections still remain in private archives without public access, for example in the collection of the (music) historian Murat Bardakçı.[48] In general, however, with the noteworthy exception of a couple of Greek books and notations,[49] Armenian manuscripts and prints (Bilal 2013), and some Ottoman treatises and notations, today most Ottoman music manuscripts, lyric anthologies (*mecmû'a*), notations, treatises, iconographic sources or European travelogues (Aksoy 2003) are more or less known, and often available in books, articles, libraries or online. Several bibliographies offer overviews of archives and libraries.[50] Today, the search for and the analysis of sources still constitutes the central field of Turkish musicology, and will probably remain so for several more years. In particular the critical edition of Ottoman music notations (which has been a central field of musicology in Europe for almost two centuries) has just began. Issues and debates on the origin or identity of music, though still repeated in popular books, have been completely replaced within the scholaraly community by detailed philological work.

A history of music print in Turkey has not yet been written (Paçacı 2010; Oransay 1978). Countless editions of the same or similar music published without dates, and a general lack of clarity on the process of edition empede an overview of the development of printed notation. Both problems not only arise with respect to manuscripts and prints of the nineteenth century, but similarly for publications of the twenties century, as for example the "*Türk Musikisi Klasikleri,*" published in a total of 180 numbers by the *Darü'l-Elhân* between 1923 and 1930 under the guidance of Rauf Yekta, Ali Rıfat Çağatay and Ahmed Irsoy (later further editions where published by the Istanbul Musicipal Conservatory, Behar 2005: 108ff). Except for some initial insights from Ralf Martin Jäger, who compared the prints with notation manuscripts on which the editions of the "*Türk Musikisi Klasikleri*" are obviously at least partly based, we still hardly understand

48 In a publication for the 25th anniversary of the publisher Pan, Bardakçı (2012) included some valuable examples from his collection, including reprints of 25 autographs of Ottoman and Turkish composers from Hafiz Post, Itrî and Hammâmîzâde Ismail Dede Efendi to Münir Nurettin Selçuk and Cevdet Cağla.

49 For example *Efterpi* 1830), *Pandora* (1843, 1846), *Armonia* (1848), *Kallifonos Seirin* (1859), *Lesbia Sappho* (1870), *Mousikon Apanthisma* (1872), *Asias Lira* (1908). Behar 2005: 244-268; Bardakçı 1993.

50 Korkmaz 2015; Behar 2005: 191-268; Paçacı 2010; Keskiner 2009; Uslu 2006; İhsanoğlu et. al. 2003 (which is the most encompasing bibliography, including in total 713 works dating from 1299-1922); Ergan 1994; Akdoğu 1989.

the porcess of compilation of these classical publications. As is widely known, Suphi Ezgi during the 1930s and 1940s "reconstructed" several "ancient" pieces. However he did so without any editorial explanation, not even in cases where he obviously completely reinvented certain pieces whose current versions were simply not to his personal taste.[51]

> 'Restoration' to its original condition' *(asıllarına irca)* is a key idea for Ezgi and Arel. Almost all notations published by Suphi Ezgi in his five-volume work are in fact 'restorations' of his own making. (Behar 2001: 108)

The main aim of these early editors was obviously to publish aesthetically convincing versions rather than historically faithful editions of compositions from a given period.

As mentioned before, some early editions of historical notations were published in articles or books already around 1900, which hardly became known among musicians.

> However, this publication had no impact on musical historiography for another fifty years. (...) In this context, it is not without significance that the Romanian-American scholar Eugenia Popescu-Judetz's articles published in the 1960s and her comprehensive book in 1973, for the first time situated Cantemir in the history of Ottoman music theory. (Aksoy 2013: 21)

Several publications of the early and middle Republican years presented parts of the repertoire of Ottoman-Turkish art music, both lyrics (e.g. the anthologies by Sadeddin Nüzhet Ergun, 1943; Ethem Ruhi Üngör, 1981, both based on a great number of manuscripts)[52] and notations, which had previously been transmitted orally (Üngör, 1965; Heper, 1979). The now famous collection of notations from Ali Ufukî, including over 400 vocal and instrumental melodies, was discovered only in 1948 in the British Museum by the historian Çağatay Uluçay, who introduced it to Arel. In 1964 Haydar Sanal published 14 compositions of the collection; later biographical details concerning Ali Ufukî were often published as well as information on the content of his collection.[53] A first facsimile became available in 1976, followed by further serious research; a full transcription was published by Muammer Uludemir in 1989. The Paris manuscript of Ali Ufukî was

---

51 Behar 2013b:10; Feldman 1990/91; e.g. '*usûl durak evferi*' first put forward by Ezgi in 1935, as a "restoration," though it did not appear in any earlier source and Ezgi obviousy created it anew. In 1946 Ezgi published a small volume containing 39 *duraks*, later Arel composed 80 further *duraks* all using Ezgis *usul durak evferi*. "*As a matter of fact, nowhere do either Arel nor Ezgi provide any significant historical or musicological argument, or even any sort of supporting evidence, in favor of the treatment they close to inflict on the durak*" (Behar 2001:107).

52 Üngör for example is based on a total of 108 prints from 1852-1975 and 26 manuscripts beginning with that of Hafiz Post (17th century). Further anthologies include Terzet 1975; Anıl & Zakoğlu 1979; Üngör 1981; Aksüt 1983; Emin, Bedia & Hakan Ünkan 1984. Wright 1996: 468, fn. 1.

53 Cevher 2003; Berthier 2001; Oransay 1964; 1972; Ergin 1968-1976; Elçin 1976; Öztuna 1969; Sanal 1964; Uluçay 1948.

described for the first time in 1932 by Rıza Nur, but only in 1990 analyzed in detail by Cem Behar. An edition of the music-related parts of the manuscript will be published in 2018 by Judith I. Haug.[54] Since the turn of the millenium the repertoire transmitted in the manuscripts of Cantemir and Ali Ufukî became part of the mainstream repertoire.

In the late 1980s, Nevzat Atlığ tried to revive the series, "*Türk Musikîsi Klasikleri*"; recently his successor as artistic Director of the State Choir for Classical Turkish music, M. Fatih Salgar, edited notations of the Mevlevi tradition, Selim III, Dede Efendi and Hacı Arif Bey with comparable claims (Salgar 2005; 2008; 2010; 2011a; b). Similar to the *Darü'l-Elhân* and *Belediye Konservatuvarı* editions, none of these later editions give any information about written sources upon which the edition might be based, nor on the process of compilation, only the editor's *meşk* teacher is mentioned. Further editions are either published by conservatories, state choirs (or its respective directors, e.g. Beşiroğlu 2008; Beşiroğlu et. al 2009) and musicians. Many more or less popular books include notations, in general again without any explanation. One of the few exceptions is a scientific edition of a historical notation, the *Ferahnak Mevlevî Ayını* by Sermüezzin Rifat Bey, edited by Bülent Aksoy in 1992.

Recently, some historical notation collections became publicly available, most important being the collection of the TRT, available online since 2013, which includes the digitalized private collections of Leon Hanciyan (1857-1947), Muallim Ismail Hakkı Bey (1865-1927), Refik Fersan (1893-1965), Şerif İçli (1899-1956), Vecihe Daryal (1908-1970) and others.[55]A number of Hamparsum collections have been transcribed in recent Turkish dissertations (Olley 2017: 20). An almost complete online edition of Hamparsun manuscripts containing Ottoman art music is conducted by the University of Münster under the direction of Ralf Martin Jäger since 2016.[56] Similarly an edition is planned of the recently discovered 4500 manuscript pages containing Ottoman (and other) music in post-Byzantine notation from the fifteenth century until 1830, as described for the first time by Kalaitzidis (2012).

Today, in practice, editions without any scientific basis dominate Turkey's musical life. The oral tradition, central for the aesthetic of Ottoman music, hence begins to pose a problem for historians, while the reconstruction of music as notated in the manuscripts of the seventeenth and eighteenth century (later even of the nineteenth century) provides a radical shift from the learing process of the *meşk*.

54 Behar 1990; 2005: 17-55; 2008; Haug 2010; 2017.

55 www.trtkulliyat.com. The private collection of Cüneyd Kosal for example consisted of around 150,000 copies of notes with more than 80,000 individual sheets and around 120 notebooks with handwritings of famous musicians of the nineteenth century. The archive contains 30,000 pages of notes and a private musical library. This archive and library today is stored at the ISAM (Islamic Research Center) library.

56 https://www.uni-muenster.de/CMO-Edition/en/index.html.

In 1977, the German music historian Carl Dahlhaus (1977/1983) discussed a comparable tension in the historiography of nineteenth century European music, between a musical piece perceived as a work of aesthetic reality on the one hand and a composition as a historical source on the other. According to Dahlhaus, musical historiography cannot ignore the contemporary aesthetic reality but must also avoid being based on aesthetic judgments. The exclusion of main parts of the musical repertoire, as a consequence of the concept of source-based music history would be more than frustrating. The edition of Ottoman music manuscripts of the nineteenth century could help contextualise the repertoire historically – not for the time when this music was composed, but rather their state in the nineteenth century when they where notated for the first time.

Similar to urban Ottoman-Turkish music, Anatolian music was also increasingly written down and edited in notations over the twentieth century, again in most cases without any account of the process and the criteria of compilation. Since the nineteenth century the earliest folk songs were collected and their notations printed by Armenian and Greek scholars (Bilal 2013; Erol 2009: 298). In 1887 the Hungarian Ignácz Kúnos collected Turkish folk songs, later Maximilian Bittner (1896/97), Friedrich Giese (1907) and others (Çiftçi 2011). Turkish folklorists began later. In order to become acquainted with the still unknown "Turkish folk music," from 1915 musicians from Istanbul, including Musa Süreyya, Ahmet Cevdet and Necip Asım began to collect folk songs while on trips to Anatolia specifically for that purpose. After the foundation of the Republic of Turkey the collecting and research expanded, as the folk songs became part of the political project of constructing a national Turkish culture. In 1920 Minister of Education, Riza Nur founded a Bureau of Culture (*Hars Dairesi*), which began to collect songs on official field trips. Since 1926 several institutions conducted expeditions to collect and edit folk music, including the Istanbul Conservatory's *Folklor Hey'eti* (folklore committee) printed in several volumes since 1926 and from the late 1930s the Ankara State Conservatory.[57] In particular songs of the *aşık* tradition were now perceived as "authentic" Turkish literature (and music). Aşık Veysel's poems were published for the first time in 1940 by Ahmet Kutsi Tecer (Yüksel 2011: 87). Non-Turkish poet-singer traditions, however, such as Kurdish *dengbêj* or the Zazaki-speaking *sa / sayir* from Dersim, the Arabic *finnên* tradition in Antakya, remained completely excluded from this Kemalist notion of Anatolian music history. Between the 1930s and the 1950s musicians and musicologists such as Muzaffer Sarısözen (1899–1963), Sadi Yaver Ataman (1906-1994), Halil Bedii Yönetken (1899-1968), and Mahmut Ragıb Gazimihal (1900-1961) traveled throughout Anatolia, and recorded and / or transcribed more than 10,000 melodies of different regions and styles.[58] Sarısözen's large collec-

57 Kolukırık 2015: 62ff; Yüksel 2011: 84; Altınay 2004: 96ff; Stokes 1992: 34ff.
58 Balkılıç 2009; ; Altınay 2004: 218ff; Öztürkmen 1998; Emnalar 1998; Elçi 1997.

tions of Anatolian folk music became the basis for the growing radio archive, in 1967, part of the new founded TRT (Television and Radio Corporation).

After the 1960s the TRT became the central institution for the collecting and compiling process, facilitating the enlargement and standardization of the official folk music repertoire. Until today, a comittee controls all notations and lyrics of newly collected songs, and possibly accepts a proposed song by awarding it an official TRT number. In addition the source person, region and transcriber are added to the standard TRT notation sheet. Hence the basic fact is widely ignored, that many folk songs might be spread over a wide region and known in different versions, even in different languages (e.g. Turkish, Kurdish, Armenian, Laz, Zaza). An additional TRT criteria is that it exclusively accepts anonymous folk songs – with the absurd consequence that for many *aşık* songs the singer-poet (and composer) is mentioned only as source person and not as composer. The specification of source person (*kaynak kişi*) and region of origin is even added in many liner notes of CDs containing Turkish folk music. Due to the political nationalistic character of the project the collections were restricted to songs in the Turkish language and the music of ethnic minorities, such as Kurds, Armenians and others remained excluded. Even Turkish lyrics were regularly changed according to the ideal of a "correct" Turkish, replacing foreign words with "pure Turkish" words (*öz Türkçe*; Balkılıç 2015:156-159). The TRT notations became the most important sources for almost all Turkish folk musicians and ensembles, including all radio ensembles and conservatories of Turkish music, founded after the late 1970s in Istanbul and in other cities. Private versions of folk music are published in particular as part of method teaching books, for instance for *bağlama* or in musicological books on the folk music of particular regions or styles, for example, "Introduction to the Music of the Region of Trabzon" by Süleyman Şenel (1994), "Songs of Muş" by Songül Karahasanoğlu (2008), or "Deyiş's in the Music of Alevi-Bektaşi" by Melih Duygulu (1997).

Important for contemporary music life is the growing amount of (more or less scientifically) edited notations of Ottoman and Anatolian music, which facilitate the public availability of music.

During the last twenty plus years a growing number of CDs with historical recordings of Turkish music on 78rpm discs, either from early commercial recordings or even field recordings, have been released.[59] To my knowledge the first historical recordings of Turkish music were published in 1994 by the US label Rounder Records with the LP "*Masters of Turkish Music*," later followed by two similar compilations. In the same year "Traditional Crossroads," directed by Harold G. Hagopian, an Armenian of Istanbul origin released "*Istanbul 1925*," and in 1995 "*Tanburi Cemil Bey*," "*Udi Hrant*" and "*The Voice of Komitas*." Later other American labels fol-

59 For the history of recording technique and historical records in Turkey see Reiggle 2013; Strötbaum 2012; 2008; 1992; Ünlü 2004; Akçura 2002; Seemann 2002: 210ff.

lowed, including Golden Horn Records with its series "Heritage," founded in 2000 (e.g. "*Mesut Cemil*"). Again in 1995, *Ocora* (Paris) published their first historical record "*Turquie. Archives de la musique turque.*" Most of these early re-editions depict a nostalgic sound image of late Ottoman Istanbul, with recordings of urban art music. In addition international musicologists edited some historical recordings, for example the recordings made by Bartok in 1936[60], or original field recordings, mostly targeting an international rather than a Turkish audience (e.g. Ocora, Musée d'Ethnographie Genève). In European archives such as the Museum for Ethnology in Berlin, further collections are stored, including recordings made by Kurt and Ursula Reinhard or by Dieter Christensen made since the mid 1950s.

In 1991, the Turkish record company *Kalan Müzik* was founded (that same year the law banning languages other than Turkish was lifted). *Kalan Müzik* began to publish its "Archive Series," initially as audio cassettes, later on CD, beginning in 2009 even with some DVDs. The editions where dedicated to famous singers of the early and mid-twentieth century (e.g. Hafız Burhan, Hafız Kemal, Hafız Sadettin Kaynak, Safiye Ayla, Kani Karaca, Zeki Müren, Sabite Tur Gülerman, Özdal Orhon), collective historical recordings (e.g. *Gazeller* 1 & 2, *Women of Istanbul*), to composers (e.g. Selahattin Pınar), famous music schools (e.g. *Üsküdar Musıki Cemiyeti*) or instrumentalists (e.g. Neyzen Tevfik, Mesut Cemil, Yorgo Bacanos, Akagündüz Kutbay, Niyazi Sayın, Cüneyd Orhon, Necdet Yaşar). Outstanding are three double CDs focusing on Ottoman-Turkish instruments (*ud*, *ney*, *kemençe*) combining rare recordings of important instrumentalists. Extended well-informed and illustrated liner notes, written by specialists such as Bülent Aksoy, Cemal Ünlü, Aziz Şenol Filiz, Osman Nuri Özpekel and others, were added to the CDs, in most cases in two or three languages (including Turkish and English).

Similarly *Kalan* released historical recordings of Anatolian music, again edited by musicologists or collectors (including Melih Duygulu, Bayram Bilge Tokel, Tahir Abacı, İlhan Başgöz, Ulaş Özdemir, Abuzer Akbıyık and Salih Turhan). CDs containing historical recordings of folk music either focused on particular famous regional singers (such as Malatyalı Fahri Kayahan, Hısarlı Ahmed, Nida Tüfekci, Muharrem Ertaş, Hasan Taşan, Muhlis Akarsu, Neşet Ertaş), or on minorities such as Pomaks (1998), Syriacs (2002), Pontos Greeks (2003), female *âşık*s (2010), Kurdish Alevi (2011), *Êzidis* (2008), nomadic *Yörük*s (2007) or Romas (2008). Historical recordings of urban minorities include "Byzantine Music: The Protopsaltis of the Holy Great Church of Christ" (research: Antonios E. Alygizakis), *Pera Laterna*, several CDs with Ladino-Jewish, and Armenian music.

Later TRT partly adopted the concept of *Kalan*, starting their own "*Arşiv Serisi.*" The series of hitherto 300 CDs predominantly edited recordings made by TRT with more or less well-known singers of both folk and art music but also

60 CD *Béla Bartók. Turkish Folk Music Collection*, Hungaroton 1996.

Figure 3: CD cover containing historical recordings of Pontos Greeks, Kalan 2003.

Figure 4: CD released by TRT in 2011 with historical recordings of the famous *ud* player Yorgo Bacanos.

some instrumentalists (e.g. Yorgo Bacanos). Different from *Kalan* music the liner notes of the TRT CDs simply present the lyrics but in general no (or only little) background information. Another CD series produced by TRT presents folk songs originating in (intentionally) all provinces in Turkey (*Il Il Türkülerimiz*), however, with new interpretations by TRT choirs, soloists and ensembles rather than with historical or fieldwork recordings.

Other labels published historical recordings only sporadicly, for example *Odeon*, *Kaf*, *Cemre*, *Boyut Sinema VCD*, *Miras*, *Çoşkun Plak* and some others more.[61] In 1998, also the bank publishing house, *Yapı Kredi* edited a box with 3 CDs of historical recordings.[62] Historical recordings of Kurdish music based on radio programs in Northern Iraq have been edited by *Seyranê* (for example recordings with Mihmed Arif Cizrawi, 2000).[63] For some important musicians such as Neşet Ertaş (*Kalan*), Ruhi Su or Şivan Perwer CD editions of complete recordings are available.

Historisation of Past and Present

The growing number of historical details and reconstructions impedes the formation of a comprehensive and comprehensible historical imagination. New knowledge resulting from rediscovered or newly analysed sources was simply added up to the already available encyclopedic knowledge on music of the past. Still today, only few academic articles offer a complete overview on the development of Ottoman music history,[64] theoretical reflections on the problem of an appropriate historiography has just begun (Behar 2012; Greve 2015).

Since around the mid twentieth century Turkish musicologists referred to historical periods for Turkish music, using terms of European music history, but defining those periods along the life spans of composers rather than on an analytical basis. The periodisation of Ercüment Berker (1988) for example reads:[65]

---

61 Some examples *Odeon* (Perihan Altındağ-Sözeri, 2008; Rıza Konyali, 2010), Kaf (e.g. Bekir Sıtkı Sezgin, three CDs, 2006; Alâeddin Yavaşça, 2001; Şerif Muhiddin Targan, 2001), *Cemre* (e.g. Rıza Rıt, 2000), Boyut Sinema (VCDs on Bekir Sıdkı Sezgin, Kâni Karaca and Salahattin Içli), Çoşkun Plak (Münir Nurettin Selçuk, Celâl Güzelses, n.y.) and many others. *Otantik halk müzigi arsiv serisi* (Yüvcel Parmakçı: *Miras*, Esen 2009).

62 CDs *Yurttan Sesler. Yeni Türkiye'nin Ezgileri / Voices from the Land* (sic!). *The Melodies of New Turkey*. Yapı Kredi Kültür Sanat Yayıncılık 1999; CDs *Geçmişten Günümüze Türk Müziği*, Türkiye Iş Bankası 2000.

63 MC Mihmed Arif Cizrawi: *Seyranê*, Kom Müzik, 2000.

64 For example Behar 2006; Pekin 2002; Aksoy et. al. in: *Dünden Bugüne Istanbul Ansiklopedisi* 1994.

65 Ercüment Berker: *Türk Musikisi'nin Toplumsal Değeri* (1988), quoted after Beşiroğlu et al. 2010: 25.

1. Period of preparation and formation (*hazırlık ve oluşma period*): from the beginning until 'Abd al-Qâdir Marâghî (d. 1435)
2. Pre-classical period: from 'Abd al-Qâdir Marâghî until Itrî (d. 1711/2)
3. Classical (*klasik*) period: from Itrî until Dede Efendi (d. 1846)
4. Neo-classic (*neoklasik*) period: from Dede Efendi until Hacı Arif Bey (d.1884)
5. Romantic period: from Hacı Arif until Hüseyin Saadettin Arel (d. 1955)
6. Reform period: from Arel until today[66]

Musical characteristics of these supposed periods, as well as the transitions between them were hardly discussed. In particular the frequent use of the term "classical" (*klasik*) is striking. With the obvious intention to construct a status of Ottoman music parallel to "Classical" European music, the term "classical" (*klasik Türk müziği*), beginning in the late 1970s, was also used for Turkish state choirs and conservatories. This unreflective adoption of Western periods was sharply criticized by scholars such as Bülent Aksoy (2015: 28) as "*fictional and a reflection of an inferiority complex in relation to Western music.*" Other periodizations simply follow centuries – in line with recent concepts in Western music history, for example M.N. Özalps "Turkish Music History," (1976 / 2000).[67] Mehmet Kaygısız' "Music among the Turks" (2000) begins with a "Short history of the Turks/ Roots of Turkish Culture," followed by a chapter on the "Roots of Ottoman Culture" (i.e. Iranian, Arabic, Shamanizm, Western, national). The periodisation of Ottoman music beginning in the sixteenth century is arranged according to centuries, and again this part mainly contains biographies. In his book "Music of the Ottoman court" (1996), Walter Feldman was the first musicologist who tried to construct periods for Ottoman instrumental music on the basis of analysis of music transmitted in historical sources. Since then, however, no further attempt has been made following this approach.

Today agreement exists only on a vague outline of Ottoman music history. Obviously crucial for its emergence was the sixteenth and seventeenth centuries. According to Feldman (2007) the time between 1580 and 1700 mark a kind of "formative period." Cem Behar (2006: 393) stated "*the earliest period to which we can trace back the inception of a specifically Ottoman / Turkish musical tradition is the second half of the sixteenth century.*" During this period some fundamental changes led to the formation of an Ottoman art music style, which remained mainly unchanged until today. These new elements included the use of Turkish song texts instead of Persian and Arabic, apparent changes in the use of *makams*, *usuls*, tempo, compositional forms and musical instruments (*tanbur*, *kopuz*, *ney*, *mıskal*,

66 The periodization in Vural Sözer's encyclopedia (1986: 794) for exampleis : "Early Classic (1640 – 1711)", "Neo Classic (1825 – 1897)" and "Romantic (1880-1955)".

67 The chapters in the *Dünden Bününe Istanbul Ansiklopedisi* (Aksoy et. al. 1994): Byzantine Music / fifteenth and sixteenth centuries / Structural changes in the seventeenth and eighteenth centuries / Musical Life outside the Palace / Music Gathering / Western Music / Light Music / *Arabesk*.

kanun, santur, kemance or *rebab, daire*) and the establishment of the *fasıl* cycle as the main form of performance (Behar 2006: 393). Another major musical innovation of the end of the sixteenth century "*perhaps in part as a compensation for the loss of a complex and sophisticated composed repertoire – was the emergence of developed improvisation, both for voice and instruments, which earned a new name – the* taksim." (Feldman 2015:116) It is this very period where a source-based music historiography begins to find more stable ground, while its prehistory remains unclear.

> Unfortunately, due to the lack of sources – and particulary of any musical notation – we do not really know what the 'antecedent' musical tradition of royal courts and city-dwellers may have sounded like.[68]

According to Feldman, after a period of decline during the sixteenth century, the most important source of the mid-seventeenth century, the *mecmû'a* of Ali Ufukî might hence be interpreted as a "*transitional stage between the decline of earlier, international music norms, and the creation of the mature Ottoman musical style and repertoire, mainly between 1670 and 1800.*" (Feldman 2015: 94)

Since the 1990s pre-Ottoman music history, that is the time before this emergence of a distinctive Ottoman art music, also attracted the interest of researchers. Research on this period could potentially connect the ideological "prehistory" of Turkish music (as mentioned above) with a source-based Ottoman music history.[69] The geographical context for appropriate historiographies of this time had to cover the territory of the Selçuk or Mongol empires, hence including almost the whole Islamic world of the period, including for instance Herat, Samarkand, Baghdad, and Cairo. Initially the focus of (music) historians was mainly on 'Abd al-Qâdir Marâghî, (d. 1435), the last of the greatest theorists of the pre-Ottoman Islamic tradition.[70] Both Yılmaz Öztuna und Murat Bardakçı wrote books on Abdülkadır Merağı, in 1983 and 1986 respectivly. Other researchers, in particular Owen Wright, Eckhardt Neubauer, Eugenia Judetz-Popescu, Recep Uslu and Nilgün Doğrusöz analyzed further sources of the period, including those of the obviously rich fifteenth century. In his recent book

68 Behar 2006: 392; "*For the most part, in the music of the Islamic civilization, it is only at this point in time – the early seventeenth century – that one can begin to wrestle with those musicological issues that are properly termed historical*". (Feldman 2015:86) "*There is not one historical document proving that Sultan Bayezid II was a composer; this fact was pointed out in serious articles, but nevertheless recent television and radio programs, featuring professional Turkish musicians, in addition to three remarkable albums, ascribed one eviç saz semaisi and two neva peşrev to Bayezid II.*" (Aksoy 2015: 22)

69 Inalcık 2010; Akdoagn 2008; 2009; Arslan 2005; Wright 1996; Neubauer 1969; 1994.

70 Abd al-Qadir al-Maraghi dedicated his celebrated book *Makasıdu'l-Elhân* to Ottoman Sultan Murad II and sent it from Samarkand to Edirne; This tradition was introduced at the Ottoman court firsthand to Istanbul by Abdulaziz, his youngest son, who was active as a composer, performer, and a writer on music during the reign of Mehmed II (1451-1481). He again was followed by his son, Mahmud, who was still active in the court of Süleyman I (1520-1566).

"Music of the Seljuk Territory" (2010), Recep Uslu gave a first comprehensive overview over the period.[71]

A possible internal periodization of the eighteenth and nineteenth centuries is still under discussion. A first phase, sometime called "first classical age", is documented by the manuscripts of Demetrius Cantemir, Osman Dede (d. 1730) and several Constantinopolitan Greek musicians and cantors such as Panagiotis Khalatzoghlou (d. 1748), Kyrillos Marmarinos (d.1756) and Petros Peloponnesios (d. 1778) (Feldman 2014:157). The most prominent composer was Itrî (d. 1711/12), and his life span is often used to define the period. It is unclear if the so-called Tulip Age (1703-30) had any parallel in music history.

Another potentially central figure of the eighteenth century was Selim III (1761-1808), himself a respected composer, who patronized numerous musicians and composers.[72] The main composer of this time was obviously Ismail Dede Efendi (1778-1846). Later it was Selim III. who commisioned Abdülbâki Nasir Dede to develop his notation. The "second classical era" hence could be 1780 until 1850 or 1876 (thus ending with the start of the reign of Abdülhamid II, 1876-1908). The later eighteenth century obviously brought the establishment of a more complex tonal system while leading the rather austere melody toward a somewhat more popular taste.[73] While *tanbur* and *ney* became the most important instruments, the *mıskal* (pan flute) and others disapeared.

For a long time, in particular among Western music historians, the nineteenth century was perceived simply as a time of degeneration. Only recently did it garner greater interest by musicologists and historians. In particular Gönül Paçacı's catalogue included numerous sources of this time, and more findings will be presented in the near future by the project *Corpus Musicae Ottomanicae* (CMO), directed by Ralf Martin Jäger, which aims to edit all available manuscripts in Hamparsum notation (Olley 2017). From the nineteenth century, Western influence on Ottoman music grew, with complex consequences. Whether the foundation of the Republic of Turkey does or does not mark a caesura in art music more influencial than the changes during the decades preceding it, is still under discussion.

While this overall outline is mainly based on data of musical life (performance practice, music theory, social history of musical life), a periodisation of the musical structures itself is still far from complete. Even worse, the historical analysis of music and musical structures has hardly been done at all, Walter Feldman's

[71] Hali Inalcık's (2010) comprehensive book on court literature (partly including music) covers a period from the Iranian middle ages tradition until the sixteenth century Ottoman Empire.

[72] For example Kücük Mehmet Aga (d. 1800?), Zeki Mehmed Aga (1776-1846); Hammamizade Ismail Dede (1778 – 1847), Tanburi Isak, violinist Kemani Miron, Santuri Hüseyin Aga; Ilya (d.1799); Corci or Yorgaki.

[73] Walter Feldman's liner notes on the CD Bezmara: *Tanbûrî Isak*, En Chordais 2005.

study on *peşrev* and *semâ'î* between the sixteenth and the early eighteenth centuries remained singular, while even that failed to provide a methodological discussion. Historiography of Ottoman-Turkish music, in particular the challenge to construct a historical narrative in fact, faces serious theoretical problems. Already the subjects of a musical historiography needs to be reflected, including music and musical structures, *makam*, *usul* and musical genres, form, instruments, tonal systems, the history of musical theory to finally the performance practice and the perception of music.

The term "Ottoman music" creates another fundamental problem. The geographical definition of the Ottoman Empire evolved over the centuries, streaching over wide parts of South East Europe, Anatolia, and the Arabic world. In order to limit and manage the scope of the field, the notion of "Ottoman music" hence requires further clearification. The music of ethnic and religious minorities potentially widens the field even further – Istanbul itself saw the co-existence of numerous styles, performances and practices of art music.

Today several Turkish music historians including Cem Behar, Ersu Pekin and Bülent Aksoy doubt that individual personal styles and even historical periods of Ottoman music make any sence at all, thus calling for a radical new conception of musical historiography. The central problem is the lack of notations, hence of sources which could pass down the music of earlier times. In particular Cem Behar (2012) has emphasized the performative character of Ottoman-Turkish art music. In a tradition without notation both composing and passing on music is impossible without performance.

> [Ottoman / Turkish] music above all is action, because its reallity cannot be found in writings or theory but rather in *meşk* and performance. Music is obviously practice and performance; it is not only imagination and thinking. The practice of music, however, can only be learned by *meşk*. (Behar 2012:35)

In his seminal book on "Without Affection there is no *Meşk*," Behar (1989/2012) describes *meşk* as a central aesthetic and pedagogic category over a period reaching from the early seventeenth century till the mid-twentieth century: "In a way, *meşk* is the music tradition itself" (Behar 2012:56).

In fact the character of Ottoman-Turkish art music, which does not fit neatly into the (at least post-renaissance) Western musical categories of fixed, "composed" elements or free, "improvised" parts, needs to be discussed before it can be analysed historically (Neubauer 1997: 345; Jäger 2015). In oral transmission music changes constantly and what remains today are almost exclusively musical versions fixed during the nineteenth and early twentieth centuries, even where sources pretend to reflect music of a much earlier period. Hence a central starting point for all analysis of Ottoman-Turkish music history is necessarily the nineteenth century, it's aesthetical, musical and social changes which led to the increasing use of notation, and thus the fixation of orally transmitted music. Only to a very limited degree and only for music composed from the late eighteenth century on, is it possible, as Behar called it, to "put history into musical works," that it to get an idea of how, when and in which version a given piece was composed (Behar 2011; Aksoy 1997). The vast majority of Ottoman music as performed today is the result of a long oral tradition, whose conditions, influences and changes still little is known. Turkish music historians are therefore in the strange situation that the main parts of the contemporary repertoire constitute a serious problem rather than a starting point.

Only since the 1990s were source-based historical approaches adapted for Anatolian folk music too. As mentioned before, the Kemalistic view of history connected recent folk music directly with prehistoric precursors, though at the price of not being able to prove this connection. Actually we hardly know how Anatolian music might have sounded some two hundred years ago. Oral history is still a comparatively new field in Turkish musicology (which has been developing since the early 1990s; Öztürkmen 2016), and written sources on folk music – in particular for earlier centuries – are rare and in general of limited value. Songs from *aşıks* such as Pir Sultan Abdal or from Kurdish *dengbêj* for example, were obviously sung and transmitted over longer periods, though only few written sources (*cönk*) preserve them (Koz 2012; Başgöz 2002). Due to missing sources it is hardly reconstructable how and to what extent the music itself (possibly differing from the lyrics) might have changed (or not). Later biographies of *aşıks* are only rarly documented by written sources, in most cases only the lyrics give some historic clues (Artun 2014; Basgöz 1994). The shift to a historical and documented approach to folk music hence has dramatic implications: instead of a history of "Turkish music" that claims to cover virtually thousands of years beginning in a mystical Central Asian prehistory, a source-based historical approach will in most cases reduce the scope of music history to some few decades with only rare and isolated insights into earlier times (as for example in the manuscripts of Ali Ufukî). The change of historiographic concepts is hence painful and troubelsome. During the last 20 years substantial research has been conducted on the ideological ballast and the dramatic changes in folk music as a result of the Kemalist cultural policies of the 1920s and 1930s. This de-ideologization is still under discussion, beyond some few specialists Kemalist ideologies still remain powerful.

Contemporary Turkish musicologists who work on the history of folk music either try to integrate data of political and cultural history, e.g. Okan Murat Öztürk in his study on *zeybek*, 2006; or work with oral history of musicians, such as Süleyman Şenel (2009a) in his two volumes on *âşık*s in Kastamonu. On the other hand, field recordings made in the early twentieth century have meanwhile become historical sources, and to a growing extent are presented and analysed as such, for example in the books by Şenel and Songül Karahasanoğlu on music in Muş, Trabzon or Kastamonu. In particular Süleyman Şenel edited a great number of documents concerning early folk song collections, including record sheets and sources on the collectors (Şenel 2010; 2009a; b; c; 1995; 1997). This development of a historiography of the nearest past, i.e. the twentieth century might be seen as an ongoing finalisation of the alienation of traditon.

In addition, over the past twenty plus years, a growing number of publications based on written sources concerning the music history of the twentieth century have appeared, such as memories and biographies (Kani Karaca, Targan, Cüneyd Orhon, Emin Ongan, Halil Can (1905-1973), Tanburi Cemil Bey, Refik Fersan, Safiye Ayla and others), or even facsimiles and re-editions of recent writings, as for example the edition of the notation prints of the *Dârü'l Elhân* on 6 CDs as part of the program of the "European Capital of Culture."[74] Already in the 1990s nostalgic music had become popular, with albums such as "*Ud ile Nostalji*," "*Kanun ile Nostalji*" (Stokes 1996). Part of this reasearch of the near past also included Western music in the late Ottoman Empire and the Republic of Turkey.

To conclude, as a result of this historization of the recent past, today almost all contemporary music might be perceived as historical, while the "present" becomes increasingly short.

Reconstructions and Revivals

In Turkey the first musical reconstructions – probably a more symbolic and ideological reconstruction rather than a historically informed one – took place in 1911, when Esad Arseven (1875-1971) revitalized a *mehter* (janissary) band, which had been disbanded in 1826. His ensemble continued until 1935. In 1952 a second attempt to found a *mehter* band was conducted by the Military Museum Istanbul, and today this music is regularly used with revived political meaning to represent Ottoman-Turkish political and military power (Sanlıkol 2011: 32ff; Tuğlacı 1986: 25-27). In 1940 Mesut Cemil founded the "Unisono Men's Choir for Historical Turkish Music" (*Tarihî Türk Musikisi Ünison Erkek Korosu*) at the still new Radio Ankara, which not only adopted the term "Turkish music" but also performed Ottoman art songs in choirs rather than by soloists (see following chapter).[75] It is not clear if the term "*tarihi*" (historical) here already indicates a historical distance from the music, which at that time was still suspected of being politically reactionary. The pretended "historical" approach might have been an attempt to hide an actual continuation of the Ottoman music tradition.

Since the late twentieth century, however, and culminating since the 1990s, a wide field of music revivals in Turkey, including aesthetically more or less convincing musical interpretations and reconstructions emerged, which attempted to

74 Kolukırık 2015; Erguner 2010; Beşiroğlu et. al. 2010; Yalgin 2009; Aksoy 2009; Güngör 2006; Uzel 2006; Kaygusuz 2006; Ünal 2000; Örter 1998; Kulin 1996; Bardakçı 1995; Cengiz 1993; Cevher 1993; Seroussi 1989; Şehsuvaroğlu 1974; Sürelsan 1972; Cemil 1947.

75 Aksoy 1985: 1211-1236; Ali 1983: 1531-1534; Oransay 1973.

reconstruct and revive diverse identities and as part of them their respective music traditions, including Ottoman court and Sufi music, Kurdish music, Alevism, music of the Black Sea Coast, of Dersim (Tunceli), Armenian music, Jewish music and other traditions. Even Western Music of the late Ottoman Empire has been reconstructed in particular by Emre Aracı (see following chapter). Most of these recent revivals attempted to reverse the effects of the strong Turkish nationalism of the early Republic – or even before – and the ensuing efforts towards nationwide standardisation of "Turkish music."

An important difference in these numerous revivals pertains to the historical distance between the imagined period of reference and the present. While the music of Ali Ufukî's manuscript for example, was written down around 1650, Armenian music culture was exterminated in 1915. Jewish and Greek cultures diminished continuosly after 1923, a result of the wealth tax in 1942-44, and the Istanbul progroms of September 1955. Dersim, today's Tunceli, lost its *de facto* independent status after massive and bloody military operations in 1937/38. As mentioned, Kurdish (as well as other non-Turkish) songs were largely excluded from all official folk song collections, and later from the offical Turkish folk music repertoire as controlled by the TRT. Only the emergence of private media such as audio cassettes opened new avenues for Kurdish music.

> In the 1960s, the introduction of the cassette player was another boost for the *dengbêj* tradition. From now on *dengbêj* recorded songs on cassettes that were recorded by individuals and distributed informally. Until 1980 the circulation of cassettes thrived, but came abruptly to a standstill in the terror of the aftermath of the 12 September military coup. And although radio and cassettes had initiated important changes, they were still marginal forms of Kurdish expression that had been overshadowed by Turkish as the language and culture of the dominant majority. (Hamelink 2016: 27)

The constitution of 1982, written by the military government of the coup of September 12, 1980, officially banned the Kurdish language. In the following years Turkish nationalism tried to assimilate Kurdish culture by force and many Kurds destroyed cassettes with recordings of Kurdish music in fear of reprisals by security forces.[76]

Other Anatolian regional music traditions, including those in Turkish, disappeared slowly since the founding of the Republic under the influence of TRT and the growing commercialization. However, in most cases at least parts are still extant. Alevism, for example, began to lose all the main elements of its social structure in the first decades of the Republic (Kehl-Bodrogi 1992). Functions traditionally attached to the religious leaders (*dede*) were transferred to national justice and administration and the migration of many Alevi from their villages to mainly Sunni-dominated Turkish cities from the 1950s further weakened reli-

76 Hamelink 2016: 203ff; During this period only some Kurdish recordings circulated (e.g. by Şakiro, Hûseynê Farê, Ayşe Şan, Meryem Xan, Îsa Perwarî), also some locally known *dengbejs* and other singers (Yücel 2009).

gious traditions. Since the 1960s, in a general atmosphere of politicization, many younger Alevis turned to left-wing political ideologies and began to view religion critically. While those remaining Alevi became a target for conservative and nationalistic Sunni Turks. Since the 1970s and in particular after the coup in 1980, the influence of Sunni Islam in Turkey grew. The compulsory religious lessons in schools did not even mention Alevism and the government build mosques in many Alevi villages. Progroms against Alevis (e.g. 1978 in Kahramanmaraş, 1980 Çorum) at the end of the 1970s further inflamed the atmosphere.

Another important factor for the emergence and success of revival movements was international support, either from diaspora communities (as in the case of the Alevi and Kurds) or by respective nation states, such as Greece, Israel or Armenia. Also the admission to the UNESCO list of Intangible Cultural Heritage (2008 Mevlevı *sema* ceremony; 2009 *aşık* tradition, 2010 alevi *semah*, 2013 Folk songs from Arguvan / Malatya) had an impact.[77]

During the twentieth and early 21st centuries, historical reconstructions and revivals are far from being specific to Turkey, but rather happened almost worldwide (Livingston 1999; Bithell & Hill 2014). In her cross-cultural theory of revivals, Tamara E. Livingston (1999:66) defined a music revival:

> ... as any social movement with the goal of restoring and preserving a musical tradition which is belived to be disappearing or completely relegated to the past. The purpose of the movement is twofold: (1) to serve as cultural opposition and as an alternative to mainstream culture, and (2) to improve existing culture through the values based on historical value and authenticity expressed by revivalists.

After an encompassing survey of music revivals she found the following basic ingredients (1999:69):

1. an individual or small group of "core" revivalists
2. revival of informants and /or original sources (e.g. historical sound recordings)
3. a revivalist ideology and discourse
4. a group of followers which form the basis of a revivalist community
5. revivalist activities (organisations, festivals, competitions)
6. non-profit and /or commercial enterprises catering to the revivalist market

Differences in the character of these basis ingredients led to a large range of revival movements in contemporary Turkey.

Reconstructing Ottoman Music

The importance of Livingston's first two points, that is core activists and sources can be seen best in the case of historically informed Ottoman court music. Here, the availability of notations and historical backgroud information as described

77 Cf. the comparable cases of Korea, Vietnam, and Georgia (Bithell & Hill 2014: 135, 160, 573).

above was the main factor for the movement. In addition the still virulent notion of timelessness, and hence of a direct continuation of the past and the imagined closeness of past musicians facilitated the openess and the felt closeness to the Ottoman musical past.

The first reconstruction of Ottoman music as transmitted only in manuscripts rather than by oral tradition was conducted by Ruhi Ayangil (b. 1953). In 1978, himself a young *kanun* player in the age of 25, Ruhi Ayangil performed three songs from Ali Ufukî's *mecmû'a*. Only ten years later he recorded some of Ufukî's *ilahi*s on the audio cassette entitled "*Uyan Ey Gözlerim,*" which he distributed privately himself. On these pioneer recordings Ruhi Ayangil played the (at that time unusual and rare) *santur*, attempting to reconstruct the historical sound the *santur* player, Ali Ufukî might have had in mind. Until today Ruhi Ayangil remains a leading figure for historically informed performance in Turkey (while at the same time being interested in contemporary music). The Ayangil Ensemble for example, reconstructed Hamparsun notations for a concert program entitled, "Ottoman Music from Istanbul. Music Manuscripts of Goethes Times," performed in 2004 at the Congress for Musicology in Weimar, Germany. Later Ayangil led an ensemble formed after the model of the *ince saz* ensemble in the 1700 mission of Ibrahim Paşa to Vienna, as described by contemporary Austrian sources. Another important impulse for historically informed performance came from the ensemble *Sarband,* directed by Vladimir Ivanoff since the 1990s (as described previously).

Another central musicians in this emerging field was Fikret Karakaya, Director of the ensemble *Bezmara*. In 1996, encouraged by the Istanbul-based *Institut Français d'Études Anatoliennes*, Karakaya, at that time *kemençe*-player at Istanbul radio, began to specialize in the repertoire of Cantemir and Ali Ufukî. On the basis of iconographic sources, and advised by music historians including Walter Feldman and Ersu Pekin, he reconstructed forgotten Ottoman instruments such as the *çenk* (harp), *kopuz* (long necked lute), *şehrud* (short lecked lute) and *mıskal* (panflute).[78] For other instruments which were curently still in use, *Bezmara* tried to adapt historical playing techniques.

Historically informed performance of Ottoman music is still impeded however, by the general lack of sources. We hardly have any detailed accounts on the construction of musical instruments, the composition of ensembles, playing techniques, tunings, melodic embellishment, and even less on singing techniques, timbre or intonation in practice (supposing they might differ from music theory). "Due to the continuation of *meşk* over centuries, the biggest loss is not that of works but rather the loss of styles." (Behar 2012: 170) Few historical instruments

---

78 Karakaya 2010; CD *17. Yüzyıl Istanbul'unda Musiki*, Güvercin 2010; CD *Tanbûrî Isak*, En Chordais (Greece) 2004, CD Bezmârâ, *Yıtık Sesin Peşinde*, Kalan 2000; Bezmârâ: *Turkey. Splendors of Topkapı*, Opus 111, 1999. Uslu 2009; Agayeva 2000; 1995; Beşiroğlu & Ergur 2009; Pekin 2003.

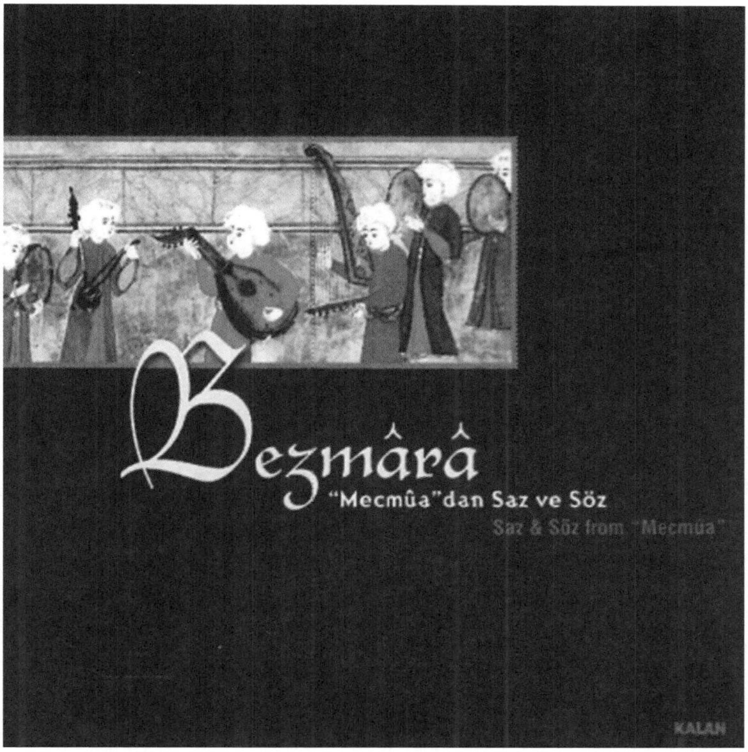

Figure 5: CD with recordings of Ali Ufukî's repertoire performed by Bezmârâ, Kalan 2004.

have survived (for example several *neys*; Tan & Çıpan 2014) and only from the later nineteenth century are at least the names of instrument makers known (in particular makers of *tanbur, kemençe* or *lavta*; Behar 1997). Obviously old instruments never achieved a particular value, and still today modern instruments are generally considered better. While *tanbur* and *ney* obviously did not change substantialy over the last three centuries, other instruments disappeared, or their construction changed. The open angular harp (*çenk*) for example, in pre- and early Ottoman times, was an important instrument, popular in a wide area reaching from Central Asia to the Middle East. Towards the end of the seventeenth century, however, the instrument disapeared from the Ottoman court. A first stimulus for a revitalisation of the *çenk* obviously came from the famous *ney* player, Niyazi Sayın, during the period of the foundation of the state conservatory (the late 1970s), when he received a celtic harp, played by Uğurtan Aksel. In 1988, a first historical *çenk* was reconstructed by Feridun Özgören (b. 1942 in Istanbul, living in the USA since 1973) in cooperation with the American musician Robert Labaree, a student of both Niyazi Sayın and the *kemençe* player İhsan Özgen.[79] For this first recon-

[79] CD Robert Laboree: Çengname. Music for the Turkish Harp, Kalan 2001.

struction Feridun Özgören added a front column, thus actually building a framed harp; the instrument hence cannot be tucked under the player's arm, but sits upright on its own stand. Furtheron Özgören added tuning-pegs to enable modulations. In later versions he used high-tension nylon strings like modern the European pedal harp and a bridge resting on a spruce sound board like the *ud*. The next attempt was realized by Feridun Obul in 1995, in cooperation with Fikret Karakaya, based on Persian and Ottoman miniatures of the fifteenth and sixteenth century and on Ahmed-i Dâî's *Çenknâme*. Once returned to the musical world, the *çenk* was soon used for different hybrid and contemporary musical projects. Already in 1991, Ihsan Özgen composed a piece called *Karadeniz* for *kemençe*, cello, *mıskal* (pan flute) and *çenk*, which was premiered at the nineteenth Istanbul Festival. In 2007 Western harpist Şirin Pancaroğlu commisioned Hasan Uçarsu to write a concert for orchestra and both Western pedal harp and *çenk*. Her later album *Çengnâme* was completely dedicated to the *çenk*. It is striking that this CD was not published at *Kalan* or any other label specializing in Turkish music but rather by *Lila Müzik*, a Turkish label for Western classical music.[80] The repertoire of the album was strictly Ottoman,[81] though some well-known Turkish art musicians, includning Derya Türkan and Murat Aydemir participated, and some Western instruments such as double bass and Western pedal harp also featured.

Other recently reconstructed Ottoman instruments include:

- *Kopuz* (the *kopuz* of Ottoman court music should not to be confused with the predecessor of the *baglama* bearing the same name) was a long-necked lute popular in the sixteenth century. Together with the *ud*, it disappeared from the Ottoman tradition. A first reconstruction was made by Sacit Gürel in 1996 following Fikret Karakaya's sketches, who had analyzed miniatures and the description of Evlia Çelebi (seventeenth century). The reconstructed instruments use four double strings, the sound is somewhat between that of *tanbur* and *lute*.
- *Şehrud*, a big lute, was popular in Persia and the Ottoman Empire during the fifteenth – sixteenth century, possibly tuned one octave lower than the *ud*. Reconstruction again by Sacit Gürel 1996 after Karakaya.
- The *ud* was popular at the Ottoman court in the sixteenth century, later it fell out of use, to reappear only during the nineteenth century. Again an historical instrument was reconstructed in 1996 by Sacit Gürel following Fikret Karakaya.

---

80 CD Şirin Pancaroğlu: *Çenknağme*, Lila Müzik 2014.

81 Except for the last piece, "A Night in Shiraz", by the Iranian composer Mahyar Tafreshipour (comissioned in Amsterdam in 2008 by Profesor Bo Lawergren, and already performed in Turkey in 2009 by Ceren Necipoğlu).

- The *kanun* until the late seventeenth century, was made completely from wood, the strings from bronze. Later gut strings where used, and the sound board covered by skin. Tuning pegs (*mandals*) where invented during the nineteenth century. A first reconstruction of the historical *kanun* was made by Ümit Bolu following Fikret Karakaya, a second attempt by Muzaffer Okumuş.
- *Mıskal* was a panflute with 22 reed pipes, used until the late eighteenth century. Two instruments are preserved in the Topkapı museum. Already in the 1980s Ihsan Özgen added a modern Greek panflute in concerts with the Bosporus ensemble, in 1996, Fikret Karakaya initiated the reconstruction of the Ottoman variant.
- *Kemançe* or *rebab* was a spike fiddle with a sound box made of coconut covered by skin; its strings were made from horse hair. The instrument was in use until the eighteenth century. Today a modernized *rebab* has gained popularity anew. Fikret Karakaya's reconstruction follows depictions from Hızır Ağa (eighteenth century).
- *Sinekeman*, i.e. the *viola d'amour* fell out of use after its last player, Nuri Duyguer, died in 1963. One instrument is stored in the Topkapı Saray Museum (Karakaya 2010:30).
- The *santur* used strings which were half bronze, half steel, streched on a trapezoidal board, in Ottoman times one string per note, today in triplets. The instrument became popular from the seventeenth century and disapeared towards the mid-twentieth century. Karakaya's reconstruction was first made in 1997.

With these reconstructed instruments *Bezmara* was able to form ensembles similar to those of the seventeenth century. Actually the fragile, unsustaining and soft sound of *Bezmara*, dominated by stringed instruments (*çeng*, *ud*, *kopuz*, *şehrud*, *kanun*, sometimes *santur*) with a noticable bass (by the *şehrud*) differs substantially from contemporary ensembles for Ottoman-Turkish art music. The *usul* is always made audible.[82] However, all details of musical interpretation, instrumentation, improvisation, tempo, rhythm, melodic embellishment, singing and playing techniques and intonation are unavoidably based on aesthetical taste and speculation of the musicians rather than on historical sources. *Taksims* therefore represent today's interpretation of *makam* rather than historical reconstructions.

A later album of *Bezmara* was dedicated to Tanbûrî Isak (1745–1814) and hence focused on music of the late eighteenth century. It was produced by the Greek music organisation, *En Chordais* in 2004, including extensive liner notes with historical backgroud, notation (based on Yekta's edition) and musical analysis, written by Walter Feldman.[83] The sound again differs from the sound of *Bezmara*'s

82 CD Bezmârâ: *Turkey. Splendors of Topkapı*, Opus 111, 1999; in Turkey released a CD Bezmârâ, *Yıtık Sesin Peşinde* (Kalan, 2000); CD Bezmara: *Mecmu'a dan Saz ve Söz*, Kalan 2004; CD *17. Yüzyıl Istanbul'unda musiki*, Güvercin Müzik 2010.

83 CD *Tanbûrî Isak*, En Chordais, 2004.

interpretations of earlier instrumental music. The singer (in betweeen also a small choir) clearly dominates, in addition the *tanbur* is clearly audible, while only rarely do other instruments play distinguishable melodic ornamentation; the *usul* is again played throughout. In 2008 Fikret Karakaya released an album under his own name, which contained his own instrumental composition "in old style" (*eski tarzda*). Most pieces were recorded with smaller ensembles, including *kemençe*, *tanbur*, *kudüm* or *daire*, *santur*, *ney*, *kanun*, violin and sometimes cello.[84]

After 2000, several ensembles performed historical reconstructions, often involving international cooperation, and sometimes in hybrid musical arrangements. Attached to Yalçın Tura's later edition of Cantemir's *edvâr* in 2001, were 2 CDs contained recordings of 25 pieces.[85] In 2004 *En Chordais* released two albums whose music was reconstructed from Ottoman-Greek composers of the eighteenth century, again with comprehensive liner notes.[86] The CD dedicated to music by Petros Peloponnesios (1740-1778), the most well-known composer of the Phanariotic traditon (Istanbul Greeks), included some pieces as transcribed from historical manuscripts by Thomas Apostolopoulos. Hânende Zaharya (d. after 1760) on the other hand, was an Ottoman-Greek composer of both Ottoman tradition and Greek Church music. Some further projects include:

- La Turchescha & Cevher-I Musiki: *Venedik'ten Istanbul'a* ("From Venice to Istanbul"), 2007.[87] An Izmir-based ensemble for Ottoman-Turkish music (including *santur* and *şehrud*) cooperated for this album with an ensemble of historical Baroque instruments (theorbe, *viéle*, viola da gamba, *colascione*, recorder, harp) directed by the musicologist and soprano, Çimen Seymen, who was already experienced in historical Barock music performance. Pieces from the *mecmû'â-ı saz ü söz* and seventeenth century collections printed in Italy were included, especially pieces whose titles refer to Turkey (e.g. Sarabande *La Turchescha*, by Girolamo Kapsberger, c.1580-1651).
- *Enderûn Terâvihi*. This was a reconstruction of the lost *Ramadan* tradition as a part of the program, "Cultural Capital of Europe," on the basis of one manuscript by Sehzâde Efendi (a grandson of Sultan Abdülaziz) and the memory of some *hafızs*, with performances in several mosques during the 2010 *Ramadan* and a printed edition including lyrics, notations and 2 CDs.[88]
- Editions of the *Dârü'l Elhân* notation prints on CD, together with recordings of anew performances directed by Mustafa Doğan Dikmen as part of the program,

[84] CD Fikret Karakaya: *Eski Musikinin Rüzgârıyla*, Güvercin 2008.

[85] Performed on *tanbur* (Murat Aydemir), *ney* (Salih Bilgin), *rebab* (Hasan Esen), *kanun* (Şehvar Beşiroğlu), *kudüm* and *daire* (Hüseyin Tuncel) Tura et al. 2001: 69.

[86] CD *Hanende Zaharya*, Kalan 2005; CD En Chordais: *Petros Peloponesios*, En Chordais 2005.

[87] CD La Turchescha & Cevher-I Musiki: *Venedik'ten Istanbul'a*, Calliope 2007 / Ak 2008.

[88] Şahin & Kemiksiz 2010; CD Şahin, Ahmed & Kemiksiz, Mehmed. *Tevhid Halkası*, Dalar 2010.

Figure 6: CD cover with music from Ali Ufukî published by the "Golden Horn Ensemble" of Ahmet Kadri Rizeli in 2009. In the following year another CD was dedicated to Dimitrie Cantemir.[89] This is contemporary interpretation of the reconstructed music, not in historical instrumentation (*kemençe*, cello, *kanun*, *tanbur*, *ney*, *daire / bendir*, *kudüm*)

"Cultural Capital of Europe." The performances of the notations are sung and played without melodic embelishments of vibrato, with a focus on clear pronounciation, partly based on historical 78rpm records.[90]

- Sanlıkol (2011): A CD attached to Mehmet Ali Sanlıkol's book on *mehter* bands contains reconstructions of *mehter* music, according to written scources, such as Ali Ufukî, Cantemir or Salomon Schweigger (1551-1622).
- A tentative reconstruction of music from the Seljuk Period, is added to a book on this issue by Recep Uslu (2010). However, most of the music is composed anew by Emrah Hatipoğlu and Ali Tan, in cooperation with Recup Uslu; the musicians are mainly from *Bezmara*, likewise the reconstructed instruments (e.g. *şehrud*, *çenk*; Uslu 2015b).
- The *Marâghî-Ensemble*, based in Venice, Italy performs music of Marâghî and of the early Ottoman repertoire.[91]

---

89 CD Golden Horn Ensemble: *Ali Ufki*, Sony 2008; CD *Dimitrie Cantemir*, Sony 2009

90 CD / DVD Mustafa Doğan Dikmen (ed.) *Dârü'l-Elhân Külliyâtı*, Istanbul Avrupa Kültür Başkenti 2010.

91 http://www.ensemblemaraghi.it/bio/ (accessed November 30, 2016).

Figure 7: CD cover with music from Dimitrie Cantemir and others, performed by Turkish and American musicians, published in 2004 by the American label Golden Horn Records.

- A reconstruction of the pre-Ottoman tradition of music therapy has been conducted since the 1970s by Oruç Güvenç (1948-2017). Relying on the theory of pentatonicizm as the historically oldest tone system, Güvenç also reconstructed historical instruments found in Central Asia and Siberia, such as angular harps and long necked lutes.[92] Recently Ahmet Hakkı Turabi, Professor of Theology at the Marmara University, is also conducting practice based reaseach on the Islamic tradition of music therapy.[93] In terms of musical interpretation no attempts at historical reconstruction are conducted but rather performances in contemporary Turkish art music style.
- The reconstructions by the French *kanun* player, Julien Weiss (1953-2015) focus the problem of historical intonation. Weiss first played Arabic, in particular Syrian music, before he became interested in Ottoman music. His main aim was to

92 Cf. The journal *Miras*, edited by *Tümata* (directed by Oruç Güvenç), e.g. issue 2012 on pre-historical music instruments.

93 CD Vakitlere Göre Müzik ile Tedavi: Şifanağme (2), Istanbul, Origami (c. 2012).

play both Syrian and Ottoman traditions on one single instrument, which at the same time pretends to be near to the pitch system of Middle Age theoretists such as Safî ud-Dîn (Pohlit 2011). The CD, "*Parfums Ottoman*" (2006) for example bears the remarkable subtitle, "Arabic-Turkish court music."[94] During the 1990s, Weiss commissioned a specific *kanun* from the Izmir-based instrument maker, Ejder Güleç, which was later followed by several continually improving models, the last one being his *kanun* No 9. Again his repertoire was mainly based on the manuscripts of Ali Ufukî and Cantemir. While his intonation was nearer to Arabic traditions than to contemporary Turkish intonation, Weiss later uses a faster tempo than most Turkish ensembles, and a forced percussion. According to Stephan Pohlits, Weiss stated that his interpretation of historic Ottoman compositions in the CD, "*Parfums Ottomans*" received mixed reactions, especially among Turkish musicians, for whom it sounded too much "like Arab music."[95]

Urban Minority Revivals

The revivals of musical traditions of contemporary urban ethnic-religious minorities offer a completely different picture. On the one hand the remaining local communities comprise at least a potentially interested audience with an esthablished social life and network. On the other hand, additional support is offered by Armenian, Greek or Jewish diaspora and nation states. As a result of the revivals, however, all three music traditions became, for the first time in the history of the Republic, part of the mainstream music in Turkey, appreciated beyond their respective communities.

Early collections of Eastern Mediterranean Judeo-Spanish folk songs began with Alberto Hemsi (1897-1975), who collected folk songs in the 1920s in Turkey, 1923 in Rhodes, and after 1928 in Egypt.[96] From the 1950s some of his notations were printed, most of them being harmonized songs. In Turkey, Jewish musicians such Izzet Bana and Jak Esim began in the 1970s to collect songs, primarily in order to perform them themselves (Kolcu 2009: 30). The group *Los Pasaros Sefaradis* released the first Turkish-Sephardic audio cassette in 1978, and continued with a further four albums until 2009. In addition the group regulary traveled for concerts to Europe, Israel and USA.[97] The last CD contained liner notes with

94 CD AL Kindi: Parfums Ottoman. Arabic Turkish Court Music, Chant du Monde 2011.

95 Pohlit 2011: 47. "Our aim here has been not merely a reconstruction with claims to historical accuracy, but also a resolutely innovative, playful, indeed exhilarating approach." Pohlit 2011: 26. Shannon 2003.

96 Díaz-Mas et. al. 1995; Dorn 1991: 146; Kolcu 2009: 24.

97 https://sephardiccenter.wordpress.com/music-2/los-pasharos-sefaradis/ (accessed August 22, 2015) 2 CDs Los Pasharos Sefaradis: *Zemirot. Turkish-Sephardic Sinagog Hymns*, Gözlem 2010.

well documented songs and musical notations.[98] Starting in the 1990s, *Kalan Müzik* released a number of CDs containing recent synagogal, half liturgical music (*maftirim*), historical recordings, for example by Algazi (1889-1950) and Ladino songs.[99] Since the 1980s and 1990s Jewish musicians tried to reconstruct traditional songs with historical instruments and voice techniques (Kolcu 2009: 28). Similarly in the mid-1980s the *maftirim* choir was revived, a tradition in urban centers of the western Ottoman empire (Salonika, Edirne, Izmir, Istanbul) with a repertoire of half liturgical hymns. David Behar, a *kanun* player in his eighties, and student of the famed *hazan* Isak Algazi (Jackson 2013: 49), sought a way to notate the currenly performed *maftirim* repertoire. Fatih Salgar (later Director of the State Choir for Turkish Classical Music) notated the repertoire and from 2005 his notations were actually used by the choir.[100]

> Founded in 2003, the Ottoman-Turkish Sephardic Cultural Research Center is Istanbul's hub for everything relating to Turkey's Jewish communities. The Center collects, archives, and documents Sephardic cultural productions to promote the survival, celebration, and academic study of religious and secular traditions, food, music, and the Judeo-Spanish language.[101]

During the early 2000s, Hadass Pal-Yarden, a doctoral student of ethnomusicology at Bar-Ilan University, Israel, conducted fieldwork and artistic research in Turkey. As a result in 2003, she released an album of urban Ladino music, including extensive liner notes based on her fieldwork and historical reseach with detailed information on written and recorded sources as well as the historical background to the songs. In her own interpretation of the songs she was accompanied by well-known Turkish musicians including the ensemble *Istanbul Sazendeler* and accordion player Muammer Ketençoğlu.[102]

Today an estimated 60,000–65,000 Armenians live in Turkey, mostly in Istanbul (Özdogan et. al. 2009: 462). In addition an unknown number of Turkish or Kurdish assimilated Armenians – or people with one or two parents of Armenian origin – live in Anatolian cites and villages, in almost all cases without speaking Armenian or having deeper knowledge of Armenian traditions. Legal or undocumented migrants have also come from Armenia to Turkey since the 1990s.

---

98 CD *Maftirim*, Kalan 2001; Şarhon 2009; Yako Taragano Synagogue Hymns Choir: *Zemırot I & II*, Ottoman-Turkish Sephardic Culture Research Centre 2002; 2008; CD Aarom Kohen: *Şevahot Lael: Allah'a Övgüler. From the Ottoman Era to the present: Jewish Liturgical Music*, Kalan 2008; CD Isak Algazi Efendi: *Osmanlı-Türk ve Osmanlı-Yahudi Musıkisinin Büzük Sesi*, Kalan 2004.

99 CD Hazan Aaron Kohen Yasak: Maftirim Ilahiler Korosu: Maftirim. Judeo-Sufi Connection, Kalan 2001.

100 Şarhon (2009) includs an introduction by Edwin Seroussi (Hebrew University of Jerusalem), and the notated repertoire of *piyyutim*, as performed by the *Maftirim* on four CDs and one DVD, sung by David Behar, Hazan Isak Maçoro, Hazan David Sevi in 1987.

101 https://sephardiccenter.wordpress.com/music-2/los-pasharos-sefaradis/ (accessed August 22, 2015)

102 CD Hadass Pal-Yarden: Yahudice. Ladino Sehir Music / Urban Ladino Music. Kalan 2003.

Figure 8: In a very personal album "*Lost Traces Hidden Memories*" (Kalan 2014), the pianist, composer and music therapist Renan Koen recounts and musically interprets the long story of her own family, beginning with her great grandmother.

Despite the genocide of 1915, a great number of Armenian sources survived, the earliest being ethnographic researches of the nineteenth century (Bilal 2013). Most important were the collections of Armenian folk music which Gomitas notated between 1890 and 1901. Some of his students later conducted similar musical research, for example Mihran Toumajan (1920–1965) among Armenian migrants and refugees in Europe and North America (Toumajan 1972ff). In addition Armenian culture – though different from that of Ottoman Armenians before 1915 – was still alive in Armenia, as well as among Armenians in America and elsewhere.

The first attempt at a reconstruction of Anatolian Armenian music in Turkey was prompted by contacts with this Armenian diaspora. A first Armenian folk dance ensemble was founded in 1971 at the *Surp Khach Tibrevank* Alumni Association, Istanbul, which learned choreographies and songs from eastern Armenian repertoires (Yıldız 2016: 71ff). The *Sayat Nova* Choir, which was officially founded in 1972 as a church choir, mainly performed Armenian folk music. From the mid-1990s, after many years of avoiding the open display of Armenian identity within broader Turkish society, in favor of a more introverted communal life, the Armenian community began making its voice heard. Armenian music of Anatolia started to attract the attention of the church choirs. Concert themes were no more determined according to musicians / composers but according to cities of origin or within a homeland perspective, such as concerts with folk songs from Muş, Yergir Nairi and Ergir (Yıldız 2016: 86).

The group *Knar* was founded in 1992 as the first music ensemble in Turkey strictly for Armenian music, created initially to accompany the dance shows of the Kumkapı Bezciyan Alumni Association (Yıldız 2016: 94ff). Their first concert took place in 1996 and a CD was published three years later.[103] Non-Armenian musicians in Turkey also became interested in Armenian music, for example Muammer Ketencoğlu and *Kardeş Türküler*.[104] In 2009, *Kardeş Türküler* gave a concert together with Onnik Dinkjian and his son Ara, in Diyarbakır / Dikranagert. Onnik Dinkjian, born 1929 in Paris in a family originating from Diyarbakır / Dikranagert, migrated to USA at an early age, where he became a well-known singer of Armenian church music (Yıldız 2016: 125ff). Ara Dinkjian is an *ud*-player, famous in world music as well as in Turkey. Accompanied by *Knar*, Turkish musicologist and singer Burcu Yıldız reconstructed Armenian songs as notated by Mihran Toumajan and Gomitas for the "Symposium on Cultural Interaction in the Ottoman Empire and Turkey," which was organized at the Bilgi University in 2010 by the Hrant Dink Foundation and included a session on Mihran Toumajan (Yıldız 2016: 96). In 2014 Yıldız together with Ari Hergel released an album with reconstructed non-Armenian songs notated by Gomitas, including Kurdish and Turkish songs and even an *ezan*, interpreted by Aram Kerovpyan, Şevval Sam, Ashug Bingyol and by Burcu Yıldız.[105] In 2010 *Kalan Müzik* released a CD with reconstructed songs from Hamparsum, at the same time the encompassing book on Armenian-Ottoman music by Aram Kerovpyan and Altuğ Yılmaz was published as part of the program "European Capital of Culture."[106] The Turkish singer Sema Moritz only coincidently found the notations of Karnik Garmiryan (1872-1947), written in Hamparsum notation, as printed in 2004; in 2016 she published a CD with her interpretation of twelve of his songs, in arrangements by Dieter Moritz.

Revival of Anatolian Music

The revival of music traditions from Anatolia, in place of the idea of a national Turkish music, offers an even more complex picture. The Turkish nationalist dis-

103 CD Anadolu Ermeni Halk Müziği, Kalan 1999

104 CD *Halklardan Ezgiler: Ermeni Halk Müzigi* ("Folk Melodies: Armenian Folk Music"), Kalan 1995, was compiled by Muammer Ketençoğlu.

105 CD Ari Hergel & Burcu Yıldız: *Gomidas Vartabed'in Ermenice, Kürtce ve Turkce derlemelerinden düzenlemeler* ("Arrangements from Armenian, Kurdish, and Turkish Songs Collected by Gomidas Vartabed"), Kalan 2014.

106 CD *Baba Hamparsum*, Kalan 2010; Kerovpyan & Yılmaz 2010.

course had already underlined the notion of "authenticity" (in spite of all the radical changes in the performance of "Turkish music", see chapter IV), as had proponents of other music traditions, for example Gomitas for Armenian music (Yıldız 2016: 101ff). As Livingston notes, the concept of "authenticity" is crucial for music revivals:

> In all music revivals, the most important components for the formation of the aesthetic and ethical code are the ideas of historical continuity and organic purity of the revived practice. The term "authentic" is most commonly employed to distinguish the revived practice from other musics and to draw attention to its supposed "time depth. (Livingston 1999: 74)

Due to the general lack of written sources for Anatolian music (in particular of non-Turkish traditions), most reconstructions are inevitably based either on fieldwork with musicians, who were supposed to have remained more "authentic," providing insight into an "older" music and performance style; or relying on historical recordings. Private music collectors became crucial for almost all Anatolian music revivals. Livingston (1999: 70) emphasises the "*the importance of historical recordings to revivalism cannot be overestimated.*"

Most music revival movements were part of larger phenomena of ethnic, religious, national or political identity discourses, e.g. Kurdish, Alevi, Laz;[107] others part of re-emerging local identities. In particular the new religious or national movements worked to establish networks of media and festivals, first among the European diaspora, and after the 1990s also in Turkey.

> In order to create a sense of community, revivalist magazines, journals, recordings and radio stations help to bring people separated by geographical space together, while festivals and competitions bring people physically together. The events are crucial to the revivalist community because revivalists meet each other face-to-face to share repertoire and playing techniques, to discuss the strengths and weaknesses of artists within the tradition, to actively learn and experience the revivalist ethos and aesthetic code at work, and to socialize among other "insiders. (Livingston 1999: 73)

However, local music traditions were also revived, even where no substantial community could support it, among them Turkish regional traditions such as music from the Black Sea Coast (Bates 2008: 70ff). Long-necked lutes, for example, were played in Anatolia traditionally in different sizes, with different numbers of frets and strings and tunings and carrying particular and local names (Picken 1975). As part of the modernisation and standardization of folk music in the TRT, however, the *bağlama* went through several modifications, including use of a plectrum (*mızrap*) instead of hands and fingers, metal strings, form and construction of the body completely made from wood, the addition of frets (in order to be able to play *makams*), and the development of standardized playing techniques and rhythms, pretending to represent regional styles (*tavır*) (Parlak 2000: 72ff; 101ff).

---

[107] Taşkın 2016; Akkaya et. al. 2008: 253ff.

During the 1990s a couple of *bağlama* players re-endevored the almost forgotten playing technique of hands on a small three-stringed *cura* (*üc telli kopuz*) among Yörük nomads in the region of Fethiye, in particular as played by the late Ramazan Güngör. Comparable techniques have been used traditionally in particular by Alevi musicians in Malatya (Arguvan), Kahramanmaraş, Gaziantep, Urfa (Kısas), Tunceli, Sivas, Tokat, Amasya, Kayseri (Sarız), Erzincan, Erzurum and Elbistan (Parlak 2000: 110). The instruments and their names again differed regionally, the three-stringed *dede sazı* or *balta sazı* was played in Malatya, Kahramanmaras, and Tunceli (called *tembur* in Zaza language), the *ruzba*, *irizba* or *ikitelli*. Well-known *bağlama* players including Talip Özkan, Arif Sağ, Erol Parlak and Erdal Erzincan visited Göngör to learn from him. Later this research was extended over Anatolia and eventually even over Central Asian lutes. As another village musician, Hayri Dev with his *üçtelli cura* and *sipsi* became well-known due to several recordings, published by Kalan Müzik. As a result, a great number of playing techniques emerged, including *pençe* (stroke by hands), *tel çekme* (picking) and *parma vurma* (tapping), which were later further improved to an unpreceded vituosity (Parlak 2001). The most well-known performers were Hasret Gültekin (1971–1993), Erdal Erzincan (b. 1971) and Erol Parlak (b. 1964, Van); and many younger musicians followed later. Around the same time, in the 1990s, Erkan Oğur began to play mainly on an old, smaller long-necked lute, which he had found among elder musicians, and which he called *kopuz*, indicating a connection with the historical *kopuz*, mentioned for example in the dictionary of Mahmud al-Kashgari (1074), in the Dede Korkut book (c. fifteenth century), or in poems of Yunus Emre (around 1300; Eroğlu 2009). Also other *bağlama* players today sometimes prefer old instruments rather than modern standardized ones, the most well-known being Cengiz Özkan. In 2003, Özkan released a CD with songs by Aşık Veysel. The CD begins with an original recording of Veysel speaking, then the instrument enters and finally Özkan's voice. The puristic interpretation in this album, without further instruments for accompaniment is very near to the Veysel's original recordings. Similarly Ertan Tekin's CD, *Demans* (2011) begins with a recording of Aşık Veysel, though the music is then arranged with strings and other instruments.

Revivals of particular Anatolian music styles or instruments were swiftly integrated into the mainstream (folk) music of Turkey, contributing to further artistic development (see chapter IV). Their initial character as revivalist music was soon lost.

> After a tradition has been "revived" the question always arises as to the balance between "preservation" of the tradition (i.e. strict adherence to revivalist stylistic parameters) and innovation, even innovation that is intended to win over a greater audience for the tradition. Frequently this tension is responsible for the break down of the revival. (Livingston 1999: 71)

Kurdish Music

In 1991, the Turkish administration under Turgut Özal amended law 2932, and hence enabled the publication of Kurdish langage in print and music recordings. In the same year Istanbul saw the opening of the "Centre for the Culture of Mesopotamia" (*Navenda Canda Mezopotamya*, NCA) and later similar centres were founded in other cities, for example the Dicle-Fırat Culture Center in Diyarbakır in 2003 (Hongur 2014: 79). The aim of these centres was to recreate the "national culture" which, it asserted, had been "destroyed" and "assimilated." In the 1990s the Kurdish scene in Turkey became highly politicized, which also led to a politicization of traditional Kurdish music.[108] All kinds of songs, for example those of the *dengbêj*, but even dance songs were interpreted as symbols of a Kurdish nation. In this atmosphere numerous politically-focussed Kurdish music groups (*koms*) were founded, including *Agirê Jiyan*, *Koma Dengê Azadî*, *Koma Amed*, which regarded music as a way to build a collective Kurdish identity (Sarıtaş 2010). Though the music of these *komas* was influenced by the politically left-wing groups of the 1980s, and therefore included European instruments and harmony (see following chapter), they were in general perceived as "Kurdish."

> In revivals of music outside of Western culture, cosmopolitan attitudes and aesthetics may be so internalized that they are reproduced in performance despite the best intentions of revivalists to remain faithful to their source. (Livingston 1999: 77)

In the early twenty first century the number of songs with politicized lyrics decreased. As the Kurdish movement's discourse began to emphasize linguistic and cultural rights, the importance of singing in Kurdish remained (Sarıtaş 2010: 7). In fact this period saw numerous efforts to revitalize traditional Kurdish music in Turkey.

> As making Kurdish folk music was perceived as a statement against cultural assimilation, the musicians in MKM implemented a project about Kurdish folk songs which have become Turkified. Two albums were released from Kom Müzik, Sahiya Stranan 1-2. In these two albums, folk songs that were collected by Muzaffer Sarısözen's team and Turkified were sung in Kurdish by MKM musicians. (Sarıtaş 2010: 120)

These albums hence aimed to document the cultural appropriation and criticize TRT's assimilation.

> There had been criticism after the first album was released, claiming that some songs were not in Kurdish originally, but rather in Armenian or other languages. After the criticism, in the cover of the second album it was indicated that there have been many exchanges between cultures of the region, and the aim was not to denote a language for folk songs. (Sarıtaş 2010: 121)

An example for a hybrid historical reconstruction of Kurdish music is the album *Muzîka Serayê ya Kurdî* ("Kurdish Palace Music") published in 2007 with ex-

[108] Hamelink 2016; Şen 2016; Aksoy 2006; Hongur 2014.

tended liner notes and complete notations.[109] The text describes Kurdish court music from the time of Ehmedê Xanî (1651–1707), author of the famous epic *Mem û Zîn*. The music, however, is composed anew by Behrûz Rezayî and is partly even polyphonic.

In 2001 the first *Diyarbakır Kültür ve Sanat Festivali* took place, later most pro-Kurdish municipalities organized comparable festivals (Yücel 2009: 10). The municipality of Diyarbakır together with the Diyarbakır-based *Dicle-Fırat* Cultural Center further organized the *dengbêj* project (*Dengbêj ve Dengbêjlik Geleneği*), funded by the European Union's Grant scheme for the promotion of cultural rights in Turkey. As a result, in May 2007 the *Mala dengbêjan* (house of *dengbêj*) opened in Diyarbakır. Hilmî Akyol played a key role, having collected *dengbêj* songs since 1979. By 2009 he had published more than ten books of collected folklore. New *dengbêj* centres were founded in other additional cities such as Van, Hakkarı and Muş. The performance of *dengbêj* began to change.

> Nowadays, the *dengbêj*s rarely sing in private houses, in the village guesthouses *(köy odaları)* or during weddings. The *dengbêj*s sing in the *dengbêj* house, during festivals, and on TV. (Yücel 2009: 14)

Performances became shorter, and in the repertoire

> 'Old' songs seem to be given more value than the new ones, as representing the 'tradition', the 'real culture.' They are often referred to as the 'classic songs'. (Yücel 2009: 10)

In 2009 the national television TRT launched its first Kurdish program TRT 6 (since 2015 *TRT Kurdî*). In addition *Med* TV from Europe and some local programs (e.g. *Müzik Diyarı, Gün TV*) broadcast Kurdish programs. As result of transnationalisation and the general increase and spread of the use of media, a number of Kurdish singers are popular nowadays across different regions and countries, e.g. Sivan Perwer (b. 1955, Urfa), Nizamettin Arıç (b. 1956, Ağri) and Ciwan Haco (b. 1957, Qamishlo, Syria; Hough 2010). In particular the recordings of Sivan Perwer, the most famous Kurdish singer since the 1980s, have been republished in their entirety in Turkey. During the 2000s Kurdish singers – such as Aynur Doğan and the group *Kardeş Türküler* – who sang Kurdish songs became popular all over Turkey (Yüksel 2011).

Alevism and its Music

The first Alevi associations had already been founded during the 1950s and 1960s.[110] Within this new Alevi movement an intellectuel elite, often with a politically left-wing background, began to dominate over the traditional *dede* families. Since the 1980s the Alevi held private and public discussions, in newspapers

---

[109] CD Muzîka Serayê ya Kurdî / Kurdish Saray Müzigi, Kom Müzik 2007.

[110] Özdemir 2016; Dönmez 2014; Çamuroğlu 1998, Väth 1993; Vorhoff 1995.

Figure 9: CD with recordings of a *cem* ceremony, Anadolu 2001.

and books, about the meaning and character of the traditional Alevilik, and even more on perspectives of a contemporary Alevilik.[111] Until today, hundreds of books, audio cassettes and CDs have been published, dozens of Alevi associations and new radio and television stations have been established (Zırh 2008: 106). Alevi identity has become part of the complex patchwork of identities in Turkey, which included cultural, religious, ethnic and regional elements.

Over the twentieth century the social character of Alevism meanwhile has changed, with traditional life in Anatolian villages rescinding and religious knowledge becoming rare. For a revival it was therefore necessary to research traditions, to mediate differing regional traditions, and to reconstruct and establish them anew, in particular among the growing Alevi diaspora in Turkish cities or even in Europe. Other factors such as migration, urbanisation, mediatization, institutionalisation, standardisation of formally regional traditions, and the struggle for public representation became important. *Cem* ceremonies, which used to be held only secretly inside Alevi villages are now held in public *cem* houses (*cemevi*), which where founded in Turkish cities such as Istanbul, Ankara or in Europe (Özdemir

[111] Massicard 2001; Vorhoff 1995: 59-74; Väth 1993: 211-222; Kehl-Bodrogi 1992.

2016). Their main function was it to enable urban Alevi communities to conduct religious practices, in particular *cems* and funerals. These new *cemevis* also had a strong impact on the character of Alevism in general. *Cemevis* in larger cities created new forms of public *cems*, which were then conducted regulary, during wintertime on a weekly basis, always in the very same building. According to modern working conditions such *cems* are often organized on weekends, in general *cems* in modern *cemevis* tend to be shorter than traditional ones. *Semahs* are performed by trained groups, wearing special costumes (Karolewski 2014; Erol 2010: 378, 385). According to Arzu Öztürkmen, it was already around the 1970s that *semahs* were performed outside of *cems* for the first time, e.g. by folk dancers and later during Alevi festivals (Öztürkmen 2005; Tambar 2010: 669).

A new element of this urban Alevism were festivals which combined symolic meaning, performance of Alevi identity and revived traditions. Since 1963 the Turkish administration allowed the organisation of an annual festival in Hacıbektaş (after the model of the Mevlevi festivals in Konya since 1953), including *cems*, concerts by Alevi singers and performances of *semah* groups. In 2009, 2011, 2014 and 2015 Kalan Müzik produced CDs entitled *Kızılbaş* I, II and *Alevilere* I and II, where several well-known folk singers interpreted Alevi songs. An example of a CD reconstructing Alevi music tradition might be *Mekteb-i Irfan* ("School of Wisdom") by Erol Köker (born in Arguvan, near Malatya), released in 2009.[112] Köker graduated from the Istanbul State Conservatory for Turkish music (ITÜ) and became a teacher of repertoire there. The linear notes of this CD contain extensive information on Alevism, including precise data on each individual song, their source person and the village where it was collected.

Music from Dersim

The case of Dersim (today's Tunceli province) whose regional identity discourses emerged in the 1990s, influenced by the previously discussed Marxist, Kurdish and Alevi discourses, presents a particular strong movement of musical reconstructions (Greve & Şahin 2017). Since the late 1970s private researchers, such as Zilfi Selcan, Daimi Cengiz, Hawar Tornêcengi, Cemal Taş, Metin and Kemal Kahraman and Mesut Özcan collected oral history and folk songs from the region. The earliest published CD with field recordings from Tunceli was released by the brothers, Metin and Kemal Kahraman under the title "Elder people sing Dersim songs" (*Yaşlılar Dersim Türküleri Söylüyor*) in 1997.[113] In addition to their

112 CD Erol Köker: Mekteb-i Irfan ("School of Wisdom"), Ak Müzik 2009.

113 Solomon 2012; Neyzi 2002. CD Metin and Kemal Kahraman: *Yaşlılar Dersim Türküleri Söylüyor*, Lızge Müzik 1997. Only one year later the similar, but much less documented CD *Kurdish bards* was released. *Traditional music from Dersim* was released by the Austrian record label *Extraplatte*, edited by Mehmet Emir, with recordings from Zeynel Kahraman, Mursaye Sıleman and Hıdır Akgül.

fieldwork, however, Metin and Kemal Kahraman integrated the recordings also in their own music production. On their CD *Sürela* (2000)[114] the Kahraman brothers presented two original instrumental and two vocal recording by the late Zeynel Kahraman (1930–2012) and Yusuf Yıldız in between their own new songs. In 2001 they released a full album with recordings of Zeynel Kahraman (*Melem Tıya*) and a second one with field recordings of the traditional duo of clarinet and drum (*Davul-Gırnata*).[115] Later also other musicians from Dersim, such as Mikail Aslan (b. 1972 in Hozat, Tunceli) or Cemil Koçgiri (b. 1980 in Duisburg, Germany) adopted the idea of integrating historical and field recordings into their own CDs.[116] Others musicians sang new interpretations of these historic recordings, like Erdoğan Emir who based a song on the recordings of Zeynel Kahrman (CD *Sad*, 2010). Metin and Kemal Kahraman later extended their research to the religion and culture of Dersim. The albums *Ceverê Hazara* (2006) and *Sae Moru/Şahmaran* (2011) are particularly good examples of the combination of field work with music. Both CDs include well-written, extended booklets, providing ethnographic and historic information on Dersim. The central focus of *Ceverê Hazara* ("The Gate of Thousands") is on Alevism in Dersim. *Sae Moru/Şahmaran* (2011) is inspired by a mythical creature, half woman, half snake. The inspiration for the project was a book with a Zaza version, collected by Mustafa Düzgün in 1993. In addition to this book the Kahramans did further interviews, which they included in original recordings on the CD. The music of both CDs, however, is not traditional but rather displays contemporary, partly even polyphonic arrangements, Anatolian and Western instruments such as violin, guitar and several international percussion instruments. One song is even sung together with the Armenian Sayat Nova Choir from Istanbul.

Two other musicians have tried to reconstruct historical music from Dersim, though in a less structured way. Cemil Koçgiri reinterpreted the song, *Cananı gördüm* following the notation of Muzafer Sarısözen (1944), but also based on a version he had found in Mazgirt, Tunceli (2007).[117] Mikail Aslan, born 1972 in Hozat, Tunceli, but living in Mainz, Germany since 1995, began at first mainly with his own composition, combining traditional Anatolian elements with Western music. In 2010, after several years of research Mikail Aslan released the CD, *Petag – Dersim Armenian Songs* (Kalan, 2010). The songs recorded there were based on historical transcriptions of Armenian music from Dersim, made between the 1930s and 1960s by Mihran Toumajan and Hampartsum Kasparyan, and on

114 CD Metin Kemal Kahraman, *Sürela*, Lızge, 2000.

115 MC Zeynel Kahraman: *Melem Tıya*, Lızge 2001; MC *Davul-Gırnata*, Lızge 2001.

116 CD Cemil Koçgiri: *Heya*, Kalan 2007: *Xan Eyledik* (Ali Ilgün), and Fırık Dede (a legendary religious leader, who had died in this very year 2007 in the age of 106): *Çekilmiş imiş*. CD Mikail Aslan: *Petag*, Kalan 2010: *Dersim dört dağ içinde* (historical recording on 78rpm by Nishan Morderos Keljikian, recorded in New York about 1929).

117 CD Cemil Koçgiri, *Heya*, Kalan 2007.

recordings from the archives of the Armenian-Dutch singer Ilda Simonian. To these generally short songs the Istanbul musician, Levent Güneş added newly composed introductory and intermediate melodies. For the interpretation, Mikail Aslan invited musicians from Armenia such as the *Akunq Ensemble.*[118] A comparison by Aslan of two interpretations of religious Alevi songs from the late religious leader, Fırık Dede, also demonstrates the growing historical awareness. On the CD, *Miraz* (2005) guitar, a deep *bağlama*, bass, violin and cello are use, the song is performed by a male and a female voice together. Only four years later, on the CD, *Kızılbaş* (2009) Mikail Aslan sings another religious song of Fırık Dede, *Dêsa Khurêsa*, as collected by Cemal Taş.[119] In this later interpretation only a traditional *tembur* (small long-necked lute) is used for accompaniment, the song remained almost completely as the original, the singular difference that it was sung by a younger and educated voice.

Eventually, after 2000, even music of a variety of early Anatolian cultures was reconstructed in several large-scale projects – despite the obvious lack of sources and hence of historical knowledge.[120] Both in Turkey and internationally most successful was the dance show "Sultans of the Dance," directed by Mustafa Erdoğan (b. 1965), premiered in 1999. In 2001, "Fire of Anatolia" (*Anadolu Ateşi*), followed, a show program including 90 dancers and musicians, which traveled through a great number of countries. The shows evoked several early Anatolian cultures, including the Mount Nemrut culture, Central Asian shamans, Zarathustriasm, Yezidi, Alevi, Mevlevi, Anatolian folk dances and others.[121] The Troy project, again by Mustafa Erdoğan, was fairly freely based on the Illias, and was presented in fantasized historical costumes, the music was newly composed by Yücel Arzen (b.1970) in the style of archaicizing film music. In addition to a Western orchestra some folk instruments, including *duduk*, *ney*, kaval, clarinet, panflute, *zurna*, *tulum*, *kemençe*, *santur*, *ud*, *kanun*, *bağlama*s, *buzuki*, harp, *didgeridoo* (!) and percussion was integrated. Among the singers, members of *Kardeş Türküler* such as Fehmiye Çelik, Ayşenur Kolibal and Vedat Yıldırım took part. In 2013 rehearsals began for "Sun of Mesopotamia," produced by the "Brotherhood of Dance" with support of the Ministry for Culture and Tourism, and directed by Sezgin Aydin. Accordingly the press in-

118 The following project of Mikail Aslan, *Pelguzar* (Kalan, 2010) is based on an epos of the Koçgiri region, north of Dersim, as collected by Tevfik Şahin (Basel, Switzerland). The music, however is predominantly newly composed by Mikail Aslan.

119 CD Mikail Aslan, *Miraz* (2005); CD *Kızılbaş* (Kalan, 2009).

120 Already in 1951, Arel played the reconstruction of a "Sumeric hymn" according to Francis Galpin in at least one concert. The program for a Concert of Turkish Music by a Group of the *İleri Türk Musikisi Konservatuvarı*, Istanbul, Çituri Biraderler Basımevi 1951; Galpin 1937.

121 Music by Fuat Saka, Taner Demiralp, Mustafa Erdoğan, Murat Uygun, Turgay Güzelcan, Serdar Yalçın.

formation the program was supposed to deal with cuneiform culture, the cultures of Göbeklitepe (10th millenium BC) and Gilgamesch.[122]

Musically more ambitious was the project on music of the Hettites, "*Hattusa,*" written and directed by Oğuz Elbaş (with the assistance of Okan Murat Öztürk), and realized in 2010 with the participation of numerous prominent musicians, including Cihat Aşkın, Okan Murat Öztürk, Özay Önal, Erdem Şimşek and the Venician folk music group, *Ensemble Calicanto*. Parts of the music were newly composed by Ertuğrul Bayraktarkartal. Based on archaeological research on music of the Hettites (Alp 1999), Oğuz Elbaş reconstructed Hettite instruments (and costumes for all musicians), Şehvar Beşiroğlu and Çağatay Akyol (both already experienced in the reconstruction of early Ottoman *çenk*) played the early Anatolian harp (Beşiroğlu & Ergur 2009; Beşiroğlu & Celasin 2006), Okan Murat Öztürk and Erdem Şimşek performed on reconstructed long-necked lutes. In addition a string orchestra, clarinet, recorder, mandolina, accordion, *gayda*, *taragot* and percussion instruments where used. The main parts of the concert were performed on *bağlama* with added choir and orchestra, and were based on folk music from the region of Çorum, where they were collected more than 3000 years after the collapse of the Hittite empire. The project gave several concerts in Ankara, Corum, Gaziantep and Kahramanmaras, but also in Evora /Portugal, Budapest and Vicenza (Italy).

Another completely different approach to music of the classical antiquity was the piece "Seikilos Epitaph" for ensemble, written by the Western composer, Evrim Demirel in 2016. Himself born in Aydın, where the famous stone including the first century notation was found in 1883, Demirel kept the original melody but added a contemporary, polyphonic, partly atonal accompaniment.

In 1993, the "Copenhagen Criteria" of the European Union called for the protection of minorities as a condition for Turkey's membership. In fact, the late 1990s and early 2000s were dominated by a liberal multicultural discourse, and many ethnic and religious minorities in Turkey formed new identities, which often included cultural revivals.

> In the 1990s, so to speak, the Pandora's Box was opened. And what had come up from that box, was not only the ethnic or religious identity issues, but also the feminist movement and the lost memories of non-Muslims appeared, which began with nostalgia of old Istanbul […]. These years also witnessed an increase in the publication and communication on these issues. Since the late 1990s with the Turkish-Greek rapprochement and in the 2000s with increasing exchange programs like Erasmus, a new generation of researchers were raised. (Öztürkmen 2015: 175)

Several "ethnic" music styles gained popularity beyond their own comunities, within the majority society, and at the same time became identity markers for emerging discourses.

---

122 www.sunofmesopotamia.com (accessed November 15, 2013).

> The cultural and musical variety which had been labelled as 'regional' (*yöre* and *bölge*) during the 'radion years' [1940s – 60s], gained a character associated directly with ethnic identities in the period following the 1980 coup d'etat. In this situation, folk music that could function as a means for integration in terms of nationalism and ethnic identity, now became an obvious discriminator for the 'other' (Öztürk 2015: 190)

Since the 1990s, a number of concerts in Istanbul attempted to stage a multicultural Ottoman musical world (Coskun 1999), e.g. the concert series "*Birlikte Yaşamak*" ("living together") including a *maftirim* group (dir. Menahem Eskenazi). Another example was the concert following the commemoration of the conquest of Istanbul by Mehmet I (May 29), which from 1995 presented singers of the jewish religious tradition, such as the *maftirim* group, an Armenian choir, and Sufi group of Taşkin Savaş, *Yakarış Müzik Topluluğu*. Similar is the concert, *Müzigin Renkleri* organized by the Foundation for Turkish History, Türk Tarihi Vakfı, or "*Istanbul'un Dans Renkleri / Yedi Bölgeden Yedi Tepe Istanbulluyuz*" as part of the 2010 European Capital of Culture.[123] The documentary film "The Lost Songs of Anatolia" (*Anadolu Kayıp Şarkılar*, Nezih Ünen, 2010) included original music recordings from all of Anatolia (though in arranged versions).

Probably the most successful ensemble of the Anatolian and Urban revivals was *Kardeş Türküler*, founded in 1993 as part of the Boğaziçi Performing Arts Ensemble (*Boğaziçi Gösteri Sanatları Topluluğu BGST*). From its inception, *Kardeş Tüküler* aimed to perform the music of Anatolia, Thrace and Mesopotamia in their original languages. The repertoire of their first concert in 1993 was composed of Turkish, Kurdish, Azerbaijani and Armenian songs. Later they turned to various other cultures, and enriched their repertoire with Laz, Georgian, Circassian, Romani, Macedonian, and Alevi songs and dances. At the same time the group was politically active in the field of human rights and tolerance of all ethnic and religious minorities. *Kardeş Türkülers* first album was released in 1997 by *Kalan Müzik*, including music from different cultures of Anatolia and Mesopotamia. The second album *Doğu* ("The East", Kalan, 1999)[124] had a more local and specific focus. The group gained at latest nationwide fame with the music to the popular film, *Vizontele* by Yılmaz Erdoğan and Ömer F. Sorak, which was awarded the honour of best film music in the Antalya Film Festival 2001. While

---

[123] In the following years numerous multireligious concerts took place, such as "Rumi and Tolerance" at CRR 2005; or the *Hatay Medeniyetler Buluşması* ("Hatay Civilisations Conference") in Antakya 2005. Further concerts were organized by the Ministry of Culture as promotional tourism for the multicultural nature of Turkey, e.g. *Hoşgörü Imperatorluğu* at CRR with the Armenian Surp Takavor church choir, a cantor from the Greek Patriachate, Ladino and Greek songs by *Los Paşaros Sefaradis* and Buzuki Orhan, an Alevi *semah*, and a group of Whirling Dervishes.

[124] In September 2000, the core group of *Kardeş Türküler* directed and arranged the music for the album *Roj û Heyv* by the famous Kurdish musician Şivan Perwer. Following this they went on to prepare the music for Yılmaz Erdoğan and Ömer F. Sorak's film *Vizontele*, and Erdoğan's *Vizontele Tuba*. The sountrack for *Vizontele* was released by the *Kalan Müzik* in 2001, followed by that of *Vizontele Tuuba* in 2004.

Figure 10: CD cover of Muammer Ketençoğlu's CD with newly arranged Turkish, Greek and Jewish music from Smyrna / İzmir, Kalan 2007

a core group including the main singers remained in the group, many instrumentalists changed over the years. *Kardeş Türküler* used a rich instrumentation including all kinds of Anatolian folk instruments, but also bass, guitar, clarinet, violin, accordion, *ud*, *buzuki*, *cümbüş*, and a strong and rich percussion group.

As part of the project, several members of *Kardeş Türküler* conducted research among Anatolian minorities. In particular the different languages of Anatolia forced the singers of the group to learn at least the pronounciation of several languages. From 1962 BÜFK (*Boğaziçi Üniversitesi Folklor Kulübü*, precursor to the BGST) edited the journal, *Folklora Doğru* ("Towards Folklore", from 1990 *Folklora Doğru / Dans-Müzik – Kültür*). For the CD, *Eyhok, Music from Hakkarı* (Kalan, 2004) Aytekin Ataş, Selda Öztürk, Vedat Yıldırım and Neriman Güneş conducted extensive fieldwork (advised by Muhsin Kızılkaya). Later several songs collected in Hakkarı were integrated in the repertoires of *Kardeş Türküler*, including a modernized version of "*Elo Dino*" on the album, *Hemavaz* (2002; Bates 2008: 66). Comparable combinations of fieldwork and new musical interpretations were conducted by the singer, Ayşenur Kolivar at the eastern Black Sea Coast. Ayşenur Kolivar left the group in 2000, but continued to sing in Lazuri, Hemşin and Georgian (Bates 2008, 68). The book, "The 15 Years Story of *Kardeş*

Türküler," released by BGST in 2008 at the fifteenth anniversary of the ensemble, discloses their influences in a remakably open and reflective way (Akkaya et. al. 2008). In addition to a documentation of the group's history it includes interviews with numerous musicians and music experts, each of which is printed in both Turkish and the respective native language of the interviewee, e.g. Laz, Kurmanji, Zaza, Georgian, Armenian, Adige and Ladino.

As we have seen, these recent music revivals not only recovered numerous music traditions which had almost disappeared, but at least to the same degree, became starting points for individual creative musical innovation. Tamara Lingiston estimated the life-spans of numerous music revivals varying from some few years to almost a century.

> I would suggest that when there is no longer an overriding concern for historical "authenticity" (i.e. style markers that are conciously employed for historical reference) and the "tradition" is felt to bee too constricting of a reference point by the majority of revivalists, that revivals break down into different styles. (80)

Conclusion

Until the nineteenth century the history of music as a description of historical development was never an issue for Ottoman music theory (and other) writers. The musical past was conceptualized as an idealized origin on the one hand, i.e. as invented or mainly shaped by person such as Pythagoras, Ptolemy, al Fârâbî, Ibn Sîna, or 'Abd al-Qâdir Marâghî; and the live stories of direct teachers and their teachers (-teachers) on the other. Ottoman sources do not testify to a conciousness of the historical development of music, musicians of the past are mentioned rather as figures of a timeless and ongoing tradition, thought of as persons of just another generation, as imagined teachers, who derserve respect, and who could be regarded as direct precursors.

In the first book on Turkish music history Rauf Yekta integrated Turkish music into the contemporary European concept of music historiography. European historiography of the nineteenth century described the development of music in demarcated steps from earlier, less developed states, ascending from "culture" to "culture" to finally reach the beginning of European music in the Middle Ages. The foundation of the Republic of Turkey in 1923 led to further changes in Turkish music historiography, in particular concerning the concept of origin. The nineteenth century European idea of cultures as prehistory was modificated to the ideologically loaded theory of an origin as "Turkish music culture." In the 1940s, Hüseyin Sâdeddin Arel tried to integrate this theory of a "Turkish origin" into the concept of cultures as prehistories, by leading musical prehistory to a "Turkish culture" rather than to European classical music. Until today most Turkish popular books on music history follow this general outline, without taking any possible influence of non-Turks into account. For the description of Ottoman music history, on the other hand, biographies, particularly of composers still dominate the imagination, while historical development (except for some Turkish music historians) is widely ignored. This narrative may be seen as the historical backgroud of most Turkish musicians until today.

It was mainly the development of notation and later that of audio recording, which led to further changes of the notion of the past and its music. Since around 1900 some connoisseurs, including Rauf Yekta, Suphi Ezgi and Hüseyin Sadettin Arel collected and revered old manuscripts (in particular notations and *edvârs*), and began to publish articles or books for the first time directly based on these written sources. The concept of given and unchanging cultures hence began to loose its unquestioned position, and for the first time differences *within* music cultures (i.e. within Ottoman-Turkish music) attracted the interest of researchers. Since about the 1990s the focus of research shifted completely to historical sources, and today, most Ottoman music notations, treatises, iconographic sources or European travelogues have been analysed or edited and thus became available. Issues and debates on the origin or identity of music, though still repeated in popular books, were completely replaced among academic scholars by detailed philological work. Similarly the publication of notation grew in scope, making more and more music of the past public available, even without the need for *meşk* lessons by a personal teacher. Since the turn of the millenium, the repertoire transmitted only in written form (as opposed to orally) by Cantemir and Ali Ufukî, became part of the mainstream repertoire. Similar to Ottoman-Turkish music, growing amounts of Anatolian music has also been written down and published in notations, again in most cases without any account of the process and the criteria of editing.

As a result of the development of historical research and pulication today, a growing amount of historical music is available. The still prevalent notion of a direct continuation of the past and the imagined closeness of its musicians facilitates the appropriation of this now free historical material, opening up a huge field of aesthetically more or less convincing musical interpretations and reconstructions. From the 1990s, reconstruction of Ottoman music became a particularly popular new field for musicians, often involving international cooperation, and sometimes in hybrid musical interpretations. The musical style of both the compositions transmitted in manuscripts and their historical performance often sounds strange to contemporary musicians and audience, which again raises the awareness of historical changes.

Comparable efforts (though to a lesser degree) also became visible in the reconstruction of Anatolian folk music since the 1990s. Due to the general lack of written sources reconstruction was inevitably based on either fieldwork with musicians, or historical recordings. Many lost music styles were reconstructed or revived by scholars, collectors and musicians. Jewish, Alevi and Kurdish music, non-Turkish songs from the Back Sea coast or from Dersim hence became publicly audible and sometimes even popular. The most popular group of this "ethnic revival" was *Kardeş Türküler*, who sang songs from different traditions in numerous Anatolian languages.

An important effect of the ongoing historicization is that traditions have lost their self-evident importance. Crucial for this alienation of traditon is the historiography of the nearest past, i.e. the twentieth century. Towards the end of the twentieth century, historical music recordings gained growing importance as a new type of source, preserving the actual sound of a recent past. During the last twenty-plus years a growing number of CDs with historical recordings on 78rpm discs have been released in Turkey, in particular since 1997 by the record company *Kalan Müzik*. As a result of this historicization of the recent past, today almost every contemporary music might be perceived as historical, while the present becomes increasingly short.

Overall the conception of music from the past as available since the late twentieth century is highly contradictory and confusing. While a growing number of sources (treatises, notations, recordings etc.) are available, only few and in many cases more ideological narratives connect these sources and form a legible history. Several projects on historical reconstruction of Ottoman music as well as the numerous revivals of ethnic, regional or religious music further confuses the picture.

The German musicologist Carl Dahlhaus (1977 / 1983), writing on European music of the nineteenth century, defined tradition as refering

> either to the legacy of the past that has survived unquestioned into the present or to a conscious assimilation of this legacy (Dahlhaus 1983: 64).

This embeddedness of the past in the present was promoted by the Ottoman *meşk* education where a student learns the repertoire, playing technique and practices, interpretation and aesthetic by imitation from his master. At best he would be able to replace him. This self-evident inbeddedness within music and musicians of the past almost got lost in modern Turkey, or at least has changed its character to become "history." According to Maurice Halbwachs, founder of social memory studies,

> History generally begins at the point were tradition ceases and the social memory dissolves. (Halbwachs 1967: 103, quoted after Assmann 2011: 30)

Ottoman-Turkish music of the past has become an object of the present, while in former times the present was perceived as a direct continuation of the past. This former uninterrupted inclusion of the past into the present (a concept of course not limited to the Middle East), which might be called "tradition," implied a secure aesthetic reference for musicians:

> Now, a sense of tradition, an undying and unquestioning faith in the authority of our legacy from the past, is not exclusively a way of looking at the past. Its concern is also – perhaps even primarily – the present and the future. Those who feel guided and shel-

> tered by standarts, institutions and habitual patterns of perception from previous centuries will likewise feel a sense of confidence in the present and, at the same time, foresee a future that differes little from the present. (Dahlhaus 1983: 109)

The historicization of music hence implies, at least to a certain degree its alienation. Dahlhaus reflected a comparable change in Europe during the nineteenth century, however, reduced the importance of this interpretation:

> By objectifying tradition, and thereby making it the object of history, we do not detach ourselves from tradition, whether this be the tradition we have grown up or a foreign tradition we wish to adopt. Rather, we gain one means of ascertaining just what it is about this tradition that gives it its distinctive character. The historian does not treat tradition as a distant object; he feels enveloped by it, caught in its sway. (Dahlhaus 1983:59)

According to Dahlhaus, the historicization rather implies serious aesthetic consequences:

> Yet by distancing himself from the past the historian clears a path for the new. It is possible without distortion to draw from the historicist thesis of the substantive historicality of works of music the conclusion that an age should look to its own music for its reflection instead of clinging doggedly to music of the past. (Dahlhaus 1983: 63)

A conciousness of music history tends to produce a canon of works that according to music historians, emphatically *"belong to history [...] in the strong sense of towering above the debris otherwhise left behind by the past."* (Dahlhaus 1983: 93) Musicians were therefore encouraged to develop music, which could represent the present, so that it might later be accepted in a still-to-be-written music history.

> However, once unreflected tradition has been tranformed into a 'reflected', or rather progressively 'more reflected' tradition, it becomes difficultto view change with customary traditionalist equanimity. Instead, we fel forced to choose between propagating change with progressive ardour, or hindering it in a conservative spirit, or even reversing it out of fondness for the old order. Naïve traditionalism metamorphoses into other forms of behaviour towards the legacy of the past. (Dahlhaus 1983: 65)

The change from a living (and of course continously changing) "musical tradition," to its historicization, led to both a growing knowledge of this now increasingly fixed and objectivated past, coupled with an increasing distance from it.

Music of the present, however, and hence also music of the future, which is not yet part of any historic canon, demands new ideas, techniques and new musical approaches. In contemporary Turkey "historical" Ottoman music is much better known and much easier available than ever before. But while this past thus became better known, both present and future became unwritten, frightening and almost unlimited, open fields.

How much ever the resort to an Ottoman musical past might be motivated by the search for a stable and confident point of reference, the resulting research on historical Ottoman music served to widen the field of artistic music in Turkey.

IV Obsessions with Hybridity

Within the rapidly changing musical world in Turkey, the ongoing aesthetic dominance of *melodies* compared to other musical elements seems to be the most solid heritage. Only a few Turkish musicians and composers have completely abandoned the composition and performance of monophone or harmonically accompanied *melodies* in favour of polyphonic music or compositions of timbre. The performance practice of melodies, however, has become enriched and diverse to an almost endless extent. Today pure melodies, performed by one single musician, sound insufficient to most listeners in Turkey. In Turkey today the focus of musical creativity is on the performance of music rather than on its composition. Over the last centrury a vast spectrum of potential realizations of melodies has developed, while the composition of new melodies has remained much less attractive for Turkish musicians. Recent performance practice includes chamber ensembles such as duos, trios and quartets, composed of a range of instruments, as well as choirs and orchestras for traditional art or folk music, up to to cross-over projects with jazz or non-Western music, such as Indian music or *flamenco*. The core group of the well-known ensemble *Yansımalar* encompasses *ney*, guitar, *tanbur*, percussion, and bass. Similarly, the group *Ince Saz* includes *tanbur*, *kemençe*, drums, bass and voice. Solo performances, or soloists heterophonically accompanied by one or two instrumentalists, have become rare exceptions. Even bağlama players, who often perform solo during their concerts, usually add further instruments into their studio recordings.

Over the entire twentieth century almost all musicians in Turkey have at least for some time tried to develop a kind of *sentez* (synthesis), of what they perceived as alternative musical worlds, that is the horizontal music of the Middle East and the vertical music of the West (in this sense beginning, say, in the early Baroque period). The notions of these "two cultures" are, of course, completely unclear. Bruno Nettl (1984: 4) gave a general description for what is perceived as Western music:

> In many of the world's cultures, the concept of a Western music is well established and in use, and the differences among various Western musics are regarded as trivial. [... Its] general traits [include]: functional harmony, along with the concept that in proper music, harmony must always be present. Then there is the idea that music is normally made by groups, the larger the better, with a form of dictatorial leadership. And further: the notion that planning is important, with the norm of the carefully composed piece, meticulously rehearsed, and performed the same way every time; the concept of radical innovation in musical content or style in composition, along with the need for precise repetition in performance; the principle of control as exhibited in notation; the concept of music as something sufficiently independent of the other domains of culture.

In particular Western orchestras have become a model for most music cultures worldwide, inspiring all kind of larger ensembles with traditional instruments.

Today the use of "hybrid" ensembles and instruments forms a central characteristic of almost all Turkish music (as is probably similar in most countries around the world). As pointed out in the introduction, this is at the same time the main reason why the terms "hybrid" and "sentez" (synthesis) are no longer helpful for the description of the musical reality of contemporary Turkey.

The historical development of this plethora of music in Turkey over the twentieth century is far too complex to be placed in a linear narrative. Rather, the following chapter tries to describe the present situation using systematic categories, each beginning with its respective predecessors. In terms of musical structures two general approaches to contemporary Turkish performance practice and composition might be distinguished, though in practice they are closely interrelated.

1. Traditional Turkish music (of any tradition) is often performed monophone without any substantial melodic, rhythmic or formal change, but played on instruments or by ensembles which were either adopted from non-Turkish (in particular European) traditions, e.g. choir, piano, guitar, orchestra, new mixed ensembles; or on improved and adjusted instruments of more or less Ottoman-Turkish tradition. Further adaptations and changes concern playing and singing techniques, in most cases again developed to enrich the timbre. Several Turkish musicians today try to adapt traditional Turkish playing techniques for Western instruments or, conversely, make technical changes to enable Western instruments to play Turkish music. In 2008, the guitarist Tolgahan Çoğulu (b. 1978) developed an *adjustable microtonal guitar*, on which he plays Anatolian folk songs and Ottoman art music as well as Western music. In 2010 he finished his Ph.D. thesis on *The Adaptation of Bağlama Techniques into Classical Guitar Performance*. The composer Onur Türkmen (b. 1972) on the other hand, wrote his Ph.D. on *Contemporary Techniques Applied to Turkish Music Instruments: Kemençe, Ud, Kanun, Ney*. Today, Western playing techniques such as differentiated articulation, glissando, vibrato, trills, tremolos, harmonics and chords are regularly used in Turkish music.

Furthermore, such changes in instruments and ensembles have an impact on the image of a performance and its performer; sometimes these aspects even dominate the musical ones. In particular, within the urban society of Turkey (as elsewhere in the world), choirs and Western orchestras are perceived as more prestigious than, for example, a single *bağlama*. In particular during the early Republic of Turkey, the state openly supported this perception.

One important precondition for this development is the rise of instrumental music, or at least of the instrumental accompaniment to singing in Turkey. The background to this development is the prestige of instrumental music in Western music since the eighteenth century. In the Ottoman Empire most musical traditions were primarily vocal rather than instrumental. However, at least at the Ottoman court of the eighteenth century, also purely instrumental concerts, *fasıl-ı sazende*, were regularly performed, including genres such as *peşrev* (which thereby developed from introductory pieces to respected compositions); *saz semai* and extended *taksims*. During the nineteenth century, exposure to Western orchestras, chamber ensembles and polyphonic instruments such as the piano, in combination with the impact of the cultural hegemony of Europe over most parts of the world, began to change the musical world also in Turkey. Around 1900 Tanburi Cemil Bey became famous for his extraordinary virtuosity and musciality on *tanbur* and *kemençe* due to his numerous 78rpm recordings. His recordings led to a new perception of the musical function of instruments, as not necessarily an accompaniment for the human voice. In the 1970s and 1980s, traditional musicians such as Niyazi Sayın, Necdet Yaşar and İhsan Ozgen, each an admirer of Cemil Bey, re-produced this perception among a younger generation of musicians.

In the field of folk music, *bağlama* players such as Ali Ekber Çiçek, Talip Özkan and Arif Sağ introduced a comparable instrumental virtuosity only much later, beginning in the 1960s. However, the aesthetic changes in Turkish folk music during the twentieth century were even more dramatic than those in Ottoman-Turkish art music. Folk music became ambitious and demanding in terms of aesthetics, intonation and virtuosity, becoming a sophisticated artificial music, substantially different from performance practices of Anatolian villages where these traditions originated.

Part of this shift of the aesthetic focus to the interpretation of traditional pieces is the fixing and formalising of these once constantly developing traditions as described in the previous chapter. The fixation (and partly also the historicization) of melodies led to a perception similar to that of "musical works" in the Western sense. Today, concerts of famous *bağlama* players often remind one of recitals of piano or violin, while at the same time, the traditional and social functions of genres such as *gelin ağlatması*, *semah* or folk dances, while to a reduced extent, still continue.

As part of these broad changes the various styles of Anatolian folk music and Ottoman-Turkish art music have merged substantially – in particular in terms of performance practice – and elements of Western music or popular music are often intermingled as well.

The adaptation of historically non-Ottoman-Turkish instruments or ensembles for Turkish music has given rise to several technical challenges. The main general problem is the intonation, hence the pitch system. While fretless string instruments such as violin or cello can easily play all kinds of micro intervals, the means for, say, piano or guitar, are limited. Often the use of Western instruments forces musicians to change the tonal system and play in Western tempered tuning. Also in terms of sound and melodic ornamentation, not every instrument fits each Turkish tradition without substantial changes, nor do all possible ensemble compositions make aesthetic sense.

2. Similarly common for Turkish music today is the use of Western functional harmony, that is, polyphonic accompaniment of traditional melodies – while again (in most cases), genre, musical form and the main melody remain un-

changed. The musical language of these added harmonizations is in general basic, hardly progressing to the rich harmonic language of the European late Romantic music (not to mention atonality, 12-tone music or other styles beyond traditional tonality) rather resonant in its harmonic vocabulary to Western popular music. As indicated above, the addition of a basic major/minor harmony as accompaniment almost always enforces the use of the Western tempered system. Both general approaches, changes in performance practice (affecting mainly the timbre) and harmonization, are therefore interdependent.

Arrangements of this second type were already being written in the nineteenth century. However, as is widely known, in Western art music the traditional major-minor tonality was abandoned at the latest after the 1920s with the Second Viennese School. Its ongoing use in Turkey led to an aesthetic isolation of Turkish Western composers; and furthermore to a Western perception of Turkish music as folkloristic or even as a kind of popular music. Today in particular Anatolian folk music targeting Turkish audiences is often performed with similar basic harmonization, while international audiences (i.e. the exoticist "world music" scene) tends to prefer either monophonic, unaccompanied – "traditional" – versions or, to a much lesser extent, polyphonic avant-garde interpretations.

In cross-cultural projects of world music (as mentioned in chapter II) musical elements of non-Western music cultures are also integrated into Turkish musical elements to varying degrees. While combinations with traditions whose tonal system (at least today) is again basically Western, e.g. flamenco, tango or klezmer, imply Western concepts of pitch system and tonality, while Indian or Japanese music for example offer different musical concepts.

Only a few Turkish musicians, composers or ensembles have seriously questioned the aesthetic dominance of melodies, mostly in the context of contemporary Western music. As already mentioned in chapter II, composers and musicians of contemporary Western music today are often interested in "cross-cultural encounters," also including those with Turkish music. On the other hand, however, contemporary Western music tends to avoid melodies, at least simple, catchy melodies. In order to meet these Western aesthetic expectations, Turkish composers have tried to change or completely avoid melody. In some cases the melody might remain as an exotic detail, in some few cases new music might respect several aesthetics (e.g. Turkish and Western) at the same time.

To my knowledge, only one musicologist so far has proposed a categorisation of "hybrid" music in Turkey, that is Yaprak Melike Uyar. In her Ph.D. thesis "Cultural Connotations and the Process of Localization" (2016), Uyar distinguishes three approaches to hybrid jazz in Turkey:

1) "Tradionalists" who refuse all kinds of fusion with traditional Turkish music, strictly remaining within the scope of traditional jazz – actually Uyar estimates this category as containing about 90 percent of Turkish jazz (Uyar 2016: 106).

2) "Eclectic synthesis," that is, musicians using traditional Turkish songs in a tempered pitch system (with *makams* such as *nihavend* or *acemaşiran*), for example interpreting well-known folk songs such as Aşık Veysel's *Uzun ince bir yoldayım*, as arranged by Baki Duyarlar and sung by Esin Afşar in 1997.

3) "Absorbed synthesis":

> A more interventionist approach to fusion can be observed especially on melodic and harmonic levels. Musicians may perform songs from either Turkish makam music or the Turkish/Anatolian folk repertoire. In this kind of synthesis, most of the time, one or more instruments with the ability to play microtones in the Turkish music system exist in the band.

Examples include Önder Focan: "Swing A la Turc," 2007, including Şenol Filiz (*ney*) in addition to a jazz ensemble; Erkan Oğur: *Çayın Öte Yüzünde*, a traditional song form Elazığ, played on a fretless guitar (Uyar 2016: 112ff).

While the difference between the latter two categories is not always clear, it seems that Uyar faced the same problem which I was not able to solve: that is, to find fully convincing and encompassing categories within an almost endless plethora of existing musical approaches in Turkey, in particular over the last 20 years.

The broadening of musical styles came in parallel with the augmentation of the repertoire of most Turkish musicians to an unprecedented degree. Concert programs and CDs came to include pieces of Turkish folk and art music, historical European art music (from a range of periods and styles) and possibly pieces from other music traditions. At his numerous concerts and on his CDs, the violinist Cihat Aşkın (until 2012 Director of the State Conservatory for Turkish Music at ITÜ), plays European classical, Ottoman and Anatolian pieces in different arrangements. His CD, "*Umutsuz* – The Desperate" (2004), for example, contains compositions by Yalçın Tura, the Armenian composer Haçadur Avedisyan, Pyotr Ilyich Tchaikovsky, Luciano Berio, Refik Fersan, in addition to Azerbaijan and Armenian folk songs.[1] Similarly wide-ranging is the repertoire of the cellist Uğur Işık[2], who on his first two albums recorded a *zeybek*, three instrumental compositions of Ottoman art music (two of them actually of ostensibly pre-Ottoman composers), *Gemiler Giresun'e* (a folk song from Trabzon, Black Sea Coast), the famous *baglama* composition *Haydar haydar*, an Armenian lullaby, *La rosa en flore* (a famous Landino song), *Kızılırmak* from the folk singer Aşık Veysel, the *Salât-Kemâliye* (a religious prayer), *Alamanti* (a Greek dance song) and finally a hymn from Alî Ufukî's collection. His second CD presents religious music from Europe and Byzantium, the third includes music by the mystic George Ivano-

1 CD Cihat Aşkın: *Umutsuz – The Desperate*, Kalan 2004. www.cihataskin.net (accessed December 4, 2012).

2 Uğur Işık: *Unveils Anatolian Spirit*, Kalan 2005; *Cello Invocations*, Kalan 2008. CD Uğur Işık: *Chess of Cello*, Kalan n.y.

vich Gurdjieff (1866-1949), Turkish folk songs, music by Jean Baptiste Lully (1632-1687), and Eric Satie (Gnossienne No. 1). The CD, "Touches" by Tahir Aydogdu (*kanun*), Bilgin Canaz (*ney*) and Hakan A. Toker (piano, akkordeon) contains traditional instrumental compositions from Çinuçen Tanrıkorur, Aleko Bacanos and Hacı Arif Bey, but also Astor Piazzola (Oblivion), Bach-Gounod (Ave Maria) and again Eric Satie (Gymnopedie No 1).[3] The group, *Ince Saz* has played, over the years, Ottoman art music, Turkish folk songs, Turkish tangos and their own compositions. On his CD dedicated to the reconstructed *çenk*, the American musician Robert Labordees included among other pieces a *teke zorlaması* (here the *çenk* replaces the *cura*); the famous bağlama piece *ötme bülbül ötme*; the *şarkı gül yüzlülerin sevkine gel* by Dede Efendi; an *uzun hava* and *halay* from Seyhan as recorded by Bela Bartok in 1936; an Alevi *sema* from Ali Ekber Çiçek; a *zeybek* dance tune; a *yayla havası*; a song from Safiye Ayla composed by Sadettin Kaynak; a *sultani yegah saz semaisi* from Nedim Ağa (d. 1850).[4] Most Turkish folk musicians try to interpret music from at least the entire area of Anatolia in their repertoire, and official teaching programs for Turkish folk music offer lessons on all regional styles. Refusing the nationalistic Turkish approach to folk music, the group *Kardeş Türküler* even combined the music from different ethnic and religious minorities, using up to 20 languages per concert (including Turkish, Greek, Kurdish, Romani, Aramaic, Zaza, Laz, Hemşin, Ladino and Arabic).

As a result of both general approaches, the diversity of musicial performances of traditional melodies as well as the repertoire of contemporary musicians has enlarged substantially.

Finally it should be remembered that both traditional and recent musical styles still continue to exist in pure forms in Turkey, including European music for piano; hymns sung during Ramadan; *türkü*s, classical Turkish music and others. New compositions, however, are almost always "hybrid," mixed, or, to put it better: individually composed music; though of course connected in numerous ways (via melody, rhythm, form or instruments) with one or often many musical traditions.

In this present chapter, I will try to describe different musical approaches for this general search for *sentez*/hybridity. At first, changes on musical instruments (and voice) will be discussed, divided into sub-chapters on Ottoman and Western instruments; *bağlama* and guitar; the voice; and percussion instruments. This part aims to describe the breathtaking enlargement of available instruments and playing techniques.

A second sub-chapter deals with the introduction and adoption of Western harmony into all kind of musical traditions in Turkey, together with the development of Western-Turkish music as including any kind of traditional Turkish

---

3 CD Tanını: *Dokunuşlar / Touches*, Kaf 2008.

4 Robert Laboree: *Cengname. Music for the Turkish Harp* (Kalan 2001);

music. A short excursus will at least provide a sketch of attempts for hybridization within the wide field of popular music and jazz.

Another important factor of Turkish music of the twentieth century is the development of new, often larger ensembles for traditional music, this being in the focus in the third sub-chapter.

The last part of this chapter describes some examples of music and musical approaches which no longer fit in any established musical tradition but rather create completely individual music.

I would like to underline once again that the following sketch does not intend to present an encompassing history of Turkish music of the twentieth/twenty-first century but rather attempts to describe the process of individualisation of music practice and composition as a result of the obsessive search for *sentez*. Further, it is not possible to mention all musical projects representing a particular approach – there are simply too many.

Instruments in Flux

Ottoman and Western Musical Instruments

For a detailed view on the development of musical performances over the twentieth century, let us begin with changes concerning musical instruments. Alterations in instruments and in their use as well as technical or musical improvements of existing instruments and their playing technique have of course always been a part of musical life. It is widely known that the formation of a particular Ottoman style of art music during the seventeenth century also included changes of ensembles and hence the sound of the music. Later the growing number of *terkîb*s and *makam*s led to the avoidance of some instruments including *çenk* (harp) and later *mıskal* (panflute), while the musical importance and prestige of other instruments, such as *tanbur* and *ney*, grew (Feldman 1996).

Let us as an example briefly follow the development of bowed instruments in the Ottoman Empire and the Republic of Turkey (Çolakoğlu Sarı 2016). Until the seventeenth century bowed instruments played a minor role at the court, compared to lutes (*ud*, *şahrud*, *kopuz*), harps (*çenk*) and psalterium (*mugni*). Only the spike fiddle of Persian origin, *kemânce* (also called *kemân* or *rebâb*), was played, an instrument with long neck and round body (Feldman 1996: 111ff; Soydaş & Beşiroğlu 2007). During the eighteenth century in Istanbul the *kemânce* was replaced by the European *viola d'amore* (Turkish *sine keman*, "breast violin") (Zümrüt 2000: 42ff; Feldman 1996: 128ff)). Around one century later the *sine keman* also disappeared, coming to be replaced by the violin which was introduced into the Ottoman Empire in the early nineteenth century, just as in many music cultures worldwide (including India, Iran and Arabic countries; Nettl 1985: 47ff). At the turn of the twentieth century violins were played in light Ottoman urban music, mainly by Armenian, Greek and Roma musicians.[5] In the following decades a number of violinists became famous as excellent *taksim* perfomers, e.g. Memduh, Nubar Tekyay, later Cevdet Çağla, Hakkı Deran, Emin Ongan, Ali Erköse, Cahit Peksayar (Ünlü 2004: 129ff). In *gazino*s a solo violin player (*solist kemani*) used to follow the solo singer on the stage and support her/him musically (Beken 1998: 190). After the 1970s the violin became the main instrument in the large orchestras of "Classical Turkish Music." Their most important conductor, Nevzat Atlığ (b. 1925) began his music carrier as violinist. Most violinists of these *klâsik* ensembles play with Western technique, while the timbre of the instrument in more popular and commercial ensembles is marked by a higher degree of noise; in particular overtones are often intentionally reinforced. In this classical style, however, few violinists gained personal fame, and the violin more and more became an instrument for *tutti*s.

Our knowledge of the introduction of the violin into Anatolian music is limited. We know that the instrument was brought by Gypsies from the Balkans to Anatolia, and that they later aided its migration from West to East. In Elazığ and Dersim (Tunceli), however, violins were most probably directly introduced to Armenians by European missionaries during the late ninteenth century.

The cello was to enter Turkish traditional music much later than the violin. During the first decades of the twentieth century Ali Rıfat Çağatay (1872-1935) und Tanburi Cemil Bey experimented with it, and the latter adapted playing techniques of the *kemençe* for cello. A student of Çağatay, Şerif Muhiddin Targan (1892–1967) gave concerts on cello even in New York (1924–1934).[6] While most of his compositions remain in the tradition of Ottoman-Turkish art music, his "*Kapris* I" (1923) for *ud* solo is a tonal virtuoso piece in the tradition of Western *Capriccio*, as is *Kanatlarım olsaydı* ("If I would have Wings", 1924). For *Koşan Çocuk* ("Running Child") Targan even wrote an elaborate piano accompaniment (Cevher 1993: 79-85). Later a few Turkish cello players became well-known, including Vecdi Seyhun (1915-1984) and Tarık Kip (1927-2000). Most of them mainly played other instruments, e.g. Çağatay (*ud*), Targan *(ud),* Tanburi Cemil Bey *(tanbur, kemençe),* Kadı Fuat *(tanbur),* or Mesut Cemil Tel *(tanbur, kemençe).* In the 1950s the instrument was used in film music (Cemal Cümbüş). The *Mevlevi* introduced celli from the 1970s. In ensembles of *klâsik* Turkish music celli are sometimes part of string ensembles, together with the less popular viola. Here, violins and celli are almost exclusively bowed rather than plucked, while bowing is never as uniform as it is in Western orchestras. The most prominent cello player today is Uğur Işık, who takes part in numerous projects with arranged Turkish

5 Armenian violinists include Kemani Tatyos Efendi (1858 – 1913), Hanciyan, Kirkor, kemani Serkis, Tekyay-Çömlekçiyan; other well-known violinists are Cevdet Çağlar (b. 1902); Emin Ongan (1906-1985), Hakkı Derman (1907-1972).

6 Cevher 1993; CD *Peygamber Torunun Müzigi: Şerif Muhittin Targan*, Kaf 2001; CD *Şerif Muhittin Targan: Bütün Eserleri*, Kalan 2007.

art music, and who has released three solo albums to date.[7] In 2008 another album presented Turkish folk songs performed (in a more Western style) on two cellos.[8] Double bass is still rare in traditional Turkish music. In contemporary Turkish ensembles the most active double bass musician is Volkan Hürsever, who studied the instrument at the State Conservatory of Mimar Sinan University and jazz theory with Neşet Ruacan. Volkan Hürsever has played with almost all Turkish jazz musicians as well as with numerous international musicians, including Alan Harris, Laverne Buttler, Marion Cowings, Billy James, Harvey Thompson and Clifford Jarvis.

Parallel to these European instruments, during the early twentieth century, a completely different bowed instrument appeared, the *kemençe*. Before this time, pear-shaped bowed instruments were mainly played as popular folk music instruments in the Aegaeian region and Thrakia. Similar instruments are the Greek *lyra* or *politiki lyra* (lyra of Istanbul) and the Bulgarian *gadulka*; while other bowed instruments are played in western, southern and eastern Anatolia (e.g. Kastamonu, Tekke, Mardin, Southeast Anatolia etc., Erkan 2014: 396, 412). The playing technique of the *kemençe* involves serious challenges: as the middle string is slightly longer than the others, the fingering on it differs from that on both outer strings. In addition the strings are not held down by the fingertips, the player rather pushes his fingernails at the side of the strings. At least since the eighteenth century the *kemençe*, together with *lavta*, was played for popular urban *köçek* and *tavşan* dance groups, mainly by Greeks (Aksoy 2005). Later the instrument was used occasionally in *rembetiko* (again under the name *lira*); one well-known player was Lambros Leondaridis (1912-?).[9] Around 1900 individual musicians such as Vasilâki (1845-1907) and Tanburi Cemil Bey (1871-1916) adapted the *kemençe* for Ottoman-Turkish art music. Well-known *kemençe* players in this field were Anastas (d. 1940?) and Aleko Bacanos (1888-1950), later also Kemal Niyazi Seyhun (1885-1967), Fahire Fersan (1900-1997) and Cüneyd Orhon (1926-2006). With the death of Aleko Bacanos in 1950 the *kemençe* in Turkey had completely lost its Greek character. Nowadays, along with *tanbur* and *ney*, it is perceived as an instrument for excellent Ottoman-Turkish art musicians.[10]

The first attempts to add a fourth string to the *kemençe* were initiated before 1926 by Vasilâki and Tanburi Cemil Bey, aiming to extend the instrument's range (Önüter 1989). In 1933, the introduction of a nut aimed to facilitate the fingering. Both innovations were made by Zühtü Rıza Tinel (Önüter 1989: 168). In this

---

7 CD Ugur Isik: *Unveils Anatolian Spirit*, Kalan 2005; *Cello Invocations*, Kalan 2008.

8 CD Şinasi Çilden & Şebnem Orhan: *Breath of Anatolia with two Cellos*, Yavuz Asöcal 2008. Another cello player who performs Turkish music is Özer Arkun (b. 1973).

9 CD *Rembetica*, Rounder 1079, Track 19; CD *Kemençe* Kalan 2005; CD Politiki Lyra. Lambros Leondaridis. Thessaloniki, En Chordais, 2006.

10 Önüter 1989: 29ff. Well-known *kemençe*-players in the 1980*s* where Ihsan Özgen and Hasan Esen, today for example Ahmet Kadri Rizeli, Derya Türkan, Sokratis Sinopoulos, Neva Özgen and Nermin Kaygusuz

very year, Arel developed the prototypes of *kemençe* quintet instruments with soprano, alto, tenor and bass *kemençe*, each with four strings of equalized length.[11] Cüneyd Orhon (1926-2006) preferred Arel's soprano *kemençe*, tuned like a violin, and after 1975 he taught this instrument at the state conservatory (Aksoy 2005; Önüter 1989: 30ff). Hadiye Ötügen (d. 1963) first learned *kemençe*, then cello (she served as cello teacher at the *Dârü'l Elhân*), later returning to *kemençe*. She adapted new playing techniques from the cello, for example changing playing positions (Aksoy 2005: 45). In 2010 the State Conservatory of the ITÜ organized the International Cüneyd Orhon *Kemençe* Symposium, for which Onur Türkmen composed a *kemençe* quintet (Sarı 2010). Further changes to the instrument were implemented outside of Turkey. In Crete, Ross Daly experimented with playing techniques of *lyra, kemençe* and also the Azerbaijan *kemanche*, and hence developed a sophisticated personal style. A new type of *lyra* was invented by the instrument maker Níkos Bras with around 18 sympathetic strings, and a new physical form to the instrument.[12]

The *yaylı tanbur*, a bowed variant of the plucked *tanbur*, was introduced into Turkish art music by Tanburi Cemil Bey in the early twentieth century. Initially the instrument was constructed with a wooden corpus; from 1930s on, influenced by the *cümbüş*, the *yaylı tanbur* was also made from aluminium (Sarı 2012: 68). The Autralian Peter Biffin finally developed an instrument called *tarhu*, based on different bowed instruments of Aegean traditions, in combination with the Ottoman *tanbur*, Iranian-Ottoman-Crete *lyra* and the Indian technique of resonance strings.

In addition some historical Ottoman instruments were still (or again) played in the twentieth century. During the 1920s Kemani Mustafa Sunar (1981-1959) experimented with changes on the *rebab* (a shorter neck, strings of guitars or mandolin instead of horse hair, with the tuning mechanisms of the guitar). However, only a few *rebab* players are known from the twentieth century, including *Aleko* Bacanos, E. Seviş, and more recently Hasan Esen and Oruç Güvenç.[13] Today *rebab* is rarely used beyond the version developed by Mustafa Sunar.[14] For the *sinekeman* over the twentieth century only one musician is known, that is Nuri Duyguer (1877-1963), who played *sinekeman* at the *Şark Musikisi Cemiyeti* and until the 1950s in the *icra heyeti* (ensemble) of the Conservatory Istanbul. *Kemane*, the sophisticated version of the bowed folk music instruments are played today for example by Cafer Naylıbaş and more recently by Mehtap Demir.[15]

---

[11] For lower instruments sometimes the finger was pressed on the strings; Önüter 1989: 170; Sarı 2012: 170f; Üniter 1989:37.

[12] Kallimopoulou 2009: 58ff, 63ff, 67ff.

[13] Twentieth century *rebab*-players include *Süreyya Baba, tanburi Cemil Bey, kemani Faik Munis Bey. Cahid Gözkan, Sabahaddin Volkan.*

[14] Aksu 1990: 25; CD Hasan Esen: *Rebab*, Kalan 2004.

[15] CD Cafer Naylıbaş: *Feryad-ı kemane*, Onearth 2013; CD Mehtap Demir: *Anadolu Kokusu / Le Parfum d'Asie Mineure*, Ahenk Müzik, 2016.

To conclude, we may summarize that both the range of bowed instrument types available and their practical use (construction, playing techniques, repertoires) have enlarged significantly, with an accelerating development over the past decades.

Similar tendencies, though not all to the same degree, may be stated for almost all instruments in Turkey. Following some general tendencies concerning the development of further instruments will be given. For the *kanun*, for example, *mandal* (tuning pegs) were introduced for the first time around 1870–80 (Sarı 2012: 102f). Rauf Yekta (1913) mentions two to three *mandal*s, whereas today's standard is nine (Sarı 2012: 126f). As one example for improved playing techniques, *kanun* players such as Hakan Güngör (b. 1973), Göksel Baktagir (b. 1966) or the New York-based Tamer Pınarbaşı, pluck the string with almost all the fingers, rather than with the index finger only. While construction of the *ud* generally remained unchanged during the twentieth century, its playing technique became influenced by Western instruments such as cello, and later, guitar. Today, chords and fast played scales are common practice, while they hardly occur on the Ottoman *tanbur*. The *ud* player and composer Münir Nurettin Beken (b. 1964), today based in Los Angeles, wrote several compositions for *ud* solo using innovative techniques. In 2005 he composed a concerto for *ud* and orchestra. According to Kyriakos Kalaitzidis, a total of six concertos have been written for *ud* and orchestra worldwide until the present day.[16] Minor changes in the construction of the *ud* include the use of African woods for the corpus. The so-called *Godin MultiOud* for example is a newly developed *ud* with eleven strings, a corpus similar to that of the electric guitar, with a decorated sound hole, and peg heads again following the model of the guitar.[17]

Over the twentieth century, playing techniques for *ney* also became highly developed due to numerous creative *neyzen*, in particular Niyazi Sayın (Erguner 1986/2002, Greve 1995). Many *neyzen* today use a footstool as is used with the guitar. While in earlier times every *ney* player would build his instrument himself, today numerous *ney* makers in Istanbul and other Turkish cities offer instruments, from cheap plastic *ney*s to expensive professional pieces. Süleyman Erguner considered for some time the construction of an additional hole with keys for *ney*. Later he reconstructed and played the smaller open flute *girift*, which was last played by Giriftzen Asim Bey (1852–1929).[18] For the growing number of cross-over ensembles which include a *ney*, several *ney* players prefer instruments where the sensible pitch *segah* is higher, hence nearer to the tempered pitch system. On the other hand, surprisingly little new music has been composed for *ney* (a few examples include short parts in Yalçın Tura's works and Fazıl Say's Concerto for *ney* and orchestra), as compared for example with the traditional Japa-

16 I am grateful to Kyriakos Kalaitzidis for this information.

17 http://www.godinguitars.com/godinmultioudp.htm (accessed August 25, 2015)

18 CD Erguner, Süleyman: *Girift*, Istanbul Büyüksehir Belediyesi, 2010.

nese flute *shakuhachi*, which has inspired numerous compositions of contemporary music (Senay 2014). The difficulty in finding appropriate instrumentalists sometimes prompts composers to allow *ney* parts to be played on Western flute instead of *ney* (e.g. Taner Akyols *An die Liegengebliebenen*, 2005). On the other hand several pieces of traditional Ottoman music have been adapted for Western flute, for examples for the flute player, Şefika Kutluer.[19]

Another instrument of European origin, the clarinet (*klarnet*, *girnata*) is widely played in Turkey today, in particular among Romas for entertainment and dance music, but also in (light) art music, and in all kinds of hybrid ensembles (Seeman 2002: 144; Duygulu 2006). Clarinets first entered the (Western) palace band at the time of Mahmud II (1808-1839).[20] In the early twentieth century the clarinet was not even played in coffee houses or music associations (*cemiyeti*). Around 1920 *klârnet Ibrahim* (d.1925) introduced the instrument at the *Üsküdar Musiki Cemiyeti*, later his student *Şükrü Tunar*, the most well-known clarinet player of his time, played it at Radio Istanbul, in *gazino*s and for film music, while more conservative ensembles still refused to accept the instrument. Still today the sound of the clarinet is associated with entertainment or light *fasıl* music rather than Ottoman art music. In interviews with Turkish Roman musicians, Seeman (2002: 144) found "*that many Roman professional families that specialise as clarinetists played* zurna *within the past three to four generations.*" Similar to the violin the clarinet migrated from western Anatolia eastward, often replacing the *zurna*. In the 1960s Ismet Sıral played microtones for the first time on tenor saxophone (Uyar 2016); recently in particular Göksun Çavdar (b. 1974) and Hüsnü Şenlendirici (b. 1976) further developed playing techniques of the Turkish clarinet. Recently musicians such as Ergün Şenlendirici and Hasan Gözetlik even performed Turkish music on trumpet and trombone respectively.

From around 1800 to the present, the piano in Istanbul mainly functioned as an instrument for Western music among the Ottoman elite (Alimdar 2016: 230ff). In 1928, a commission directed by the historian Fuat Mehmet Köprülü proposed, among other reforms, the installation of organs in mosques (this never was realised; Lewis 1961: 408). As far as we know *taksim*s were played on piano only from the early twentieth century on (e.g. by Feyzi Aslangil[21]). Pianists were active at the *Şark Musiki Cemiyeti* or the *Üsküdar Mûsikî Cemiyeti* in the 1920s and pianos are audible on several recordings by singers such as Münir Nurettin Selçuk or Perihan Altındağ-Sözeri (O'Connell 2013; Greve 1995). After the 1950s the piano again fell out of use among serious Turkish ensembles for traditional music. In Turkish

[19] CD Sefika Kutluer: *Mevlana Rumi*, Lausanne: Gallo 2008, including Ilyaş Mirzayevs (b. 1961) Flute Concerto "From Mevlana to Today", citing Dede Efendi's 4th salute of the *Sema*; *Saz Semai* from Tanburi Cemal Bey (1873-1916).

[20] Picken 1968: 511; Zümrüt 2000: 47; Alimdar 2016:432f.

[21] CD Feyzi Aslangil, *Piyano ile Saz Eserleri ve Taksimler / Turkish music on the Piano (1910-1965)*, Kalan 2000.

light music, however, it remains popular until today. Since the 1980s the so-called *orgs*, that is keyboards, together with a soft voice singing became typical for the *taverna* style. Over the past twenty plus years, numerous CDs have been published, containing reduced versions of Ottoman-Turkish art music with simple harmonic accompaniment played on piano. A sophisticated version of this approach might be heard in the duo of *kanun* (Göksel Baktagir) and piano (Ceyhun Çelikten).[22] Several contemporary editions offer notation of Turkish music arranged for piano.[23] Linking with historical keyboard instruments in Europe of the sixteenth-twentieth centuries, several Turkish piano makers meanwhile tried to enable the instruments to play microtones, for example Oz (2011), or the recent *Ultratonal Piyano* of Ozan Yarman. The "Haken Audio Company" today offers a "Continuum," a keyboard without keys, constructed for the performance of infinitely variable pitches (as used for instance by the composer and Jazz pianist Evrim Demirel). Since around 2000, several classical Turkish pianists such as Fazıl Say, Birsen Ulucan, Seda Roda, Renan Koen and Aylin Aykan have become interested in Turkish music as well, commissioning hybrid compositions including traditional music for piano, e.g. Birsen Ulucan, İnci Yakar and Evrim Demirel (2010), or composed by themselves (Say, Koen, Aykan).[24] The piano and *kanun* duo of Esra Berkman (*kanun*) & Nazlı Işıldak (piano) plays composition and arrangements of Western piano music by Armenian composers such as Haçatur Avetisyan (1926-1996) or new compositions commissioned by Turkish composers, including Uğraş Durmuş or Tolga Zafer Özdemir.

Similarly harp players such as Ceren Necipoğlu (1972–2009), Şirin Pancaroğlu and Natalia Mann played arrangements of Turkish art music and commissioned new works, as for example the Concerto for *Çenk*, Harp and Orchestra by Hasan Uçarsu, written for Şirin Pancaroğlu.[25]

Bağlama*s and Guitars*

It is only since the 1960s that the *bağlama has* shifted from being an instrument to accompany singing to a solo instrument with rapidly developing playing

22 CD *Boğaziçi*, Akustik Müzik, n.y.

23 For example Çağrıhan Erkan & Ali Dinge: *Piyano için Saz Eserleri*, Albüm 1, Izmir: Berke 2003 including *Çeçen Kızı* by Tanburi Cemil Bey; Kevser Hanım: *Nihavend Longa*; Refik Fersan: *Nikriz Sirto*; Santuri Ethem: *Şehnaz Longa*. The small book by Zülfikar Yavuz Özer (2011) discusses limitations of the piano for the tonal system of Turkish music.

24 CD Birsen Usucan: *Masallar, Rüyalar, Fısıltılar*, Istanbul: Lilamüzik 2011.

25 For example CD Ceren Necipoğlu: *Bir Kitap Gibi*, Kalan 2009; CD Şirin Pancaroğlu: *Istanbul'un Ses Telleri*, including *Yerebatan* (Cistern) for *kemençe*, bass and harp by Arda Ardaşes Agoşyan (b. 1977) and *Istanbul'un Ağaçları* (The Trees of Istanbul) for harp, *kemençe*, *kanun* and *ud* by Turgay Erdener (b. 1957); arrangements of Turkish folk and art music on the CD Şirin Pancaroğlu & Meriç Dönük & Jarrod Cagwin: *Elişi*, Kalan 2011; CD Sirin Pancaroglu: Çenkname, 2011 with musicians such as Ilhan Yazici (voice), Derya Türkan, Yurdal Tokcan, Fahrettin Yarkın.

techniques.[26] The *âşıks*, including the famous ones such as Âşık Veysel or Davut Suları, as well as most of the *zakirs* (those who play *bağlama* during Alevi rituals, *cem*), in general used to play a basic accompaniment while aesthetically more central were the lyrics and hence the voice. Village instruments regularly exhibited flexible fretting, with regional variation in the size of the instruments (*divan*, *tanbura*, *çöğür*, *cura* etc.), the number of strings and frets, and the tuning.[27] Since the 1940s the TRT presented the long-necked *bağlama* as a kind of national Turkish instrument, mostly used in small ensembles (*saz orkestrası*). Since the 1960s the E-*saz* emerged, following the model of the E-guitar. In the 1970s Özay Gönlüm constructed an instrument with three necks, uniting *tanbura*, *bağlama* and *cura* in one body. Since then, the appearance of the *bağlama* has changed further. Its design and decoration have been enhanced and the headstock with the pegs was angled in order to raise the tension of the strings and thus achieve a higher and more accurate sound. During the 1960s and 1970s *bağlama* players such as Ali Ekber Çiçek (1935-2006) and Talip Özkan (1939-2010) developed new playing techniques and experimented with new tunings. *Zeybek* (dance tunes from the Aegeans), for example, were traditionally played on *davul-zurna*, but from the 1960s Talip Özkan adapted such pieces for *bağlama*. In particular in his famous piece *Haydar Haydar*, Ali Ekber Çiçek presented new plucking techniques.[28]

From the 1980s the group *Muhabbet*, with Arif Sağ (b. 1945), Musa Eroğlu (b. 1946), Yavuz Top (g. 1950) and Muhlis Akarsu (1948-1994), gained fame with mainly Alevi songs, in particular from the region of Sivas-Erzincan. In terms of melodic structure most of the songs follow comparable patterns, many songs exhibiting short descending sequences, mainly in the scale of *hüseyni*. The fingering and hence also the melodic embellishments are similarly typical. Aside from solo introductions most of the pieces were performed together strictly in monophone. Arif Sağ, the most famous *bağlama*-player among this new *bağlama* style played on a short-necked variant of the *bağlama* in the so-called *bağlama* tuning, as it was used traditionally, in particular among Alevis. Soon both replaced the long necked variant with *kara* and other tunings, as they have been preferred at TRT since the 1940s. Eventually even TRT adapted the short necked *bağlama*,

---

26 Only few Anatolian instruments have gained a comparable status as solo instruments, for example *kaval* (e.g. Sinan Celik), mey (e.g. Ertan Tekin), (*kabak*) *kemane* (e.g. Özgür Celik, Mehtap Demir) or the Black See *kemençe*. CD Özgür Çelik: *Öznağme*, Z Müzik 2012. CD Mehtap Demir: *Anadolu Kokusu*, Ahenk 2016. Since the 1960s, the *mey* began to to be integrated into Turkey's professional music world. Development of this instrument includes the use of different sizes (large – *ana*, medium – *orta*, and small – *cura*); the use of an adapter (*boğaz*) to raise and lower the pitch of the *mey* by a major second; and from the late 1970s production of full diatonic sets of instruments (Karahasanoglu & Skoog 2011: 203). CD Ertan Tekin: *Demans*, Kalan 2011.

27 Gazimihal 1975; Picken 1975; Markoff 1986; Kurt 1989; Akdoğu 1994; Parlak 2000, Koç 2016 (a, b); Öztürk 2016.

28 Erzincan 2006; CD Talip Özkan: *The Dark Fire*, Island Records, 1992; CD Talip Özkan: *Yağar yağmuş*, Kalan 1997.

with the consequence that long necked instruments such as *divan sazi*, *meydan sazi* or the smaller *cura* have seemed to almost disappear. It is noteworthy that the rise of the short necked *bağlama* occurred in parallel to the revival of Alevism. While melodies on the long necked variant are mainly performed on the highest string, on the short necked *bağlama* players uses all three strings equally, which enables the musician to play faster. On the other hand, the options for drones are reduced (one result of the different tunings). In particular Arif Sağ's long, virtuosic and introvert solo improvisations, which he played as introductions to the songs, went far beyond the *açış* (opening) of village musicians in the past but rather exhibit an artistic claim of their own. His music (and that of *Muhabbet* as well as that of many of his followers) became concert music with purely artistic ambitions. Today many professional folk musicians (e.g. Erdal Erzincan, Erol Parlak, Erkan Oğur and Cengiz Özkan, to name just a few of the most well-known) think of themselves as artists in an emphatic sense and their concerts tend to follow the model of Western art music recitals.

Since the end of the 1970s, state conservatories in Turkey have offered regular programs with *bağlama* as the main subject, which has led to a further rise in the technical and musical level for that instrument. Several efforts have been made to standardize the size, tuning and names of the numerous instruments of the *bağlama* family (Terzi 2017; Parlak 2017). The commercial success of folk music offered a lucrative market for *bağlama* players of studio and *türkü bars*. In the 1990s Çetin Akdeniz (b. 1967), a graduate of the ITÜ conservatory, became the most famous studio musician; he introduced extremely fast scales, influenced by guitar technique.[29] Another recent innovation was the introduction of the capodaster, again adapted from the guitar. The group concept of *Muhabbet* furthermore led to several chamber ensembles combining different *bağlama* types *(cura, tanbura, bağlama, divan sazı, mezdan sazı)*, without levelling out the individual instrument as in the TRT *saz orchestras*, e.g. the trio *Bengi Bağlama Üçlüsü* (since 1988) or Erol Parlak's *bağlama* quintet (2000–2012).[30] Over the last two decades a number of new types of *bağlama* have been constructed, e.g. the bass *bağlama*, the *kopuz* in the mid-1990s (actually based on old village instruments, Akkaya et. al 2008: 282) and slightly later the six-stringed *Oğur Sazı* (both built by Kemal Eroğlu) as played by Erkan Oğur, Sinan Cem Eroğlu and Erdal Yapıcı (Eroğlu 2009). Zeki Çağlar Namlı (b. 1981) constructed an instrument with a second resonance body at the neck of the *bağlama*.[31]

---

29 Even faster played the Bielefeld-based (Germany) Ismet Topçu (b. 1966), who in the early 1980s developed a four stringed *bağlama* tuned *D A E A*.

30 For example CD Bengi Bağlama Üçlüsü: *Sel Gider... kum kalır...*, Kalan 2001; CD Bengi Bağlama Üçlüsü: *Günes Bahçesinden Ezgiler*, Kalan 1999.

31 CD Zeki Çağlar Namlı: *La Lune / Köy*, 2006; CD Zeki Çağlar Namlı & Dominique Di Piazza: *Face to Face/Yüzyüze*, Istanbul: Lir 2011.

Since the 1990s younger players have further enriched the instrument's playing techniques, either adapted from the guitar or from related Anatolian or Central Asian lutes. In particular Arif Sağ, Erol Parlak and Erdal Erzincan adapted the so-called *şelpe* or *pençe* technique. The *şelpe* technique (in fact a general term for numerous plucking and tapping techniques) was initially inspired by the late Ramazan Güngör from Fethiye and his regional playing technique on a small three stringed *cura* (Erkan 2014, I: 223, 263; II: 173ff). In particular Erol Parlak and Erdal Erzincan's technique went far beyond that of Arif Sağ; the timbre of Parlak's instrument (which is individually constructed according to his suggestions) is soft and refined, and his performance focuses almost exclusively on timbre rather than melody.[32] In concerts of Erol Parlak's *bağlama* quintet (2000-c.2012), there are long passages with almost no perceivable melodic or rhythmic development, while the timbre constantly changes due to the changing playing techniques.[33] Later even Mozart's *Alla Truca* or Ali Ekber Çiçek's *Haydar Haydar* (once famous for its innovative plucking techniques) might be played in *şelpe* technique.[34] Today playing techniques that produce noise-like sounds and tones are continuously explored by younger players such as Barış Güney, Zeki Çağlar, Erkan Cankçı, Erdem Şimsek, Kemal Dinç and many others.[35] New playing techniques include:

Left hand: fingering of the guitar including change of hand position, finger vibrato, similar tones consecutively produced on different strings (hence with changing timbre), numerous new tunings with new fingerings, extended *glissandi* (clean or with noise);

Right hand: guitar-like picking by individual fingers, percussive beating on all parts of the instrument, stopped pickings and strikes, natural and artificial flageolet tones, *sul ponte* playing, combinations of *mizrap* (plectrum) and finger picking, and scratching of the string.

New playing techniques are also performed on prepared instruments, for example by clamping small objects below strings (e.g. by Kemal Dinç). Some of the new teaching books focus on these new techniques (e.g. by Erol Parlak 2000, Erdal Erzincan & Arif Sağ 2013), while others develop new pedagogical concepts for the instrument, for example with exercises (several volumes by Ali Kazım Akdağ; Attila Özdek 2014 or Zeki Atagür 2013, the latter even contains fingering lists of polyphone chords). First compositions of new Western music for the *bağlama* include the "*Concerto di Berlinbul*" for *bağlama*, guitar and chamber orchestra by Carlo Domeniconi (1988) and a suite for *bağlama*, violin and piano by Hay-

---

32 CD Erol Parlak: *Pervâne*, ASM 1998; CD Erol Parlek: *Katre*, Akkiraz n.y.; CD Erol Parlak: *Yalınkat*, Arda Müzik 2007; Erol Parlak: *Har*, Anadolu 2011; .

33 CD Erol Parlak *Bağlama Beşlisi*: *Eşik*, Akkiraz 2003.

34 E.g. played by Adem Tosunoğlu.

35 CD Barış Güney: *Tohum*, Kalan 2007; CD Barış Güney: *Düşlere Yolculuk*, Kalan 2009. CD Kemal Dinç: *Bağlama için Denemeler*, Kalan 2012.

rettin Akdemir (1989).[36] Recently composers such as Taner Akyol, Kemal Dinç, Helmut Zapf and Erdem Şimşek have written further new music, mainly for *bağlama* solo (Akyol 2017). In Taner Akyol's, *Hatırlamalar* for string quartet and *bağlama* (2006) he applies melodies and embellishments of the *bağlama* to Western stringed instruments.

Parallel to the progress of playing techniques, instrument making has developed in terms of decoration, form and construction. The tendency is towards a clearer and new timbre through the use of new exotic woods, positioning a bass bar inside the instrument, changes to the sound hole (bigger, smaller, new form, round, with keys to open or close it, position at the side or in the front of the instrument, etc.). On the other hand, tuning has been made better and easier by adopting the pegs or the whole headstock of mandolina or guitar. Some *bağlama* players (such as Ahmet Aslan) experiment with strings from other instruments, e.g. *kanun*, *ud* or flamenco guitar; or with removing or adding bass strings to the traditional chorus. Numerous previously forgotten traditional tunings are in use today, together with newly invented ones. Ahmet Aslan and luthier Süleyman Aslan recently developed an instrument between guitar and *bağlama,* which Ahmet Aslan called *Di-Tar.*

With this recent concentration of *bağlama* music on timbre, Western notation, with its focus on melody and rhythm, has reached its limits. Several *bağlama* players including Erol Parlak and Erdal Erzincan proposed additional signs for a notation of the numerous new techniques (see figure 11). This challenge (which is still under development) is reminiscent of that of composers of contemporary Western music, whose scores often include several explanatory pages about their individually invented or developed notation.

Just like the piano, the classical guitar is actually unsuitable for traditional Turkish music. Its frets are fixed according to the Western pitch system and its playing technique was developed primarily for polyphonic music. The microtones – pitches outside of the traditional Western tone system – are almost impossible to achieve on guitar. Nevertheles the guitar, perceived as a kind of "modern *bağlama,*" has become an "*in general important if not principal instrument in the Turkish music scene.*" (Dawe & Eroğlu 2013: 51) Since 1975, Middle East Technical University, Ankara established the first guitar department in Turkey (with Ahmet Kanneci), later to be followed by the state conservatory of ITÜ and other academies. Today the instrument is well established within teaching programs and concerts all over Turkey.

Turkish guitarists have pursued three different approaches to deal with the challenges of the Turkish pitch system. The first and by far most common approach is to simply skip or adjust all microtones and play within the tempered

36 Adil Arslan: *Üryan* (Tempo, 1992); Carlo Domeniconi: *Concerto di Berlinbul* (Raks, 1993).

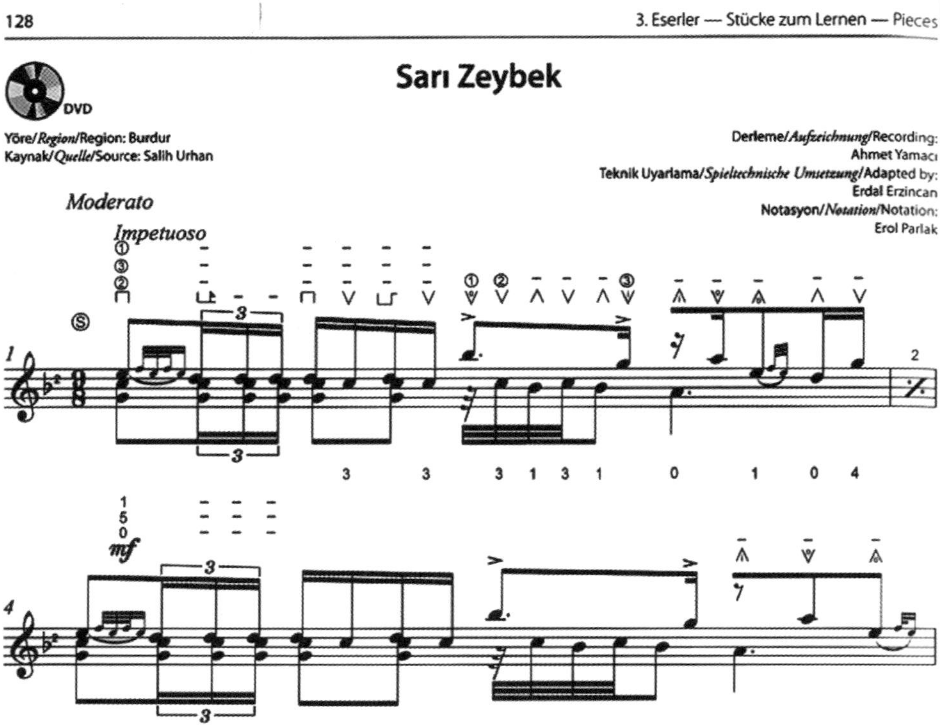

Figure 11: Notation for *bağlama* by Erol Parlak (2011: 128)

pitch system. Today numerous well-known Turkish guitarists play Western, popular and Turkish music, for example Hasan Cihan Örter (b. 1958).[37]

The second, not less radical approach, is to remove the frets of the guitar. The fretless guitar was introduced into Turkish music by Erkan Oğur (b. 1954, Ankara) as early as 1976 (Dawe & Eroglu 2013: 62-68), but until today few guitarists have adopted this instrument (e.g. Sinan Cem Eroğlu or Cenk Erdoğan[38]). On this guitar not only can all traditional *makams* be played but even more transpositions of all *makams* on all *duraks* (tonics). In addition, playing techniques of the fretless guitar have been enlarged substantially (Eroğlu 2017). The timbre is softer than that of the classical guitar with a broad range of possible vibrati. The fretless guitar allows the adaptation of left hand techniques of instruments such as *bağlama*, *tanbur* and *ud*, including traditional fingering (such as moving up and down along one string only) and all kinds of melodic embellishments. The duo

[37] Others include Bekir Küçükay (b. 1958); or Cem Duruöz (CD *Anadolu Hazineleri / Treasures of Anatolia*, Ak Müzik 2009).

[38] CD Sinan Cem Eroglu: *Tesadüf*, 2012; CD *Hane-i Akustik*, 2011; CD Cenk Erdoğan: *ARC*, Jazzschool Records 2010.

of Erman Şenol & Ali Kireşçi plays Turkish folk songs and original compositions arranged for fretless guitar and fretless bass. As a next step, Erdinç Aksaç and others have begun to experiment with a fretless *bağlama*.

A third way to improve the guitar was developed by the classical guitarist Tolgahan Çoğulu (b. 1978, Ankara)[39], who added further frets to the traditional guitar, thus making microtones available. In his "Adjustable Microtonal Guitar," which he developed in 2008, the position of *all* frets are flexible, hence all microtones are available – those used in traditional Turkish *makam*s as well as any traditional or artificially constructed tone system worldwide. In addition to technical innovations concerning the intonation, Tolgahan Çoğulu tried to extend the playing techniques of his new guitars. In 2001, he wrote his PhD thesis on "The Adaptation of *Bağlama* Techniques to Classical Guitar." He arranged traditional Anatolian *türkü* songs (e.g. Asik Veysel's *Kara Toprak*) for his instrument and also for classical Ottoman-Turkish compositions (e.g. Abdülkadir Marâghî's *Rast Nakış Beste*) and contemporary Western music (e.g. Lou Harrison's "Sonata in Ishartum").

Today hence, these two most popular instruments in Turkey, the *bağlama* and the guitar, exhibit the widest enlargement in their musical possibilities.

Voice

While almost all Turkish music is vocal music, little research has been done on Turkish vocal techniques and styles. The most encompassing research, conducted by John O'Connor, focuses on the singer Münir Nurettin Selcuk (1899-1981), while other scholarship examines the recitation of the Qur'an. The again obvious dramatic development of singing techniques over the twentieth century have hardly been analysed yet, and consequently only some crucial turning points will briefly be mentioned here.

While we know of a number of non-Muslim instrumentalists at the Ottoman court (e.g. Greeks such as Tanbûrî Angelos, d. 1690; Petraki, 1730–1777; or Jews such as Tanbûrî Isak, 1745-1814), most of the singers began in an Islamic education, that is as *imam*, Qur'an reader or muezzin.[40] Western singing techniques only later entered Ottoman music, mainly after the foundation of the Republic of Turkey. An early pioneer obviously was *Nedim Bey (d. 1910)* (O'Connell 2013: 48). Around 1900 the most popular urban singing style was the religious style (*hâfiz uslûbu*), or *goygoy* (nasal timbre) style, with a rich use of glottal vibrato, trills, melismatic embellishment and glissandos (Doğrusöz 2008: 150; O'Connell 2001: 784).

39 www.tolgahancogulu.com (accessed September 28, 2016)

40 An exception was Zaccharias (d. c. 1740), cantor of the Byzantine patriarch but also singer at the court of Ahmed III.

The most important change in the solo singing of Turkish art music was initiated by the singer Münir Nurettin Selçuk. In his youth as singer at the court, Selçuk, from 1926 on, first made recordings on HMV (still in this old style), later he sang live at radio concerts, and eventually from 1954-1976, he became director of the Istanbul Conservatory ensemble (*icra heyeti*). Selçuk's voice technique changed substantially after a short stay in Paris around 1928, though not in terms of an adaptation of Western classical voice technique but rather by developing an individual vocal style. His voice exhibited a clear control of breath and legato, a pure singing style with clear diction and nuance, varieties of vibrato, diaphragm control and a few larynx techniques. O'Connell described Selçuk's interpretation of the *gazel L'âl Olursun* (*nihavend*) as follows:

> In imitation of a 'western' precedent, the vocalist articulated each ornament (such as grace notes and trills) with great care. In imitation of coloratura, he thoughtfully prepared each gesture, executing every descending run, melodic sequence, cadential motif and melismatic passage with exquisite taste and exemplary skill. In contrast to other *gazel* performers, Selçuk exploited here the dynamic possibilities of electronic recording that enabled him to perform the softest pianissimos (especially during the zemin) and the loudest fortissimos (especially during the *miyan*) without upsetting the clarity of the text or the character of the mode. Selçuk choosing to add rubatos for effect, usually at the end of a poetic foot and sometimes to mark in English a dominant note or in Turkish a *güçlü*. Usually, Selçuk even included a programmatic element by replicating a cry when singing the word *ağlarsın* (you cry). Selçuk's use of vocal techniques in the performance of this *gazel* was also not traditional. Avoiding the nazalized timbre and glottalized character of other gazel performers, Selçuk adopted the full range of chest and head register yet strictly controlling vocal production and larynx oscillation. (O'Connell 2013: 43f)

At the same time Selçuk was the first to present this music as a soloist, standing in front of his audience. During his famous concert at the French Theatre (Fransiz Tiyatrosu) on February 22, 1930:

> [he] was the first vocalist to perform *alaturka* as a soloist. Standing (rather than sitting) on stage, he was also the first artist to present *alaturka* following a 'western' convention rather than a traditional format. His manner of presentation was also different. Accompanied by a selected group of musicians (including a pianist), dressed in tails and performing in a established venue for 'western' music, he sought to enshrine *alaturka* within the hallowed walls of an *alafranga* edifice, the concert hall. (O'Connell 2013: 109f)

In the early Republic for the first time female singers such as Safiye Ayla, Hamiyet Yüceses and Müezzen Senar gained fame in Ottoman-Turkish art music. Later developments of vocal techniques and styles, in particular at TRT, still deserve detailed research. In general the singing style of art music became clearer and less embellished. With the further popularisation of *şarkıs* (art songs) from the 1950s, singing techniques again changed substantially, as in the case of Zeki Müren or Bülent Ersoy.

> Zeki Müren was considered by many to have a new kind of voice. It was a voice that resisted traditional musical processes of reckoning relation to teachers and mentors. (...) So part of the newness of Müren's voice was registered in terms of this broad institutional change in Turkish vocal culture: singers increasingly learned repertoire and technique from audio and other sources, rather than from institutionalized musical authorities. It was also registered in terms of technological changes. For some contemporaries, Müren was the first to use the mirorphone as an expressive device, holding it at varying distances to capture different vocal nuances, and using it as a stage prop. (Stokes 2010: 60f).

Unfortunately the numerous regional Anatolian singing styles have also hardly been described and analysed yet by musicologists. The standardization of these styles at TRT from the 1940s on is still known only approximately.

The main figure who characterizes the introduction of Western singing techniques into Turkish folk music is Ruhi Su (1912–1985). As a reaction against the aesthetic of TRT choirs and ensembles, Ruhi Su developed a completely new singing style for folk music. Trained as a Western opera singer, from 1942 until 1952 Ruhi Su sang as bass-baritone at the State Opera, Ankara. In the early 1940s he began to sing folk songs on the radio, including many Alevi songs. From 1952 until 1957 he was imprisoned for political reasons, following which Ruhi Su completely devoted himself to folk music. His strong, but soft opera-trained voice with careful and controlled vibrato was usually accompanied by a simple *bağlama*, which intervened short, simple motifs or melodies between the sung parts. In the mid-1960s in Istanbul he recorded his first albums with this new style, which in their reduced timbre differed substantially from the overloaded versions of TRT ensembles. A CD series with his complete recordings, mainly released after his death, is still available today. Ruhi Su's aesthetic influenced a number of singers, including Hasan Yükselir (b.1955).

After the 1980s, as a result of the popularization of folk music but similarly of its artificialisation, folk music singing styles and techniques changed further. Singers such as Arif Sağ and Musa Eroğlu sang in a softer, more expressive and dramatic style than traditional *aşık* singers until the 1950s (Reinhard/de Oliveira Pinto 1989: 167). Just as for folk instrumentalists, Turkish folk singers today are expected to master melodic styles and larynx techniques of all major areas in Anatolia, though most singers still specialize in the region of their own origin.

Percussion

Unlike Indian musical culture for example, Ottoman-Turkish music had no tradition of solo percussion playing. Drummers are generally poorly regarded in folk music, and only *davul* players during village festivals had some solo functions. Most Turkish percussion instruments are used for accompaniment: *kös* (bass drum), *nakkare* (kettle drum), *davul* (large cylindrical drum), *hile* (*zil*) (cymbals); *def* (frame drum with cymbals), *bendir* (larger frame drum without cymbals), *kud-*

düm (double kettle drum), *darbuka*, *koltuk davulu* (*nagara*) (small drum) and in eastern Anatolia, primarily among Kurds, the *erbane* (large frame drum).

In Ottoman-Turkish art music the rhythmic patterns (*usûl*) are constitutive for the structure of all compositions.[41] During all performances, both singer and instrumentalists must continually keep the *usûl* in mind. Similarly central is the function of *usûl* for the *meşk*, where the first step in learning a new composition is to beat its *usûl* on the knees. However, together with the formation of larger ensembles and choirs (see below) the dominance of the rhythm pattern has substantially declined. In the classical Turkish music style *usûl*s are not usually played but only implicitly structure the melody. In most Turkish classical music choirs the percussionist (if there is one at all) is placed in the background of the ensemble.

> Especially since the further developments of choral performance under the State Turkish Music Chorus and Dr. Nevzad Atlığ in the 1960s, the musical 'gestures' implicit within Ottoman vocal compositions have been accentuated, often obscuring any relationship with *usûl* structures. Since the late 1980s this has also led to a 'reaction' among tradition-conscious musicians to reinstate percussion, but by this late date often without much command of the usûl melodic relations as they had been understood by earlier Ottoman composers. (Feldman 2017: 155)

Only in some Sufi ensembles did the *kuddüm* player still function as musical director until the late twentieth century, while in most cases, conductors or players of melody instruments took over this position (Greve 1995: 225).

The only exception to the limited role of percussion in Ottoman music were the *mehter* ensembles, where drums played a central role. A few recent projects have focused on the more sophisticated parts of this repertoire, e.g. Kudsi Erguner's project, *Osmanli Davulları* / Ottoman Drums (CD Imge 2002).

In folk music, on the other hand, the role and importance of percussion rose remarkably towards the end of the twentieth century. As mentioned in Chapter II, world music with its focus on dance music and percussion opened new avenues and musical experiences for Turkish percussionists. In particular the asymmetric rhythms of Anatolian music with five, seven or nine beats, often even with different or even changing internal structures, provide serious difficulties for Western musicians and audiences. Hence Turkish percussionists were perceived as musicians with a particular competence, and percussionists such as Okay Temiz (b. 1939), Burhan Öçal (b.1959) and Mısırlı Ahmet (b.1963) became internationally succesful.[42] At the same time, percussion instruments from Africa, Latin America, and Asia entered Turkish music, including congas, *berimbao*, tabla, *udu*,

41 On the history and structure of *usûl* in the Islamic world, see Helvacı, Jäger and Olley 2016.

42 MC Aka Gündüz & Okay Temiz: *Zikr*, n.y.; MC Oriental Wind & The Karnataka College of Percussion: *Sankirna*, 1984; Okay Temiy & Karnataka College of Percussion: *Mishram*, Raks 1995; MC Okay Temiz & Group Zourna, Ada Müzik 1998; *Mısırlı Ahmet*, Ak Müzik 2005.

gatham, talkingh drum, mouth harp, *cajón* and *djembe*. In 1994 the brothers Fahrettin and Ferruh Yarkınlar founded the *Yarkın Türk Ritm Topluluğu* (Yarkın Turkish Rhythm Ensemble) which subsequently published four albums, probably the first purely percussion albums in Turkey. *Kardeş Türküler* are known as a rich and strong percussion group.[43] Another well-known percussionist today is Türker Çolak (b. 1986), who studied percussion at the State Conservatory of the Istanbul University and played as soloist at the State Symphony Orchestra Istanbul. In addition to classical orchestral percussion, Türker Çolak has played Latin American, Brazilian, African and Iranian percussion instruments. He was involved in dance performances of "My Dream," an ensemble of handicapped Chinese musicians; and in the groups of *Yansımalar*, *Ince Saz*, *Mızrabın Nefesi*, the percussion groups *Gürkey Vurmalı Çalgılar* and *Istanbul Vurmalı Çalgılar Topluluğu*, the Cemal Reşid Rey Symphony Orchestra, and the Student Orchestra of the State Conservatory of Istanbul University.

Today, to repeat and widen the conclusion already made for bowed instruments and long-necked lutes as above, many more instruments and playing techniques are available in Turkish music than ever before in history. Numerous excellent and innovative musicians, both singers and instrumentalists, still continually work to broaden the means of musical expression. In many cases instruments have overcome the limitations of particular traditions and have been adapted to almost all musical styles in Turkey. Consequently, also the composition of ensembles for traditional music has changed substantially, mainly by opening up for a growing number of instruments which have never before performed the respective tradition.

However, before we continue to analyze how instruments and voices are combined into transformed or newly founded ensembles for traditional music, I will briefly describe the historical development of harmonization in traditional music in Turkey.

Western Harmony

The arrival of Western music into the Ottoman Empire in the early nineteenth century led to the establishment of Western musical institutions such as military bands, operas, symphonic concerts and music academies, but also introduced Western musical structures, including functional tonality, counterpoint and Western forms and genres.[44] This Western music of the late Ottoman period was re-

43 According to Eliot Bates (2008: 3, Fn. 6), in 1992, members of the group first became acquainted with *udu* percussion pot drums (of Nigerian origin), which later became a standard percussion instrument in Turkish ensembles, during a concert of the Japanese musician Kitaro in Istanbul.

44 Alaner 2017 (a), Aracı 2006; Kosal 2003; Uslu 1999; And 1989: 13ff; Aksoy 1985: 1212.

discovered only twenty years ago, by musician-musicologists such as Vedat Kosal (2003), Selçuk Alimdar (2016) and Emre Aracı (2006, 2010a, b); Aracı has meanwhile recorded much of this long forgotten music with his *London Academy of Ottoman Court Music*.[45]

Until today, however, harmony has been used almost as a vocabulary, fixed in the state in which it was adopted from Europe around or shortly after 1800, rather than being perceived as a living tradition, open to further development. Only a few Turkish composers have approached the musical language of their contemporary European and American peers, going beyond folkloristic approaches to develop their own harmonic grammar.

Already at an early stage musicians in Istanbul began to experiment with combinations of Western and traditional Ottoman music. Giuseppe Donizetti (1797-1856) was Director of the newly formed (Western) military band *mızıkay-ı hümâyûn* at the Ottoman court from 1828, and hence the key figure for the introduction of Western music to Istanbul. He learned *hamparsum* notation, harmonized around 40 *peşrev* and *şarkı* for piano and composed two *peşrev*, a "*Cansone Mussulmana*" for choir, solo singer and piano, and a *medhiyye*.[46] After 1826 the *mızıkay-ı hümâyûn* included two ensembles, called *fasl-i atîk* and *fasl-i cedîd* respectivly (old vs. new concert). Unfortunately almost nothing is known about the latter, which obviously combined instruments of European origin such as flute, trombone, mandolin, violin or cello with traditional Ottoman instruments.[47] From 1856 to 1858 and again from 1868 until the end of the 1890s, Callisto Guatelli (1819–1900), served as Director of the *mızıkay-ı hümâyûn*. Among his purely Western compositions, some marches are based on *makam* scales; in addition he again harmonized traditional art songs (*şarkı*), the first already published before 1850.[48] Another comparable collection of *Airs Orienteux* was printed in Istanbul by two Armenian singing teachers, Arisdaguès Hohanessian and Gabriel Eramian, in 1858.[49] From Murat V. (1840-1904), the most productive composer of the Ottoman family, about 500 pieces for piano have survived, among them several plain harmonized folk melodies, such as an "*Aydın Havası*" for piano (Kosal 2003: 33f, 42ff; Alimdar 2016: 15). After him for example Abdülmecid II. (1868–1944, ruled 1922–24) composed an arrangement of

45 CD Emre Aracı & Prag Senfoni Oda Orkestrası: Sultan Portreler, Kalan 2004; In 1999 Kalan music published a CD containing late Ottoman marches on 78 rpm recordings (1903-1923).

46 *Sevkefza Peşrevi* in *Musiki Mecmuası* 70, 1953: 29ff; Aracı 2006: 125ff., 134; Aracı 2010a: 10, 15. Further examples in Yöre 2015: 917f.

47 Gazimihal 1955: 99-103; on the effects of Western music on the melodies of traditional Turkish music cf. Yahya Kaçar, 2012: 149-160.

48 Kosal 2003:93; Alimdar 2016: 94; For a reconstruction of his compositions for guitar and *kanun* see CD Bekir Küçükay & Tahir Aydoğdu, *Yüzyıllık Şarkılar*, Ateş Müzik 2006.

49 CD Emre Aracı: *Guatelli Pasha and his Musical Portrait Album of the 19th Century Royal Family*, CD Emre Aracı & Prag Senfoni Oda Orkestra: *Sultan Portreler*, Kalan 2004.

Figure 12: Arif Bey: *Şarkı "Ne blesse pas mon coeur brulant comme la flame"*, harmonized probably by the Editor, Emin Efendi; Print: K. Zartarian No. 10, Istanbul, c. 1870s

the famous *tekbir* from Itrî (d. 1712) in G major (Kosal 2003: 58). Many of the musical works which Hacı Emin Efendi (1845-1907), a former student of Guatelli, published from 1876 on, were again pieces of Ottoman/Turkish music with piano accompaniment, mainly written for the Levantine and European public of Istanbul and in particular the district of Pera.[50]

The harmonic language of this late Ottoman salon music is much simpler than contemporary (hence late Romantic) music in Europe, and the attempts at harmonization of traditional melodies even more basic (see figure 12). Ralf Jäger (2006) describes a "*Chant Turc,*" which was edited in 1894 by Hacı Emin Efendi in a *fasıl* booklet as a supplement to the journal, *Malumat* (with predominantly *şarkı*s). The song was based on a *muhayyer şarkı* from Hacı Arif Bey (1831-1884), arranged by (an elsewhere unknown) Osman Efendi for piano. While the right hand plays the melody, the left hand adds a simple major-minor accompaniment, sometimes unexpectedly shifting to related harmonic regions. In an arrangement of a *hüseynî şarkı* from an unknown Rıza Efendi by Melik Efendi, the melody is notated separately, hence it might have been performed by a melody instrument, while the

50 Other printed works include marches, polka, mazurka and other pieces for piano. Behar 2013: 3; Jäger 2006: 67; Alimdar 2016: 508f; Doğuduyal 2016:157ff.

melody in the right hand constantly varies. The harmonization presents triads, open fourths, octaves, fourth-fifths or fifth-fourth chords, emphasizing the structural tones of *makam hüseyni* in an almost drone-like manner.

Around the same time, among the Christian minorities in Istanbul, polyphonic music became a practiced technique but also a much debated issue.

> In the second half of the nineteenth century, Greek Orthodox churches in various cities of Europe moved away from the traditional monophonic music of the Eastern Orthodox Church and adopted a liturgical music which was modernized according to the rules of European polyphony. More specifically, the general practice was to harmonize the existing ecclesiastical chants, re-composing them for four voices accompanied by the piano. (Erol 2009: 85)

> The first ecclesiastical music school in Greece was founded in 1826 on the island of Aegina (…) In the 1830s, the teacher of the school, Athanasios Avramiadis (...) followed western musical models and established "tetratonic" chanting in the choir of the church of the Orphanage of Aegina. However, the debates around the introduction of the polyphonic or "tetraphonic" music into the church of Greece gained vehemence in the years 1868-1870. In 1869, during the Easter service, the choir of the Cathedral of Athens attempted to chant several hymns in "tetraphonic" music (Erol 2009: 131)

Eventually in 1878, polyphonic music was introduced at the Church of Eisodion (Pera/Istanbul) (Erol 2009: 232); but several musicians and intellectuals rejected what they perceived as the invasion of Western music including tempered intervals, which "*could damage the familiarity with and the ability of hearing the small intervals of eastern music.*" (Erol 2009: 253) Around the mid-1870s, the "Greek Literary Society of Constantinople" encountered European – in this period, especially French – composers and musicians. For example, the composer Louis Albert Bourgault-Ducoudray (1840–1910) was sent by the French Ministry of Public Education to do research on Greek ecclesiastical and popular music and subsequently to collect popular songs in Constantinople, Smyrna and Greece (Erol 2009: 204f). In 1876 Ducoudray published Greek popular songs which he had collected from Smyrna and Athens, arranged with piano accompaniment.

Similarly, though later, the Armenian church also introduced polyphony.

> "In the late nineteenth century, young European- and Russian-educated Armenian musicians adapted Armenian music to Western temperament and polyphony, starting with liturgical music. The *Surp Badarak* (Holy Liturgy) was first polyphonized in 1885 by Kristafor Gara-Murza, followed by Amy Akpar in 1896 and Levon Chilingiryan in 1906, but these versions were not officially recognized by the Armenian Apostolic Church. Magar Yegmalyan's 1896 harmonized version was the first *badarak* to receive widespread official acceptance. Gomidas' four-part contrapuntal *badarak* arrangement was published in Paris in 1933, and later rearranged in three parts by his student, Vartan Sarkisyan. This reformist movement within liturgical music led to a polarization among the *tıbir*s (cantors). The number of those who rejected notation – believing that it would damage the oral tradition – decreased over time, but the real conflict emerged around the issue of polyphony and westernization." (Yıldız 2016: 114f)

Early Ottoman opera would later come to include hybrid music (Spinetti 2010; Aracı 2010b). Dikran Çuhacıyan (1837-1898) for example, composer of early Ottoman operettas, also arranged Turkish art songs polyphonically (Alimdar 2016: 509). In the context of Ottoman theater *kanto* developed. The term itself derived from the Italian word *canto*, meaning singing, chant, or song. *Kanto* emerged around 1870 in the entertainment neighborhood of Galata as "*Turkish appropriation of Western European-derived light strophic songs.*"[51] Between the acts of theater pieces songs were performed solo or duo on European instruments (violin, trumpet, trombone, trap drum, cymbals), based on *makam*s that were close to Western modes (*e.g. rast, hüzzam, hicaz, hüseyni, nihavend*). A first period of *kanto*s ended in the early twentieth century, a second one reached it peak in the 1920s. This second phase is documented on several 78 rpm records; composers include Kaptanzade Ali Rıza Bey, Refik Fersan, Dramalı Hasan, Sadettin Kaynak and others. In this later phase Turkish instruments such as *cümbüş* and *ud* were also used, and in the music the foxtrot or Charleston were integrated, as well as light Western songs and Turkish *şarkı*s.[52] *Kanto*s were composed of simple melodies based on common urban *makam* or Western melodic scales. The later period (1923-45) "*demonstrated a more extensive and consistent attention to a variety of classical Turkish* makam*s*" (Seeman 2002: 178). Most of the performers, in particular the singer, were non-Muslims, including Armenians, Jews and expecially Greeks (Beken 1998: 114).

During the early Republic of Turkey the focus of Western oriented Turkish composers (if interested in traditional Turkish music) completely switched from urban art songs to Anatolian folk songs, while the general approach of harmonization based on functional harmony continued. The new government strongly reinforced support for public Western musical life in Turkey. Orchestras, opera houses and ballets were founded, in Ankara from the 1930s and later also in Istanbul and Izmir.[53] The political project of this period was the replacement of traditional Ottoman art music with a new synthesis of Anatolian-Turkish and Western music. During the early Republican period, folklorism was explicitly encouraged by the political authorities, required by Mustafa Kemal Atatürk himself, and almost impossible to reject. Several composers sought inspiration in subjects from Turkish folk literature, as for example Saygun in his operas and many songs. While in Saygun's and Erkin's early compositions the aesthetic influence of French impressionism was still visible, later Hindemith's neoclassicism also became important. In particular during the 1920s and 1930s, many traditional Turkish art musicians

51 Seeman 2002: 178; Meriç 2011; Hiçyılmaz 1999; CD *Kantolar (1905-1945)*, Kalan 1998.

52 Cemal Ünlü, liner notes to CD *Kantolar (1905-1945)*, Kalan 1998: 44.

53 State Opera Ankara 1948, Conservatory Izmir 1958, State Opera and Ballet Istanbul 1969, State Conservatory Istanbul 1971, State Symphony Orchestra Istanbul 1972, State Conservatory Izmir 1984, State Conservatory Gaziantep 1988, in addition several municipal conservatories and music departments at state universities in Istanbul, Eskisehir, Adana (1987-89) Akdemir 1991: 38ff.; Zimmermann-Kalyoncu 1984; Oransay 1983; Say 1993b; Jäger 1998: 1072; Filarmoni Derneği 1982; Deleon 1986; 1988; Altar 1989.

learned Western art music. At this time also light "European" music (of varying degrees) became popular, including genres such as the foxtrot, tango or jazz.[54]

In particular during the 1930s, after the return from their studies in Europe, almost all composers of the so-called first Turkish generation, such as the "Turkish Five" (*Türk Beşler*) tried to combine Turkish folk music with Western tonality and within the framework of Western music, just as both Ziya Gökalp and Hindemith had proposed.[55] While arrangements of *şarkı* and other genres of Ottoman art music were no longer written (with the remarkable exception of Hasan Ferid Alnar) almost all Turkish composers of this period (1930s and 1940s) harmonized Anatolian melodies. The first simple arrangements were written for choirs, followed by pieces for voice and accompaniment (piano, chamber ensemble, orchestra), almost always preserving the original folk melody. Beginning in the 1940s the arrangements became more and more sophisticated, a clear departure from the strict traditional melodic material.

An early example for this folkoristic approach are the *12 Anadolu Türküsü* (1926) by Cemal Reşit Rey for piano and voice.[56] During his years of education in Paris and Genf (1913-1923) Rey wrote songs in French with piano accompaniment. It was only after his return to Turkey in 1923 that he also composed instrumental music such as the sonata for two pianos (1924). Influenced by Turkish nationalism he included traditional Turkish folk melodies in many of his compositions, including:

- 12 *Anadolu Halk Türküler* (12 Anatolian Folk songs) for choir (1926);
- *Zeybek* (an Aegean folk dance), opera (1926);
- *Anadolu Dansları. Halk Ezgileri üzerine Türk Manzaraları / Scènes Turque* (*Türk Manzaları*), 8 pieces for piano (1928; four parts arranged for orchestra, 1932);
- *Bebek Efsanesi / La légende du Bebek*, symphonic poem for orchestra (1928);
- *Anadolu İzlenimleri / Impressions d'Anatolie*, sonata for violin and piano (1928)
- *İki Anadolu Türküsü* (two Anatolian songs) for voice and orchestra (1930);
- *Karagöz, Poème Symphonique en Forme de Suite*, for orchestra (1932).[57]

The most important Turkish composer of the period was Ahmet Adnan Saygun (1907-1991), who at the same time did extensive fieldwork on Anatolian folk music as inspired by Bartók, with whom he traveled on his fieldwork trip to south Turkey in 1936 (figure 13).[58] Saygun's numerous songs for choir, or accompaniments for

[54] Akgün 1993; Uyar 2016; Özpazarcık 1998; CD Seyyan Hanim (1913-1989): *Tangolar* (Kalan, 1996), CD Ibrahim Özgür (1910-1959): *Tangolar. The Bel Ami of Turkish Tango* (Oriente Rien, 1999); CD *Yurttan Sesler. Yeni Türkiye'nin Ezgileri* (Yapı ve Kredi Kültür Sanat Yayıncılık, 1998); Seeman 2002: 326ff; Yaprak 2016.

[55] Deniz 2015; Hindemith 1935/1983: 102; Behar 1987: 103; Pack 1977: 65ff.

[56] Ilyasoğlu 1997: 111ff; Aydin 2003; Kütahyali 1981: 109.

[57] Ilyasoğlu 1997: 306ff; Kütahyalı 1981: 108ff; Woodard 1999.

[58] Aydın 2003: 122-143; Vikár & Saygun 1976; Bartók 1976; CD Béla Bartók: *Turkish Folk Music Collection*, Hungaroton, 1996.

Figure 13: Ahmet Adnan Saygun: *Sivas Düz Süit*, op. 23, No. 4, 1955 (Saygun 1955: 1)

piano or orchestra, are direct arrangements of folk songs, even many of his piano compositions are based on traditional melodies (e.g. *Anadolu'dan*, 1945) or rhythms, e.g.:

- Suite for Orchestra, op 14 (1937), based on folk melodies;
- Sonatina for piano solo, opus 15 (1937), the third part is a free *horon* dance;
- Sonata for violin and piano, op 20 (1941), the second part is a *horon*;
- *Anadolu'dan* ("From Anatolia") for piano, op. 25 (1945);
- *Demet*, Suite for violin and piano, op 33 (1956), largely based on folk tunes; the first part a free *uzun hava*, the second part a *horon*; the third part a *ağır zeybek*, the fourth part *sepetçioğlu*, a dance from Kastamonu;

- *Aksak Tartılar üzerine on etüd* for piano, op 38 (1964), *Aksak Tartılar üzerine on iki Prelüd*, op 45 (1967), *Aksak Tartılar üzerine* 15 parça, opus 47 (1971); *Aksak Tartılar üzerine on taslak*, op 58 (1976);[59]
- *Halay* for orchestra, opus 24 (1942-1944);

Saygun's *Töresel Musiki, Okuma Kitabı op 40* ("Traditional Music, a Reading Book", 1967), written for singing lessons at the Conservatory, was a close synthesis of folk music research and composition. The collection includes 150 sight reading exercises, newly composed fictitious folk music melodies, typologically arranged according to contemporary ideas of cultural history from "pre-traditional" over three tone and pentatonic melodies to church modes and eventually free modal melodies.[60] In his Yunus Emre Oratorium (1942) based on lyrics of Sufi mystic, Yunus Emre (thirteenth century), elements of Turkish art music are audible, which in the following years became more important for Saygun. The Oratorium includes quotes from *ilahis*, *nefes* and *uzun havas*; in aria No 4, as an alternative for flute and tam tam, *ney* and *kudüm* may be used. Also his first concerto for piano partly uses *makams* (Aydin 2003:128-136). The Partita for solo violin (op.36, 1961) for example, uses *uşşak*, the melody changing between b and b flat, while in traditional art music it should have been lowered by one *koma*. The fourth part, on the other hand, includes an *ağır zeybek* as well as an *uzun hava* (Giray 2002: 20ff). In Saygun's later compositions, however, folk and art music merged into a complex personal style, distinct from the contemporary music in Europe and America. Though Saygun remained interested in folk music, his orchestrations became richer and the arrangements of folk material more free. In Turkey, Saygun opened the way for the next generation, which eventually became connected with the Western avantgarde. His students include composers such as Kemal İlerici, İlhan Usmanbaş, Muammer Sun, Cengiz Tanç, İlhan Baran and others.

The titles of many of Necil Kazim Akses' (1908-1999) works also indicate a similar close relationship to folk music, e.g. *Çiftetelli* (dance) for orchestra, 1934.[61] In his many vocal compositions, folk songs are often the starting point, e.g. *Türküler* ("Folk Songs", ca. 1937) and *On Türkü* ("10 Folk Songs"), 1964, both for mixed choirs. At the end of the 1960s Akses became interested in traditional art music; for example in his Concerto for Viola, 1977 (the second movement in *makam bestenigar*). In *Itri Neva Kar'ı üzerine Scherzo* ("Scherzo over the *Kar* in *makam Neva* by Itri") for orchestra (1970), Akses arranged a famous art song of the late seventeenth century. The music is almost monophonic with sparse harmonic accompaniment and few counterpoints, while formally the melody is freely arranged. Similarly,

59 Maral & Lindley 2011: 19ff; Aracı 2001.

60 In 2005 Özkan Manav wrote *Saygun'la Yüz Yüze: 'Töresel Musiki'den beş Parca üzerine Çoğaltmalar* for violin, "Variations on Five Melodies from Sayguns *Töresel Musiki*".

61 Özkoç 2012. For analyses of several compositions and the *makams* used in them, see Aydin 2003:157-175.

Ulvi Cemil Erkin's (1906-1972) main inspiration was Turkish folk music.[62] In particular his effective and powerful compositions on Anatolian asymmetric rhythms became famous, such as the well-known *Köçekçe* (a popular dance) for orchestra (1943).[63] Erkin sometimes imitates sounds and playing techniques of folk music instruments, for instance of the bowed instrument *kemençe* (String quartet, 1935/1936, fourth movement) or of the flute *kaval* (*Beş Damla*, second movement, left hand). Only rarely did Erkin use *makams* of the traditional art music, and if so, only as scale material. Unlike other composers of his generation Hasan Ferid Alnar (1906-1978) was initially educated in traditional Turkish art music; in his youth he was a successful performer of the *kanun* (at the respected *Dârüt-Tâlîm-i Mûsikî*) and composed at least 10 *saz semâîsi* and two *peşrev* (1927), and *şarkı*. Some 78rpm records of the early 1920s prove his ability on the *taksim*. In his concerto for *kanun* and string orchestra, he quotes the *Rast Peşrevi* by Giriftzen Asim Bey (1852-1929) and also in his Cello Concerto (1943–47) *makam hicaz* is used in the first and third movements.[64]

Beginning in the 1940s Turkish composers tended to compose larger forms than before, and used folk music in a freer way. Already in the 1930s, Cemal Reşit Rey turned away from folklorism and wrote music for orchestra, again more influenced by French impressionism. These tendencies can be seen in *Enstaneler* ("Moments") for orchestra (1931), *Concerto Cromatique* for piano and orchestra (1933) and the *Poème* for *Ondes Martenot* and string ensemble (1934).[65] The music is often mono- or heterophone, while counterpoint plays a minor role. Most parts rather serve the enrichment of the orchestra timbre with ostinati and short accompaniment figurations, without displaying their own melodic character (in this sense reminiscent of Debussy). Sometimes the orchestration becomes grandiose in a late romantic manner, for instance when basic melodies on violins are accompanied by very simple harmony. On the other hand, there are moments

---

62 Aydin 2003:94-115; Most of Erkin's songs and choir pieces are arranged folk songs (e.g. *Yedi Türkü* (seven folk songs, for bass baritone and piano, 1936; *Yedi Türkü* for mixed choir, 1945; *On Türkü* (Ten folk songs) for mixed choir, 1963. They directly quote folk music, often monophonic parts or those whose harmonic development is reduced by long drones or ostinati.

63 Other examples include the "Piano Quintet" (1943, second movement 7/8, fourth movement 5/8), "Sinfonietta" (1951), the third movement 3+2+2+3/8). Also Erkin's violin concerto (1947), the first and the second symphony (1947; 1948/1951) as well as the Symphony Concertante (1966) are among the most popular Turkish compositions of the twentieth century, and were also performed abroad.

64 CD *Bir Cumhuriyet Çınarı: Ferid Alnar*, Türk Hava Yolları, 2009, musical director CD Rûhi Ayangil. Ferid Alnar: *Peşrev'den Konçerto'ya*, Kalan 2014. For the use of *makam* in Alnar's compositions see Aydin 2003: 61-88. Already in 1935 Alnar composed *Emprovizasyon*, a free adaptation of a *taksim* for piano. Also the *10 Yunus Emre Ilâhîsi Koro Süiti* (1970) use *makams*. CD Rûhî Ayangil, *Ferid Alnar*, Istanbul 2010.

65 A later exception is the *Bir Istanbul Türküsü Üzerine Çeşitlemeler* (Variations over an Istanbul folksong, 1960/61) on the well-known song *Kâtibim*. Still in 1976 he wrote *Üc Anadolu Türküsü* for voice and orchestra. Ilyasoglu 1997

when *makam* inspired melodies seem to impede Western tonality. Formally many of Rey's compositions display a sequence of short sections. Rey himself called the time after 1950 his "fantasy" period. He was occupied with Sufi mysticism and thoughts about death. His monumental orchestra pieces, *Çağrılış* ("Invocation", 1950) and *Fatih* ("Conqueror", i.e. Mehmet II., 1953) present a far-reaching reduction of his harmonic language, differing from earlier works in the integration of conterpoint passages at formaly important positions.

Western-Turkish music of the 1940s and 1950s, though aesthetically much more advanced than that of the 1930s, moved into a period of national isolation, which was reinforced by ongoing orientalistic expectations of the Western audience. It should be remembered that Western-oriented Turkish composers began to compose during a period in which the art music language in Europe went through a fundamental structural change, eventually leaving the concept of tonality. Compared to this music Western Turkish music of the nineteenth and early twentieth centuries displays a simplified classic or romantic musical language. As a result, the gap widened between Turkish Western music and contemporary Western music, which led to the growing international aesthetic isolation of Turkish composers. Seen from the West, Turkish composers remained in a conservative position and did not follow the international trends of their time. In terms of both aesthetics and the structure of their music hardly anything connects the so-called Turkish Five with Western composers of the same generation, such as Pierre Luigi Dallapicola (b. 1904), Olivier Messiaen (b. 1908), Pierre Schaeffer (b. 1910) and John Cage (b. 1912).

In Turkey most composers more or less continued to follow the folkloristic tradition, combining it with neo-classicist or impressionist influences. Composers such as Okan Demiriş (b. 1942), Muammer Sun (b. 1932), Bülent Tarcan (1914-1991), Nevit Kodallı (b. 1924-2009), Ferid Tüzün (1929-1977), Ilhan Baran (1934-2016) and others further developed the synthesis of Anatolian folk music and Western tonality and thus tried to remain comprehensible for a broader Turkish audience. Beginning in the 1940s Kemal İlerici (1910-1986) began to construct a system of harmony which was supposed to unite Turkish folk music and Western polyphony. A final version was published in 1970 (figure 14).[66] The basic scale (*anadizi*) of his system was that of *hüseyni*, which is the most common scale for Anatolian folk music. Other scales were also introduced into his system, in particular including pitches outside the Western tempered system. Within the scales İlerici separated the tones (I, IV and V) from others. The basis of his polyphony are stratifications of fourths; harmonically the most important three degrees are in distances of thirds from each other. According to İlerici, within the basic scale the tones E-A-D (V-I-IV) sound stable (*durucu*), while G-C-Fis-B2 (VII-III-VI-II) are unstable (*yürüyücü*) (İlerici1981: 24f). His system includes a complex canon of

[66] İlerici 1970; Bayraktar 1993; Aydin 2003:69.

Figure 14: *Ferahfezâ Saz semaisi* by Tanburî Cemil Bey, the higher voice is Tanbur Cemil Bey's original melody, while the lower one was added by Kemal İlerici (İlerici1981: 248)

chords with resolutions and counterpoint. İlerici's book includes numerous notation examples from both Turkish folk and art songs, even including religious hymns such as *salâti* and *tevsih*. He explains his system in detail for numerous *makams*; later chapters focus on traditonal forms and rhythms (pp. 393ff).

Even before the publication of İlerici's developed system in 1970, a number of Turkish composers had adapted it for their music, including İlhan Baran (1934-2016), Muammer Sun (b. 1932), Sabahattin Kalender (b. 1919), Nevit Kodallı (b. 1924-2009), Bülent Tarcan (1914-1991) and Cenan Akın (b. 1932). Muammer Sun's (b. 1932) "Orchestra Suite Colours of the Homeland" (*Yurt Renkleri*, 1953-1983), includes melodies, though not original folk music, composed according to İlerici's system.[67] While Turkish folkloristic music remained estranged from contemporary Western music, and was hardly taken seriously and rarely performed in Europe and America, at the same time in Turkey hope diminished that a synthesis of Turkish folk music and European music could gain acceptance among a broader Turkish audience. Folkloristic Turkish music was appreciated by well-educated Kemalists, while the large majority in Turkey did not understand nor appreciate it (İlyasoğlu 2009: 89). Of course not all Western-Turkish composers in the second half of the twentieth century composed folkloristic music (and certainly none did it exclusively); rather a rich music scene developed, whose history still remains unwritten except for a few monographs and articles on individual composers or works.[68]

Since the 1950s a small group of Western oriented Turkish composers began to give up traditional concepts of Western harmony and melody, approaching the international avant-garde of their time (Köksal 2015). In Turkey, however, it took until about twenty five years after Arnold Schönberg had developed his twelve-tone technique for Ilhan Usmanbaş to become the first Turkish composer to write a piece in this technique, namely, "Music No. 1" for cello and piano (1950). The previous "Music No. 2" for cello and piano had been composed according to the harmony of İlerici. When the Turkish Five wrote their major works, a younger generation, including Bülent Arel (1918-1990), İlhan Usmanbaş (born 1921), Ertuğrul Oğuz Fırat (born 1923), Ilhan Mimaroğlu (1926-2012), later also Cengiz Tanç (1933-1998) and Ali Dogan Sinangil (b. 1934) were studying the music of the Second Viennese School and the music of their own generation, such as Iannis Xenakis (1922-2001), György Ligeti (1923-2006), Luigi Nono (1924-1990), Morton Feldman (1926-1987) and Karl-Heinz Stockhausen (1928-2007). In 1953, a group of composers, musicians and intellectuals (including Usmanbaş, Ilhan Mimaroğlu, Ertuğrul Oğuz Fırat, Arel, Faruk Güvenş and Bülent Ecevit) founded the *Helicon* association in Ankara with its own string orchestra, to study, discuss and even perform contemporary Turkish music. *"The Helicon society stood firm for the new music*

67 Sun 2008; 2011: 283ff ; CD Hande Dalkilic: Muammer Sun: *Yurt Renkleri / Country Colors*, Kalan 2004.

68 E.g. Ilyasoglu 2000; 2006; 2009; Ali 2002.

aesthetics in the face of an iron-willed conservative majority" (Yürür 1995:2). The most important composer of this generation was Ilhan Usmanbaş (b. 1921). Usmanbaş began to study composition with the so-called Turkish Five in 1941 (Ilzasoğlu 2000; Manav & Nemutlu 2011). In 1950 Usmanbaş read "*Schönberg et son École*" by René Leibowitz (1947), and one year later he studied with Kemal İlerici. In his compositions in twelve-tone technique he was mainly influenced by Alban Berg (*Lyrische Suite*, *Wozzeck*) and Schönberg's *Pierrot Lunaire*. In 1952 he studied in the US with Luigi Dallapiccola, and again in 1957-58 with Milton Babbit, Henry Cowell, and Morton Feldman. After his first attempts with twelve-tone technique in the 1950s, Usmanbaş composed serial music, influenced by composers such as Karel Goyvaerts, Boulez, Stockhausen, whose music he had encountered in America.[69]

In the 1960s, a few young Turkish composers wrote aleatoric music (Usmanbaş, Fırat), compositions focusing on timbre (Usmanbaş, Tanç) and electronic music (Arel, Mimaroğlu). Traditional music did not play any substantial role for these composers. Ahmet Yürür (b. 1941), who studied in Ankara and Paris, then later with Saygun and Erkin, and from 1978 on in the USA (Indiana and Maryland), might be seen as the first Turkish postmodern composer. At the same time an ethnomusicologist, Yürür traveled to India to do fieldwork for his PhD. (Doğuduyal 2016) However, several contemporary international music styles and composers hardly reached Turkey at all; particularly notable in their absence were Fluxus, John Cage, George Crumb and later Minimal Music. In 1995 Ahmet Yürür wrote:

> Turkey has remained immune to the turn-of-the-century movements in music such as futurismo, bruitisme, serialism, electronic, non-Western and alternative sounds, etc. (…) Saygun was a devout fighter against new music which he claimed as an ephemeral fad. So, atonality was never considered worthy of being taught in music schools. (Yürür 1995:1)

MIAM (*Müzik İleri Araştırmalar Merkezi* / Center for Advanced Studies in Music), founded in 1999 and attached to the Conservatory for Turkish Music of the Technical University Istanbul provided further international contact for young Turkish composers and musicians. During the last fifteen years, in particular around MIAM (but also beyond, for example at Yıldız University) a young scene of New Music, electronic, lounge and world music has emerged, also including some autodidacts, sometimes near to popular music.[70] Only few of these musicians (in

69 In the 1960s and '70s he composed with aleatoric elements and graphical notations. *Keman ve Piyano için 5 Etüd* (1953-55) for example uses a series for dynamics. His piano pieces *Ölümsüz Deniz Taşlarıydı* (Ankara, 1965) have no indication for rhythm hence leaving the pianist a great deal of interpretation. In spite of violent clusters the music is timeless, lost, suspended. Similarly,, the String Quartet (1970). During the 1970s Usmanbaş began to include elements of *makams* (Stringquartet, Saxophone Quartet, 1970; 3. Symphony, 1979); in the 1980s Usmanbaş even partially wrote minimal music (3. Sympohony, Violin Partita).

70 Website www.newmusicistanbul.com (accessed September 12, 2012), managed by the pianist Seda Röder, numbers a dozen contemporary Turkish composers more or less of this scene. www.cagdasturkbestecileri.com/besteciler.html (accessed November 12, 2012); Rei-

particular in the fields of lounge or world music) made their way into the Turkish market, e.g. the *Yakaza* Ensemble, which for their ethnic lounge music use instruments such as the Afghan *rebab*, *shakuhachi*, *saron*, *dombra*, *mbira*, *ney*, *yaylı tanbur*, cello, *tar*, *kudüm*, saxophone, bass and electronics[71], or the *Nevcivan Özel* Project with instruments such as *tar*, *kemence*, indian *tabla* and double bass.

While serious composers of folkloristic and in particular those of contemporary international Western music remained unknown in Turkey, light classical music often became successful, as for example Ferhat Livaneli and Zülfü Livaneli's *New Age Symphony* (1999) or several compositions by Can Attila (b. 1969).[72] Some more examples:

- CD Murat Malay: *Canakkale 1915 Symphony*, 2010.[73] The orchestra includes *bağlama*, *ney*, *kaval.*
- CD *Senfonik Istanbul*, Istanbul Büyüksehir Belediyesi, 2015; including orchestrations of well-known Istanbul songs by Tuğrul Karataş and Cemil Sağyaşar.
- CD *Royal Philharmonic Orchestra plays Sezen Aksu*, Universal 2016. Arrangements by Erdal Kızılçay.
- Tuluyhan Uğurlu (b. 1965): Symphony Turk / *Senfoni Türk* for orchestra, including a *mehter* ensemble, *rebab*, *ney*, *tambur*, *ud*, *bağlama*, *bendir*), 2002.[74]
- Anjelika Akbar, pianist, born in in Kasachstan, degree at Hacetepe State Conservatory Ankara; several projects with light, sometimes slightly "Turkified" Western piano music.[75]

Today numerous CDs and notations of Turkish folk and art music arranged in simple tonality for piano or guitar are available (e.g. Toptaş 2016) (see figure 15).

A final example again demonstrates that the audience today is hardly used to unaccompanied melodies anymore. Nezih Ünen's film, *Anadolu'nun Kayıp Şarkıları* (2010) was initiated with the aim to "record authentic music, dance and rituals at the place where they reside." (Introduction of the film). However, these recordings were arranged in a studio with added sound, percussion and harmony accompaniment. The obvious contradiction did not prevent the success of the film.

---

gle & Whitehead 2008. CD *Anthology of Turkish Experimental Music 1961-2014*, Sub Rosa/Alife, 2016. The CD series *Müzik Hayvanı* comprises low budget produced CDs distributed on the basis of free donations in a few CD shops in Istanbul; they contain electronic music most of which was produced at MIAM (http://muzikhayvani.com), sometimes including some Western or other instruments.

71 CD Yakaza Ensemble: *A'mâk-ı Hayâl*, Ak Müzik, 2010; CD *İçbükeydış*, Ak Müzik, 2012; CD Nevcivan Özel Project: *Taristan*, Ak, 2010.

72 Zülfü Livaneli: *New Age Symphony* (IDA 1999), with the London Symphony Orchestra, conducted by Francis Shaw; CD Ferhat Livaneli: *Lâlezâr. Chamber Music* (Emi, 1990).

73 Murat Malay: *Canakkale 1915 & Palestine Symphony*, 3Adim 2010.

74 http://www.tuluyhanugurlu.com/ (accessed October, 13, 2016); see also MC Tuluyhan Uğurlu: *Kutsal Kitaplardan Ayetler* ("Verses from holy books") for piano, BMG 1993.

75 CD Anjelika Akbar: *Bach a lÒrientale*, 2003.

Figure 15: *Nihavend Sazsemâi* by Hasib Dede, arranged for piano by Çağrıhan Erkan (Erkan & Dinge 2003: 6)

As we have seen, in most newly composed "Western music" by Turkish musicians, Turkish folk or art music was integrated. While this was done mainly by simple harmonization, many composers also implemented elements of traditional Turkish music in a more creative and individual way.

Excursus: Popular Music and Jazz

Musical approaches similar to the folklorists of the 1930s and 40s, that is, the harmonization of Turkish folk or sometimes art songs performed on Western instruments and ensembles, are practiced (though in general much more simply) within the larger field of popular music. Popular Turkish music in fact encompasses a large field of completely diverse music scenes. There are hardly any commonalities, for example, between jazz, *arabesk* or political protest songs. A comprehensive history of popular music in Turkey has unfortunately not been written yet, in particular to bridge the first half of the twentieth century (including operetta, early jazz, tango, kanto, etc) with more recent styles. Here only a few points concerning musical hybridity will be contributed.

In the late 1950s the popular singer Tülay German (b. 1935) performed the folk song *Burcak Tarlası* ("Vetch Field") at the Balkan Festival in Yugoslavia. In the 1970s, she recorded chansons and folk songs together with Francois Rabbath, who added a pure, unembellished accompaniment on a bowed double bass.[76] Later, in the 1970s and '80s, the singer Esin Afsar (1936-2011) similarly performed folk songs as chansons. In the late 1960s (the time of the famous *Altın Mikrofon* pop song competition) the so-called *Anadolu Rock* (Anatolian Rock) developed, with groups and soloists such as *Moğollar* (The Mongols, 1967-76), *Üç Hürel* (the Three *Hürel* brothers), *Kardaşlar* (The Brothers), *Dervişan*, Erkin Koray (b. 1941), Cem Karaca (1945-2004) and Barış Manço (1943-1999) (Skoog 2012). Reaching their peak in the 1970s these musicians performed folk songs in the style of rock music.

In parallel, politically left wing music groups began to emerge in Turkey (Gündoğar 2005: 247). Initially, most groups arranged folk songs for guitar, while later orchestration and harmonization gained importance, and instruments like bass guitar, guitar and drums were were used alongside folk instruments such as *cura, kaval, mey* and *zurna* (Sarıtaş 2010: 33; Hasgül, 1996b: 59).

> Like the Republican cadres, for a majority of the political musicians of 1960s and 70s, polyphonic music meant innovation. They modernized the folk songs in a way that local styles were lost. (Hasgül, 1996b: 72; Sarıtaş 2010: 34)

In the repertoires of political musicians of the 1960s and '70s international as well as recently composed marches and elegies (*ağıt*s) were added to politicized

---

[76] CD Toulai et Francois Rabbath: *Le Chant des Poètes*, Arion, 1998 (original LP: 1980); LP Toulai et Francois Rabbath: *Hommage a Nazim Hikmet*, Arion 1982.

folk songs (Kahyaoğlu, 2003: 63, 94; Sarıtaş 2010: 35). The songs recounted past struggles and called for mobilization, with the main political intention being the popularization of the jargon and ideas of the left wing movements.

Again around the same time, a completely different form of popular music gained prominence, *arabesk*, a melange of folk music with Western and Lebanese popular music arrangements.[77] Orhan Gencebay (*Bir Teselli Ver,* "Give me Consolation," 1968) is considered to be the first singer of *arabesk*. The lyrics and later the related *arabesk* films dealt with the pain of unhappy love, suffering, the coldness of modern metropoles, the destiny of fate and despair. Some of the later singers, such as Ibrahim Tatlises or Emrah sang mostly folksongs in *arabesk* arrangements. The ensembles to accompany the singers, however, became much larger than in any other popular music style of the time. Martin Stokes (1992: 90) described the band of Müslüm Gürses in 1990 as consisting of eight violins, *ney*, *ud*, *kanun*, electric bass, synthesizer, *darbuka*, *def*, and *davul* and electro *bağlama*. Ayse Mine in 1986 used percussion, three violins, bass, *ud*, accordion, *kanun*, and *darbuka* (Stokes 1992: 171).

Some few years after the coup d'état of 1980, political songs again became popular, now under the label *özgün müzik* (original music). While some musicians and groups perpetuated the music of the left wing movements of the 1970s, others became more and more influenced by *arabesk* (Kahyaoğlu, 2003: 116). The most prominent singer Ahmet Kaya, for example, became particularly significant for the Kurdish movement which had begun to grow. In 1985 the *Grup Yorum* was founded, until today the most successful politically left wing music group of Turkey. Similar to other comparable groups, such as *Grup Ekin*, *Grup Munzur*, *Kızılırmak* and *Grup Baran*, their songs had explicitly political lyrics rather than giving space to individual feelings and expression. In the early 1990s, Kurdish political music groups (Kurdish *koma*) began to separate from Turkish groups, including *Koma Denge Azad*, *Koma Amed*, *Koma Ciya*, or *Koma Agirê Jiyan* (Hongur 2014; Gündogar, 2005). Their music and lyrics, but also their stance as organized *(örgütlü)* musicians, referenced leftist Turkish groups. Since the 1970s, the Kurdish movement had begun to rise, from the 1980s on dominated by the PKK. Again, albums of the *komas* were mainly composed of either harmonized folk songs or new songs with direct political lyrics (Sarıtaş 2010: 5).

While the new Turkish pop music of the 1990s initially brought Turkish popular music closer to international pop sounds, several Turkish pop singers have at least from time to time performed Turkish folk or even art songs, e.g. Sezen Aksu on her album *İşik Doğudan Yükselir* (Foneks, 1995), Tarkan (*Çile Bülbülüm*), Kubat, Sertab Erener together with the Kurdish singer Aynur (*Güzelliğin on Para etme*), or Şevval Sam, who sang light art and folk music from the Black Sea Coast. I have already mentioned hybrid music in the field of lounge and world music, which

---

77 Güngör 1990; Özbek 1991; Stokes 1992; Tekelioğlu 1996.

emerged in the early twenty-first century. Internationally the most successful musician in this field is Mercan Dede, who has released 10 albums since 1998, many of which have topped the world music charts. Other groups such as Orient Expressions, in cooperation with the folk singer Sabahat Akkiraz, have followed his lead, using electronics, percussion and excellent guest musicians.[78] Also the American-Iranian group, *Niyaz* with trance electronic Sufi music, cooperated with traditional Turkish musicians, including Ulaş Özdemir and recently Sinan Cem Eroğlu (*kaval*, frettless guitar).[79] In their 2008 album "Nine Heavens" *Niyaz* interprets the well-known song "*beni beni*" by Aşık Dertli (eighteenth century).

Jazz musicians, on the other hand, from the 1950s on, have tried to synthesize Turkish traditional music and jazz. The saxophone player Ismet Sıral experimented with local melodies in jazz in the 1950s, and during the 1960s cooperated with the famous *ney* player Aka Gündüz (Uyar 2016: 97; Meriç 1999: 162). İlham Gencer performed his composition *Hicaz Caz* at the TRT in 1954 or 1955 (Uyar 2016: 98).

> During the 1970s, more organized attempts of fusion emerged. Trumpeter Maffy Falay moved to Sweden, where he had the opportunity to work with many local Swedish jazz musicians. With percussionist Okay Temiz, they formed a group called Sevda, which is one of the first bands trying to fuse Turkish music elements into the jazz idiom. They released an album in 1972. (Uyar 2016:p.100)

Also in Sweden, Okay Temiz's band "Oriental Wind" worked with flute, clarinet, saxophone, double bass, piano and Turkish instruments such as *ney*, *kaval*, *sipsi*, *zurna* and *bağlama*.[80]

After a period of stagnation in the 70s and 80s (Uyar 2016: 79), the 1990s saw some new attempts at synthesis of Turkish music and jazz. "*The group Asia Minor, led by electric bass player Kamil Erdem and including saxophonist Yahya Dai, kanun player Tahir Aydogdu and drummer Cem Aksel performed a style that combined electric jazz with Turkish music influences.*" (Uyar 2016:101) On Senem Diyici's album, *Tell me Trabizon* (Buda Musique, 1998), one song is dedicated to Ruhi Su, another to the New Music singer Cathy Berbarian. In particular during the past fifteen years as part of an expansion of jazz in Turkey (Uyar 2016), a growing number of attempts for synthesis of jazz and traditional Turkish music have been conducted. Some CDs include[81]:

---

78 CD, Külliyat, Doublemoon 2006. Another example is the CD Minor Empire: *Second Nature*, Z Yapim, 2014.

79 Ulas Özdemir on *Sumud* (Musicaction, 2012), Sinan Cem Eroglu, Ömer Avci (percussion) and Didem Basar (kanun) on "Nine Heavens" (Six Degrees, 2008), and "Fourth Light" (Dokuzsekiz, 2015).

80 Uyar 2016: 100. In 1971, the Erol Pekcan Quintet released the single *Kabağı da Boynuma Takarım* and *Nihavent Longo* (Uyar 2016:100).

81 For a comprehensive list of Turkish jazz albums, see Uyar 2016:147-163.

- Barbaros Erköse: *Cazname*, Kalan, 1997;
- Önder Focan: Swing a la Turca, Kalan 2007;
- Ahmet Kadri Rizeli (*kemençe*): *Jazz alla turca*, Sony 2008;
- Baki Duyarlar & Derya Türkan: *Kemenjazz*, Ada 2012, jazz composed by Baki Duyarlar featuring Derya Türkan (*kemençe*) and the singer Dilek Turkan, in addition to trumpet, drums, piano.
- Güç Başar Gülle: *Ilk Renk*, Ak Müzik 2010; double bass, percussion, and *ud*;

Most of these syntheses keep the traditional melody and add a harmonisation and jazz phrasing.[82] Only few musicians such as Nail Yavuzoğlu, Baki Duyarlar or Erkan Oğur have tried seriously to integrate *makam*, rather than just simple melodies, scales or instruments, into jazz. In the *Evrim Demirel Ensemble* instruments such as piano (or *Continuum*), double bass and drums are combined with the Turkish art singer Özer Özel, who also plays *yaylı tanbur*. In addition to Evrem Demriel's jazz compositions the group arranged the well-known song *Çün sana gönlüm müptela düştü* by Hafız Post (d. 1694).[83]

*

Today, a wide range of musical styles in Turkey (folk or Ottoman-Turkish art music, popular music) at least occasionally include harmonic accompaniment, though in general this is limited to a basic functional tonality. While the harmonic language itself has hardly developed, but rather has remained a stable musical vocabulary, polyphony has enriched the already endless variety of new ensembles and arrangements of traditional music.

Let us now take a look at the emergence of these more or less new forms of ensembles for traditional music.

New Ensembles for Traditional Music

The formation of new types of ensembles for Turkish music began in the early twentieth century. Before that time, Ottoman/Turkish art music was mostly performed by small instrumental ensembles of some four to eight musicians, accompanying usually one singer, who at the same time might play a small frame drum (*def*). Larger ensembles were formed on exceptional occasions, for example for important public festivals, or in the *cumhur ilahi* genre, which was sung by a small group of *hafiz* chanting in unison. During the last years of the Ottoman Empire, these so-called *ince saz* groups included instruments such as *kanun, ney,*

---

82 Uyar 2016: 109ff. Comparable jazz groups including traditional instruments may be found in Greece, for example with the ney player, Harris Lamprakis or the Sokratis Sinopoulos Quartett (including *lyra=kemençe*), piano, double bass, drums), CD Sokratis Sinopoulos Quartet: *Eight Winds*, ECM, 2015.

83 http://evrimdemirel.com/Atrium.mp3.

ud, tanbur or violin (*keman*), and rarely *lavta, kemençe, santur, def* or *kudüm*. Similar ensembles are recorded on the first 78rpm records until the 1920s and 1930s, accompanying famous singers such as Hafız Kemal, *Hafız Burhan* or *Münir Nurettin Selçuk*. Complete *fasıl*s were performed within associations such as the *Şark Musiki Cemiyeti* (from 1918 onwards*), Üsküdar Mûsikî Cemiyeti* (existing in some form from 1915, officially founded in 1923), or the *Dârü't Tâlîm-i Mûsikî* (1912-31 and 1934-39); and in addition by a small ensemble of the president of the Republic (*Riyâset-i Cumhûr İnce Saz Hey'eti*) in the later 1920s and 30s, or at private amateur gatherings as late as the 1940s (Feldman 1996: 76).

As far as we know it was Ali Rifat Çağatay who, in 1920, for the first time set up choral performances of Turkish art songs (Aksoy 2008b: 196). Further early choral recordings were made by the *Dârü't Tâlîm-i Mûsikî Heyeti* and the *Riyaseti Cumhur İncesaz Heyeti* before 1925. Similarly in the 1920s first attempts were made with the conductor standing upright before the ensemble, rather than being an integrated member of it. Early conductors such as *Ismail Hakkı* obviously stood with their back to the musicians, hence facing the audience, similar to the practice in Europe during the nineteenth century.

> (...)"Muallim" İsmail Hakkı Bey was a significant influence in the realm of concert convention. He was not only the first music director to expand the number of choristers in a fasıl ensemble, he was also the first to insist that each performer wear the same attire. For example, a picture reproduced in the journal *Şehbal* (1913) shows the entire cadre of *Mûsikî-i Osmanî* dressed in formal dress. Hakkı Bey as director is seated prominently in the center of the troupe. Further, Hakkı Bey required his singers to stand (rather than sit) during a performance. Here, he organized the musicians into a semicircle, at first directing the ensemble with a def and later conducting the ensemble with a baton. In contrast to traditional practice, he required all musicians to read music during a concert performance. (O'Connell 2017: 264)

The significant rise of choirs began at Radio Ankara, where Mesut Cemil (1902-1969) in 1939 founded the "Unisono Men's Choir for Historical Turkish Music" (*Tarihî Türk Musikisi Ünison Erkek Korosu*). In addition, during the 1940s and 50s a lighter *fasıl* style was performed regularly at Radio Ankara with a smaller instrumental ensemble group of soloists instead of a choir (Aksoy 2008b: 198). Shortly after, the singer Münir Nurettin Selçuk, and the still youthful Nevzat Atlığ (b. 1925), also began to conduct choirs for Turkish art songs (Özkahraman 2010). Particularly during these early years, most instrumental ensembles still did not differ much from former *ince saz* ensembles. From 1940 until 1950, however, the size of the *icra heyeti* ensemble of the Conservatory Istanbul increased, and by 1950 it included (at least for some concerts) four violins (one partly also *sinekeman*), three *tanbur, two ney*, one of each *santur, kemençe, kanun, ud*, and eight singers (Greve 1995: 255). Eventually it also adapted the choral performance practice. In 1951, Mesut Cemil moved to Istanbul, where he founded the *Küçük Koro* ("Small Choir"). After Mesut Cemil's death in 1963, Nevzat Atlığs followed him as director of this choir until 1975, and while in Ankara, Ruşen Ferid Kam also became director of similar choirs. The ultimate establishment of the choral style occurred in 1975 with the foundation of the State Choir for Classical Turkish Music with Nevzat Atlığ as its director. In the same year, the State Conservatory for Turkish Music Istanbul was founded, again directed by Nevzat Atlığ.[84] Graduates of this conservatory later founded further conservatories in Anatolia (e.g. Ankara, Izmir Bursa, Samsun, Elazığ, Diyarbakır), or worked at similar choirs at the state radio in Ankara, Istanbul, Izmir and Erzurun (Emnalar 1992: 159ff). During the 1980s and 1990s choral performance practice became mainstream for Ottoman-Turkish art music, and even in Turkish communities in Europe many amateur choirs were founded for this now so-called "Classical Turkish Music" (*Klasik Türk Müziği*). Today the leading ensemble is the Classical Choir of the President of the Republic (*Cumhurbaşkanlığı Klasik Türk Müziği Korosu*) directed by Fatih Salgar. The choirs were accompanied by growing ensembles, and from the 1970s on by larger ensembles and orchestras, where in addition to Ottoman instruments such as *kanun*, *kemençe*, *ud*, *tanbur* und *ney*, European string instruments dominated. The exact size, composition and even arrangement of the ensembles and choirs differed widely.[85] Ensembles at popular *gazino*s in general preferred instruments such as violin, *ud* and *kanun*, while elite Ottoman-Turkish instruments such as *tanbur*, *ney* or *kemençe* were rarely used. The exact composition varied between different gazinos, for example in the *Caddebostan gazino* there were several violins, a clarinet, *ney*, one or two *ud*s, one or two bowed *tanbur* (*yaylı tanbur*), a *kanun*, a *darbuka*, a *tef*, a *bendir*, three female and two male vocalists (Beken 1998: 98).

In the orchestra style melodies remained monophone, while a strict and well-trained unisono replaced the traditional heterophony. The former almost additive combination of individual musicians turned to carefully arranged and rehearsed ensembles, whose musical interpretation of compositions mainly depended on the conductor. Mesut Cemil's choir still made little use of dynamics and agogics.[86] Beats on the *kudüm* enforced his interpretation, only the ends of

84 The main actors in this phase were Yılmaz Öztuna, Nevzat Atlığ and Ercüment Berker. In particular Öztuna, at that time member of the governing *Adalet Partisi* (under prime minister Süleyman Demirel) and advisor at the Ministry of Culture, prepared the political ground (Akdoğu 1990: 21ff). Even the series *Türk Musikisi Klasikleri* was revived in this period, while the directors of the editing committee were Atlığ and Öztuna.

85 Greve 1995: 162ff. In Mehmet Ihsan Özer's interviews in 1988, several well-known choir directors of the time explained their ideal size of choir: Nevyat Atlığ – 20-25 each of men and women; Ruhi Ayangıl – according to the piece to be performed: for Marâghî oder Itri, 80-100; for III Selim or Hacı Arif Bey, 25-30, chamber choir, 3-20, large choir, beginning with 20; Teoman Önaldi – at least 40; Rıza Rit – 40-60; Bekir Sıdkı Sezgin – ideal 7 each of men and women, in total not more than 20; Necdet Varol – from 9 singers on, ideal 16 (Özer 1988: 68ff).

86 Columbia RT 17 462; CD *Yurttan Sesler. Yeni Türkiye'nin Ezgileri*, Yapı ve Kredi Kültür Yayıncılık, 1998; *Fethi Kopuz*, son of *Fahri Kopuz*, a leading member of the *Dârü't Tâlîm-i Mûsikî* reports that this ensemble already employed dynamics and agogik (Say 1985: 743).

musical phrases were slightly emphasized by ritardandi, though much less than by the large orchestras beginning in the 1980s. Later conductors more and more carefully worked out melodic lines, and for the first time in Turkish music dynamics and agogics became important means of expression, in particular aiming to elucidate the form, e.g. by terraced dynamics at repetitions or broad ritardandi before cadences. The sound of the orchestras with their string instruments and the complete abandonment of any realisation of the *usûl* rendered them not dissimilar to a Western symphony orchestra. *Kemençe*s melt in the general string timbre and plucked instruments such as *ud* or *tanbur* are at best audible in occasional chords; also the *ney*s are less present in the general sound. Embellishments typical for particular instruments, such as trills on *ney*, figuration on *tanbur or ud*, or arpeggios on *kanun*, are hardly played in this style. During concerts, in between choral performances some art songs might also be sung solo, also variations from choral to solo within songs are common arrangements. Only a few soloists of this style, however, became successful in the CD market, including for example Münir Utandı (b. 1952).

Similarly, the repertoire and the concert programs changed. Until the middle of the twentieth century all compositions of a *fasıl* began and ended in the same *makam*, later folk songs would also enter the repertoire.

> A concert by Hakkı Bey in Istanbul is remarkably similar to a concert by Fersan and Selçuk in Ankara. Presented in the *Union Française* on Friday, 23 January (1925), the concert by Hakkı Bey with the *Şark Musiki[si] Şubesi* (of the *Dârü'l Elhân*) is divided into five sections. In the first, 3 *fasıl*-s in the makam-s *Mâhur*, *Kurdî* and *Eviç* are detailed. While the first and third fasıl were traditional in terms of modal integrity and metric organization, the second features a number of folk songs performed by a female soloist. In the second section, Hakkı Bey directed a medley of folksongs, 7 *türkü*-s framed by an opening *medhal* and a closing dance (called "*zeybek havası*"). In the third section, a fourth *fasıl* in the makam *Rûhnevâz* featured contemporary compositions. With the exception of a fantezi in the makam Suznâk by H. Sadettin Arel (1880-1955), the medley was composed by Öztoprak and consisted of 2 *şarkı*-s and 2 *longa*-s. A *küşad* and a *zeybek* were also included (O'Connell 2017: 265).

During the 1950s (beginning with Mesut Cemil) modulations (*geçiş taksim*) became common, later even into totally unrelated *makams* (Feldman 1990/91: 76). Commercial *fasıl* of the 1960s included *sirto* and *longa* dance tunes (instead of *saz semaisi*), later also *ayın* (hymns) of the *Mevlevi* tradition might be played in concerts, detached from all ritual or religious context. Still, the form of *fasıl* remains feasible, e.g. in the sequence *peşrev* – several *şarkı* – *türkü*, several dance tunes (e.g. *longa*). The most frequently performed art songs derive from the Ottoman secular tradition, in addition compositions from the Mevlevi and other Sufi orders or popular *şarkı* of the nineteenth and early twentieth century might be sung. The exact concert planning of course differs between choirs.

Parallel to the ban on Ottoman art music, and the later rise of choirs and orchestras, the tradition of smaller chamber ensembles for Turkish art music continued in particular at Radio Ankara. In addition to Mesut Cemil's choir a *fasıl* ensemble of Şerif İçli or Fahri Kopuz, musicians such as Mesut Cemil, Ruşen Kam, Vecihe Daryal, Cevdet Kozanoğlu and many others performed Ottoman-Turkish instrumental music in duos, trios or quartets (Aksoy 2008: 193ff).

> In the early 1950s, one particular programme of Istanbul Radio played a crucial role in re-enabling an appreciation of the *ney* sound by wider audiences. This was the weekly "Instrumental Pieces on the *Ney*" *(Neylerle Saz Eserleri)* programmed by neyzen Süleyman Erguner (1902-53) accompanied by his son, Ulvi Erguner and neyzen Niyazi Sayın. (Senay 2014:415)

Traditional Ottoman-Turkish art music continued throughout the 1960s, mainly due to Ulvi Erguner and later singers such as Rıza Rıt (1925-2016), Bekir Sıdkı Sezgin (1936-1996) or Alaaddin Yavaşça (b. 1927). From 1953 until 1991 the *Mevlana* festival in Konya was the main event for music of the *mevlevi* tradition. Every year in December, the best musicians traveled to Konya to perform on the anniversary of Mevlana's death, the *Şeb-i Aruz,* in small ensembles, music of the *Mevlevi* tradition in a style similar to that of the late Ottoman Empire. The musical directors were Halil Can and Sadettin Heper, who had been educated by the last *Mevlevi* of the late Ottoman Empire. However, even here the size of the ensembles grew over time. From 1967 on the *tanbur* was introduced and from the 1970s, the cello.

Since the 1970s, in particular in Istanbul, several ensembles performed especially ambitious art music, among their members were all the main instrumentalists of their time, including Ihsan Özgen (*kemence*), Necdet Yaşar (*tanbur*), Hurşit Ungay (*kudüm*), Niyazi Sayın (*ney*), Nezih Üzel (*kudüm, bendir*), the *Erguner* brothers (*ney*), Hasan Esen (*kemence*), Abdi Coşkun (*tanbur*), Fahrettin Çimenli (*yaylı tanbur*), Çinucen Tanrıkorur (*ud*) and others. Here, individual musicians remained free in their interpretations and embellishments (of course within the framework of tradition). In this sphere during the 1970s at Radio Istanbul the practice of *beraber taksim* emerged, an interactive form of the traditionally solo improvised introduction to a *makam*, developed by instrumentalists such as Niyazi Sayın, Ihsan Özgen and Necdet Yaşar. Later other musicians adapted the form, in particular the Bosphorus Ensemble of Ihsan Özgen in the late 1980s.[87] At the turn of the twenty-first century, traditionalist performing groups such as *Lalezar* and *Bezmara* recorded serious Ottoman courtly repertoire; respected ensemble and chorus leaders include Ruhi Ayangil, Ahmet Kadri Rızeli, Murat Salim Tokaç and Fikret Karakaya.

Since the 1980s and in particular the 1990s, several new ensembles have released CDs of instrumental Ottoman-Turkish art music: the Nezih Üzel Ensemble, later the *Emirgan* Ensemble, the Duo *Ahenk* with *tanbur* and *kemençe* (Murat Aydemir and Derya Türkan), *Nevâ* with *tanbur* and *ney* (Murat Aydemir and Salih Bilgin)

---

87 Frederic Stubbs 1994: 246; Feldman 1989.

and several (more popular) CDs by Burhan Öçal (with Arif Erdebil or the "Istanbul Oriental Ensemble").[88] At the end of the 1990s the ensemble *Istanbul Sazendeleri* ("Istanbul Instrumentalists") was founded, again specializing in Ottoman instrumental music. The most prominent musicians were Göksel Baktagir and Yurdal Tokcan.[89] Later at Labyrith workshops in Crete the ensemble *Seyir* was augmented with internationals, with the participation of Ross Daily and others. The concept of the *ud* player Mehmet Bitmez and his ensemble, *Istanbul Sazkâr Toplulugu* ("Istanbul Instrumentalist Ensemble") was similar (CD, AK Müzik 2010). The Derya Türkan Trio included double bass (Renaud Garcia-Fons), cello (Uğur Işık) and *kemençe*.[90] Recently, several new types of large ensembles for Turkish art music have been formed for individual and often short-lived projects; for example:

- *3Dem*, ensemble founded in 2004 with three *ud* (Bekir Şahin Baloğlu, Bilen Işıktaş and Sami Dural; CD *Geç*, Seyhan 2013).
- *Mizrabin Nefesi* ("Breath of the Plectrum") with three *tanburs*, three *neys*, percussion and two *hafiz*,' predominantly instrumental music and *ilâhi* (CD, Kalan, 2007).
- *Kırk Ney Bir Nefes* ("40 *Neys*, one Breath"), concert program from 2009 on, with 40 *ney* players organized by Aziz Şenol Filiz.[91]
- *Sekiz Tanbur* ("Eight *Tanburs*"), concert program at *Sepetçiler Kasrı* Istanbul on September 29, 2010 (Birol Yayla, Murat Aydemir, Fahrettin Yarkin – percussion – and others).
- *5 Ney 1 Kemençe* directed by Ahmet Kadri Rızeli (CD, Pera 2010).
- *Tellerin Niyâzi*, concert program on October 17, 2011 at Cemal Reşit Rey concert hall, Istanbul by Ihsan Özer's *Kanun* Ensemble, with ten *kanuns*, percussion and voice.
- *Ayangil Acapella Korosu*, directed by Ruhi Ayangil, first public concert on April 8, 2015 in Istanbul.

Similar to the development of Ottoman-Turkish art music, Radio Ankara also became the starting point for choral interpretations of Turkish folk music. Before the 1940s Turkish folk music used to be either soloistic or performed by two or very few musicians. Only some urban Anatolian traditions, in places such as Izmir, Urfa or Elazığ, developed ensembles with more instruments.[92]

88 CD Emirgan Ensemble: *Klasik Osmanlı Müziği*, Kalan 1995;CD *Ahenk. Turkish Classical Music*. Kalan 1998; CD *Ahenk 2*. Golden Horn 2006 (Kalan, n.Y.); CD Bilgin & Aydemir: *Nevâ*, Golden Horn 2004.

89 E.g. CD Istanbul Sazendeleri: *Sazende Faslı 1*, KAF 2008.

90 CD *Ministrel's Era*, Kalan 2006; the following project was CD Renaud García & Derya Türkan: *Silk Moon*, M&MT 2014

91 *Ney* players included Arif Erdebil, Ender Dogan, Salih Bilgin, Aziz Şenol Filiz, Ahmet Kaya, Ömer Erdoğdular, Sadrettin Özçimi, Ahmet Kaya, Volkan Yılmaz, Fikret Bertuğ, Ümit Gürelman, Murat Salim Tokac, Burcu Karadağ and others.

92 Sungurluoğlu 1968; Abacı 2000; Akbıyık 2006.

> For example, in Laurence Picken's survey of Anatolian ensemble formations, based primarily on Halil Bediî Yönetken's Folklore Archive collecting trips conducted from 1937 to 1952, with few exceptions regional ensembles contained no more than two different instrument types. (Bates 2008: 41)

From the 1940s, Radio Ankara broadcast the program "We learn a folk song" (*Bir Halk Türküsü Öğreniyoruz*) twice a week for half an hour each time. Under the direction of Muzaffer Sarısözen a choir called "Voices of the Homeland" (*Yurdun sesler*) sang folk songs from all over Anatolia accompanied by a small *bağlama* ensemble (usually four *divan sazı*, seven *bağlama*, one *cura*; Stokes 1992: 70f)). Successors to this choir were founded in several Turkish cities, in 1953 at Radio Izmir (director Mustafa Hoşsu) and in 1954 at Radio Istanbul (director Ahmet Yamacı). In 1950, Sadi Yaver Ataman founded another "Vocal and Instrumental Union for Melodies of the Home Country" *(Memleket Havaları Ses ve Saz Birliği)* at Radio Istanbul (Şenel 1995; Koç 2016a). During the 1960s and 70s at Radio Istanbul Neriman and Nida Tüfekçi were particularly important as directors of choirs, soloists and teachers, and from 1976 they were also at the new State Conservatory for Turkish Music at the Technical University Istanbul (Tüfekçi & Tüfekçi 1964). The musical basis of the folk music choirs were notations of earlier official folk music collections. Just as in Turkish art music, in Turkish folk music the size of the choirs and ensembles grew over time, including a greater number of *bağlama*s and later also *baglama*s in different sizes (*cura*, *bağlama*, *divan sazı*), in addition to instruments such as *kaval* (flutes), *zurna* and *mey* (both double reed instruments), bowed *kabak kemane*, sometimes even the Azerbaijan long-necked lute *tar*, frame drums (*def*, *mazhar*) or the goblet drum *darbuka*.[93] In folk music, however, the role of solo singers remained stronger than in art music, even at TRT. Already at Radio Ankara during the 1940s a number of folk singers performed as "local artists" *(mahalli sanatçı)*, including Osman Pehlivan (1847-1942), Hisarlı Ahmet (1908-1984), Muharrem Ertaş (1913-1984) and Sadi Yaver Ataman (1906-1994; Şenel 1995).[94] In the 1950s, Ruhi Su performed folk songs in an aesthetic protest to the TRT, sung by one single Western-trained voice and accompanied by one plain *bağlama*. In 1971, however, even Ruhi Su founded the *Dostlar Korosu* ("Choir of Friends"). By this time, most private music schools (*dershane*) which offered folk music had began to adopt *saz orkestra*s and folk music choirs based on the notations of TRT. The composition of Erdal Erzincan's recent Saz-Orchester includes four first *şelpe*; four second *şelpe*; three third *şelpe*; two first plucked *bağlama*; four second plucked *bağlama*; two *divan bağlama*; one cura *bağlama*; and one *bass bağlama*.[95] In 2000, a monumental con-

---

93 Stokes 1992. The fiddle *kemençe* of the Black Sea Coast rarely occurs within TRT ensembles (Stokes 1993: 27-45).

94 Many singers and instrumentalists of this ensemble later became well-known stars of Turkish folk music: Neriman Altındağ, Muzaffer Akgün, Sarı Recep, from 1953 on Nida Tüfekçi (1926-1993), from 1960 on Cemil Demirsipahlı (b. 1933) Elçi 1997; Yılmaz 1996.

95 Erdal Erzincan: *Bağlama Orkestrası*, Kalan 2013

cert organised by the European Federation of Alevi Associations in Cologne, entitled *Bin Yılın Türküsü* – Saga of the Millenium brought together 1246 *bağlama* players from all over Europe, and the Cologne Symphony Orkestra conducted by Betin Günes.

While public radio and television TRT continued to broadcast folk music with choirs or soloists accompanied by small folk music orchestras, since the 1960s the commercial MC (later CD) market preferred completely different ensembles. Initially audio cassettes presented local singers and styles as they had continued to be performed locally, while later professional music production increasingly rearranged music for a growing commercial market. In the 1980s the folk music group *Muhabbet* reduced the large TRT ensembles and choirs to three or four *bağlamas* and singers. The group was perceived as a combination of well-known soloists, rather than as an ensemble or orchestra of almost anonymous musicians such as at TRT. In the 1980s and 90s *bağlama* players and singers such as Mahsuni Şerif, Arif Sağ, Muhlis Akarsu, Ali Eber Çiçek and Musa Eroğlu became stars, as did female singers including Belkis Akkale, Sabahhat Akkıraz and Nuray Hafiftaş. During the 1990s a standard for studio production of folk music developed, which partly endures until today. The main instrument is a *bağlama*, which accompanies the melody in the background of the sung parts, and, much more audibly adds short instrumental passages between the vocal phrases. The background is provided by keyboard, rhythm and bass (which also roughly follows the melody); introductions are sometimes played on *kaval* or *mey*. Rhythmic acompaniment is provided either by electronic drums or Turkish percussion instruments, such as *bendir*, *asma davul*, *erbane* or others. Similar to the use at TRT the *zurna* has been separated from its traditional duo combination with *davul* and used as a solo instrument, often featuring before the whole ensemble (including strong percussion) plays towards the end of lively songs. *Uzun hava* songs are in general accompanied by a drone, often played by several instruments together. Elements of local styles still continue: *karadeniz* music arrangements for instance include local instruments from the Black Sea Coast such as *kemençe*, *tulum*, *garmon*; for central and eastern Anatolian music *ney*, *zurna* and *kaval* are preferred. Even Ottoman-Turkish art instruments (*klasik kemençe*, *kanun*, *yaylı tanbur*), Western classical instruments (clarinet, violin, flute), and contemporary Western electric /electronic instruments (keyboards, electric guitar) have entered folk music arrangements (Bates 2008: 191). In popular productions the influence of *arabesk* has also became audible, for example in high voices or by the acompaniment of string ensemble (or imitations of them on keyboard), which perform the musical function of the *bağlama*.

With the unexpected success of the group *Muhabbet* in the 1980s, and the rise of a Turkish youth culture in the 1990s, folk music became an important part of popular music, which opened a new market for studio musicians, and for live singers in *türkü bars*. In live performances of the 1990s, some singers used to accompany themselves on a *bağlama* and pre-programed keyboard simultaneously.

Similarly, in *Türkü Bars*, the accompaniment of folk songs with the combination of *bağlama* and guitar (sometimes enhanced by violin, clarinet, *kaval*, percussion or keyboard) became a common practice. Several notation editions offer easily accessible material similar to (and often mixed with) Turkish art music arranged for instruments such as piano or guitar.

One example of an extraordinarily expensive production of commercial folk music might be the CD *Boyut* by the female folk singer Zara (Ulus Müzik, 2000). The arrangements include numerous instruments such as *tar*, *garmon*, classic *kemençe*, Black Sea *kemençe*, viola, cello, piano, *ney*, oboe, *kaval*, *mey*, *balaban*, several *bağlama*s, trumpet, trombone and others. In addition to the CD a DVD was attached with video clips of the songs recorded in various regions of Anatolia. The unique approach of the group *Kardeş Türküler*, with a great number of Anatolian instruments including strong percussion and several singers (not to forget the large dance ensembles during the group's concerts) has already been mentioned (Bates 2008: 56, 68). On the CD *Çocuk Haklı* (Kalan 2011) *Kardeş Türküler* used the following instruments: *ud*, *kamançe*, *kemençe*, violin, viola, cello, *bağlama*, *kopuz*, *divan bağlama*, *bas bağlama*, *cura*, *tar*, *lavta*, banjo, bass guitar, *panduri*, electric guitar, e-bow, *kaval*, *zurna*, *duduk*, *tulum*, clarinet, saxophone, trumpet, accordion, harp, *darbuka*, *bendir*, *tef*, *asma davul*, *udu*, *kanjira*, talking drum, and *hollo*. During the 1990s (influenced by political music groups since the 1960s), the group used harmonic accompaniment either by Western functional harmony (provided by a guitar or vocals), or by riffs, that is, repeated ostinati as accompaniment for melodic or rhythmic solos (Akkaya et.al. 2008: 120) (see figure 16).

Another important factor affecting the performance practice of Turkish folk music was the development of sophisticated playing and timbre techniques in particular for the contemporary *bağlama* as described before. The album *Ah Istanbul* by the *bağlama* player and singer Cengiz Özkan (b. 1967) for example presents popular but aesthetically ambitious folk songs covering a wide repertoire (CD Kalan, 1997). Each song is arranged carefully in its regional style, e.g. Arguvan (on a single *bağlama*), Rumeli-Üsküp (together with the accordionist Muammer Ketençoğlu, in addition to *davul* and *zurna*), Gaziantep (*kanun*, violin, *ud*, percussion and vocals), Kırşehir (*bağlama* and *kaval*), Rize (*tulum*, *kemençe*, percussion), İstanbul (together with *tanbur*, *kaval* and Erkan Oğur on fretless gitar). Comparable in their elite musical approach are, for example, Erdal Erzincan, Erol Parlak, Okan Murat Öztürk and others. Since the 1990s the duo of Erkan Oğur & Ismail Hakki Demircioğlu[96] performs folk songs on *kopuz* and *divan sazı*, sung by two voices. Similarly trios and larger chamber ensembles for several *bağlama* ensembles developed as a kind of chamber folk music. The most well-known groups are Erol Parlak's *bağlama* quintet, the *bağlama* trio *Bengi* of Okan Murat Öztürk and the trio of Adnan Koç, Cihangir Terzi and Deniz Güneş.

96 E.g. CD *Gülün Kokusu vardi*, Kalan 1998; Beşik, Kalan 2000.

SîYA ŞAPERAN

Figure 16: *Sîya Şaperan* from the album *Kardeş Türküler: Hemawas*, (CD Kalan 2002; Akkaya et al 2008: 119)

As part of the deep changes in traditional ensembles, all styles of traditional Turkish (art and folk) music have moved towards each other. In Turkey it is a much debated issue whether folk and art music need to be seen as one single or two different traditions, in particular the issue of potentially common roots has been debated over decades (see Chapter III). Although folk and art music obviously share many common elements, ranging from the simple fact that both are primarily monophonic, modal vocal music, in most cases even an unexperienced listener will immediately understand if a given piece of music is Anatolian folk music or Ottoman-Turkish art music. On the other hand, numerous urban Anatolian music styles, in the Aegean region as well as in Eastern Anatolia (Urfa,

Elazığ, Diyarbakır) share instruments, forms and musical structures with Ottoman-Turkish art music as practiced in Istanbul, hence they resist a notion of different music worlds. Over the last two or three decades the use of Turkish art music instruments in contemporary Anatolian music has become more common, and in parallel, folk songs have become part of today's Turkish art music repertoire. Even *taksim* and *açış* (of folk music) have grown together substantially. Several small ensembles or individual musicians combine both art and folk music; to mention just three examples:

- Erdal Akkaya (*bağlama*) and Ara Dinkjian (*ud*), concert program in Aya Ireni in 2009;
- Coşkun Karademir (*bağlama*) and Özer Özel (*yaylı tanbur*): *Seslerin Camî* in 2016.
- *Dem Trio* with Okan Murat Öztürk (*bağama*), Murat Salim Tokaç (*tanbur*, *ney*), and Cenk Güray (*bağlama*), later with Derya Türkan (*kemençe*).

A conclusion of this short sketch of changing and newly founded ensembles for traditional Turkish music links to the discussion of the development of musical instruments in the previous part: today, just as with musical instruments, also ensembles exist with an unprecedented diversity. No remaining standard of performance practice stabilizes musical life; rather almost every concert and every CD presents a new type of ensemble, composed of improved, changed, newly adapted, or (originally) non-Turkish instruments.

Taking together the three general aspects which have been described so far, that is 1) the improvement of instruments and their playing techniques; 2) the introduction of Western tonality and harmonic accompaniment; and 3) the emergence of numerous new forms of ensembles for traditional music; all of these have led to an almost infinite variety of musical performance, questioning all existing notions of separate musical traditions.

Melting Traditions

In particular since the 1990s–but partly even before–arrangements, music projects, compositions and ensembles blend musical elements of different traditions to a degree that it becomes impossible to categorize them according to established musical traditions. It is for this non-homogenous and individualized field of disintegration of musical traditions that I initially proposed the term "post-traditional" music, as explained in the introduction. Musicians such as Erkan Oğur, Derya Türkan, Murat Aydemir, Uğur Işık (but also a great number of still less famous musicians) repeatedly form new ensembles, new combinations of sounds and repertoire, mostly for one concert or a single CD. At this point any attempt at a comprehensive narrative tends to end and pass over to unconnected individual examples. I will only shortly describe some few of these individual approaches, ignoring many others in order not to distract from my main argument, that is, that individual musical projects today more and more replace coherent musical traditions. Only exceptionally do these individual musical projects share common elements; in most cases they might be described as individual combinations of elements of diverse musical traditions.

Already in the 1940s, Hüseyin Sadeddin Arel had developed a new concept of Turkish chamber music based on a Western model. He composed numerous pieces in *makam* for duo, trio, quartet and small chamber ensembles composed of Ottoman-Turkish instruments, for example for *kemençe* quartets. In 1977, Timur Selçuk (b. 1945), son of the celebrated singer Münir Nurettin Selçuk and known mainly for his political songs, founded the Istanbul Chamber Orchestra (*Istanbul Oda Orkestrası*) for harmonized versions of Turkish art songs, including those of his father.[97] In 2010 at the Cemal Reşit Rey Concert Hall, Istanbul, the program, *Muniristanbu,l* presented songs of Münir Nurettin Selçuk played by an ensemble of about 100 musicians consisting of a symphony orchestra, a choir for Turkish music and Turkish musical instruments in addition to five soloists, conducted by Timur Selçuk. Similarly Cihat Aşkın has arranged over the last 20 years both art and folk songs for orchestra and violin or for smaller ensembles. A completely different and unique approach involving the polyphonization of Turkish art music was developed by Kudsi Ergüner on his CD *Sufyan* (Equinox 2011). The piece *Vals*, in fact a *taksim*, is played by two *neys* and accompanied by drone chord held by several further *neys*. *Fuga* (on the same album) is a study in counterpoint with fugato-like beginnings in three *ney* parts, alternating with solos, again over drones. Also the late Ihsan Özgen wrote several polyphonic compositions, in particular for his daughters Neva Özgen (*kemençe*) and Yelda Özgen (cello), for example *Uzak* for *kemençe* and cello (2003) (Reigle & Whitehead 2008).

The first attempts at polyphonic arrangements within folk music were conducted in the late 1970s, for example by Arif Sağ. Since 1979, Adil Arslan in Berlin collaborated with the guitarist and composer Carlo Domeniconi, in 1986 Arslan released the album *Batı-Doğu Divanı* which included alevi *semah*s arranged for *bağlama* and chamber orchestra, composed of flute, English horn, *bağlama,* guitar, percussion, two violins, viola, cello and double bass (CD Tempo, 1986). From 1990 the Berlin-based *bağlama* player Sıddık Doğan wrote comparable accompaniments for the orchestra or string quartet of the municipal music school, where he was teaching. Similarly other Turkish musicians cooperated with non-Turkish musicians, e.g.:

- The albums of the Germany-based Kurdish musician Nizamettin Arıç (b. 1956), in particular "*Kurdish Ballads 1-2*" (2001, 2002) and "*Dayê*" (1987) display a mix of several eastern Anatolian instruments including *mey*, *zurna*, *kaval*, *cura*, *tambur*, *erbane*, often arranged pholyphonically, even with sound collages.[98]

---

97 A recent recording is the CD, *Babamın Şarkıları*, Balet Plak, 2004; cf Stokes 2010:173ff.

98 CD *Images, Dreams / Wêneyên Xewnan*, Teyra n.d.; reedited Ses, 1993; Şen 2016.

- Nilüfer Akbal: *Ray'e / Road / Yol*, Ada 2002, including flamenco guitar, keyboard, *tabla*, Turkish and latin percussion, trumpet, saxophone, strings, *bansuri* (Indian flute), *ney*, *kabak kemane*, *kanun*, *bağlama*, and accordion. Most musicians are Germans, some are Turks and it was recorded in Hamburg.
- *Trio Mara*, with the Vienna-based Kurdish singer Sakîna, Nurê Dilovanî (violin), and Nazê Îşhan (piano), CD *Derî / Behind the Doors*, Ahenk Müzik, 2013.
- Taner Akyol Trio, with the Berlin-based *bağlama* player and composer Taner Akyol, pianist Antonis Anissegos and percussion player Sebastian Flaig.

There are also several projects without any non-Turkish participation, as for example the *Anadolu* Quartet, a string quartet which plays Anatolian folk songs arranged by violinist Ahmet Tirgil (b. 1982).[99]

In 1990, the group *Yansımalar* ("Reflections") was founded by two well-known musicians of traditional Turkish art music, Şenol Filiz (*ney*) and Birol Yayla (*tanbur*, guitar). In addition percussion and double bass are used, and for concerts and on CDs occasionally other instruments feature, such as cello, *kanun*, or *yaylı tanbur*. The group has released eight albums, and made music for several Turkish movies. In April 2011 *Yansımalar* gave a concert with the Istanbul Opera Orchestra, with arrangements written by the conductor, Serdar Yalçın.

Similarly *Incesaz* was founded in 1997 by Murat Aydemir (*tanbur*), Derya Türkan (*kemençe*) and Cengiz Onural (guitar), a former member of the popular music group *Yeni Türkü*. To date *Incesaz* has released eight albums including a variety of different musical concepts and has cooperated with several guest musicians, such as the Turkish art music singer Melihat Gülses (CD *Iki. Eylül Şarkıları*, Kalan, 2002), Cengiz Özkan (CD *Elif*, Kalan, 2007) Sezen Aksu, Zuhal Olçay, Cengiz Özkan, Cihat Aşkın, Leman Sam, Münip Utandı, Aşkın Nur Yengi and Muammer Ketençoğlu. The third album (*Istanbul'a*, Kalan 2004) focused on instrumental music, including a string quartet; the fourth one (*Mazi Kalbimde*, Kalan, 2005) on Turkish tangos of the 1930s-50s. For the 75th anniversary of Turkish Airlines *Incesaz* released the CD *Yollar* ("Ways"), together with the Hungarian Symphony Orchestra, composed by Cengiz Onural and orchestrated by Oğuzhan Balcı and Cengiz Onural.

A number of individual musicians could be mentioned here, just to give some few examples:

- Sema (b. 1956) is an Istanbul based singer who has realized numerous music projects, including Turkish tangos and songs of the early 20th centry; *ilahi*s arranged for a harpsichord, piano, electronics, *ney*, bass and drums; the musical theater *Ashura* together with the *5. Sokak Tiyatrosu* (direction: Mustafa Avkiran, Övül Avkiran), in Armenian, Hebrew, Turkish, Arabic and other languages.[100]

99 www.anadoluquartet.com/kayitlar

100 http://semamoritz.com.

- Saadet Türköz (b. 1961 in Istanbul, of Kazakh origin) is a singer of free improvisation, based in Zurich. Türköz has performed traditional Kazakh and Turkish songs (both folk and art) as well as avant-garde music, mostly together with free improvising jazz musicians, including Elliott Sharp (guitar), Joelle Léandre (cello), or Werner Luedi (saxophone). Her versions of traditional songs are completely alienated by experimental voice techniques.[101]
- Microtonal Guitar Duo with Sinan Cem Eroğlu (fretless guitar) and Tolgahan Çoğulu (microtonal guitar); in some concerts enlarged by Erdem Şimşek (bağlama). The repertoire consists of all kinds of Anatolian music ranging from Aşık Veysel to Kurdish and Georgian folk songs to the song *kele kele* by the Armenian composer and musicologist Vartabed Gomitas. In all arrangements the guitar almost inevitably adds Western polyphony to the traditional (or newly composed) melodies. There are even some compositions originally written for piano that are part of the repertoire, for example pieces by Eric Satie and Frédéric Chopin of the twentieth and nineteenth centuries respectively, or the jazz ballad "Our Spanish Love Song" by the jazz bassist Charlie Haden.[102]

Several music projects have arranged Western classical compositions for Turkish instruments, including several times, for example (just as the Microtonal Guitar Duo), Eric Satie's piano pieces *Gymnopedies* and *Gnossiennes*:

- Sertab Erener (*Sarı Beni*, 1999);
- Sarband (CD *Danse Gothique*, Jaro 2000);
- Tahir Aydogdu (*kanun*), Bilgin Canaz (*ney*) and Hakan A. Toker (piano, accordion) (CD "Touches", Kaf, 2008);
- Uğur Işık (CD, *Cello Invocations*, Kalan 2008);
- Erkan Oğur for fretless guitar and piano for the filk *Mommo* (2009); and for fretless guitar and vocals (CD *Dönmez Yolu*, Kalan, 2012).[103]

Some other examples for a comparable approach include the Erol Parlack Quintet performance of the famous, "Rondo alla Turca" from Mozart's Piano Sonata No. 11 in A major (KV 331), the "Rachmaninov Anatolian Project" with piano (Güldiyar Tanrıdağlı), *duduk* (Ertan Tekin), and fretless guitar/*yaylı tanbur* (Cenk Erdoğan);[104] further arrangements by Engin Düzyol (Tchaikovsky's Swan Lake for Turkish art ensemble) or Ahmet Baran (Nocturne C sharp Minor by Chopin

---

[101] Saadet Türköz: *Kara Toprak* (Amori, 1994); Saadet Türköz: *Marmara See* (Intact, 1999). Saadet Türköz: *Urumchi*, Intact record 2005 (traditional Kazakh music); *Urumchi Nar(r)*, Leo Records 2012. www.saadet.ch/index-flash.html.

[102] CD *Atlas*, 2012 Kalan; CD with Sinan Cem Eroğlu: *Microtonal Gitar Duo*, Kalan 2015

[103] CD Sarband: *Danse Gothique*, Jaro 2000; CD Tahir Aydogdu, Bilgin Canaz & Hakan A. Toker: *Touches*, Kaf, 2008; CD Uğur Işık: *Cello Invocations*, Kalan 2008; CD Erkan Oğur: *Dönmez Yolu*, Kalan, 2012; CD Sertab Erener: *Sertab Erener*, Sony 1999.

[104] CD *Rachmaninov Anatolian Project*, Kalan 2015

on *kanun*) or Gürol Ağırbaş.[105] The Berlin-based musician Nevzay Akpınar composed a fictional Baroque composition for *bağlama* entitled *A la baroc.*[106]

Avant-garde and Tradition

Numerous contemporary Turkish composers of Western music at least occasionally include elements of Turkish music in combination with modern approaches to Western art music, hence breaking with the folkloristic and tonal approach of the early and middle Republican period. Also more and more Turkish instrumentalists of Western music seem to be interested in traditional music; pianists such as Birsen Ulucan, Tahsin Kamil Sökmen and Aylin Aykan, or harpists such as Ceren Necipoğlu (1972–2009) and Şirin Pancaroğlu (b. 1968)[107] have performed arrangements of traditional Turkish music. Many compositions are written for individual ensembles, often initiated by personal contacts with traditional instrumentalists who are willing and able to perform particular pieces, on occasion with commission. In 2016 the Berlin-based Neophon Ensemble, together with the composer Stefan Pohlit initiated commissions for four compositions and a competition for compositions, which should include a *kanun* as constructed by the late Julien Jalâl Ed-Din Weiss (1953-2015). Among more than 200 entries, Konstantin Heuer, Catherine Lamb, Arash Yazdani, Ezequiel Menalled, Klaus Lang and Stefan Pohlit himself were selected for concerts in Berlin, Ankara and Istanbul with the Neophon Ensemble, percussion and *ney* player Osman Öksüoğlu and *kanun* player Tolga Volkan Kılıç.

Below are a few examples of these compositions, listed here following the date of the composers birth:[108]

- Cengiz Tanç (1933-1997): Nine Turkish folk songs in "Suite I for String Orchestra" arranged for Western instruments and *bağlama* (1974).

---

105 CD Gürol Ağırbaş: *Köprüler. Iki Dünya.* Ada Müzik 2006. The CD contains Maurice Ravel's Bolero, Vivaldi's Four Seasons; Johannes Brahms' Hungarian Dances, Carl Orff's Carmina Burana and other popular classic pieces on *arabesk* string orchestra and diverse Turkish instruments. Similarly the international well-known rock songs, including "Englishman in New York" (Sting), "Smoke on the Water" (Deep Purple), "Billie Jean" (Michael Jackson), "La Isla Bonita" (Madonna) and others on mixed Western and Turkish instruments (including *kanun*, Turkish percussion, *ney* and others) by the group Dolapdere Big Gang.

106 Nevzat Akpinar: *Melez Yollarda*, Akkiraz 2009

107 For example the CD, Ceren Necipoğlu: *Bir Kitap Gibi*, Kalan 2009; Şirin Pancaroğlu: *Istanbul'un Ses Telleri*, including *Yerebatan* (cistern) für *kemençe*, bass and harp by Arda Ardaşes Agoşyan (b. 1977) and *Istanbul'un Ağaçları* (The Trees of Istanbul) for harp, *kemençe*, *kanun* and *ud* by Turgay Erdener (b. 1957); arrangements of both folk and art music for two harps to be found on the CD, Şirin Pancaroğlu & Meriç Dönük & Jarrod Cagwin: *Elişi*, Kalan 2011. Aylin Aykan composed the piece *Sesler, gölgeler* commissioned by Deutschlandfunk Radio (2007), on the well-known Istanbul song *Kâtibim.*

108 The data is mainly based on Ilyasoğlu 2007 and the web pages of the composers.

- Yalçın Tura (b. 1934), a composer and musicologist, specialist in Ottoman music history, he often uses elements of this musical tradition in his compositions. Most of his music is tonal, the melody remains central; *Şey Galib'e Saygı* ("Homage to *Şey Galib*"), a cantata for soprano, tenor, choir and orchestra (1972–1975), written for the *Ayangil Türk Müziği Orkestrası ve Korosu* (strings, *ney*, *kemençe*, *kanun*, *ud*, *tanbur*, *kudüm*, *bendir*); *Oyun Havaları* ("Dance Tunes") for violin and chamber orchestra (1959-1972-1993); *Hüseyni Saz Semaisi* for *ney*, *kemençe*, *tanbur* (1972); *Tulum Havası* for three oboes (1972); Concertino for *Kemençe*, Violino Picolo and Orchestra of Five Instruments 'In Honor of Kantemiroğlu' (2000).[109]
- Betin Günes (b. 1957), based in Cologne: "Turkish Dance" for trombone quartet, 1984; *Karadeniz Sahillerinde* ("Along the Black Sea Coast", 1987) for chamber orchestra; *Haydar Haydar* for Orchester (2000) after the famous composition for *bağlama* by Ali Ekber Çicek (1935–2006); *Ben Mevlanayım* ("I am Mevlana") for great orchestra and tenor solo, bass, *ney*, piano (2008).[110]
- Aydın Karlıbel (b. 1957), used elements from traditional music in several compositions for piano solo, including *Hasan Efeni'nin Salat-ı Ümmiye'si üzerine Parafraz*; *Eski Istanbul'a dair Resimler* (Pictures of Ancient Istanbul").[111]
- Meliha Doğuduyal (b. 1959), based in the Netherlands: *Anatolian Suite* for orchestra (1997); *Taksim* for *ney* with or without *electronic band* (2007).[112]
- Kamran İnce (b. 1960) born in Montana, USA, of Turkish-American parents; studied at the Oberlin Conservatory as well as at the Eastman School of Music. Ince is professor of composition at the University of Memphis and at MIAM, Istanbul Technical University: *Nihavent Longa* (traditional dance tune in *makam nihavent*) for wind instruments (2007); *Concerto for Orchestra, Turkish Instruments and Voices* (2009); *The Invasion* for winds, percusions, *ney*, *kemençe*, *bağlama*, *zurna*s(2011); *Asumani* for cello and *ney* (2012); opera "Judgement of Midas" (CD Albany, 2015), for Western orchestra including *ney*, *kemençe*, *ud*, *kanun*, *bağlama*.[113]
- Münir Nurettin Beken (b. 1964), several chamber pieces for Ottoman-Turkish instruments since 1979, e.g. *Damlalar* ("Water Drops", 1982) for *kemençe*, *kanun* and *ud*); several etudes for *ud* (since 1986); Suite for *Ud* and Orchestra (2005); Concertino for *Ud* and Orchestra (2005).
- Hasan Ucarsu (b. 1965), *Eski Istanbul'un Arka Sokaklarında* ("In the Side Streets of Old Istanbul") for *kanun*, cello, clarinet, harp and percussion (2001); *Davet-*

---

109 CD Ayangil Türk Müziği Orkestra ve Korosu'nun Yalçın Tura'ya Armağanı: *Şey Galib'e Saygı*; Syncron 1999; CD *Sensoy plays Tura*, Kalan 1999.

110 CD *Ich will Dir was sagen*, Telos Music 2005; www.betingunes.de (accessed December 4, 2012).

111 CD Aydın Karlıbel: *Transcriptions and Original Works*, Kalan 2007.

112 http://melihadoguduyal.com/biography.html (accessed December 4, 2012); Doğuduyal 2016.

113 www.kamranince.com (accessed December 4, 2012).

siz Misafirler ("Uninvited Guests") for harp, *çeng* (Ottoman harp) and orchestra (2007-2008).

- Özkan Manav (b. 1967): *Beş Anadolu Ezgisi* ("Five Anatolian Melodies", 2013). *Bölüm* 3 (2001), *Bölüm* 4 (2001) and *Bölüm* 5 (2006) for piano partly use *makams*; *Bölüm* 6 for piano (2009) uses microtones.[114]
- Fazıl Say (b. 1970), pianist and composer. Say composes music in a wide stylistic spectrum reaching from international contemporary music and jazz to chanson. Most of his recent compostions deal with traditional elements in a free way. *Dances of Nasreddın Hodja* (1990) on rhythms of Ottoman art music (1. *Devr-i Turan*; 2. *Devr-i Hindî*; 3. *Bektaşi Raksanı*; 4. *Şark-ı Devr-i Revâni Velvelesi*); *Kara Toprak* ("Black Earth", 1997) for piano, inspired by a song from Aşık Veysel (1894-1975). In the beginning the damped piano imitates an opening (*açış*) of a *bağlama*, later the piano improvises virtuosically on motives of the song with harmonic accompaniment; *Yine bir Gülnihal* for piano (1998) after Dede Efendi's song; *Uzun İnce Bir Yoldayım*, on another song by Aşık Veysel for piano, voice and orchestra (2004); *Istanbul Senfonisi* (2009), some parts inspired by traditional music, in *Tarikat* the phrase "*la ilahe illalleh*" includes *ney* and *kuddüm*, before the orchestra enters with imitation of the *ney* melody; in "Oriental night" a *kanun taksim* enters, followed by a dance, citing the art song "*Dök Zülfünü Meydane Gel*" ("Let down your hair and come to the square"); later a *köçekçe* dance; *Hezarfen* – Concerto for *Ney* and Orchestra (2011). The third part, *Perpetuum mobile*, uses a motive from a Black Sea Coast dance, imitating a Black Sea *kemençe*. The untitled fourth part is inspired by the folk song *Odam Kireçtir Benim*; *Mezopotamya Senfonisi* (2012); Concerto for piano and chamber orchestra No. 2 "Silk Road" (1993), the last movement is inspired by the folk song *Ankara'nın Taşına Bak* ("See the Stone of Ankara"). Further projects together involved the percussionist Burhan Öçal and *ney*-player Kudsi Ergüner.[115]
- Onur Türkmen (b. 1972), based in Ankara: *Music for Kemençe Quintett* (2010); *Hat* ("Calligraphy") for *kemençe* and strings (2011); *5 Short Pieces* for *ney*, *kanun*, *kemençe*, cello (2012); *Minyatür* for *kemençe* and alto *kemençe* (2012); *Dilsiz Şeytan* for voice, *kaval* and tenor saxophone (2013).[116]
- Tolga Yayalar (b. 1973), studied in Boston and Harvard, currently based in Ankara: *Lucia di Ombre* (2005), material based on Byzantine modes, including microtones; *Lachrymea* (2013) for *kemençe* and microtonal guitar.
- Evrim Demirel (b. 1977), composer and jazz pianist based in Istanbul: *Zeybek* (a folk dance) for wind instruments and percussion (2004); *Saz Semaisi No. 1* for

---

114 http://ozkanmanav.com/ (accessed October 13, 2016).

115 CD Fazıl Say: *Dervish in Manhattan* (2000): Fazıl Say & Kudsi Ergüner Quartett (piano, *ney*, bass, drums). http://fazilsay.com (accessed December 4, 2012), CD Fazil Say: *Istanbul Senfonisi*, Ak Müzik 2010.

116 www.onurturkmen.info (accessed December 4, 2012)

clarinet, violin, piano (2004); "Ottoman Miniatures" for orchestra (2004); "*Saba* in Istanbul" for *setar*, *ud*, cornet, viola da gamba, *bendir*, *tombak* (2005); *Saz Semaisi No. 2* for E-flat clarinet, violin, cello, harp piano (2004); "Cross-Linked" for two violins, viola, two cellos, double bass, harp, three percussionists, bass clarinet, piano (2005); *Makamsız* for recorder, *kanun*, viola da gamba, cello, marimba, *darbuka* (2005); *Fasıl No:1* for Turkish ensemble and orchestra (2010); *Four Folksongs From Anatolia* for traditional Turkish singer and ensemble (2010).[117]

- Eray Altınbüken (b. 1975): *Kumdakı kan* ("Blood in the Sand") for *kemençe*, guitar and cello (2003; Reigle & Whitehead 2008: xviii).
- Taner Akyol (b. 1977), *bağlama* player and composer based in Berlin: Concerto for *Baglama* and Ensemble (2002)[118]; *An die Liegengebliebenen* for string trio, alto flute (or *ney*) and *bağlama* (2005); *Hatırlamalar* ("Memories") for string quartet and *bağlama* (2006); *Taksim'de Üç Ağaç ve Çapulcular* for *bağlama* and chamber ensemble (2013); Children's opera "*Ali Baba und die 40 Räuber*" (2011) using traditional material, including *makam*s *hicaz*, *karcıgar* and *kürdi*, folksongs, *bağlama*, *asma davul*, *zurna*, *kaval* together with Western orchestra.[119]
- Uğras Durmuş (b. 1978), composer who studied in the Netherlands, based in Istanbul: *Imece* for *ney*, *kanun*, *kemençe*, *tanbur*, percussion, clarinet, violin and cello (2008); *Haliç'te* ("At the Golden Horn") compositions for *kanun* and piano (since 2011); *Uzun Hava 1* for piano and clarinet (2009), *Uzun Hava 2* for chamber ensemble (2016); *Kaval* for *kanun*, *kaval* and *kuddüm*, contemporary Western music on Ottoman-Turkish instruments (2013); *Uyan ey Gözlerin* for choir.[120]
- Ataç Sezer (b. 1979): *Peschrev* (sic) for *ney*, e-bass and *electronics* (2008), *Mirage* for *ney* and E-piano (2013).[121]

It is noteworthy that a number of these young Turkish composers spent at least some time abroad, and several of the mentioned compositions have been written

117 www.evrimdemirel.com (accessed 4 December 2012)

118 www.tanerakyol.com (accessed 4 December 2012).

119 Libretto: Cetin Ipekkaya & Marietta Rohrer-Ipekkaya, 2012; Yavus 2014: 122f. "*Through the motivic relations, Akyol sometimes searches a way to integrate bağlama with the orchestral timbre. In this direction bağlama sometimes becomes a member of different groups and is put into interrelations. Such a section can be found in the first act and first scene between measures 64 and 75.. Here bağlama respectively plays in unison with piano, strings, marimba, and contrabass; or the bağlama part is supported by harp and piano. Thus in the eleven-measure section, bağlama and other instruments create different orchestral timbres*" (Yavus 2014: 164). CD *Birds of Passage / Göcmen Kuslari*, Enja 2007; Newly composed folk songs arranged for chamber orchestra, including Anatolian instruments (mainly the *bağlama*), but still remaining songs with main melodies; CD *Maria Farantouri sings Taner Akyol*, Enja 2010.

120 www.ugrasdurmus.com.

121 www.newmusicistanbul.com/composers/atac-sezer (accessed 26 January 2012); www.atac sezer.com (accessed 14 June 2017).

as commissions of European ensembles.[122] Further non-Turkish composers based in Turkey should be mentioned, in particular Michael Ellinson and Stefan Pohlit.

- Michael Paul Ellison (b.1969), after many years in Istanbul, he is now based in Bristol and co-director of Hezarfen Ensemble. *Karşılama* (2002) for *kemençe*, voice, *kanun*, *ud*, cello, *mey*, *bendir*; *Elif* (2003, revised 2016), for Turkish traditional voice, *ud*, *kemençe*, violin, bass clarinet, cello; "'Turkish' Concerto" (2008) for *ney*, *kemençe*, *kanun*, *ud*, *bendir*, cello and orchestra; "Say I am You-Mevlâna" (2012), opera for three soloists, chorus, Turkish instruments and ensemble; "Round *Evcara*" (2015) for *kemençe* and cello; Opera *Deniz Küstü* ("The Sea-Crossed Fisherman", 2016), based on the novel of Yaşar Kemal, for orchestra including *ney*, *kemençe* and *kanun*.[123]
- Stefan Pohlit (b. 1976), studied in Saarbrücken, Karlsruhe (Germany) and Istanbul, based in Izmir: *piš-raw* for large orchestra (2006); "4 Experimental Approaches to Compositions from the Ottoman Court Repertoire" for lyric soprano and ten instrumentalists (2006)

These ever mulitplying new compositions display a wide range of both aesthetic approaches and compositional techniques. Here only some general and preliminary remarks can be included.

The most common cross-cultural approach for Western trained composers is the integration of traditional Turkish instruments into a basically Western ensemble. The traditional instrument adds an exotic element, but sometimes also elements of Turkish music are integrated, including melodic embellishment, or scales reminiscent of *makam*s or rhythms. Constellations of this kind – with a traditional instrument which essentially replaces a comparable Western instrument inside a Western genre – do not provide serious musical or technical problems. The benefit, however, is limited to a new timbre and to what is mostly perceived as a rise of traditional instruments into the canon of Western classical music.

Especially attractive for musicians, composers and the audience is one of the largest forms, the concerto for orchestra and solo instrument. The earliest model for this approach is Hasan Ferid Alnar's concerto for *kanun* (1951). A number of projects combine the *bağlama* with Western orchestra, mostly again with folkloristic harmonizations, as for example in *Anadolu* (Anatolia) for *bağlama* and or-

---

122 e.g. Meliha Doğuduyal, Evrim Demirel, Uğraş Durmuş, Gökçe Altay and Selim Doğru in the Netherlands; Betin Güneş, Fazıl Say, Ataç Sezer, Ahmet Altınel, Füsün Köksal, Taner Akyol, İnci Yakar, Zeynep Gedizlioğlu in Germany, the Netherlands or France; Mehmet Can Özer in Switzerland; Kamran Ince, Hasan Uçarsu, Özkan Manav, Tolga Yaylar, Taylan Cihan and Turgut Erçetin in the USA. Evrim Demirel for example wrote *Telvin* for Nieuw Ensemble, Ottoman Miniatures for orchestra and Four Folk Songs From Anatolia for Atlas Ensemble, *Makamsiz* for the Dutch Ziggurat Ensemble.

123 Reagle & Whitehead 2008:xxff; https://ellisonotes.com/works/ accessed November 16, 2016.

chestra by Sanar Yurdatapan, premiered in Köln 1986 (soloist: Orhan Temur, conductor: Betin Güneş), formally a suite-like sequence of Anatolian songs and dance melodies.[124] Two years later in Cologne the Concertino for three *bağlamas* and Orchester (1988) was premiered. More recent are projects by the *bağlama* player Erdal Akkaya with the Duisburger Philharmonic and later the Kammersymphonie Berlin (2014), again arranged folk songs;[125] the *Remayisê Munzuri* (2005) arranged by Gerhard Fischer-Münster in cooperation with Mikail Aslan; or Yavuz Bingöl's *Bin Yılın Ozanları "Karacaoglan"* with chamber orchestra (2016), and similar projects by Cengiz Özkan with the *CRR Senfoni Orkestrası* (2016). Concertos in a contemporary Western musical language, based mainly on new musical material rather than on folk melodies include Carlo Dominiconi's *Concerto di Berlinbul* for *bağlama* and chamber orchestra (1988, Yavus 2014: 122f), and the concertos for *bağlama* and orchestra composed by Taner Akyol (2002), Kemal Dinç (2013), and Sinem Altan (2013).[126] Recently comparable concerti have been composed also for Ottoman-Turkish instruments and orchestra, for *ud* (Münir Nurettin Beken, 2005), *kanun* (Turgay Erdener, 2015; Ahmet Baran, 2015), *ney* (Fazıl Say, 2012), two *kemençe*s (Münir Nurettin Beken, 2017), *kanun*, *ud*, percussion and orchestra (Enver Yalçın Özdıker, 2017) and *çenk* / harp (Hasan Uçarsu, 2007/08). It is noteworthy that this recent interest in solo concertos is not limited to Turkey, as several of concertos for traditional instruments have been composed in many Middle Eastern countries, including:

- Iraq: Concert for *ud* and Orchestra by Rahim Alhaj;
- Lebanon: Concerto for *ud* and Orchestra (2002) by Marcel Khalife (b. 1950); Concerto for *kanun* & Orchestra (2012) by Marcel Khalife (b. 1950);
- Israel: Concerto for *ud* and Orchestra by Michale Wolpe (b. 1960); Concerto for *kanun* and Orchestra by Nabil Azzam
- Egypt: two concerti for *ud* and orchestra by Atia Sharara (1922-2014), and Ammar El Sherei (1948-2012), one for *nay* and Orchestra by Atia Sharara;[127]
- Greece: Kyriakos Kalaitzidis: Concerto for *ud* and Orchestra 2015; Concerto for Orchestra and Traditional Clarinet by Theodoros Antoniou;
- Armenia: two concertos for *kanun* and Orchestra (1954, 1987) by Khachatur Avetisyan (1926–1996);[128]
- Azerbaijan: Concerto for *ud* and Orchestra and Concerto for *kamancha* and Orchestra by Haji Khanmammadov (1918-2005)

---

124 MC Melike Demirağ / Şanar Yurdatapan: *Istanbul'da olmak / Anadolu*, Ada, 1989.

125 MC Arif Sağ Trio: *Concerto for Bağlama* (ASM, 1998).

126 Sinem Altan: *Concert for Baglama and Orchestra. „Beni baglama – don't bind me"*, Berlin: Ries & Erler 2013.

127 I owe most of this data to Kyriakos Kalaitzidis, recordings of most concerts might be found on youtube.

128 CD Karine Hovhannisyan: *Classical Music for the Armenian Kanun*, Traditional Crossroads 2007

Ilyas Mirzayev (b. 1961), Azerbaijani composer and jazz musician, based in Turkey, has composed his symphony "Sufi" in cooperation with the *ney* player Ercan Irmak, similarly his Concerto for *ney* (2002) (which in its harmonized version quotes an *ayin* of Ismail Dede Efendi [1782–1846] and a *saz semai* from Tanburi Cemil Bey [1873–1916]); further, his *Dede Efendi Gülnihal* for flute and Orchestra (2000).[129] For the Turkish *Tekfen Filarmoni Orkestrası* Mirzayev further wrote the Triple Concerto for *kanun*, *ud*, and *ney* (2016) as well as the *Karadeniz Rapsodi* for *Tulum* and Orchestra (2012).

In smaller ensembles elements of traditional music inevitably become more audible, and hence most composers try to blend timbre, scales (sometimes even different intonations) and rhythms. In Taner Akyol's *Hatıralamalar* for string quartet and *bağlama*, Akyol adapted the traditional melodic pattern of the *bağlama* for strings without quoting any traditional melody. In trios or duos it becomes impossible to give the ensemble a clear characterization of either Western or Turkish tradition. The duo for piano and *kanun* by Esra Berkman (*kanun*) & Nazlı Işıldak (piano, initially Ayça Daştan) for example is balanced between both worlds.[130] Most pieces try to use playing techniques and timbres common to both instruments (as for example arpeggi).

Another musical approach is it to detach traditional musical elements and combine them anew in an abstract soundscape. *Lir ve Ateş* for string quartet, piano and *bağlama* by Kemal Dinç consists of three movements, with extensive improvisations for piano or *bağlama* inserted between. The first movement begins with quiet *bağlama* and plucked piano tones. Later intensifying three-tone motives emerge, which build a soundscape rather than clear melodies. Gradually the melody broadens, changing the *makam* repeatedly, in between short resorts to a *zeybek* or an alevi *semah*. More and more the string quartet attracts the audience's attention, supported by the piano. Some lighter parts again turn to expressions of pain. Towards the end the sound weave intensifies and eventually ends in tutti. Kemal Dinç's music is abstract, with no melodies, no clear harmonic language but rather constantly changing *makam*s. The musical form is often hard to detect. Short, amorphous and minimalistic motifs determine the music, imitations are passed from one instrument to another, building dense, rhythmically and dynamically intensifying weaves. Repeatedly the music seems to stop and the intense weaves are detached by broad, calm fields of sound. In particular with respect to the *bağlama*, every now and then remnants of folk music are audible, in melodies, in the playing technique and in particular in asymmetric rhythms. Whenever an Anatolian element seems to be present, however, Dinç

---

[129] CD Sefika Kutluer: *Mevlana Rumi*. Gallo 2008.

[130] Their repertoire includues Tolga Zafer Özdemir (b. 1975): *Kesitler* (2010); Enis Günüş (b. 1982): Arrangement of the piece, *Başına Bağlamış Astar*; Ugraş Durmuş *Haliç'te* 1 and 2 ("At the Golden Horn") for *kanun* and piano (2011; 2016). CD Esra Berkman & Nazlı Işıldak, *Uyanış. Haçatur Avetisyan*. Kalan 2013.

alienates the playing technique and rhythm, modulates, changes motifs, creating confusing soundscapes. A similar focus on timbre and sound characterizes Dinç's solo pieces for *bağlama*, Denemeler ("Essay", 2012, see figure 17)

Again asymmetric rhythm seems to be the only remaining Anatolian element in this music, except for some short alienated melodic quotes (e.g. in *Ay ve Mavi Tilki* / "The Moon and the Blue Fox") or in remnants of *makam saba* at the end of *Denemeler I.* Titles such as *Mezxana* (a name for Diyarbakır used by Armenians and Kurds) or the dedication of *Ay ve Mavi Tilki* to the region of Dersim, are more homages to personal inspiration rather than quotes of regional styles. The music is strangely emotional and disjointed; there are only a few distinguishable melodies. In place of these, the motion diminishes and gives way to short amorphous repetitions in changing variants before fading out. Some pieces are heavily dominated by abstract noise, but later move into quick, rhythmic transitions. Most often, the same pitches are played on different strings and positions, producing a rich fabric of texture and sound in which melodic passages flow and blend. Particulary in the case of the *bağlama*, one unavoidably expects a return to the drone and hence to the initial mode, and the rejection of such musical security creates a sense of emptiness and loneliness in Dinc's music.

The general use of Anatolian rhythms has already has been mentioned several times, for instance in the framework of world music. Also many Western-Turkish composers prefered this approach to musical hybridity or identity markers, beginning with the early Turkish folklorists to recent composers such as Fazıl Say. Ottoman forms have also been adapted for contemporary music, as for example by Stefan Pohlit in Ikaros (2006) and "*Der zerrissene Orpheus*" ("The Torn Orpheus"; 2006/2015) or by Demirel (*Saz Semaisi* No 1 & 2).

The integration of the Turkish concept of melody, however, is much more challenging. One approach is the free addition of the *taksim* by adding a (tonal or not) acompaniment to a monophone *taksim*-like melody. During his education in Paris in the 1930s, the young Ulvi Cemil Erkin wrote an "Improvisation" (for violin and piano). Similarly Hasan Ferid Alnar in 1935 (see figure 18) and much later Ertugrul O Firat. The *Ney Taksim* in Yalçın Tura's cantata *Sey Galib'e Saygı* (1972-75) is already less tonal and much nearer to an Ottoman-Turkish *taksim*, while just a soft drone on the strings is added for accompaniment.[131]

In other cases *taksim* is perceived purely as an inspiration for free compositions. *Mugam Sayagi* by the Azerbaijan composer, Franghiz Ali-Zadeh (b. 1947)[132] is a meditation on long held tones rather than a traditional *makam* realisation. Sparse, amorphous melodies rise from low to higher pitch levels, forming layers

131 CD Ayangil Türk Müziği Orkestra ve Korosu, *Galib'e Saygı*, Türkiye İş Bankası, 1999.

132 Born in Baku, Azerbaijan Ali-Zadeh studied piano and composition in Baku. 1993-96 she served as director of the choir of the municipal opera in Mersin, later as teacher for piano and music theory in the same city. Since 1999 she has been based in Germany.

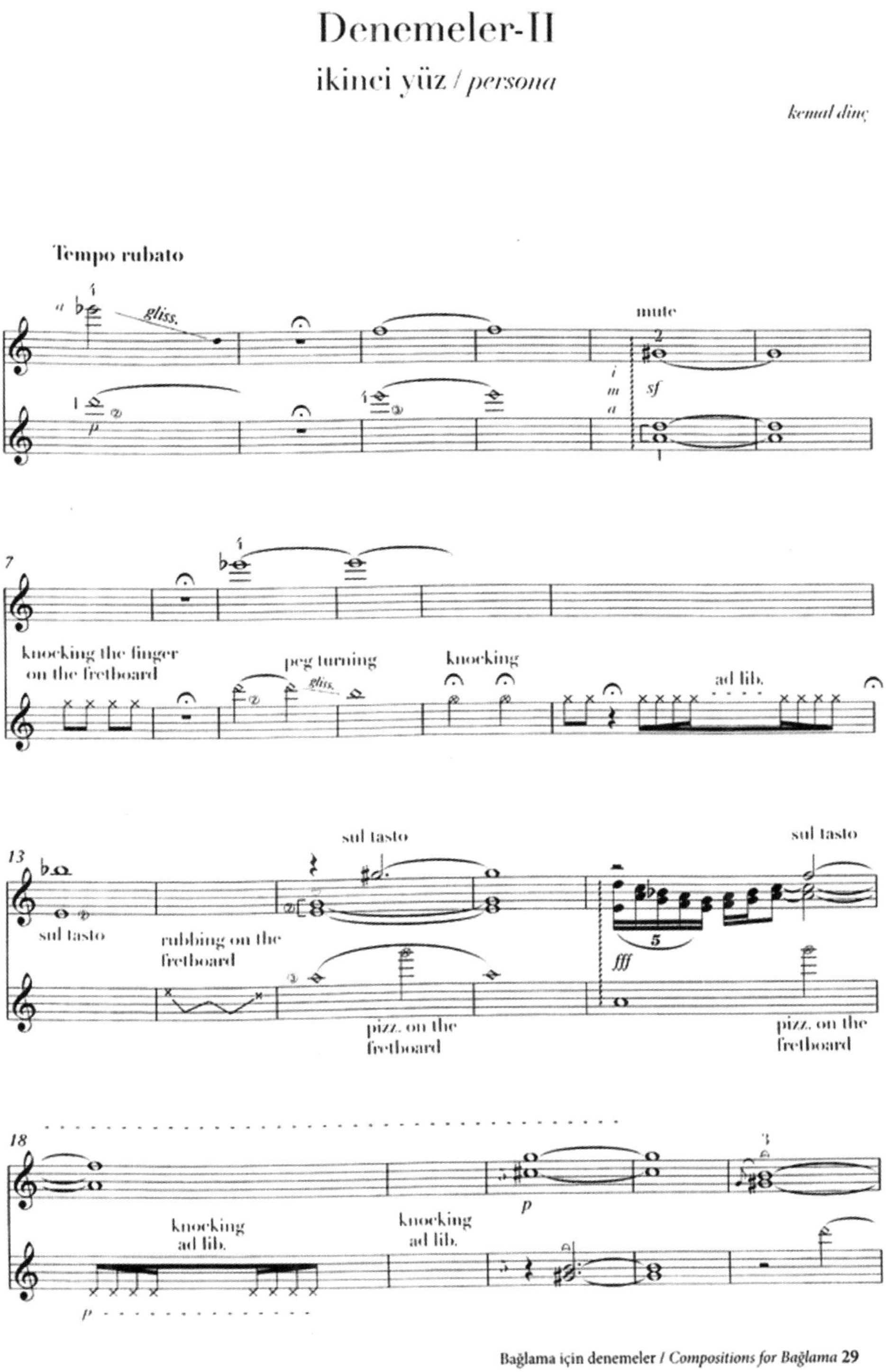

Figure 17: Kemal Dinç: Denemeler II (Dinç 2012: 29)

Figure 18: Hasan Ferid Alnar: Improvisation (1935)

of movable drones and extremely slow melodies. The title of Onur Türkmen's (b. 1972) piece, *Hat* for *kemençe* and Western chamber ensemble (2011, commissioned by *kemençe* player Nermin Kaygusuz) is derived from calligraphy (Turkish: *hat*), and literally means line. "*Yet, composing a piece of music within the* hat *concept is all about revealing a 'line' of* makams *penetrating and merging into each other,"* Türkmen wrote about this composition. "*No quotations are used in* hat *but only ambiguous remnants through* makams *and yet its melodic associations.*" In fact partly free *taksim*-like *kemençe* solos are interrupted by other instruments, mostly at the same pitches adding different timbres, hence creating soundscapes of the melodies resting, as coloring a lost and unreal *taksim* by means of contemporary timbre and dissonant composition.

The general rule for the integration of microtone, hence the Ottoman-Turkish pitch system, into polyphonic music is that tempered pitches needs to be avoided (also in the accompanying instruments) in case a near but non-tempered pitch is performed (for example by a traditional instrument).

Evrim Demirel:

> For example let's say we have the *uşşak koma* – la si-with-koma do re mi fa sol – you should not touch this si note in this part, no si at all. All harmonies before and after need to be adjusted accordingly.

A remarkable musical approach to this problem is *Bölüm 6* ("Sixth Movement") for piano by Özkan Manav (b. 1967), part of a series of independent compositions for piano. In dreamlike passages the piano repeatedly leaves the temperate pitch system and changes to *makam* such as *neva*, *segah* and *hüzzam*. Necessarily some notes of the piano (b, d#, f#) have to be retuned in advance. In most cases these unusual, retuned notes are touched individually, softly and very carefully, as though the music itself is not sure of these notes. The composition is dedicated to the memory of the late Ottoman composer Hacı Ârif Bey (1831–1885).

Another way to avoid the problems of different pitch systems is it to separate the different musical languages into different sections. The Project *Medcezir* ("Tides," 2008) by Selim Doğru (b. 1971, based in the Netherlands) follows this strategy. The Axyz Ensemble performed new compositions by Çağlayan Yıldız, Gökçe Altay, Oğuz Büyükberber and Selim Doğru, each alternating with traditional music played by Kemal Dinç (*bağlama*), Murat Tokaç (*tanbur*), Erkan Oğur (*kopuz*, voice) and Fahrettin Yarkın (percussion).

The project *Turquoise* of the *Nederlands Blazers Ensemble* (2006) confronted new compositions for orchestra by Kamran Ince with Kurdish songs such as *Ahmedo* or *Kece Kurdan* performed by the Kurdish singer Aynur Doğan, which were mainly accompanied only by percussion, or monophonic small orchestra sounds (*Dewo dewo*). In Hasan Uçarsu's concerto *Davetsiz Misafirler* the soloist switches from movement to movement between Western and Ottoman harp (*çeng*). In particular the parts of the *çeng* are only sparseley accompanied by the orchestra in order to avoid clashes of the Ottoman-Turkish and the Western intonation (Pohlit 2011: 193f). Marc Sinan (b. 1976) in his last three large compositions even visually separates traditional Turkish and Western music, though they continue to interact. In *Hasretim–Journey to Anatolia* (2013) most of the Turkish sounds are provided by video recording. The attached film depicts impressions from a journey along the Black Sea Coast, with recordings of regional folk music. The Dresden Symphony Orchestra together with some traditional musicians – Güç Başar Gülle (*ud*), Ömer Can Satır (*kaval*), Onur Şentürk (*kemençe*), Erdem Şimşek (*bağlama*) – on the other hand perform live newly composed music.[133] A subsequent project entitled *Dede Korkut*, realized again with the Dresden Symphony Orchestra in 2015, focused on Central Asian music, including musicians from Central Asia; *Aghet* by Marc Sinan, Zeynep Gedizlioğlu, Helmut Oehring, and the Armenian composer Vache Sharafyan, is dedicated to the Armenian composer, singer and musicologist Gomitas.[134]

In *Variations on Dertli Kaval* for piano, viola and violin (commissioned by the pianist Birsen Ulucan in 2019) the composer İnci Yakar (b. 1981) explicitly composed a transition from a traditional folksong, the Turkish folksong *Dertli Kaval* ("Painful Flute"), from the Bulgarian region of Deliorman, where the pianist Birsen Ulucan grew up, to contemporary music. The piece begins with an old recording of Ulucan's grandfather singing the song. After about one minute a viola takes the melody, later a simple counterpoint is added to the violin. Beginning with the third stanza the piano frames the melody with free atonal soundfields. The melody gets more and more abstract, more expressive and dissonant, the texture turns to a free composition of timbre.[135]

The development of New Music in the West further expanded the alternative ways to compose timbre or soundscapes, which are much easier to combine with modal melodies than with polyphonic or harmonic music. Here, both musical traditions are structured separately, that is, a soundscape of contemporary Western music functions as background for a Turkish melody.

Pure sound collages are the technically and aesthetically least complicated expression of this trend. Mehmet Can Özer's piece *Siyah Kalem Dansı* ("Dance of the Black Pen") for *bağlama* and live electronics (2007) for example uses alienated *bağlama* recordings within abstract soundscapes. In another piece (*In the Arctic Cave*, 2006) it is piano and *ney* instead, though ultimately the choice of instrument does not make too great a difference.[136] *Anadolu'dan Dört Halk Türküsü*

---

133 In an earlier CD (Marc Sinan & Julia Hülsman: *Fasıl*, ECM 2009) only the album title and the title of the first piece, *Peshrev*, is reminiscent of Ottoman music, not the music itself, which is jazz and new Western music. CD/DVD Hasretim, ECM 2013. http://www.marcsinan.com.

134 For the political discussion on this project see http://www.spiegel.de/kultur/gesellschaft/streit-um-dresdner-musikprojekt-die-tuerkei-hat-laengst-eine-grenze-ueberschritten-a-1089177.html

135 CD *Salon Romantique Turque*, Özcan, Birsen und Ayşen Ulucan, Regensburg: Spektral, 2009. Also in a later composition Inci Yakar included a traditional folk song, *Ağlama / Don't cry* (2009) by Aşık Daimi (1932 – 1982).

136 CD Mehmet Can Özer, *Siyah Kalem Dance*, AK Müzik 2009; Mehmet Can Özer: Dictionary of War (2003; Reagle & Whitehead 2008:259; CD).

("Four Folk Songs from Anatolia") by Evrim Demirel was originaly written in 2004 for the Atlas Ensemble as a suite for Western voice and cross-cultural chamber ensemble. The composition is based on traditional songs from different Turkish regions: *Yağmur Yağar* from Kütahya, *Yayla Yollarından Yürüyüp Gelir* from Burdur, *Ferayidir Gızın Adı* from Muğla and *Batum* from Sinop. The composition begins with a free soundscape from which the melody emerges (bar 32, see figure 19).

In 2010 Evrim Demirel revised his former composition for Birsen Ulucan, changing its instrumentation and replacing the Western singer with the Turkish art music singer Özer Özel. While the earlier version was clearly Western music – although including strong elements of Turkish music – it became a hardly classifiable intercultural art music ranging equally over several traditions. Together with the traditional Ottoman-Turkish singing technique by Özer Özel the Turkish pitch system now became clearly audible, sometimes in tension with the Western tempered intonation. The main instrument has become the piano, used here in the unfamiliar function as a bridge between Turkish and Western music: in dense polyphonic duos with the *kanun* the piano transports Western contemporary tonality into the environment of Turkish music. Later the piano returns to a more Western musical structure. In particular the second and the fourth songs are almost piano songs, somewhat reminiscent of arrangements from the "Turkish Five" in the 1930s and '40s. Jazz elements in the piano however, for instance the rich syncopation, reveal the jazz experience of the composer. Towards the end of the piece the piano becomes more and more percussive and playful – however still creating free atonality. The other instruments, both Western and Turkish, provide a rich variety of musical colours. Here melodies are hardly used, the composition is made up mainly of sound and timbre. The central and recurring element is the piano with its differing textures. Only the traditional song melodies remain unchanged and clearly perceptible, and are never reduced to an exotic quotation. All other musical elements are constantly in transition. It is this dense and colourful musical space which allows so many different musics to melt together. The third song, for instance begins with a kind of *taksim* played on the *kemençe* before the musical background of free atonality, and leading to a free, clearly Anatolian melody.[137]

[137] In his *Symphony of Dialogue* (commissioned by the *Nederlands Fonds voor Podiumkunsten*) Demirel similarly combined an orchestra with Muslim, Jewish and Christian singing traditions. Promotion-DVD with the Symfonnieorkest De Philharmonie, conducted by Daan Admiral, soloists Selma Harkink, Halil Necipoğlu, Ken Gould 2010.

Anadolu'dan Dört Halk Türküsü
♩ = 66
Evrim Demirel
Kanun
Percussion
Büyuk Def Bendir (zilli) Büyük Zil Trampet
Piano
Clarinet in B♭
Bass Clarinet in B♭
Violin
Kemence
Yayli Tanbur
Violoncello
Double Bass
Pno. 1
Cl.
B. Cl.
Vln.
Y. Tanbur
Vc.
Db.

Kanun
Pno. 1
Ped.
Cl.
B. Cl.
Vln.
Kemence
Y. Tanbur
Vc.
Db.

Figure 19: Evrim Demirel: *Anadolu'dan Dört Halk Türküleri*, 2010 Version.

Conclusion

Throughout the entire twentieth century and into the beginning of the twenty-first, almost all musicians in Turkey have made some attempt to develop a kind of synthesis of what they perceived as different musical worlds, that is the horizontal music of the Middle East and the vertical music of the West. As a result Turkey in general did not become part of the "Western music world," rather art music in Turkey has become radically individualized and diverse. Today, musical instruments, ensembles and arrangements exist in unprecedented and inextricable diversity. There are no standards of performance practice to stabilise musical life, rather almost every concert and every CD presents a new type of ensemble, performing a new repertoire with new arrangements. The amount of available instrument types, their practical use (construction, playing techniques, repertoires) and their combination into ensembles have expanded dramatically, with an accelerating development over the past two decades. While the harmonic language in general remained surprisingly limited, melodies compared to other musical elements still dominate Turkish art music. Only a few Turkish musicians and composers have completely given up composing and performing monophone melodies in favour of polyphony or compositions of timbre.

Today, traditional Turkish music is often performed on instruments or by ensembles which were either adapted from non-Turkish (in particular European) traditions, e.g. choir, piano, guitar, orchestra, new mixed ensembles; or developed, changed or sometimes entirely re-invented instruments of more or less Ottoman-Turkish-Anatolian tradition. Parallel to the augmenting of musical styles, the repertoire of most Turkish musicians expanded to an unprecedented degree, including pieces of both Turkish folk and art music, as well as historical European art music (of a range of periods and styles) and sometimes also other music traditions. For several well-known Turkish songs (art and folk) a great number of contemporary arrangements have been made, ranging from traditional performance and historical reconstruction, to jazz, *arabesk*, rock and contemporary Western music.

As part of these extensive developments the numerous styles of Anatolian folk music and Ottoman-Turkish art music have moved substantially closer to each other, in particular in terms of performance practice. In addition, elements of Western music or popular music are also often intermingled. Today, a large field of "Turkish music" exists, reaching from light popular interpretations by mixed ensembles, solo instruments such as piano or guitar, and orchestras to sophisticated, highly individual interpretations of an again mixed repertoire of traditional music. Today the use of hybrid ensembles and instruments forms a central characteristic of almost all Turkish music. While the idea of musical traditions, such as folk music, Ottoman-Turkish art music, regional Anatolian styles, *tekke* style or others, is still imagined as existing by the audience as well as for most musicians, in fact all of these traditions have disintegrated to a large extent. Instead Turkish musicians today tend to develop individual musical projects, for which they draw upon an unprecedentedly large range of instruments, playing techniques, ensemble types, musical genres and repertoires.

The pace of development of instruments, arrangements and ensembles has led to serious challenges for Turkish musicians. In order to be able to play in as many individual musical projects as possible, a musician is expected to master both a wide range of musical and technical skills and instruments, and to be flexible in his or her ability for different musical styles and aesthetics.

> Studio musicians need to be able to play their instrument in tune with instruments in several different tuning systems: Western equal tempered (common in pop productions featuring synthesizers or electric guitars), *Orta-Anadolu halk* [Central Anatolian folk music], *Osman sanat* [Ottoman art music], and other less formalized regional traditions. [...] Consequently, studio musicians bring a large instrument inventory to a tracking session. Eyüp Hamis brings over 100 *ney*s and *kaval*s, while Ertan Tekin has at least 40 *ney/duduk/balaban* instruments, many optimized for contemporary studio contexts. (Bates 2008: 197)

In addition to the challenging training in their main instrument and musical style, contemporary traditional musicians are expected to have at least a basic knowledge in and experience with other musical traditions in Turkey, that is folk music, Ottoman-Turkish art music, as well as Western music and its harmonic language, jazz and sometimes even contemporary Western music. The main problem for younger composers is to find traditional musicians who are able to play their individual music, in terms of playing technique and notation reading, and who are in addition open to experimental or sometimes atonal music. The 60 year old concerto for *kanun* by Alnar has only ever been performed by three soloists to date, that is Rûhi Ayangil, Tahir Aydoğdu and Halil Altınköprü.[138] In addition the French *kanun* player, Julien Jâlal Eddine Weiss must be mentioned, as well as Esra Berkman, who played arrangements and new compositions for *kanun* and piano and performed in the *Istanbul Contemporary Music Ensemble.* There is no comparably large number of cross-cultural experienced musicians for any other traditional Turkish instrument. For the *ney,* in almost all related projects, *ney* players Burcu Karadağ or Kudsi Ergüner are involved. On *tanbur* for new Western and jazz music, Özer Özel is the sole active musician (in particular in the *Evrim Demirel Ensemble*), and in numerous cross-cultural ensembles and projects Murat Aydemir is present. Violinist Cihat Aşkın was already mentioned, while the sisters Neva Özgen (*kemençe*) and Yelda Özgen Öztürk (Cello) are active in many music projects from Greek to Western music. For *kemençe* in particular Derya Türkan and Nermin Kaygusuz are active in several cross-cultural music

[138] Ayhan Sarı, "Geleneksel Türk Müziginde ile 'kanun', 'bağlama', 'ney' Koncertoları", in: *Musîki Dergisi*, www.musikidergisi.net/?p=2122 (accessed December 1, 2012)

projects. Even more extreme in its restricted range of competent artists is the situation concerning Turkish folk instruments. New cross-cultural music for *bağlama* has mainly been performed by just a few players, including Kemal Dinç, Taner Akyol and Erdem Şimşek in Istanbul. Outstanding of course is the *kopuz* and fretless guitar player Erkan Oğur. From 2015-2020, the Istanbul-based Hezarfen Ensemble is conducting a large project entitled *Beyond East and West* (financed by the European Research Council) including seminars and workshops with traditional musicians, with the long-term goal of integrating Turkish traditional instruments and voices into contemporary music.

In today's musical life in Turkey hence, musicians are actually in a much stronger position than composers, who, more than ever in history, strongly depend on the former. Many new compositions are directly composed by commissions of musicians, due to personal contacts, or by the members of individual ensembles or projects themselves. Even stronger than the role of composers is that of arrangers–though in general they remain unknown; most often musicians arrange music just for themselves.

To summarize concisely, we might state that new post-traditional Turkish music today is comprised of individually arranged monophonic melodies, with sophisticated timbres, possibly including harmony, contemporary composition techniques, traditional embellishments or (traditional, jazz-like or free) improvisations, arranged for cross-culturally experienced and highly individual musicians, mostly personally known by the composer or the arranger.

V The Failing Struggle for Standards

The Impact of Kemalism

On first sight it seems to be surprising that the Republic of Turkey, with its authoritarian administration, offered musicians the freedom to expand the stylistic range of Turkish music almost infinitely. Actually in its early years, the new Republic of Turkey even articulated an exceptionaly explicit vision of how its music should sound: a combination of national "Turkish folk music" arranged in the musical language of the West. President Mustafa Kemal Atatürk saw music as an important part of his vision for Turkey, and on several occasions explained his ideas of "Turkish music," culminating in his often quoted speech on November 1, 1934 before the Grand National Assembly.[1] Over the decades, numerous Turkish intellectuals, musicologists, historians and musicians have described and analyzed Mustafa Kemal's personal approach towards music, together with the musical reforms (*müzik inkılâbı*) of the 1930s and '40s, while cultural politics (in particular those concerning music) after the 1950s have hardly been analyzed at all.[2] Relying mainly on the leading theorist of Turkish nationalism, Ziya Gökalp (1876-1924), Atatürk saw Ottoman music as non-national (*gayrimillî*), rooted in Byzantine music, and influenced by Arabic and Iranian music. Anatolian folk music on the other hand, according to Gökalp (and Mustafa Kemal) was perceived as a central aspect of "Turkish culture."

Consequently, the Republic of Turkey perpetuated and enforced the support for Western classical music already granted by the later Ottoman Sultans, now with the aim of becoming a full member of the Western musical world. The general overestimation of the potential for this musical transformation was expresssed most clearly by Ahmet Adnan Saygun, who compared the discarding of

---

1 The most quoted passage of this speech reads as follows: *"Friends! I know how you desire the youth of the nation to be accomplished in all the fine arts. This is being done. But, in my opinion, first and foremost to be carried forward among them is Turkish Music. The measure of change in a nation is her acceptance and comprehension of the change in music. The music that we have been listening to is far from having worth to imbue pride. We must know this in all our being. It is necessary to collect sublime folk idioms – sayings that depict national affections, and embroider them according to the general principles of music as soon as possible. Only then may Turkish National Music rise, and take its place within Universal Music."* (Yarman 2007: 135).

2 Akkaş 2015; Öztürk 2015; Akkaş 2015; Ayaz 2014; Deniz 2015: 30ff; Bartsch 2012; Erol 2012; O'Connell 1996; 2000; 2005; 187-92; Üngör 2011: 31; Yarman 2010; Paçacı 1999; Kahramankaptan 1998, 39f; Tekelioğlu 1996; Stokes 1992: 25ff; Refiğ 1991; Ataman 1991; Aksoy 1985; 1989; Behar 1987b: 93ff; Markoff 1986; Say 1985, "Atatürk ve Müzik", Say 1991: 115-118; Aksoy 1985; Zimmermann-Kalyoncu 1985: 15, 157; Ali 1983: 1531; Saygun 1981.

Arabic letters from the Turkish alphabet to tempering the traditional intervals.[3] The government invited Western experts such as Paul Hindemith, Ernst Praetorius, Max Reinhardt and Carl Ebert to help establish and nurture a Western music life in Turkey; from the 1930s institutions for music education including music academies and the "People's Houses" (*Halkevleri*) were founded; scholarships for musical education abroad were granted (Kahramankaptan 1998); state and municipal ensembles, orchestras, chamber music ensembles, solists, choirs and operas were supported, and, from 1926, Western musical education was introduced in schools.[4] As a result, today, the general knowledge of Western musical instruments, ensembles, aesthetics, harmony and notation has become common in Turkey. Until recently, this state support for Western music was never seriously challenged or reduced, nor even politically controlled. However, the official support of Western music never included all musical styles, only the music of the late Baroque, Classic and Romantic periods. Hence neither earlier music (such as music of the Renaissance or the Middle Ages), nor contemporary music (as composed from the early twentieth century on) were included.[5] With the exception of teaching positions for some Turkish composers at state or municipal music academies, still today, contemporary music hardly receives financial support by the state. Most concerts with contemporary Western music in Istanbul take place in private concert halls (such as *Borusan Müzik Evi* or *Akbank Sanat*), with the only exception of the MIAM, which is attached to the state conservatory of the ITÜ.

To a lesser degree, Turkish folk music also benefited from Kemalism, even though being laden with a strong Turkish nationalism and under strict political control. As mentioned in chapter III, Kemalism deeply influenced the perception of history in Turkey, in particular via the nationalistic theory of an "origin" of a "Turkish music." The political aim of Kemalist cultural policies was the creation of a homogeneous Turkish culture, rather than the support of an aesthetically convincing music.[6] Already the former Committee of Union and Progress (CUP) even tried to influence the structure of the Anatolian population through demographic engineering, culminating in the genocide of the Anatolian Armenians in 1915 (Üngör 2011; Dündar 2008). "*The genesis of the Young Turk educational philosophy was rooted in Ziya Gökalp's belief that reshaping society was necessary and desirable.*" (Üngör 2011: 172) The Kemalist state in particular discriminated and

---

3 Ahmet Adnan Saygun, "Yeni Türk Musikisi", *Eser Dergisi*, Ankara, Nisan 1948: 17, quoted after Paçacı 1999: 23.

4 Ayas 2014; Ada & Ince 2009; Katoğlu 2009: 25-79; Özeke 2003; Akdemir 1991; Zimmermann-Kalyoncu 1984: 20-63; Oransay 1983; Hindemith 1935/1983; Ali 1983; Pack 1977; Okyay 1973:16ff.

5 With the exception of some few eastern European composers such as Bartók or Stravinsky.

6 Similar effords to standardize regional culture were conducted in many new national states all over Asia and Africa, for example in Indonesia after its independence in 1945 / 49, cf. Mack 2004.

prohibited non-Turkish folk music, attempting to educate non-Turks towards Turkishness (Üngör 2011: 170ff). "*A major component of Kemalist cultural policies in the East was music. Şükrü Kaya [Director of the Settlement of Tribes and Migrants during World War I, 1927-37 Minister of Interior] had proudly declared that 'music is an element of national upbringing'.*" (Üngör 2011: 198) As a consequence, research on folk music, in particular the collection of folk tunes, gained strong official support, both in order to construct and strengthen the idea of a homogenous Turkish folk music, and at the same time with the practical objective of creating a repertoire of national Turkish music.[7] New institutions would implement the education in Western and Turkish music, including the "Turkish Hearths" (*Türk Ocaklar*), the "Association for the Knowledge on the Turkish People" (*Türk Halk Bilgisi Dernegi*), and, from 1932 the "People's Houses" (*Halkevleri*, similarly *köy odaları* and *köy enstitüleri*). In 1931 a first *âşık* festival took place in Sivas, another one followed in 1938 in Bayburt. Later famous *âşık*s were invited to concerts and to teach in People's Houses (*halkevleri*) nationwide.

The main aesthetic idea of Kemalist culture politics was the combination of folk music with Western classical music (Katoğlu 2009: 68ff). In his influencial book, "The Principles of Turkism" (1923), Ziya Gökalp proposed:

> *If we collect these [folk music melodies] and harmonize them in the western manner, we shall have both a national and a European music. [...] This, essentially, is the Turkist program in the field of music; the rest is up to our national musicians.* (Gökalp 1923/1968: 99)

In fact, as seen in the previous chapter, over the entire twentieth century and through to the beginning of the twenty first century, almost all musicians in Turkey tried to develop some kind of synthesis at least for some time. How exactly this musical synthesis should be achieved and how it should sound was left to the musicians, reflecting an underestimation on the part of the state as to the almost endless possibles musical approaches. While the music of composers such as Saygun or Erkin was probably closer to Mustafa Kemal's vision, many other musicians developed completely different and unexpected forms of music. In addition it should be reminded that neither Gökalp nor Mustafa Kemal initiated this search for synthesis, which already began in the mid-nineteenth century, with its prehistory going back to European travelers of the eighteenth and nineteenth century (Ayas 2014: 105).

Musical restrictions, on the other hand, during the first years of the Turkish Republic mainly affected Ottoman-Turkish and religious music, as for example through the closure of the Sufi lodges in 1925 and of the Turkish department of the Conservatory Istanbul one year later. In 1926, the Ministry of Education released a directive to all schools prohibiting *alaturca* music. In 1934/35, several private music associations dispersed and state support for Ottoman-Turkish music all but ceased.

---

7 For folk music researchers in Turkey cf. Emnalar 1998: 747-930.

However, even during this period of the most intense Kemalist efforts, the state never succeded in gaining control over the entire national music life, but rather only over state institutions. The development of a public music life since the later nineteenth century (as described in chapter II), with the introduction of public concerts, public institutions for education (private associations and schools, municipal and later state convervatories) had resulted in an increase in the number and influence of actors within Turkey's musical scene. The growing importance of media including notation (since the early nineteenth century), the printing of notation (since 1876), books on music, method teaching books, newspapers, journals, and since around 1900, 78rpm discs records, opened up a public music life, mainly outside the influence of the state. During the founding years of the Republic, private musicians and scholars such as Yekta, Arel and Ezgi published the most important editions of notations (at the Conservatory Istanbul), and wrote fundamental theoretical writings, intending to standardize issues such as intervals, notation, *usul* and *makam*. Sadeddin Nüzhet Ergun (1942) similarly inventorized the religious repertoire. At the commercial record and *gazino* market in the 1930s and '40s, for the first time female singers of classical Ottoman-Turkish songs such as Safiye Ayla, Perihan Altındağ-Sözeri and Hamiyet Yüceses became succesful. Carrying on the tradition of musical gatherings of the late Ottoman period, members of the Ottomanist elite regularly hosted private musical gatherings. In his biography, the singer and composer of Turkish classical music, Alâeddin Yavaşca, stresses the educational importance of these gatherings and provides detailed descriptions of some of those he participated in, together with a list of the major regular gatherings which took place in Istanbul.[8] Apart from music, which was the central focus of these events, the participants entertained themselves with poetry readings and discussions on history and aesthetics. Furthermore, the building of musical instruments always remained a private buisiness (with the single later exception of the influencial Department for Music Technology at the State Conservatory for Turkish music of the ITÜ, which was established in 1979). Consequently, as seen in the previous chapter, no standards emerged in this field, not even for the short-necked variant of the *bağlama,* which is now popular almost nationwide.

The strict Kemalist music policy continued only for less than twenty years. From the 1940s and '50s, Kemalist cultural politics became less consistent, and in particular the efforts to educate the people towards "Turkish culture" decreased. Some reforms were completely withdrawn, for example the Turcification of the *ezan* (McPherson 2011: 5; Kusi´c 1996: 168f)

> Around 1940 a radical change concerning Turkish folk music started. While until then Turkish folk music was perceived only as raw material, which needed to be polyphonized with Western techniqus, it was now seen as an art, which was to be spread among the masses. (Bartsch 2012: 54)

---

8 Şen 2001: 37–39, 51, 353; Ayas 2014: 309ff; Poulos 2011; Erguner 2000.

From 1938, the central instrument for the political influence on Turkish music was Radio Ankara, which from 1938-1949 was the only radio station in Turkey (except for a short attempt to revive Radio Istanbul in 1943-44).[9] Until at least the 1940s, only a few radio sets were available in Turkey, and radio programs broadcast in Istanbul and Ankara could only be received in some limited parts of Anatolia.[10] Even by 1964, only 36.8 percent of the country could receive broadcasts from the now several Turkish radio stations (Bartsch 2012: 75).

With the commissioning of Radio Ankara in 1939, the situation of folk music changed. Although the radio played mainly Western popular and classical music, other programs presented Turkish music, mostly played live. Here, local folk musicians (*mahalli sanatçı*), including for example Osman Pehlivan (1847-1942), Hisarlı Ahmet (1908-1984), Muharrem Ertaş (1913-1984) or Sadi Yaver Ataman (1906-1994), were presented to a growing audience. In 1940, Mesut Cemil began to perform Ottoman-Turkish songs at Radio Ankara with his "Choir for Historical Turkish Music" (see chapter IV). In a new program called "Songs of the Homeland" (*Yurttan Sesler*) from 1941, on this choir sung folk songs (Bartsch 2012: 131ff), and in the program "We learn a Folk Song" (*Bir Halk Türküsü Öğreniyoruz*) folklorist Muzaffer Sarısözen explicitely introduced regional folk songs to a national audience.[11] In 1947, Sarısözen founded his own folk music choir at Radio Ankara, called *Yurttan Sesler*, which soon found followers in Istanbul and Izmir. In these years a number of musicians worked at the radio, either as regular staff (in 1943 for example, 64 musicians just for Turkish music) or as guest musicians.[12] Musicians were selected by entrance exams, and educated further through a number of compulsory lectures, including classical Turkish music, folk music, music theory, voice care (*ses sağlığı*), ear training (*kulak terbiyesi*), Turkish and text reading (*Türkçe ve metin okuma*).[13] "Folk musician" became a serious profession, and in the following decades the technical and artistic level of folk music rose. The development of Radio Ankara and Istanbul and later TRT created a nationwide standardization of regional traditions, in particular concerning the choir and orchestra performances of both folk and Ottoman-Turkish Music.

Simaltaneously the strong rejection of Ottoman music weakened. In 1940 the municipal Istanbul Music Academy, revived its ensembles for Ottoman-Turkish

9 Bartsch 2012: 71. In addition several radio stations from neighboring countries gained some popularity in Turkey (Bartsch 2012: 76).

10 For this reason the ban of Ottoman-Turkish music on Turkish radio from 2 November 1934 – 6 September 1935 did not have any serious impact. In 1935 only 6.082 radio receivers were registered in Turkey, 3,244 of which were in Istanbul (Kocabaşıoğlu 1980:55; Bartsch 2012: 77ff). In the same year Radio Istanbul broadcast only 270 minutes daily, Radio Ankara only 90 minutes (Kocabaşıoğlu 1980: 58). Tekelioğlu 2001: 114; Yarman 2010: 1. I am obliged to Elif Damla Yavuz for bringing this point to my attention.

11 Paçacı 1999: 124; Yılmaz 1996; Şenel 1995; Sarısözen 1952.

12 Kütükçü 2012; Aksoy 2009; Bartsch 2012: 95ff.

13 Bartsch 2012: 100; Aksoy 2002: 332–333; Kozanoğlu 1988: 22.

music (*icra heyeti*), which then gave regular concerts, some of which were broadcast over the radio. In 1943 the Turkish department of this music academy re-opened, directed by Arel.[14] Beginning in the 1950s a general atmosphere of cultural liberalisation commenced, leading to the admission of political parties, elections, and a return of the visibility of Islam. "*In 1950 the state-forced music revolution in fact ended*" (Bartsch 2012: 41). Already in 1947 religious education had been re-introduced into schools and in 1949 an Islamic-theological faculty was founded in Ankara. Although the nationalistic incrimination of Ottoman-Turkish music continued during the 1950s, the newly founded Radio Istanbul included Ottoman-Turkish music in its program. In 1962, *divan müzik* already comprised 26 percent of the programming of Radio Ankara, folk music only nine percent, Western light music 25 percent, and Western classical music 14 percent (Kocabaşıoğlu 1980: 392). In 1953 in Konya the first *Mevlevi* festival was held. As already mentioned, the notation archive of TRT became a central resource for both folk and Ottoman-Turkish music.[15]

> The period from 1950-1970, except for a short time after the military coup in 1960, might be characterized as a kind of "soft politic" or "politic without politics" period, in which in cultural policy an understanding of *laissez faire* became effective, and in which some practices of the first quarter of the Republic ended. (Ada 2009: 90)

It was also in these years that folk music was included in school music books for the first time, whereas school education had previously been focused on Western music. The "People's Houses," on the other hand, the main institution for Kemalist cultural education, were closed in 1950.

While during the first decades of the Republic, cultural and musical politics were dominated by the idea of education, from the 1970s the dominant theme was the protection of music. In 1970, after the military coup, within a cabinet of technocrats, Talat Sait Halman became the first culture minister of the Republic. The following years wittnessed a number of important changes in Turkey's music life. In 1976 the state, mainly following the aesthetic ideas of Arel, founded the first state choir for "Classical Turkish Music," as well as the first conservatory for Turkish music, offering study programs for both Turkish "classical" and folk music. Politically influential was the (music) historian Yılmaz Öztuna, at that time member of the *Adalet Partisi* of Prime Minister *Süleyman Demirel* (Akdoğu 1990: 21ff). On the other hand, in 1973, the private "Foundation of Culture and Arts" IKSV, for the first time initiated the annual Istanbul Festival. A number of professional associations in the field of Turkish music were also founded during the following years.[16]

---

14 Aksoy 1985: 1211-1236; Ali 1983: 1531-1534; Oransay 1973.

15 The fourth edition of TRT's repertoire catalogue of classical Turkish music in 1983 already included 10,000 compositions (Kip 1983).

16 MESAM (*Türkiye Musiki Eseri Sahipleri Meslek Birliği*); MSG (*Musiki Eseri Sahipleri Grubu Meslek Birliği*; MÜYOR-BIR (*Müzik Yorumcular□ Meslek Birliği*); MÜZIKBIR (*Baglantılı*

After the 1980s coup, state control of music was further reduced (Yazıcıoğlu 2010: 241), however, with the important exception of an even stricter nationalistic control of folk music (Stokes 1992: 65f). All non-Turkish music was excluded, in particular Kurdish music, but also *arabesk* music from state institutions and media.

> The censorship was double edged. While some members of the [TRT] commission controlled the lyrics, others monitored the music. You could not use phrases reminiscent of Greek themes. You could not use the *saz* and piano together. You could never use *bouzouki*, *balalaika* or *cümbüş*. They were totally forbidden. (Yurdatapan 2016:24)

The main targets were politically left-wing lyrics and non-Turkish songs. In particular Kurdish music had been barred from public media such as radio and later TRT already earlier, while Turkish language Kurdish singers, including Malatyalı Fahri Kayan (1918–1969) and Diyarbakır'lı Celâl Gülses (died 1959) became famous. Later Kurdish *arabesk* singers such as Müslüm Gürses, Mahsun Kırmızıgül, Emrah and Ibrahim Tatlises were similarly successful. Only the emergence of audio cassettes in the late 1960s, enabled private local amateur reseachers to record music and the oral history of ethnic minorities.[17] The constitution of 1982, written by the military government of the September 12, 1980 coup, officially banned the Kurdish language and many Kurdish musicians were imprisioned. In the following years the Turkish government again tried to assimilate Kurdish culture by force, many Kurds even destroyed cassettes with recordings of Kurdish music in fear of reprisals by security forces.[18] The strict ban was lifted only in 1991.

In 1983, culture was addressed by the Ministry of Culture and Tourism (minister then Ilhan Evliyaoğlu), whose approach prioritised economics over either political ideology or culture as a value in its own right.[19] "*This last period [1980-2000] is marked by globalization and the parallel privatization of the culture industry.*" (Ince 2011: 194) The state monopoly on radio and TV ended in the 1990s, opening a period of neo-capitalist freedom which lasted until around 2013, when the APK returned to a model of greater state control of public and private media. Not only the state, but also municipalities became active in sponsoring culture. "*Today, in big cities like Istanbul, Izmir, Bursa and Kocaeli, the municipalities exist on the supply side of the cultural arena with investment in libraries, and in cultural, artistic and youth cultures.*" (Ince 2011: 195) Today, a number of ensembles for both Ottoman-Turkish music and Turkish folk music are directly attached to (and financed

Hak Sahibi Fonogram Yapımcıları Meslek Birliği); MÜ-YAP (*Mü-Yap Baglantılı Hak Sahibi Fonogram Yapımcıları Meslek Birliği*); MÜYA-BiR (*Baglantili Hak Sahibi Fonogram Yapımcıları Meslek Birliği*) Council of Europe 2013: 136f.

17 For private regional researchers see for example: for the Teke region Erkan 2014: 13-45; for Trabzon: Şenel 1994: 112ff, 2009a; and for Dersim (Tunceli): Greve & Şahin 2017.

18 Hemlink 2016: 203ff; During this period only some Kurdish recordings circulated (e.g. by Şakiro, Hûseynê Farê, Ayşe Şan, Meryem Xan, Îsa Perwarî), also some localy known *dengbejs* and other singers (Yücel 2009).

19 From 1991-2003 again a Ministry for Culture existed.

by) the Ministry of Tourism and Culture. In addition the Ministry and municipalities sponsor concert venues, and (to a smaller extent) the production of CDs and books.[20] Compared to other European countries, however, the financial resources which the Turkish government allocates to culture are relatively low: In 2010, the budget of the Ministry for Culture was 690 million Euros, the equivalent of 10 Euros per person. At the same time Greece (already in a deep financial crisis) spent 32 Euros per person; Russia, 30 Euros, Germany, 101 Euros and France, 197 Euros (Radikal, 18 April, 2011).

Looking back to the Kemalist music reforms, we might conclude that in spite of serious political efforts, at the end of the twentieth century no clearly definable "Turkish Music" style had come into being, rather music in Turkey had become radically individualized and diverse. Even Western Turkish music, in particular after the Second World War, was only rarely performed outside of Turkey and most Turkish composers remained internationally unknown. In a period when in Europe and America new avant-garde music styles emerged, most Western Turkish composers continued to write tonal and folklore music. Instead of contributing to the integration of Turkey into the Western world, Turkish Western folklore music became an indicator of its cultural isolation.

The reason for this failure of the Kemalist vision of music are of course complex and cannot be discussed here in detail. In general, however, one can hardly escape the assessment that the early Kemalist state largely overestimated its potential impact on music, musicians and music life. Its approach to music was too ideological, too abstract, and insufficiently based on knowledge of music and music life to allow any of its intended changes to become reality. Furthermore, the ongoing influence of nationalist and "westernizing" ideologies (as for example in the AEU system or the nationalist notion of "Turkish folk music," – see below) ultimately impeded any potentially more flexible or pragmatic responses to developing global influences.

An obvious indicator of the general uncertainity in contemporary music life in Turkey, a consequence of Kemalist ideology, is the confusing categorisation of music together with its terminology, beginning with the term for "music" itself. "Music" might be expressed by the Ottoman (originally greek) *mûsikî*, or by the newer word *müzik* of French origin; in earlier writings (mainly by Gültekin Oran-

---

[20] The sub-structure of the Ministry of Tourism and Culture includes general directorates of Fine Arts, State Turkish Sufi Music Community, State Historical Turkish Music Community, State Modern Dance Community, State Modern Folk Music Community, State Polyphonic Music Chorus, State Folk Dance, Ankara Turkish World Music Community, State Turkish World Dance and Music Community, Presidential Symphony Orchestra, State Symphony Orchestra (six orchestras), State Classical Turkish Music Chorus (eight choirs), State Folk Music Chorus (five choirs), State Turkish Music Community, State Turkish Music Research and Practice Community. Affiliated is further the General Directorate of State Opera and Ballet. Council of Europe 2013: 122ff.

say) the much less comon *küğ* is used, said to be of old Turkish origin. The background to this situation are the radical language reforms implemented from 1932 by the Society for Research on the Turkish Language (*Türk Dili Tetkik Cemiyeti*), which aimed to replace Arabic and Persian words and gramatical structures with "pure Turkish" ones.[21] Already in 1928 Arabic scripture had been replaced by the Latin alphabet. From 1941 new dictionaries were published, which introduced further neologisms and attempted to standardize the new Turkish language. A musical dictionary compiled with the participation of Ahmed Adnan Saygun in 1954, was not very influencial,[22] though around the same time the use of language for school education seems to have been standardized (Levand 1972: 462, 468). Non-Turkish languages spoken in Turkey, on the other hand, such as Arabic, Kurdish, Armenian or Laz were widely surpressed, and Kurdish after 1980 even forbidden.

As part of these reforms the language used to describe music also changed. The Arabic-Ottoman term, *îqâ'* (rhythm), for example, still used in the early notation editions of the Istanbul conservatory, was completely replaced by the similarly Arabic-Ottoman word, *usûl*; the word *pest* for lower octaves was replaced by the Turkish *kaba*. In particular when referring to Western music, a great number of terms of mainly French origin entered into the Turkish language (Steuerwald 1963: 124), and even in traditional Turkish music several terms were adapted from Western music (e.g. *form, teori*), and often used in parallel to Ottoman terms or neologisms. Later, some of these foreign words again became turkified, for example *akompanye* (accompany) to *eşlik*; *düo* (duo) to *ikileme*; *triole* to *üçleme*; *interpret* to *yorum*; *period* to *dönem* (Gedikli 1987: 9ff).

Around the early 1950s the official reformation of the Turkish language came to an end. While the goal of creating a pure Turkish failed, despite considerable efforts by the Turkish state, the reforms created a deep divide between contemporary musicians and listeners, and the (even late-) Ottoman writings on music. The access of Turkish readers to literature on Ottoman music had been impeded for decades, which also explains the widespread interest in the editions of Ottoman sources since the 1990s, as described in chapter III. Even the language of books on the early Republican period (including for example the seminal books of Suphi Ezgi) today appears antiquated and difficult to understand. Ottoman Turkish in the Republic of Turkey became a difficult language written in an unusual script.

As a result, there are at least two or three terms in use for any component of Turkish music theory today, which regulary causes confusion. Parts of *şarkı* might be called *zemin* or *ayrıltak*; *nakarat* or *kavuştak*; *meyan* or *coştak*; composed *makams* either *mürekkeb or birleşik makam*; the entrance tone of a given *makam* either *giriş* or *iptada*; melodic developments of *makams* either *çıkıcı* or *sâit* and *inici* or

21 Steuerwald 1963; Korkmaz 1974; Levend 1972: 355.

22 Steuerwald 1963: 38f. Türk Dil Kurumu (ed.): *Terim Anketleri: Müzik*, Ankara 1954 (Tansuğ 1991).

nazi respectively. In Özkan's theory book (1984/2003) even the table of contents includes several different terms, for example the third chapter "*şed* (*transposition = Göçürüm*)." In addition, here, the words *modülasyon*, *geç* or *makam değiştirme* might be used. However, as this last example demonstrates, issues of language sometimes obscure theoretical differences. In fact, changing a *makam* within a composition or a *taksim* is not the same as a modulation in classic-romantic – hence harmonic – Western music; and transposition again is something different. Of course, further, all theoretical concepts changed significantly over the time.

> Cantemir's treatise does not possess a single term to describe any form of "modulation" other than "transposition" (*şedd*). Modern Turkish music uses the term *geçki* (from *geç* = to pass) for "modulation," but this seems to be of twentieth century origin. [...] Modulation had a different role in the seventeenth century from the role it holds in the repertoire and practice of 19th-20th centuriy, i.e. "modern" Turkish music. The repertoire of modern Turkish music features modulation of a variety of types in all but the simplest compositions [...] In addition [Turkish music] uses fleeting modulations and single-note alterations very frequently. Sometimes variant versions of the same item may introduce these smaller modulations, and today choral directors and radio musicians commonly introduce them where they feel they might enhance the written score from which they are playing. (Feldman1993: 15f).

The diverse terms mentioned above may thus refer to different issues within a complex musical field, ranging from "modulation" to "transposition," "alteration" of single tones, or short extensions or changes of *makams*. In Ezgis theory, moreover the scales of several *makam*s are explained as transpositions (*göçürülmüş makam*; *şed makam*) of so-called "basic" *makam*s, as for example *nihavend* as *buselik* on g; *acemaşiran* as *çargâh* on f; *mahur* as *çargâh* on g.

Even more problematic is the terminology for Anatolian folk music. Until at least the mid-twentieth century no standard terminology existed in the villages, with regional differences combinging with a variety of Anatolian dialects and languages to resist standardization. Together with the growing collection of folk songs and the rise of folk music, this field's inclusion in general music education made the need for clear terminology urgent. The numerous sizes and forms of long-necked lute types in Anatolia, for example, used to be referred to by specific names, as for example *cura*, *çöğür*, *bağlama*, *tambura*, *divan*, *balta sazı*, *bulgar(î)*, *ikitelli*, *üçtelli*, *ırızva* or *thembur*.[23] Today the word *bağlama* is widely used as a general term for all types, while specifications of the different types and sizes are still not standardized (Terzi 2017). In many cases the attemps at terminological standardization of folk music simaltaneously implied their Turkification. None of the most well-known dictionaries for Turkish folk music even mention the Kurdish words for the poet-singers, *dengbêj* or for their songs (*kılam*).[24]

---

23 Duygulu 2014: 66ff; Gazimihal 1975; Picken 1975: 209f.

24 Duygulu 2014; Özbek (1998) 2014; Önaldı 1977; Gazimihal 1961.

Serious ideological and terminological problems also impede the description of musical styles. Even for clearly definable musical styles, no concensus exists on their ascribed vocabulary. About half a dozen terms (more or less in use) today describe the music tradition of, say, Itrî or Dede Efendi, each with differing historical or ideological implications: *geleneksel Türk müziği* ("traditional Turkish music"), *sanat müziği* ("art music"), *türk sanat müziği* ("Turkish art music"), *geleneksel Türk sanat müziği* (" Traditional Turkish art music"), *divan müziği* (music of the *divan* poetry), "*saray müziği*" or "*enderûn müziği*" ("court music"), *Osmanlı müziği* (Ottoman music), "*Osmanlı / Türk müziği*" ("Ottoman/Turkish music"), "*edvâr müziği*" ("*makam* theory book music"), "*makam müziği*", or "*klasik Türk müziği*" ("classical Turkish music") (Sahin 2009: 21). Unfortunatly none of these terms is completely convincing, rather each of them is problematic in its own way. The term "Turkish music" for example, employed before the twentieth century mainly by European writers, became widespread in Turkish publications beginning with Rauf Yekta's pioneering article in the *Encyclopédie Lavignac* (1922), up to Öztuna's *Encyclopedia of Turkish Music* (1976/90) and in many recent Turkish books on music. However, the term potentially excludes ethnically non-Turkish musicians (or at least puts them on the periphery). Morover, one might doubt in general if political, linguistic or ethnic categories – such as the term "Turkish" – necessarily meet with musicological categories. Comparable difficulties are encountered for example, with the similarly political term, "Kurdish music." Due to the great lack of musicological research in this field, we do not know if a musical stylistic area, comparable to the ethnic or linguistic borders of Kurdishness (and possibly other westiranian languages), exists.[25] Together with the rise of historical approaches, further doubts arose concerning the use of the term "Turkish music" for music before the foundation of the "Turkish" Republic in 1923, reminiscent of the different, even pejorative use of the term "Turkish" before the Republic's establishment. The potentially historically more appropriate term "Ottoman music," however, also implies problematic geographic and historic limitations. The music of all Ottoman territories, (including most of todays Arabic countries as well as the Balkans) in no way comprise a musical unit. In addition, a music history defined by the political-

25 Kurdish folk dances and epic singers show similarities over different regions. In addition, however, several regional or religious froms of song and recitation exist. The music of, say, Hakkâri, differs significantly from that in eastern Dersim or Northern Iran (as far as we know today). Similar musical phenomena might be referred to differently in different regions (Allison 2001: 114ff), while elsewhere similar terms might carry different meanings. *Kilam / kılam / kalâm* for example is a term for the songs of the *dengbêj*, the Zaza songs in Dersim (often with instrumental accompaniment) or the religious hymns of the *Ahl-e Haqq* in Iran. Again, insufficient research impedes clear statements on stylistic boarders. Just as many Kurds speak neighbored languages such as Turkish, Persian or Arabic, for many folk songs versions in more than one laguage are known, while it is impossible to prove one given version or even language as primary. In cities such as Diyarbakır, Mardin, Elazığ, Urfa in Turkey, Erbil and Sulaimaniye in Iraq, or Mahabad and Sanandaj in Iran, music is deeply influenced by neighbor music styles, melodies, instruments or performance practice anyway.

historical Ottoman period would set a frame from the fourteenth until the early twentieth century. Here, the question requires clarification, as to whether a political caesura such as the establishment or the collapse of an empire necessarily also implies a break in music history.

Terms implying social definitions, such as "Ottoman / Turkish court music" present new problems. As Cem Behar repeatedly underlined, the music in question was not only performed at the Ottoman court, but often also in numerous urban sites including dervish lodges, and houses of the upper but also of the lower social stratas. The term "Classical Turkish Music" (*Klâsik türk müziği*; recently sometimes also "classical Ottoman music"[26]), which became widespread after the late 1970s, obviously implys a comparison with, or rather the claim of equal value to the "classical" music of the West. Today, "Classical Turkish Music" is mostly understood as a nomination of a particular performance practice, that is by large choirs and orchestras.

If even the terminology of a historical and musically clearly definable style is in confusion, no consensus can be expected concerning the nomination of musical substyles, not to speak of the overwhelming musical plurality of the present. Under the impact of Kemalist ideology in particular, the term "Turkish folk music" (*Türk halk müziği*), its scope and limits over decades was one of the most politically sensitive issues in Turkey. In the late ninteenth century, both European and Ottoman intellectuals and musicians supposed the existence of two cultural and hence musical worlds, that is *alaturka* (*şark*) and *alafranga* (*garp*). This division included multiple elements of culture and lifestyle, for example, styles of dress, eating habits, beliefs, behaviours and of course music (O'Connell 2000; 2005). The term *Alafranga*, that is "occidental" way, introduced already during the *Tanzimat* period around 1850, hence encompased Western arts, life style, operetta, *kanto*, later tango and march music. Both supposed musical worlds were often compared with each other, and the idea of a musical synthesis was discussed and practiced.[27] Within this setting, towards the end of the ninteenth century, the idea emerged that Anatolian folk music would be the "true" Turkish music, as opposed to Ottoman art music. The field of *alaturka* hence divided into two subfields, defined by nationalist ascriptions rather than by musical criteria.[28] During the early Republic, Ottoman music even became a symbol for reaction, seen as being "foreign" to the "Turkish people." Several scholars, such as Yekta, Ezgi and Arel tried to decribe Ottoman music as being similarly "Turkish" music. The most elaborate ideological defence of Ottoman-Turkish music was Sâdettin Arel's article series, "To whom belongs Turkish music" (*Türk Musikisi Kimindir*).[29] Arel's idea, that Turkish folk and art music would share the same "Turkish roots," though con-

26 E.g. CD Emirgan Ensemble: *Klasik Osmanlı Müziği*, Kalan1995.
27 Behar 1987b: 87; Aksoy 1985.
28 Balkılıç 2009; Şenel (ed.) 2000; Öztürkmen 1998; Behar 1987: 93ff; Aksoy 1985; 1989: 2.
29 1939/1940 (1969); Ayas 2015: 329-344; Behar 1987.

stantly challenged and discussed, has generally remained dominant until today. Contemporary scholars, such as Okan Murat Özkan and Cenk Güray even reject terms such as "Turkish folk music" and "Turkish classical music," and prefer an approach of "integrated traditional music."[30] In his recent Ph.D. thesis, Okan Murat Özkan (2014), for the first time tried to prove this approach by extended and detailed musical analysis. In general, however, while musicological research on musical styles and stylistic differences based on musical analysis is a widely neglected field in Turkey, the debate over styles was (and still is) dominated by ideology. This sensitive and ideological discussion even affects the terminology and general approach of music theory. Since no research on folk music was ever practiced before the early twentieth century, early Turkish folk music researchers were forced to develop a terminology anew, and hence adapted the concepts and terminology of either Western musicology or Ottoman music theory. In Anatolian villages, a terminology for the melodic or rhythmic structure of its music, for example, hardly existed. Gazimihal in his book "*Usûls* of Turkish Folk Music" (*Türk Halk Musikisi Usûlleri*, 1929 / 1962), used the Ottoman term *usul* (the term for a complex system of form and rhythms in Ottoman music) also for Anatolian rhythm, while his categorisation of "*usul*" as basic, mixed and combined meters (1. *Ana usûller ve üçerli şekilleri*, 2. *Birleşik usûller*. 3. *Karma usûller*) substantially differed from the Ottoman concept, hence underlining the difference between Turkish folk music and Ottoman music, which in his time was still viewed with discrimination.[31] However, what would have made more sense? The adaption of Western concepts and terms, as for example "rhythm," "meter," "bar" or "beat" would imply even more different concepts. Similar discussion exists concerning the pitch system or the concept of *makam*. As a pendant of *makam*, the concept of *ayak* (literary "foot," a term of folk poetry) was developed in the 1950s by Arseven and Yönetken.[32] A generally accepted canon for concepts and terms for Turkish folk music still does not exist.

The question of musical styles and substyles raises similarly ideologically sensitive issues. In fact, "folk music" between Thrakia and the Caucasia includes a great number of musical (sub) styles, sometimes in close contact with the music of neighboring areas outside of Turkey. Turkish *zeybek* and Greek *zeibekiko* are interconnected, as are Kurdish folk dances and *dengbêj* in, say, Hakkarı and Kurdish Iran. Many genres of Anatolian folk music could be compared with traditions

---

30 Öztürk 2014; Şahin 2009: 22f.

31 Terzi 2015; Öztürk 2015: 182; Gazimihal 1961: 215-244. Similar classifications of "folk" rhythms": İlerici 1981: 253: *Küçük* [minor] *usûller* (2, 3, 4, 5, 6/8, 9/8, 12/8, 7, 8, 9, 10); *Büyük* [major] *usûller* (11 and more); Arseven 1957: basic meters (2, 3, 4); mixed meters: (6/8, 9/8, 12/8); additive meters: (5, 7, 9,10); Sarısözen 1962: *Ana* [basic] *usûller*: (2,3,4 and 6/8, 9/8, 12/8); *Birleşik* [compound/additive] *usûller*: (5,6,7,8,9); *Karma* [mixed] *usûller*: (10 and more).

32 Niyazi Yılmaz (1996); for example *müstezat ayağı = rast makamı; garip ayağı = hicaz makamı* usw. Emnalar 1998: 548ff.; Markoff 2001: 84ff.; Stokes 1992: 50ff.; Akdoğu 1994.

outside of Turkey, for example in the Balkans, Armenia, Iran, and as far as Central Asia. Over decades, Kemalist politics attempted to construct the concept of a homogenous "Turkish folk music," and all claims of regional or even ethnic differences were perceived as cultural separatism. As an attempt to moderate the obvious regional differences, in particular for the long-necked lutes, today a standard of "regional styles" (*yöresel tavırlar*), implying patterns of melodic ornamentations, plectrum movements, and in particular left-hand movements and rhythms is widely established as a regular part of teaching programs.[33] Well-known *tavır*s include that of the Aegians, Thrakia, Ankara, Kırşehir, Yozgat, Konya, Kayseri, Silifke, Teke, Azerbaijan, and songs and ritual dances of Alevism (*deyiş* and *semah*). However, little research has been conducted to prove or describe these styles.

> Patently made-up is *tavır*, having recently come into existence. An example of this is '*Karadeniz tezenesi*,' the Black Sea plectrum pattern. This simply consists of adding a *çiftleme* (doubling) to any *aksak* rhythm. It is agreed by all, and particulary by *bağlama* players in Trabzon and the Eastern Black Sea lowland, that no such thing exists, even though is has been granted the status of *tavir* by Yener's recent *bağlama* method (1987)... (Stokes 1992: 78f)

Most musicological publications on regional music styles define the scope of their research along provincial borders, for example music in Muş, music in Trabzon, music in Gaziantep or music in Elazığ. Without any discussion of the limits of musical styles, they hence rely completely on political or administrative borders. Only few scholars have seriously tried to analyse commonalities or differences between substyles, an approach which could replace the ongoing ideological debate. The widespread lack of a source-based historical perspective on folk music, not to speak of the general exclusion of Armenian music before 1915 as a possible factor, further complicates the situation. As a result of the dearth of research due to the influence of Kemalism, the ideologically crucial question of whether "Turkish folk music" and "Turkish art music" are part of one music style or two, cannot be answered scientifically. On the one hand, obviously no clear musical border divides urban music in Istanbul or Izmir from the regions surrounding them. Music of the Aegean area, and even urban music from Elazığ or Urfa in south-east Anatolia, obviously share strong structural similarities with "Ottoman art music." On the other hand, instruments such as the *bağlama* are used exclusively in Anatolian music (though by far not everywhere), and it has never been able to perform the subtle intonations of Ottoman-Turkish music. Historically a possible division of folk and urban music again is even more difficult to describe, as for example in the repertoire of Ali Ufukî (Feldman 2015). To conclude, from a purely musicological point of view, the concept of "Turkish folk music" is simply an ideological construct, which needs to be replaced by a much more detailed raster of musical styles and traditions.

[33] Aksoy 1989: 1; Stokes 1992: 50ff, 76ff; CD Coskun Gülâ, Kalan, 1999.

To summarise, if even for the wide field of more or less "traditional" music (including "Ottoman-Turkish art music," and "Turkish folk music") an appropriate terminology is widely missing, the plethora of individual music as described in chapter IV is completely beyond the scope of contemporary musical terminology. Kemalism is one causative factor in the extreme expansion of musical (sub) styles, while its ideology simultanesouly seriously impeded the perception and understanding of music.

On the other hand, as has been underlined before, most developments leading to the recent disintegration of musical traditions had already begun before the foundation of the Republic of Turkey. A general explanation hence has to go back further in history.

Education and Transmission

Within a larger historical framework, a crucial element in the development of music from the ninteenth until the early twenty first century, is the slow but ongoing decline of the *meşk*, resulting in a fundamental change in musical transmission and education. Since at least the early seventeenth century both the repertoire and its performance practice was transmitted exclusively by *meşk*, hence under the strict control of music masters (Behar 2012). Music theory books (*edvâr*) described pitches, *makam* and *usûl*s, but never intended to teach the music itself.

> Of course music history and theory can be learned from books *(edvâr)*. But this theory on its own is useless. Music first of all is action, since its reality does not exist in writings or in theory but in *meşk* and in performance. Evidently music is practice, it is performance; it is not only imagination or thought. The practice of music, however, can only and is only to be found in *meşk*. (Behar 2012: 35)

In contrast to the teaching of calligraphy for example, which often was done by exchange of assignments without personal contact, the interaction of music pupil and master was always both direct and physical (Behar 2012: 16). This direct contact implied a strict control of the correct performance of transmitted pieces, in addition to the transmission of the piece itself. In fact, both were inseparable and mutually connected. In Ottoman times compositions could only remain or even become famous if their composers managed to transmit them to other musicians, hence by performance in the *meşk*. To become a good musician without strong memory was simply impossible, similarly to compose without performing the new composition (Behar 2012: 63). The relationship of apprentice and master continued over months or even years – the learning of long and complex works alone might have taken weeks or even months (Behar 2012: 37). In addition to the transmission of compositions and their performance style, *meşk* included regular conversations (*sohbet*) on aesthetics, ethics, religion, and all aspects of music (Senay 2015b). A separate curriculum of, for example, vocal techniques or music history, as far as we know, was never practiced. Theoretical issues such as *makam* and *usul* were integral parts of the transmission of the repertoire, and not taught theoretically or with the help of written material (again, as far as we know today). *Meşk* was practiced widely in the urban context, while we know much less about teaching and the transmission of music in the countryside.[34] We can assume that teaching there was probably less organized, and more significantly, without the formalized beating of *usul*.

The emergence of new media in the nineteenth century, that is Hamparsum, Greek and Western staff notation for practical use,[35] printed books (the earliest known printed anthology of song lyrics was *Biblios Kaloumeni Evterpi* printed in Galata in the 1830s, the first in Turkish the *mecmûa* of Haşim Beys 1852/53; Behar 2012: 43), and eventually the print of staff notation from 1876 on, intially affected only slowly the structure of music transmission. Later, the printing of notation grew both in quantity and scope, making more and more music available, even without the need for *meşk* lessons with a personal teacher. Ismail Hakkı Bey (1866-1927) was the first musician who used staff notation both for education and for his own composition in a systematic way (Behar 1987: 44). In addition, around the beginning of the twentieth century, printed self-teaching books facilitated new approaches to music education.[36] In his treatise, "The Notation Teacher" (*Nota Muallimi*) published in 1883, Notacı Hacı Emin Efendi propagated the practical advantages of staff notation:

> In our country the science of music is taught in two ways, one of which being *alaturka*, hence the memorisation of the names of notes and *düm tek*, the other being European notation. If a person who is enthusiastic about learning the science of music via the Turkish method starts his education in his youth with a talented music teacher and engages in it to the utmost, he/she can acquire considerable amount of knowledge about it. However, a student who starts his/her education in the *alafranga* way, thus with notation, can within some months acquire the notes and the beats of the *usûl* by reading notations. Within a few years he/she will learn which notes the *makam*s of *peşrevs*, *semaî* and *şarkıs* he/she performs are built upon, and how the notation of a şarkı he/she had listen to has to be arranged. In the end he/she will learn the science of music perfectly."[37]

34 On of the few exceptions is Kalyoncu & Özata 2012, a case study on instrumental teaching in Bolu. For the education of *aşık* cf. Artun 2014.

35 Olley 2017; Ayangil 2008; 2010; Khalil 2009; O'Connell 2010

36 Alimdar 2016: 436; 326ff; Ayangil 2010:44ff; Paçacı 2010; early teaching books include Ali Salâhi Bey, *Hocasız Ud Ögrenmek Usûlu*, 1910; Mu'allim Ismâ'îl Hakkı Bey, *Usûlât, Solfej, Makâmât ve Ilâveli Nota Dersleri*, Istanbul 1925; Tanburi Cemil Bey, *Rehber-i Musıki*, Constantinople 1903; Mehmet Zati, *Nazariat-i Musıki ve Talim-i Kiraat-ı Musıki*, Istanbul c. 1905; Hasan Tahsin, *Gülzar-i Musıki*, Istanbul 1903/04; Kazim Zu, *Musikî Istilâhatı*, Istanbul 1894 (Ankara 1964). Behar 2012: 40; Greve 1995: 127f; Kalender 1978; Oransay 1973: 1501f; Borrel 1928: 520.

37 Paçacı 2015: 156ff; 2010: 116f; Erol 2003; Behar 2012: 79.

On the other hand, until the twentieth century, a strong and continuing opposition rejected notation as the "enemy of the science of music" (*fenn-i musiki düsmani*; Behar 2012: 18), accusing notation of reducing memory and the sence for *usûl*.

The introduction of notation for folk music began much later than for Ottoman-Turkish art music, that is in the early twentieth century, and the transformation to a written music culture is still in progress. However, the enlargement of the available repertoire due to the introduction of new media is even more obvious in the case of Anatolian folk music. While before the introduction of notation and sound recordings, musicians could learn songs other than their own either from a teacher (if there was one accessible), or from fellow musicians; today, thousands of pieces are available in the archive of TRT, whose copies widely circulate in digital forms). As mentioned before, TRT tried to control this repertoire by allowing only a strict selection of songs determined by committees according to political, literary-linguistic and musical criteria (Birdoğan 1992; Stokes 1992: 65f). The growing role of MC, CD and the internet, however, reduced the monopoly of TRT and hence the effectiveness of the control.

The growing importance of notation further created a closer relationship between music theory and musical practice, as elements such as pitch system and rhythm are necessarily and inseparately implicit in notation. In the later nineteenth century, some leading Mevlevi in Istanbul were interested in music theory, that is Hüseyin Fahreddin Dede (1854-1911), Atâullah Dede (1842-1910) and Celâleddin Efendi (1848-1907). Their pupils Rauf Yekta, Suphi Ezgi, Sâdeddin Arel and Ahmed Avni Konuk later became dominant in Turkish music theory of the early twentieth century. Between 1913 and 1920 Yekta, Ezgi and Arel Artikel published articles on music theory in several journals including *Şehbal*, Millî and *Tetebbular Mecmuası*, while after 1923 the physician, Sâlih Murad Uzdilek replaced Yekta. This later group published their theoretical writings beginning in the 1930s. The seminal works of Rauf Yekta (1914) and Suphi Ezgis (1933-53) might be perceived as a phase of codification and (at least attempted) standardization of Ottoman-Turkish music.

> The rationalization, theorization and subsequent standardization of traditional Ottoman/Turkish music was a vast enterprise, initiated towards the end of the last century by Rauf Yekta Bey (1871-1935), and brought to fruition in the 1940s and 50s by two of his colleagues and contemporary composers and musicologists: Hüseyin Sadettin Arel (1880-1955) and Dr. Subhi Zühtü Ezgi (1869-1962). Pitch, scale, intervals and *makams* were standardized and adapted to western staff notation. Rhythmic patterns (*usûls*) musical genres and pieces were classified and systematized. (Behar 2001: 97)

The pitch system and notation developed by Arel, Ezgi and Uzdilek (generally known as the Arel-Ezgi-Uzdilek system, AEU) includes 24 unequal intervals per octave, the whole tone (8:9, 204 cent) is divided into nine intervals of equal size, the so called *koma* of almost 23 cent (Arel 1991; Uzdilek 1944). Only five positions out of these nine are in fact used: *koma* (23 cent), *bakiye* (90 cent), *küçük mücennep* (114 cent), *büyük mücennep* (180 cent) and *tanini* (204 cent). In line with Ottoman music theory and practice, notations of the nineteenth century and similarly the notation system of Rauf Yekta, used the scale of *makam rast* as a general scale, which means that accidentals were needed for all pitches outside of *rast.* [38] For almost half a century, from 1875-1928, notation print progressed with only the two accidentals of staff notation (# and b), although in practice, Ottoman music had many more intervals. The exact intonation was simply deduced from the *makam.* Arel and Ezgi radically changed this notation system, taking the Western diatonic C major scale as general scale, which they claimed to be based on *makam çargâh*, although the traditional *makam* of this name had a completely different interval structure. The main impact of this change concerns the note placed on the middle line of the notation system, which would be *segâh* or (in AEU) the slightly higher tone *bûselik*, which is equivalent to the Western b flat. Since in Ottoman-Turkish music *segâh* is much more frequent than *bûselik*, the older system made more musical sense. However, as a consequence, the interval below the middle staff line would be smaller than the one above it. Similar inconsistencies, however, already exist within Western music notation, where for example (with a G clef) the interval between the middle staff lines and its higher intervening space is only a minor second, while the one below the middle staff line is a major second. In Yekta's system, however, the b would indicate different intervals, depending if it is placed before *segâh* or before any other tone. The AEU system further introduced additional accidentals, shaped in the model of Western accidentals, in order to make all pitches clearly readable, independent from the *makam.* These new accidentals, however, still contained the potential for misunderstandings. The Western # and b flat, here, look more "conventional" – as looking similar to Western use – than the new ones, while in musical practice no such preference exists.

Contemporary standard notations of folk tunes use, in addition to the Western accidentals, two more accidentals, that is *b²* / #², indicating tones lowered / raised by two *komas*. Again practical intonation in Anatolian might differ regionally. In most lectures for *bağlama*, the teachers prefer solmization syllables (do, re, mi, fa, so, la, si, do), and the singing of melodies on their respective solfege syllables are a regular part of folk music education.

The main problem with all attempts at notation, however, is even deeper. The intonation of certain tones within some *makams* changes according to the melodic environment. According to Banu Şenay, the well-known *ney*-Player Salih Bilgin (b. 1960), himself a student of Niyazi Sayın (b. 1927), explained during his *meşk*:

---

38 Say 1985 "Türk Müziği Yazıları", p. 934. The ground tones of the most popular fifteen *makams* are on the general scale of *rast*: D – *yegah* (*yegah, sultani yegah, şedaraban*); E – *yegah* (*hüseyni-aşiran, suzidil*); F – *acemaşiran* (*acemaşiran*); F# – *ırak* (*ırak, eviç*); G – *rast* (*rast, mahur, nikriz, nihavend*); A – *dugah* (*uşşak husseyni nevâ, hicaz, bûselik, kurdi, saba, beyati, isfahan*); B – *segâh* (*segâh, hüzzam*).

> We need to think of pitches as zones *(bölge)*. The pitch *dik kürdi*, for example, has its own territory. (…) If we take Turkish music as a music of relationship *(münasebet musikisi)*, the essential thing we need to grasp is each pitch's relationship to another. The secret of learning this music lies in understanding those relationships. (…) Music theory calls that distance 'interval' *(aralık)*. But if we think of that distance as 'interval', we will never become free from the rules of theory. If we treat that distance as relationship, then we might be able to search for those spiritual relationships between sounds." (Senay 2015b: 532)

These details of intonation are frequent issues of discussion among musicians.

> The perceptive listener to Turkish classical music will often observe discrepancies, both small and large, in the performance of the 'same' pitch – whether by two different musicians, or by the same musician at two different points in time. Intonation is often a personal matter of opinion. Two outstanding musicians performing together can continuously play the pitch Puselik (h) so out of tune with each other as to cause discomfort. (Signell 1977: 44)

In some *makams* hence pitches outside of Arel's system are used (for example in *uşşak* or *sabâ*)[39], some of them do not even carry a name. Salih Bilgin emphasized the importance of "pitch sensibility " (*perde hassasiyeti*), that is,

> the ability to hear/discern and articulate correctly the pitches and intervals in a certain melodic line. (…) Although there are twenty-four tones in an octave, in the playing of a *makam* there may be many more. These intervals and pitch inflections are not captured in the notation system; they are learned through listening and performing. (Senay 2015b: 532).

This problem of correct intonation and the theoretical number and sizes of intervals is further problematic in a historical perspective, as mentioned in chapter III.[40] Today, a general consensus exists that the Arel-Ezgi-Uzdilek (AEU) interval and notations system, in fact standard in Turkish music, fits neither the musical practice nor to theoretical calculations, and urgently needs to be reformed. Over the twentieth century several scholars proposed alternative pitch and notation systems, though no new consensus was reached.[41] Turkish music theorists today do not even agree on the number of intervals for Turkish music (17, 24, 29, 30, 41, or 53; Ayangil 2010:54f; Yarman 2007). Some attempts to measure the intonation have not coalesced into a final result, but rather demonstrated the complexity of intonation and the lack of standards.[42] In July 2011, the music academy of the ITÜ decided to use the new notation developed by Nail Yavusoğlu (2008; 2013), however, a general consensus among musicians on this decision again does not exist.

---

39 Signell 1977: 37ff; Oransay 1973: 1498.

40 Feldman 1996: 217-18. In fact, intonation at the time of Cantemir might have been nearer to the practice in contemporary Iran than to Turkey (Feldman 1996). Only the French-Syrian *kanun* player Weiss has tried to perform Cantemir according to this historic intonation (Pohlit 2011: 44ff).

41 Oransay 1959; Karadeniz 1965/ 1984 (based on Abdülkadir Töre (1873–1946)); Zeren 1978, Tura 1988; recently Yarman 2007.

42 Signells 1977: 153-159; Bozkurt, Yarman, Karaosmanoğlu & Akkoç 2009.

In addition to the alterations in the basic scale and the additional accidentals, the absolute pitch of the notation also changed. While *Yekta* defined *dugâh* as Western d, *dügâh* was later interpreted as a = 440 Hz. In musical practice, however, pitches change according to tuning systems and the range of the singer. "*Since there is no* akord *in which everybody is at home, transposition is a necessary and normal part of musical practice.*" (Stubbs 1994: 90) And again, even worse is the situation of absolute and relative pitches in Turkish folk music. While in actual performance of professional ensembles the absolute pitch might change, and it is far from fixed in village performances, in contemporary Turkish notation practice, all folk tunes are notated with a finalis on a (=la). This issue of transposing notation together with proposals for its reformation have been discussed intensively among Turkish musicians, with little consensus reached.

Another central issue for music theory in Ottoman times and in the early twentieth century, is the desription of *makams*. Ezgi constructed *makams* focusing on their scale, as constructed by tetrachords and pentachords. His system includes thirteen basic *makams* (*basıt makam*), compound (*mürekkep*) and transposed *makams* (*sed*). In addition, every *makam* is characterized by its melodic behavior (range / *tessitura*), its hierachy of tones (at least tonic, and *güclü*), its melodic direction (*seyir*), its melodic gestures, phrases (*çeşni*), modulations to other *makams*, and often its intonation of certain tones. Again, a standardization has not been achieved, and actually would be far from musical reality.

> Within the tradition I have seen practiced by my teacher, the character of a single *makam* is manifest in great variety. Most musicians would agree that the concept of *makam* is defined by a structure and a progression, though the particulars of the precise structure and seyir is a matter open to much debate. (Stubbs 1994, 124f)

Over the twentieth and early twenty first centuries, a number of encompassing descriptions of *makams* have been published, which include theoretical descriptions, but often even more extended notations of composition, which relate their approach to the traditional concept of *meşk*.[43] Today, *makam* is at least partly learned as music theory and on the basis of written (and printed) theoretical explanations, and not, as before, as part of a repertoire.

The formal institutionalization of music education in Turkey began in the Second Constitutional era in 1908, when a general liberalization made the foundation of private music associations and schools possible (*Musikî-i Osmanî, Dârü'l Mûsikî Osmani*, a few years later *Darüt-talim-i Musiki*, *Şark Musiki Cemiyeti*, *Gülşen-i Musiki Mektebi* and *Darülfeyz-i Musiki*). Most of these *cemiyetis* offered music lessons in the form of *meşk*, organised concerts, some even published printed nota-

43 Aksoy 2000; Yekta (1922), Ezgi (1933-53), Arel (1991 (1943-48), Karadeniz 1983 (begun 1965), Özkan 1984, Kutluğ 2000 (8 vol), Aydemir 2010, Ederer 2011 and Yavuzoğlu 2011. Printed books on music theory, including Ezgi (1933-53), Karadeniz (1965/1984), Özkan (1984/ 2000) untill Yahya Kaçar (2012).

tion (*Dârü't Tâlim-i Mûsikî*).[44] In particular public conservatories then gradually introduced Western models of music education.[45] In 1914 the theater academy *Darü'l Bedâyi* was founded with a music department, which in 1917 became *Darü'l Elhân*, the first conservatory in Turkey with programs for both Western and Turkish music.[46] In parallel, a conservatory was founded in Ankara, which offered study programs in Western music. In other Turkish cities, music academies or departments for educating music teachers were founded later. After 1973 conservatories became integral parts of universities. In 2015, there were 39 state conservatories in Turkey.[47]

> The "School for Music Teachers" (Musiki Muallim Mektebi, 1924), "Istanbul Municipal Conservatory" (Istanbul Belediye Konservatuarı, 1925), Gazi Terbiye (1928), the "Ankara Conservatory" (1936), "Izmir Conservatory" (1954) and the "State Conservatory for Turkish Music" (Türk Musikisi Devlet Konservatuarı, 1975) were considered as important milestones in terms of the institutionalization of musical life. Thus in Turkey, one single type of education based on Western lines, but two types of conservatories were established: conservatories for Western music and those for Turkish music respectively. Moreover, even Turkish music conservatories had basic programs, which were equipped with a structure and functions that imitated Western musical conservatories and adopted the latter as role models. A remarkable number of the programs were based on Western musical education. In fact, Western ideology founded a hegemonic and hierarchical model and this model was appropriated politically by everyone. (Öztürk 2015: 184)

Among musicians of Ottoman-Turkish music, however, *meşk* continued to be practiced. Traditional performers, including for example Alâeddin Yavaşça (b. 1927) and Bekir Sıdkı Sezgin (1936-96) organised *meşk* outside the conservatory education (Behar 2012: 189). From 1939 on, Radio Ankara offered regular lessons for professional musicians working there, both in folk and Ottoman-Turkish music, the latter mainly in form of *meşk*. Teachers included Muzaffer Sarısözen for folk music; and for Ottoman-Turkish music in 1966 for example, Cüneyd Orhon, Alâeddin Yavaşça, Cevdet Çağlar, Ercüment Berker, Hakkı Derman, Münir Nurettin Selçuk, Necdet Yaşar, Nevzat Atlığ, Niyazi Sayın and Şefik Gürmeriç (Aksoy 2009: 179; Beken 1989: 128). Even many teaching books, including those for *ud* by Mutlu Torun (1996) or for *ney* by Süleyman Erguner (1986/2002), stress the importance of a personal teacher in addition to written material (Behar 2012: 186).

In the case of Ottoman-Turkish art music, the incorporation of recordings in the learning process is documented almost as early as the emergence of the Turkish recording industry, from around the first quarter of the twentieth century until today.[48] While some musicians (mainly in the post World War II era) created

44 Alimdar 2016: 422ff; Behar 1998: 140–142; 2012: 174; Ergin 1977: 1053ff; Oransay 1973.

45 Akkoç 2015, Ayangil 2008: 403; Poulos 2011; Behar 2012.

46 Alimdar 2016: 422; Kolukırık 2015; Akçay 1993: 20; Aksoy 1985: 1235; Özalp 1984: 81-87; Ergin 1977: 1271-1280; 1309-1320; Oransay 1973; Sürelsan 1971.

47 http://muzikegitimcileri.net/universite/konserve.html, accessed January 26, 2017.

48 Behar 2012: 191; Poulos 2011: 9; Bates 2011: 44.

transcriptions of recorded *taksims* –especially those of Tanburi Cemil Bey (d. 1916)– most serious musicians learned many of these *taksims* by repeatedly listening to the original recording, rather than from transcriptions.

The today most important conservatory for Ottoman-Turkish and folk music is the State Conservatory for Turkish Music, (attached to the ITÜ), which opened in 1975. Its seven principal departments include basic knowledge for music teachers (*temel bilim*), musicology, composition, instrument making, vocal education, music instruments, and folk dance. Since their foundation, similar conservatories for Turkish music struggle with the challenge to integrate traditional approaches of teaching into an institution and didactic concepts imported for the West. Conservatories, in general, separate the holistic traditional education into disciplines such as instrumental playing techniques, voice training, music theory, repertoire, music history etc.

The education of professional folk musicians within a music academy even had to be developed anew, as an institutionalized education for folk music never existed before. Still today, no consesus exists on approach and methods, and hardly any academic didactic on the education for *bağlama* exists (Özdek 2016; Akdag 2017). Even more unclear is the education for singers of folk music. In particular since the 1990s numerous teaching books for *bağlama* have been published, most of which have a similar structure: Following a short introduction into (an adapted) staff notation system, the main part of the book includes notations of compositions, in between some advice on playing technique and *tavır*. A developed didactic methodology is only rarely attempted, most books directly mirror the personal teaching style of experienced teachers. Today an experienced *bağlama*-player is expected to be familiar with a large number of tunings, styles and *tavır*s on different types of lutes (*bağlama*, *cura*, bass *bağlama* etc); and have the ability to improvise introductions in different regional styles. Most professional musicians are excellent prima vista performers, though the aesthetic value of knowing a large repertoire by heart is still high. In addition to the already challenging education in their main instrument and musical style, contemporary traditional musicians are expected to have at least basic knowledge of other musical traditions in Turkey, that is folk music or art music respectively, as well as Western music and its harmonic language, jazz and sometimes even contemporary Western music. At ITÜ, students of Turkish music have to also attend compulsory lessons in piano, harmony and counterpoint over their years of study. In addition to traditional instruments, the music academy of the ITÜ also offers lecture for Turkish music students in chello, viola, violine, clarinet and double bass.

In addition to formal music academies, contemporary lessons in traditional Turkish music are offered by numerous education centres of the Greater Istanbul Council and local municipalities, private associations or teaching centres (*dershane*), and furthermore by numerous teaching books, CD, DVD or VCD with teaching programs, or in online lectures.[49] Several non-Turkish musicologists, reported their personal experience of lessons in Turkish music, in most cases an individual combination of *meşk*, notation and other materials and methods.[50] O'Connell for example describes a lesson of vocal performance with Dr. Alâeddin Yavasca in the early 1990s:

> When teaching a semi-classical song *(şarkı)*, Dr. Yavasca first performed the whole piece without interruption from a musical score, often using his own transcription of the piece and sometimes being accompanied by a student on the plucked zither *(kanun)*. Subdividing the song into discrete poetic units (in this instance: *zemin*, *nakarat*, *meyan* and *nakarat*), he asked all the students to perform after him each section of the work using the Turkish system of solfège *(solfej)*. The whole procedure was then repeated with meter *(usûl)*, students beating the rhythmic cycle on their knees *(usûl vurmak)*. When this operation was accomplished to his satisfaction and when he had clarified significant points concerning tuning and accuracy, he introduced the song text *(güfte)*. Here, he translated words not used in modern Turkish and pointed out potential difficulties with regard to pronunciations. Puncuating the lesson with musical insights, literary comments and historical anecdotes, he finally asked the students (both individually and collectively) to perform the whole piece by integrating the melody and the text following the didactic sequence outlined above. (O'Connell 2010: 23)

It is noteworthy that in Turkish musicology a wide range of related issues has only recently begun to be researched, for example the perception and reception of music, music psychology, sociology of music, and possibly most important: the didactic of music.[51]

Today it is impossible to become a master musician solely via traditonal *meşk* (Behar 2012: 183). Meanwhile the complete repertoire of Ottoman-Turkish music is available in written form, composers even write down new works directly. However, it is still important for musicians to perform from memory rather than from notations. The state choir of the Presidency for example, has a repertoire of about 3000 pieces, mainly known by heart. On the other hand all singers are experienced sight readers of notations. Similarly good folk musicians are still revered acording to their large repertoires which they know by heart. Many contemporary musicians play from digitilised notation as stored in tablet computers, which again expands the available notations.

---

49 Senay 2015b: 527f; 2014: 407; Stokes 1992: S:43ff.

50 For example Klaser's (2001: 62ff) description of "learning the *makam*" with Yusuf Ömürlü at *Kubbealtı Müzik Akademisi*.

51 Musicology is still a new field in Turkey. The first institute for musicology was founded by Gültekin Oransay (1930-1989) at the Ege Üniversitesi in Izmir in 1976, followed by institutes at Mimar Sinan State Conservatory (1983), İTÜ, Ankara State Conservatory of Hacetepe University (1986). In 2000s already 20 departments for musicology existed all over Turkey (Çolakoğlu Sarı 2015: 6). Introductions into the field in Turkish include Karahasanoğlu & Yavuz 2016; Kaplan 2005; Özer 2002; 1997; Uslu 2006.

This loss of the primacy of performance (as in the *meşk*) to written notation and some decades later to audio recordings, resonates what Walter Benjamin described in 1935 in his famous essay, "The Work of Art in the Age of Mechanical Reproduction" (*Das Kunstwerk im Zeitalter seiner technischen Reproduzierbarkeit*), as the loss of the "presence in time and space," the loss of "authenticity" or "aura" of works of art, hence the loss of their unique aesthetic authority. As described in chapter III, the decline of *meşk* and the growing importance of written sources changed the notion of music of the past, and historical notations could become objects of the present. The self-evident inbeddedness of contemporary music in music of the past hence has almost been lost in modern Turkey, or at least changed its character to become "music history."

Main reason for the recent individualization of musical traditions, then, is the loss of aesthetic control by experienced music masters as a consequence of the decline of *meşk*. *Meşk* densely controlled both the repertoire and its performance together, its standardizing power obviously was much stronger than later that of notation, which only saved the composition, but not its realisation, interpretation and aesthetics. Printed notation and even more audio recordings hence became accessible and amenable to all kind of musical interpretation.

Conclusion

This book began with impressions of the music life in Istanbul in 2010, with its amazing diversity of musical practices. Istanbul today is a global music city where numerous individual, more or less professional musicians live and work, most of them internationally well-connected. Abundant music projects are domminated by elements of numerous musical traditions, while these music traditions as discrete units have widely disintegrated. This Turkish music life today is hence characterized by an advanced process of individualization. This development is the result of both global and national factors.

1. The emergence of new media, such as notation, printed books and the technology of audio recordings, led from the early ninteenth century to a slow and still ongoing decline of the *meşk*, the traditional system of music transmission and education. This development had a deep impact on musical aesthetics, music theory, didactics, the musical repertoire, and the notion of the musical past. Musicians today do not necessarily perceive themselves as part of one music tradition, that is a direct and personal heritage, characterized by the control of repertoire and musical quality, which does not ask for personal decisions or innovation. The strict control of muscial transmission by music masters has weakened, while the available repertoire enlarged substantially to include every music which can be bought, copied or uploaded in any form of notation or sound recording. Today, music of the past has become an object of personal interpretation.

The adaption of notation further influenced music theory, which also had to reflect upon appropriate forms and uses of this new technique. Until today the numerous inconsistencies in the Western staff notations adapted for Ottoman-Turkish music are a much discussed issue in Turkey, without no general consensus beyond a deep dissatisfaction with the Arel-Ezgi-Uzdilek system of notation and intonation, which nevertheless still forms the (almost) only standard in Turkish music today. Except for the issue of notation, however, Turkish music theory continued to be written mainly within the Ottoman tradition of reflection and calculation of intervals, tone system, *makam* descriptions and (to a minor degree) *usul* and metric. Hardly any theorist has addressed aesthetics or musical-technical issues related to contemporary music. Kemal İlerici was the only theorist who attempted to develop an adaption of polyphony / harmony for traditional Turkish music. Similarly no specific method for instrumentation or arrangement has been written, almost nothing on musical form and no theory of composition.

As a didactic method, until today, *meşk* has not been completely replaced by Western models of music education, though music academies regularly offer separate lectures in issues such as instrument / vocal technique, music theory, music history etc., instead of the traditional holistic teaching. In most cases various combinations of *meşk* and Western approaches, including lectures or written teaching materials are practiced. Even more complicated is the search for an appropriate teaching methodology for folk music, where prior to the early Republic hardly any standard of education ever existed. It is noteworthy, that within the field of Turkish musicology, which in general has developed impressively over the last decades, issues such as psychology of music and moreover didactics of music have hardly been scientifically researched.

Globalisation, closer international relations, increased feasability of travel and the emergence of an international Turkish diaspora, all contributed to enlarge the scope of Turkish musical life and at the same time the range of available music styles. Emigration from the Ottoman Empire to America and Europe, hence out of the Islamic world, began in the later nineteenth century. Until the mid-twentieth century migration in Turkey mainly influenced Western Turkish music. But over the last twenty-plus years historical neighbors such as Iran, countries, which were in the past part of the Ottoman Empire such as Greece or Bulgaria; and finally countries, such as Armenia and Israel, founded partially by former Ottoman minorities, intensified their musical interactions with Turkey.

In general, migration, international mobility, as well as the growing global mediascape expanded the available individual experiences and available musical styles to an unprecedented degree. In particular so-called world music led to the emergence of a plethora of individual musicians and ensembles, among them also many who performed (among others) more or less Turkish music. Since the late 1980s the market for all kinds of traditional music in Europe and America grew: Islamic music; rhythmical and instrumental music; cross-cultural encounters of Indian, Flamenco and many other music traditions with Turkish musicians; early European music in dialogue with Middle Eastern traditions; and contemporary Western music integrating elements of traditional Turkish music.

Both the repertoire of "Turkish music" and musical practice, including arrangement, instrumentation and harmonisation developed what might be called "Turkish music" or "traditional music in Turkey" to an unprecedented level.

2. In addition to these global changes, which more or less affected all music cultures worldwide, local and national factors in Turkey also influenced music and music life. Most important was the deep influence of Kemalist ideology and cultural politics. Probably more than any other state in the world, the Kemalist Republic of Turkey, at least during its first two decades, used great force to attempt to realize an explicit vision of its music and music life. While this vision of a national Turkish music, to be created by the arrangment of folk music within Western musical structures did not become reality, state policies still had a great impact in their strong support of Western music, which led to a well-established and rich Western music life in Turkey, numerous good composers, performers and compositions.

As another consequence of Kemalism, the political and aesthetic value of Anatolian folk music substantially increased. New institutions such as the radio, later TRT, music academies and numerous performance ensembles established folk music in Turkey as both popular and artistic music. The main problem in Kemalist music policy was its focus on nationalistic ideology, which largely dominated over concrete knowledge of music, and led to a naïve overestimation of the political influence on music. The foundation of conservatories and the implementation of music eduction in schools did not replace traditional *meşk*, but only added further didactic methodologies, hence fostering diverse, mostly hybrid didactic approaches. Hardly any scientific reflection has dealt with transitions or combinations of the diverse didactic methodologies. Even more underestimated was the potential range of musical syntheses between Turkish and Western music traditions, which led to immense musical diversity. Kemalist ideology further influenced terminology and the notion of music styles, for example the artifical separation of "Turkish art music" and "Turkish folk music."

The impact of numerous individual Turkish musicians, composers or scholars, too often ignored or underestimated as a factor, must also be taken into account. Persons such as Tanburi Cemil Bey, Rauf Yekta Bey, Hüseyin Saddetin Arel, Münir Nurettin Selçuk, Ahmet Adnan Saygun, Muzaffer Sarısözen, Nevzat Atlığ, Zeki Müren, Kudsi Erguner, Erkan Oğur, Arif Sağ, Fikret Karakaya or Derya Türkan (just to mention a few) in one way or another influenced Turkish music merely through their own musical and intellectual personality. Private spheres in many diverse fields preserved music, where the state tried to control or even prohibit it, including music of the Mevlevi, the Ottoman court tradition, Kurdish music, Armenian music, or numerous local folk traditions, hence constantly propelling the musical field to be larger and broader.

On the whole, Kemalism never achieved its aim of the complete control of the field of music, and instead of a clearly perceivable style of "Turkish music" a strong individualisation of music took place, with the emergence of individual musicians, individual music pieces, individual life experiences, identities and approaches to music, individual musical projects, individual CDs and concerts, even individual concepts of music theory, conferences or research projects. While the available repertoire constantly grew, both internationally and nationwide, and similarly the plurality of musical practices, the position of composers weakened compared to musicians and arrangeurs. During the last twenty-plus years, most music projects repeatedly rearranged "traditional" melodies in new combinations and arrangements of a growing variety of musical instruments.

Today, Kemalist ideology has widely lost its force; during the AKP period (hence over the last 15 years), more and more Kemalist ideas have been questioned. Recently many Western Turkish musicians and composers have included traditional music (of some sort) without any ideological scruples and fear of raising suspicions of reactionary tendencies. The result is no return to Ottoman music, but rather a further hybridization and individualization.

Both global and the local developments in Turkey have therefore led to a growth in available cultural and musical experiences, musical repertoire and musical practices. This last chapter has described, as a complementary factor, the story of numerous healthy and fruitful failures in standardization. Despite strong efforts by the Turkish state, its institutions such as conservatories and the TRT, the forces of Turkish nationalism, but also those of numerous individual theorists, musicians, and musicologists, almost all aspects of traditional music and music life including performance practice, repertoire, musical education and transmission, and even the field of music theory have diversified to endless individual approaches. As an obvious – and pleasant – conclusion to this last chapter we might say, that musical creativity is obviously difficult to control.

*

In contrast to historians, who are free to decide rationally on the time frame for their research, cultural / music anthropologists, writing on the (wider) present, have firm ground only concerning the beginning of the period of their research. Its end necessarily remains open: The time frame simply ends at the very moment when the author lays down his pen. It is tempting to estimate a future more convincing end of the studied time frame. The internationalisation of Turkish music, as part of a general globalisation, has developed continuously since at least the early nineteenth century, and even the process of individualization will most probably continue. These developments, which have been decribed in this book, did not began with Mustafa Kemal Atatürk, and most probably will not end with Recep Tayyip Erdoğan. At least in the field of music, Kemalism sought too much, which some eighty years later, resulted in a kind of aesthetic chaos. The starting point for a possible future music politic of the "New Turkey" is hence even more complex and confusing than that of the Republic of Turkey. For musicians, composers and arangeurs the contemporary quietly chaotic situation has opened almost endless space for creativity towards the end of Kemalist Turkey. If we accept globalisation as being the more important factor than Kemalism, we might for the long term, expect a continuation of the process of individualisation, whatever form "New Turkey" will take.

VI References

Abacı, Tahir, 2000, *Harput / Elazığ Türküleri*, Istanbul, Pan Yayıncılık.

Abtuman, Elif 2012, "Talkin Drums", *The New Yorker*, 9 July 2012 (http://www.newyorker.com/culture/culture-desk/talking-drums (24 October 2015).

Abu-Lughod, Lila 1991, "Writing against Culture", *Recapturing Anthropology*, ed. Fox, R.G, Santa Fe, New Mexico, pp. 137-162.

Serhan Ada (ed) 2011, *Istanbul'un Festivalleri*, Istanbul, Istanbul Bilgi Üniversitesi Yayınları.

- 2009, "Bir Yeni Kültür Politikası için", Ada & İnce 2009: 81-109.

Ada, Serhan & İnce, H.Ayca (ed.), 2009, *Türkiye'de Kültür Politikalarına Giriş*, Istanbul, Bilgi Üniversitesi Yayınları.

Agayeva, Sureya, 1995, "Ortaçağ Görsel Sanatlarında Nefesli Çalgılar Örnekleri", *Musiki Mecmuası*, CDL.

- 1999, "Türk Musikisinde Edvar", *Musiki Mecmuası*, CDLXIII.
- 2000, "Abdülkadir Meragi'de Türk Çalgıları", *Musiki Mecmuası*, CDLXVII.
- 2006, "Osmanlı Saraylarında Azerbaycan bilgin ve müzisyenleri", *Osmanli Dönem Türk Musikî Sempozyumu*.

Agayeva, Sureya & Uslu, Recep 2009, *Ruhperver*, 2009, Vol. 1, Ankara: Ürün Yayınevi.

Akbıyık, Abuzer, 2006, *Şanlıurfa Sıra Gecesi*, Şanlıurfa, Elif Matbaası.

Açın, Cafer, 2000, *Bağlama Yapım Sanatı ve Sanatçıları*. İstanbul, Emek Basımevi.

Akçay, Ismail, 1993, "Musiki Tarihinden Belgeler (1): Musiki Encümeni ve Dar-ül-Elhan Talimatı Suretidir, *Musiki Mecmuası*, No. 437, pp. 13-24.

Akçura, Gökhan, 2002, *Gramofon Çağı*, Istanbul: Om Yayınevi.

Akdağ, Ali Kazım, 2017, "Strukturprobleme der Bağlama-Ausbildung in der Türkei und Bağlama-Lehrbücher im Rahmen der Lehrplan-Entwicklung", Çiftçi & Greve, forthcoming.

Akdemir, Hayrettin, 1991, *Die neue türkische Musik*, Berlin, Hitit.

Akdoğan, Bayram 1996, "Hüccetü's-Semâ' adli Musikî Risâlesi ve Ankaravî Ismail B. Ahmed'in Mûsikî Anlayışı", Ankara Üniversitesi İlahiyat Fakültesi: *Ankara Dergisi*, 35, 477-505.

- 1999, "15. Yüzyıl Osmanlı Dönemininde Türk Mûsikîsi"; *Diyanet Ilmi Dergi*, vol. 35, 1, 135-170.
- 2008, "Türk Din Musikisi Tarihine bir Bakiş", *Ankarana Üniversitesi Ilahiyat Fakültesi Dergisi*, 1, 151-190.
- 2009, Fethullah Şirvânî ve Mûsikî Risâlesi (Mecelletun Fi'l-Mûsîka), Ankara, Bilge Ajans ve Matbaası.
- 2009, İsmâil-i Ankaravî ve Mûsıkî Risâlesi, İstanbul, Rağbet.

Akdoğu, Onur 1989a, *Türk Müzigi Bibliografyası (9.yy – 1928)*, Izmir, E.Ü. Devlet Türk Musikisi Konservatuvarı Yayınları No. 89.

– 1989b, *Taksim Nedir Nasıl Yapılır*, Izmir.

– 1990, *Tarihçi Müzikolog Yılmaz Öztuna*, Izmir, Reform Matbaasi.

– 1990, *Lemi Atli, Hayati ve Eserleri*, Ankara, Kültür Bakanlığı.

– (ed.) 1992, *Nâyî Osman Dede ve Rabt-i Tâbirât-i Mûsikî*, Izmir.

– 1994, *Türk Müziğinde Perdeler*, İzmir.

Akgün, Fehmi 1993, *Yıllar Boyunca Tango 1865-1993*, Istanbul, Pan.

Akkaş, Salih, 2015, *Türkiye'de Cumhuriyet Dönemi Kültür ve Müzik Politikaları (1923–2000)*, Ankara, Son Çağ.

Akkaya, Ayhan, Özer, Diler, Çelik, Fehmiye & Uncu, Ülker (ed.) 2008, *Kardeş Türküler 15 Yılın Öyküsü*, Istanbul, bgst Yayınları.

Aksoy, Asu, 2009, "Zihinsel Değişim? AKP Iktidarı ve Kültür Politikası", Ada & Ince, pp. 179-198.

Aksoy, Bülent, 1985, "Tanzimat'tan Cumhuriyet'e Musiki ve Batılılaşma", *Tanzimat'tan Cumhuriyet'e Türkiye Ansiklopedisi*, vol. 5, Belge, Murat (ed.), Istanbul, 1211-1236.

– 1989, "Is the Question of the Origin of Turkish Music not redundant?", *Turkish Musical Quarterly*, 2, 4.

– (ed.), 1992, *Sermüezzin Rifat Bey'in Ferahnak Mevlevî Ayını*, Istanbul, Pan.

– 1997, "Sultan III. Selim'in Öldürülmeden bir gece önce bestelediği Şarkı", *Türklük Arastırmaları Dergisi* 8, Istanbul, Marmara Üniversitesi Fen-Edebiyat Fakültesi, Türk Tarihi Kurumu Matbaası.

– 2000, Makam Tanıma Doğru, *Musikişinas*, Vol. 4, pp. 71-87.

– 2005, CD *Kemençe*, liner notes, Kalan 2005.

– 2008a, *Avrupalı Gezginlerin Gözüyle Osmanlılarda Musiki*, Istanbul, Pan.

– 2008b, *Geçmişin Musıki Mirasına Bakışlar*, Istanbul, Pan.

– 2009, *Cüneyd Orhon anlatıyor: Radyo Günlerim*, Istanbul, Pan.

– 2010, "Musical Relationships between Italy and Turkey through Turkish Eyes", Spinetti 2010, 61-77.

– n.d., „Ottoman Music within the Makam Traditions of Middle-Easter art Music: An Overview", (http://www.bulentsavas.com/english/althtml/ottoman musicwithin.htm (accessed 15 September 2016).

– 2015, "Prelimınary Notes on the Possibility (or Impossibility) of Writing Ottoman Music History", Greve (ed.), 2015: 16-31.

Aksoy, Bülent, et al., 1994, "Musiki Hayatı", *Dünden Bugüne Istanbul Ansiklopedisi*, vol. 5, Istanbul, Kültür Bakanlığı ve Tarih Vakfı Ortak Yayınları, pp. 521-540.

Aksu, Sema, 1990, *Türk Musıkisinde Rebab üzerine bir Araştırma*, thesis, İstanbul, İTÜ.

Aksüt, Sadun 1983, *Musikisi Güfteleri*, Istanbul.

– 1967, 500 *Yıllık Türk Musikisi Antolojisi*, Istanbul.

- 1993, *Türk Musikisinin 100 Bestekârları*, Istanbul.
- 1994, *Tanbur Metodu*, Istanbul, Inkilâp Kitabevi.
- (ed.) 2011, *Şevkı Bey. Yâdigârı Şevk (Mahsûbi Tabiat)*, Istanbul, ITÜ TMDK Yayınları.

Akyol, Taner, 2017, "Bağlama und Zeitgenössische Klassische Musik", Çiftçi & Greve (eds.), 2017.

Alaner, Bülent, 1986, *Music Publications from Ottoman Empire Up Today, 1876-1986, Osmanlı İmperatorluğu'ndan Günümüze Belgelerle Müzik Yayıncılığı (1876-1986)*, Ankara.

- 2017 (a) "Osmanlı İmparatorluğu'nda Çok Sesli Müziğin Gelişimi", Tarih Tarih Yayınevi, https://www.tarihtarih.com/?Syf=26&Syz=353046 (accessed 14 June 2017).
- 2017 (b), "Cumhuriyet Döneminde Çok Sesli Müzik", Tarih Tarih Yayınevi, https://www.tarihtarih.com/?Syf=26&Syz=353046 (accessed 14 June 2017).

Ali, Filiz, 1983, "Türkiye Cumhuriyeti'nde Konservatuvarlar", Belge, Murat (ed.), *Cuhuriyet Dönemi Türkiye Ansiklopedisi*, Istanbul, pp. 1531-1534.

- 2002, *Bülent Arel. Elektronik Müziğin Öncüsü*, Istanbul, Türkiye İş Bankası Yayınları.

Alimdar, Selçuk, 2016, *Osmanlı'da Batı Müziği*, Istanbul, İş Bankası Kültür Yayınları.

Almanya Alevi Birlikleri Federasyonu (ed.), 2000, *Bin Yılın Türküsü. Das Epos des Jahrtausends. Saga of the Millenium*, Köln AABF.

Alp, Sedat, 1999, *Hititlerde Şarkı, Müzik ve Dans, Hitit Çağında Anadolu'da Üzüm ve Şarap*, Ankara, Kavaklıdere Kültür Yayınları No: 6.

- 2000, *Song, Music, and Dance of Hittites* (trans. Yaprak Eran), Ankara, Kavaklıdere Cultural Publications.

Altan, Ali , Doğrusöz, Nilgün & Uslu, Recep, 2012, *Itri Izleri*, Istanbul, Balat Yayınları.

Altan, Sinem 2013, *Beni bağlama – don't bind me. Konzert für Bağlama und Orchester*, Berlin, Ries & Erler.

Altar, Cevad Memduh, 1989, *Opera Tarihi*, vol. 4, Istanbul, Kültür Bakanlığı Yayınları.

Altınay, Reyhan, 2004, *Cumhurriyet Döneminde Türk Halk Müziği. Kitaplar, Makaleler, Nota Yayınları*, Meta Basım, Izmir.

Altınay, Yeşim, 2010, *Turkish Music Instruments*, Istanbul, İstanbul Avrupa Kültür Baskenti Ajansi.

Altschiller, Donald, 1995, "Turkish Americans", Galens, Judy, Sheets, Anna & Young, Robyn V. (ed.), *Gale Encyclopedia of Multicultural America*, vol. 2, New York, Gale Research, pp. 364-1373.

Ambros, A.W., 1968, *Geschichte der Musik*, vol. 1, (Leipzig 1862-1878), Hildesheim.

And, Metin, 2004, *Başlangıcından 1983'e: Türk Tiyatro Tarihi*, Istanbul, İletişim Yayınları.

- 1976, *A Pictorial History of Turkish Dancing: From Folk Dancing to Whirling Dervishes-Belly Dancing to Ballett*, Ankara, Dost 1976.
- 1982, *Osmanlı Şenliklerinde Türk Sanatları*, Ankara, Kültür ve Turizm Bakanlığı Yayınları.
- 1989, *Türkiye'de Italyan Sahnesi, Italyan Sahnesinde Türkiye*, Istanbul, Metis.

Anıl, Avni & Zakoğlu, Bünbey, 1979, *Güfteler, Türk Sanat Musikisi Sözlü Eserler*, Istanbul.

Andrews, Peter Alford, 1989, *Ethnic Groups of Turkey*, Wiesbaden, Reichert, pp. 142-147.

Anhegger, Robert, 1982, "Die Deutschlanderfahrung der Türken im Spiegel ihrer Lieder. Eine Einstimmung", Birkenfeld, H. (ed.), *Gastarbeiterkinder aus der Türkei. Zwischen Eingliederung und Rückkehr*, München, Beck.

Apostolopoulos, Thomas, 2005, "The Socio-Cultural Context", Feldman, Walter, Guettat, M., Kalaitzides, Kyriakos (eds.), *Music in the Mediterranean*, Volume I *History*, Thessaloniki, En Chordais, Project MediMuses in the context of European Union programme Euromed Heritage II., pp.477-484.

Apostolopoulos, Thomas & Kalaitzidis, Kyriakos, 2015, "Konstantinopolis'in Bizans öncesi ve Bizans sonrası Müzik Mirası", Yılmaz, Coşkun (ed.), *Büyük İstanbul Tarihi*, Istanbul, İSAM, 20-35.

Aracı, Emre, 2001, *Ahmed Adnan Saygun. Doğu-Batı Arası Müzik Köprüsü*, Istanbul, YKY.

- 2006, *Donizetti Paşa. Osmanlı Sarayının İtalyan Maestrosu*, Istanbul YKY.
- 2010a, "From Napoleon to Mahmud: The Chequered Career of the Other Donizetti", Spinetti 2010: 3-16.
- 2010b, *Naum Tiyatrosu. 19. Yüzyıl İstanbulu'nun İtalyan Operası*. Yapı Kredi Yayınları.

Arel, Hüseyin Sadeddin, 1951, "300 Küsur Senelik Nota Mecmuası Hakkında", *Musıki Mecmuası*, No 45.

- 1969 (1939/49), *Türk Musikisi Kimindir*, Türk Musikisi Araştırma ve Değerlendirme Komisyonu Yayınları 1, Istanbul.
- 1991, *Türk Musikisi Nazariyatı Dersleri*, Ankara.

Arna, Sibel, 2006, "Ermeni sanatçı konuşuyor, Azeri meslektaşı tercüme ediyor", Interview with Ilyas Mirzayev, Hürriyet, 1 July 2006, http://www.hurriyet.com.tr/cumartesi/4637746.asp (accessed 25 August, 2015).

Arnaud-Demir, Françoise, 1996, *Littérature Populaire: En Suivant les Âşık*, Montreuil, Ankara.

Arseven, Veysel, 1957, "Türk Halk Müziğinde Metrik Sistem", *Türk Folklor Araştırmaları Dergisi* 100/101, 1590.

Arslan, Fazli, 2001, "Qur'ân's Tacwîd at Qutb Al-Dîn al Shirâzî's Music Notation", *International Journal of Humanities and Social Science*, vol. 1, No. 10; 209-216.

- 2005, "Safiyyüddîn Abdülmümin el-Urmevî'nin er-Risâletü'ş-Şerefiyye'sinde Mûsikî Matematiği", *AÜIFD* XLVI (2005), No II, 267-304.
- 2009, "Müzik Kuramcısı ve Efsanevi Kişilik olarak Safiyyüddîn-i Urmevî", *Sosyal Bilimler Dergisi*, no. 26, 165-179.

Arsunar, Ferruh, 1937a, *Anadolu'nun Pentatonik Melodileri Hakkında Birkaç Not*, Istanbul, Numune Matbaası.

- 1937b, *Tunceli-Dersim Halk Türküleri ve Pentatonik*, Istanbul, Resimli Ay Matbaası.

Artun, Erman 2014, *Aşıklık Geleneği ve Aşık Edebiyati*, Istanbul, Kitabevi.

Arzruni, Şahan, 2001, USA, European Traditional Music, Armenian, Sadie, Stanley (ed.), *The New Grove Dictionary of Music and Musicians*, Vol. 26, London, MacMillan.

Aşkın, Cihat, 2010, "Murat Bardakcı'nın bir Yazışı Üzerine Çeşitlemeler", *Yeşilgazete*, 11 November 2010.

Aslan, Üzeyir, (ed) 2007, *Molla Cami – Hoca Neş'et: Ney'in Feryadı*, Istanbul, Sufi Kitap.

Assmann, Jan, (1997) 2011, *Cultural Memory and Early Civilization. Writing, Remembrance, and Political Imagination*, Cambridge, Cambridge University Press.

Atagür, Zeki, 2013, *Bağlama Egzersizleri*, Ankara, Sonsöz Gazetecilik Matbaacılık.

Atalay, Adnan, 1984, "Müzik Yazısı", Say, Ahmet (ed.), *Müzik Ansiklopedisi*, Ankara.

Ataman, Ahmet Muhtar 1928, *Musiki Tarihi*, Istanbul, Develt Matbaasi.

Ataman, Sadi Yaver, 1991, *Atatürk ve Türk Musıkisi*, Atatürk Dizisi 31, Ankara, Kültür Bakanlığı Yayınları 1291.

Atilgan, Halil, 1992, "Halk Müziğimizde Anonimlik ve Beste Meselesi", Turhan, Salih (ed.), *Türk Halk Musikîsinde Çeşitli Görüşler*, Ankara, Kültür Bakanlığı, pp.163-173.

Avrupa Kültür Başkenti, 2010, *Klasik Türk Müziği. Program Kitapçığı*, Istanbul.

Ayan, Dursun, 2011, *Béla Bartók'un Türk Halk Müziği Derlemeleri üzerine Çalışmaları*, Istanbul: Kitabevi.

Ayangil, Ruhi, 2008, "Western Notation in Turkish Music", *Journal of the Royal Asiatic Society*, Vol. 18, 4, pp. 401-447.

- 2010, "Western Notation: A Debatable Matter in Turkish *Makam* Music Contributed by Guiseppe Donizetti Pasha", Spinetti 2010: 39-57.

Ayas, Güneş, 2014, *Mûsiki İnkılâbı'nın Sosyolojisi. Klasik Türk Müziği Geleneğinde Süreklilik ve Değişim*, Istanbul, Doğu Kitabevi.

- 2015, *Müzik Sosyolojisi. Sorunlar, Yaklaşımlar, Tartışmalar*, Istanbul, Doğu Kitabevi.

Aydin, Yılmaz, 2003, *Türkiye'de Avrupa ile Müzik İlişkileri Işığında Türk Beşleri*, Ankara, Müzik Ansiklopedisi Yayınları.

Aydemir, Murat, 2010, *Turkish Music Makam Guide* (translated by Erman Dirikcan), Istanbul: Pan; (Greek translation by S. Kompotiati, Athens, Fagotto books 2012).

Aydın, Yılmaz, *Türk Beşleri*, Ankara, Müzik Ansiklopedisi Yayınları.

Aytar, Volkan & Parmaksızoğlu, Kübra, 2010, *Istanbul'da Eğlence*, Istanbul, Istanbul Bilgi Üniversitesi Yayınları.

Bachir-Loopuyt, Talia, 2013, *Une Musique du Monde faite en Allemagne? Les compétitions Creole et l'idéale société plurielle dans l'Allemagne d'aujourd'hui*, Ph.D. Thesis EHESS Paris.

Bakbaşa, Ceyda, 2011, "Istanbul'da Sanat Fuarları", Ada 2011: 115-129.

Balkılıç, Özgür, 2009, *Cumhuriyet, Halk ve Müzik*, Ankara, Tan.

Balkır, Canan & Kaiser, Bianca, 2015, "Türkiye'de Avrupa Birliği Vatandaşları", Erdoğan & Kaya, 2015, 223-241.

Bardakçı, Murat, 1986, *Maragali Abdulkadir*, Istanbul, Pan.

- 1993, *Fener Beyleri'ne Türk Şarkıları*, Istanbul, Pan.
- 1995, *Refik Fersan ve Hatıraları*, Istanbul, Pan.
- 1997, *Sultanî Besteler. Osmanoğulları'nın son Padişahı Mehmed Vahideddin'in. Eserleri*, Istanbul, Pan.
- 2000, "Derviş es-Seyyid Mehmed Efendi'in Tanbur Perdeleri Risalesi", *Musikişinas*, p. 6-39.
- 2010, "Musiki Inkılâbi ve Başarısızlık", *Habertürk*, 8 November 2010.
- 2012a, "Itrî Yılı", *Habertürk*, 1 February 2012.
- 2012b, *25 Yıla 25 Besteci*, Istanbul, Pan.
- 2012c, *The Treatise of Ahmed Oglı Şükru'llah and Theory of Oriental Music in the 15th Century*, Harvard (Doğu Dilleri ve Edebiyatlarının Kaynakları 51. Türkçe Kaynaklar XLIV).

Bartók, Béla, 1976, *Turkish Folk Music from Asia Minor*, ed. Benjamin Suchoff, Princeton.

Bartsch, Patrick, 2012, *Musikpolitik im Kemalismus. Die Zeitschrift Radyo zwischen 1941 und 1949*, Bamberg, University of Bamberg Press.

Başeğmezler, Nejat, 1992, *Necil Kâzım Akses'e Armağan*, Ankara, Sevda-Cenap And Müzik Vakfı Yayınları.

Basgöz, Ilhan, 1979 (1994), *Âsik Ali Izzet Özkan*, Istanbul, Indiana Üniversitesi.

- 2002, "Turkish Folk Literature", Inalcık, Halil & Renda, Güncel (eds.), *Ottoman Civilization*, Ankara, Ministery of Culture, pp. 597-623.

Beşikçi, Ismail, 1977, *Türk-Tarih Tezi ve Kürd Sorunu*, Ankara, Komal.

Bates, Eliot, 2008, *Social Interaction, Musical Arrangements, and the Production of Digital Autio in Istanbul Recording Studios*, PhD Dissertation University of California, Berkeley.

- 2011, *Music in Turkey. Experienting Music, Expressing Culture*, Oxford, Oxford University Press.

Baumann, Max Peter (ed), 1985, *Musik der Türken in Westberlin*, Kassel, Yvonne Landec.

Baydar, Evren Kutlay, 2010, *Osmanlı'nın Avrupalı Müzisyenleri*, Istanbul, Kapı.

Bayley, Amanda, (forthcoming), "Cross-cultural Collaborations with the Kronos Quartet", Clarke, E. and Doffman, M., eds. *Creativity, Improvisation and Collaboration: Perspectives on the Performance of Contemporary Music.* Oxford and New York: Oxford University Press.

Bayraktar, Ertuğrul, 1993, "An Outline of Kemal Ilerici Harmonic System", Say, Ahmet (ed.), *The Music Makers in Turkey*, Ankara, pp. 51-54.

Beck, Ulrich, 1983, "Jenseits von Stand und Klasse", R. Krechel (ed.), *Soziale Ungleichheiten*, Göttingen, Schwarz Verlag.

Begian, Harry, 1964, *Gomitas Vartabed: His Life and Importance to Armenian Music*, Ph.D. Thesis, University of Michigan.

Behar, Büsra Ersanlı, 1992, *Iktidar ve Tarih: Türkiye'de 'Resmi tarih' Tezinin Oluşumu. (1929-1937)*, Istanbul, AFA.

Behar, Cem, 1987a, 18. *Yüzyılında Türk Müziği*, Charles Fonton, Istanbul.

- 1987b, *Klasik Türk Musıkisi üzerinde Denemeler*, Istanbul, Bağlam.
- 1990, *Ali Ufkî ve Mezmurlar*, Istanbul, Pan.
- 1997, "Manol of the Ud, Baron of the Kemençe: Turkish Musical Instruments and Makers"; *Music & Art*, Vol 7.
- 2001, "The Technical Modernization of Turkish Music: The Case of the Durak". Hammarlund, Olsson & Özdalga 2001, pp. 97-109.
- 2005, *Musıkiden Müziğe, Osmanlı / Türk Müziği: Gelenek ve Modernlik*, Istanbul, Yapı Kredi Yayınları.
- 2006, "The Ottoman Musical Tradition", *The Cambridge History of Turkey*, Vol. 3 (*The Later Ottoman Empire, 1603–1839*), Cambridge, Cambridge University Press, 393-408.
- 2008, *Saklı Mecmua. Ali Ufkî'nin Bibliotheque Nationale de France'taki (Turc 292) Yazması*, Istanbul, Yapı Kredi Yayınları.
- 2010, *Şeyhülilâm'in Müziği. 18. Yüzyılda Osmanlı/Türk Musikisi ve Şeyhülislâm Es'ad Efendi'nin Atrabü'l-Âsâr'i*, Istanbul, Yapı Kredi Yayınları.
- 2012 (1998), *Aşk Olmayınca Meşk Olmaz. Geleneksel Osmanlı / Türk Müziğinde Öğretim ve İntikal*, Istanbul, Yapı Kredi Yayınları.
- 2013a, "Dede Efendi'nin Eserlerine Tarih Koymak", *Musikişinas* 11, pp. 20-50.
- 2013b, "Text and Memory in Ottoman/Turkish Musical Tradition", Pennanen et.el. 2013: 3-11.
- 2015, *Osmanlı / Türk Musıkisinin Kısa Tarihi*, İstanbul, Yapı Kredi Yayınları.

Beken, Münir Nurettin, 1998, *Musicians, Audience and Power: The Changing Aesthetics in the Music at the Maksim Gazino of Istanbul*, PhD Theis University of Maryland.

Benjamin, Walter, (1935) 1939, "Das Kunstwerk im Zeitalter seiner technischen Reproduzierbarkeit", Schöttker, Detlev (ed.), Walter Benjamin. *Das Kunstwerk im Zeitalter seiner technischen Reproduzierbarkeit. Kommentar.* Frankfurt a.M., Suhrkamp Verlag, 2002: 7-50.

Berkman, Esra, 2012, *Kanun Virtüözü, Besteci ve Eğititci Haçatur Avetisyan (1926-1996) ve Kanun Çalgısı özelinde Ermenistan Sovyet Sosyalist Cumhuriyet'inde (1920-1991) Müziğin Dönüşümü*, Ph.D. thesis Yıldız Teknik Üniversitesi.

Berliner Institut für Vergleichende Sozialforschung, 2005, *Türkische TV-Sender in Deutschland*, Berlin.

Berthier, Stephanos & Annie (ed.), *Topkapı Sarayı'nda Yasam. Albertus Bobovius ya da Santuri Ali Ufki Bey'in Anıları. (1669)*, translated bz Ali Berktay, Istanbul, Kitab Yayınevi.

Beşiroğlu, Şehvar (ed.), 2008, *III Selim*, Istanbul, ITÜ Türk Musikisi Devlet Konservatuvarı Yayınları, ITÜ Bestekârlar Serisi 3.

Beşiroğlu, Şehvar & Ergur, Ali, 2009, "Modern Disappearance and Postmodern Rebirth of the Ceng", *CIM*, 09, 2009 (http://cim09.lam.jussieu.fr/CIM09fr/Actes_files/Besiroglu-Ergur.pdf, accessed 3 December, 2013).

Beşiroğlu, Şehvar & Celasin, Cenk, 2006, "Hitit Medeniyeti Müzik Kültürünün Analizinde Arkeolojik Verileri Rolü", *İTÜ Dergisi*, 2006, Vol. 3, 2, pp. 35-46.

Beşiroğlu, Şehvar, Çolakoğlu, Gözde, Tohumcu, Z. Gonca & Küçükaksoy, F. Merve (ed.), *Prof. Ercüment Berker ve Yazıları*, İTÜ Türk Musikisi Devlet Konservatuarı Yayınları.

Betzwieser, Thomas, 1993, *Exotismus und "Türkenoper" in der französischen Musik des Ancien Régime*, Neue Heidelberger Schriften zur Musikwissenschaft, Vol. 21, Laaber.

Bhabha, Homi K., 1990, "The Third Space", Rutherford, J. (ed.), *Identity: Community, Culture, Difference*, London, Lawrence & Wishard.

Bilal, Melissa, 2013, *Thou Need'st not Weep, for I have wept full score: An Affective Genealogy of the Armenian Lullaby in Turkey*, Ph D Thesis, Chicago, Illinois.

Birdoğan, Nejat, 1992, "Halk Ezgilerimizdeki Söz Sakatlıkları", Turhan, Salih (ed.), *Türk Halk Musikîsinde Çeşitli Görüşler*, Ankara, Kültür Bakanliği, pp. 174-191.

Bithell, Carole & Hill, Juniper, 2014a, "An Introduction to Music Revival as Concept, Cultural Process, and Medium of Change", Bithell & Hill 2014b, pp. 3-42.

- 2014b, (eds.), *The Oxford Handbook of Music Revival*, Oxford University Press.

Bohlmann, Philip V., 1987, "The European Discovery of Music in the Islamic World and the "Non-Western" in the 19th-Century Music History", *The Journal of Musicology*, Vol. V, 2, pp. 147-163.

- 1988, *The Study of Folk Music in the Modern World*, Bloomington, Indiana University Press.
- 2013, *Cambridge History of World Music*, Cambridge University Press.

Bora, Emine, 2010, *Klasik Osmanlı Müziğinde Ermeni Bestekârlar*, Istanbul, Avrupa Kültür Baskenti.

Borrel, Eugene , 1928, "Contribution à la Bibliographie de la Musique Turque au XXe Siècle", *Revue des Etudes Islamiques*, pp. 513-527.

Bozkurt, Barış, Yarman, Ozan, Karaosmanoğlu, M. Kemal, Akkoç, Can, 2009, „Weighing Diverse Theoretical Models on Turkish Maqam Music against Pitch Measurments: A Comparison of Peaks Automatically Derived from Frequency Histograms with Proposed Scale Tones", *Journal of New Music Research*, Vol. 38, No. 1, pp. 45-70.

Brandl, Rudolf Maria, 1989, "Konstantinopolitanische Makamen des 19. Jahrhunderts in Neumen: Die Musik der Fanarioten", Jürgen Elsner (ed), *Maqam, Raga, Zeilenmelodik. Konzeptionen und Prinzipien der Musikproduktion. Materialien der 1. Arbeitstagung der Study Group „maqâm" beim Internationalen Council for Traditional Music*, Berlin, ppç 156-169.

Broughton, Simon, Ellingham, Mark & Trillo, Richard (ed.), 1999, *World Music. The Rough Guide*, London, Rough Guides.

Budak, Ogün Attilla, 2000 / 2006, *Türk Müziğinin Kökeni-Gelişimi*, Ankara, Phoenix.

Bunzl, John, 1989, *Juden im Orient: Jüdische Gemeinschaften in der islamischen Welt und orientalische Juden in Israel*, Wien, Junius.

Burada, Teodor T, 1911, *Scrierile Muzicale ale lui Dimitrie Cantemir*, Bukarest.

Caner, Yusuf, 2009, *Benim Bağlama / Meine Bağlama*, Duisburg, Verlag Hubert Nogatz.

Castles, Stephan & Miller, Mark J., 1993, *The Age of Migration. International Population Movements in the Modern World*, New York, The Guilford Press.

Celasin, Cenk, 2007, *Orta Tunç Çağı'ndan Roma Dönemi'ne Anadolu Müzik Kültürünün Analizi*, Ph.D. thesis, İTÜ, Istambul.

Cengiz, Halil Erdoğan (ed.), 1993, *Yaşanmış Olaylarla Atatürk ve Müzik. Riyâset-i Cumhûr İnce Saz Hey'eti Şefi Binbaşı Hâfız Yaşar Okur'un Anıları (1924–1938)*, Ankara, Müzik Ansiklopedisi Yayınları.

Cevher. M. Hakan, 1993, *Şerif Muhiddin Targan. Hayatı – Besteciliği – Eserleri*, Izmir.

- 2003, (ed.), *Hâzâ mecmûa-i sâz ü söz*, Izmir 2003.
- 2004, *Rûh-Perver. İnceleme, Günümüz Türkçesi, Çeviriyazım, Esas Metin*, Istanbul, Saade.

Ceyhan, Adem, 1997, *Bedr-i Dilsad'in Murâd-nâmesi*, Ankara, Milli Eğitim Bakanlığı.

Chiannis, Sotirios & Brandl, Rudolf M., 2001, "Greece, §IV: Traditional Music", Sadie, Stanley & Tyrell, John (eds.), *The New Grove Dictionary of Music and Musicians*, 2nd edition, London, Macmillan, Vol. 10, pp. 353-9.

Coggins, Peter, 1995, "The Experience of Turkish and Turkish Cypriot Life in the United Kingdom", de Tapia, 1995, pp. 125-145.

Cohen, Judith, 1999, "Jewish Music, Sephardic", Broughton, Ellingham & Trillo, 1999, vol. 1, pp. 370-377.

Coplan, David B., 1993, "Ethnomusicology and the Meaning of Tradition", Blum, Stephen, Bohlman, Philip V. & Neuman, Daniel M. (eds.), *Ethnomusicology and Modern Music History*, pp.35-48.

Çoşkun, Zeki, 1999, "Azınlık Sesleri", Pacacı, Gönül (ed.), *Cumhuriyet'in Sesleri*, Istanbul, Tarih Vakfı Yayınları.

Çağlar, Ayşe, 1998, "Verordnete Rebellion: Deutsch-türkischer Rap und türkischer Pop in Berlin". Mayer, Ruth, Terkessidis, Mark (ed). *Global Kolorit. Multikulturalismus und Populärkultur*. St. Andrä/Wördern: Hannibal.

Raha Çamuroğlu 1998, "Alevi Revivalism in Turkey", in T. Olsson, E. Özdalga & E. Raudvere (Hrsg.), *Alevi Identity: Cultural Religious and Social Perspectives*, Swedish Research Institute in Berlin, Istanbul, pp. 79-84.

Celik, Ece, 2013, "Yaptığım Müzik Hikâyelerden Etkileniyor"; Interview with Yinon Muallem, *Radikal*, 4 July 2013.

Çevik, Mehmet, 2013, *Türkü ve Algı. Türkü Kültüründe Değişim Süreci*, Ankara, Ürün Yayınları.

Çiftçi, Nevzat, 2011, "Vom Nomadeninstrument zum Weltinstrument: Die Emanzipation der türkischen Langhalslaute Bağlama (Saz)", unpublished paper read at the *Conference of the German National Comitee of the ICTM*, February 11-12, 2011 in Hildesheim (Germany).

– 2017, "Zur Geschichte der Baglama in Europa", Çiftçi & Greve 2017.

Çiftçi, Nevzat & Greve, Martin &, forthcomming 2017, *Das Erste Baglama Symposium in Deutschland*, Berlin, Ries & Erler.

Çine, Hamit, 1997, "Boğaz Havaları ve Üçtelli Bağlama", *V. Milletlerarası Türk Halk Kültürü Kongresi. Halk Müziği, Oyun Tiyatro*, Ankara 1997, pp. 100-103.

Çolakoğlu Sarı, Gözde, 2015, *1. Müzikoloji Bölümleri Çalıştayı*, Istanbul, İstanbul Teknik Üniversitesi Türk Musikisi Devlet Konservatuvarı Yayınları.

– 2016, *Anadolu'dan Balkanlara Kemençe*, Saarbrücken, Türkiye Alim Kitapları.

Dahlhaus, Carl, 1977, *Grundlagen der Musikgeschichte*, Köln, Gerig (*Foundations of Music History*, Cambridge University Press 1983).

Daniszâde, Sevket Gavsi, 1914, "Tarih-i Musik-i Sultan Selim", *Peyam Dergisi*.

Dawe, Kevin & Eroğlu, Sinan Cem, 2013, "The Guitar in Turkey: Erkan Ogur and the Istanbul Guitarszene", *Ethnomusicology Forum*, 22, 1, pp. 49-70.

Değirmenci, Koray, 2013, *Creating Global Music in Turkey*, Lanham, Lexington Books.

Deleon, Jak, 1986, *Bale Tarihi*, Istanbul, Imge.

– 1988, *Osmanlı'dan Cumhuriyete Türk Balesi*, Istanbul, Dönemli.

– 1996, *The White Russians in Istanbul*, Istanbul, Remzi Kitabevi.

Deniz, Ünsal, 2015, *Millî Mûsiki ve Türk Beşleri. Türk Beşleri tarafından Çokseslendirilmiş Olan Türkülerin Armoni Anlayışı Bakımdan İncelenmesi*, Malatya, Gece.

Nur Derviş, 1989, "Cinuçen Tanrıkorur et la Tradition du Ud Turque", *Cahiers de Musique traditionelles* 2, 255-262.

De Zeeuw, Hans, 2009, *De Turkse Langhalsluit of Bağlama*, Amsterdam, self publishing.

Díaz-Mas, Paloma, Pedrosa, José Manuel & Romero, Elena (ed), 1995, *Alberto Hemsi: Cancionero Sefardí*, Jerusalem, The Jewish Music Research Centre, The Hebrew University of Jerusalem.

Dietrich, Eberhard, 1987, *Das Rebetiko. Eine Studie zur Städtischen Musik Griechenlands*, (Beiträge zur Ethnomusikologie 17), Hamburg, Wagner.

Dinç, Kemal, 2012, *Bağlama icin Denemeler*, Istanbul, Pan.

– 2014, *Kelebek in Konzert. Rhythmische Übungen für die Musikpraxis mit Kindern*, Düsseldorf, Ministerium für Familie, Kinder, Jugend, Kultur und Sport NRW.

Djani-Zade, Tamila, 1998, "Music of Azerbaijan", Nettl, Bruno, Danielson, Virjinia, Stone, Ruth M., Porter, James & Rice, Timothy (eds.), *The Garland Encyclopedia to World Music*, Garland Publ., pp. 921-933.

Dikmen, Mustafa Dogan & Türk Musikisi Vakfi, 2010, *Dârü'l-Elhân Külliyâti*, Istanbul Avrupa Kültür Baskenti.

Dogrusöz, Nilgün, 1993, *Hâfiz Post Güfte Mecmuası (Türkçe Güfteler)*, Yayınlanmamış Yüksek Lisans Tezi, Istanbul Teknik Üniversitesi.

– 2007, *Harîrî bin Muhammed'in Kirsehrî Edvari üzerine bir İnceleme*, Ph.D. Thesis, Istanbul Teknik Üniversitesi.

– 2008, "The Architecture of Turkish Vocal Music: Münir Nurettin Selcuk", Reagle & Whitehead, 2008, pp. 149-165.

– 2012, *Mûsikî Risâleleri (Ankara Milli Kütüphane, 131 Numaralı Yazma)*, Istanbul, Bilim Kültür ve Sanat Derneği.

– 2015, "From Anatolian *Edvâr* (Musical Theory Book) Writers to Abdülbâkî Nâsır Dede: An Evaluation of the History of Ottoman/Turkish Music Theory", Greve 2015: 77-86.

Doğuduyal, Meliha, 2016, *Müzikten Söze*, İstanbul, Bağlam.

Dorn, Pamela J., 1991, *Change and Ideology: The Ethnomusicology of Turkish Jewry*, Ph.D. Thesis Indiana University, Ann Arbour, UMI.

Dönmez, Banu Mustan, 2014, *Alevi Müzik Uyanışı*, Istanbul, Gece Kitaplığı.

Duygulu, Melih, 1995, *Gaziantep Türküleri*, Istanbul.

– 1997, *Alevî-Bektaşi Müziğinde Deyişler*, İstanbul, Sistem Ofset.

– 2006, *Türkiye'de Çingene Müziği*, Istanbul: Pan.

– 2014, *Türk Halk Müziği Sözlüğü*, Istanbul, Pan.

Dündar, Fuat, 2008, *Modern Türkiye'nin Şifresi: İttihat ve Terakki'nin Etnisite Mühendisliği (1913-1918)*, Istanbul, İletişim.

– 2014, "Deportation Demos, Militarizing Natios: Forced Migration and Conflicts in the Ottoman Empire and Modern Turkey (1908-1947)", Karaçay, Aysem Biriz & Üstübici, Aysem (ed.), *Migration to and from Turkey: Changing Patterns and Shifting Policies*, Istanbul, The Isis Press, pp. 39-72.

Ederer, Eric Bernard, 2007, *The Cümbüş as Instrument of "the Other" in Modern Turkey*, MA Thesis, University of California, Santa Barbara.

– 2015, *Makam and Beyond. A Progressive Approach to Near Eastern Music Theory*, Santa Barbara, Plum Loco Publishing.

Ediboğlu, B.S., 1962, *Ünlü Türk Bestekarları*, Istanbul.

Moritz Eggert, 2011, Interview with Stefan Pohlit, http://blogs.nmz.de/badblog/2011/02/25/in-der-fremde-1-stefan-pohlit/, (25.2.2011).

Eker, Süer, 2010, "The Place of Dimitri Kantemiroglu's Turkish in 18th Century Ottoman Turkish", Bibliothèque Métropolitaine Bucarest, ed., *Travaux de Symposium International le Livre. LaRoumanie. L'Europe 2010*, Vol. IV, Bucarest, 69-78.

Ekici, Savaş, 2001, "Ramazan Güngör'ün Türk Halk Müzigi Içerisindeki Yeri ve Önemi", *Toplumbilim* 12, 65-68.

Ekinci, Mehmet Uğur, 2012, "The Kevserî Mecmûası Unveiled: Exploring an Eighteenth-Century Collection of Ottoman Music", *Journal of the Royal Asiatic Society (third Series)*, Vol. 22, 2, pp. 199-225.

– 2015a, "Kantemiroğlu Notalarının Bilinmeyen Bir Nüshası", *Musikişinas*, Vol. 13, 75-125.

– 2015b, *Kevserî Mecmuası. 18. Yüzyıl Saz Müziği Külliyatı*, Istanbul, Pan.

Elçi, Armağan Coşkun, 1997, *Muzaffer Sarısözen (Hayatı, Eserleri ve Çalışmaları)*, Ankara, T.C. Kültür Bakanlığı.

Elçin, Şükru, (ed.) 1976, *Ali Ufki, Mecmua-i Saz u Söz*, Kultur Bakanlığı Yayınları, Ankara.

Elflein, Dietmar, "Vom neuen deutschen Sprechgesang zu Oriental Hip Hop – einigen Gedanken zur Geschichte von Hip Hop in der BRD", Annette Kreutziger-Herr und Manfred Strack (ed.), *Aus der Neuen Welt: Streifzüge durch die amerikanische Musik des 20. Jahrhunderts*, Hamburg, pp. 283-296.

Élias, Nicolas, 2012, *Lavta, Étude pour un Lute d'Istanbul*, (Les Cahiers du Bosphore LXVII), Istanbul, Les Editions Isis.

– 2015, *L'Usage Communal des Sons Dans Les Montagnes Pontiques (Turquie)*, Ph.D. Thesis, l'Université Paris Ouest Nanteree La Défense.

Elschek, Oskár, 1985, "Die historische Erforschung mündlich, teilschriftlich und schriftlich überlieferter traditioneller Musikkulturen", *Beiträge zur Musikwissenschaft*, Vol. 2, 103-109.

Emnalar, Atınç, 1992, *Türk Müziğinde Koro*, Izmir.

– 1998, *Tüm Yönleriyle Türk Halk Müziği ve Nazariyatı*, İzmir.

Enlil, Zeynep & Evren, Yiğit, 2011, *Yaratıcı İstanbul. Yaratıcı Sektörler ve Kent*, Istanbul, Istanbul Bilgi Üniversitesi Yayınları.

Erdener, Yıldıray, 1995, *The Song Contests of Turkish Ministrels. Improvised Poetry Sung to Traditional Music*, New York & London, Garland Publishing.

Erdoğan, M. Murat & Kaya, Ayhan, 2015, *Türkiye'nin Göç Tarihi. 14. Yüzyılından 21. Yüzyıla Türkye'ye Göçler*, Istanbul, Bilgi Üniversitesi Yayınları.

Erdoğan, Esra Kaya 2011, "Hizmet, Girişim, Kültür Ekseninde Istanbul'da ilçe Festivalleri", Ada 2011: 79-97.

Ergan, Mehmed Salih, 1994, *Türkiye Müzik Bibliyografyası – Kitaplar, Notalar (1929-1993)*, Konya.

Ergin, Cafer 1968-1976, "Hazâ Mecmua-i Sâz ü Söz (Ali Ufkî Edvarı)", *Musiki Mecmuası*, no. 233, 235-237, 239-243, 245-249, 250-259, 261-269, 270, 272-275, 277, 279-281. 285-289, 291-293, 296, 298, 300, 303, 308-309, 316, 318-320, 322-324.

Ergin, Nihat, 1999, *Yıldız Sarayında Müzik*, Ankara, T.C. Kültür Bakanlığı Yayınları.

Ergin, Osman, 1977, *Türk Maarif Tarihi*, Eser Kültür Yayınları.

Ergun, Sadeddin Nüzhet, 1943, *Türk Musikisi Antolojisi,* Vol. 1, *Dini Eserler*, Istanbul, Rıza Koşkun Matbaası.

Erguner, Kudsi, 2000, *La Fontaine de la Sèparation. Voyages d'un Musicien Soufi*, Aris, Le bois d'Orion.

Erguner, Süleyman, 1986 / 2002, *Ney "Metod"*, Istanbul, Ergüner Müzik.

– 2003, *Rauf Yektâ Bey. Neyzen – Müzikolog – Bestekâr*, Istanbul, Kitabevi.

– 2010, *Şehrimini*, Istanbul, Heyamola Yayınlar.

Ergür, Cumhur Enes, 2011, *Salâhî Dede. Salâhaddîn Demirtaş, Hayatı ve Eserleri*, Istanbul, Istanbul Kitabevi.

Erkan, Cağrıhan & Dinge, Ali, 2003, *Piyano icin Saz Eserleri, Albüm 1*, Izmir, Berke.

Erkan, Yusuf, 2014, *Cumhuriyet Döneminde Teke Yöresi. Burdur Sanatçıları (Geleneksel Kuşak – Genç Kuşak)*, Istanbul; Narçiçeği Yayıncılık.

Eroğlu, Sinan Cem, 2009, *Orta Asya'dan Anadolu'ya Kopuzun Gelişimi ve Türk Halk Müziği'ndeki Yeri ve Önemi*, İstanbul MA Thesis İTÜ.

– 2017, "Die Stellung der *kopuz* in der Türkischen Volksmusik", Çiftçi & Greve 2017.

Erol, Ayhan, 2012, "Music, Power and Symbolic Violence: The Turkish State's Music Policies During the Early Republican Policies", *European Journal of Cultural Studies*, 15, 1, pp. 35-52.

Erol, Merih, 2003, "Türkçe Matbu Nota ve Solfej Kitabı: Hacı Emin Efendi ve Nota Muallimi (1885)", *Müteferrika*, No. 23.

– 2009, *Cultural Identification of the Greek Orthodox Elite of Constantinople: Discourse on Music in the Nineteenth and Early Twentieth Centuries*, Ph.D. Thesis, Boğaziçi University.

– 2015, *Greek Orthodox Music in Ottoman Istanbul. Nation and Community in the Era of Reform*, Indiana University Press.

– 2017, "The Greek-Turkish Musical "Rapprochement" of the 2000s and Approaches to Ottoman Musical Heritage", *Turkish Journal of Sociology*, 37 (forthcomming).

Ersanlı, Büşra 2003, *İktidar ve Tarih. Türkiye'de 'Resmî Tarih' Tezinin Oluşumu (1929–1937)*, Istanbul, İletişim.

Ersoy, Özgür, 2013, *Lehrbuch für Baglama*, Berlin, Ries & Erler.

Ertan, Deniz 2007, "Cycles and Peripheries: An Ottoman Kitâb el Edvâr", *Asian Music*, vol. 38, 1, 31-60.

Esen, Orhan, 2005, "Learning from Istanbul. Die Stadt Istanbul: Materielle Produktion und Produktion des Diskurses", Esen, Orhan & Lanz, Stephan (ed.), *Self Service City: Istanbul*, Berlin, b books, pp. 33-52.

Ertaylan, I. 1958, *Gazi Giray Han, Hayatı ve Eserleri*, Istanbul.

Erten, Oğuz, 2010, "Sanat piyasasında modern, klasik geçti", *Radikal*, 11.8. 2010: 20.

Erzincan, Erdal & Sağ, Arif, 2013, *Bağlama Metodu / Bağlama Method*, Istanbul: Pan.

Erzincan, Mercan, 2006, *Türk Halk Müziğinde Uyarlama Kavramı ve Bağlama Uyarlayan Dört Zeybek Ezgisi üzerinde Müzikal Analiz*, MA Thesis, Istanbul, Haliç Üniversitesi.

Ezgi, Suphi, 1933–1953, *Türk Musikisi, Nazari ve Ameli*, Istanbul.

Faist, Thomas, 2000, *Transstaatliche Räume. Politik, Wirtschaft und Kultur in und zwischen Deutschland und der Türkei*, Bielefeld, Transkript Verlag.

Farmer, Hanry George, 1937, "Turkish Instruments of Music in the Seventeenth Century", *Collection of Oriental Writers on Music*, Glasgow, The Civic Press.

Featherstone, Mike, Lash, Scott, & Robertson, Roland (eds.), 1995, *Global Modernities*, London, Sage.

Feldman, Walter 1989, "Record Review: Classical Turkish Music in Greece", *Turkish Music Quarterly*, pp. 8-10.

– 1990 / 1991, "Cultural Authority and Authenticity in the Turkish Repertoire", *Asian Music*, pp. 73-111.

– 1993, "Ottoman Sources on the Development of the Taksîm", *Yearbook for Traditional Music*, vol. 25, 1-28.

– 1996, *Music of the Ottoman Court: Makam, Composition and the early Ottoman Instrumental Repertoire* (= Intercultural Music Studies 10), Berlin.

– 2001, "Structure and Evolution of the Mevlevî Ayîn: The Case of the Third Selâm." Hammarlund, Anders, Olsson, Tord & Ozdalga, Elisabeth (ed.), *Sufism Music and Society in Turkey and the Middle East*, Istanbul, Swedish Research Institute in Istanbul, pp. 49-59.

– 2007, "Ottoman Music", *Oxford Music Online*, Oxford University Press.

– 2015, "The Musical 'Renaissance' of Late Seventeenth Century Ottoman Turkey: Reflections on the Musical Material of Ali Ufkî (ca. 1610-1675), Hâfiz Post (d. 1694) and the ‚Marâghî' Repertoire', Greve 2015: 87-138.

– 2017, "The Art of Melodic Extension Within and Beyond the Usûl", Helvacı, Olley & Jäger 2017: 153-176.

Ferid, Rusen, 1933, *Bestegâr – Sair Nazîm. Hayatı, Eserleri hakkında Tetkikat*, Istanbul, Hilâl Matbaası.

Filarmoni Derneği (ed.), 1982, *Atatürk Türkiye'sinde Müzik Reformu Yılları. Opera, Bale, Senfonik Müzik*, Istanbul.

Freemuse (ed.), 2016, *The Freemuse Files: Turkey*, Copenhagen, Freemuse.

Frith, Simon, 2000, " The Discourse of World Music", Born, Georgina & Desmondalgh, David (eds.), *Western Music and its Others. Difference, Representation, and Appropriation in Music*, University of California Press, pp. 305-323.

Fuchs, Martin & Rüpke, Jörg, 2015, "Religious Individualisation in Historical Perspective", *Religion*, 45:3, 323-329, DOI: 10.1080/0048721X.2015.1041795.

Fuhrmann, Malte, 2009, "Down and Out the Quays of Izmir: 'European' Musicians, Innkeepers, and Prostitutes in the Ottoman Port-Cities", *Mediteranean Historical Review*, Vol. 24,2, pp. 169-185.

Galpin, Francis, 1937, *The Music of the Sumerians.*

[Gazimihal], Mahmut Ragıp 1927, "Aperçus préliminaires sur l'origine asiatique de quelques instruments turque", *Bilten Inst. za prousavanje folklora sarajevo*, Sarajevo.

– 1928, *Anadolu Türküleri ve Musıki Istikbalımız*, Marifet Matbaası.

– 1929, *Şarkî Anadolu Türküleri ve Oyunları. Istanbul Konservatuarı Folklôr Hey'eti'nin dördüncü Tetkik Seyahatı Münasebetiyle*, Istanbul.

– 1939, *Türkiye-Avrupa Musiki Münasebetleri: 1600-1875*, Istanbul: Numune Matbaası.

– 1955, *Türk Askerî Muzikaları Tarihi*, Istanbul, Maarif Basımevi.

– 1958, *Asya ve Anadolu Kaynaklarında Iklığ*, Ankara.

– 1958 / 1975 / 2001, *Ülkelerde Kopuz ve Tezeneli Sazlarımız*, Ankara, T.C. Kültür Bakanlığı.

– 1961, *Musıki Sözlüğü*, Istanbul, Milli Eğitim Basımevi 1961.

Gedikli, Necati, 1987, "Müzik Araştırmacısı ve Folklorcu olarak Ahmet Adnan Saygun", Göğüsö M. Tuğrup (ed.), *Ahmed Adnan Saygun Semineri*, Izmir, Mars.

Giray, Selim, 2002, *Ahmed Adnan Saygun'un Keman Yapıtlari: Bir Kemancıya Rehber*, Ankara: T.C. Kültür Bakanlığı.

Glick-Schiller, Nina et al., 1997, "From Immigrant to Transmigrant: Theorizing Transnational Migration", Pries, Ludger (ed.), *Transnationale Migration*, (Soziale Welt, Sonderband 12), Baden-Baden, Nomos, pp. 121-140.

Gökalp, Ziya, 1923 (1968), *Türkçülüğün Esâsları*, Ankara; (English): *The Principles of Turkism*, Translated by Robret Devereux, Leiden.

Göktepe, Salâhattin, 1971, *Büyük Müzisyenler Ansiklopedisi*, Izmir.

Göktürk, Deniz, Soysal, Levent & Türeli, Ipek, 2009, *Orienting Istanbul. Cultural Capital of Europe?*, Oxfordshire, Routledge.

Gölcen, Ilhami, 2007, *Rauf Yekta. Fransızca Musıki Yazıları (Fransızca Metinlerin Tıpkıbasımı ile)*, Ankara, Ürün.

Gölpınarlı, Abdülbâki, 1953, *Mevlânadan Sonra Mevlevîlik*, Istanbul.

Görgün, Ayten, 2000, "Kadınlar Mevlevileri böldü", *Hürriyet*, 13.1.2000: 22.

Greve, Martin, 1995, *Die Europäisierung Orientalischer Kunstmusik in der Türkei*, Frankfurt a.M: P. Lang.

- 2003, *Die Musik der imaginären Türkei. Musik und Musikleben im Kontext der Migration aus der Türkei in Deutschland*, Stuttgart, Metzler.
- 2008, "Turkish Music in European Institutions", Hemetek, Ursula & Sağlam, Hande (ed.), *Music from Turkey in the Diaspora*, Universität für Musik und Darstellende Kunst Wien (Klanglese 5, Institut für Volksliedforschung und Ethnomusikologie), pp. 89-95.
- (ed.) 2015, *Writing the History of „Ottoman Music"*, Würzburg, Ergon.
- (2002) 2016, "Writing against Europe: On the Necessary Decline of Ethnomusicology", translated by Férdia J. Stone-Davis, Ethnomusicology Translations, https://scholarworks.iu.edu/journals/index.php/emt/article/view/22461.

Greve, Martin & Kaya, Ayhan, 2004, "Islamic Force, Takım 34 und andere. Identitätsmixturen türkischer Rapper in Berlin und Istanbul", Kimminich, Eva (ed.), *Rap: More than Words, Welt – Körper – Sprache*, vol. 4, pp. 161-179.

Greve, Martin & Şahin, Özay, forthcomming 2017, *The Sound of Dersim. Dersimli Müzisyen Anlatıyor*, Bilgi Üniversitesi Yayınları.

Gronow, Pekka, 1981, The Record Industry comes to the Orient, *Ethnomuicology*, pp. 251-284.

Gündogar, Sinan, 2005, *Muhalif Müzik. Halk Şiirindeki Protesto Geleneğinden Günümüz Politik Şarkıları*, İstanbul: Devin Yayınları.

Güngör, Necati, 2006, *Safiye Ayla'nın Anıları*, Istanbul. Heyamola.

Güngör, Nazife, 1990, *Arabesk. Sosyokültürel Açıdan Arabesk Müzik*, Istanbul, Bilgi.

Güntekin, Mehmet, 2010, *Istanbul'un 100 Musikisinasi*, Istanbul'un Yüzleri Serisi 17, Istanbul, Istanbul Büyükşehir Belediyesi Kültür Yayınları.

Güray, Cenk, 2012, *Bin Yılın Mirası, Makam Var Eden Döngü: Edvar Geleneği*, Istanbul, Pan.

Gürler, Mehmet, 2015, *Islâmda Mûsikî ve Son Asır Osmanlı Musıkı-Şinasları*, Istanbul, Sebil Yayınevi.

Hagopian, Harold, 1999, "Armenia: The Sorrow Sound"; Broughton, Ellingham & Trillo 1999, pp. 332-337.

Halbwachs, Maurice, 1967, *Das kollektive Gedächtnis*, Frankfurt.

Hall, Leslie, 1982, "Turkish Musical Culture in Toronto", *Canadian Folk Music Journal*, 10, pp. 48-53.

Hammarlund, Anders, 1993, *Yeni Sesler – Nya Stämmor. En väg till Musiken i det turkiska Sverige*, Stockholm, Stockholm University.

Hamelink, Wendelmoet, 2016, *The Sung Home. Narrative, Morality, and the Kurdish Nation*, Leiden, Brill.

Hannerz, Ulf, 1987, "The World in Creolization", *Africa*, 57, 4, pp. 546-559.

- 1989, "Culture between Center and Periphery: Toward a Macroanthropology", *Ethnos*, 54, 3-4, 200-216.

Hasgül, Necdet, 1996, "Türkiye popüler müzik tarihinde 'Anadolu Pop' akımının yeri, *Folklore Doğru*, Vol. 62, pp. 51-74.

Hassanpour, Amir, 1997, "MED-TV, Grossbritannien und der türkische Staat: Die Suche einer staatenlosen Nation nach Souveränität im Äther". Borck, Carsten, Savelsberg, Eva & Hajo, Siamend (ed.): *Ethnizität, Nationalismus, Religion und Politik in Kurdistan*, Münster: Lit, vol 1, pp. 239-278.

Haug, Judith I., 2010, *Der Genfer Psalter in den Niederlanden, Deutschland, England und dem Osmanischen Reich (16.–18. Jh)*, Tübinger Beiträge zur Musikwissenschaft, 30, Tutzing, Hans Schneider Verlag.

- 2017, "Representations of Usûl in Alî Ufukî's Manuscrips", Jäger, Olley & Helvacı (eds.), 2017: 91-107.

Hein, Carola, 2010, "The European Capital of Culture Programme and Istanbul 2010", Göktürk, Soysal & Türeli, 2010: 253-266.

Helvacı, Zeynep, 2007, *Lirin Tarihi: Eski ön Asya ve Yunan Uygarlıklarında kullanılan Lirlerin Karşılaştırılması*, Ph.D. Thesis, Baskent Üniversitesi, Ankara.

Helvacı, Zeynep, Jacob Olley & Jäger, Ralf Martin (eds.), 2017, *Rhythmic Cycles and Structures in the Art Music of the Middle East*, Würzburg, Ergon.

Hemetek, Ursula & Sağlam, Hande (eds.), 2008, *Music from Turkey in the Diaspora* (= Klanglese 5), Wien, Institut für Volksmusikforschung und Ethnomusikologie.

Heper, Sadettin (ed.), 1979, *Mevlevî Âyinleri*, Konya, Konya Turizm Derneği Yayını.

Hiçyılmaz, Ergun, 1999, *İstanbul Geceleri ve Kantolar*, Istanbul, Sabah Kitabları.

Hindemith, Paul, 2013, *Vorschläge für den Aufbau des türkischen Musikleben*, Düsseldorf, Staccato Verlag, (Turkish translation by Elif Damla Yavuz: *Hindemith Raporları 1935/1936/1937*, Ankara: Sevda-Cenap And Vakfı Yayınları 2013).

Hobsbawm, Eric & Ranger, Terence, 1983, *The Invention of Tradition*, Cambridge, Cambridge University Press.

Hoffmann, Judith (ed.), 2007, *Partnerschaft im Wachsen. Die deutsch-türkischen Kulturbeziehungen. Bestandsaufnahme und Empfehlungen*, Stuttgart, IFA.

Holst, Gail, 1975/1979, *Rebetika. Lieder einer griechischen Subkultur*, Berlin, Gerhardt.

Hongur, G., 2014, *Politics, Struggle, Violence, and the Transformation of Expressive Culture: An Ethnography of Kurds' Musical Practices in Turkey*, Ph.D. thesis, Istanbul.

Hough, Christina 2010, "Obscured Hybridity: The Kurdishness of Turkish Folk Music", *Pacific Review of Ethnomusicology*, vol. 15.

İçduygu, Ahmet, 2015, "Türkiye'de Yönelen Düzensiz Göç Dalgaları İçinde 'Transit Göç'", Erdoğan & Kaya 2015: 279-294.

Idelsohn, A.Z., 1913, "Die Maqamen der arabischen Musik", *Sammelbände der internationalen Musikgesellschaft*, 15, pp. 1-63.

İhsanoğlu, Ekmeleddin, Şeşen, Ramazan, Gündüz, Gülcan & M.Serdar Bekar (ed.), 2003, *Osmanlı Mûsikî Literatürü Tarihi*, Istanbul, Islam Tarihi, Sanat ve Kültür Araştırma Merkezi IRCICA.

Ilerici, Kemal, 1980 (1970), *Bestecilik Bakımdan Türk Müziği ve Armonisi*, Istanbul, Milli Eğitim Basımevi.

Ilyasoğlu, Evin, 1997, *Cemal Reşit Rey. Müzikten ibaret bir Dünyada Gezintiler*, Istanbul, Yapı Kredi Yayınları.

– 2000, *İlhan Usmanbaş. Ölümsüz Deniz Taşlarıydı*, İstanbul, Yapı Kredi Yayınları.

– 2006, *Bülent Tarcan. Bir Hekimin Senfonik Öyküsü*, Istanbul, Dünya.

– 2007, *71 Türk Bestecisi / 71 Turkish Composers*, Istanbul, Pan.

– 2009, *Mersin'den Yükselen Çağdaş Bir Ses: Nevit Kodallı*, Istanbul, Pan.

İnal, Ibnülemin Mahmut Kemal, 1958, *Hoş Sadâ. Son Asır Türk Musikişinasları*, Istanbul, Maarif Basimevi.

İnalcik, Halil, 2010, *Has-Bağçede 'ays u tarab. Nedîmler Sâirler Mutribler. Seçme Eserleri: III*, Istanbul, Türkiye İş Bankası Kültür Yayınları 2010.

İnanç, Zeri, 2016, *Erivan Radyosunda Kürt Sesi*, Istanbul, İsmail Beşikçi Vakfı Yayınları.

İnci, Ayça, 2011, "Cultural Policy in Turkey Today: İntroduction and Overview", Ada, Serhat (ed.), *Turkish Cultuar Policy Report. A Civil Perspective*, İstanbul: Bilgi Üniversitesi Yayınları, pp. 191-200.

Independent Commision on Turkey, 2004, *Turkey in Europe: Moore than a Promise*. www.independentcommissiononturkey.org/report.html.

Istanbul 2010, 2010a, *Program: Müzik Projeler*, Istanbul.

– 2010b, *Klasik Türk Müziği. Program Kitabcığı*, Istanbul.

– 2010c, *Ramadan Istanbul 2010*, Istanbul Kültür Baskent.

Istanbul Belediyesi, 2010, *Ramadan Istanbul 2010*, Istanbul Kültür Baskent.

Ivanoff, Alexandra, 2013, "In Retrospect: Istanbul's Classical Music Scene in 2013", *Today's Zaman*, 24 December 2013.

Jackson, Maureen, 2013, *Mixing Musics. Turkish Jewry and the Urban Landscape of a Sacred Song*, Stanford Studies in Jewish History and Culture, Stanford, California, Stanford University Press.

Jäger, Ralf Martin, 1996a, *Türkische Kunstmusik und ihre handschriftlichen Quellen aus dem 19. Jahrhundert*, Eisenach.

– 1996b, *Katalog der hamparsun-notası-Manuskripte im Archiv des Konservatoriums der Universität Istanbul*, Eisenach.

– 1997, "Die türkische Janitscharenmusik: Mehterhane", in: *Die Musik in Geschichte und Gegenwart*, vol. 9, Kassel, Bärenreiter, pp. 1318-1329.

– 1997a, "Türkei", "IX: Ausbildungsstätten, Bibliotheken, Ensembles", *Die Musik in Geschichte und Gegenwart*, vol. 9, Kassel, Bärenreiter, pp. 1070-1076.

– 2006, "Osmanische Musikkultur zwischen Orient und Okzident: Der Beginn der kompositorischen Auseinandersetzung mit Europa an der Schwelle zum 20. Jahrhundert", Christ, Heidi (ed.), *Musik verbindet uns. Festschrift für Marianne Bröcker* (Veröffentlichungsreihe der Forschungsstelle für fränkische Volksmusik der Bezirke Mittel-, Ober- und Unterfranken 62), Uffenheim, pp. 51-62.

– 2015, "Concepts of Western and Ottoman Music History", Greve 2015: 33-50.

Kahramankaptan, Şefik, 1998, *Ismet Inönü ve Hârika Çocuklar*, Ankara: Ümit.

Kaiser, Bianco, 2013, Living in Turkey as a Foreigner: Insights from the Perspective of German", Paper read at the Conference *Perceptions of International Migration in Turkey*, Istanbul Bilgi University, April 12, 2013.

Kalaitzidis, Kyriakos, 2005, – 2005, "Instrumentarium", Feldman, W., Guettat, M., Kalaitzides, Kyriakos (eds.), *Music in the Mediterranean*, Volume II *Theory*, Thessaloniki, En Chordais, Project MediMuses in the context of European Union programme Euromed Heritage II, pp. 111-117.

– 2012, *Post-Byzantine Music Manuscripts as a Source for Oriental Secular Music 15th – 19th Century*, Istanbuler Texte und Studien 28; Würzburg: Ergon Verlag.

Kalender, Ruhi, 1978, "Yüzyılımızın Başlarında İstanbul'un Musiki Hayatı", *Ankara Üniversitesi İlâhiyat Fakültesi Dergisi* 23, Ankara, pp. 411-444.

Kaliviotis, Aristomenis, 2013 (original 2002), *İzmir Rumalarının Müziği 1900–1922, Eğlence, Müzik Dükkanları, Plak Kayıtları*, translated by Yılmaz Okyay, Istanbul, Yapı Kredi Yayınları.

Kalkan, Şenay (ed.), 2004, *Muhalif Bağlama. „Arif Sağ Kitabi"*, Istanbul, Türkiye İş Bankası Kültür Yayınları 2004.

Kallimopoulou, Eleni, 2009, *Paradosiaká: Music, Meaning and Identity in Modern Greece*, Surrey, Ashgate.

Kalyoncu, Nesrin & Özata, Cemal, 2012, Instrument Teaching in the Context of Oral Tradition: A Field Study from Bolu, Turkey, *Oral Tradition*, 27/2, pp. 363-380.

Kaplan, Ayten, 2005, *Kültürel Müzikoloji*, Istanbul, Bağlam.

Karadağ, Burcu, 2013, *Meşkte Ney Eğitimi. Teaching the Ney with the Mesk Method*, Istanbul, Pan.

Karadeniz, Ekrem, (1965) 1984, *Türk Musikisinin Nazariye ve Esasları*, Istanbul, İş Bankası Yayınları.

Karahasanoğlu, Songül, 2008, *Muş Türküleri ve Oyun Havaları*, Istanbul, Yalın Yayıncılık.

Karahasanoğlu, Songül & Skoog, Gabriel, 2011, "Innovative Neglect: Contextual Divergence and the Development of the Mey in Turkey", *The Galphin Society Journal*, LXIV, 2001-2008.

Karahasanoğlu, Songül & Yavuz, Elif Damla, 2015, *Müzikte Araştırma Yöntemleri*, İstanbul, İTÜ.

Karakaya, Fikret, 2010, *Unutulmuş Osmanlı Sazları*, Istanbul, Avrupa Kültür Başkent.

Karolewski, Janina, 2014, "Ritual Text and Music in Turkish Alevism. Dimensions of Transmission and Bearers of Knowledge", Schulze, Henrik (ed.), *Musical Text as Ritual Object*, Turnhout.

Karomatov, F.M. , Meskeris, V.A. & Vyzgo, T.S., 1987, *Mittelasien; Musikgeschichte in Bildern*, vol. II: *Musik des Altertums*, Lieferung 9, Leipzig, Deutscher Verlag für Musik.

Karaosmanoğlu, Defne, 2009, "Eating the Past: Multiple Spaces, Multiple Times Performing „Ottomanness" in Istanbul", *International Journal of Cultural Studies*, 12, 339-358.

Karpat, Kemal H., 1995, "The Turks in America", Tapia, Stéphane de (ed.), 1995, *Turcs d'Europe et d'Ailleurs*, Paris, Institut National des Langues et Civilisations Orientales, pp. 231-252.

Kartomi, Margaret J., "The Process and Results of Musical Culture Contact: A Discussion of Terminology and Concepts", *Ethnomusicology*, pp. 227-249.

Kartomi, Margret J. & Blum, Stephen, (ed.), 1994, *Music-Cultures in Contact. Convergences and Collisions*, Basel, Gordon and Breach.

Katoğlu, Murat, 2009, "Cumhuriyet Döneminde Yüksek Kültürün Kamu Hizmeti Olarak Kurumlaşması", Ada & Ince (ed.), 2009: 25-79.

Kaya, Ayhan. 2000. *'Sicher in Kreuzberg' Berlin'deki Küçük Istanbul. Diyasporada Kimliğin Oluşumu*, Istanbul, Büke.

Kaygısız, Mehmet, 2000, *Türklerde Müzik*, Istanbul, Kaynak Yayınları.

Kaygusuz, Nermin, 2006, *Muallim Ismail Hakki Bey ve Mûsikî Tekâmül Dersleri*, Istanbul, ITÜ Vakfi Yayınları.

Kehl-Bodrogi, Krisztina, 1992, *Vom revolutionären Klassenkampf zum 'wahren' Islam. Transformationsprozesse im Alevitentum in der Türkei nach 1980*, Sozialanthropologische Arbeitspapiere Nr. 49, Berlin, Das Arabische Buch.

Kerovpyan, Aram & Yılmaz, Altuğ, 2010, *Klasik Osmanli Müziği ve Ermeniler*, Istanbul, Avrupa Kültür Başkenti.

Keskiner, Bora, 2006, "Risâle-I Edvâr: Kadı-zade Mehmed Tirevî (Süleymaniye Kütüphanesi / Reşid Efendi 1059/5", *Musikişinas*, p. 33-46.

– 2009, Arap Harflı Türkçe Süreli Yayınlarda Türk Musikisi Teorisi Bibliyografyası, *Türkiye Araştırmaları Literatür Dergisi* 7/14, pp. 375-415.

Keupp, Heiner, et. al., 1999, *Identitätskonstruktionen. Das Patchwork der Identitäten in der Spätmoderne*, Reinbeck, Rohwolt.

Keyder, Çağlar (ed.), 1999a, *Istanbul. Between the Global and the Local*, Lanham, Rowman, Littlefield.

– 1999b, "The Setting", Keyder (ed.) 1999, 3-28.

– 2010, "Istanbul into the Twenty-First Century", Göktürk, Soysal & Türeli 2010.

Khalil, Alexander Konrad, 2009, *Echoes of Constantinople: Oral and Written Tradition of the Psaltes of the Ecumenical Patriarchate of Constantinople*, unpublished Ph. D. Thesis, University of California, San Diego.

Kip, Tarık (ed.), 1983, *TRT Türk Sanat Musikisi Sözlü Eserler Repertuvarı*, Ankara, TRT.

Kiesewetter, R.G., 1842 / 1968, *Die Musik der Araber*, Leipzig 1842, Reprint Wiesbaden.

Kishibe, Shigeo, 1940, "The Origin of the Pipa", *Transactions of the Asiatic Society of Japan*, 2nd series Vol. xiv: 259-303.

Kim, Jin-Ah, 2016, "Cross-Cultural Music Making: Conditions and Perspectives", unpublished paper read at the Confernce "Integrative Approaches to Contemporary Cross-Culturall Music Making", at the DHI Rome, Rome, 18-19 March, 2016.

– 2014, "Musik und Kulturtransfer. Ideen zu einem musikwissenschaftlichen Forschungsbereich", Kim, Jin-Ah & Riva, Nepomuk (ed.), *Entgrenzte Welt? Musik und Kulturtransfer*, Berlin, Ries & Erler, 9-56.

Kişmir, Celâlettin, 1967, "Avrupa'da Mevlâna Sevgisi", *Mevlana Güldestesi*, Konya, 26-31.

Klaser, Rajna, 2001, *From an Imagined Paradise to an Imagined Nation: Interpreting Şarkı as a Cultural Play*, unpublished Ph.D. Thesis, University of California, Berkeley.

Klebe, Dorit, 2008, "The Festival Türkgünü [Turkish Day] in Berlin and its Musical Forms of Expression", Hemetek & Sağlam pp. 61-76.

Kocabaşoğlu, Uyğur, 1980, *Şirket Telsizinden Devlet Radyosunaç TRT Öncesi Dönemde Radyonun Tarihsel Gelişimi ve Türk Siyasal Hayatı İçindeki Yeri*, Ankara, Ankara Üniversitesi Siyasal Bilgiler Fakültesi Yayınları No. 442, S.B.F. Basın ve Yayın Yüksek Okulu Basımevi.

Kolcu, Julia Aylin, 2009, *Judeo-Spanische Musik vom Osmanischen Reich bis zur heutigen Musikpraxis in der Türkei.* MA Thesis, Leuphana Universität Lüneburg.

Kolukırık, Kubilay, 2015, *Türk Müzik Tarihinde Dârü'l-elhân ve Dârü'l-elhân Mecmuası*, İstanbul, Barış Kitap.

Komische Oper Berlin (ed.), 2014, *Selam Opera! Interkultur im Opernbetrieb*, Leipzig, Henschel.

Korkmaz, Harun, 2015, *The Catalog of Music Manuscripts in Istanbul University Library*, Sources of Oriental Languages and Literatures 118, The Department of Near Eastern Languages and Civilizations, Harvard University.

Korkmaz, Zeynep, 1974, *Cumhuriyet Döneminde Türk Dili*, Ankara, Ankara Üniversitesi Dil ve Tarih-Coğrafya Fakültesi Yayınları.

Kosal, Vedat, 2003, *Westliche Klassische Musik in dem Osmanischen Reich*, Istanbul.

Kocabaşoğlu, Uygur, 1980, *Şirket Telsizinden Devlet Radyosuna*, Ankara, A. Ü. Siyasal Bilgiler Fakültesi Yayını.

Koç, Adnan, 2016a, "Teknolojik Gelişmeler ve Sosyokültürel Değişimler Sarmalında Günümüzde Bağlama İcracılığı", Koç 2016 (b): 112-123.

Koç, Adnan, 2016b (ed.), *1. Uluslararası Nida Tüfekçi Bağlama Sempozyumu*, Istanbul, İstanbul Teknik Üniversitesi Türk Musikisi Devlet Konservatuvarı.

Koz, M. Sabri 2012, "Cönk ve Mecmûa Zapraklarında Aşık Aramak", Hatice Aynur et. al. (Eds.), *Mecmûa: Osmanlı Edebiyatının Kırkambarı*, Istanbul, Turkuaz 2012, pp. 157-200.

Kulin, Ayse, 1996, *Bir Tatlı Huzur. Fotograflarla Münir Nurettin Selçuk'un Yaşam Öyküyü*, Istanbul, Sel.

Köksal, Aykut, 2015, "Elliler Modernizmi ve İlhan Usmanbaş", Köksal, Nemutlu & Şenürkmez 2015: 13-28.

Köksal, Aykut, Nemutlu, Mehmet & Şenürkmez, Kıvılcım Yıldız, 2015, *Perpetuum Mobile. İlhan Usmanbaş'ın Yapıtı*, İstanbul, Pan.

Kozanoğlu, Cevdet, 1988, *Radyo Hatıralarım*, Ankara, TRT Yayınları.

Kutluğ, Yakup Fikret, 2000, *Türk Musikisinde Makamlar*, Istanbul, Yapı Kredi Yayınları.

Kurt, Irfan, 1989, 1989, *Bağlama Düzen ve Pozisyon*, Istanbul, Pan.

Kuyumjian, Rita Soulahian, (2001) 2010, *Deliliğin Arkeolojisi Gomidas. Bir Ermeni Ikonun Portresi*, Istanbul, Birzaman.

Kütahyali, Önder, 1981, *Çağdaş Müzik Tarihi*, Ankara, Varol Matbaası.

Kütükçü, Tamer 2012, *Radyoculuk Geleneğimiz ve Türk Musikisi*, Istanbul, Ötüken.

Lo, Jasqueline, 2000, "Beyond Happy Hybridity: Performing Asian-Australian Identities", Ang, Ien, Chalmers, Sharon, Law, Lisa & Thomas, Mandy (eds.), *Alter/Asians: Asian-Australian identities in art, media and popular culture*, Annandale, NSW, Australia, Pluto Press, pp. 152-168.

Levend, A.S., 1972, *Türk Dilinde Gelişme ve Sadeleşme Evreleri*, Ankara, Türk Dil Kurumu.

Lewis, Bernhard, 1961, *The Emergence of Modern Turkey*, London.

Livingston, Tamara E., 1999, "Music Revivals: Towards a General Theory", *Ethnomusicology*, Vol. 43, No. 1, pp. 66-85.

Lucas, Ann E., 2012014, "Ancient Music, Modern Myth: Persian Music and the Pursuit of Methodology in Historical Ethnomusicology", McCollum & Hebert 2015: 175-196.

Lundberg, Dan, 1994, *Persikoträdgårdarnas musik*, Stockholm Universitet.

Macar, Elçin, 2015, "Yunanistan'dan Anadolu'ya Göç: Nüfüs Mübadelesi", Erdoğan & Kaya, pp. 173-190.

Mack, Dieter, 2004, *Zeitgenössische Musik in Indonesien: zwischen lokalen Traditionen, nationalen Verpflichtungen und internationalen Einflüssen*, Hildesheim, Olms Verlag.

Manav, Özkan & Nemutlu, Mehmet, 2011, *Müzikte Alımlama*, Istanbul, Pan.

Maraqa, Salah Eddin, 2015, *Die traditionelle Kunstmusik in Syrien und Ägypten von 1500 bis 1800. Eine Untersuchung der musiktheoretischen und historisch-biographischen Quellen*, Tutzing.

Maral, Alper & Lindley, Mark, 2011, *Techniques of 20th-Century Turkish "Contemporary" Music. An Introductory Survey*, Istanbul.

Marett, Allan, 1987, "Turkish Folk Music in Sidney. A Preliminary Investigation". *Transplanted European Music Cultures*, Adelaide, Pagel, pp. 80-89.

Markoff, Irene Judith, 1986, *Musical Theory, Performance and the Contemporary Bağlama Specialist in Turkey*, Ann Arbour.

– "Aspects of Turkihs Folk Music Theory", 2001, Danielson, Virginia, Marcus, Scott & Reynolds, Dwight (eds.), *Garland Encyclopedia of World Music*, vol 6, *The Middle East*, pp. 77-87.

Martin, Robert, 1988/89, Charles Fonton, *Turkish Musical Quaterly*, 1/2 –2/1.

Massicard, Elise, 2001, "Alevismus in der Türkei: Kollektive Identität ohne starken Inhalt?" Rammert, Werner et al. (ed.), *Kollektive Identitäten und kulturelle Innovationen. Ethnologische, soziologische und historische Studien*, Leipzig, Leipziger Universitätsverlag, pp. 155-174.

McCollum, Jonathan & Hebert, David G., 2014, *Theory and Method in Historical Ethnomusicology*, Lanhan, Lexington Books.

McPherson, Eve, 2011, "Political History and Embodied Identity. Discourse in the Turkish Call to Prayer". *Music & Politics* 5, Number 1.

Mendívis, Julio, 2009, *Making Music History: Strategien der Historisierung „geschichtsloser" Musikkulturen – Der Fall der Musik aus den Anden (Bolivien, Ecuador und Peru)*, unpublished Habilitationsschrift, Hochschule für Musik und Theater Hannover, Köln.

Meric, Murat, 1999, "Türkiye'de Caz: Bir uzun Serüven", Paçacı 1999: 160-167.

– 2011, "Cumhurriyet Dönemi İstanbul Eğlence Hayatına bir Bakış", Aytar & Parmaksızoğlu 2011.

Merkt, Irmgard, 1993, "Das Eigene und das Fremde. Zur Entwicklung interkultureller Musik-Erziehung", Böhle, Reinhard (ed.), *Möglichkeiten der Interkulturellen Ästhetischen Erziehung in Theorie und Praxis. Beiträge vom 1. Symposium zur Interkulturellen Ästhetischen Erziehung an der Hochschule der Künste Berlin*, Frankfurt am Main, IKO, pp. 141-151.

Milli Eğitim Bakanlığı, 2009, Ortaöğretim Genel Müdürlüğü (ed.), *Güzel Sanatlar ve Spor Lisesi Geleneksel Türk Müziği Tarihi Dersi Öğretim Programı*, Ankara.

Mimaroğlu, Ilhan, 1991, *Elektronik Müzik*, Istanbul, Pan.

Nettl, Bruno, 1985, *The Western Impact on World Music*, New York, Schirmer Books.

Neubauer, Eckhard, 1969, "Musik zur Mongolenzeit in Iran und angrenzenden Ländern", *Der Islam*, 45, pp. 233-261.

- 1985/1986, "1750 Charles Fonton: Essai sur la musique orientale, Istanbul", *Zeitschrift für Geschichte der Arabisch-Islamischen Wissenschaften* 2, 277-324 / 3, pp. 324-377.
- 1986, *Codex on Music* (Fethullah Mümin Sirvânî, *Mecelle fi'l-Musiki*), Frankfurt a.M., Institut for Arabic-Islamic Science der Johann Wolfgang von Goethe Universität.
- 1994, "15. ve 16. Yüzyıllarda Istanbul'da Musiki Hayatı", *Dünden Bügune Istanbul Ansiklopedisi*, Vol. 5, pp. 523-533.
- 1997, "Zur Bedeutung der Begriffe Komponist und Komposition in der Musikgeschichte der islamischen Welt", *Zeitschrift für Geschichte der arabisch-islamischen Wissenschaften* 11, pp. 307-363.
- 2000, "Glimpses of Arab Music in Ottoman Times from Syrian and Egyptian Sources", *Zeitschrift für Geschichte der Arabisch-Islamischen Wissenschaften*, 13, pp. 317-365.

Neuhoff, Hans, 2017, "Weltmusik studieren – unterrichten – vermitteln", Leggewie, Claus & Meyer, Erik (eds.), *Global Pop*, Stuttgart, J.B. Metzler, pp. 222-230.

Neumark, Fritz, 1980, *Zuflucht am Bosporus. Gelehrte, Politiker und Künstler in der Emigration 1933-53*, Frankfurt am Main, Knecht.

Neyzi, Leyla, 2002, "Metin-Kemal Kahraman'ın Müziği: Yaşlı Kuşağın Belleği Yoluyla Dersimli Kimliğinin Yeniden Keşfi", *Toplum ve Bilim* 92, pp. 163-175.

Noordink, Marianne, 2010, "The Execution of Melody on Arab and Turkish Ney: Another Story?", unpublished Article.

O'Connell, John Morgan, 1996, *Alaturka Revisited: Style as History in Turkish Vocal Performance*, PhD dissertation, University of California, Los Angeles.
- 2000, "Fine Art, Fine Music: Controlling Turkish Taste at the Fine Arts Academy in 1926", *Yearbook for Traditional Music*, Vol. 32, pp. 117-142.
- 2001, "From Empire to Republic: Vocal Style in Twentieth-Century Turkey", Danielson, Virginia, Marcus, Scott & Reynolds, Dwight (eds.), *Garland Encyclopedia of World Music*, vol 6, *The Middle East*, pp. 781-787.
- 2005, "In the Time of Alaturka: Identifying Difference in Musical Discouse", *Ethnomusicology*, Vol. 49, 2, pp. 177-205.
- 2008, "War of the Waves: Cypriot Broadcasting in the United Kingdom", Hemetek & Sağlam, 2008, pp. 119-130.
- 2010, "Alabanda: Brass Bands and Musical Methods in Turkey", Spinetti 2010: 19-37.
- 2013, *Alaturca: Style in Turkish Music (1923-1938)*, Farnham, Ashgate.
- 2017, "Usulsüz: Meter in the Concerts of Münir Nurettin Selçuk (1923-1938)", Helvacı, Olley & Jäger 2017: 247-276.

Okyay, Erdoğan, 1973/74, "Die Schulmusikerziehung in der Türkei. Ihre geschichtliche Entwicklung und ihr heutiger Zustand", *Mitteilungen der deutschen Gesellschaft für Musik des Orients*, Berlin, Vol. 12, pp. 6-39.

- 2009, *Atatürk Devrimlerinin Simgesi Cumhurbaskanlığı Senfoni Orkestrası'na Armağan*, Ankara, Sevda Cenap And Vakfı Yayınları.
- 2012, *Ankara Devlet Konservatuvarı'na Armağan*, Ankara, Sevda Cenap And Müzik Vakfı Yayınları.

Olley, Jacob, 2017, *Writing Music in Nineteenth-Century Istanbul. Ottoman Armenian and the Intention of Hampartsum Notation*, unpublished Ph.D. thesis, King's College London.

Oransay, Gültekin, 1959, "Das Tonsystem der Türkei-Türkischen Kunstmusik", *Die Musikforschung* Vol. 10, pp. 250-264.

- 1964, *Die traditionelle türkische Kunstmusik*, Ankara, Küğ.
- 1965, *Batı Tekniğiyle Yazan 60 Türk Bağdar*, Ankara, Küğ.
- 1966, *Die melodische Linie und der Begriff Makam der traditionellen türkischen Kunstmusik vom 15. bis zum 19. Jahrhundert*, Ph.D. Thesis, München, Ankara, Türk Tarih Kurumu.
- 1972, *Ali Ufkî ve Türk Dini Musikisi*, unpublished doçentlik thesis, Ankara.
- 1973, "Cumhuriyetin ilk Elli Yılında Geleneksel Sanat Musıkimiz", in: Öner, N. (ed.), *50.Yıl*, Ankara, Ankara Üniversitesi Ilâhiyat Fakültesi Yayınları.
- "Türkiye'de Defter ve Dergi Biçiminde Fasıl Yayınları 1875-1876", *İlâhiyat Fakültesi Dergisi* XXII, Ankara.
- 1983, "Çoksesli Müzik"; Belge, Murat, (ed.), *Cumhuriyet Dönemi Türkiye Ansiklopedisi*, Istanbul, Iletişim, pp. 1517-1730.

Oransay, Melâhat & Gültekin, 1969, *Çağdaş Seslendiricilerimiz ve Küğ Yazarlarımız*, Ankara, Küğ Yayını.

Osman, Ali Osman, 2001, *Alamanya Türküleri. Türk Göçmen Edebiyatinin Sözlü/öncü kolu*, Ankara, T.C. Kültür Bakanlığı Yayınlığı.

Dr. Oz, 2011, *Miktrotonal Klavye Tasarımları*, unpublished broshure.

Ölmez, Niyazi, 2008, *Sesler Hazinesi*, Istanbul, Turkuaz Yayınları.

Önaldı, Şenel, 1977, *Türk Halk Musikîsi Ansiklopedisi*, Istanbul, Alfa Matbaacılık.

Öner, Oguz, 2009, "Istanbul 2010 European Capital of Culture: Towards a Participatory Culture?", Göktürk, Soysal & Türeli, 267-278.

Önüter, Fatos, 1989, *Kemençe'nin Tarihi Gelişimi, Kemençe üzerine Araştırma ve Düşünceler*, Master Thesis, İTÜ, Istanbul.

Örter, Erol, 1998, *Buzuki Erol*, Pan.

Özalp, M.N., 1976 / 1986 / 2000, *Türk Musikisi Tarihi*, Istanbul / Ankara, TRT / Istanbul, MEB Yayınları.

Özbek, Mehmet, (1998) 2014, *Türk Halk Müziği El Kitabı I Terimler Sözlüğü*, Ankara: Atatürk Kültür Merkezi.

Özbek, Meral, 1991, *Popüler Kültür ve Orhan Gencebay*, Istanbul: Iletişim.

Özdek, Attila, 2014, *Bağlama için Etüt, Egzersiz ve Eserler*, Ankara, Plaka Matbaacılık.
- 2016, "Günümüzde Bağlama Eğitiminde Görülen Problemler ve Çözüm Önerileri", Koç, Adnan (ed.), *1. Uluslararası Nida Tüfekçi Bağlama Sempozyumu*, İstanbul, İTÜ, pp. 177-207.

Özdemir, Ulas, 2007, *Su Diyar-i Gurbet Elde, Aşık Mücrimî'nin Yasamı ve Şiirleri*, Pan.
- 2016, *Kimlik, Ritüel, Müzik Icrası, İstanbul Cemevlerinde Zakirlik Hizmeti*, Istanbul, Kolektif.

Özdogan, G., Üstel, F., Karakaslı, K. & Kentel, F., 2009, *Türkiye'de Ermeniler: Cemaat-Birey-Yurtta*. Istanbul, Istanbul Bilgi Üniversitesi Yayınları.

Özeke, Sezen, 2003, *A History of Music Teacher Education in the Republic of Turkey, 1982–1998*, unpublished PhD thesis at the Arizona State University.

Özer, Mehmet Ihsan, 1988, *Ses Cinsleri ve Çeşitli Akortlar açısından Klasik Türk Müziğinde Koro*, Thesis, İTÜ, Istanbul.

Özer, Zülfikar Yavuz, 2011, *Türk Mûsikîsinde Piyano Kullanılır mı?* Izmir, Ege Üniversitesi Yayınevi.

Özer, Yetkin, 1997, *Bilim Perspektifinde Müzik*, Izmir, Eylül 1997.
- 2002, *Müzik Etnografisi. Alan Çalışmasında Yöntem ve Teknik*, Izmir, Dokuz Eylül Yayınları.

Özkahraman, Hikmet, 2010, *Basında Nevzat Atlığ '1949'dan Günümüze*, Istanbul, Üstün Eserler.

Özkan, Derya (ed.), 2014, *Cool Istanbul. Urban Enclosure and Resistance*, Bielefeld, Transcript.

Özkan, İsmail Hakkı, 1984/2003, *Türk Mûsıkîsi Nazariyatı ve Usûlleri*, Ankara, Ötüken.

Özkoç, Önder, 2012, "Necil Kazim Akses'in "Neva Kâr" üzerine Scherzo'su", paper presented at the symposium "Itrî ve Dönemine Disiplinlerarası Bakışlar", Istanbul 3.12.2012.

Özpazarcık, Ismail, 1998, *Alaturka Hayatlar Alafranga Masallar*, Istanbul, Altın Kitaplar.

Özpekel, Osman Nuri, 1979, *Hafiz Post Güfte Mecmuası*, Istanbul, İstanbul Üniversitesi.

Öztuna, Yılmaz, 1949 / 1955, Türk Musikisi Lugatı, *Musiki Mecmuası*, 15, 1949-91, 1955.
- 1969, Türk Bestecileri Ansiklopedisi, Istanbul.
- 1969 / 1974 / 1976 / 1980 / 1990, *Türk Musikisi Ansiklopedisi*, Ankara, Kültür Bakanlığı.
- 1983, *Abdülkaadir Merâğî*, Ankara, Kültür ve Turizm Bakanlığı Yayınları.
- 1986, *Sâdeddin Arel*, Ankara, Kültür ve Turizm Bakanlığı Yayınları.
- 1987a, *Dede Efendi*, Ankara, Kültür ve Turizm Bakanlığı Yayınları.
- 1987b, *Itrî*, Ankara, Kültür ve Turizm Bakanlığı Yayınları.
- 1987c, *Türk Mûsikîsi. Teknik ve Tarih*, Istanbul, Türkpetrol Vakfi Lâle Mecmuası.

- 1988, *Abdülkaadir Merâgi*, Ankara, Kültür ve Turizm Bakanlığı Yayınları.

Öztürk, Ali Osman, 2001, *Alamanya Türküleri*, T.C. Kültür Bakanlığı Yayınlığı, Ankara.

Öztürk, Okan Murat, 2006, *Zeybek Kültürü ve Müziği*, Istanbul, Pan.

- 2014, *Makam Müziğinde Ezgi ve Makam İlişkinin Analizi ve Yorumlanması Açısından Yeni bir Yaklaşım: Perde Düzenleri ve Makamsal Ezgi Çekirdekleri*, Ph.D. thesis, İstanbul Teknik Üniversitesi.

- 2015, "An Effective Means for Representing the *Unity of Opposites*: The Development of Ideology Concerning Folk Music in Turkey in the Context of Nationalism and Ethnic Identity", Greve 2015: 177-193.

- 2016, "Geleneksel Bağlama İcrasında Gelişiminde Üstadlık Kültürünün ve Belirleyiciliği", Koç, Adnan 2016 (b): 127-142.

Öztürkmen, Arzu, 1998, *Türkiye'de Folklor ve Milliyetçilik*, Istanbul, İletişim.

- 2005, "Staging a Ritual Dance out of its's Context: The Role of an Individual Artist in Transforming the Alevi Semah", *Asian Folklor Studies*, 64, pp. 247-260.

- 2016, "Günhan Danışman (1943-2009): XII Oral History Conference in Istanbul, 2000," Santacana, Carles & Vilanova, Mercedes (eds.), *Many Voives of Oral History*, Barcelona, Icaria, pp. 34-40.

Özyıldırım, Murat, 2013, *Arap ve Türk Musikisinin XX. Yüzyıl Birlikteliği*, İstanbul, Bağlam.

Pack, William D., 1977, *Paul Hindemith in Turkey: Some Contributions to Music Education*, Ph.D. Thesis Brigham Young University.

Paçacı, Gönül, 1999 (ed.), *Cumhuriyet'in Sesleri*, İstanbul, Tarih Vakfı.

- 2010, *Osmanlı Müziğini Okumak. Neşriyât-i Musık*, Istanbul, İstanbul 2010 Avrupa Kültür Başkenti.

- 2015, „Changes in the Field of Turkish Music during the Late Ottoman/Early Republican Era", Greve 2015: 151-165.

Parlak, Erol, 2000, *Türkiye'de El ile (tezenesiz) Saz Çalma Geleneği ve Çalış Teknikleri*, Ankara, T.C. Kültür Bakanliği.

- 2001, *Şelpe Tekniği Metodu 1*, Istanbul, Maket Matbaacılık.

- 2011, *Bağlama Schule*, Acoustic Music, Oldenburg.

- 2013, *Garip Bülbül Neşet Ertaş. Hayatı, Sanatı, Eserleri*, Istanbul, Demos.

- 2017, "Standardisierung und Notation der Bağlama von der Republiksgründung bis zur Gegenwart", Çiftçi & Greve 2017.

Pekin, Ersu, 2003, "Surname'nin Müziği: 16. Yüzyılda İstanbul'da Çalgılar", *Dipnot*, pp. 52-90.

- 2004, "Theory, Instruments and Music", Inalcık, Halil & Renda, Günsel (eds.), *Ottoman Civilization*, Ankara , Ministery of Culture and Tourizm, Vol. 2.

- 2015, "Neither Dates nor Sources: A Methodological Problem in Writing the History of Ottoman Music", Greve 2015: 57-74.

Pennanen, Risto Pekka, 2008, "Lost in Scales: Balkan Folk Music Research and the Ottoman Legacy", *Musicology*, 8, 127-146.

– 2004, "The Nationalization of Ottoman Popular Music in Greece", *Ethnomusicology*, Vol. 48, 1, pp. 1-25.

Pennanen, Risto Pekka, Poulos, Panagiotis C. & Theodosiou, Aspasia (eds.) 2013, *Ottoman Intimacies, Balkan Musical Realities*, (Papers and Monographs of the Finnish Institute at Athens, vol. XIX, Helsinki.

Perchinig, Bernhard, 2008, "Eine kurze Geschichte der türkischen Einwanderung nach Zentral- und Westeuropa", Hemetek & Sağlam, pp. 11-19.

Peres de Silva, Glaucia, 2017, "Weltmusik: Ein politisch umstrittener Begriff", Leggewie, Claus & Meyer, Erik (eds.), *Global Pop*, Stuttgart, J.B. Metzler, pp. 9-16.

Picken, Laurence, 1975, *Folk Music Instruments of Turkey*, London, Oxford University.

Pierini, Marc, 2011, "General Remarks", Ada, Serhan (ed.), *Turkish Cultural Policy Report. A Civil Perspective*, Istanbul, İstanbul Bilgi Üniversitesti Yayınları, pp. 159-162.

Petropoulos, Elias, 2000, *Songs of the Greek Underworld*, London, Saqi.

Pieterse, Jan Nederveen, 1995, "Globalization as Hybridization", Featherstone, Mike, Lash, Scott & Robertson, Roland (eds.), *Global Modernities*, London, Sage, pp 45-68.

Pohlit, Stefan, 2010a, "Musical Life and Westernization in the Republic of Turkey. Schismogenesis and Cultural Revisioning in Contemporary Music", Paper presented at the conference "Europe in Opera – Musical Compositions of an Identity" at Casa de Mateus (Porto / Portugal).

– 2010b, "Dialog mit der Türkei. Interkulturalität in Neuer Musik", *Neue Zeitschrift für Musik*, 5, pp. 58-61.

– 2011, *Julien Jalâl ed-Dine Weiss – A New Qanun System: Its Application in the Performance Practice of the Ensemble "Al-Kindi" and in Contemporary Western Music*, Ph.D. Thesis, Istanbul Technical University.

Pries, Ludger, 2010, *Transnationalisierung. Theorie und Emperie grenzübergreifender Vergesellschaftung*, Wiesbaden, VS-Verlag.

Popescu-Judetz, Eugenia, 1973, *Dimitrie Cantemir, Cartea ştiinţei muzicii*, Bukarest, Editura musicalã a uniunii compozitorilor (*Prince Dimitrie Cantemir*, Istanbul, Pan, 2000).

– 1981, *Studies in Oreintal Arts*, Pittsburgh, Pennsylvania, pp. 99-170.

– 1996, "Trends in Musical Notation", Popescu-Judetz, Eugenia, *Meanings in Turkish Music*, Istanbul, Pan, pp. 11-48.

– 1998, *XVIII. Yüzyıl Musiki Yazmalarından Kevserî Mecmuası Üstüne Karşılastırmalı bir İnceleme* (Turkish translation by Bülent Aksoy), Istanbul, Pan.

– 1999, *Prince Dimitrie Cantemir*, Istanbul, Pan.

- 2002, *Tanburî Kücük Artin. A Musical treatise of the eighteenth Century*, Istanbul, Pan.
- 2007a, *A Summary Catalogue of the Turkish Makams*, Istanbul, Pan.
- 2007b, *Beyond the Glory of the Sultans. Cantemir's View of the Turks*, Istanbul, Pan.
- 2010, *Three Comparative Essays on Turkish Music*, Istanbul, Pan.

Popescu-Judetz, Eugenia & Neubauer, 2004, Eckhard, *Seydî's Book on Music – A 15th Century Turkish Discourse*, (The Science of Music in Islam – Volume 6), Frankfurt am Main, Institute for of Arabic-Islamic-Science.

Popescu-Judetz, Eugenia & Sirli, Adriana Ababi, 2001, *Sources of 18th Century Music, Panayiotes Chalatzoglu and Kyrillos Marmarinos' Comparativ Treatises on Secular Music*, Istanbul, Pan.

Poulos, Panagiotis C., 2005, *Apostolos Konstas'ın Nazariyat Kitabı*, Ph.D. Thesis, İTÜ.
- 2011, "Rethinking Orality in Turkish Classical Music: A Genealogy of Contemporary Musical Assemblages", *Middle East Journal of Culture and Communication* 4, pp. 164-183.

Racy, Ali Jihad, 1977, *Musical Change and Commercial Recording in Egypt, 1904-1932*, PhD, University of Illinois, 1977.

Rasmussen, Anne, 1992, "An Evening in the Orient. The Middle Eastern Nightclub in America", *Asian Music*, xxiii, 2, pp. 63-88.

Reents, Edo, 2006, "Der Sultan des Swing", *Tagesspigel*, 15. December 2006.

Refiğ, Gülper, 1997, *Atatürk ve Adnan Saygun. Özsoy Operası*, Istanbul, Boyut Müzik.

Reigle, Robert, 2013, "A brief History of Kurdish Music Recordings in Turkey", *Hellenic Journal of Music, Education, and Culture*, vol. 4, 2 (www.hejmec.eu).

Reigle, Robert & Whitehead, Paul (ed), 2008, *Spectral World Music. Proceedings of the Istanbul Spectral Music Conference*, Istanbul, Pan.

Reinhard, Kurt, 1972, "Grundlagen und Ergebnisse der Erforschung türkischer Musik", *Acta Musicologica*, xliv, 266-280.
- 1984, "Das Na't des Itrî und seine Versionen", *Jahrbuch für musikalische Volks- und Völkerkunde*, Vol. 2, pp. 9-30.

Reinhard, Ursula, 1987, "Türkische Musik. Ihre Interpreten in West-Berlin und in der Heimat. Ein Vergleich", *Jahrbuch für Volksliedforschung*, pp. 81-92.

Reinhard, Ursula & Pinto, Tiago de Oliveira, 1989, *Sänger und Poeten mit der Laute. Türkische Âşık und Ozan*, Berlin, Staatliche Museen Preussischer Kulturbesitz. Museum für Völkerkunde Berlin.

Robertson, Roland (ed.), "Glocalization: Time-Space and Homogenity-Heterogenity", Featherstone, Mike, Lash, Scott & Robertson, Roland (eds.), *Global Modernities*, London, pp. 25-44.

Roda, Frank, 1985, *Wir singen zusammen. Neue Lieder für türkische und deutsche Kinder*, Berlin, Express.

Rona, Mustafa, 1962, *50 Yıllık Türk Musikisi*, Istanbul 1960.

- 1970, *20. Yüzyıl Türk Musikisi*, Istanbul.

Ruskin, Jesse D. & Rice, Timothy, 2002, "The Individual in Musical Ethnography", *Ethnomusicology*, vol. 56, no. 2 (spring / summer 2012), pp. 299-327.

Ryker, Harrison, 1991, *New Music in the Orient. Essays on Composition in Asia since World War II*, Buren.

Sağ, Arif & Erzincan, Erdal, 2009, *Bağlama Metodu / Bağlama Method*, Istanbul, Pan.

Sağlam, Hande, 2017, "Musikalische Vermittlungsmöglichkeiten der MigrantInnen aus der Türkei in Österreich/Wien", Çiftçi & Greve 2017.

"Sahne Cağdas Sanatın", *Radikal*, 24.11.2011: 42.

Salgar, M. Fatih, 2005, *50 Türk Müziği Bestekârı*, Istanbul, Ötüken.

- 2008, *The Music of Devine Love. Mevlevî Âyînlari*, Istanbul, Ötüken.

- 2010, Dede Efendi, *Hayatı, Sanatı, Eserleri*, Istanbul, Ötüken.

- 2011a, *Selim III. Hayatı, Sanatı, Eserleri*, Istanbul, Ötüken.

- 2011b, *Haci Arif Bey, Hayatı, Sanatı*, Eserleri, Istanbul, Ötüken.

Salomoni, Fabio, 2014, "Just beyond the border: Azerbaijani and Armenian Migrants in Turkey", Karacay, Ayşem Biris & Üstübici, Ayşen (eds.), *Migration to and from Turkey: Changing Patterns and Shifting Policies*, Istanbul, Isis Press, pp. 121-170.

Sanal, Haydar, 1964, *Mehter Musikisi*, Istanbul.

Sanlıkol, Mehmet Ali, 2011, *Çalıcı Mehterler*, Istanbul, Yapı Kredi Yayınları.

Sarı, Mehmet Ali, 2013, *Kur'ân-ı Kerîm ve Dinî Mûsıkî*, Istanbul, Marmara Üniversitesi Fakültesi Vakfı Yayınları.

Sarı, Ayhan, 2012, *Türk Müziği Çalgıları*, Istanbul, Nota.

- 2010, "'Asrı Kemençe' yazması ve 'damla kemençe'ye geliştirme bakışı", paper presented at the *I. Cüneyt Orhon Kemençe Sempozyumu*, 2010 at İTÜ TMDK, İstanbul (http://www.musikidergisi.net/?p=2408 accessed October 21, 2016).

- 2012a, "Geleneksel Türk Müziginde ile 'kanun', 'bağlama', 'ney' Koncertoları", Musîki Dergisi, www.musikidergisi.net/?p=2122 (accessed 1 December, 2012).

- 2015, II. Kanun Sempozyumu ve Festivali ardından, Musiki Dergisi = http://www.musikidergisi.com/yazar-94 ii._kanun_sempozyumu_ve_festivali_ardindan ....html (accessed 2 November, 2016).

Sarı, Özgür, 2010, *Tourism as a Tool for Development: The Case of Mawlana Tourism in Konya*, unpublished Ph.D. Thesis Middle East Technical University.

Sarısözen, Muzaffer, 1952, *Yurttan Sesler*, Ankara, Akın.

- 1962, *Türk Halk Müziğinde Usulleri*, Ankara, Resimli Posta Matbaası.

Saritas, B. Siynem Ezgi, 2010, *Articulation of Kurdish Identity through politicized Music of Komas*, Master Thesis, Ankara, Middle Eastern Technical University.

Say, Ahmed, 1985, *Müzik Ansiklopedesi*, Ankara.

- 1995, *The Music Makers in Turkey*, Ankara, Music Encyclopedia Publication.

– 2014, “Türkiye’de Müzik Eğitimi Kurumlarına Genel Bir Bakış”, Say, Ahmet: *Müzik Yazıları*. Ankara, Müzik Ansiklopedisi Yayınları.

Saygun, Ahmet Adnan, 1936, *Türk Halk Mûsıkîsinde Pentatonizm*, Istanbul.

– 1937, *Rıze, Artvin ve Kars Havalisi Türkü, Saz Oyunları hakkında bazı Malûmat.*

– 1951, “Authenticity in Folk Music”, *International Folk Music Journal*, vol. 3, 7-10.

– 1955, *Sivas Düz Halayı*, Ankara, Devlet Konservatuvarı Yayınları.

– 1981 (1987), *Atatürk ve Musıki*, Ankara, Sevda – Cenap And Müzik Vakfı Yayınları.

Schedtler, Susanne, 1999, *Das Eigene in der Fremde. Einwanderer-Musikkulturen in Hamburg*, Münster, Lit.

Schneider, Albrecht, 1976, *Musikwissenschaft und Kulturkreislehre. Zur Methodik und Geschichte der Vergleichenden Musikwissenschaft*, Bonn-Bad Godesberg, Verlag für systematische Musikwissenschaft.

Seeman, Sonia Tamar, 2002, *'You're Roman!' Music and Identity in Tukrish Roman Communities*, Ph.D. Thesis, UCLA.

Sefarad Kültürü Araştırma Derneği, 2009, *Türk Sefarad Sinagog Ilahileri / Turkish-Sephardic Synagogue Hymns / Kantas de Sinagoga Turko-Sefardi*, Istanbul: Sefarad Kültürü Araştırma Derneği 2009.

Sels, Liselotte, 2014, *Türkü and Halay Between Ghent and Turkey. An Ethnographic Study of Turkish Folk Music in a Transnational Context*, Unpublished Ph.D. Thesis, University Ghent.

Senay, Banu, 2014, “The Fall and Rise of the Ney: From the Sufi Lodge to the World Stage”, *Ethnomusicology Forum*, Vol. 23, 3, pp. 405-424.

– 2015a, “Artists, Antagonisms and the *ney* in the popularization of 'Sufi Music' in Turkey”, *European Journal of Cultural Studies*, Vol. 18, 1, pp. 52-69.

– 2015b, Masterful Words: Musicianship and Ethics in Learning the Ney, *Journal of the Royal Anthropological Institute (N.S.)*, 21, pp. 524-541.

Seroussi, Edwin, 1989, *Mizmirat Qedem: The Live and Music of Rabi Isaac Algazi from Turkey*, Jerusalem, „Renanot“, The Institute for Jewish Music.

Sezen, Armağan, 1992, *Türk Müziğinde Nota Yayıncılığı (1875-1928)*, Master thesis İTÜ 1992.

Shamilly, Gultekin, 1992, “Mirza-Bey's 'Treatise on Music'”, *Turkish Music Quaterly*, 5,2/3, pp. 1-11.

Shannon, Jonathan H., 2003, “Sultans of Spin: Syrian Sacred Music on the World Stage”, *American Anthropologist*, 105, 2, pp. 266-277.

Siebert, Daniel, 2015, *Musik im Zeitalter der Globalisierung. Prozesse – Perspektiven – Stile*, Bielefeld, Transcript.

Signell, Karl, 1977, *Makam: Modal Practice in Turkish Art Music*, Seattle, Asian Muic Publishing.

Skalla, Eva & Amiri, Jemima, 1999, “Kurdish Music. Songs of the Stateless”. Broughton, Ellingham, & Trillo 1999, vol. 1, pp. 378-384.

Skoog, Gabriel, 2012, *On Strange Shepherds, Golden Microphones, and Electric Guitars: Genre, Scene, and the Rise of Anadolu Pop in the Republic of Turkey*, Ph.D. Thesis, University of Washington.

Slobin, Mark, 1992, Micromusics of the West: A Comparative Approach, *Ethnomusicology*, pp. 1-85.

Solmaz, Metin, 1996, *Türkiye'de Pop Müzik. Dünü ve Bügünü ile bir Infilak Masalı*, Istanbul.

Solomon, Thomas, 2005, "'Living underground is tough': authenticity and locality in the hip-hop community in Istanbul, Turkey", *Popular Music*, vol 24, 1, pp. 1-20.

– 2005, "'Listening to Istanbul'. Imaging Place in Turkish Rap Music", *Studia Musicologica Norvegica*, vol 31, pp. 46-67.

– 2006, "Hardcore Muslims: Islamic Themes in Turkish Rap in Diaspora and in the Homeland", *Yearbook for Traditional Music*, 38, pp. 59-78.

– 2007, "Articulation the historical moment: Turkey, Europe, and Eurovision 2003", Raykoff, Ivan & Tobin, Robert (eds.), *A Song for Europe: Popular Music and Politics in the Eurovision Song Contest*, Aldershot, Ashgate, pp. 135-145.

– 2015, "Theorising Diaspora, Hybridity and Music", Solomon, Thomas (ed.), *African Musics in Context: Institutions, Culture, Identity*, Kampala, Fountain Publishers, pp. 319-360.

Soydaş, Emin, 2007, *Osmanlı Sarayında Çalgılar*, Ph.D. Thesis, İTÜ.

Soydaş, Emin & Beşiroğlu, Şehvar Ş., 2007, Osmanlı Saray Müziğinde Yaylı Çalgılar, *İTÜ Dergisi/b*, vol. 4, No. 1, pp. 3-12.

Sözer, Vural, 1964 / 1986, *Müzik ve Müsisyenler Ansiklopedisi*, Istanbul.

Spinetti, Federico (ed.), 2010, *Guiseppe Donizetti Pasha. Music and Historical Trajectories between Italy and Turkey*, Bergamo, Fondazione Donizetti.

Steering Committee for Culture, Heritage and Landscape (CDCPP) (ed.), 2013, *Cultural Policy in Turkey – National Report*, Council of Europe, Strasbourg.

Steuerwald, Karl, 1963, *Untersuchungen zur Türkischen Sprache der Gegenwart. Teil I Die Türkische Sprachpolitik seit 1928*, Berlin, Langenscheidt.

Stock, Jonathan, 2001, "Ethnomusicology and the Individual", *The World of Music*, vol. 43,1.

Stokes, Martin, 1992, *The Arabesk Debate. Music and Musicians in Modern Turkey*, Oxford, Clarendon.

– 1996, "History, Memory, and Nostalgia in contemporary Turkish Musicology" www.umbc.edu/MA/index/number1/stokes1/st1.htm (1.November 2013).

– 1999, "Turkey: Sounds of Anatolia", Broughton, Ellingham & Trillo 1999: 396-410.

– 2010, *The Republic of Love. Cultural Intimacy in Turkish Popular Music*, Chicago Studies in Ethnomusicology, Chicago, The University of Chicago Press.

– 2013, "New Islamist popular culture in Turkey", Salhi, Kamal (ed.), *Music, Culture and Identity in the Muslim World*, Abingdon, Routledge, pp. 15-34.

Strassberger, Katinka, 1984, "Frischer Wind aus dem Orient. Ein Gespräch mit dem türkischen Schlagzeuger Okay Temiz", *Fachblatt Musikmagazin*, 5, pp. 90-95.

Strötbaum, Hugo, 1992, "Seventy-eight Revolutions per Minute in the Levant. Discography of Favorite's Oriental Recordings". *De Turcicis Aliisque Rebus Commentarii Henry Hofman dedicati* , Utrecht, Institut voor Oosterse Talen en Culturen, pp. 149-189.

– 2008, "Favorite Revisited: An Update". *9. Diskographentag*, Utrecht.

– 2012, "Goulash, Wiener Schnitzel and Şiş Kebap: Premier Record", *Gesellschaft für historische Tonträger: Lindström Projekt*, Vol. 4, pp. 1-38.

Stubbs, Frederick W., 1994, *The Art and Science of Taksim: An Empirical Analysis of Traditional Improvisation from 20th Century Istanbul*, Ph.D. Thesis Wesleyan University.

Su, Ruhi, 1985, *Ezgili Yürek. Şiirler Yazılar Konuşmalar*, Istanbul, Adam.

Sürelsan, Ismail Baha, 1971, "Istanbul Konservatuvarina dair I-IV", *Musiki ve Nota*, year 2, 1971, Vol. 16 (p.4-6), 19 (p.26-29), 22 (p.4-5), 23 (p.4-5).

– 1972, "Rauf Yektâ Bey'in '1932 Kahire Şark Musıkîsi Kongresi'ne dair Notları", *Musıki ve Nota*, 3, p. 28.

Sun, Sinemiş Adige, 2011, *Muammer Sun'a Armağan*, Ankara, Sevda-Cenap And Müzik Vakfı Yayınları.

Sun, Muammer, 2008, *Çoksesli Halk Türküleri*, Sun.

Sungurluoğlu, İ., 1961, *Harput Yollarında*, Ankara, Elazığ Kültür ve Tanıtma Vakfı Yayınları, no. 2, vol. 3.

Şahin, Nevin, 2009, *Contested Belongings; Understanding the Meaning of Turkish Classical Music among Young Women in Germany*, MA Thesis, Ankara, Middle East Technical University.

Şahin, Ahmed & Kemiksiz, Mehmet, 2010, *Ramazan: Enderûn Terâvihi ve Cumhur Müezzinliği*, http://www.enderunteravihi.com/, accessed November 22, 2016.

Şarman, Kansu, 2005, *Türk Promethe'ler. Cumhurriyet'in Öğrencileri Avrupa'da (1925–1945)*, İstanbul, Türkiye İş Bankası Kültür Yayınları.

Şen, Besime, 2016, *Devlet, Piyasa, Parti. Nizamettin Ariç ve Kürt Müziği*, Istanbul, Avesta.

Şenel, Süleyman, 1994, *Trabzon Bölgesi Halk Musikisine Giris*, Istanbul, Anadolu Sanat Yayınları.

– 1997, *Kastamonulu Aşık Yorgansız Hakki Çavuş*, Istanbul, Zafer Matbaasi.

– 1995, *Sadi Yaver Ataman*, Istanbul.

– 1999, "Cumhuriyet Dönemi'nde Türk Halk Müziği Araştırmaları", *Folklor / Edebiyat* Vol 17, pp. 99-128.

– 2000 (ed.), "Béla Bartók'un Türk Halk Müziği Çalışmaları İçindeki Yeri", Şenel, Süleyman (ed.), Türkiye'ye *Gelişin 60. Yıldönümü Anısına. Béla Bartók Paneli Bildirileri*, Istanbul, pp. 26-36.
– 2009a, *Kastamonu'da Âşık Fasılları*, Kastamonu, Kastamonu Valiliği.
– 2009b (ed.), *Adnan Ataman, Bu Toprağın Sesi*, İstanbul Büyükşehir Belediyesi.
– 2009c (ed.), *Adnan Ataman: Safranbolu Türküleri ve Oyun Havaları*, Istanbul, Safranbolu Kaymakamlığı.
– 2010, *Istanbul Cevresi Alan Araştırmaları*, Istanbul, Istanbul Avrupa Kültür Başkenti.
– 2015, Ottoman Türkü, Greve 2015: 195-209.

Şehsuvaroğlu, Bedi N., 1974, *Halil Can*, Istanbul, Hüsnütbiat Matbaası.

Şekeryan, Aris (ed), 2012, *Kemani Sarkis Efendi Suciyan. Hayatı ve Eserleri*, Istanbul, Aras.

Sener, Halil Ibrahim & Sari, Mehmet Ali, 1979-1980, "Muradname, Transliterated & Comments", *Musiki Mecmuası*, pp. 362-364, 370-371.

Tambar, Kabir, 2010, "The Aesthetics of Public Visibility: Alevi Semah and the Paradoxes of Pluralism in Turkey", *Comparative Studies in Society and History*, 52(3), pp. 652-679.

Tan, Ali & Çıpan, Mustafa, 2014, *Ney...*, Konya, Konya Valiliği İl Kültür ve Turizm Müdürlüğü.

Tanrıkorur, Çinuçen, 1998, "Ezikliğimiz Soruyor: 'Sizin Konserlerinize Yabancılar Geliyormuş'", Tanrıkorur, Çinuçen (ed.), *Müzik Kimliğimiz üzerine Düşünceler*, Istanbul, Ötüken, pp 161-175.
– 2001, "Bir Yarışma, Bir Cevap", Tanrıkorur, Çinuçen, *Biraz da Müzik*, Istanbul, Zaman Kitab, pp. 60-62.

Tansuğ, Feza, 1991, "Ahmed Adnan Saygun (1907-1991), The Loss of a Pioneer", *Turkish Music Quaterly* 4,2, pp. 9-11.

de Tapia, Stèphane, 1995, *Turcs d'Europe et d'Ailleurs*, Paris, Institut National des Langues et Civilisations Orientales.

Taşkın, Nilüfer, 2016, *Bu bir İsyan Şarkısı Değil! Lazlar, Kimlik, Müzik*, Istanbul, İletişim.

Tekelioğlu, Orhan, 1996, "The Rise of a Spontaneous Synthesis: The Historical Background of Turkish Popular Music", *Middle Eastern Studies*, Vol. 32, 2, pp. 195-215.
– 2001, "The Inner History of 'Turkish Music Revolution' – Demise of a Music Magazine", Hammarlund, Anders, Olsson, Tord & Ozdalga, Elisabeth (ed.), *Sufism Music and Society in Turkey and the Middle East*, Istanbul, Swedish Research Institute in Istanbul, pp. 111-116.
– 2011, "1940'li Yıllardan Itibaren Istanbul'un Caz Mekânları", Aytar & Parmaksızoğlu, pp. 105-126.

Tekin, Gönül Alpay, 1992, *Cengnâme, Ahmed-i Daî: Inceleme, Tenkidli Metin*, Cambridge, Harvard University Press.

Tel, Mes'du Cemil, 1975 / 2002, *Tanbûrî Cemil'in Hayâtı (1947)*, Istanbul, Kubealtı Nesriyâtı.

Terzet, Ahmet Şevket, 1975, *Klâsik Türk Musikisi Antolojisi*, Istanbul.

Terzi, Cihangir, 2015, *Türk Halk Müziğinde Metrik Yapı. Nota Örnekleriyle Ölçüler ve Düzüm Sistematiği*, Istanbul, İstanbul Teknik Üniversitesi Türk Musikisi Devlet Konservatuvarı Yayınları.

– 2017, "Klassifizierung der in Anatolien gespielten Bağlama-Familie in terminologischer, typologischer und tonräumlicher Hinsicht", Çiftçi & Greve 2017.

Tkachenko, Paul Steven, 2009, "The Musical Activities of the Young Turkish – Speaking Community in London: Identity and Nationalism", Kucukcan, T & V Gungor (eds)., *Turks in Europe: Culture, Identity, Integration*, Amsterdam, Türkevi Research Centre.

Tohumcu, Z. Gonca Girgin, 2006, *Müziği Yazmak. Müzik Notasyonunun Tarih içinde Yolculuğu*, Istanbul, Nota Yayıncılık.

Toptaş, Barış, 2016, *Türk Müziği Etütleri*, 2 Vols.

Torun, Mutlu, 1996, *Ud Metodu: "Gelenekten Geleceğe"*, Istanbul, Çağlar Yayınları.

Toumajan, Mihran, 1972ff, *Hayreni Yerg ou Ban*, Yerevan.

Tuğlaci, Pars, 1986, *Mehterhane'den Bando'ya / Turkish Bands of Past and Present*, Istanbul, Cem Yayınevi.

Tura, Yalçın, 1976 / 2001 (ed.), *Kantemiroğlu (Dimitrie Cantemir), Kitab-i 'Ilmul-Musiki 'ala vechi'l-Hurufat*, Istanbul, Yapı Kredi Yayaınları.

– 1988, *Türk Mûsıkîsinin Mes'eleleri*, Istanbul.

– 2006, *Tedkîk ü Tahkîk. Inceleme ve Gerçeği Araştırma*, Istanbul, Pan.

Tura, Yalçın, Aksoy, Bülent, Behar, Cem, Ayangil, Ruhi & Beşiroğlu, Şehvar, 2001, "Kantemioğlu ve Osmanlı Müziğinde Yorum Sorunu Üstüne", *Sanat Dünyamiz*, 79, pp. 69-85.

Turabi, Ahmet Hakkı, 2005, *Gevrekzâde Hâfız Hasan Efendi ve Mûsikî Risâlesi*, Istanbul, Ragbet Yayınları.

Tüfekçi, Neriman & Nida, 1964, *Memleket Türküleri*, Istanbul, Hakan.

Tüfekçioğlu, Zeynep, 2016, "Contemporary Literary Depictions of the Ottoman Past: Neo-Ottomanism or Ottomania?" Paper presented at the Turkologentag 2016, 16 September, 2016 in Hamburg.

TÜIK, 2006, http://www.turkstat.gov.tr/icerikgetir.do?istab_id=171.

Türk Musikisinin Araştırma ve Uygulama Grubu, 1985, *Tarih içinde Türk Musikisi*, Istanbul, Istanbul Üniversitesi Güzel Sanatlar Bölümü.

Ulu, *Esin, 2014, Kültürlerarası Hümanizmanın Müzikteki Simgesi. Çağdaş iki oratoryo: A. Adnan Saygun'un Yunus Emre ve Michael Tippett'in Zamanımızın Çocuğu Oratoryolarının Yapı, Stil ve İçerik Yönlerinden Karşılaştırmalı İncelemesi*, Ankara, Gece Kitaplığı.

Unbehaun, Horst, 1995, "Migration Professionelle des Turcs vers le Proche-Orient, la Russie et L'Asie Centrale", de Tapia 1995: 279-309.

Uluçay, Çağatay, 1948, "Mecmûa-i Sâz ü Söz", *Türk Musıki Dergisi*, 14.

Uludemir, Muammer, 1989, *Mecmua-i Saz u Söz: Bildiriler*, Izmir, Bornova.

Uslu, Recep, 1999, "Osmanlılarda Batı Musikisi Teorisi Eserleri", *Orkestra*, 307, 41-53.

- 2001, *Mehmet Hafid Efendi ve Musiki*, Istanbul, Pan.
- 2006, *Müzikoloji ve Kaynakları*, Istanbul, İTÜ Vakfı.
- 2007, *Fatih Döneminde Musiki ve Semsi-i Rûmî'nin Mecmûa-i Güfte'si*, Istanbul, İstanbul Fetih Cemiyeti.
- 2008, "Müzik Tarihi Açısından Es'ad Efendi'nin Atrabü'l Âsâri", *Musikisinas*, 10, pp. 192-233.
- 2009 / 2014, *A Violinist in Ottoman Court: Saraydaki Kemancı*, Istanbul / Ankara 2014 (www.academia.edu).
- 2010, *Selçuklu Topraklarında Müzik*, Konya, Konya Valiliği Kültür İşleri.
- 2015a, *Meragi'den II. Murad'a Müziğin Maksatları. Makâsidu'l-Elhân*, Ankara, Atatürk Kültür Merkezi Başkanlığı.
- 2015b, "Is an Echo of Seljuk Music Audible? A Methodological Research", Greve, 2015: 241-246.

Uslu, Recep & Dogrusöz Disiacik, Nilgün, 2009, *Abdülbâki Nâsir Dede'nin Müzik Yazısı 'Tahrîriye'*, Türk Musikisi Devlet Konservatuarı Yayınları, Istanbul.

Utz, Chrstian, 2002, *Neue Musik und Interkulturalität von John Cage bis Tan Dun*, (Beihefte zum Archiv für Musikwissenschaft), Stuttgart.

- 2014, *Komponieren im Kontext der Globalisierung*, Bielefeld, Transcript.
- 2015, "Verflechtungen und Reflexionen. Transnationale Tendenzen neuer Musik seit 1945", Hiekel, Jörk Peter & Utz, Christian (eds.), *Lexikon Neue Musik*, Stuttgart, Metzler/Bärenreiter, pp. 135-154.

Uysal, Sabri, 2001, *Zum Musikleben der Türken in Nordrhein-Westfalen*, Gräfelfing, Gräfelfing Buchverlag.

Uyar, Yaprak Melike, 2016, *Jazz in Turkey: Cultural Connotation and the Process of Localization*, Ph.D. Thesis IÜT Istanbul.

Uyar, Yaprak Melike & Beşiroğlu, Ş. Şehvar, 2012, "Recent Representations of the Music of the Mevlevi Order of Sufism", *Journal of Interdisciplinary Music Studies*, Vol. 6, 2, pp. 137-150.

Uz, Kazim, 1894 /1964, *Musiki Istilahatı*, Oransay, Gültekin (ed.), Ankara, Küğ Yayını.

Uzcan, Nihat (ed.), 1978, *Başlangıçtan Günümüze Kadar Türk Bestekârları Ansiklopedisi. Şarkı Güfteleri ve Türküler*, Istanbul, İtimat Kitabevi.

Uzdilek, S.M., 1944, *Ilim ve Musiki ve Türk Musikisi üzerinde Etüdler*, Istanbul.

Uzunçarşılı, Ismail Hakkı, 1977, "Osmanlılar Zamanında Saraylarda Musiki Hayatı", *Belleten*, xli.

– 1986, "Osmanli Sarayinda Ehl-i Hiref (sanatkârlar) defteri", *Türk Tarih Kurumu – Belgeler Dergisi*, vol. xi, 15, pp. 23-77.

Ünal, Fehamet, 2000, *Emin Ongan. Ömrünü Musıkiye Adayan İnsan*, Istanbul, Pan.

Üngör, Etem, 1965, *Türk Marşları*, Ankara, Türk Kültür Araştırma Enstitüsü Yayınları.

– 1981, *Türk Mûsikîsi Güfteler Antolojisi*, Istanbul, Erenler Yayınları.

Üngör, Ugur Ümit, 2011, *The Making of Modern Turkey. Nation and State in Eastern Anatolia 1913-1959*, Oxford, Oxford University Press.

Ünkan, Emin, Bedia & Hakan, 1984, *Türk Sanat Musikisinde Temel Bilgiler*, Istanbul.

Ünlü, Cemal, 2004, *Git Zaman Gel Zaman. Fonograf – Gramofon – Taş plak*, Istanbul, Pan.

Ülkütaşır, M.Şakir (ed..), 1973, *Türkiye'de Folklor ve Etnografya Çalışmaları*, Ankara.

Üniter, Fatos, 1989, *Kemençe'nin Tarihi Gelişime. Kemençe üzerine araştırma ve düşünceler*, Master thesis ITÜ.

Ünver, O. Can, 2015, "Azerbaycan Türkleri Örneğinde Avrasya Coğrafyasından Türkiye'ye Yönelik Yüksek Nitelikli İnsan Göçü", Erdoğan, M. Murat & Kaya, Ayhan (eds.), *Türkiye'nin Göç Tarihi: 14. Yüzyıldan 21. Yüzyıla Türkiye'ye Göçler*, Istanbul, Bilgi Üniversitesi Yayınları.

Üzel, Nezih, 2006, *Radyoda bir Gün*, Istanbul, Pan.

Vansina, Jan, 1985, *Oral Tradition as History*, Madison.

Väth, Gerhard, 1993, "Zur Diskussion über das Alevitentum", *Zeitschrift für Türkeistudien*, 2, pp. 211-222.

Verlan, Sascha & Loh, Hannes, 2000, *20 Jahre Hiphop in Deutschland*, Höfen, Hannibal.

Verband deutscher Musikschulen, 2012, *Lehrplan Bağlama*, Kassel, Gustav Bosse Verlag.

Vervelde, Leo & Greve, Martin, 2008, "The World in Sounds. The Academy for World Music", *Musikforum*, 2, p.48-50.

Vicente, Victor A., 2007, *The Aesthetics of Motion in Musics for the Mevlana Celal Eddin Rumi*, unpublished PhD dissertation, University of Maryland.

Vikár, Laszlo & Saygun, A. Adnan, 1976, *Béla Bartók's Folk Music Research in Turkey*, Budapest.

Vorhoff, Karin, 1995, *Zwischen Glaube, Nation und neuer Gemeinschaft: Alevitische Identität in der Türkei der Gegenwart*, Berlin, Klaus Schwarz.

Vural, Feyzan Göher, 2011, *Islamiyet'ten önce Türklerde Kültür ve Müzik. Hun, Kök Türk ve Uygur Devletleri*, Istanbul, Cizgi.

Waltron, Jeremy F., "Practices of Neo-Ottomanism: Making Space and Place in Istanbul", Göktürk, Soysal & Türeli 2010: 88-103.

Weich-Shahak, Susanna (ed), 2014, *Judeo-Spanish Songs for the Life Cycle in the Eastern Mediterranean*, (Anthology of Music Traditons in Israel), The Hebrew University of Jerusalem. Jewish Music Research Center.

Welsch, Wolfgang, 1992, "Transkulturalität. Lebensformen nach der Auflösung der Kulturen", *Informative Philosophie 2*, pp. 5-20.

Woodard, Kathryn, 1999, *Creating a national music in Turkey: The solo piano works of Ahmed Adnan Saygun*, ProQuest Dissertations & Theses (PQDT).

Wright, Owen, 1988, "Aspects of Historical Change in the Turkish Classical Repertoire", *Musica Asiatica* 5, pp. 1-108.

- 1992a (ed), *Demetrie Cantemir. The Collection of Notations*, London 1992 / 2000, London: Ashgate, Aldershot.
- 1992b, *Words Without Songs*, London.
- 1994, "17. ve 18. Yuzyıllardaki Yapısal Değişimler", *Dünden Bugüne Istanbul Ansiklopedisi*, vol. 5.
- 1994/1995, "Abd al Qadir al-Maraghi and Ali B. Muhammad Bina'i: Two Fifteenth-century Examples of Notation", *Bulletin of the School of Oriental and African Studies*, vol. 57, pp. 475-515, vol. 58, pp. 17-39.
- 1996a, "Middle Eastern Song-Text Colletions", *Early Music*, 24, pp 454-469.
- 1996b, "On the Concept of a 'Timurid' Music", *Oriente Moderno*, 15 (74), 2.

Wurm, Maria, 2006, *Musik in der Migration. Beobachtungen zur Kulturellen Artikulation Türkischer Jugendlicher in Deutschland*, Bielefeld.

Yahya Kaçar, Gülçin, 2011, *Gülzâr-ı Mûsikî*, Ankara: Maya Akademi Yayınları.

- 2012 (2009), *Türk Mûsikîsi Rehberi*, Ankara, Maya Akademi.
- 2012, *Türk Mûsikîsi Üzerine Görüşler (Analiz ve Yorumlar)*, Ankara, Maya Akademi.

Yalçın, Gökhan, 2016, *Hâşim Bey Mecmuası*, Ankara, Atatürk Kültür Merkezi.

Yalgin, Mahmet (ed.), 2009, *Biraz Hayat Biraz Sanat Kemençeci bir Avukat, Nihat Doğu Kitabi*, Izmir, Ege Üniversitesi Yayınevi.

Yarman, Ozan, 2007, *79-Tuning & Theory for Turkish Maqam Music. As A Solution to the Non-Conformance Between Current Model And Practice*, Ph.D. Thesis ITÜ.

- 2010, „Alaturka Müziğinin Yasaklanmasında Atatürk: Belgeler Zemininde bir Çözümleme", https://www.academia.edu (acessed 17 June, 2017).

Yavasca, Alâeddin, 2002, *Türk Mûsikîsi'nde Kompozisyon ve Beste Biçimleri*, Istanbul, Türk Kültürüne Hizmet Vakfı.

Yavuz, Elif Damla, 2014, *Communities Within Individual in a Transcultural Work: Ali Baba und die 40 Räuber*, Unpublished Ph.D. Thesis, Istanbul Technical University.

Yavuzoğlu, Nail, 2008/2010, *21. Yüzyılda Türk Müziği Teorisi*, Istanbul, Pan.

- 2011, *Türk Müziğinde Makamlar ve Seyir Özellilleri*, Istanbul, Pan.
- 2013, *Türk Makam Müziği ve Yani Notasyon*, Istanbul, İnkilâp.

Yazıcı, Ümit, 2011, *Tanbûri Ali Efendi. Hayatı ve Eserleri*, İzmir, Dokuz Eylül Üniversitesi Yayınları.

Yazıcıoğlu, E. Taçlı, 2010, "Contesting the Global Consumption Ethos: Reterritorialization of Rock in Turkey", *Journal of Macromarketing*, 30, 3, pp. 238-253.

Yedig, Serhan, 2007, "Erdal Erzincan'ı, Yo-Yo Ma'ya İpekyolu projesi için önereceğim. Interview with Kayhan Kalhor", January 2007, http://www.muzik soylesileri.net/cms/index.php?option=com_content&task=view&id=177&Item id=43 (accessed 25 August, 2015).

Rauf Yekta, 1318/1902, 2000, *Esâtîz-i Elhân, Hâce Abdülkadir el-Merâgî*, İstanbul, Mahmud Bey Matbaası, Nuri Akbayar (ed.), Istanbul, Pan.

- 1915 "Eski Türk Musikisine Dair Tetebbu'lar", *Milli Metebbular Mecmuası*, 3.
- 1924, *Şark Mûsikîsi Tarihi*, Istanbul, Mahmud Bey Matbaası.
- 1913-1922, "La Musique Turque", Lavignac (ed.), *Encyclopédie de la Musique*, vol. V, pp. 2945-3064.

Yiangou, Christiana, 2005, *Smyrna and Asia Minor Revolution: The Birth of the Rembetiko Song*, Master Thesis, California State University Dominguez-Hills.

Yıldırım, Imam, 2013, *Bağlama, Band 1, Jedem Kind ein Instrument*, Mainz, Schott.

Yıldız, Burcu, 2016, *Experiencing Armenian Music in Turkey: An Ethnography of Musicultural Memory*, Würzburg, Ergon.

Yılmaz, Altuğ & Kerovpyan, Aram, 2011, *Klasik Osmanlı Müziği ve Ermeniler*, İstanbul, Avrupa Kültür Başkent.

Yılmaz, Niyazi, 1996, *Türk Halk Müziğinin Kurucu Hocası Muzaffer Sarısözen*, Ankara, Ocak.

Yılmaz, Zeki, 1988 (1973) *Türk Musikisi Dersleri*, Istanbul.

Yöre, Seyit, 2015, The European Innovations in Ottoman Music Culture in the Context of Musical Composition, Uyanık (et. al. eds), *International Conference on the Changing World and Social Research I, Vienna 2015, Proceedings Book*, Konya: Palet.

- 2011, "Kültürleşmenin bir Parçası olarak Osmanlı'da Opera'nın Görünümü", *Zeitschrift für die Welt der Türken*, Vol. 3,2, pp.53-69.

Yurdatapan, Sanar, 2016, "Turkey: Censorship Past and Present", *Freemuse* 2016: 22-29.

Yücel, Clémence Scalbert, 2009, "The Invention of a Tradition: Diyarbakirs's dengbêj Project". *European Journal of Turkish Studies*, 10, http://ejts//revues.org/index4055.html.

Yücesoy, Eda Ünlü, 2011, *Istanbul'da Medya. Çoğrafi Dağılım ve Üretim*, İstanbul Bilgi Üniversitesi Yayınları.

Yüksel, Metin, 2011, *Dengbêj, Mullah, Intelligentsia: The Survival and Revival ot the Kurdish-Kurmanji Language in the Middle East, 1925–1960*. Ph.D. Thesis Chicago, Illinois.

Yürür, Ahmet, 1995, "Processes in New Music in Turkey", http://www.turkishmusic.org/cgi-bin/d?processes_7.htm (accessed October 25, 2016).

Zelepos, Ioannis, 2010, "Städte als Projektionsflöchen im griechischen Popularlied des 20. Jahrhunderts am Beispiel Istanbul, Izmirs und Thessalonikis", Tischler, Ulrike & Zelepos, Ioannis (ed.), *Bilderwelten – Weltenbilder. Die Gegenwart der Ver-*

gangenheit in postosmanischen Metropolen Südosteuropas: Thessaloniki, Istanbul, Izmir, Frankfurt, Peter Lang, pp. 63-99.

Zeren, M.Ayhan, 1978, *Müzikte Ses Sistemleri: Genel Diziler*, Ankara.

Zırh, Besım Can, 2008, "Euro-Alevis: From Gastarbeiter to Transnational Communiy", Anghel, Remus Gabriel, Gerharz, Eva, Rescher, Gilberto & Salzbrunn, Monika (ed.), *The Making of World Society. Perspectives from Transnational Research*, Bielefeld, Transcript, pp. 103-131.

Zimmermann-Kalyoncu, Cornelia, 1985, *Deutsche Musiker in der Türkei im 20. Jahrhundert*, Frankfurt a.M. Peter Lang Verlag.

De Zorzi, Giovanni, 2008. "Learning the ney flute in Italy. A seven years "field" experience", Hemetek & Sağlam 2008, 107-118.

– 2010, *Musiche di Turchia*, Mailand, Ricordi.

Zümrüt, Mehmet Emin, 2000, "Türk Musikisi'nde Batı Etkisi ve Batı Musikisi Aletlerinin Kullanılması – II", *Musikişinas*, 2000, Vol. 4, pp. 41-51.

Audio and Visual Sources.

2000 Pasaporte Latino. *Latin türküler*. DMC. 2000 (audio cassette).

Ahenk. *Turkish Classical Music*. Kalan 1998 (CD).

Ahenk 2. *Golden Horn*. 2006 / Kalan, n.Y. (CD).

Ajamlar. Compositions Attributed to Abdoqâder Marâqi. Showqnâme. Mohammad-Rezâ Darvishi. Mahoor. 2011 (CD).

Akdeniz, Çetin. *Bağlama Virtüozu*. Duygu Müzik. 1995 (audio cassette).

Akkaya, Erdal & Maya, Jeronimo. *Endülüs & Anadolu Buluşmalar*. Ahenk. 2014 (CD).

Nevzat Akpinar. *Melez Yollarda*. Akkiraz. 2009 (CD).

Sezen Aksu. *İşik Doğudan Yükselir*. Foneks. 1995 (CD).

–. *Düğün ve Cenaze*. Plaza. 1997 (audio cassette).

Aktaş, Osman. *Ana*. Kalan 1998 (CD).

Aleviler'e I / II. Kalan. 2014 / 2015 (CDs).

Isak Algazi Efendi. Osmanlı – Türk ve Osmanlı-Yahudi Musıkisinin Büzük Sesi. Kalan. 2004 (CD).

Al Kindi. *Parfums Ottoman. Arabic Turkish Court Music*. Chant du Monde. 2011 (CD).

Alnar, Ferid. *Peşrev'den Konçerto'ya*. Kalan. 2014 (CD).

–. *Bir Cumhuriyet Çınarı*. Türk Hava Yolları. 2009 (Kitap, CD).

Perihan Altındağ-Sözeri. *Anısına Saygı*. Odeon. 2008 (CD).

–. *Perihan Altındağ-Sözeri'den Seçmeler TRT*. 2011 (CD).

De Amsterdam Klezmer Band & Galata Gypsy Band. *Katakofti*. Kalan 2003 (CD).

Anadolu Ermeni Halk Müziği. Kalan. 1999 (CD).

Anadolu Ninnileri. Kalan. 2006 (CD).

Anthology of Turkish Experimenal Music 1961-2014, Sub Rosa/Alife, 2016 (CD).
Aracı, Emre & Prag Senfoni Oda Orkestra. *Sultan Portreler*. Kalan. 2004 (CD).
–. *Guatelli Pasha and his Musical Portrait Album of the 19th Century Royal Family*, Kalan (CD).
Aracı, Emre & The London Academy of Ottoman Court Music Ensemble: *European Music at the Ottoman Court*, Kalan 2000 (CD).
Aras Quintet. *Mevlana Instrumental*. Aras. c. 1970 (33rpm record).
Arifa. *Anatolian Alchemy*. Mundus. 2012 (CD).
Arslan, Adil. *Üryan*. Tempo. 1992 (audio cassette).
Aslan, Mikail. *Miraz*, Kalan 2005 (CD).
–. *Zernkut*. Kalan. 2008 (CD).
–. *Pelguzar*. Kalan. 2010 (CD).
–. *Petag. Dersim Ermeni Halk Şarkılar*. Kalanç 2010 (CD).
Aslangil, Feyzi. *Piyano ile Saz Eserleri ve Taksimler (1910-1965)*. Kalan. 2000 (CD).
Asya Içlerinden Balkanlardan Saz. Kalan. 1998 (audio cassette).
Aşkın, Cihat. *Umutsuz – The Desperate*. Kalan. 2004 (CD).
Ayangil Türk Müziği Orkestra ve Korosu'nun Yalçın Tura'ya Armağanı. Şey Galib'e Saygı. Syncron. 1999 (audio cassette).
Ayangil Türk Müziği Orkestra ve Korosu Solistleri. *Bestekâr III. Selîm Hân*, İstanbul Büyükşehir Belediyesi, 2008 (CD).
Yorgo Bacanos'dan Taksimleri (1950–1953). Istanbul Radyosu Kayıtları. TRT. 2011 (CD).
Yorgo Bacanos (1900-1977). Kalan. 1997 (CD).
Bach & Itrî. Kalan. 2013 (CD).
Bağlama-Symposium in Deutschland / Manufacturing of a Baglama with Carvel-Built Body, Ethnologisches Museum Berlin. Staatliche Museen zu Berlin 2014. Erstes Baglama-Symposium Berlin. Özay Şahin, Berlin: Ethnologischen Museum der Staatlichen Museen zu Berlin Abteilung Musikethnologie. 2014 (DVD).
Baktagir, Göksel. *Enstrumental Türk Müziği*. Akustik. 2008 (CD).
Baktagir, Göksel & Çelikten, Ceyhun. *Boğaziçi*. Akustik Müzik. N.y. (c. mid 2000s) (CD).
Béla Bartók. *Turkish Folk Music Collection*. Hungaroton. 1996 (CD).
Bektaşi Nefesleri. Cemre. 1997 (CD).
Bengi Bağlama Üçlüsü. *Güneş Bahçesinden Ezgiler*. Kalan. 1999 (CD).
–. *Sel Gider... Kum Kalır...* Kalan. 2001 (CD).
Berkman, Esra & Işıldak, Nazlı. *Uyanış. Haçatur Avetisyan*. Kalan. 2013 (CD).
Bezmara. Turkey. *Splendors of Topkapı*. Opus 111. 1999 (CD; in Turkey released as *Yıtık Sesin Peşinde*. Kalan. 2000).
–. *Tanbûrî Isak*. En Chordais. 2004 (CD).
–. *Mecmu'a dan Saz ve Söz*. Kalan. 2004 (CD).
–. *Ali Ufki Bey'in Tanıklığıyla. 17. Yüzyıl Istanbul'unda Musiki*. Güvercin. 2010 (CD).

Bilgin, Salih & Aydemir, Murat. *Nevâ*. Golden Horn. 2004 (CD).
Bosphorus, United Nations High Commissioner for Refugees, 1990. *Osmanli Imparatorlugu'nda Müzik. Music in the Ottoman Empire. Live 31 May 1990 Herod Atticus*. 1990 (CD).
Buddha Bar, 1999-2015 (18 CDs).
Buhûrizâde Mustafa Itrî Efendi. Bilinen ve Bilinmeyen Yönleri ile. Istanbul Büyükşehir Belediyesi. 2013 (CD).
Büyüközteki, Sami & Akaçca, Ali. *Düşler*. Akustik. 2003 (CD).
Cantemir Ensemble. *Music in Istanbul and Ottoman Empire around 1700*. Golden Horn Records. 2004 (CD).
Cizrawi, Mihmed Arif. *Seyranê*. Kom Müzik. 2000 (CD).
Concerto Köln & Sarband. *Dream of the Orient*. Deutsche Grammophon. 2003 (CD).
–, *The Waltz. Ecstasy and Mysticism*. Archiv Produktion. 2005 (CD).
Constantinople. *Musique du Moyen Âge et de la Renaissance*. Atma Classique. 2001 (CD).
Courtois, Vincent & Andrieux, Gilles. *Turkish Blend*. Al Sur. 1995 (CD).
Cumhurbaşkanlığı Klasik Türk Müziği Korosu. *Itrı*. Kaf. 2012 (CD).
Çalgija. Music of the Balkan and Anatolia 2. Pan. 1992 (CD).
Çelik, Özgür. *Öznağme*. Z Müzik. 2012 (CD).
Çelik, Sinan. *Kaval / Anadolu Ezgiler*. Duygu. (o.J.) (CD).
–. *Kaval. Açışlar / Doğaçlamalar*. Duygu (o.J.). (CD).
Çınar, Feyzullah. *Fazilet*. Kalan 2003.
Çiçek, Ali Ekber. *Haydar Haydar*. TRT. 2010.
Çilden, Şinasi & Orhan, Şebnem. *Breath of Anatolia with two Cellos*. Yavuz Asöcal. 2008 (CD).
Dalkılıç. Hande. *Muammer Sun: Yurt Renkleri / Country Colors*. Kalan. 2004 (CD).
Davul-Gırnata, Lızge. 2001 (audio cassette).
Dede Efendi Mevlevi Sesler. Istanbul Büyükşehir Belediyesi. 2007 (CD).
Demir, Mahmut & Françoise. *Garip ile Senem*. Bayar. 1987 (audio cassette).
–. *Yar Bağında*. Kalan. 1995 (CD).
Demir, Mehtap. *Anadolu Kokusu*. Ahenk. 2016 (CD).
Demirağ, Melike / Yurdatapan, Şanar. *Istanbul'da olmak / Anadolu*. Ada. 1989 (audio cassette).
Evrim Demirel Ensemble. *Ada*. Kalan. 2012 (CD).
Destination: Istanbul. Dynamic / Bar de Lune. 2006 (CD).
Dikmen, Mustafa Doğan: *Dârü'l-Elhân Külliyâtı*, Istanbul Avrupa Kültür Başkenti 2010.
Dinç, Kemal. *Lir ve Ateş*. Kalan. 2006 (CD).
–. *Bağlama için Denemeler*. Kalan. 2012 (CD).
Dertli Divani. Hasbıhâl. Kalan. 2005 (CD).

Doğan, Aynur. *Hevra / Together*. Sony. 2013 (CD).
Doğan, Sıddık. *Çoban Yıldızı*. Duygu. 1999 (CD).
Erkan Oğr, Derya Türkan & İlkin Deniz. *Dokunmak*. M & MT. 2014 (CD).
Domeniconi, Carlo. *Concerto di Berlinbul.* Raks. 1993 (audio cassette).
During, Sjahin. *Afro Anatolian Tales*. Doublemoon. 2008 (CD).
Duruöz, Cem. *Anadolu Hazineleri / Treasures of Anatolia*. Ak Müzik. 2009 (CD).
Emir, Erdoğan. *Sad*. Kom Müzik. 2010 (CD).
Emre Ensemble Istanbul. *Yunus Emre. Lieder des türkischen Sufi-Dichters*. Silkroad. 1998 (CD).
En Chordais. *Petros Peloponesios*. En Chordais. 2005 (CD).
–. *Music of Asia Minor and Constantinople*. Ocora. 2008 (CD).
Ensemble Galatia. Ortaçağ Şarkıları / Medieval Music from 13th–15th Century. Kalan. 2013 (CD).
Erçetin, Candan. *Çapkın*. Topkapı. 1997 (audio cassette).
Erdoğan, Cenk. *ARC*, Jazzschool Records 2010 (CD).
Erguner, Kudsi. *Sufi Music of Turkey*. Times Square Music. 1990 (CD).
–. *The Turkish Ney*. Unesco. 1990 (CD).
–. *Tasavvuf'tan Flamenko'ya / L'Orient de l'Occident*. Al Sur. 1995 (CD).
–. *Ottomania*. ACT. 1999 (CD).
–. *Islam Blues*. ACT. 2001 (CD).
–. *Taj Mahal*. Equinox. 2001 (CD).
–. *Ney-Zen*. Imaj. 2002 (CD).
–. *Osmanlı Davulları*. Imaj. 2002 (CD).
–. *Taj Mahal*. Equinox. 2004 (CD).
–. *Sufyan*. Equinox. 2011 (CD).
Ergüner, Kudsi & Bellenger, Xavier. *Ney et Kena. Conférence de Roseaux*. Ocora. 1984 (LP).
Erguner, Süleyman. *Girift*. Istanbul Büyüksehir Belediyesi. 2010 (CD).
–. *Anadolu Nefesi*. Çınar. 2014 (CD).
Erguner Topluluğu. *Sufî Music. Türk Tasavvuf Musikîsi*. Kalite. Early 1990s (audio cassette).
Sinan Cem Eroğlu. *Hane-i Akustiki*. Beğeni Müzik. 2011 (CD).
–. *Tesadüf*. Ahenk. 2012 (CD).
Eroğlu, Sinan Cem & Çoğulu, Tolgahan. *Microtonal Gitar Duo*. Kalan. 2015 (CD).
Erzincan, Erdal. *Girdab-i Mihmet*. Kalan 2011 (CD).
–. *Bağlama Orkestrası*. Kalan. 2013 (CD).
Erzincan, Erdal & Kalhor, Kayhan. *The Wind*. ECM. 2006 (CD).
–. *Tahran Konseri*. Kalan. 2012 (DVD).
–. *Kula Kulluk Yakışır Mı?* ECM. 2013 (CD).
Erzincan Türküleri. TRT / Kalan. 2010 (CD).
Erzincanlı Hafiz Şerif. Kalan. 2004 (CD).

Esen, Hasan. *Rebab*. Kalan. 2004 (CD).
Eyhok (Hakkari). Kalan. 2004 (CD).
Forabandit. Buda Musique. 2012 (CD).
–. *Port*. Buda Musique. 2014 (CD).
Galata Mevlevi Musik und Sema Ensemble. *Lost in Ecstasy*. Heaven and Earth. 1999 (CD).
Garcia-Fons, Renaud. *Oriental Bass*. Enja. 2002 (CD).
Geçmişten Günümüze Türk Müziği. Türkiye Iş Bankası. 2000 (3 CDs).
Golden Horn Ensemble. *Ali Ufki*. Sony. 2008 (CD).
–. *Dimitrie Cantemir*. Sony. 2009 (CD).
Gülâ, Coşkun. *Bağlama tezene tavırları*. Kalan. 1999 (audio cassette).
Gündüz, Aka & Temiz, Okay. *Zikr*. EMI. 1989. (audio cassette).
Güneş, Betin. *Kompositionen*. Temur Musik. 1992 (CD).
–. *Premiere für den Frieden*. Eigenart. 1994 (CD).
–. *Izmir Konzert für Altposaune und Orchester*. Audite. 1995 (CD).
–. *Ich will Dir was sagen*. Telos Music. 2005 (CD).
Güney, Barış. *Tohum*. Kalan. 2007 (CD).
–. *Düşlere yolculuk*. Kalan. 2009 (CD).
Güzelses, Celâl. Coşkun Plak, n.y. (audio cassette).
Christodoulos Halaris. *Pandora. Music of the Post-byzantine High Society*. Vol. II. Orata. n.y. (CD).
Halklardan Ezgiler. Ermeni Halk Müziği. Kalan. 1995 (CD).
Baba Hampartyum. Kalan. 2010 (CD).
Hanende Zaharya. Kalan. 2005 (CD).
Helvacıoğlu, Erdem & Bandit, Ros. *Black Falcon*. Positif. 2010 (CD).
Hergel, Arı & Yıldız, Burcu. *Gomidas Vartabed'in Ermenice, Kürtçe ve Türkçe Derlemelerinden Düzenlemeler*. Kalan. 2014 (CD).
Hesperion XXI. *Orient-Ocident 1200–1700*. Alia Vox. 2006 (CD).
–, *Istanbul. Dimitirie Cantemir, 1673–1723*. Alia Vox. 2009 (CD).
–, *La Sublime Porte. Voix d'Istanbul 1430–1750*. Alia Vox. 2011 (CD).
Hovhannisyan, Karine. *Classical Music for the Armenian Kanun*. Traditional Crossroads. 2007 (CD).
Inspirations. *Rotterdam Concert*. Kalan. 1995 (audio cassette).
Istanbul Connection. Kalan. 2006 (CD).
Istanbul Sazendeleri. *Sazende Fasli 1*. Kaf. 2008 (CD).
Istanbul'dan Yeni Müzik. I. Uluslararası Müzik Festivai. Leyla Pınar. 1993 (audio cassette).
Işık, Uğur. *Unveils Anatolian Spirit*. Kalan. 2005 (CD).
–. *Cello Invocations*. Kalan. 2008 (CD).
–. *Chess of Cello*. Kalan. 2015 (CD).
JazzEastern – an Osman Ismen Project. Columbia. 1998 (audio cassette).

Judeo-Spanish Songs from Eastern Mediterranean. Inedit. 1994 (CD).
Kaçar, Gülçin Yahya. *Abdülkâdir-I Merâgî Besteleri*. Atatürk Kültür Merkezi Başkanlığı. 2015 (CD).
Kadın Aşıklar. Kalan. 2010 (CD).
Kahraman, Metin Kemal. *Yaşlılar Dersim Türküleri Söylüyor*. Lızge. 1997 (CD).
–. *Ferfecir*. Ses Plak. 1999 (CD).
–, *Sürela*. Lızge. 2000 (CD).
–, *Cevere Hazara*. Lizge. 2006 (CD).
–, *Sae Moru/Şahmaran*. Lızge. 2011 (CD).
Kahraman, Zeynel. *Melem Tıya*. Lızge. 2001 (audio cassette).
Kalhor, Kayhan. *Silent City*. World Village. 2008 (CD).
Kandiralı, Mustafa & Ensemble. *Caz Roman*. Network Medien. 1992 (CD).
Kantolar (1905-1945). Kalan. 1998 (audio cassette).
Karaca, Kâni. Boyut Sinema. (1980) (VCD).
Karadağ, Burcu. *Neyzen*. Mega. 2012 (CD).
Karademir, Coşkun, Kartal, Emirhan & Doğan Sevinç, Hatice. *Dönüş Yolu*. Ak Müzik. 2011 (CD).
Karakaya, Fikret. *Eski Musikinin Rüzgâriyla*. Güvercin. 2008 (CD).
Kardeş Türküler. *Kardeş Türküler*. Kalan. 1997 (CD).
–. *Doğu*. Kalan. 1999 (CD).
–. *Vizontele*. Kalan. 2001 (CD).
–. *Hemâvâz*. Kalan. 2002 (CD).
Vizontele Tuuba. Kalan. 2004 (CD).
Bahar. Kalan. 2005 (CD).
–. *Çocuk Haklı*. Kalan. 2011 (CD).
Karlıbel, Aydın. *Transcriptions and Original Works*. Kalan. 2007 (CD).
Kecskes Ensemble. *Ancient Turkish Music in Europe*. Hungaroton. 1984 (LP).
Kemençe. Kalan. 2005 (CD).
Ketençoğlu, Muammer. *Smyrna Recollections*. Kalan. 2007 (CD).
Kızılbaş I / II, Kalan 2009, 2011 (CDs).
Klasik Bektaşi Nefesleri / Bektaşi Hymns. EMI-Kent. 1995 (audio cassette).
Koç, Dilek. *Souvenir de Salonique*. General Music / Sony. 2015 (CD).
Koçgiri, Cemil. *Heya*. Kalan. 2007 (CD).
Hazan Aaron Kohen Yasak, Maftirim Ilahiler Korosu. *Maftirim. Judeo-Sufi Connection*. Kalan. 2001 (CD).
Kohen Yasak. *Şevahot Lael: Allah'a Övgüler. From the Ottoman Era to the Present: Jewish Liturgical Music*. Kalan. 2008 (CD).
Konyali, Riza. Odeon. 2010 (CD).
Köker, Erol. *Mekteb-i Irfan*. Ak Müzik. 2009 (CD).
Kronos Quartett. *Mugam Sayagi: Music of Franghiz Ali-Zadeh*. Nonesuch.

Kurdish Alevi. Ocax û xwelî Zêmarên kurdên elewî / Ocak ve Kül Kürt Alevi Ağıtları. Kalan. 2011 (CD).

Kurdish bards. Traditional music from Dersim. Extraplatte. 1998 (CD).

Kutluer, Şefika. *Mevlana Rumi.* Gallo. 2008 (CD).

Küçükay, Bekir & Aydoğan, Tahir. *Yüzyıllık Şarkılar.* Ateş Müzik. 2006 (audio cassette).

Laboree, Robert. *Çengname. Music for the Turkish Harp.* Kalan. 2001 (CD).

La Turchescha & Cevher-I Musiki. *Venedik'ten Istanbul'a.* Calliope. 2007 / Ak. 2008 (CD).

Les Fin'Amoureures: *Marions Les Roses.* Alpha. 2005 (CD).

Let my Love be Roman. Musics of Turkey's Roma. Kalan. 2008 (CD).

Livaneli, Ferhat. *Lâlezâr. Chamber Music.* Emi. 1990 (CD).

Livaneli, Zülfü. *New Age Symphony.* IDA. 1999 (CD).

Malay, Murat. *Çanakkale 1915 & Palestine Symphony.* 3Adim. 2010 (CD).

MacCrimmon, Brenna. *Kular Misafiri. Events in small Chambers.* Kalan. 2009 (CD).

Crimmon, Brenna Mac & Sesler, Selim. *Karşılama.* Kalan. 1998 (CD).

McKennith, Loreena. *An Ancient Muse.* Quinlan Road. 2006.

Mısırlı Ahmet. Ak Müzik. 2005 (CD).

Minor Empire. *Second Nature.* Z Yapim. 2014 (CD).

Moradi, Ali Akbar & Özdemir, Ulaş. *The Companion.* Hermes Records. 2007 (CD).

Moritz, Sema. *Bir Beyoğlu Bestekârı. Karnik Garmiryan.* Boyut. Boyut (CD).

Muallem, Yinon. *Klezmer for the Sultan.* Oriente Music. 2005 (CD).

–. *The Way it is.* Kaf. 2008 (CD).

Music of Cyprus. Kalan. 2007 (CD).

The Music of Islam. Vol. 9 Mawlawiyah Music of the Whirling Derwishes. Celestial Harmonies. 1997 (CD).

Music Therapy According to the Time (Vakitlere Göre Müzik ile Tedavi): Şifanağme 2. Origami. c. 2012 (CD).

Muzîka Serayê ya Kurdî / Kurdish Saray Müzigi. Kom Müzik. 2007 (CD).

Mürtezaoğlu, Cavit & Öney, Feryal. *From Tabriz to Taurus / Tebriz'den Toros'a.* Kalan. 2012 (CD).

Namlı, Zeki Çağlar. *La Lune / Köy.* Akkiraz. 2006 (CD).

Namlı, Zeki Çağlar & Di Piazza, Dominique. *Face to Face.* Lir. 2011 (CD).

Naylıbaş, Cafer. *Feryad-ı kemane.* Onearth. 2013 (CD).

Necipoğlu, Ceren. *Bir Kitap Gibi.* Kalan. 2009 (CD).

Nederlands Blazers Ensemble, Aynur. *Turquoise.* NBE. 2006 (CD).

–. *Zeibekiko. The Greek Concert.* NBE. 2007 (CD).

Nefes. *Fasl-ı Nefes.* Güvercin. 1996 (CD).

Nevcivan Özel Project. *Taristan.* Ak. 2010 (CD).

Erkan Oğur, *Fretless.* Feuer und Eıs. 1994 CD).

–. *Gülün Kokusu Vardı.* Kalan. 1998 (CD).

–, *Hiç*. Kalan. 1999 (CD).
–, *Anadolu Beşik*. Kalan. 2000 (CD).
Oğur, Erkan & Gasparyan, Djivan. *Fuad*. Kalan. 2001 (CD).
Oriental Wind & The Karnataka College of Percussion. *Sankirna*. Sonet. 1984 (LP).
Ottoman marches on 78 rpm recordings (1903-1923). Kalan. 1999 (CD).
Ottoman Sounds. Magnificant Ottoman Composers. Boyut Music. 2008 (CD).
Öcal, Burhan. *Turkish Folk Music Vol. 1*. Soundways. 1992 (LP).
Öçal, Burhan & Istanbul Oriental Ensemble. *Sultan's Secret Door*. Network. 1997 (CD).
–. *Orient Secret*. L'empreinte digitale. 1998 (CD).
–. *Caravanserai*. Network. 2000 (CD).
Öçal, Burhan & Istanbul Oriental Orchestra & Züricher Kammerorchester. *Concerto Alla Turca*. Universal Music. 2006 (CD).
Öçal, Burhan & Namlook, Pete. *Sultan – Osman*. PW. 1998 (CD).
Öçal, Burhan & Seda Oriental Band. *Seda Oriental Band*. Konnex. 1998 (CD).
Öçal, Burhan & Tacuma, Jamaaladeen featering Natacha Atlas. *Groove alla Turca*. Doublemoon. 1998 (CD).
Öçal, Burhan & Edebil, Arif. *Demedim mı? Musique Savante et Musique Soufi*. Amori. 1995 (CD).
Özdemir, Ulaş. *Ummanda. Maraş Sinemilli Deyişleri*. Kalan. 1998 (CD).
–. *Bu Dem / This Breath*. Kalan. 2008 (CD).
Özer, Mehmet Can. *Siyah Kalem Dance*. AK Müzik. 2009 (CD).
Özgür, Ibrahim. *Tangolar. The Bel Ami of Turkish Tango*. Oriente Rien. 1999 (CD).
Özkan, Aşık Ali Izzet. *Mecnun Leylamı Gördüm*. Kalan. 2000 (CD).
Özkan, Cengiz. *Ah Istanbul*. Kalan. 1997 (CD).
–. *Aşık Veysel Türküleri. Saklarım gözümde güzel güzelliğini*. Kalan. 2003 (CD).
Özkan, Talip. *Yağar yağmuş*. Kalan. 1997 (LP).
–. *The Dark Fire*. Island Records. 1992 (CD).
Öztürk, Okan Murat. *Aşk Adami söyletir. Anadolu sevda türküleri*. Rec müzik. 2007 (CD).
Özyürek, Hande. *Face to Face/Yüzyüze*. Kalan. 2007 (CD).
Pal-Yarden, Hadass. Yahudice. Ladino Sehir Music / Urban Ladino Music. Kalan. 2003 (CD).
Pancaroğlu, Şirin. *Istanbul'un Ses Telleri*. Kalan. 2010 (CD).
–. *Çenknağme*. Lila Müzik. 2014 (CD).
Pancaroğlu, Şirin & Dönük, Meriç & Cagwin, Jarrod. *Elişi*. Kalan. 2011 (CD).
Parlak, Erol. *Ah bu türküler*. ASM. 1995 (CD).
–. *Pervâne*, ASM. 1998 (CD).
–, *Göç Yolları*. ASM. 1998 (CD).
–, *Katre*, Akkiraz 2003 (CD).
–, *Har*. Anadolu. 2011 (CD).

Erol Parlak Bağlama Beşlisi. *Eşik*. Akkiraz. 2003 (CD).

Parmakçı, Yücel. *Miras*. Esen. 2009 (CD).

Pera Güzeli Laterna. Istanbul 2010 Avrupa Kültür Başkenti. 2010 (Book, CD. DVD).

Polat, Mehmet. *Desire*. Reinmusic. 2011 (CD).

Mehmet Polat Trio. *Next Spring*. Homerecords. 2014 (CD).

Pomak Göçmenlerde Müzik ve Pesna. Kalan. 1998 (CD).

Pontos Şarkıları. Recordings of 1930. Kalan. 2003 (CD).

Rachmaninov Anatolian Project. Kalan. 2015 (CD).

Rappaport, Sylvain & Micenmacher. Youval. *Turkish Songs*. Al Sur. 1997 (CD).

Rembetica. Historic Urban Folk Music from Greece. Rounder. 1992 (CD).

Rembetika. Kalan. 1993 (audio cassette).

Rembetika II. Izmir ve Istanbul'dan Yıllanmış Şarkılar. Kalan. 1996 (CD).

Rıt, Rıza. Cemre. 2000 (CD).

Arif Sağ Trio. *Concerto for Bağlama*. ASM. 1998 (audio cassette).

Sarband. *Cantico*. Jaro. 1990 (LP).

–. *Music of the Emperors*. Jaro. 1992 (LP).

–. *Llibre Vermell de Montserrat. Medieval Pilgrim Songs from Spain*. Jaro. 1994 (CD).

–, *Sepharad. Songs of the Spanish Jews in the Mediterranean and the Ottoman Empire*. BMG. 1995 (CD).

–, *Sephardic Songs. In the Hispano-Arabic Tradition of Medieval Spain*. Jaro. 1996 (CD).

–, *Yehudi: Jewish Music from the Seraglio*. Teldec. 1996 (CD).

–, *Gerusalemme Liberata*. Teldec. 1999 (CD).

–, *Alla Turca*. Teldec. 1999 (CD).

–, *Fantasies from Hindoostan*. Teldec. 2000 (CD).

–, *Danse Gothique: Music by Satie & Machaut*. Jaro. 2000 (CD).

Sarısözen, Muzafer. TRT. 2002 (CD).

Say, Fazıl. *Istanbul Senfonisi*. Ak Müzik. 2010 (CD).

Selanik'tan Trabzon'a Köprü. Güvercin. 2013 (CD).

Münir Nurettin Selçuk. Çoşkun Plak. N.y. (audio cassette).

Seyyan Hanim (1913-1989). *Tangolar*. Kalan. 1996 (CD).

Bekir Sıtkı Sezgin. Klasikler I, II. Kaf. 2006 (CD).

Bekir Sıdkı Sezgin. Boyut Sinema. (1980) (VCD).

Sinan, Marc & Hülsman, Julia. *Fasıl*. ECM. 2009 (CD).

Sinopoulos, Sokratis & Türkan, Derya. *Letter from Istanbul*. Golden Horn Recods. 2001 (CD).

Sokratis Sinopoulos Quartet. *Eight Winds*, ECM, 2015 (CD).

Söz Saz Istanbul, Yenikapi Mevlevîhanesi 1597–1925. Itrî 300. Yılı anısına. TFM Müzik. 2012 (CD).

Sufi's Secret Vol 2. Indie Europe. 2010 (CD).

Sufi Müzik'ten Flamenko'ya / From Sufi Music to Flamenco. Kalan. 2000 (CD).

Süryani, Kalan. 2002 (CD).
Şahin, Ahmed & Kemiksiz, Mehmed. *Tevhid Halkası*. Dalar 2010 (CD).
Şensoy plays Tura. Kalan. 1999 (audio cassette).
Tanburi Cemıl Bey, Kalan 2016.
Tanini. *Dokunuşlar / Touches*. Kaf. 2008 (CD).
Targan, Şerif Muhittin. *Bütün Eserleri*. Kalan. 2007 (CD).
–. *Peygamber Torunun Müzigi: Şerif Muhittin Targan*. Kaf. 2001 (CD).
Tatyan Havaları. Kalan. 2008 (CD).
Tébrizizadeh, Mahmoud & Erguner, Kudsi. *Oriental Dreams*. Sunset France Playasound. 1994 (LP).
Tekbilek, Ömer Faruk & Keane, Brian. *Süleyman the Magnificent*. Celestial Harmonies. 1988 (audio cassette).
Tekbir, Durak, *Naat ve Salatlar. Islamic Religious Music*. Kent. 1993 (audio cassette).
Tekin, Ertan. *Demans*. Kalan. 2011 (CD).
Telvin, Kalan. 2006 (CD).
Temiz, Okay & Karnataka College of Perkussion. *Mishram*. Raks. 1997 (audio cassette).
Temiz, Okay & Group Zourna. *Karşılama*. Ada. 1997 (audio cassette).
Ali Murtaza Topal Dede. Kalan. 2003 (CD).
Torun, Mutlu. *Buluşmalar-Sana Siirler Okuyacağım*. Kalan. 2001 (CD).
Toulai & Francois Rabbath. *Hommage a Nazim Hikmet*. Arion. 1982 (LP).
–. *Le Chant des Poètes*. Arion. 1998 (org. 1980, LP).
Turquie. Musique des Troubadours. Ethnic Auvidis. 1992 (CD).
Nida Tüfekçi.TRT. 2001 (CD).
Derya Türkan. *Ministrels Era*. Kalan. 2006 (CD).
Türköz, Saadet. *Kara Toprak*. Amori. 1994 (CD).
–, *Marmara See*. Intact. 1999 (CD).
–, *Urumchi*. Intact record. 2005 (CD).
Ulucan, Özcan, Birsen und Ayşen. *Salon Romantique Turque*. Spektral. 2009 (CD).
Urfa'dan üç Musiki Ustası – Kel Hamza, Mukim Tahir, Bekçi Bakır. Kalan. 2004 (CD).
Urfalı Tenekeçi Mahmut Güzelgöz. Kalan. 2007 (CD).
Urfali Camil Cankat, Ahmet Cankat. Kalan. 2011 (CD).
Uğurlu, Tuluyhan. *Symphony Turk / Senfoni Türk*. Doğan Music. 2002 (CD).
Birsen Uslucan. *Masallar, Rüyalar, Fısıltılar*. Lila Müzik. 2011 (CD).
Üzel, Nezih. *Ilahiler (Sufi Music)*. Kent. (c. end 1980s) (audio cassette).
–. *Mevlana Rubailer. Selected Masterpieces of Mevlevi Music*. Kent. (c. end 1980s) (audio cassette).
Yakaza Ensemble. *A'mâk-ı Hayâl*. Ak Müzik. 2010 (CD).
–. *İçbükeydış*. Ak Müzik. 2012 (CD).
Yako Taragano Synagogue Hymns Choir. *Zemırot I & II*. Ottoman-Turkish Sephardic Culture Research Centre. 2002; 2008 (CDs).

Yansımalar & Suren Asaduryan. *Vuslat.* 2001 (CD).
Yarınıstan, Papageorgiou, Vassiliki & Öngör, Taner. *Bizim Adalar.* Ak. 2014 (CD).
Alâeddin Yavaşça. KAF. 2001 (CD).
Yayla, Kalan. 2007 (CD).
Yezidiler. Kalan. 2008 (CD).
Yörüklerde Müzik ve Boğaz Çalma. Kalan. 1998 (CD).
Yurttan Sesler. Yeni Türkiye'nin Ezgileri. Yapı ve Kredi Kültür Sanat Yayıncılık. 1998 (CD).
Yüksel, Levent. *Adi Menekşe.* Plaza. 1998 (CD).
Yükselir, Hasan. *Herkes Gibisin, Ayrılık.* Güvercin Müzik. c. 1991/92 (audio cassette).
–. *Su Türküler.* Su Arts. mid 1990s (audio cassette).
Zikir. Islamic Ritual Music. Kent. 1993 (audio cassette).

ORIENT-INSTITUT
ISTANBUL

ISTANBULER TEXTE UND STUDIEN

Alle erschienenen Titel sind auch als E-Books erhältlich. Sechs Jahre nach Erscheinen sind sie kostenfrei über www.ergon-verlag.de abrufbar.

1. Barbara Kellner-Heinkele, Sigrid Kleinmichel (Hrsg.), *Mīr ʿAlīšīr Nawāʾī. Akten des Symposiums aus Anlaß des 560. Geburtstages und des 500. Jahres des Todes von Mīr ʿAlīšīr Nawāʾī am 23. April 2001.* Würzburg 2003.
2. Bernard Heyberger, Silvia Naef (Eds.), *La multiplication des images en pays d'Islam. De l'estampe à la télévision (17-21 siècle). Actes du colloque* Images : fonctions et langages. L'incursion de l'image moderne dans l'Orient musulman et sa périphérie. *Istanbul, Université du Bosphore (Boğaziçi Üniversitesi), 25 – 27 mars 1999.* Würzburg 2003.
3. Maurice Cerasi with the collaboration of Emiliano Bugatti and Sabrina D'Agostiono, *The Istanbul Divanyolu. A Case Study in Ottoman Urbanity and Architecture.* Würzburg 2004.
4. Angelika Neuwirth, Michael Hess, Judith Pfeiffer, Börte Sagaster (Eds.), *Ghazal as World Literature II: From a Literary Genre to a Great Tradition. The Ottoman Gazel in Context.* Würzburg 2006.
5. Alihan Töre Şagunî, Kutlukhan-Edikut Şakirov, Oğuz Doğan (Çevirmenler), Kutlukhan-Edikut Şakirov (Editör), *Türkistan Kaygısı.* Würzburg 2006.
6. Olcay Akyıldız, Halim Kara, Börte Sagaster (Eds.), *Autobiographical Themes in Turkish Literature: Theoretical and Comparative Perspectives.* Würzburg 2007.
7. Filiz Kıral, Barbara Pusch, Claus Schönig, Arus Yumul (Eds.), *Cultural Changes in the Turkic World.* Würzburg 2007.
8. Ildikó Bellér-Hann (Ed.), *The Past as Resource in the Turkic Speaking World.* Würzburg 2008.
9. Brigitte Heuer, Barbara Kellner-Heinkele, Claus Schönig (Hrsg.), *„Die Wunder der Schöpfung". Mensch und Natur in der türksprachigen Welt.* Würzburg 2012.
10. Christoph Herzog, Barbara Pusch (Eds.), *Groups, Ideologies and Discourses: Glimpses of the Turkic Speaking World.* Würzburg 2008.
11. D. G. Tor, *Violent Order: Religious Warfare, Chivalry, and the* ʿAyyār *Phenomenon in the Medieval Islamic World.* Würzburg 2007.

12. Christopher Kubaseck, Günter Seufert (Hrsg.), *Deutsche Wissenschaftler im türkischen Exil: Die Wissenschaftsmigration in die Türkei 1933-1945.* Würzburg 2008.

13. Barbara Pusch, Tomas Wilkoszewski (Hrsg.), *Facetten internationaler Migration in die Türkei: Gesellschaftliche Rahmenbedingungen und persönliche Lebenswelten.* Würzburg 2008.

14. Kutlukhan-Edikut Şakirov (Ed.), *Türkistan Kaygısı. Faksimile.* In Vorbereitung.

15. Camilla Adang, Sabine Schmidtke, David Sklare (Eds.), *A Common Rationality: Muʿtazilism in Islam and Judaism.* Würzburg 2007.

16. Edward Badeen, *Sunnitische Theologie in osmanischer Zeit.* Würzburg 2008.

17. Claudia Ulbrich, Richard Wittmann (Eds.): *Fashioning the Self in Transcultural Settings: The Uses and Significance of Dress in Self-Narrative.* Würzburg 2015.

18. Christoph Herzog, Malek Sharif (Eds.), *The First Ottoman Experiment in Democracy.* Würzburg 2010.

19. Dorothée Guillemarre-Acet, *Impérialisme et nationalisme. L'Allemagne, l'Empire ottoman et la Turquie (1908 -1933).* Würzburg 2009.

20. Marcel Geser, *Zwischen Missionierung und „Stärkung des Deutschtums": Der Deutsche Kindergarten in Konstantinopel von seinen Anfängen bis 1918.* Würzburg 2010.

21. Camilla Adang, Sabine Schmidtke (Eds.), *Contacts and Controversies between Muslims, Jews and Christians in the Ottoman Empire and Pre-Modern Iran.* Würzburg 2010.

22. Barbara Pusch, Uğur Tekin (Hrsg.), *Migration und Türkei. Neue Bewegungen am Rande der Europäischen Union.* Würzburg 2011.

23. Tülay Gürler, *Jude sein in der Türkei. Erinnerungen des Ehrenvorsitzenden der Jüdischen Gemeinde der Türkei Bensiyon Pinto.* Herausgegeben von Richard Wittmann. Würzburg 2010.

24. Stefan Leder (Ed.), *Crossroads between Latin Europe and the Near East: Corollaries of the Frankish Presence in the Eastern Mediterranean (12th - 14th centuries).* Würzburg 2011.

25. Börte Sagaster, Karin Schweißgut, Barbara Kellner-Heinkele, Claus Schönig (Hrsg.), *Hoşsohbet: Erika Glassen zu Ehren.* Würzburg 2011.

26. Arnd-Michael Nohl, Barbara Pusch (Hrsg.), *Bildung und gesellschaftlicher Wandel in der Türkei. Historische und aktuelle Aspekte.* Würzburg 2011.

27. Malte Fuhrmann, M. Erdem Kabadayı, Jürgen Mittag (Eds.), *Urban Landscapes of Modernity: Istanbul and the Ruhr.* In Vorbereitung.

28. Kyriakos Kalaitzidis, *Post-Byzantine Music Manuscripts as a Source for Oriental Secular Music (15th to Early 19th Century).* Würzburg 2012.

29. Hüseyin Ağuiçenoğlu, *Zwischen Bindung und Abnabelung. Das „Mutterland" in der Presse der Dobrudscha und der türkischen Zyprioten in postosmanischer Zeit.* Würzburg 2012.

30. Bekim Agai, Olcay Akyıldız, Caspar Hillebrand (Eds.), *Venturing Beyond Borders – Reflections on Genre, Function and Boundaries in Middle Eastern Travel Writing*. Würzburg 2013.
31. Jens Peter Laut (Hrsg.), *Literatur und Gesellschaft. Kleine Schriften von Erika Glassen zur türkischen Literaturgeschichte und zum Kulturwandel in der modernen Türkei*. Würzburg 2014.
32. Tobias Heinzelmann, *Populäre religiöse Literatur und Buchkultur im Osmanischen Reich. Eine Studie zur Nutzung der Werke der Brüder Yazıcıoğlı*. Würzburg 2015.
33. Martin Greve (Ed.), *Writing the History of "Ottoman Music"*. Würzburg 2015.
34. A.C.S. Peacock, Sara Nur Yıldız (Eds.), *Islamic Literature and Intellectual Life in Fourteenth- and Fifteenth-Century Anatolia*. Würzburg 2016.
35. Burcu Yıldız, *Experiencing Armenian Music in Turkey: An Ethnography of Musicultural Memory*. Würzburg 2016.
36. Zeynep Helvacı, Jacob Olley, Ralf Martin Jäger (Eds.), *Rhythmic Cycles and Structures in the Art Music of the Middle East*. Würzburg 2017.
37. Karin Schweißgut, *Das Armutssujet in der türkischen Literatur des 20. Jahrhunderts*. Würzburg 2016.
38. Stefan Hanß, *Die materielle Kultur der Seeschlacht von Lepanto (1571). Materialität, Medialität und die historische Produktion eines Ereignisses*. Würzburg 2017.
39. Martin Greve, *Makamsız: Individualization of Traditional Music on the Eve of Kemalist Turkey*. Würzburg 2017.